Praise for *Eleano*

"The completion of Blanche Wiesen Cook's monumental and inspirational life of Eleanor Roosevelt [series] is a notable event. . . . Volume 3 continues the story of Eleanor's 'journey to greatness.' Keeping the focus on her actions and reactions, Cook skillfully narrates the epic history of the war years."
—*The New York Times Book Review*

"A monumental biography [and] an exhilarating story, as well as undeniably melancholy one. In her relentless efforts to push American democracy to fulfill its promises, Eleanor Roosevelt was ahead of her time. As we ponder our curdled political culture . . . it's not at all clear that we have yet caught up to her."
—Maureen Corrigan, NPR's *Fresh Air*

"More than a presidential spouse, however, or feminist icon, the Eleanor Roosevelt who inhabits these meticulously crafted pages transcends both first-lady history and the marriage around which Roosevelt scholarship has traditionally pivoted."
—*The Wall Street Journal*

"The final installment in Blanche Wiesen Cook's trilogy of biographies of Eleanor Roosevelt . . . finds the first lady increasingly comfortable in her own skin. . . . As these remarkable volumes chronicle, Roosevelt found her voice and her calling as an advocate—for peace, women's rights, and the disadvantaged."
—*O, the Oprah Magazine*

"Reads like the great history that it is . . . The monumental achievement of this current volume . . . is the rich depiction of the period's contextual history."
—*San Francisco Chronicle*

"In the third and final volume of Blanche Wiesen Cook's magisterial biography of ER . . . [Cook's] perspective, through ER's eyes, is vigorous and fresh, the comparisons with our own darkening world subtle and yet potent."
—*Minneapolis Star Tribune*

"[A] sweeping and detailed look at the first lady about whom more books have been written than any other, with the exception of Jacqueline Kennedy . . . Today, she is acclaimed not only as an inspirational first lady of the United States but also of the world—and as one of the twentieth century's great humanitarians. Cook's trilogy, and this volume in particular, eloquently defines her legacy and its continuing relevance."
—*Richmond Times-Dispatch*

"Magisterial . . . Cook captures the headlong energy of those years perfectly. Readers will encounter in these pages an intimate, touchingly human Eleanor Roosevelt—an icon they can both admire and genuinely like."
—*Christian Science Monitor*

"Exhaustively researched and beautifully written . . . gives us a sympathetic but very human portrait of this 'First Lady of the World' . . . Anyone interested in the life of this towering figure in twentieth-century history will want to read this book."
—*BookPage*

"Illuminating . . . A magnificent capstone to Cook's decades-long evaluation of Eleanor Roosevelt."
—BBC.com's *Between the Lines*

"Fascinating reading, and . . . highlights for students of history how the world has changed since [Eleanor Roosevelt]'s time. And how it has not."
—*Booklist* (starred review)

"Outstanding . . . A winning concluding volume in a series that does for Eleanor Roosevelt what Robert Caro has done for Lyndon Johnson."
—*Kirkus Reviews* (starred review)

"Superb . . . Cook skillfully weaves her subject's active and emotional life among friends and family members into the depiction of her public role."
—*Publishers Weekly*

"Highly readable and richly detailed . . . Cook succeeds in demonstrating how Eleanor's political ideas regarding human rights, economic insecurity, and the plight of refugees echo today."
—*Library Journal*

PENGUIN BOOKS

ELEANOR ROOSEVELT VOLUME 3

Blanche Wiesen Cook is distinguished professor of history and women's studies at John Jay College and Graduate Center; City University of New York. In addition to her biography of Eleanor Roosevelt, her other books include *The Declassified Eisenhower* and *Crystal Eastman on Women and Revolution*. *Eleanor Roosevelt Volume One* was a winner of the *Los Angeles Times* Book Prize, and Volumes One and Two were *New York Times* bestsellers.

BLANCHE WIESEN COOK

Eleanor Roosevelt

The War Years and After

VOLUME THREE

1939–1962

Penguin Books

This book is dedicated to all those activists and agitators who resist tyranny, challenge authority, fight for peace, freedom, and Human Rights—as we continue our journey for One World: no borders, no boundaries, no walls.

PENGUIN BOOKS
An imprint of Penguin Random House LLC
375 Hudson Street
New York, New York 10014
penguin.com

First published in the United States of America by Viking,
an imprint of Penguin Random House LLC, 2016
Published in Penguin Books 2017

Photo credits

FRONTISPIECE: © Yousuf Karsh

INSERT: *p. 1* (top and bottom): Library of Congress; *p. 2:* Franklin Delano Roosevelt Library; *p. 3* (top): Library of Congress (bottom); Franklin D. Roosevelt Library; *p. 4* (top): Tenschert Photograph Company/Franklin D. Roosevelt Library; (bottom) University of Pennsylvania; *p. 5* (top and bottom): Library of Congress; *p. 6* (top and middle): National Archives; (bottom) Library of Congress; *p. 7:* Air Force Historical Research Agency; *p. 8* (top and bottom): National Archives; *p. 9* (top): National Archives; (bottom) Franklin D. Roosevelt Library; *p. 10* (top): Franklin D. Roosevelt Library; (bottom) Courtesy of Peggy Bok Kiskadden; *p. 11* (top): Library of Congress; (bottom) Courtesy of Victoria Klose; *p. 12* (top): Roosevelt House at Hunter College; (bottom) Pandit family archives; courtesy of Manjari Mehta and the Pandit family; *p. 13* (top): Roosevelt House at Hunter College; (bottom) David J. Bort; *p. 14* (top): Franklin D. Roosevelt Library; (bottom) Smithsonian Institution Archives, Image #SIA 20009-2477; *p. 15* (top): Franklin D. Roosevelt Library; (bottom) Roosevelt House at Hunter College; *p. 16:* Dorothy Norman

THE LIBRARY OF CONGRESS HAS CATALOGED THE HARDCOVER EDITION AS FOLLOWS:
Cook, Blanche Wisen.
Eleanor Roosevelt, Volume One 1884–1933 / Blanche Wiesen Cook.
Eleanor Roosevelt, Volume Two 1933–1938 / Blanche Wiesen Cook.
Eleanor Roosevelt, Volume Three 1939–1962 / Blanche Wiesen Cook.
p. cm.
Includes bibliographical references and index.
ISBN 067080486X (volume 1, hardcover)
ISBN 9780670844982 (volume 2, hardcover)
ISBN 9780670023950 (volume 3, hardcover) / ISBN 9780735221185 (e-book)
ISBN 9780143109624 (volume 3, paperback)
1. Roosevelt, Eleanor, 1884–1962. 2. Presidents—United States—
Wives—Bigraphy. I. Title.
E807.1.R48C66 1992
973.917'092—dc20
[B] 87-40632

Printed in the United States of America
1 3 5 7 9 10 8 6 4 2

Set in Adobe Garamond Pro   Designed by Francesca Belanger

Contents

PREFACE AND ACKNOWLEDGMENTS   ix

Introduction: "Lady Great Heart"   1

Chapter One: "We All Go Ahead Together, or We All Go Down Together"   17

Chapter Two: "You Cannot Just Sit and Talk About It, You Have to Do Something"   39

Chapter Three: Tea and Hot Dogs: The Royal Visit   58

Chapter Four: "We Must Think of the Greatest Good for the Greatest Number"   84

Chapter Five: "If They Perish, We Perish Sooner or Later"   113

Chapter Six: "We Have to Fight with Our Minds"   131

Chapter Seven: Red Scare, Refugees, and Racism   155

Chapter Eight: The Politician and the Agitator: New Beginnings   187

Chapter Nine: Radical Youth and Refugees: Winter–Spring 1940   202

Chapter Ten: "When You Go to War, You Cease to Solve the Problems of Peace": March–June 1940   227

Chapter Eleven: "If Democracy Is to Survive, It Must Be Because It Meets the Needs of the People"   255

Chapter Twelve: "The World Rightly Belongs to Those Who Really Care": The Convention of 1940   279

Chapter Thirteen: War and *The Moral Basis of Democracy*   303

Chapter Fourteen: "Defense Is Not a Matter of What You Get, But of What You Give"   320

Chapter Fifteen: "Heroism Is Always a Thrilling Thing":
   The Politics of Race   353

Chapter Sixteen: "Isolationism Is Impossible": The Politics of Rescue   369

Chapter Seventeen: "To Know Me Is a Terrible Thing":
   Friendship, Loyalties, and Alliances   405

Chapter Eighteen: "Golden Footprints":
   A Permanent Bond in War and Peace   439

Chapter Nineteen: "The White Heron of the One Flight":
   Travels in the Pacific and Beyond   479

Epilogue: ER's Legacy: Human Rights   543

LIST OF ARCHIVES   571

NOTE ON SOURCES AND SELECTED BIBLIOGRAPHY   573

NOTES   587

INDEX   655

A SECTION OF PHOTOGRAPHS FOLLOWS PAGE   272

Preface and Acknowledgments

Eleanor Roosevelt never stopped growing and changing, organizing and inspiring. Called "a woman for all seasons," she generated movements for peace and freedom, for human rights and dignity, worldwide. Throughout my journey with ER I have been fortunate enough to be part of many movements inspired by her vision and legacy. This study could not have been completed without the individuals who have illuminated my understanding and enriched my life. Above all, in our lives committed to activism and creativity, Clare Coss—my primary coconspirator—has profoundly broadened my understanding and contributed dramatically to every aspect of this work. We first met at a Women's International League for Peace and Freedom meeting in 1966, to organize protests against the war in Vietnam. Since then, the women of WILPF and the global women's peace and human rights movement have been central to my work.

In June 1988, I was privileged to be part of a U.S. delegation to the First International Conference on Women, Peace, and the Environment in Moscow.* The conference, sponsored by the Soviet Women's Committee and comprising representatives from over twenty-four nations, occurred while the democratic changes of perestroika and glasnost were getting under way—shortly after the ecological tragedy of the Chernobyl nuclear power plant. The conference was a harmonic convergence that confronted the dire facts of radiation poisoning, militarism, and the ongoing drilling and dumping of industrial toxins—and sought ways to pursue international paths to ecology and health. The Green Party activists, Friends of the Earth, and various peace groups at that meeting were in unanimous agreement: "The environment has no borders," and, in the words of Cora Weiss—then the international coordinator of SANE/Freeze—"a world without waste is a world without want or war." The conference resulted in

---

*Historian and Women Strike for Peace activist Amy Swerdlow and I represented the National Council for Research on Women, funded by the Russell Sage Foundation—thanks to Alida Brill.

permanent friendships and new networks of activism to pursue specific goals—all of which are more urgently needed than ever.

Shortly after that meeting, Bella Abzug and Mim Kelber founded WEDO, the Women's Environmental and Development Organization, to save Mother Earth from pollution and poverty. From 1990 on, the women of WEDO, representing fifty-four nations, worked at the UN and transnationally to create an Earth Summit and build a global sisterhood for justice and peace. With Charlotte Bunch's extraordinary team at the Center for Women's Global Leadership at Rutgers University and many allied groups around the world, the campaign for Women's Rights as Human Rights was under way. Bunch's work continues to flourish, and the CWGL—along with AWID, DAWN, MADRE, NESRI, Outright, and such organizations as Urgent Action Fund—is bringing healing and hope to people across this planet, where currently 64 million refugees face a frightening future.

During the UN decade devoted to women and change, I worked with my U.S. friends and Margarita Papandreou's team of activists—united in Women for a Meaningful Summit, followed by Women for Mutual Security. The inspiring first lady of Greece patterned her career after Eleanor Roosevelt—whose spirit was entirely present during our Moscow discussions and in our subsequent meetings. I am forever grateful to Margarita, and to Leonore Forestal and Hilkka Pietilä, then secretary general of the Finnish UN Association and subsequently author of *Engendering the Global Agenda: The Story of Women and the United Nations* (New York: UN Non-Governmental Organization Liaison Service, 2002), a book that is basic to our understanding of the work of these NGOs and the UN.

Many friends have offered hospitality and insights through the many years of my ER research. I continue to be grateful to those named in Volumes I and II, and I apologize for names involuntarily omitted. I am thankful to Celia Morris, in Washington, D.C.—and to her friends in Houston, Bill and Diana Hobby. Bill's memories of his mother, Oveta Culp Hobby—a life member of the NAACP—changed my understanding of her many contributions, from World War II to Eisenhower's cabinet, in which she served as the first secretary of the Department of Health, Education and Welfare.*

In Arizona, Esther Lape's friends Harold Clarke and Burt Drucker were

---

*While we await a full biography of Oveta Culp Hobby, see Melanie Gustafson's essay in Susan Ware's *Notable American Women* (Cambridge, MA: Belknap, 2005).

fountains of information, and gifted me with several boxes of Lape's papers, including correspondence with ER, which will go to the Franklin Delano Roosevelt Library (FDRL) in Hyde Park. Also in Arizona, Clare and I enjoyed hospitality and conversations with Annette Kolodny and Dan Peters, and with Judith McDaniel and Jan Schwartz; and in Cambridge, Massachusetts, with Betty Burkes and Cathy Hoffman. Amazing times were spent at Bernard Baruch's Hobcaw Barony in Georgetown, South Carolina, to launch SCETV's interactive Web site *Between the Waters*. Project director Betsy Newman and the Belle Baruch Foundation hosted splendid conferences highlighted by discussions of race and change, informed by scholars and such notable former residents as educator Minnie Kennedy.

A unique weekend in Skowhegan, Maine, with Senator Margaret Chase Smith expanded my understanding of ER's partisanship. Because I'd been invited to be the third Margaret Chase Smith Lecturer, the senator wanted me to know when her friendship with ER ended. On 4 November, the Sunday before the Eisenhower–Stevenson election of 1956, they were the first women ever invited to debate the presidential election on national television. Pleased to be part of ER's press conferences, although she wrote only a weekly column for her local paper, and subsequently allied on many issues, Senator Smith, a liberal Republican, considered ER a friend. She was mostly subdued, and ER dominated the debate until she denounced Eisenhower for his opposition to the Suez Crisis, and his efforts to get Israel, Britain, and France to withdraw from their invasion of Egypt. She accused Eisenhower of "supporting the Kremlin and an Egyptian dictator against our oldest and strongest allies." Shocked, Senator Smith countered that Eisenhower was a patriot who did not support Communists, Nasser, or dictatorship. He sought to avoid World War III—which indeed seemed imminent. ER rejected Smith's words and shouted that Eisenhower was "Weak! Weak!" At the end, she refused to shake Margaret Chase Smith's hand, turned her back, and stormed out of the studio. They never spoke again. I knew how competitive ER was; but until this conversation, I did not realize she could be rude.*

*Margaret Chase Smith gave me the tape of their CBS *Face the Nation* debate, which will go to the FDRL. She also wrote about their friendship, up until that debate; see *Declaration of Conscience* (New York: Doubleday, 1972), 203–11. For Eisenhower's successful negotiations and UN support for withdrawal—and amity—during one of the most dangerous episodes of the ongoing Middle East

Many friends, historians, and biographers have generously shared resources, suggestions, and information. From Phoenix, Al Vinck sent me details regarding ER's Easter 1943 visit to the Gila River Internment Camp—and the enduring impact of her concern on the many Japanese-Americans Vinck interviewed who attended Gila Camp reunions. Al and Linda Bouchey of the Wilderstein Historic Site, the home of Margaret Lynch (Daisy) Suckley, have been helpful in myriad ways. The vigorous staff at Hunter College's Roosevelt House, Deborah Gardner and Harold Holzer, and Uri Perrin of the Eleanor Roosevelt Center at Val-Kill, keep ER's flame brightly lit—as does Judith Hope's Eleanor's Legacy, splendidly administered by Brette McSweeney—to support women for public office. I am grateful to Alston Kastner for his memories and tour of the Emergency Rescue Committee.

In addition to those named in Volumes I and II, I am grateful to the members of our women's biography seminar. Over the years, Maureen Beasley, Fran Burke, Mindy Chateauvert, Kathleen Dalton, Carole Fink, Judith Friedlander, Catherine Foster (aka Cate Fosl), William Loren Katz, Richard Lieberman, Annette Rubenstein, Pierre Sauvage, Scott Sandage, Anne Firor Scott, Greg Robinson, Pat Sullivan, Robert Cohen, Marilyn Young, Gloria Steinem, Kate Stimpson, Will Swift, Fred Jerome, Geoff Ward, and Dorothy Zellner have been continually helpful and inspiring. In addition to her family memories, I am grateful to Susan Curnan for ER-related delectables; to David Woolner, John Sears, and other FERI visionaries who worked so hard to reinvigorate the Universal Declaration of Human Rights and Bring Human Rights Home. Ingrid Winther Scobie shared Lorena Hickok's correspondence with Helen Gahagan Douglas at the University of Oklahoma, which transforms our understanding of Hick's later life—her important work and close friendships with Helen Gahagan Douglas, Esther Lape, and others. Subsequently, Linda Boyd Kavars, JoAnne Myers, Patsy Costello, and others forged a Lorena Hickok Memorial and Scholarship Fund to bury Hick's ashes with a named plaque and bluestone bench under a dogwood tree. See Kavars's interview, "Eleanor Roosevelt and Her Legacy," in *The Hudson River Valley Review*, Autumn 2009, p. 85.

crisis, see David A. Nichols, *Eisenhower 1956: The President's Year of Crisis, Suez and the Brink of War* (New York: Simon & Schuster, 2011).

Allida Black, Christopher Brick, and their team have bestowed upon us the Eleanor Roosevelt Papers Project, online and in print. I deeply appreciate their assistance over time. Profound gratitude to journalist and hero Ruth Gruber—whose many conversations and eighteen books have enhanced my journey with ER in countless ways. Illuminating discussions with Jos Barnes, Harry Belafonte, Anita Nayar, Claire Reed, Dorothy Norman, Patti Kenner, Peggy Bok Kiskadden, Eva Kollisch, Naomi Replansky, and Frances Goldin have broadened my scope and enlarged my heart. Endless gratitude to Joan Ormont, whose wisdom shepherded me through layers of unknowns as I struggled to complete this work; to virtuoso of chi Edith Lee, who keeps the energy flowing and in balance; to Melania Clavell, responsible for all digital tasks regarding computers— enhanced by her administrative expertise and supportive good cheer. Appreciation for our ongoing "Hunter Gang" (Kathleen and Maeve D'Arcy; B. J. Kowalski; Rosetta Capotorto) and thanks to Andy Lancet, WNYC's and NPR's archivist, for many references—and ER's voice. I also thank Trent Duffy for his input and time.

Biographers depend on documents, and I applaud the congenial staffs and splendid archivists of the FDRL, the Schlesinger Library at Radcliffe, Columbia University's Oral History Collection and Manuscript Library, the Swarthmore College Peace Collection, the Library of Congress, and the New York Public Library manuscript collections. This book was mightily informed by Jane Clark Chermayeff, who connected me to Elaine and Peter Pratt—who generously loaned me boxes of Trude Pratt Lash's papers. Special acknowledgment to my State Department "boss," Bill Slany, who walked with me through the U.S. archives in search of ER's Papers when I served on the State Department's Historical Advisory Committee to declassify documents and pursue the Freedom of Information Act. We found 198 boxes, declassified in 1988. William Z. Slany was then editor in chief of the *Foreign Relations of the United States* series, and one still hopes a FRUS volume may be forthcoming.

I am profoundly grateful to Michelle Martin and Cornelia Jane Strawser for most illuminating conversations about their mothers, Tiny (Maryris Chaney) and Ruby Black. Finally, it has been my privilege to meet with ER's nieces and several Roosevelt grandchildren—whose work continues ER's legacy. In California, I am thankful to the late Eleanor Roosevelt II and Diana Roosevelt Jaicks, and to Janet Roosevelt Katten—for their hospitality, recollections, and many resources over the years. Frank and Jinx Roosevelt shared perspective and memories; David and Manuela Roosevelt, now activists for ER's legacy, noted that Eleanor listened to Gregorian chants while she waited for her sons and grandchildren to return from their late-night dates. Kate R. Whitney and Sara R. Wilford, both progressive educators in ER's tradition, have deepened my perspective in multiple ways—thanks are due to Sandra Robinson for arranging dinner with Sara Wilford. I particularly appreciate Julius C. C. Edelstein—journalist, diplomat, public citizen—who as CUNY vice chancellor gave us open enrollment and the SEEK program and, as our mutual friend, connected me with Kate Whitney. Over the years, Kate, Julius, and I enjoyed regular lunches that inspirited our work and friendship. Julius Edelstein's motto continues to inform our lives: "It is better for everybody when it is better for everybody."

Charlotte Sheedy, forever friend and agent, was always available with sage advice and astute counsel. At Viking, thanks to Wendy Wolf for her patience, enthusiasm, and steadfast support and to her assistant, Georgia Bodnar. My special gratitude and genuine awe for Beena Kamlani's brilliance—she edited this volume with passion, fierce intelligence, a honed vision, sharp creative sensibilities, and profound political discernment. I honor her total commitment, her immense labor, and the enormous time she spent during every phase of this project.

I want to thank my friends and students at John Jay and the CUNY Graduate Center who have enhanced my life over the decades and the History and Women's Studies departments—Manu Bhagavan, Sandi Cooper, Renate Bridenthal, Roscoe Brown, Tanya Domi, Mary Gibson, Jim Cohen, Carol Groneman, Ed Paulino, Frances Fox Piven, Arthur Schlesinger, and Neil Smith and Barbara Welter; Elizabeth Small and Marilyn Weber; the Lost & Found team; and Bob Isaacson and the CUNY TV community. Former graduate students and researchers Eileen Clancy, Page Delano, Frances Madesen, Melanie Gustavson, Deb Schultz, Jean Mills, Miriam Molnar, John Stern, Marci Gallo, and Kelly Anderson have been helpful in countless ways. I am filled with gratitude for the enduring friendship and generous support of Alice KesslerHarris and Gerald Markowitz, who read each draft of ER I, II, and III, offering insightful commentary, unwavering encouragement, and happy times through the years.

Fortified and sustained by the loving support of our family of heart and hearth, I thank: Harold and Bill Coss, Marjorie D. W. Lessem, Daniel Wayne Lessem and Orlando Zavala, Douglas Jed and Stefanie Lessem, Clare Coss McGuire, Katie Marie McGuire Rolon, Elizabeth LordeRollins and Judy Boals, Jonathan and Judy Rollins, Ann Cammett and Marcia Gallo, and all the beautiful grands and great-grands.

Many close friends have traveled with us and marched with us shoulder to shoulder as we seek to fortify movements for women's rights and human rights. Their contributions have mightily informed this project. This volume is in part dedicated to the memory of Rhonda Copelon, Deborah Ann Light, Ronnie Gilbert, Jane Marcus, Frances Clayton, Michael Ratner, and Alison Bernstein, whose legacies continue to embolden the world. In 2015, Charlotte Bunch, Roxanna Carrillo, and Lepa Mladjenovic were with us at The Hague for WILPF'S 100th anniversary meeting, and then we traveled to Croatia—to Split, along the Dalmatian Coast, and Supetar, once war zones, now peace trails. For the joy along every activist step, and in pursuit of each word, my heartfelt and most profound gratitude to Clare Coss.

21 July 2016

Introduction

"Lady Great Heart"

Admired and beloved, scorned and reviled, influential, controversial, and timeless, Eleanor Roosevelt changed history. As first lady in wartime, she insisted on civil rights, liberty, democracy, and economic security for all. While President Franklin Delano Roosevelt was obligated to southern Democrats for support against mostly isolationist Republicans, and therefore needed to juggle, he allowed his wife a measure of independence regarding domestic issues. As educator, journalist, and prescient activist/public citizen, ER had a profound and enduring impact. She was a democratic socialist, or social democrat, who believed all change required a vigorous, informed, popular movement. She and her allies introduced the debates that offered hope for the future then and that still do today, as struggles for peace and freedom, democracy and justice, dignity and human rights continue worldwide.

She crossed class and race divides, built bridges and forged remarkable friendships. The playwright, journalist, and Republican congresswoman Clare Boothe Luce noted that ER was among the world's "best loved women" for many reasons, but above all: "No woman has ever so comforted the distressed—or distressed the comfortable." The African-American poet, activist, teacher, and priest Dr. Pauli Murray, called a "Firebrand" by ER, was inspired by their friendship and described how ER modeled what women could do. ER, she wrote, was not only "the First Lady of the World . . . she was also the Mother of the Women's Revolution."

Everywhere she went, ER offered hope. Her interest and concern empowered impoverished communities and healed the wounded. Tell me, she asked, what do you want, what do you need? She traveled to war zones as cannons blazed and bombs fell, visited hospitals in every state and factories and mines both at home and abroad. She identified with, and worked especially for, people in want, in need, in trouble.

In the miseries of those in pain or in need, she saw the sufferings of her own parents and sought to alleviate them. Forever hurt by her mother's disregard, ER remained devoted to an illusory, alcoholic father. Her mother died at twenty-nine, when Eleanor was eight; her father died two years later at thirty-four. During these solemn years she lived with her grandmother and her difficult uncles and aunts. ER remained forever haunted by the ravages of alcoholism, a family disease.

At fifteen, she was released from her gloomy lonely childhood when she embarked on a three-year journey of study and travel under the tutelage of Marie Souvestre, brilliant headmistress of the Allenswood Academy in England. Souvestre recognized her many talents, and she experienced "attention and admiration" for the first time: "Attention and admiration were the things throughout all my childhood that I most wanted, because I was made to feel so conscious of the fact that nothing about me would attract attention or would bring me admiration!"

Her mother called her "Granny" when she was six and told her that since she was so "plain," she had best develop "manners." ER was haunted by those words of shame. But at Allenswood she learned self-worth, and it changed her life. French-speaking upon arrival, she was an ardent student and was encouraged to be creative, independent, and bold. She was a popular leader among her classmates and Marie Souvestre's special favorite, and her confidence grew and her eager spirit flourished. She excelled at music and became proficient at playing the piano and violin. She quickly demonstrated her gift for languages by mastering German and Italian. She danced and played games and enjoyed sports and competition. To the end of her life, she credited her years at Allenswood with her sense of social responsibility and political activism, highlighted by the cultured cosmopolitan teachings of Marie Souvestre: "Whatever I have become since had its seed in those three years of contact with a liberal mind and a strong personality."

Educators open doors, reveal paths to creativity, and inspire their students to reach for the best in themselves. After a lifetime of creativity and achievement, ER affirmed that "the happiest day of my life was the day I made the first field hockey team at Allenswood School." Marie Souvestre had recognized ER's profound gifts, encouraged her talents, and forever emboldened her quest for independence, competition, and a life of endless learning, passionate intensity, and surprising romance.

ER's deepest affiliations were with people, those she met across the country and around the world. Her great friend Lady Stella Reading, who became director of the Women's Voluntary Service in wartime London, observed most clearly that "Eleanor Roosevelt cares first and always for people." They are her "interest . . . her hobby . . . her preoccupation . . . her every thought is for human beings. . . . I believe that the basis of all her strength is in her profound interest in them and her readiness to share with them the agony of experience and the fulfillment of destiny."

She responded to public acclaim with self-deprecating humility. In 1939 more than a thousand activists and educators she admired honored her at New York's Hotel Astor as an "apostle of good-will" whose wisdom helped "resolve the maladjustments in the social order." Journalist Dorothy Thompson said "few people received universal admiration, and virtually nobody universal affection. . . . I doubt if any woman in the whole world is so beloved." ER was grateful but bewildered. After all, she responded, she did nothing extraordinary, just what came to hand. Anyone would have done what she had done, she claimed, "given the opportunity." Her modesty was an abiding quality. Indeed, her humility seemed to grow in proportion to the attention she received.

ER's profound love of people, and for the world, was fortified by cherished friendships. While she accepted Marie Souvestre's mantra "Never be bored, and you will never be boring," she was easily bored and often impatient. Although loyal to those she loved, she was always open to promising new relationships. Over time, her life filled with several unusual romances.

ER returned to New York at eighteen, to "come out" into society—and in 1905, at twenty, she married her distant cousin Franklin Delano Roosevelt. Their marriage, forged by love, was maintained by shared visions and political goals. To appreciate ER's public life and many contributions, it is necessary to reconsider her formative years, which enabled her to conquer the loneliness she experienced during her childhood and the early years of her marriage. In 1918, stunned by evidence of her husband's betrayal with her friend and social secretary Lucy Mercer, ER confronted depression, rejected suicide, and determined to live fully, with ardor and purpose. Her marriage became a generous partnership—mutually supportive, respectful, and affectionate.

Although ER never wrote the truth about her heart and erased Lucy Mercer and her husband's subsequent infidelities from the public record, we know that over the decades she escorted all her friends to a sheltered green holly grove to view the statue in Rock Creek Cemetery she called *Grief.* Commissioned by Henry Adams, that sanctuary of mourning and resistance had been created by the sculptor Augustus Saint-Gaudens to honor Adams's late wife Marian Hooper Adams, known as Clover. A pioneering woman photographer, linguist, and learned "bluestocking," Clover was a gracious and popular hostess whose translations and research were important to Henry Adams's early histories. He never credited her work, and forbade the sale of her acclaimed portraits when they were to be published. When she learned of Henry's affair with her friend Elizabeth Cameron in 1885, she committed suicide by drinking photographic (prussic) acid.

For hours on end, alone and in despair, ER sat upon the stone benches, designed by Stanford White, to face that hooded robed figure and consider the lives of women. She felt connected to generations of Washington wives who had so much to contribute but who were so routinely ignored, belittled, and humiliated. In the quiet of that holly grove, ER moved beyond pain and suicide. She was thirty-five, and her five children ranged in age from three to thirteen. She did not want them to suffer the cold embrace of her own mother's legacy and was determined to move beyond her frozen gloom. Her mentors offered examples of courage, understanding, and strength. There were alternative roads to hope, love, and forgiveness. She would forgive, but she would never forget. On her desk ER kept a copy of the poem Cecil Spring-Rice had written about the bronze statue she visited repeatedly over the years. It was among her bedside papers at her death:

> O steadfast, deep, inexorable eyes
> Set look inscrutable, nor smile nor frown!
> O tranquil eyes that look so calmly down
> Upon a world of passion and of lies!

Restored by her contemplations of grief, ER forged with FDR one of history's most powerful and enduring partnerships. She understood his needs, forgave his transgressions, buried her jealousies, and embarked on her own independent career. She left the role of dutiful, submissive wife at the altar of *Grief* in Rock Creek Cemetery. She became an activist, journalist, radio commentator, and teacher, a woman with power who enjoyed manipulating power. FDR encouraged her independence and when he silenced her did so for reasons of state. Unfortunately, as World War II progressed, many reasons of state emerged—generally regarding issues of race and rescue about which ER cared profoundly, a primary theme of this volume.

Inspired by Marie Souvestre, ER became a great teacher and prolific writer, dedicated to continual learning and adventure. Indeed she identified herself as an adventurer. In 1960, she wrote:

> Learning and living. But they are really the same thing, aren't they? There is no experience from which you can't learn something. . . . And the purpose of life, after all, is to live it, to taste experience to the utmost, to reach out eagerly and without fear for newer and richer experience.
>
> You can do that only if you have curiosity, an unquenchable spirit of adventure. The experience can have meaning only if you understand it . . . if you have arrived at some knowledge of yourself, a knowledge based on a deliberately and usually painfully acquired self-discipline which teaches you to cast out fear and frees you for the fullest experience of the adventure of life.
>
> My own life has been crowded with activity and, best of all, with people. I have seen them wrest victory from defeat; I have seen them conquer fear and come out strong and free. . . .
>
> I honor the human race. When it faces life head-on, it can almost remake itself. . . . In the long run, we shape our lives and we shape ourselves. The process never ends until we die. And the choices we make are ultimately our own responsibility.

ER's life as an adventurer was enhanced by her partnership with FDR, and strengthened by her intimate circle of friends, who during the 1920s helped forge her public career and remained her primary and most trusted support network. Esther Lape, a scholar, activist, and director of the American Foundation who fought for the World Court, and her life partner, the international lawyer Elizabeth Read, were ER's mentors and lifelong confidantes. She trusted them, and her traveling companion and secretary Malvina "Tommy" Thompson, above all. Tommy, born in the

Bronx, a stenographer with a grand sense of humor, became ER's personal secretary in 1928. Dedicated to ER, she was brilliant, critical, perceptive, and fun to be with.

During the 1920s ER was intimate with Nancy Cook and Marion Dickerman. They worked together to build women's influence in the Democratic Party and created Val-Kill, where they lived. Cook ran the Val-Kill furniture factory and with Caroline O'Day purchased the Tod-hunter School for Girls, where Dickerman was headmistress and ER was associate principal and most popular teacher. ER was delighted by this friendship until it shattered bitterly in 1938. Tensions and jealousies had intensified as ER's circle widened. Cook and Dickerman despised Earl Miller, the state trooper whom FDR assigned to protect his "Lady" in 1929 and who became ER's great companion; and they could not stand the journalist Lorena Hickok, called "Hick," who was ER's primary companion after the 1932 election. Hick considered Cook and Dicker-man "self-absorbed snobs" and for years refused to visit ER at Val-Kill. In 1938 Nancy Cook verbally assaulted ER with her fantasy that she and Dickerman had "created" ER and were responsible for her public achieve-ments. Although her precise words are unknown, they wrecked the friendship. ER was devastated. The partnership that had sustained Val-Kill, which had once been filled with so much joy and creative energy, was now marked by an icy, emotionally empty divide. It was over. ER moved into what had been the furniture factory, remodeled so that Tommy and her beloved Henry Osthagen also had an apartment there. The school was sold; ER settled money on Cook and Dickerman and expected them to move, which they refused to do until 1947. For many years, toxic tensions at Val-Kill were all that remained of their once cre-ative friendship.

Disillusioned by her former friends, ER plunged into gloom. Frantic with worry, Tommy telephoned Esther Lape and Elizabeth Read to report that ER was depressed, had taken to her bed, refused to see anybody, and simply turned "her face to the wall." She slowly recovered as her steadies rallied around her. She returned to her work, grateful for her growing circle of friends, and moved on. Cook and Dickerman were invited to major events and family gatherings, but they remained beyond ER's emo-tional scope. Always correct and courteous, but forevermore cold and uninterested, every event for them was agony. Tommy wrote to ER's daughter, Anna, with relief that her mother's life "is so completely changed she does not need to depend on them for any companionship."

While she must have been aware of the jealousies that swirled around every aspect of her life and the rivalries that marked her many friendships, ER never overtly acknowledged them. There were tensions between Hick and Joe Lash; between Trude Pratt Lash and Elinor Morgenthau; and between Joe Lash and ER's last great friend, the physician Dr. David Gurewitsch. Unpleasant upsets erupted among her children, and eventually Tommy disparaged almost everybody. In correspondence with her only confidantes, Esther Lape and Elizabeth Read, Tommy was often privately critical. Once, when publicly critical, she wrote Trude with remorse about her irate words: certainly ER "has every right to invite anyone she wishes. I am a mean disagreeable old woman and can't seem to do anything to improve myself."

Happily, the live-in steadies of ER's court—Tommy, Earl Miller, and Hick, her core emotional team in New York and the White House—trusted one another and seemed harmonious whenever they were together. Although their roles were different, and their contributions to ER's heart and hearth varied, they each put ER's needs first and promoted her interests. Always the squire, Earl sought to protect his Lady from "chiselers and users." He personally vetted each new friend, every newcomer to ER's table.

Orphaned and homeless at twelve, a wild child of many gifts, Earl Miller had wandered about, a self-creation: boxer, gymnast, and circus acrobat. He played the piano and sang, much as her father had. The most attentive and generous companion of her middle years, he delighted ER. With him she was carefree and frolicsome. Physically, Earl reenergized ER, coached her tennis game, taught her to shoot rifles and pistols, and gave her a chestnut mare named Dot, who became her favorite horse, the one she rode every morning for many years.

He introduced her to his show business friends, especially the innovative dancer Mayris Chaney, called Tiny, who quickly entered ER's circle of intimates. In 1943, when ER moved into her Greenwich Village apartment on Washington Square, she refused John Golden's offer of a piano, noting that she preferred to have Earl's, "for purely sentimental reasons."

There is no doubt that he brought restorative elements—music and athletics—to ER's life, enhancing her joy in her leisure hours. But the scope of their relationship remains an ongoing mystery because their correspondence has disappeared—we have no diaries, memoirs, or letters for detail and nuance. There are rumors that a vast correspondence was purchased and then destroyed. In 1971 Joe Lash wrote that there were many ER letters to Earl "full of warmth and affection," but he wrote in 1982 that they "have disappeared."

The only other reference to this correspondence is in the 1947 divorce proceedings between Earl and his third wife, Simone Miller. After a packet of "endearing" letters was introduced and sealed by the court, Simone was awarded a considerable but undisclosed settlement and custody of their two children, Earl Jr., six, and Anna Eleanor, three. ER was godmother to both children but remained unnamed in the rather sensational divorce. On 13 January 1947 the New York *Daily News* columnist Ed Sullivan noted, "Navy Commander's wife will rock the country if she names the co-respondent in her divorce action!!!"

Whatever the boundaries of their relationship, it was lifelong—and the subject of controversy and jealousy among ER's closest friends.

As for Hick, early in their relationship, she and ER explored their feelings about romantic love and unbridled jealousy. "You are right," ER once wrote her. "There are only two ways to beat jealousy. One is not to love enough so as not to care if someone gives you less than you thought they might, the other is to love so much that you are happy in their happiness and have no more room for thoughts of yourself, but that is only possible to the old!"

By 1945, those words defined ER's feelings about FDR. She even forgave her mean-spirited cousin Laura (Polly) Delano for telling her about Lucy Mercer's many visits with FDR. ER's subsequent friendship with Polly, as revealed in William Turner Levy's celebration of ER, is rather a puzzle. Indeed, the contours and depths of many of ER's friendships remain incompletely known. She and Broadway producer John Golden met for lunch every week when ER was in New York. The financier Bernard Baruch was also one of her intimates and startled ER when he suggested they marry. She wrote Esther Lape, "Have you heard? Bernie has proposed marriage! Isn't that controlling!" History awaits a biography of Esther Lape, who devoted her life to movements for world peace and universal health care.

Joseph Lash, whom she met when he was an activist in the American

Youth Congress (AYC), also became a dear friend. He brought a keen intellect, vision, and passion to his relationship with ER, and their friendship deepened when he married Trude Pratt, whose many contributions to the first lady's activism during the war years remained long unacknowledged.* ER's deep interest in Trude and Joe Lash's romance was in part about love across barriers and divides and the ways they bridged religious and national differences. Their relationship enhanced ER's life, in many ways shaped her wartime efforts, and inspired her hopes for the future. During and after the war, ER and Trude worked together on projects for civil rights and human rights, and opposed discrimination in housing and segregation in the city's schools. Their friendship endured many changes and was framed by daily morning phone conversations, wherever both of them happened to be.

ER's quest for peace and justice expanded during the war years, 1939–1945, as she struggled to influence domestic and international policies, not merely as first lady but also as lobbyist, journalist, public critic, and activist power broker. Joseph Lash noted, during the 1984 centennial celebrations of her birth, that ER was "infinite"—and the impact of her work incalculable. "She went to great lengths to deny and conceal her influence," Lash said, partly to avoid charges of "petticoat rule" from political enemies and thereby protect her husband. While she was pleased when FDR adopted her words and ideas, she was aware that he never publicly acknowledged "her role in his life." She understood he needed her presence among the American people and abroad, where she became his goodwill ambassador for the United States and was beloved by so many.

However unacknowledged, history's most active and controversial first lady appreciated their partnership and was grateful for every opportunity actually to influence policy from a position of power. Although many have observed the tensions between them, which grew during the war, others observed their mutual reliance. ER's friend Justine Wise Polier emphasized the intensity of all they shared, their different observations, and fully

---

*A private person, Gertrud von Adam Wenzel Pratt Lash denied her courageous activities, including her efforts on behalf of refugees from Germany and her influence on ER, which enabled the Varian Fry rescue operation, until shortly before her death in 2004. Subsequently her son Dr. Peter Pratt encouraged me to go through ten boxes of papers Trude had carefully annotated. While some of the material appears in this book, one awaits a full biography.

explored disagreements. Polier was sometimes present at the White House dinners, or when FDR phoned his wife, and she observed their discussions during urgent crises. While they "both grew individually . . . in very different ways," they grew together "throughout their marriage." To the end, they confided in and trusted each other, even as they increasingly traveled separately.

ER was frequently hurt by FDR but remained loyal to his vision and respected his political acumen. They disagreed profoundly about strategies to end racial violence and segregation and also about efforts to rescue Europe's endangered refugees. Whenever she was silenced, she deferred to his judgment about what was politically needed and feasible. She was his conscience, and she knew it.

Chester Bowles, director of the Office of Price Administration during the war and subsequently a member of Congress from Connecticut and ambassador to India, was close to ER, whom she credited for his political career. Bowles agreed with Polier about the increasingly tense Roosevelt partnership but concluded that ER retained an enduring influence. ER told Bowles that when FDR traveled, she generally spoke to him on the telephone each morning: "I have learned by experience to recognize the point at which the President's patience is about to give out and he will begin to scold me. At that moment I hurriedly say Franklin, my car is waiting, I must be on my way, I shall call you again tomorrow."

Bowles believed the views and ideas of FDR's "remarkable wife" were found throughout his policies and speeches. ER, he wrote, "deserved a major share of credit for all that he succeeded in doing. She helped bring to the surface his compassion, his concern for people and for human dignity. . . . She brought the American people to him and encouraged him to give himself to the people."

ER was a proud card-carrying member of the Newspaper Guild. She brought union members, both rank-and-file and officers, into the White House to dine and to meet the president, and she encouraged them to use their meetings to lobby, agitate, and make their causes known. After one White House weekend, a notable unionist was interviewed. She recounted that she had awakened in the middle of the night, stunned by her surroundings: "Imagine me Feigele Shapiro, sleeping in Lincoln's bed."

ER's ties to her labor colleagues remained strong during the years on the scholarship committee of the Women's Trade Union League (WTUL).

Rose Schneiderman of the International Ladies' Garment Workers' Union (ILGWU) was "like a sister," according to the historian Brigid O'Farrell; ILGWU head David Dubinsky was a good friend, and United Auto Workers leader Walter Reuther was "like a beloved son."

ER believed union rights, civil rights, and human rights would help create a peaceful world defined by economic security, housing, health, and freedom for all humanity. She lived in service to these ideals. But today, seventy years after the end of World War II, as we embark on a new era of intensified racism and conflict, ER's vision remains embattled. To reconsider her efforts, to review what she considered at stake in our fight for liberty, dignity, and security, is to reignite hope and recall notable successes. Throughout the 1940s she helped young interned Japanese-Americans leave their camps to attend schools, colleges, and universities, and she worked for their right, women and men, to enlist in the military. On Easter Sunday 1943, after visits to the Gila River and other Japanese internment camps, she changed public opinion by her columns.

Throughout the war, ER agitated for black recruits and nurses in all services and for an end to the most discriminatory segregation practices—at public events, in officers' clubs and dining halls, and on public transportation. Her enthusiasm for the skills of the Tuskegee pilot Charles Alfred Anderson, with whom she flew, resulted in the successful training and deployment of more than 990 Tuskegee Airmen. Throughout the war she monitored the activities of the heroic black fighter pilots, who were finally sent into combat in April 1943 after she protested their prolonged idleness.*

ER also lobbied for the full participation of black and white women in the military. In 1944, when James Forrestal replaced Frank Knox as secretary of the navy, black women were finally accepted into the WAVES (Women Accepted for Volunteer Emergency Service). Two were selected for officer's training—ER's student activist friend Harriet Ida Pickens,

---

*According to the historian Gail Buckley, the first Tuskegee combat pilots, who comprised the heroic 99th Pursuit Squadron, named her mother Lena Horne "Queen of the 99th." In her splendid history, *American Patriots*, and in her family memoir, *The Hornes*, Buckley provides succinct details of their many exploits and awards, as well as vital statistics: "Black engineers built Burma's Ledo Road, China's Stilwell Road, and the Alcan Highway. . . . There were 165,000 black sailors (all messmen or stewards); 17,000 black marines, 5000 black Coast Guard, 4000 black WACs and WAVEs." Only the Merchant Marines were integrated.

daughter of NAACP officer William Pickens, and Hunter College graduate and social worker Frances Wills Thorpe.*

Thurgood Marshall, who became director of the NAACP's legal
defense fund in 1938 and shepherded the most significant integration
cases through the courts during the 1940s and 1950s, called ER "Lady
Big Heart." Appointed by Lyndon Baines Johnson to the Supreme Court,
Justice Marshall credited ER for the hope that sustained race activists
throughout the decades. He told his biographer, the diplomat-journalist
Carl Rowan, that "Eleanor Roosevelt did a lot; but her husband didn't do
a damn thing." She became "a great force for justice" and was "one dream
maker" who empowered Marshall and gave "the NAACP a reach that
exceeded the mean clutches of all the racists" who dominated U.S. politics and so limited FDR's efforts.

In 1957 Rowan sought to learn why Justice Marshall considered ER
"one of the greatest of dream makers." When he called her for an interview, she replied, "What a coincidence. I am this moment reading your
new book, *Go South to Sorrow*," and she invited him to her New York
apartment. The interview turned into a prolonged visit at Hyde Park,
during which she told Rowan the story of her childhood and of the legacy
of her many struggles. "All my life I have fought fear—physical fear, and
the fear of not being loved," she remarked candidly. Her privileged childhood offered prestige and money, but affluence did not "shield her from
the agony of watching her fathers and uncles drink themselves to death."
Unloved, dressed in ill-fitting "hand-me-down" clothes that her aunts
had discarded, young ER had known she was "different from the other
girls" and confided to Rowan: "I never lost a feeling of kinship for anyone
who is suffering." For ER, there were no inferior children; there were only
new pathways to love, education, and respect.

During his two-week visit, Rowan became mightily impressed with
ER. They spent many long evenings after dinner alone on the porch "listening to frogs croak from the lily pads of Val-Kill Creek," as ER shared
private and political confidences "openly and honestly." She said she never
had real differences with FDR "on racial and social reforms, but there was
conflict over timing. She always wanted to move faster than Franklin

*I am grateful to our Sag Harbor Initiative friend Bill Pickens, who shared his
grandmother's letters with me, including those from ER. See Thorpe, *Navy Blue*.

did." He insisted that "a democracy moves slowly," and he required the political support of Congress. He juggled but encouraged ER to say and do what she believed necessary.*

After FDR's death, when she represented the United States at the United Nations, she too juggled. Opposed by Dixiecrats and McCarthyites, limited by State Department restraints and Cold War tensions inflamed by aggressive Soviet propaganda, she seemed to follow FDR's political strategy precisely—and moved differently than she might have were she not in the government. Profoundly anti-Soviet, but condemned as a Communist by U.S. politicians, ER compromised. But her brilliant diplomacy resulted in the passage of the Universal Declaration of Human Rights on 10 December 1948. From that day to this, the declaration remains the single most important document of worldwide hope for peace and justice.

Subsequently, ER's activities for civil rights intensified. During her final meetings with northern student activists in 1961 and 1962, she encouraged boycotts and sit-ins, as well as demonstrations for integration. She advised, "Go South for Freedom."†

While ER's legacy regarding civil rights and human rights remains "infinite," this volume focuses on the infinitely controversial war years, 1939–45. To learn about her efforts, especially regarding race discrimination and the failure to rescue refugees in flight from Nazi horror, is only to intensify the controversies. ER's struggles regarding race and rescue enable us to understand history's slow, still ongoing movement toward international justice and human rights.

Debates over FDR's "indifference" to the Jewish slaughter will surely

---

*Rowan was moved and inspired by ER's memories. When he departed on 3 July 1957, she compared his visits to the "Man Who Came to Dinner"—Alexander Woollcott's prolonged residence at the White House—and said: "'I'm pleased that you stayed longer than Woollcott did.'" Carl Rowan left "Lady Great Heart" grateful and convinced that for "Thurgood Marshall and his cause, ER helped mightily to keep the dream alive." Rowan, *Dream Makers*, pp. 131–42.

†In 1961 I was Hunter College student council president and followed ER's advice. After she spoke at Roosevelt House, we organized two buses of student activists to participate in the extraordinary events under way in North Carolina. In 1962, when I was student affairs vice president of the National Student Association, I and my colleagues were again moved by her words—and vigorously supported the Student Non-Violent Coordinating Committee.

continue. Those who argue that FDR did "everything possible" are contradicted by ER's assertion that nobody did all they could have. In 1946 she visited displaced persons camps in Germany, and when she returned to the United States, she addressed the women's division of the United Jewish Appeal: "We let our consciences realize too late the need of standing up against something that we knew was wrong. We have therefore had to avenge it—but we did nothing to prevent it. I hope that in the future, we . . . remember that there can be no compromise . . . with the things we know are wrong."

In 2003, Arthur Schlesinger suggested that he and I meet for dinner to discuss, as he put it, "our differences" regarding FDR, which had been aired mostly at the Graduate Center for several years. After a cordial evening, during which we agreed about all contemporary issues, our final exchange was illuminating. I said, "I know what ER proposed and FDR rejected. How can you argue that FDR did everything 'possible' to rescue and save the perishing?" Schlesinger answered by pointing to the politics of FDR's position: U.S. anti-Semitism. Look at the numbers, he said. Thirty percent of the U.S. population was German-American; the Democratic Party was Irish, Italian, and southern. There was no congressional support to save the Jews, no movement to save them, and intense division among Jewish leaders—many of whom remained silent throughout. Silence. Denial. Complicity.

Our understanding of the U.S.-British failure is complicated by ER's silence regarding Eleanor Rathbone's parliamentary efforts to "rescue the perishing"—despite the fact that ER's friend Lady Stella Reading was a member of Rathbone's committee. The full story remains to be told.

Subsequently, ER became an optimistic Zionist. She visited Israel three times, accompanied by David Gurewitsch, Ruth Gruber, and Trude Pratt Lash. She was concerned about Jewish refugees languishing in displaced persons camps mostly in Germany, as well as about Palestinian refugees newly removed from their homes who languished in camps mostly in Jordan, Lebanon, and Syria, under conditions ER pronounced entirely unacceptable. She saw why violence had escalated as it did in the 1948 war but tended to absolve Israel for the Nakba, the flight or removal of 800,000 Palestinian refugees. "The truth is the Arab authorities are to a large extent responsible for this wholesale flight. Mass evacuation was apparently a part of their strategy," to be followed by a quick victory of the Arab armies and restoration of all property. ER concluded that responsibility "must be shared" by all parties, including the British, and that to avoid endless war throughout the region, all parties must pursue peace—repatriation or resettlement—through UN negotiations.

Because in war there are no final victories, and every war sows the seeds for the next, ER's vision for a permanent just peace is urgently needed now. She brought to the United Nations two convictions: that humanity was connected now as never before, and that liberal democracy was essential to humanity's survival. As FDR said in 1940, "We will have a liberal democracy, or we will return to the Dark Ages." In 1943, she concluded the time had come for "world thinking" to ensure a postwar economy of creativity, education, abundance, and full employment. It was a theme that she had expressed vigorously since 1934 and now brought to the world stage for global impact.

> To deny any part of a population the opportunities for more enjoyment in life, for higher aspirations is a menace to the nation as a whole. There has been too much concentrating wealth, and even if it means that some of us have got to learn to be a little more unselfish about sharing what we have . . . , we must realize that it will profit us all in the long run. . . . I think the day of selfishness is over; the day of really working together has come . . . all of us, regardless of race or creed or color. We must wipe out any feeling . . . of intolerance, of belief that any one group can go ahead alone. We all go ahead together, or we go down together.

Today, as poverty, inequality, and neoslavery return across the United States, as women and children are condemned to bondage and refugees are in flight worldwide, ER's words are urgently needed. Her prescience can serve to embolden U.S. politicians finally to discuss and ratify the Economic and Social Rights Covenant of the Universal Declaration of Human Rights, and the inspiration of her life can be a guide for healing and restorative movements worldwide.

Chapter One

"We All Go Ahead Together, or We All Go Down Together"

The events of 1938 had left ER's world, all that she cared about personally and politically, in disarray. Now on every front, 1939 ushered in a dangerous and frightening reality. She began the year with the clear recognition that the times called for fortitude and boldness.

At home, things continued to spiral downward. Over ten million Americans were still unemployed, farm prices were low, and recession conditions prevailed, yet every domestic program the Roosevelts supported had come under vicious attack. It seemed to ER and her allies that America "had become 'bored with the poor, the unemployed, the insecure.'"

Indeed, congressional opposition to New Deal reforms had intensified. FDR's effort to purge conservative Democrats during the 1938 midterm elections, especially in the South, had backfired as anti–New Deal Democrats and Republicans won major victories. There were now 13 new Republican governors, 8 new Republican senators, and 81 new Republican congresspeople (up from 88 to 170), representing the first significant GOP gains in ten years. Although Democrats maintained a two-thirds majority in the Senate and a significant congressional majority, they were severely divided among themselves. Fortified by the election of right-wing politicians, members of both parties declared war on FDR, his progressive vision, and the very idea of a permanent New Deal. ER became the obsessive focus of vitriolic commentary, especially concerning her support for civil rights, racial justice, working women, and radical youth.

Internationally, global peace was endangered as fascists triumphed in Europe. Brutal dictators led by "the mad dog of Europe," as Adolf Hitler was increasingly known, orchestrated war, war everywhere. In Spain, General Francisco Franco's forces, aided in part by the Anglo-American arms embargo, were in ascendance over the Loyalists. In Munich in September 1938, British and French appeasers sought to ensure "peace in our

time" by sacrificing democratic Czechoslovakia to Hitler's demands. The
United States was becoming more isolationist, yet FDR was certain that
catastrophe was imminent.

But life went on during the December 1938 holidays as the White
House filled with children, grandchildren, and extended family. A rare
debutante party for ER's eldest niece, her brother Hall's daughter Eleanor
(known to history as Eleanor Roosevelt II), was scheduled for two days
after Christmas.

For this first White House debutante dance since Helen Taft's party
in 1910, ER planned a festive occasion. ER was delighted to celebrate her
niece, in part to atone for having suddenly recalled her from Paris in
October. ER II had begun a year of study abroad, but due to FDR's fears
of impending crisis in Europe, her aunt and uncle had "ordered" her
home. Deeply disappointed, nineteen-year-old Eleanor had returned to
the home of her mother, Margaret Richardson Roosevelt Cutter, in Dedham, Massachusetts. But when Eleanor offered to host her coming-out
ball, joy returned. In Washington, surrounded by cousins (Roosevelts,
Delanos, Alsops), the children of cabinet members, and her two brothers,
Henry and Daniel, ER II, charming and elegant in an "all white ruffled
frock of French organdy," was escorted to the "sparkling east ballroom"
by her father and her aunt. As Benny Goodman's band played, "Aunt
Eleanor danced with my father. They were a striking pair, both of them
tall and good dancers." It was "all very thrilling and wonderful."

ER was subsequently annoyed to learn that Charles Graves, a British
journalist, had attended the party under false pretenses. A guest of her
unsuspecting godmother, cousin Susie Parish, he wrote a derisive account
of the event for the *Washington Post*. In a harsh letter to Graves, ER noted
that it had been a private party, as he certainly had known. His intrusive,
rude behavior might seem a trifle, but it gave U.S. journalists "a feeling of
injustice that I would allow you to come as a reporter, which, of course,
was not my intention, when they were barred."

ER was particularly upset about the episode, she explained, because it
endangered friendly U.S. feelings "toward England and the English people." Indeed, ER and FDR were eager to improve U.S. public opinion
regarding the United Kingdom and had worked together for months on
arrangements for an unprecedented royal visit in June. The very week ER
wrote her letter of reproach to Graves, the president had sent a letter to

King George VI detailing various outings he thought the royals might enjoy. The Roosevelts were determined to create a new climate of friendship and support, especially in the face of recent Gallup polls indicating that over 70 percent of Americans disapproved of any economic or military aid to Great Britain.

ER planned an intimate New Year's Eve that featured a Gary Cooper western. Before dinner, she wrote a New Year's Day message on youth and democracy addressed to the United States and the world. "I hope adults everywhere, particularly women, will emphasize the value of the contribution which youth can make" to help solve the "problems of all nations." She called for "all assistance possible" to help young people work for "the value of democracy," which depended on the commitment of "every individual to take an active part in his government."

After dinner ER II chose to watch the western with her aunt and uncle while her contemporaries went out to party. At 11:45 the household gathered in the Oval Office, where a dozen stemmed glasses awaited FDR's daiquiri cocktails. ER II described the scene: "Aunt Eleanor proposed the first toast—'To the United States of America, [may] our union promote peace and freedom on the earth.' After we 'drank to her heartfelt wish,' she raised her glass again: 'To the president of the United States. May he remain in good health, and may God help him to lead this nation forward, as it is his wish to do, into better times for every citizen, young or old, of every color or faith, male or female, as our democracy struggles to establish a democratic way of life throughout the earth.'" There followed an hour of lively conversation and toasts to "absent family and friends."

For ER, the evening was marred by a serious security breach when two brazen sixteen-year-olds, one disguised as a girl, and pretending to be invited guests, sauntered into the family's private quarters, accompanied by the doorman. When he announced the girl as Joan, Henry Morgenthau's daughter, who was expected, ER demanded to know the truth. The two boys had broken in on a dare, for an autograph. But ER was horrified by their complete lack of consideration and frightened for her husband, so vulnerable in his wheelchair. "They came up the back stairs" to FDR's study, she told her press conference. "I never saw such nerve."

Sara Delano Roosevelt, FDR's mother, had been at the White House since before Christmas and intended to stay for another week, for the christening of her newest great-grandson, FDR III. While ER had been happy to ride her horse each morning and festivities had gone on apace, the household was so filled that there had been considerable tension. SDR particularly disapproved of Hall and was routinely rude to his children. ER looked forward to getting away to New York for diversion and a brief respite.

Her "flying trip" to New York on 2 January turned out to be unusually trying. Cousin Susie, once her close confidante, had suffered for years from various maladies, exacerbated by an addiction to painkillers and antidepressants; ER found her company tedious. And the Broadway play she had looked forward to seeing—*Oscar Wilde*, with Robert Morley in the title role—disturbed her profoundly. "I said I would tell you something about the play which I went to see with our two youngest sons and their wives," she wrote in *My Day*. "It was beautifully cast and beautifully acted, but . . . to me his story is unpleasant and the end was tragic. . . . Since I am not obliged to know him as an individual, I think I would rather forget him and enjoy only what he has left us in literature, which can be enjoyed and leaves no bad taste behind."

In New York she stayed at the apartment she had rented since 1935, a private refuge from her public life as first lady. The third-floor walk-up was in the Greenwich Village townhouse of life partners Esther Lape and Elizabeth Read, her political mentors and advisers. While in her Manhattan hideaway, ER was stunned to learn that Bill Dana, owner of Hick's beloved sanctuary, the Little House, in Mastic, had died suddenly of a heart attack. He was only forty-five and had seemed in robust health. Everybody who knew him was devastated. ER sent her best thoughts to Hick: "Bill was so fond of you that I know what this means to you personally aside from your sympathy for Ella & the complications which may arise about the place," a reference to his widow Ella Dana's possible need to rent out the big house, which would render Hick's future in the Little House uncertain.

As for her own household complications, ER wrote Hick, "I'm playing a rather mean trick tonight, pleaded a headache and sent Mama [FDR's mother, SDR] down to sit as hostess at the Diplomatic dinner! She told everyone at lunch today how much she disliked having to sit so far down the table so I thought this was a good way to put her at the top & I've had one and a half hours of sleep so I'll really be able to enjoy the music for a change!"

Besides ER's concerns about FDR, who looked older "this winter & seems to me to mind the social things more," her former boon companion and bodyguard Earl Miller had been sick, she wrote to her daughter Anna, bringing fresh anxiety.

Politically, she had one good thing to report: on 21 January the Supreme Court upheld the constitutionality of the Tennessee Valley Authority (TVA), which "made Pa very cheerful this morning." But that good news was overshadowed by the Senate's cut in funding for the WPA, the New Deal's most useful Works Progress Administration. FDR lost by one vote, and ER believed Vice President John Nance Garner, who had presidential ambitions for 1940, was responsible. She wished WPA supporters, and all the writers, artists, and unionists involved in it, "would demonstrate at the Capitol but they won't, they will write to me & I won't be able to do much from now on."

Internationally, on 26 January 1939, General Francisco Franco took Barcelona and moved on to Madrid. The fascist onslaught in Spain involved appalling casualties. Mussolini sent 100,000 Italian troops to support Franco, and the Nazis tested every new plane in their arsenal against the Loyalists. The bombing raids were merciless. Pablo Neruda, Chilean consul and poet, wrote from Madrid, "And through the streets the blood of children flowed / Simply, like the blood of children." ER wrote Anna, "Father is very gloomy. . . . He thinks Spain lost to Franco which means Hitler-Mussolini domination & then he thinks gradual infiltration into South America & inevitable closing in on us. He thinks England and France go this spring. It is not cheerful." ER's secretary, Malvina "Tommy" Thompson, also wrote Anna, "At the moment your mother is hoarse explaining that she cannot lift the embargo on Spain, and has nothing to do with the WPA cuts."

ER tried to cheer herself up by experimenting with new hairstyles: "I bobbed my hair yesterday & learned how to use make up . . . & find it a great care & time consumer!" But even such inconsequential private decisions offered her critics ammunition. When the press first reported that ER used lipstick, "at the insistence of her daughter," for example, religious fanatics and the Roman Catholic Church slandered her viciously, accusing her of leading adolescent girls ("hot bloods") astray. Such issues became ever more the stuff of controversy as religious fundamentalists attacked her for her commitment to women's rights, especially women's rights to work and to receive birth control information.

As ER confronted each petty and large disturbance of heart and hearth, domestic and global, she was encouraged by one dominant fact: FDR was in a fighting mood. Her husband's renewed vigor delighted her. He had made up his mind to demand significant changes in U.S. policy and spent every available minute during the holidays writing what he had determined would be one of the most important speeches of his presidency. When he read his wife various drafts, ER, his best critic, usually wanted more, but this time they were in accord.

FDR's sixth State of the Union, delivered to Congress on the morning of 4 January, sent a prescient warning to the nation. America could not possibly sail alone, aloof and uninvolved, through the world's turbulent waters.

FDR described his concept of the role of religion in public life more specifically than ever before. Religion was "the source" of democracy and the guarantor of international good faith. "Religion, by teaching man his relationship to God, gives the individual a sense of his own dignity and teaches him to respect himself by respecting his neighbors. Democracy, the practice of self-government, is a covenant among free men to respect the rights and liberties of their fellows. International good faith, a sister of democracy, springs from the will of civilized nations . . . to respect the rights and liberties of other nations." Modern civilization depended upon and required all three.

> Where freedom of religion has been attacked, the attack has come from sources opposed to democracy. Where democracy has been overthrown, the spirit of free worship has disappeared. And where religion and democracy have vanished, good faith and reason in international affairs have given way to strident ambition and brute force.

FDR went on to make two specific demands: for immediate military preparedness in the face of lawless aggression, and for changes in the 1935 Neutrality Act, which he had initially championed. ER had consistently opposed the act because its arms embargo clause served to support Germany, Japan, and Italy. The connectedness of all people in time of war was a theme she had been insisting upon in private letters and in her public writings for many years. On 5 April 1938 she had written, "Of course the trouble is that most people in this country think that we can stay out of wars in other parts of the world. Even if we stay out of it and save our own skins, we cannot escape the conditions which will undoubtedly exist in other parts of the world and which will react against us. . . . The best we can do is to realize nobody can save his own skin alone. We must all hang together."

Now in his 1939 State of the Union, FDR acknowledged that "our neutrality laws may operate unevenly and unfairly—may actually give aid to an aggressor and deny it to the victim. The instinct for self-preservation should warn us that we ought not to let that happen anymore." His concept of preparedness went beyond rearmament to include national unity and the development of every sector of the economy. The New Deal, "our program of social and economic reform," was "part of defense, as basic as armaments themselves." He promoted a conservation movement for "land, water power, forests"; he invoked the continuing need to "provide food, shelter, and medical care for the health of our population" and "new opportunities for work and education" for youth; and he called for a commitment to sustain "our obligation to the aged, the helpless, and the needy"—all of which were integral to our strength and "common destiny." "Above all," he asserted, the people of the nation needed to come together, so that "differences of occupation, geography, race, and religion no longer obscure the nation's fundamental unity in thought and action."

FDR wanted to expand Social Security and create better health security measures. He wanted a permanent Civilian Conservation Corps and public works programs. The race to "make democracy work" required yet more federal spending. But to "balance the budget" he wanted to cut federal spending by one-third. At that point the Republicans in the audience, hitherto silent and stony-faced, broke into enthusiastic applause. Smiling grimly, the president acknowledged this outburst and concluded with the words of Abraham Lincoln: "This generation will nobly save or meanly lose the last best hope of earth. . . . The way is plain, peaceful, generous, just—a way which if followed the world will forever applaud and God must forever bless!"

In her column, which she evidently wrote immediately upon returning from the Capitol, ER assessed FDR's historic address from the point of view of his enemies. Seated in the executive gallery, she had observed "a solid block of people beneath us who were opposed on general grounds" to everything FDR might say. Occasionally one or another nodded in agreement to the truth of a statement. But they were so determined to maintain their silence that, with one exception, they refrained from applause even when they were in agreement. "When it ended, I doubt if anyone in the room remained entirely cold."

Her husband's words about democracy in an era of mounting Communism and fascism generated a national conversation that ER joined. She told her regular press conference, "There can be no real democracy unless there are three basic things. 1. Economic security sufficient to give at least some minimum to make living worthwhile. 2. Sufficient education to understand the problems before the country and to help solve them. 3. The sources of information must be free—press, radio, movies." To remain free, she insisted, "we have to watch other factors . . . such as bankers, subscribers and advertisers. They have to be watched by the people as carefully as government is watched."

At that press conference, ER was asked her opinion of George Gallup's polls, since in the most recent one she had achieved a higher approval rate than FDR (68 to 51 percent). "Where you have no official position and no responsibility," she replied, "it is much easier to be popular." But she hated "to see us put so much trust in polls. After all, they don't represent reasoned thought, and we may be influenced in our thinking by what is said in a poll."

She did, however, enjoy one poll taken by members of the Dining Car Employees Union, which named her "the most generous tipper among women riders on the country's railroads." According to the *New York Times*, women generally tipped "much less" than men, but ER redeemed her sex. She was, the *Times* headlined, "a Leader in Tipping."

Shortly after his State of the Union, FDR made a momentous telephone call to his friend and mentor, Harvard Law School professor Felix Frankfurter, with the news that he intended to name him to the Supreme Court, to replace Justice Benjamin Cardozo. Stunned, Frankfurter whispered that he wished his "mother had been alive to see this day."

Justice Cardozo had died in July 1938, thereby vacating the "scholar's seat" that had previously belonged to Justice Oliver Wendell Holmes. For six months legal scholars and New Dealers had been lobbying FDR on behalf of Frankfurter. But FDR had resisted, intending to name instead a legal scholar from the West in order to achieve geographic balance on the

Court. He did favor putting Frankfurter on the Court eventually but planned to wait until after Justice Louis Brandeis retired so there would not be two Jews on the Court at the same time. It is unclear why, after six months of inaction, he changed his mind.

The rising anti-Jewish feeling may have bolstered his decision. Several years earlier Sam Rosenman—FDR's counsel, chief speechwriter, and editor of his presidential papers—and his wife, Dorothy, had initially declined to join FDR on his 1936 campaign for fear that "two Jews on the train," as it went through the Bible Belt, would inflame opposition, but FDR had replied, "That's no way to handle anti-Semitism. The way to handle it is to meet it head-on." Sam and Dorothy Rosenman had joined the train.

The pressure against Frankfurter was great. Senator Patrick McCarran (D-NV) launched a crude anti-Semitic campaign against him, while delegations of prominent Jews descended on him to demand that he refuse the nomination, worrying that it would intensify anti-Jewish feeling in the United States. He replied, "So you would create your own ghetto!"

The three days of confirmation hearings degenerated into an anti-Semitic circus filled with "witnesses" who decried the impending loss of Christian America. Dean Acheson, Frankfurter's former student who accompanied him throughout the hearings, observed that all the witnesses "were fanatical and some were very definitely mental cases." Senator McCarran's "vicious mis-representation of Felix's views and undisguised anti-Semitism" were sheer spectacle, since McCarran was determined to paint Frankfurter as "a dangerous radical, if not a Communist." The committee chair, Senator Matthew Neely (D-WV), asked Frankfurter point-blank whether he had ever enrolled in the Communist Party. The candidate replied forcefully, "I have never been enrolled and have never been qualified to be enrolled, because that does not represent my view of life, nor my view of government."

With that, the hearings were over. The gavel banged down, and a great roar of approval came from the crowded room. Frankfurter's appointment to the Supreme Court was approved unanimously that day.

The ugliness of the hearings might have served as a warning of things to come. But initially FDR's circle was relieved, and Frankfurter's friends were ecstatic. Although ER never particularly liked or trusted Frankfurter, she approved of FDR's appointment of him as a stand against bigotry, so dangerously on the march throughout Europe and the United States.

Indeed, the outspoken Frankfurter had been a prescient opponent of fascism. His words had been useful as ER and the leadership of the American Friends Service Committee (AFSC) struggled to generate concern about victims of fascism and especially about the fate of refugees from Germany, Austria, and Spain. In 1933 and 1934 he had written to FDR from Oxford and Palestine, warning of looming horrors. "That things should be happening . . . in the land of Goethe, Schiller, Lessing, Kant and Beethoven requires a complete re-orientation of one's sense of reality as well as one's historical sense." He worked ardently for refugee sanctuary within the United States and in Palestine, and also battled the rising tide of anti-Semitism in American universities, including Harvard Law School, where his own dean, Roscoe Pound, was a Nazi apologist who argued that Hitler "was saving central Europe from 'agitators.'"

On the refugee issue, ER and her allies in and out of government— notably Caroline O'Day, New York's member of Congress at large, and Secretary of Labor Frances Perkins—were particularly hopeful about the passage of the Wagner-Rogers bill. Introduced on 9 February 1939 by Senator Robert F. Wagner Jr. (D-NY), and Congresswoman Edith Nourse Rogers (R-MA). The bill proposed to admit twenty thousand German refugee children under the age of fourteen over and above the official German quota. A wide array of bipartisan supporters, ranging from Herbert Hoover, Alfred Landon, and George William Cardinal Mundelein to AFL-CIO labor leaders, endorsed the bill. The AFSC, chaired by Clarence Pickett, agreed to supervise the children's travel and their adoption. Within days of the bill's introduction, forty thousand families of all faiths volunteered to adopt the children.

For the first time, ER endorsed a piece of pending legislation at her press conference. When asked for her views on the Wagner-Rogers bill, she replied, "with permission to quote," that she hoped it passed. "I think it is a wise way to do a humanitarian act. Other nations take their share of the child refugees, and it seems a fair thing to do."

But public opinion and many government officials were hostile to allowing more refugees into the country. Opinion polls in 1939 revealed that 94 percent of Americans disapproved of Nazi policies regarding Jews, and 97 percent disapproved of Nazi policies regarding Catholics, yet 83 percent wanted nothing done to assist them.

To ER's chagrin, FDR did and said nothing to change public opinion. When she argued that he might perhaps exercise his executive leadership to save some children who were already guaranteed homes, he replied that to do so would jeopardize other programs. On 28 February the first lady explained to her friend, the family court judge Justine Wise Polier, that FDR did not object to her supporting the bill but also did not want her to get involved "at the present time."

Interior Secretary Harold Ickes, Frances Perkins, Francis Biddle, and ER spoke earnestly and often in support of the Wagner-Rogers bill, but within the administration some vigorously opposed it. FDR's cousin Laura Delano Houghteling, Uncle Fred Delano's daughter and the wife of James Lawrence Houghteling, commissioner of immigration and naturalization, had told Assistant Secretary of State Jay Pierrepont Moffat at a cocktail party that the trouble with the Wagner-Rogers bill was that twenty thousand "charming children" all too quickly "grow into 20,000 ugly adults." Moffat, friends with FDR since Groton and Harvard, agreed with her.

Although it is unclear to what extent Laura Delano Houghteling's views represented her family's feelings, FDR's State Department was clearly dominated by a toxic mix of isolationist, appeasing, and anti-Semitic sentiments. Moffat, of the Division for European Affairs (1933–40), had consistently opposed sanctions against Germany and argued for business as usual with Hitler. In 1934, when Harvard's president James Conant withdrew an invitation to Nazi official Ernst Hanfstaengl, who was to have been honored at the commencement, Moffat had objected, saying that good Cambridge fellows ought to resist the pressure of "all the Jews in Christendom [who] arose in protest." Moffat was consistent. When posted to Warsaw, where he met the Soviet foreign minister Maxim Litvinov, he reported that Litvinov had "the malevolent look of an untidy Jew."

U.S. ambassador to France William Bullitt, presumed in some circles to be in part Jewish, had a long history of making anti-Semitic outbursts. His correspondence with FDR and his colleagues continued to be sprinkled with comments about Jews, often unsubstantiated and generally "poisonous" in tone.

In Congress, sixty anti-alien bills had recently been introduced to

further limit the immigration quotas established in 1924. One bill sought
to end immigration entirely for the next ten years. Meanwhile the White
House held its fourth conference on the needs of children, which cast a
spotlight on dreadful Depression conditions that persisted throughout
the United States. Both ER and FDR hoped the conference would build
support for federal aid to education and for expanding school health programs. FDR said lectures on nutrition meant nothing unless good food
was available for compulsory school attendance. Agriculture Secretary
Henry Wallace challenged the growing enthusiasm for eugenics, lament-
ing the tendency "to condemn whole groups of people as unworthy." IQ
was not about "the blood stream by economic status." ER condemned
sectional and racial inequalities and insisted that "with the country growing so close together by the development of transportation and communication, the people can no longer afford to be sectional." She agreed
entirely with Frank Graham's enduring message, presented to over five
hundred of the nation's leading educators and social workers: "We do not
have a democracy in America when we put $220 in one child's education
annually, and less than $20 in another child's." Federal aid to education
would ensure equality of educational opportunity.

But conservative politicians, formerly willing to ignore issues of poverty, now emphasized the needs of American children as never before,
under a new political banner: America First. According to Senator Robert
Reynolds (D-NC):

> America's children are America's responsibility, and refugee children
> in Europe are Europe's responsibility. . . . Here are the grim facts:
> Every State . . . has a tremendous number of children in want. . . .
> Millions of starving, halfnaked children of 8,000,000 tenant
> farmers, scattered throughout all parts of the US, live in hovels. Their
> tumble-down shacks have no windows. They sleep on rags. . . . They
> have no medical care. . . . They are unschooled.
> Shall we first take care of our own children, or shall we bestow
> our charity on children imported from abroad?

Reynolds and other conservative politicians now used the economic
problems facing America as a pretext for vehement opposition to the
acceptance of more refugees, who were "coming in ship after ship, and

finding employment," and causing Americans to lose their jobs. The fact that the Wagner-Rogers bill concerned children younger than fourteen did not matter to these new isolationists, who said that with 600,000 young Americans already facing a jobless future, there were too many refugees in this country.

Congressman Jacob Thorkelson (R-MT) represented yet another congressional tendency. An anti-Semitic bigot, he simply despised the new refugees. To his mind, they were internationalists, Communists, money changers, and grotesqueries. He celebrated Germany because it had "discovered the insidious wiles" of these people. "In the US, the same crowd [Jew-Communists], filled with hatreds, has organized over a thousand anti-Nazi leagues. . . . They do not seem to consider that 120,000,000 Gentiles or Christian Americans may not agree with them." His arguments and those of other members of Congress reflected the profound and growing fascist sentiment within the United States.

The atmosphere during the debate on the Wagner-Rogers bill remained unchanged by international events. On 15 March 1939 Hitler invaded Prague and took over Czechoslovakia, whereupon refugees streamed out of that once-democratic country and joined the Spanish, German, and Austrian refugees seeking asylum.

All this time, despite ER's best public and private efforts, FDR said not one word about Wagner-Rogers. Various entertainers and public figures campaigned for it, particularly Helen Hayes and Eddie Cantor, but their efforts met with little response. Cantor made a personal appeal to the president via his secretary Marvin McIntyre. McIntyre replied that even those who were most sympathetic to the bill shared "a general feeling" that it would "be inadvisable" to try to increase quotas or change our immigration policies at that moment. "There is a very real feeling that if this question is too prominently raised in the Congress during the present session we might get more restrictive rather than more liberal laws and practices."

In June, Congresswoman Caroline O'Day sent FDR a memo demanding to know his position on Wagner-Rogers. O'Day was not only FDR's friend and most loyal supporter in Congress but ER's closest friend in Washington—one of the four partners with whom she had co-owned Val-Kill and Todhunter School in the 1920s. But FDR failed to answer O'Day and wrote on her memo, "File, No Action." She walked into FDR's

study one day and demanded to know the reason for his continuing
silence about the children's refugee bill. FDR replied, "They are not
our Jews."

The Wagner-Rogers bill was amended to prioritize the children but
count them fully as refugee quota numbers.* At that point Wagner withdrew it, announcing in June that he preferred "to have no bill at all."

ER's efforts on behalf of refugees were not limited to children; she sought
protection for all the victims of Hitler. She worked closely with journalist
Dorothy Thompson and Nobel Prize–winning novelist Pearl Buck, who
were active with the American Committee for Christian German Refugees and the Non-Sectarian Committee for German Refugee Children,
and responded to all their requests for assistance. On 24 January 1939,
when Thompson was honored for her championship of refugees at a fundraising banquet hosted by Albert Einstein, Carrie Chapman Catt, and
Henry Sloane Coffin, ER sent a message of profound gratitude for her
"courage and zeal." Pearl Buck concluded the event by noting, "In Germany the Jew is merely a symbol, and when he is gone the attack will
continue against all who dissent."

ER believed that the inclination toward appeasement among democrats in France, England, and the United States had endured with such
vigor for so long because Hitler promised to wipe out Communists first.
Not until Kristallnacht in November 1938 was there more widespread
opposition to Nazi atrocities. Even Hitler's takeover of Czechoslovakia on
15 March 1939 met with virtually no State Department opposition.
Within days, thousands of Czechs were imprisoned or transferred to Germany to perform forced labor. Universities were closed, anti-Jewish
Nuremberg Laws were imposed. Jews were disenfranchised, their businesses were confiscated, and Czech culture was suppressed.

Everything that had been done at Versailles allegedly to limit German
militarism was now being undone, yet few believed that opposing Hitler
was worth another world war. ER had long argued that the World Court

---

*Even within the rigid quotas established in 1924, fully 1,250,000 slots remained
unfilled between 1933 and 1943. On the Wagner-Rogers bill and the protracted
committee hearings, see Wyman, *Paper Walls,* pp. 75–98.

should condemn war as murder, but that was between 1924 and 1935, when there was still hope that the United States might join the Court, and when she still imagined the Court and the League of Nations would be able to maintain peace.

By 1939 she was convinced that war was imminent. Still, domestic support even for an economic blockade that could limit German military might was virtually nil. To build up an opposition, ER worked to promote respect for those groups that Nazis and fascists condemned and degraded—Jews, unionists, and political women dedicated to social reform. Hitler's categories of people whose lives were "not worth living," whom he labeled "useless eaters," included "single infertile women" and a range of handicapped or imperfect people.

ER focused some of her first efforts on the group that included her husband—victims of polio and other disabling diseases. The March of Dimes, a new charity founded by Eddie Cantor, sought to inspire a nationwide door-to-door campaign on behalf of handicapped children. It urged every American to donate ten cents to "fight infantile paralysis." On 30 January, in a moving radio address in honor of FDR's fifty-seventh birthday, ER praised the opportunities provided for "afflicted" children and adults at Warm Springs, and pointed to the need for other "havens of refuge and rehabilitation." They were "a source of healing for crippled bodies; a veritable fountain of courage and hope," places where youngsters might be taught "to dance on crutches" and play in orchestras. Young musicians, encouraged by their love of music, performed well and happily there and "become entirely unaware of their handicaps. . . . It is as important to mend spirits as to mend bodies." She enlisted for the crusade her close allies on all issues of justice: Edith Nourse Rogers, Mary Margaret McBride (known to radio fans as Martha Deane), Cornelia (Leila) Bryce Pinchot, wife of Gifford Pinchot, the conservationist and former governor of Pennsylvania, and other notables.

ER became ever more outspoken in her support for a federal anti-lynching law. Efforts to pass such a bill had had a long history. For generations, southern women led by black journalist Ida B. Wells had called for protection against white mob violence. Between 1882 and 1933, sixty-one anti-lynching bills had been introduced into Congress. During FDR's first administration, the NAACP had championed an anti-lynching bill co-sponsored by Senators Robert Wagner and Edward Costigan (D-CO).

ER had asked for FDR's support, but he would say nothing on its behalf. Southern Democrats with seniority controlled the Senate and had threatened a filibuster that would block all New Deal efforts. FDR believed that the success of his programs depended on placating the old-line southerners. The Wagner-Costigan bill died. From 1934 to 1940, 130 more anti-lynching bills were introduced, and every effort was resisted.

ER understood the power of the forces lined up against passage of an anti-lynching bill, but she refused to be silent. On 13 January 1939, at the National Conference on Problems of the Negro and Negro Youth, she took questions on the current bill "on the clear understanding that I am speaking for myself, as an individual, and in no other sense." The bill should be passed, she said, "as soon as possible." It was the first time she had clearly announced her position. In these perilous times, it would be "a gesture, it would be a step in the right direction. . . . It would put us on record against something we should certainly, all of us, anywhere in this country, be against." Clearly she agreed with Walter White of the NAACP that the United States could no longer stand before the world and "lecture other countries without being derided as hypocrites unless we first put our own house in order." America's ongoing refusal to ensure even the most basic civil right—the freedom from legally sanctioned murder—for black Americans provided the country's enemies with a considerable propaganda weapon. And in 1939 White called FDR's silence the "greatest single handicap" against the bill.

In February ER resigned from the Daughters of the American Revolution (DAR) because her continued membership might seem to signify agreement with "a policy of which she disapproved," as the *Times* reported.*

In January, V. D. Johnston, treasurer of Howard University, had applied to the DAR for use of Constitution Hall, a four-thousand-seat

---

*ER had joined the DAR in April 1933, after the organization requested that she do so when she became first lady. She became life member "National Number 281,200" on the basis of a long list of revolutionary ancestors, only six of whom would have been considered sufficient: Jacob Roosevelt, captain; Jacobus J. Roosevelt, soldier in Commissary Department; Cornelius Van Schaack, major, Albany County Militia; Daniel Stewart, soldier, Georgia troops; Thomas Potts, deputy to Provincial Congress; Archibald Bullock, president and commander in chief of Georgia, 1776–77. *New York Times*, 21 April 1933. Since 1933 ER had invited the DAR leadership to tea at the White House annually.

auditorium that the DAR owned tax-free; it was the largest concert space in Washington. Marian Anderson, a world-famous contralto whom renowned conductor Arturo Toscanini had called "the voice of the century," had returned from her annual tour of European capitals and hoped to perform there on Easter Sunday, 9 April. But the DAR told Johnston that Constitution Hall expressly prohibited Negro artists, whereupon he published letters of protest in several newspapers. The result was a spontaneous and robust campaign on Anderson's behalf.

ER, who had invited Anderson to sing at the White House in 1936, resigned from the DAR very publicly, thereby striking a blow against race traditions previously regarded as sacrosanct. Her resignation was overwhelmingly popular across partisan lines throughout most of the country. "Prejudice," the *Washington Herald* editorialized, "rules to make the capital of the Nation ridiculous in the eyes of all cultured people and to comfort Fuehrer Hitler and the members of our Nazibund."

Her action spurred an avalanche of letters and editorials from musicians, stars, leading public citizens, and Americans from every walk of life. Enthusiastic letters of support even came from unexpected sources, including her brother Hall's second wife, the noted Cleveland pianist Dorothy Kemp Roosevelt. "How kind of you to write your approval of my stand on race prejudice," ER replied to her. "It seems incredible when we are protesting the happenings in Germany to permit intolerance such as this in our own country."

In San Francisco, Anderson herself observed, "I am not surprised at Mrs. Roosevelt's action because she seems to me to be one who really comprehends the true meaning of democracy. I am shocked beyond words to be barred from the capital of my own country after having appeared in almost every other capital of the world." Sol Hurok, Anderson's manager, considered ER's resignation "one of the most hopeful signs . . . for democracy. . . . By her action Mrs. Roosevelt has shown herself to be a woman of courage and excellent taste."

But it was not ER's first such protest—she often matched her convictions with actions. In May 1934 at a meeting of America's educators she had made a speech supporting the passage of a resolution against school segregation. She had demanded equality in education and opportunity for all children, concluding, "We will all go ahead together, or we will all go down together." Then in November 1938 she again challenged

America's "race etiquette" when she sat alongside a key civil rights leader, Mary McLeod Bethune, at the opening of the Southern Conference for Human Welfare in Birmingham, Alabama, making a personal protest against segregation. When Sheriff Bull Connor's policemen ordered her to leave the black section, she moved her chair to the aisle between the two segregated sections.

An alternative venue for the Marian Anderson concert, the Central High School auditorium, was proposed—but then was vetoed by Washington's Public School Board. ER was outraged. At this point Howard University, the NAACP, and the Society of Friends, in an effort to find another venue, formed a citizens' committee that quickly garnered five thousand supporters. The first lady telegraphed the committee, "I regret exceedingly that Washington is to be deprived of hearing Marian Anderson, a great artist."

She joined NAACP chair Walter White and Oscar Chapman, assistant secretary of the interior, in an effort to secure a space for an outdoor public concert that would be open to everyone. When Chapman decided to use the Great Mall at the base of the Lincoln Memorial, he notified his boss, Interior Secretary Harold Ickes, who called the president. FDR shouted into the phone, "Bully for Oscar! She can sing from the top of the Washington Monument if she wants to!"

ER declined to chair the event since she was scheduled to be on a lecture tour of the West Coast in April, but she enlisted some of her closest friends to support the concert. Caroline O'Day and Isabella Greenway, both members of the committee, worked closely with Chapman and Ickes on all details. Her friends Leila and Gifford Pinchot, aware of Washington's segregated restaurants and hotels, agreed to host Anderson and her party.*

On 9 April 75,000 Americans attended Marian Anderson's Freedom Concert, which was broadcast live across the country. The unprecedented, entirely integrated audience extended the length of the mall, from the

---

*More than three hundred prominent Americans served as sponsors of the Freedom Concert, including Chief Justice Charles Evans Hughes and Justice Hugo Black, Tallulah Bankhead and Clare Boothe Luce, Henry Morgenthau and other cabinet members, many members of Congress, and Attorney General Frank Murphy. Katharine Hepburn telegraphed Caroline O'Day that she could not attend, but said to "use my name freely in regard to this matter." See Allida Black, "Eleanor Roosevelt and the Marian Anderson 'Freedom Concert,'" *Presidential Studies Quarterly* (Fall 1990), p. 727.

base of the Lincoln Memorial to the Washington Monument and beyond. Harold Ickes considered it "one of the most impressive affairs that I have ever attended." Chapman and O'Day escorted Anderson onto the stage, and when Anderson "faced the enormous crowd," Chapman said, "she was almost overcome." She paused to focus upon all the newsreel equipment and the six microphones of the major radio networks. "I had a feeling," she later reflected, "that a great wave of good will poured out from these people, almost engulfing me."

Ickes introduced Anderson, later considering his two-minute introduction "the best speech I have ever made":

In this great auditorium under the sky, all of us are free. . . .
   When God gave us the sun and the moon and the stars, He made no distinction of race, creed, or color. . . .
   Genius, like Justice, is blind. For Genius with the tip of her wings has touched this woman, who, if it had not been for . . . the great heart of Lincoln, would not be able to stand among us today a free individual in a free land. Genius draws no color line. She has endowed Marian Anderson with such a voice . . . a matter of exultant pride to any race.

Anderson sang arias, classical favorites, and spirituals. She performed "America the Beautiful," all verses. After her encore, "Nobody Knows the Trouble I've Seen," she told the audience, "I am so overwhelmed. . . . I can't tell you what you have done for me today. I thank you from the bottom of my heart again and again." She then turned to her accompanist, Kosti Vehanen, who bowed and kissed her hand. Then the short white man and the tall black woman walked back toward the monument, arm in arm. The *Times* reported that Anderson's devoted mother was present.

That brief concert, which began at five p.m. and lasted less than an hour, has endured in the nation's memory. The power of art and ethics had embraced, and the message was clear: concerned decent people would no longer ignore public insults to black Americans. The time to stand up and be counted had arrived. A long process had begun. The Freedom Concert was broadcast to millions of Americans, north and south. America had taken a first step toward respect.

For all the joy and hope inspired by that event, Washington's public spaces—its parks and playgrounds—remained segregated. While 200 black and white notables sat together in reserved seats on the platform at Lincoln's feet, 75,000 Americans in their Easter finery stood together to hear Marian Anderson. To stand together was somehow acceptable to the segregated, and ongoing, norms of the capital.

For ER, America's future, and the future of the world, depended on how people responded to the cruelties of bigotry. Race and respect, the long struggle against discrimination, was moved to the forefront of her agenda. As early as 16 January 1939, she had agreed to present Anderson with the NAACP's Spingarn Medal that July. She planned to have integrated talent to perform for the British king and queen during their June visit. She now announced that Marian Anderson "will sing for them at the White House."

During her West Coast tour, ER had time to be in Seattle with her daughter Anna, who on 1 April had given birth to her third child, John Boettiger Jr. In an unusually introspective column, ER considered the psychological ordeal that precedes childbirth: "No matter how many times we have seen babies come safely into the world, we always think before the event of all the dreadful possibilities that surround all human ventures." Once Anna was safely returned to her own room, and the baby was brought in for careful inspection, the sun returned to the world "as far as all the people who love Anna were concerned." ER was especially pleased that the president was telephoned before the press found out about the birth.

ER's relief and delight stimulated her deepest thoughts about love:

> When you love people very much, isn't it grand to be able to join in their happiness? Like everything else in the world, however, there is a price to pay for love, for the more happiness we derive from the existence and companionship of other human beings, the more vulnerable we are. . . . It takes courage to love, but pain through love is the purifying fire which those who love generously know. We all know people who are so much afraid of pain that they shut themselves up like clams in a shell and, giving out nothing, receive nothing and therefore shrink until life is a mere living death.

The next day she wrote to Esther Lape and Elizabeth Read, "Anna is doing very well, the baby is grand and life is quite serene out here!" On a personal note she confided that her many concerns about Anna's troubled husband, John Boettiger, were lifted: Anna "is a grand person and what she has done for John is really remarkable. A really narrow person has broadened out beyond belief! He was always lovable even at his most bitter and cynical stage, but life with Anna has completely changed him."

Only two weeks later, on 18 April, tragedy struck at the heart of her family. ER's nephew Daniel Stewart Roosevelt and his friend Bronson Harriman "Pete" Rumsey were killed when their airplane crashed in Mexico.* The plane belonged to Pete but had been piloted by Danny. Both boys had flying licenses. Danny's father, ER's brother Hall, flew to the border to bring their bodies home. For the first time in her relentless lecture career, ER canceled three speaking engagements to be with her brother during this unbearable tragedy, from which he never fully recovered.

Hall was crushed by his son's death and ER was staggered by it. She had admired Danny—the previous year he had accompanied his father on a trip to Europe to try to get planes to the Loyalist forces in Spain. U.S. ambassador to France William Bullitt, working to negotiate a French-German agreement, had stopped their courageous effort. The vicious blockade against aid to the Loyalists, imposed by England, France, and the United States, had ensured the triumph of the fascists, ER was sure: Madrid had fallen to them on 28 March. The final betrayal, only weeks before Danny's death, had occurred on 3 April 1939, when the United States officially recognized fascist Spain. ER always referred to the U.S. role in Franco's victory with shame and anger.

On 9 February 1939, in recognition and thanks for her support for the Spanish Loyalist cause, the Spanish government had presented ER with a

---

*According to newspaper accounts, Daniel Roosevelt and Bronson Rumsey were killed when their plane crashed during a storm twelve thousand feet above a mountain near Guadalupe Victoria, Puebla, en route to New York. The two Harvard students, both twenty-one, were trapped in the front seat and burned to death. The sole survivor, Carlota Constantine, a Sarah Lawrence graduate and daughter of INS reporter Arthur Constantine, was thrown clear with serious fractures and was rescued by Indians, who transported her on a litter of poles and skins to their village, while others ran miles to phone for help. Carlota later recounted that before leaving the airport, they had been told the weather was so bad that even freight planes were grounded. She had urged her friends to delay their flight. But "one of the youths said impossible" since he was to be a wedding usher that weekend and they had taken off anyway.

book of Goya's nineteenth-century etchings taken from the painter's original plates in Madrid.* Ignoring all objections, ER sent the etchings to the Corcoran Gallery in Washington for a public exhibition, which opened to great excitement. She also displayed them at the White House.

Coincidentally, the day she left for Dedham for Danny's funeral, the *New York Times* reported that Joseph Goebbels had attacked her for accepting "presents" from the "Red Spanish government" of Barcelona. ER treasured the prints, and as she stood beside her brother at her nephew's burial, she surely pondered Goya's images of death—the senseless random suffering of war, the cruel petty hatreds of tyrants, the rivers of blood, and the islands of love that made life bearable.

Danny's death seemed connected to so much loss, so much suffering—in Spain, in her own family, in the world. Surrounded by adverse publicity over the Goya prints, ER returned to Washington resolved to help restore democracy where it was lost and to strengthen it where it might still survive.

*The set of Goya's famous series *Los Proverbios*, eighteen etchings drawn from the original plates in Madrid, was completed on 9 November 1937. According to *Times* columnist Herbert Matthews, "The idea of this edition was primarily to raise foreign currency for the hard-pressed Loyalists, but also to prove that reverence for Spanish art was as great among the so-called 'Reds' as among their critics abroad. So, the famous engraver Adolfo Rupérez had been commissioned to make 150 sets of the four great Goya series." The first five of these, on Antique Japan paper, were accompanied by a map of Madrid to indicate "where bombs had dropped while the work was being done." After the war Matthews visited Rupérez, who told him what he knew of the etchings' whereabouts, long shrouded in mystery. One of the five sets went to Spanish Republican president Manuel Azaña, who died in Switzerland during the war. Set number two went to Eleanor Roosevelt, who kept it—despite the most amazing public protests when she accepted the gift. Herbert Matthews, *New York Times*, 8 September 1954.

Chapter Two

"You Cannot Just Sit and Talk About It, You Have to Do Something"

Since childhood, ER had accepted what she considered life's primary lesson: joy is forever stalked by uncertainty and disappointment, even tragedy. As she boarded the train home from her nephew's funeral, her heart was filled with grief. Plunged in gloom for the fate of young people as the world returned to war, she recalled her tour of Europe twenty years before, when she had witnessed the result of the most bitter carnage, with millions dead and "every other woman in a black veil to her knees." Everything she had hated about 1919—the tragedies of war, the brutalities of the Red Scare—seemed to be poisoning everything she most cared about now. The world seemed caught in a web of military madness, controlled by a shrieking lunatic who had no regard for life, for children, for the beauty of spring.

On 14 April 1939, in an effort to avert war, which would certainly bring "common ruin," FDR issued a public message to Hitler and Mussolini. Political, economic, and social problems, he insisted, could reasonably be negotiated "at the council table." New trade agreements could relieve the world from fear and the fiscally "crushing burden of armaments," so that all nations might "buy and sell on equal terms" and obtain raw materials and products essential to "peaceful economic life." In exchange for such agreements, FDR sought an "assurance" that Hitler and Mussolini would not invade the "territory or possessions" of thirty-one independent nations in Europe and the Middle East.* He hoped the two dictators could adhere to this promise of "assured nonaggression" for "ten years at the least."

Mussolini scorned the message as the result of the weak president's

---

*The thirty-one nations were Finland, Estonia, Latvia, Lithuania, Sweden, Norway, Denmark, the Netherlands, Belgium, Great Britain, Ireland, France, Portugal, Spain, Switzerland, Lichtenstein, Luxembourg, Poland, Hungary, Romania, Yugoslavia, Russia, Bulgaria, Greece, Turkey, Iraq, the Arabias, Syria, Palestine, Egypt, and Iran.

"infantile paralysis," while Hitler responded with a blistering two-hour Reichstag rant. Hitler thundered that the United States had been the first to demonstrate contempt for treaty accords and the League of Nations. To resist "encirclement," he now canceled the naval treaty with England and a 1934 pact with Poland in exchange for Polish territory to permit Germany's pathway to East Prussia, "the Polish Corridor." His speech left little doubt that war with Poland was imminent.

Worldwide, mistrust and suspicion prevailed. U.S. diplomatic circles feared that Britain might form an alliance with Hitler and hand over interests in South America, while others feared that the United States would maintain its isolation and thereby doom antifascist European nations. Still others feared that Japan would move from Chinese to Soviet territories in Asia. And still others feared that Germany and the Soviet Union would ally, at everybody's expense.

The Soviet Union had been "ostentatiously excluded" from the 1938 Munich Conference. Nonetheless all winter and spring Foreign Minister Litvinov had intensified his efforts to forge a real alliance against Hitler that would include Britain, France, Poland, Romania, Hungary, and the Soviet Union. Litvinov, who was Jewish, was married to British literary scholar and writer Ivy Low Litvinov, who failed to accompany him to Washington because she was so busy with her own work.

He found support from Harold Nicolson* and from Winston Churchill, but otherwise the response in England was tepid. Others expressed no interest at all. On 20 March, Romania agreed to give Germany "exclusive use" of over half its considerable oil production. Subsequently, King Carol confided to Hitler that he was "against Russia" and would never consent to Russian troop passage through Romania. Hungary, ethnically diverse and politically divided, feared above all a recurrence of its 1919 Communist revolution. Now led by fervent anti-Communist nationalist Admiral Miklós Horthy, Hungarians sought an independent road above the fray, with a preference for Hitler's Germany. In April, Hungary issued its own anti-Jewish laws and soon joined Germany, Italy, and Japan in the Anti-Comintern Pact.

ER approved of Litvinov's call for a Grand Alliance against Hitler. In

*Harold Nicolson, member of Parliament, a journalist and historian, is remembered today mainly as Vita Sackville-West's husband and Virginia Woolf's confidant.

1933, she had been delighted when the United States recognized the Soviet Union (in large part because of the good work of Esther Lape and her committee). She liked Litvinov personally and looked forward to meeting his independent wife. She had frequently spoken against appeasement and against all those who preferred to sacrifice Austria, Czechoslovakia, and Spain to Nazi-fascist brutality on the grounds that Hitler was allegedly the bulwark against Communism. The anti-Communist crusade had corrupted the Roman Catholic Church into supporting fascism, even in the United States, where Detroit's "radio priest" Father Charles Coughlin spewed the most hateful anti-Jewish bile every Sunday. More recently, Congressman Martin Dies (D-TX) protected Nazis while crusading against "un-Americans," by which he meant liberals, ER, and her friends, all alleged Communists. The entire world was now at risk, and it seemed to ER unnecessary, if not insane.

She was also puzzled by America's refusal to acknowledge the agonies that Japanese violence inflicted on China. Hostilities between the two countries had broken out in July 1937. Japan and the Soviet Union, she understood, were in competition and conflict from Manchuria to Mongolia to the western Asian borderlands; the Soviet Union was aiding China as it had aided Spain. Was that the reason for America's silence concerning China? she wondered. Was that why the U.S. failed to offer China any support or to oppose Japan?

According to the U.S. diplomat Norman Davis, the State Department had "two schools of thought." One believed Japan would conquer China, then move on to British, French, Dutch, and U.S. possessions in the Pacific—rendering war inevitable. The other believed China could not be conquered, and that Japan's futile effort to do so would exhaust it and render it puny. In either case, Japan would be obliged "to trade with us . . . and we have no interests in the Far East that would justify war." FDR told Davis that he agreed with the first precept. But there was a third consideration: just as appeasers, in the words of General Alan Brooke, had fantasized "a Nazi-Soviet war that would enable Britain to preside over an exhausted Europe," certain U.S. diplomats fantasized a Russo-Japanese war that would benefit U.S. influence throughout Asia.

In November 1937 the Brussels Conference on the Far East was convened to find a way to end the Japanese-Chinese conflict. For the last time Britain, France, the United States, and the Soviet Union met to discuss the world situation. FDR explicitly instructed Norman Davis, the U.S. delegate to Brussels, to "do nothing that would entail American initiative to curb Japan." Davis suggested that the United States suspend the Neutrality Act "to alarm Japan and hearten the Chinese," but FDR refused. He wanted no binding agreement. In the end, the conference merely issued a weak appeal to China and Japan to cease fighting. Davis returned to Washington depressed and disgruntled.

In the intervening two years, Japanese atrocities mounted, and the United States missed more opportunities for engagement. On 17 March 1938 Soviet foreign minister Litvinov appealed for a conference to discuss resistance to Germany and Japan. Washington ignored him. U.S. secretary of state Cordell Hull, who generally despised Japan, counseled against waging even economic warfare against it, arguing that it would harm U.S. business interests; Japan was a primary importer of U.S. cotton, steel, and oil.

On 16 April 1939 Litvinov urged the Soviet Union, Britain, and France to form a three-power military alliance, but the allies hesitated. Then in May, Winston Churchill, long a committed anti-Communist, made a startling speech in Parliament, calling on His Majesty's Government to accept "the full co-operation of Russia." On 19 May, he gave another speech and qualified his earlier statement: "Without an effective Eastern front there can be no satisfactory defence of our interests in the West, and without Russia there can be no effective Eastern front."

But it was too late. The Jewish, pro-Western Litvinov had failed to achieve his goal of an anti-Hitler alliance. On 4 May Soviet leader Joseph Stalin had named Vyacheslav Molotov to replace him as Soviet foreign minister. It was the end of an era, and some believed it was the end of everything. As soon as Litvinov's departure was announced, Harold Nicolson wrote in his journal, "The left-wing people are very upset." Many believed that with Litvinov gone, Stalin was ready to "make a neutrality pact with Germany. I fear this terribly."

In this harrowing context, ER faced the possibility of renewed bloodshed and the bombing of densely populated cities across increasingly meaningless borders. Spain remained her moral equator. She loathed war, but her views were increasingly complicated. What could be done? What might she do? She was first lady of the United States, and her husband had just recognized Franco's Spain. She set her mind on islands of hope for understanding and international amity in a sea of violence. The New York World's Fair was to open on 30 April—perhaps it would inspire protest against the waste of humanity's best creative impulses. And England's attractive young royals, King George VI and Queen Elizabeth, were to visit in June. Perhaps their visit would inspire public support for international efforts to derail fascism's rolling thunder.

She loved her brother Hall's children and was proud of their achievements. Her niece and namesake earned her first public recognition as a costume and jewelry designer through the prism of Danny's death. The *New York Times* reported on 22 April that "costumes and accessories fashioned from printed silk fabrics that represent the first efforts of Miss Eleanor Roosevelt" had been previewed at Arnold Constable, a leading Manhattan department store. "Some of the prints are patriotic and others futuristic, since Miss Roosevelt based her collection on a World of Tomorrow motif keyed to the World's Fair themes."

ER's gardens took her away from the world of wars, carnage, politics, and vested interests. She was proud of her spectacular plantings and each week sent fresh cut flowers from the White House to Hick for her city apartment and for her office at the World's Fair, as well as to other special friends. When she considered the impending visit of Britain's royals, she counted on William Reeves, her head gardener, to arrange a "profusion of beauty" and called upon her friends to send their favorite floral tributes. "England is a land of beautiful gardens and flowers," she acknowledged, but they did not have the splendid "magnolia tree planted by Andrew Jackson," whose astonishing blossoms would be "opened wide" for their visit.

In her press conferences and her columns, she spoke out where others were silent; she spoke bluntly where others punted and parried. She rejected the possibility of isolation, in a dangerous world dominated by brute force and fascist vitriol. Rather, the survival of decency must depend on international cooperation—economic, political, and military alliances. She vigorously defended her husband's decision to sell planes to France. When former president Herbert Hoover objected that the sale endangered U.S. neutrality, ER bluntly rejected her old ally's "partisanship." She was aghast that a former president would criticize her husband's foreign policy and dismissed Hoover's remarks as "a tempest in a teapot," stirred up because the United States allowed a French pilot to test-fly a U.S. plane, "which

France quite legally was going to buy. . . . It was an open transaction . . . pure commerce between two friendly nations."

Significantly, journalists and opinion makers who had previously trivialized or dismissed her efforts now applauded her commitment. The journalist Charles Hurd wrote a rhapsody to "Rugged Roosevelt Individualists," a family "both unconventional and unpredictable" that "marries, divorces, makes money and subscribes to no definite rules." Led by the matriarch and "family catalyst" eighty-four-year-old Sara Delano Roosevelt, the heterodox Roosevelts differed from one another in public and in politics while cherishing their freedom and their family. The article examined their individuality. Anna was compared to Katharine Hepburn: "tall and thin," she favors "careless clothes," and her speech is as "direct, as sharply critical." ER, "the busiest member of the family," is independent and rule-free. She travels alone and writes what she thinks. She "does not always agree with her husband," but she is also a dutiful first lady, who fits "her personal routine" to the needs of the White House. "Not even the President," Hurd concluded, "compares with her in vigor."

Surely ER was most surprised when the editors of *Time* celebrated her positions in the spring of 1939. Owned by Henry Luce, *Time* had not been kind, or even polite, to the scribbling first lady who had criticized Clare Boothe Luce's play *The Women*. Partly because Luce's own antifascist commitment was now so closely in accord with ER's views, and almost as an apology for previous articles, *Time* now wrote a panegyric to ER. Datelined 17 April 1939, it asked, "Where is foreign policy made?" According to *Time*, "a gracious, energetic, long-legged lady" made foreign policy in small, almost unnoticed ways. Agreeing with ER's commitment to forge an Anglo-American alliance, *Time* rhapsodized that when Mrs. Roosevelt and Queen Elizabeth met,

> one will be looking at the world's most symbolically important lady, the other at the world's foremost female political force. Britain's Queen, whoever she may be, will remain superlative so long as the British commonwealth retains throne and crown. The present first lady of the U.S., on the other hand, is superlative in her own personal right. She is also a woman of unequaled influence in the world, but unlike Cleopatra, the great Elizabeth, Pompadour, or Catherine of Russia, her power is not that of a ruler. She is the wife of a ruler but

her power comes from her influence not on him but on public opinion. It is a self-made influence, and, save for a modern counterpart in modern China, unique for any woman to hold.

Six years ago the tall, restless character who moved into the White House with Franklin Roosevelt was viewed by large portions of the U.S. public with some degree of derision if not alarm. They caricatured her, joked about her, called her "Eleanor Everywhere." They couldn't believe that any woman could sincerely embrace the multiplicity of interests which she added to being a wife, mother, and White House hostess.

Today enough people have met Mrs. Roosevelt, talked with her at close range, checked up on her, to accept her for what she is: the prodigious niece of prodigious, ubiquitous, omnivorous Roosevelt I. They have judged her genuine and direct. Sophisticates who used to scoff, now listen to her. They read with measurable respect her books, magazine articles, daily column which are among the most popular in America with over "four million five hundred thousand total circulation."

She confronts controversies, avoids platitudes, and recently challenged "the entire U.S. economic system" (*Time*, March 6). "I believe in the Social Security Act . . . in the National Youth Administration, never as a fundamental answer. . . . These are stop-gaps. We bought ourselves time to think. . . . There is no use kidding ourselves. We have got to face this problem. . . . This goes down to the roots of whether civilization goes on or civilization dies."

Henry Luce's flagship journal noted approvingly that the first lady was "even more vocal" concerning international relations: "Mrs. Roosevelt is no warmonger. For years she has talked and worked for peace. Four years ago she argued that 'the war idea is obsolete.' She hoped humanity would progress to the day there would not be armies, just a world police force." But she was now convinced "it may be necessary to use the forces of this world in the hope of keeping civilization going until spiritual forces gain sufficient strength everywhere to make an acceptance of disarmament possible." ER identified isolationism with appeasement and wondered "whether we have decided to hide behind neutrality? It is safe, perhaps, but I am not sure that it is always right to be safe."

In short, Mrs. Roosevelt, oracle to millions of housewives, would bring them face to face with Right and Wrong as a world issue. "Not to do so," she says, "would be, for me, not to live, but to have a sort of oyster-like existence." If nothing else would preserve Right, she would approve war.

ER's public life was devoted to persuasion, a politics of example. She believed in the power of the written word and in the goodwill of most people. She dedicated herself to presenting her messages to the greatest possible audience, in the simplest possible terms. She deplored scholar-politicians whose views might be exemplary but whose words revealed an underlying contempt for the general public.

As the world hurtled toward war, her commitment to democracy in the fascist era emboldened her in profound and permanent ways. On such critical questions as bigotry, race hatred, anti-Semitism, and the plight of Europe's refugees, she realized that it was up to her to speak and write precisely what she thought. She could depend on nobody else in her household to advance the issues that increasingly dominated her days.

Although millions of Americans read ER's words and were influenced by her integrity, simplicity, and passionate intensity, a well-orchestrated army of detractors assailed every word she wrote. They attacked her both for what she said and for what she did not say. They attacked her for what she wore, how she looked, how she traveled, and what she believed. Politicians and pundits found an endless array of false and fraudulent personal issues upon which to pillory the most outspoken first lady in U.S. history.

She was attacked for affirming the right to divorce for various reasons, including incompatibility: "Divorce is necessary and right, I believe, when two people find it impossible to live happily together." In the new context of fascist propaganda and Nazi laws, which sought total authority and control, and the subjugation of women, personal decisions were now political issues. Nazi slogans were crudely specific: Start with "the cradle and the ladle," and the state can achieve total domination. In Germany, matters of clothing and style, romance, choice, work, and recreation were narrowly defined and closely supervised. Barred from the university and most professions, women were compelled into forced breeding situations for a vast, experimental eugenics program.

Hitler was as direct about women as he was about Jews. One Nazi propagandist argued that the Enlightenment had generated "the insane dogma of equality" and the "emancipation" of Jews and women. Women must return "to the holy position of servant and maid," and Jews must be "eliminated."

The Nuremberg Laws of 1935 stripped unmarried women of their citizenship and consigned them to an underclass, *Staatsangehöriger*, a category they shared with Jews, homosexuals, political undesirables, the crippled and the enfeebled. Among those were the psychopathic and diseased, targeted for final destruction.

As assaults on women hardened, ER steadily revealed her support for women's choice and public health services. She had previously acknowledged that "I have been a long time member of the Birth Control League."* During a 1940 press conference she asserted that she did not oppose family planning and supported "the use of public funds for birth control clinics." While she had privately contributed to the maintenance of birth control clinics in New York for many years, she concluded that America appreciated diversity, and "I do not wish to impose my views on others."

ER's commitment to birth control led to FDR's support for it as well. In June 1941 ER was pleased to tell Mary Lasker that—encouraged by the enthusiasm of Ross McIntire, the surgeon general of the navy; the U.S. surgeon general Dr. Thomas Parran; and Katherine Lenroot of the U.S. Children's Bureau—FDR had agreed to a policy of public information for servicemen and would "get the whole thing moving" despite "certain repercussions from the Catholic Church."

But ER also had an ever-growing and appreciative public, which included many liberal Catholics who protested gross and "unfair attacks" against her and supported birth control. Slammed in the Catholic press for her stance on birth control, a professor at Catholic University in Washington wrote, "Like your many other Catholic friends, I regret deeply the impertinence of this editorial, which does not reflect the sentiment of most Catholics. . . . However the lunatic fringe is a bit more vociferous than the rest of the membership."

Many, including her children's friends, noticed ER's new boldness. Katherine Littell, wife of the assistant attorney general Norman Littell,

---

*In May 1942, it changed its name to the Planned Parenthood Federation. ER's endorsement led to state medical associations' support of public health service "child-spacing" programs.

wrote her friend Anna Roosevelt Boettiger of an evening she had spent at the White House:

> The President was in top form—gay, witty, sparkling, and I remembered what you'd told me of his ability to put harassing cares aside at meal time, and relax. There has *never* been such a pair in the White House. It seems incredible that one reared as your mother was should have developed into such an incarnation of Social Justice—and that she could make even the most intolerant see her point of view. She is beyond all doubt one of the truly great women of the world. . . . She is unique in her greatness in that she has achieved her place without ever compromising the eternal verities. Where Elizabeth was devious and dissimulating, Catherine the Great under-handed and grossly immoral, Catherine de Medici scheming and inhumanly calculating, Lady Mary Wortley Montagu . . . devilish in her malice.

Over the winter, even Hick, who had been ER's toughest and most trusted critic, celebrated her writing skills. "I wonder if you realize how much better your stuff is (at least in my humble opinion) than it was three or four years ago." Then in March, when asked to comment on an article ER had drafted for *Look* magazine, she elaborated,

> It is magnificent! Bravo! Again and again. . . . I haven't a single suggestion to make. . . . My dear—I can't tell you how proud I am of you! You certainly have found your stride. . . .
>
> Just for the fun of it, sometime next summer when you *may* have time, get out some of your earlier stuff, back about 1932 and 1933, and compare it with some of the things you've done in recent months. You'll be amazed, I think. And you'll understand, too, I think, why I never used to be really satisfied with what you wrote those days— and why I am so darned pleased and so proud of you now. ·
>
> Of course, one thing you have developed is a much greater facility in writing—a style, I guess you might call it. And that, my dear, comes only with hard work. You've *earned* it.

"Conquer Fear and You Will Enjoy Living," which appeared in *Look* on 23 May 1939, was a call for personal courage in the battle against bigotry and prejudice. The difference between bravery and cowardice, ER believed, lay in the ability to dominate fear. Once a person conquered fear, it was possible to act boldly in the face of opposition, even defeat or disaster. "Many a soldier has told me that when he came to a crisis all he really wanted to do was to run away from his particular responsibility but in having to think of others, he forgot his own fears and habits of thought and action reasserted themselves."

Now there was a need for national courage, so essential to "the growth of a nation." It "is the individual's courage which makes the nation's courage." She explained, "Our economic troubles today are largely due to our fears. We will not risk our money if we have it because the possible returns are not great enough. . . . If we have a job we dare not help a youngster to learn that job for fear he will do it better than we can and we will be thrown aside. As a nation we hate to give up any little advantage we may have over our neighbors because we cannot see where it would profit us and we dare not be generous."

ER specifically deplored the "newly formed patriotic societies" that had embarked on a crusade against everything "foreign." By waving an American flag and spewing hate, these organizations created an "antagonism to foreign groups in our midst under the guise of proclaiming their allegiance to age old principles of Americanism. Americanism must be flexible to meet the changes of civilization and we should remember our past and not allow ourselves to be carried away by our fears to the point of hysterical so-called patriotism."

A rising xenophobia faced refugees and immigrants who sought a haven from fascism. This cruel inhospitality, she wrote, resulted in "grave injustices. . . . Sending home a few hundred thousand aliens will not solve the unemployment problem. We need something more fundamental than that, but our hysteria on this subject is one of the evidences of national fear."

Unemployment remained the primary emergency. It "undermines the morale of our people, saps their strength and breaks their spirit. This is the question which should be at least considered today. How do we distribute the gains of modern invention so it benefits *all* the people?" Instead of facing this challenge, we fling about labels to crush what we fear. "We cry that labor has become communistic . . . we cry that we are on the way to dictatorship."

ER's simple, heartfelt essay was read by millions. In the pages of *Look*, her message of courage and resistance was accompanied with graphic illustrations of the violence that marked America in 1939: images of state violence and vigilante violence, a Nazi anti-Jewish rally festooned by American flags and swastika banners. There were also images of hope—of WPA projects and Mormon women organizing for community health. The goal was to stir Americans into action to achieve security and dignity for all.

Surrounded by history and the turbulent past in the White House, Eleanor confided to an audience in Texas that while she worked late at night in her office, which was once Lincoln's study, she occasionally had "a curious feeling" that she was not alone. Even though she did "not believe in ghosts," she felt the room get cold, the atmosphere change; odd noises emerged, and she "visualized" Lincoln either pacing about the room or leaning upon the window, "staring out at the Washington landscape meditating on affairs of state." Her ruminations evoked an appreciative *New York Times* editorial:

> There is nothing discomforting in this. The White House is built of memories. . . . It will remain a haunted house as long as it stands, but only in the benign sense that unseen presences may still be watching the destiny of the Republic. . . . What American, passing by that great pillared residence, in time of stress, could fail to feel reassured to sense the shadowy figure of Lincoln, just as Mrs. Roosevelt describes him, gazing thoughtfully from a window?

During the winter and spring of 1939, ER wrote long essays, spoke to countless groups, and traveled continually. In San Antonio, on her thirty-fourth wedding anniversary, she "laughingly admitted at a press conference that she had forgotten" the date; she would "have to add up" to recall the number of years involved. The press noted that she subsequently was "reminded of the anniversary by a telephone call from Washington, presumably from the President."

A few days earlier, in Dallas, Texas governor W. Lee O'Daniel had introduced ER as a faultless person responsible for FDR's best efforts: "Any good things he may have done during his political career are due to her, and any mistakes he may have made are due to him not taking up the matter with his wife." ER denied such influence and insisted, "A president's wife does not see her husband often enough to tell him what to do."

Whatever the truth to ER's denial, by the spring of 1939 she clearly believed she had more influence on public opinion than on her husband. FDR and his advisers conducted their protracted discussions about a third term, for example, entirely without her input. When a young scholar sent ER the transcript of a college debate on FDR's candidacy, she responded:

> I think my own real objection to a third term is that at the present time it is very bad for a democracy to feel that the ideas they believe in can only be administered by one man. The citizens should feel their individual responsibility. . . . In an era of dictators it seems a pity for us, the greatest democratic nation, to acknowledge that we have no other leader who can carry out the ideas in which the majority of people believe. . . . However, it does not matter very much what I think as I have nothing to say about it.

War as unavoidable combat and its alternatives continued to preoccupy her. In *Photoplay*, a movie magazine, she addressed the question: "Why do nations go to war? Why do people let themselves be led into war?" Perhaps, she wrote, it was "greed," the ambition to dominate, control, and own what belonged to others. People argue that we need war because "man is never satisfied! The whole history of civilization is the history of dissatisfied man." That argument defends envy and greed and ultimately poses war as creative and good, generating new discoveries, even progress.

ER rejected that view, since in war there were no final victories, as the fate of the Versailles Treaty of 1919 plainly revealed to the citizens of 1939. She counseled, therefore, "a change in the whole make up of man. Instead of a desire to acquire something for himself or his particular group, he must become a cooperative animal, one who is willing to share what he knows, and what he has, with other human beings around the world." In her first truly global essay, she argued that such a "tall order" required a fundamental change in our value system and "a long period of education." People needed to have more to live for than to die for. They must sense that all human beings have a stake in the condition of all other human beings. We must change "the way we measure success." If, for example, great new medical discoveries were "given to the world for the benefit of humanity," and were not restricted "for the use of a few," then "our world would begin to change."

The new motion picture industry showed potential, she suggested—it could lead the way to a worldwide education campaign, raising awareness about economic conditions around the globe. Americans must realize that their country was part of an interdependent world, "no matter how hard we try to keep our eyes turned inward on ourselves alone."·

In her personal life, while she and Hick remained close, much of the romance had gone out of their relationship. Hick wrote on 15 February, "Your valentine came last night dear. And I loved it. I completely forgot Saint Valentine this year!" Perhaps her forgetfulness involved finances. Listing her household expenditures in four detailed budgets that enumerated her income and outlay to the penny, Hick explained that she had no extra money at all. She acknowledged that she might seem self-indulgent, but she was in debt to her three luxuries: the Little House (the house she was renting in Mastic from Bill Dana), her new car, and her beloved dog, Prinz.

When ER questioned her debts and suggested she use her salary raise to finance her new car, Hick, in a short-lived regression, waxed positively suicidal. She acknowledged that it was "silly" and even "insane—really—for a woman of forty-five . . . without a cent in the world . . . to hang on to these three luxuries." But they meant everything to her; in fact they defined her being.

> Living—just going on living—simply doesn't mean a God damned thing to me, dear. I'm being perfectly honest when I say I'll be relieved when it's over, provided the actual ending isn't too painful. You are always horrified when I say that I wish it had happened when I had that automobile accident out in Arizona. But I still do. I'd have died happy, as happy as I've ever been in my life.

Rather than respond to Hick's aggressive, self-indulgent letter, ER's attitude was to try to do everything possible to help her. She lent her money for the new car and sent her extravagant and useful presents. Her generosity was unlimited: "Please take the 100 for your birthday. I really can give it without feeling it—I don't want you to worry about returning any of it!"

Hick was grateful but felt guilty. "I'll not even pretend that I didn't get a kick out of the raincoat. Of course you shouldn't have done it, and I hope you didn't pay too much for it. But I'm suspicious. 'Made in England for Abercrombie & Fitch' hardly sounds cheap. Well—it's a grand raincoat."

She did what she could to return ER's generosity. "I'm getting two more books of tickets [for the World's Fair] for you and having them sent to the apartment, since you say they are for Hall."

As Hick's good work for fair publicity and arrangements mounted and were fully appreciated, her depression abated. "Things are a little better with me. . . . You'll never believe it, dear, but I heard myself described the other day as 'a human dynamo'! If I'm a human dynamo, my dear, how would one describe you?"

While ER was in Seattle to be with Anna for the birth of her newest grandson, Johnnie Boettiger, her friend Dorothy Canfield Fisher wrote an essay that asked, "Where do we go from here?" which inspired ER to address America's 1939 graduates in an article. All high school and college graduates faced an era of unprecedented peril and danger. It was, she wrote, also a time of unlimited opportunity and adventure—entirely new frontiers and resources to develop.

New Deal critics to the contrary, great hydroelectric projects were not mere instances of "government extravagance." They represented, rather, "magnificent achievements" that looked far into the future toward development and planned growth. But she cautioned against waste and urged Americans to consider conservation: "You cannot drain the strength from your land by planting only one crop. You cannot let the top soil run away with the spring rains, or the floods which your lack of care for your forests has brought about. You young people must have the courage to take hold of your country, conserve it physically and own it for yourselves. It must not be owned by financial interests. It must not be owned by politicians."

ER emphasized the "need for housing, decent housing in which children can grow up healthily. In our haste we have been wasteful of our human resources." Now urgent changes were required: "It is costing us more to bring up children in surroundings which breed criminals, drug addicts, victims of tuberculosis, of venereal disease, of heart disease, than it would cost us to set ourselves squarely to the task of wiping out these mistakes on a long range, planned, basis."

The graduates of 1939, she wrote, should dismiss the notion that experts had all the answers. People in every community understood their situations and needed to solve their problems democratically and directly. She was especially contemptuous of business and financial interests that sought to reduce taxes, allegedly to stimulate industry and business. She rejected what is now called "trickle-down economics" and insisted that "the freeing of certain timid capital by a change in certain tax laws" was insufficient. Instead, she called upon young people to organize new political movements for real societal and economic change: "You have to set a new standard of values."

The call to a new standard was just a beginning. Full employment, real skills, decent housing, guaranteed pensions for all old people, and "medical care which every family needs" were necessities, as was "recreation which is part of life when lived in a normal way." Through her article, she set forth both challenges and new agendas for America's youth and asked them to consider inequality at home.

These were critical, death-dealing times. Lynchings in the South had increased in number since 1936. State terrorism—burning, looting, torture—was on the rise. Race hatred and brutality underlay the international epidemic of brownshirts and white sheets. The causes of violence needed to be addressed: "War will not be averted by a passive attitude which is afraid to make any decision for fear of offending other people. You cannot just sit and talk about it, you have to do something!"

ER had great faith in the vision of the organized youth movement. She defended its radicalism even while she deplored the Communist leanings of some young people. It was possible, she believed, to forge a radical vision within the democratic mandate of American history and theory. But democracy worked only when every individual assumed the burden of responsible citizenship.

In conclusion, she said that graduates were right to ask her for "one concrete thing you might do to start you out at once on your program as citizens." The Works Progress Administration, the National Youth Administration, and the Civilian Conservation Corps were the essence of a caring democracy at work. Those who dismissed these agencies as too costly or too radical were foolhardy—they paid for themselves over and over in opportunity, services, and hope. ER even suggested that every young person be asked to give a year of her or his life to national service. That way, "at the end of the year, [volunteers] will all know something of their nation" and be better prepared to fight national disasters—floods, fires, medical emergencies, even war.

In closing, she hailed the graduates, whom she called "explorers who must now harrow where your forefathers plowed." Her call for a national peacetime draft shocked many, but she insisted that raw individualism did nothing for democracy. Her idea would build an understanding of the nation's needs and provide the privileges and benefits of training, skills, and service. Many dismissed such solutions as fascistic or communistic. But for ER, a year of service was merely patriotic.

The 1939 New York World's Fair, with its theme "The World of Tomorrow," celebrated extraordinary achievements in science and technology, architecture and culture. High-speed technology was not just for creating faster bomber planes but could also be used for developing innovative communications—international telephone service, advanced radio reception, and something called television. The fair was meant in part to internationalize America's vision for the future—instant communication, global tourism, and peaceful human connectedness. ER considered it a splendid educational demonstration of alternative uses for humanity's brilliance.

Festive and inspiring, amazing and popular, the fair was built on twelve hundred acres of recycled wasteland in Flushing Meadows. Everything about it was grand and utopian. A seven-hundred-foot tower called a Trylon was connected to a two-hundred-foot globe, called the Perisphere, by a giant escalator called Helicline. By riding halfway up the Trylon, one entered the Perisphere to view urban and rural American neighborhoods of the future, called Democracity. Fifty-eight nations and thirty states had their own pavilions.

Hick, whose work on the fair had occupied her for three years, regularly reported to ER with enthusiasm:

> Do you know, my dear, I think there are going to be several things at this Fair you will like very much. . . . Last night, for the first time really, I got out around the grounds and saw this place. They had it fully lighted. . . . It is very, very beautiful dear. The big white globe looks like a giant, transparent iridescent soap bubble! . . . And the colors and the reflections in the pools—gorgeous! I was very much thrilled.

The fair officially opened on Sunday, 30 April, the 150th anniversary of George Washington's first presidential inauguration in New York City.

FDR arrived to give the opening speech. He was accompanied to the dais by his mother, as well as by Crown Prince Olav and Crown Princess Martha of Norway, who had just spent two nights with the Roosevelts at Hyde Park.

Minutes later ER made a grand entrance "in a costume of printed silk whose motif was the Perisphere and Trylon. . . . The tiny printed pattern was in white against a background of luggage tan and was designed by her niece, Eleanor Roosevelt 2nd." The first lady invited notable women leaders to join her on the receiving line, including Senator Hattie Caraway (D-AR), Representative Mary Norton (D-NJ), Ellen Woodward of the Social Security Board, and her cherished friend Isabella Greenway, a former Arizona member of Congress.

Making his first public statement since Hitler mocked his plea for peace, FDR said he opened the fair "as a symbol of peace." He dedicated his speech to the Four Freedoms that defined America: "freedom of speech, freedom of the press, freedom of religion, and freedom of assembly."

He acknowledged the nation's failures, including the "unhappy trial" of Prohibition and the Civil War. But the United States had "ended the practice of slavery," he observed, and "made our practice of government more direct, including the extension of the franchise to the women of the nation." And in recent years "the people of every part of our land acquired a national solidarity of economic and social thought such as had never been seen before."

Despite current racial conflicts, he asserted, America's good fortune was due to its form of government—and "to a spirit of wise tolerance which, with few exceptions, has been our American rule. We in the United States . . . remember that our populations stem from many races and kindreds and tongues."

Acknowledging the "gesture of friendship and goodwill" that so many nations had made by their presence, their messages, and their grand exhibits, the president noted that the wagon of America "is still hitched to a star," the star of "friendship . . . of progress for mankind . . . of greater happiness and less hardship, a star of international goodwill, and, above all, a star of peace. . . . And so, my friends . . . I declare the New York World's Fair of 1939 open to all mankind."

FDR's speech was the first to be televised. With his words, television made "its formal bow." The ceremony was beamed to an audience at

Radio City Music Hall, and to the fair on twelve television receivers at the Radio Corporation of America (RCA) pavilion. The transmission "was flashed eight miles to the Empire State Building and back again to Flushing on ultra-short waves." Television receivers would go on sale in New York stores the next day. According to the *New York Times*, 30 April 1939 would go down in history with "the same significance as 2 November 1910," when radio broadcasts began.

After the speech, the Roosevelts had little time to visit any of the sights, since they had to return upstate immediately. Another set of royal guests, Crown Prince Frederick and Princess Ingrid of Denmark, were to spend the night at Hyde Park. Genuinely enchanted by the fair, ER would return as often as possible. She would bring her grandchildren, family groups, and various guests, and host a large group in honor of Marian Anderson's Freedom Concert at the fair.

Chapter Three

Tea and Hot Dogs: The Royal Visit

From January to June, Congress passed only one piece of significant legislation: the Rearmament Act, a multimillion-dollar military appropriations bill. The rearmament program called for urgent air, sea, and land defenses; new heavy and light artillery; gas masks, flight training, and thousands of new airplanes. FDR achieved cross-sectional support for this legislation. ER supported the act, believing that a fortified nation is a protected nation.

Her friends in the Women's International League for Peace and Freedom, however, believed that weapons-building programs encouraged war and criticized her for it. ER explained that given the European situation, "I should think we would all of us realize that there are times when an adequate defense enables us to preserve a just peace," while "an inadequate defense obliges one to accept injustices [and compels] future insecurity."

Indeed, since the defeat of Spain's democratically elected Loyalists and the abandonment of Czechoslovakia, an entirely new era had emerged, demanding entirely new responses. "Each American family must snap out of its secure little circle and face stirring problems at home and abroad," she told an audience. "The price of keeping our personal liberty is that we shall have to think for ourselves. We are going to have to be willing to face many situations that we have never been willing to face before."

Still, as she and FDR had consistently argued, rearmament represented only part of America's defense needs. That spring of 1939 she was particularly dismayed by the stalled effort to democratize, and actually integrate racially, the Social Security Act of 1935—specifically, to include all the still-uncovered farmworkers, domestic workers, government workers, and employees of "private non-profit religious, charitable and educational institutions." Indeed, all efforts to fortify New Deal programs concerning health, education, housing, and jobs were stalled in a climate of political acrimony, which included white supremacist bluster.

Americans had to be secure against the ravages of poverty, sickness, and old age. The Social Security Board itself had recommended increases in old-age benefits and a new "triangle tax to be borne equally by employer, employee and government"; that "federal grants for aid to dependent children be raised to the level of those for the aged and the blind"; and that unemployment coverage be extended. All spring, in her lectures and writings, ER supported these urgent recommendations.

While FDR increasingly concentrated on the international situation, ER attended to the nasty backlash against her husband and the New Deal. She specifically campaigned for Senator Robert Wagner's public health bill, drafted after years of research with the involvement of her closest allies in the American Foundation led by Esther Lape. FDR agreed that "the health of the people is a public concern," but little was done.

Wagner's bill called for the restoration of the old Sheppard-Towner grants for maternal infant and child health services;* medical services for handicapped children; improved public health services nationwide, including federal grants to states for dental services; and construction of general, mental, and tuberculosis hospitals. The bill would ensure "all services and supplies necessary for the prevention, diagnosis, and treatment of illness and disability" state by state.

ER also worked vigorously for the Harrison-Thomas bill to provide federal aid for education—including grade and high schools, adult education, junior colleges, special education for the handicapped, rural library services—and for children "on federal reservations and at foreign stations."

Above all, she championed Senator Wagner's 1939 urban renewal bill, which sought to provide funds for slum clearance and low-rent housing construction. She saw it as an extension of her own work in the creation of Arthurdale, West Virginia, in 1934—now one of twenty-nine American communities administered by the Farm Security Administration. She considered the creation of affordable homes for America's industrial and farmworkers among the New Deal's greatest triumphs. Senator Wagner had a devoted

---

*Pioneered by ER's great mentors Jane Addams, Florence Kelley, Lillian Wald, and Julia Lathrop of the U.S. Children's Bureau, the Sheppard-Towner Infant and Maternity Act had been signed by Warren Harding in 1921. Vigorously opposed by right-wing groups and the American Medical Association, it was repealed in 1929. The Social Security Act of 1935 had restored the guarantee of prenatal education and infant care, but national infant health services remained underfunded.

supporter in ER when he said, "Of all the programs for the rehabilitation of our people and the development of our physical resources there is none which has a smaller effect upon the national debt and which yields a larger return in economic benefits and human welfare than the housing program."

ER's crusade for enhancing "the human side of government" was fueled by the unemployment crisis. Congress's stingy attitude toward the WPA, especially toward its training and work, education, and arts programs, seemed horrifying when over ten million people were still unemployed. In one city alone, four thousand women applied for twelve civil service positions that paid a modest annual salary. In the face of such demonstrable need, ER wondered, how could elected leaders be so shortsighted and actually cruel?

She wanted to see public protests and organized community efforts. She wanted her husband to speak more bluntly to reactionaries in Congress and in his own party. But it was an election year, and FDR preferred his diplomatic approach, even as he warned: We will have a liberal democracy, or we will return to the Dark Ages.

She went across the country to defend the New Deal, and relentlessly agitated for greater support for those who were sliding deeper into financial crisis without work or adequate shelter. It was as if she no longer considered her own needs, suspending many of her own friendships and simple pleasures. One day after a lecture in Massachusetts, she and Tommy stopped in Connecticut for a flying visit of less than an hour with Esther Lape and Elizabeth Read. Tommy explained to Lape that the visit had necessarily been brief because "Thursday she spends all day with the South Americans!"

She was referring to the entourage of Nicaragua's president, the dictator Anastasio Somoza, who arrived on 5 May. His controversial visits to Washington, New York (for the World's Fair), and New Orleans were entirely financed by the U.S. government. American companies had long dominated Nicaragua's economy—its banks, railroads, gold mines, mahogany forests, and plentiful stores of coffee and bananas.* FDR

---

*In 1927 ER wrote a front-page article in the *Women's Democratic News* called "Banks and Bayonets in Nicaragua," with the question "Do We Deserve the Hatred of the World?" It was a blistering protest against Calvin Coolidge's military invasion of Nicaragua to destroy the popular independence movement led by Augusto Sandino, the charismatic hero who struggled to create a Nicaragua "unpolluted" by

supported Somoza in the interests of the hemispheric alliance to resist Nazi incursions. FDR's famous line "He is a son of bitch, but he's our son of a bitch" became an even more urgent aspect of U.S. policy as Hitler's emissaries swarmed Latin America and trade with Germany and Japan increased.

On the morning of 5 May, in Washington's spring heat, ER watched U.S. troops pay homage to the Franco of Nicaragua. A dutiful first lady, she accepted a medal from him and stood beside him during the military parade and reception. In a published photo of her, wearing a white fox around her neck, her expression of distress and distaste recalls her cold "Griselda moods" of silent rage. She hewed to her obligations as first lady, even when her personal beliefs were at odds with administration policy.

The Nicaraguan dictator left the capital with a $2.5 million loan from the Export-Import Bank and promises of more. There is no record of what FDR requested in return from the ruler of the most underpopulated nation in the western hemisphere, who had specifically refused to accept refugees (especially merchants and intellectuals) at the 1938 Evian Conference. On his return to Managua, Somoza renamed the main street "Avenida Roosevelt," removed a "composite picture of himself and Adolf Hitler" from his office wall, and replaced it with "four portraits of FDR." Clearly U.S. support countermanded German inroads.

All spring ER continued to be dismayed by FDR's failure to respond to the mounting refugee crises. On 1 April she wired him from Seattle, where she was visiting their daughter Anna: "Just received wire signed Einstein, Dorothy Thompson, etc., about important leaders trapped in

---

U.S. military control and ownership. For decades, from her uncle TR's "big stick" policy to Taft's "dollar diplomacy" through Coolidge's escalated marine presence, Nicaragua had been a strategic military base and occupied colony. Finally on 3 January 1933 the twenty-year occupation ended when President Hoover pulled U.S. troops out of Nicaragua. Sandino called for peace and national unity. But on 21 February 1934 Sandino and his brother Socrates were brutally murdered, and hundreds of unarmed families in the Sandinista community were massacred. When civil war broke out in May 1936, the State Department refused to "interfere." With military efficiency and stunning corruption, Somoza and his family would control Nicaragua "as a private fiefdom" until the Sandinista uprising of 1979.

Madrid. Are you or State Department doing anything? All well here. Love." FDR telegraphed back the same day from Warm Springs, "State Department doing everything possible in Spain. . . . Much love to all six of you."

ER knew better. The State Department was doing nothing for refugees. In February, her old friend Nan Wood Honeyman, former member of Congress from Oregon, had appealed to her on behalf of a constituent for advice about where to turn for help with Jewish refugees. "The truth is," ER had replied, "most of the work being done for refugees is being done through the Quakers and the Jewish Refugee Committee." She suggested that Honeyman's constituent contact Clarence Pickett of the AFSC. Her own work for refugees was done through those groups, notably the current campaign to provide sanctuary for children.

Meanwhile the House passed a bill that would actually require the "detention of certain aliens" pending their deportation. Introduced by Congressman Sam Hobbs (D-AL), it targeted refugees without papers—notably those from countries recently absorbed into Hitler's Reich. Unable to obtain passports, they were now suspect and were to be detained for unspecified duration, without charges or hearings, despite all due process requirements of American law and custom.

ER's closest friends and allies spoke vigorously against the bill, which they believed was unconstitutional, un-American, and totalitarian. In the debate on the House floor, Caroline O'Day invoked Sinclair Lewis's 1935 novel *It Can't Happen Here*, in which "the United States, the greatest democracy in the world, became a totalitarian state, not overnight or all of a sudden . . . but because its citizens neglected to guard their civil liberties. Through carelessness or indifference they relinquished those liberties one by one until such time as a ruthless minority seized the reins of government and established a totalitarian state." O'Day compared the current political situation to Lewis's fictional state, and argued:

It can happen here. And if this bill becomes law we will have taken the first step. . . . [This bill] is a negation of every idea and policy and principle that our country holds most dear. I can imagine with what satisfaction Hitler will learn that his emissaries in this country have so influenced Congress that it is following his example and setting up detention or concentration camps during peacetime. . . . They are called detention camps, but Hitler knows as well as anyone how swiftly a detention camp can be transformed into a concentration camp. This bill is a vicious and un-American bill and should be defeated.

Supporters of the bill argued that it specifically targeted Communists, anarchists, and immoral agitators. "The American people do not want these . . . promoters of communistic philosophy creating disturbances and trouble in this country. Our people want to send them back from whence they came."

Despite opposition by congressional leaders Emanuel Celler, Jerry Voorhis, and Louis Ludlow, the House passed the Hobbs bill on 5 May 1939, by 289 to 61, with 80 not voting.*

FDR was concerned about the plight of refugees, but he simply had too little congressional support even for his favorite projects. When he sought, for example, to make the CCC a permanent agency, Congress voted against it. He wanted to put things off until after the 1940 elections, which promised a more liberal outcome. In the meantime he sought alternative solutions for the refugee crises. ER had letters from people who had suggested underpopulated states, like Montana and Utah, as potential havens. When she sought her friend Bernard Baruch's advice, he was uninterested and wanted to avoid exacerbating the "Jewish problem" in America.

When Baruch commended FDR for his 14 April letter to Hitler, the president cabled his gratitude, and noted, "The big thing we talked about is by no means dead. It will revive if Hitler and Mussolini do not slam the door in our faces!"

The "big thing" was Baruch's plan for the creation of a United States of Africa for all refugees—for people "of all faiths and nationalities whom Hitler had marked for destruction." He envisioned locating the colony in

*Although it did not pass the Senate in 1939, the Hobbs bill was repeatedly reintroduced and finally passed both houses in August 1950. After 2002, during the "war on terror," Congress passed "enemy alien laws" that enabled the Guantánamo Bay military prison and extraordinary rendition.

the Belgian Congo, Portuguese Angola, Kenya, and Tanganyika. Baruch saw it as a democratic and diverse alternative to a "Jewish homeland" in Palestine, which he feared could only become an embattled ghetto. Baruch intended to raise $500 million to create the sanctuary. He imagined that it would become a British protectorate and thereby would obtain British support. He enlisted Herbert Hoover to accept "leadership" for the engineering and technical aspects of the project, and he approached FDR, who "sketched a map of Africa . . . outlining the temperate, largely unpopulated areas where such a scheme might be put into effect." Evidently FDR also sent emissaries to discuss the project with Hitler. But King Leopold had rebuffed the idea "because the land belonged to the natives." "You see," Baruch told the king, "no one wants them."

Unlike Baruch, FDR believed that Britain's promise to Jews regarding Palestine, initiated by the 1917 Balfour Declaration, represented a hopeful strategy for escape and haven.* He was dismayed in May 1933 when the United Kingdom issued a new White Paper that asserted that Palestine should not "be converted into a Jewish state against the will of the Arab population" and that severely restricted Jewish immigration to 75,000 over the next five years, never to exceed one-third of the total population. On 17 May FDR wrote to Cordell Hull that this policy change betrayed England's pledge to create a "national home for the Jewish people in Palestine." Hull agreed—the United States would not officially recognize this shift in British policy.

Frustrated by a lack of progress on issues that concerned her deeply, ER confided to Hick on 20 May, "I have been admonishing FDR like a Dutch Uncle lately and he's been good about it but I can't bear to have Congress go home with nothing done!" She was also frankly disappointed by his recent speech regarding the arms embargo: "It doesn't seem much

*Endlessly contested, the November 1917 letter from the British foreign secretary Arthur Balfour to Lord James de Rothschild was clear and simple: "His Majesty's Government view with favor the establishment in Palestine of a national home for the Jewish people, and will use their best endeavors to facilitate the achievement of this object, it being clearly understood that nothing shall be done which may prejudice the civil and religious rights of existing non-Jewish communities in Palestine, or the rights and political status enjoyed by Jews in any other country." See Grose, *Israel*, p. 65.

good to me, same old thing and no real suggestions for what should be done and these are things that must be done. Well, it is easy to criticize when you don't carry the responsibility."

That was the strained political dimension in which the White House prepared for the unprecedented visit of Britain's King George VI and Queen Elizabeth. In the battle against isolationist sentiment, the first lady increasingly considered her primary public relations activity to be hosting ceremonial receptions for heads of state who visited America for alliance and support. She and FDR believed that their honored guests could personify and humanize Europe's tragedy, perhaps inducing isolationists to join their defense team.

No diplomatic visit received as much thoughtful attention to detail, time, and effort as did the heralded journey by Britain's royals. With their own quest for alliances against fascism paramount, the king and queen had planned to journey to Canada to encourage the support of "every citizen in their dominions." FDR invited them to the United States because he believed, as ER put it, "we all might soon be engaged in a life and death struggle, in which Great Britain would be our first line of defense." For all the isolationist feeling in the United States, Americans shared a bond of language, custom, and ideals with the British. Both ER and FDR hoped the royal visit would spark concern among Americans and even stir a sense of unity with the British—especially among those stubbornly removed from the international situation.

When ER returned from her southern lecture tour on 31 May, she walked into a maelstrom of tension between FDR and his mother over room arrangements for the royals. Sara had been a guest of King George V and Queen Mary at Buckingham Palace. Now their son was to visit her son, and the first mother wanted lofty standards fully observed. But FDR rejected stiff formalities. He behaved, ER later recalled, "as though we were simply going to have two very nice young people to stay with us. I think he gave some of the protocol people, both in the State Department and in the entourage of the king and queen, some very difficult moments." The president and his mother had argued for days, until FDR took to his bed. ER wrote to Anna, "Pa was annoyed every minute and developed sinus Tuesday & went to bed with a temperature of 101/2 tonight. . . . I say a little prayer to live through the 11th," when the royal visit was scheduled to end.

For her part, ER was determined to create an environment of warm gracious comfort and to fulfill her mother-in-law's formal expectations. She consulted with the State Department's chief of protocol, her knowledgeable social secretary Edith Helm, and her girlhood friend Elisabeth Cameron Lindsay, now Lady Lindsay, wife of the British ambassador Sir Ronald Lindsay. Daughter of Henry Adams's great friend Elizabeth Cameron, Lady Lindsay had been a member of ER's flamboyant biweekly "air our minds" luncheons during FDR's first term. She was trustworthy, had a grand "sense of humor," was "keen" and occasionally wicked. We "looked at things from more or less the same point of view," ER wrote.

Some people believed SDR and her son disagreed about ER's plans for the White House entertainment, but the family agreed on issues of race and justice—civility, opportunity, dignity for all—and that "we should give the king and queen something they would not have at home." ER made it clear that Marian Anderson would indeed "be presented to the King and Queen of England." That meant they would shake hands, and perhaps dine together. It was all unprecedented and, for some reporters at her regular press conference, "shocking." The program would also feature baritone Lawrence Tibbett and the popular singer Kate Smith. Alan Lomax would perform western cowboy songs. There would also be a "North Carolina Negro chorus" of thirty men and women from the Federal Music Project; the Coon Creek Girls, a "white non-WPA" group from the Kentucky mountains; several square dance and folk dance groups.

ER also wanted to emphasize to the press that there were more important issues to discuss than "etiquette" and new mattresses for the White House. The real issue before America, and the world, she declared, was the survival of democracy, which depended on "freedom and security." Freedom involved opportunity and work, education and gainful employment. Security involved the quest for peace. War now threatened democracy's very survival.

That was the urgency behind the royal visit, as well as ER's commitment to create positive newsworthy events that would transform public opinion. The press and most popular magazines anticipated the royal visit for weeks. ER appeared on the cover of *Life* magazine, as the "Queen's Hostess." The cover article featured the royal stay at Hyde Park, with extraordinary photographs by Margaret Bourke-White. Every room the royals might enter was accounted for and assessed: "Hyde Park is no castle but it is one of America's most charming homes. . . . It is an old shoe of a place—worn, scuffed and scratched, polished into shape. . . . It is most emphatically American because its owner cared nothing about having a fancy house to show off and a great deal about a good house to live in." ER was pleased that FDR insisted no changes would be made: the king and queen would see Hyde Park as it always was. They would enter a hall that featured prints of American victory over "British men of war" during the naval battles of 1812.

Despite her harried schedule, ER had agreed to an extraordinary interview and portrait session with S. J. Woolf of the *New York Times*. Woolf was treated to the fullness of one ER White House afternoon. ER gave Woolf only one hour to sketch her portrait and less than thirty minutes for questions. At three-thirty Tommy arrived to take dictation for ER's column, while Woolf sketched. She allowed him to sit in as she dictated her column to Tommy. The result was the deepest glimpse into the heart of the first lady published to date. He had intended to focus on the royal visit but was so impressed by ER's hectic life and contagious enthusiasm that he celebrated her "energy" instead. "All formality was forgotten," Woolf wrote, "as this tall, lithe woman with a gracious smile entered . . . with [her] air of naturalness and hospitality which converted a cold public building into a home."

ER's "astonishing energy and absorbing curiosity," Woolf learned, were fueled by her love for people. Her work satisfied her, helping people pleased her, and she never worried about making mistakes. She credited her splendid staff for doing much of the work for which she was complimented. She received, for example, 90,000 to 300,000 letters a year—her secretary of seventeen years, Tommy Thompson, and a team of assistants were responsible for sorting her mail. ER was particularly interested in reading critical letters, many of which taught her things she needed to know, and letters that appealed for help, most of which were sincere.

ER was moved by the story of a very poor young girl with a spinal injury, for whom she arranged hospital care. ER became close to the girl and her family. She was cured and now "is happily married living a normal life."* The encounter was a perfect illustration of her belief that communal prosperity was fully realized when disadvantaged individuals triumphed: "Every time some one rises above what appears to be an insurmountable difficulty and wins out I feel that we all ought to profit by it. If they can win, we can all win."

That, ER noted, was the message of Arthurdale. In that small West Virginia community, "people have the opportunity to make homes and livings for themselves." Although government support for the community continued to be criticized as wasteful and foolish, ER asserted that every penny was well spent "if it brings some happiness to those who need it, some security where before the future held nothing but terror."

At four o'clock, ER rushed out to change into a "pink afternoon gown" to greet three hundred waiting people. Tommy confided to Woolf that in all her years with ER, "she was always the same, never ruffled, never angry, always understanding." Then ER returned to finish dictating her column. Then another change, another reception, this time for four hundred people. Woolf completed his drawing and departed—refreshed and energized.

The day the royals left for North America, 8 May 1939, the radio press dispatches FDR received dramatically detailed the urgency of fortifying Anglo-American alliance:

Milan: Germany and Italy "converted the Rome-Berlin Axis into an outright military alliance."

Moscow: Speculation was reported "on the possibilities of German-Soviet friendship resulting from the resignation of Maxim Litvinov."

Madrid: "A flotilla of German warships" cruised Spain's coast "in honor of general Francisco Franco and the Fuehrer Adolf Hitler to mark the victory of the nationalists in the civil war."

*ER's reference is to Bertha Brodsky and the Brody family. See Cook, *Eleanor Roosevelt*, pp. 1:329–30, 619.

Berlin: Germany asserted the Italo-German military alliance "is a destroying blow to an aggressive encirclement policy. . . . Statements [about the pact] were coupled with a blunt warning to Poland that she must shoulder full blame for all that is coming."

London: The Archbishop of Canterbury appealed to Pope Pius XII "to assume leadership of a united front of 'all Christendom' to work for world peace."

Capetown, South Africa: The German South African Party— "comprised of naturalized German ex-servicemen"—opposed Adolf Hitler, rejected Nazi philosophy, asked "South Africans to remember the pre-Hitler Germany where 'right and justice were the supreme law.'"

At sea: The *Empress of Australia*, "this big passenger liner," served "temporarily" as the royal yacht for King George VI and Queen Elizabeth "on their way to become the first British ruling couple ever to visit Canada and the United States."

The king and queen arrived in Quebec on 17 May and spent eighteen days journeying across Canada.

On 4 June, as they prepared to travel to the United States, the Hamburg–American liner SS *St. Louis*, with 936 Jewish refugees aboard, was anchored "in the tropic heat" of Havana's harbor. Although the refugees had purchased their visas from Cuban consuls in Germany, President Federico Laredo Brú, who had previously welcomed five thousand refugees, now required additional payment and new papers for asylum seekers. He ordered the ship to return to Hamburg. Captain Gustav Schröder announced that there had already been two suicide attempts, and he feared a "collective suicide pact." Forced to leave Cuban waters, Captain Schröder slowly sailed up and down the U.S. coast, while urgent efforts for sanctuary were pursued.

That same week ER absorbed press reports of an American fascist movement revealed by the testimony of retired major general George Van Horn Moseley before Martin Dies's House Committee Investigating Un-American Activities. Dies insisted that Communist interest groups, Communist "transmission belts," and Communist fronts were everywhere, especially within New Deal agencies. Dies demanded "sterilization for refugees admitted to the United States" and called for "vigilante groups" to battle a "Jewish-led Communist revolution being plotted" by

FDR and his friends. Despite calls for the Dies Committee to investigate Moseley and his ties to world fascism, Dies rejected them and announced instead his intention to focus on the arts and theater efforts of the WPA, youth and labor organizers in general, and ER's friends and allies.

The only really good news of the week was the opening of the Czecho-Slovak Pavilion in Exile at the World's Fair, which ER was moved to attend. The stirring speech by former president Edvard Beneš was broadcast nationwide and carried by short-wave radio to Europe. The flag of the conquered dissolved republic flew at half-mast, a promise of restored self-rule.

After leaving the World's Fair, ER returned to her Greenwich Village apartment alone, to find the telephone ringing. Her youngest son, John, was calling with the news that his wife, Anne, was in distress, and they feared a miscarriage. Immediately ER dashed uptown to catch the night train to Boston. Anne Clark Roosevelt did lose her baby. But ER was certain the couple would recover and be strengthened by their ordeal. "Like all other disappointments and sorrows, it will probably make them more conscious that, in the real things in life, everyone stands on the same level and God sends us disciplines in order that we may better understand the sufferings of other people." Their situation recalled her own lost baby who died at seven months. According to Mollie Somerville, a White House assistant, ER never stopped "mourning the loss of her second child. . . . She once told me, 'The child you have carried under your heart, you will always carry in your heart.'"

ER returned to Washington with only two days to finish preparations for the arrival of the king and queen. She sought to put the entire nation at ease. So many people asked her how to greet their majesties, she recounted the story of a Yosemite park ranger who guided "King Albert and the Queen of the Belgians" through the park shortly after World War I. He had been "carefully coached . . . as to the proper way of addressing royalty." But when they met, he forgot the rules, and as he told ER, "I just said 'Howdy King' and held out my hand." Since they "were a charming royal couple," ER was certain that would be good enough for them. She wanted the country to relax and enjoy the royal visit, she told the press.

The next morning, 7 June, she held her regular press conference. In the afternoon she was scheduled to speak to the Workers' Alliance, the

WPA union vilified as Communist by congressional opponents of the New Deal.

Almost every hour was scheduled. There was to be a diplomatic reception as soon as the king and queen stepped off the train in Washington; then luncheon; then a small tea for about twenty prominent New Dealers, in addition to children and several of ER's ten grandchildren; then the formal state dinner and a musicale. ER assured the press that all guests at the musicale would be presented to the king and queen. After visiting Washington, the royals were to go to New York City, the World's Fair, and on to Hyde Park. "If you want a press conference at Hyde Park," ER told reporters, "I'll arrange to have one."

ER arrived at the national congress of the Workers' Alliance at twelve-thirty. Her twenty-minute "extemporaneous" talk was front-page news. "Delegates from all parts of the country stamped and cheered their approval" as the first lady spoke. They might differ on some things, ER said, "but I am certainly in sympathy with the meeting of any group of people who come together to consider their own problems" and work to achieve betterment. She did not fear radicalism among young people as much as she feared the "rut of hopelessness."

After her address, the Workers' Alliance gave her honorary membership, and she "left the platform with her arms full of flowers presented to "the greatest lady in the world." In that climate of rancor and division, politics and hope, she readied to greet the royals.

Once their train crossed the border at Niagara Falls into the United States, King George VI and Queen Elizabeth were greeted everywhere by huge cheering crowds. Accompanied by Canada's prime minister Mackenzie King and an entourage of numerous attendants, the king and queen arrived at Washington's Union Station on Thursday, 8 June. FDR said, "At last I greet you." After the long formal welcome, the two couples were surrounded by over 600,000 people who had turned out to cheer their slow drive to the White House. "It was a gay and happy crowd in spite of the sun and [94 degree] heat," ER wrote. "Their Majesties themselves made such a gracious impression . . . you could feel the enthusiasm growing."

ER was pleased because the public's reaction, despite all her efforts, had hitherto remained uncertain. Anna reported from Seattle, "According to press stories the King and Queen have been worried stiff as to whether the U.S. would give them a cheering welcome or one mingled with boos. I can well imagine that all of those who had anything to do with the preparations will be terribly near collapse." Vastly relieved, ER acknowledged the success of her publicity campaign.

Pageantry surrounded their arrival and the procession to the White House, which FDR enjoyed immensely. In support of the International Wool Growers of Australia, South Africa, New Zealand, and the United States, who had "combined" to promote their industry, ER and the queen were to wear matching fabrics. "I took it off as soon as I could," she later wrote. "The Queen could not bear to wear hers . . . for she was already suffering from the unusual heat." The queen sat upon a cushion "which I afterwards discovered had springs to make it easier for her to keep up the continual bowing."

ER's sons James (Jimmy), Elliott, and Franklin and their wives were part of the weekend. John and Anne remained in Boston; Anna and her family were in Seattle. "Luncheon was a very quiet meal with just the guests in the house and our own family, and for once my boys were subdued to such a degree that the President noticed it and remarked to the Queen that it was rare when something did not bring about a vociferous argument in our family."

That afternoon there was a drive around the city to see the Lincoln Memorial, the Cathedral Church of St. Peter and St. Paul, and Rock Creek Park. ER and Queen Elizabeth used the time to speak intimately and undisturbed. ER was relieved to learn that they agreed about major issues: the "Queen endeared herself to me by saying suddenly, 'I saw in the paper that you were being attacked for having gone to a meeting of the WPA workers. It surprises me that there should be any criticism, for it is so much better to allow people with grievances to air them; and it is particularly valuable if they can do so to someone in whom they feel a sense of sympathy and who may be able to reach the head of the government with their grievances.'"

Their long walks and many talks engendered in ER a deep respect for her new friend:

It was interesting to me to find how understanding and sympathetic was the Queen's attitude toward the social problems faced today by every one. It is quite evident that no nation is without these problems and that their solution is of world-wide interest. These sovereigns are young [fifteen years younger than the Roosevelts], and though the weight of responsibility matures people early, still one does not always find in sovereigns such ability or even desire to comprehend the problems which confront so many people in every country today, and which must be solved before we can feel that the average man and woman can have security and liberty.

Thursday evening was the state dinner at the White House. There were "a few harrowing moments," ER acknowledged years later. The receiving line was slowed down because at one point the queen felt faint from the heat and exertion of the day. Then the program was rearranged at the last minute to let Kate Smith sing first so she would not be late for her radio broadcast. Marian Anderson hesitated to sing Negro spirituals, "but we discovered it in time to persuade her [our guests] from England would want to hear the music that above all else we could call our own." An anonymous tipster wrote the FBI that the musicologist Alan Lomax, who was to sing country and cowboy songs, was "a communist or bolshevik and likely to do something dangerous." So Lomax was "frisked" by both the Secret Service and Scotland Yard and "apparently was so frightened he could hardly sing."

Before she went to bed that night, ER wrote Hick a short note: "Well, one day is over and fairly well over. The Queen reminds me of Queen Victoria! He is very nice and doesn't stutter badly when speaking aloud and not at all in quiet conversation. The entertainment went very well tonight, I think, and Marian Anderson was divine." But the heat was "oppressive," and ER was "weary."

The next morning ER told her press conference, "The Queen seems to be particularly interested in social conditions. For one so young she is extremely compassionate and understanding of the conditions that push people to desperation," and the queen was personally kind. When seven-year-old Diana Hopkins, Harry Hopkins's young daughter who was then living at the White House, expressed a desire to meet the "fairy queen" with "crown and scepter," a special meeting was arranged before dinner at the British embassy—with, ER said, "true understanding [for] the child."

Their majesties had agreed to meet the women of ER's press conference. The journalists made a double line in the corridor, and ER presented them. According to Bess Furman, Queen Elizabeth, regal in white, said only, "'There are a lot of them, aren't there?'" The king merely smiled "as he ran the feminine gauntlet."

The oppressive heat continued as the Roosevelts and the royals boarded the presidential yacht *Potomac* for a luncheon cruise to Mount Vernon, George Washington's home, where the king laid a wreath on the first president's tomb. In the afternoon, they toured a Civilian Conservation Corps camp and visited Arlington National Cemetery, where they placed wreaths at the Tomb of the Unknown Soldier and at the Canadian Cross. As they stood contemplating past and future wars, taps was played. "I was not the only one who stood with a lump in my throat," ER wrote. "Arlington was the unforgettable moment of the whole day."

The royals' Washington visit climaxed with a gala dinner at the British embassy, after which they boarded their train for New York City, and the Roosevelts took another train to Hyde Park. The two couples would rendezvous late on Saturday at the Roosevelt home. ER dashed off a brief report to Hick: "Dearest, This day . . . has gone well, even FDR is content and I am glad for him." There was good, substantial, and wide-ranging conversation at dinner, and the king told ER that "he felt he had learned a great deal." The queen was interested in every issue, and ER "was fascinated by the Queen, who never had a crease in her dress or a hair out of place." She was unhurried and emotionally unruffled no matter the circumstance. "I do not see how it is possible to remain so perfectly in character all the time. My admiration for her grew every minute she spent with us."

Jane Ickes described Washington events in more detail to Anna: "You know, Anna, this city stinks (I promised Harold that I would never more use that vulgar term, but it is the only one which adequately expresses my indignation). . . . Such hate, greed, envy, knifing, pettiness." For Jane, ER and FDR were really the story: "Anna, how lucky America is to have as hosts your mother and father. . . . They are so much more regal than royalty. . . . Really Anna, [Harold and I] just stared and felt ourselves swelling with pride and thankfulness."

The first couple arrived at Hyde Park shortly after nine in the morning and had the day to prepare for a most extraordinary twenty-four hours. This was for FDR the highlight of the visit: "My husband always loved taking people he liked home with him. I think he felt he knew them better once they had been to Hyde Park." ER was mostly pleased by the arrangements. She brought the White House staff along and butlers she trusted. Because they were African-American, however, SDR's English butler left. There is no record of what SDR thought about his impertinence, or the fact that he would not be there to advise the White House staff about the specific vagaries of the house. When SDR's butler "heard that the White House butlers were coming up to help him," ER later recalled, "he was so shocked that the King and Queen were to be waited on by colored people that he decided to take his holiday . . . in order not to see [their majesties] treated in that manner!"

Meanwhile the king and queen arrived in New York to be greeted by three million cheering people. Governor Herbert Lehman and Mayor Fiorello La Guardia led a motorcade of fifty cars from Manhattan to the fairgrounds in Queens. A grand fireworks reception was held at the British pavilion. The Magna Carta, the great charter of personal and political liberty obtained from King John in 1215, was on display, alongside George Washington's family tree. Washington was not only descended from several signers of the Magna Carta; he was also directly related to the queen. Indeed, according to genealogists, Queen Elizabeth was also a distant cousin of Robert E. Lee. Much was made about shared Anglo-American culture, heritage, and democratic traditions.

After the World's Fair, the royal couple traveled back to Manhattan to be received by Nicholas Murray Butler at Columbia University, which had been chartered as "King's College" by George II in 1754. The royals were by then running behind schedule, but en route upstate they called the Roosevelts to report their whereabouts. According to ER, "We sat in the library . . . waiting for them. Franklin had a tray of cocktails ready in front of him, and his mother sat on the other side of the fireplace looking disapprovingly at the cocktails and telling her son that the King would prefer tea. My husband, who could be as obstinate as his mother, kept his tray in readiness." When the royals finally arrived, FDR said, "My mother does not approve of cocktails and thinks you should have a cup of tea." The king replied, "Neither does my mother," and took a cocktail.

After everyone was relaxed, changed, and settled, the dinner guests arrived. Almost thirty people—local friends, neighbors, family, and Canadian prime minister Mackenzie King, who continued to accompany the royals—attended the formal dinner. But there was "a jinx" on the evening, ER wrote in her column. "Just exactly what happened to our well-trained White House butlers that night, I shall never know." Tommy reported the mishaps to Esther Lape: "I must tell you first that the City of Limoges gave the President a very complete set of really beautiful china—with his crest, etc. He sent it to his mother because she did not have enough sets for such big dinners. . . . The butlers, during dinner, were piling up the service for the next course when the table they used collapsed. Mrs. R. said the racket was terrifying. All the dishes were smashed into bits." ER noted, "Mama tried in the best-bred tradition to ignore it, but her step daughter-in-law [Helen Astor Roosevelt], from whom she had borrowed some plates for the occasion, was heard to say, 'I hope none of my dishes were among those broken.'" ER noted that the broken dishes were all "part of a set my husband had been given; none of the old family china suffered."

Since SDR's butler had decamped without warning anyone about the unexpected steps between the kitchen and service areas, mishaps continued. After dinner, a butler slipped as he entered the library with a tray of glasses, brandy, soda, water, bowls of ice, and so on. He "fell down the two steps leading from the hall and slid right into the library," ER recalled, smashing everything on the tray and "leaving a large lake of water and ice cubes at the bottom of the steps. I am sure Mama wished that her English butler had stayed." ER wrote about it in her column, "because I thought it was really funny, but my mother-in-law was very indignant with me for telling the world about it and not keeping it a deep, dark family secret." But at each upset "their Majesties remained completely calm and undisturbed," which she interpreted as a sign of tranquillity and hope in a fractious world.

After dinner, which ended late, everyone retired—except the king and FDR, who spoke together for hours. The next day Mackenzie King told FDR that after their talk the king knocked on his door to chat. He asked, "Why don't my ministers talk to me as the president did tonight? I felt exactly as though a father were giving me his most careful and wise advice." FDR encouraged the young king, who had never wanted to be king, to be bold, to take charge, to speak out, and to reassure his people.

On Sunday, 12 June, before the household left for church, a butler at breakfast "fell with a whole tray of eggs, dishes, etc." But the church service was moving and memorable, and all Hyde Park lined the roads to greet the royals. FDR, who had personally prepared the guest list and seating arrangements, subsequently wrote New York's Episcopal bishop Henry St. George Tucker, "I think the service was perfect in every way," and the king and queen were interested to learn that it was "substantially the same" as services in the Church of England. "I think last Sunday will always be remembered by them as the only quiet family day of their entire trip."

Back at the Big House, ER reported, everyone rushed to change into their "picnic clothes" for the most famous hot dog picnic in American history. The queen telephoned her two young daughters, Elizabeth and Margaret, at Buckingham Palace, who were "much amused" that she was to go to lunch while they were ready for bed. In addition to the hot dogs, which were to cook on "an outdoor fireplace," there was "smoked turkey, which Their Majesties had not tasted before, several kinds of ham cured in different ways . . . salads, baked beans, and strawberry shortcake with strawberries from Henry Morgenthau's farm." The program introduced Native American artists to the king and queen, including Ish-Ti-Opi, "a quite remarkable actor and singer," and Princess Te-Ata, "a real princess from an Oklahoma tribe, I knew well." The stage was built around old-growth trees FDR was so proud of, "and the setting was quite perfect for the Indian songs and legends."*

After the picnic the royals were invited to relax around the pool under the shade trees at ER's cottage. The president and the king swam, but ER and her guests sat with the queen and "looked on." ER "discovered" that a queen "cannot run the risk of looking disheveled," and evidently ER, who always swam, could not persuade her to enjoy the moment.

After a quiet dinner at the Big House on their last evening, the royals, FDR, and ER left for Hyde Park Station. A crowd of more than a thousand people greeted the procession of cars despite "a very heavy thunderstorm" that had come through earlier. The king said, "It's been a long week-end,

---

*Ish-Ti-Opi's "song of the last weaving," ER noted, "when the old woman is putting into her blanket the end of her life, has much of the sadness which one feels in the songs and stories of both Negroes and Indians. A proud people, our American Indians, and I liked the grace with which both these representatives of the first inhabitants of our land carried themselves when they were presented to Their Britannic Majesties." *My Day*, 13 June 1939.

but a short visit." As the royals waved from the rear platform of the train, FDR shouted, "Good luck to you! All the luck in the world!"

As they departed, "the people who were gathered everywhere on the banks of the Hudson and up on the rocks suddenly began to sing 'Auld Lang Syne.'" ER later wrote: "There was something incredibly moving about this scene—the river in the evening light, the voices of the many people . . . the train slowly pulling out with the young couple waving good-bye." Then "we stood and waved, but my mother-in-law reminded us of the old superstition that one must not watch people out of sight, so before they turned the bend, we were back in our cars."

ER "thought of the clouds that hung over them and the worries they were going to face . . . and left the scene with a heavy heart."

Britain prepared a "monster welcome" for the royal return. The *New York Times* monitored British enthusiasm for the demonstrable good and many successes of the king and queen and the goodwill they had inspired. Much was made of the king's new self-confidence and his robust and relaxed manner. With gratitude for what the royals had achieved, Harold Nicolson described their reception at Parliament Square:

> Such fun yesterday. . . . The bells of St Margaret's began to swing into welcome and the procession started. . . . There were the King and Queen and the two princesses. We lost all our dignity and yelled and yelled. The King wore a happy schoolboy grin. The Queen was superb. She really does manage to convey to each individual in the crowd that he or she have had a personal greeting. . . . We returned to the House with lumps in our throats.

As ER reflected on her time with the king and queen in terms of "the changed conditions which we are facing all over the world," she was relieved that "this country will have a kindlier feeling toward the English nation. . . . May it bring us peace for many years to come." She reported to Hick, "FDR was satisfied and all went well. I liked them both but what a life! They are happy together however and that must make a difference even in the life they have to lead." Mackenzie King was "jubilant over the whole trip. I should think it might give Hitler and Mussolini food for thought." The king and queen "undoubtedly made friends."

ER wrote nothing about the big question of the picnic: did the queen in fact eat an American hot dog? Stories abounded. The fullest description was in Assistant Attorney General Norman Littell's letter to Anna. Littell and his wife, Katherine, were among Anna's closest friends. He and a group of subcabinet liberals met with FDR to consider strategy for 1940. As conversation "drifted" to the royal visit, he repeated FDR's account. When offered her first hot dog, the queen had said, oh no, she could not possibly, her mouth was too small. According to FDR, she tried, but her mouth really was too small. He explained, you just push it in and chew, and she "tried hard but simply could not get around the hot-dog and bun and had to put it down and cut up the famous Roosevelt hot-dog. The King, on the other hand, devoured [several] with gusto."

Littell wrote Anna that "your father particularly commends the King 'as the real personality of the two.'" FDR explained that the king "is very much in love with the Queen, and is proud to have her in the foreground." Littell also noted that both royals "struck a few blows . . . for Liberal government in this country, by their casual remarks about our catching up with reforms which were really old in England." The king's statement that power had been removed from "the capitalists quite some time ago in England" had been much quoted in the Washington papers.

Indeed, FDR wrote his Republican cousin Nicholas Roosevelt that the king and queen

> are very delightful and understanding people, and, incidentally, know a great deal not only about foreign affairs in general but also about social legislation. Actually they would qualify for inclusion in that famous book, which is constantly quoted by some of *your friends—not mine*—to the effect that Eleanor and I are Communists!

After the royal visit, FDR urged Congress to repeal the arms embargo in the 1935 Neutrality Act and reconsider America's role in the event of war. While there is no record of what FDR and the king discussed, we know each day they read the newspapers—filled with headline stories and editorials about ships afloat and stranded refugees.

The Roosevelts and the royals might have discussed the many headline stories and editorials about refugees that were appearing every day that June in the major newspapers. Because the new British White Paper limited Jewish immigration to Palestine, many ships with refugees were moving from port to port in the Mediterranean, and the situation was becoming critical. The *Liesel*, with 906 Jews on board who were not allowed to enter Palestine, reportedly dumped many of its refugees on barren Mediterranean islands.

In the western hemisphere the biggest daily headline concerned the luxurious steamship SS *St. Louis*. Its affluent and privileged passengers were refugees from Berlin and Breslau—they had been fired from their universities and orchestras, removed from their offices and shops, and forbidden to enjoy the simplest pleasures, even the right to saunter through a park or dine at a café. Initially they found their trip to Cuba to be restful, even happy. They had valid passports stamped with a red J.

But a new Cuban policy barred most refugees from disembarking from such ships. Already three other liners had gone from port to port seeking shelter for their passengers.* While the *St. Louis* waited in the harbor, representatives of the Joint Distribution Committee (JDC), a Jewish refugee aid group, went to Havana to negotiate a fiscal aid package: the JDC was authorized to post a significant bond to guarantee that none of the passengers would become an economic burden. But Cuba ignored this appeal.

Captain Schröder then turned the *St. Louis* for the United States, sailing very slowly while the JDC worked feverishly. The frantic negotiations included the offer of a significant bribe for President Brú, who requested that the ship's passengers purchase their safety. Brú gave the JDC forty-eight hours to raise the money. The *St. Louis* anchored first off the South Carolina coast, then along the Florida coast. There it was shadowed by a Coast Guard vessel to make sure nobody swam ashore. The JDC deposited $500,000 in a Cuban bank, but Brú demanded more. Additional haggling ensued until it became clear that Brú would not be satisfied.

While 734 of the 936 passengers had quota numbers for eventual admission into the United States, they were told they might have to wait three months to three years until their quota space came up. So the passengers and sympathetic U.S. citizens appealed "to the President and Congress to grant the refugees emergency asylum as a mark of international good-will at the time of the visit of the British King and Queen," and a committee of

---

*The *Caporte*, the *Monte Olivia*, and the *Mendoza* went from Montevideo to Buenos Aires to Mexico City to Paraguay. At the same time Costa Rica expelled an untold number of Jews whose ninety-day permits had expired.

passengers sent an "appeal to President Roosevelt for last-minute intervention." Their wireless message: "Help them, Mr. President, the 900 passengers, of which more than 400 are women and children."

But the United States sent no word of concern. FDR did not consider issuing an executive order to allow the ship to dock; nor did he send a telegram to influence any of his Latin American allies to take in the refugees. The State Department rejected all appeals to admit passengers temporarily—and informed the JDC that no Central or South American nation would allow the ship to dock.

It was over. The *St. Louis* sailed for Europe, filled with refugees in quest of a temporary haven. They "could see the shimmering towers of Miami rising from the sea," the *New York Times* reported, "but for them they were only the battlements of another forbidden city. . . . Germany, with all the hospitality of its concentration camps, will welcome these unfortunates home."

Aboard the ship, Captain Schröder overheard two small boys playing guards, surrounded by a barrier of deck chairs. Other children lined up to appeal for permission to pass and enter.

"'Are you a Jew?' asked one guard.

"'Yes,'; replied the child.

"'Jews not admitted.'

"'Oh, please let me in. I'm only a very little Jew.'"

Negotiations continued throughout the trip back. The JDC sought refuge for the passengers in Belgium, the Netherlands, Great Britain, and France. Dutch queen Wilhelmina accepted 181 passengers. Louise Weiss, secretary general of the Central Refugee Committee in Paris, negotiated with the French foreign minister Georges Bonnet, who authorized the admission of 224. Belgium took 214, and the U.K. accepted 287. The *St. Louis* passengers were safe, for the moment.*

The voyage of the *St. Louis* served to highlight the U.S. government's capacity for inaction and cruelty. Its haunting silence in the face of the *St. Louis* resounded everywhere. To date, not one word about the *St. Louis*

---

*Only the passengers in England were actually safe. When the Nazis invaded Belgium, France, and the Netherlands, 216 of 619 of the passengers were among those rounded up. Most of that group perished. At least 460 *St. Louis* passengers ultimately arrived in the United States, while others achieved sanctuary in Argentina, Australia, and elsewhere. After the war, the West German government honored the gallantry of Captain Gustav Schröder.

has been found in ER's writings. Ironically, her staunch friend bodyguard
Earl Miller was in Florida as the *St. Louis* sailed slowly beyond Miami
and around the Keys. Miller cabled ER in distress: surely something
might be done, he pleaded—this was not a decent thing. But ER's correspondence with Miller has been lost, so we have no idea how she answered
his urgent messages regarding the *St. Louis*.

Miller referred to that event decades later. ER, he knew, had talked
with FDR. When he inquired about her silence, she told him that FDR
had handed the matter over to the State Department. There was at the
time nothing she could do.*

Hitler made full use of the tragic voyage. That very week Germany
expelled its Polish Jews, thousands of whom had been in Germany for generations. East Prussia expelled its remaining eleven thousand Jews. Leipzig
expelled four thousand Polish Jews. Some were ordered to leave within a
month, others within hours. Those without valid passports or visas were
arrested. Dresden, Breslau, Kassel, Hanover, Kiel, Bremen, Nuremberg,
Würzburg, and Cologne all issued orders of expulsion. Ordered "to leave or
go to concentration camps," they appealed for visas, admission, or haven
anywhere.

ER pondered these developments. With her full participation, the
United States had sent two specific messages to Nazi Europe. There was
to be a strengthened Anglo-American alliance; this she hoped would give
Hitler pause. And there would be no official protest, no governmental
response to Hitler's crusade against the Jews.

With congressional opinion vitriolic regarding refugees, FDR refused
to take a stand. He would spend none of his political currency defying
public or congressional sentiment concerning Jews. His priority was to
end the arms embargo and promote defense measures. It is impossible to
know what words were spoken to ER to keep her so uncharacteristically
silent on an issue that concerned her. In the wake of the *St. Louis*, she
must have been relieved when Chile and Bolivia declared that they would
uphold "the inviolability of the right of asylum" and promised haven.
China announced plans to build a colony to welcome 100,000 refugees
from Europe in Yunan Province, in south-central China.

---

*Subsequently in 1940, when a similar fate confronted the SS *Quanza*, ER was
determined to intervene. See Chapter 13.

ER was relieved by these signals of hope, but dismayed by the dominant attitudes that surrounded her. Angry at being silenced and worried about the future, she worked ever more closely with the American Friends Service Committee (AFSC) to confront bigotry. With so many ships stranded upon the high seas, the Quakers issued *Refugee Facts*, a pamphlet that called for a new policy to enable Christians and Jews, dissenters and unionists, to escape Hitler's terror. The AFSC observed that between 1933 and 1938 the United States had admitted only 26 percent of its German quota. While 241,962 immigrants from "all parts of the world" had entered the country, 246,000 people had left permanently, "a decrease of almost 5000." AFSC chairman Clarence Pickett pointed out that 31 percent of German refugees admitted to the United States were Christian. New alliances would be necessary, ER realized, to counter indifference and end the deadly silence surrounding the refugee crisis.

Chapter Four

"We Must Think of the Greatest Good for the Greatest Number"

After the royals left, ER had two weeks of relative calm, mostly alone at Val-Kill, to replenish her energies. She swam, rode, wrote her columns and longer articles. The worse things got, the harder she worked; it made her feel better, and she had occasional victories. In her 16 June column, she noted that New York governor Herbert Lehman had signed a bill introduced by "Jane H. Todd, Republican, which makes it permissible to have equal representation of the sexes on all political committees" of the New York legislature. Equal representation for women and men on all committees had been a Democratic Party goal for many years. Seventeen states actually had fifty-fifty rules by 1939. She was pleased that New York had taken this step toward "equal representation . . . and I congratulate Miss Todd and the Governor."

But in the same column, ER noted with dismay that her stand on working wives was again the subject of criticism. For her, the right of women—married or single—to work was not a partisan matter; it was a "basic right of any human being to work." It was far better to create more jobs than to exclude "any group." To limit women's freedom to work represented a step toward fascism, for "as soon as you discriminate against one group that discrimination . . . cannot be controlled and spreads to others."

This was an old debate, which ER had considered settled. In February 1936 she told a town hall meeting that once "the children are grown and at school, there is nothing much of interest to do in the home." Now, three years later, Florence Birmingham, president of the Massachusetts Women's Political Club, was spearheading a campaign to bar married women from state jobs—such legislation had been introduced in twenty states. Birmingham challenged the first lady to a debate.

ER refused, but urged a national campaign to defeat all state and local efforts to throw married women out of jobs. Not only did many women need to work for their survival, but ER encouraged affluent women to work. Indeed, she agreed with her friend Helen Rogers Reid, publisher of the *New York Herald Tribune*, who advised the Todhunter graduates of 1939 to do the best work they could do, "if not for your own sakes, then for your husbands, because it is bad for men to feel superior to the women they marry. It makes them quite insufferable."

William Felker, the irate mayor of Northampton, Massachusetts, had ordered married women who worked to resign and resented ER's opposition. He urged her to "attend to your own knitting" and behave like his "more discreet" and mostly silent neighbor Grace Coolidge. The *New York Times* editorialized in support of ER: "How can any woman knit without talking?"

During the summer of 1939 ER's intimate friendships were rather frayed. Hick was preoccupied by her work at the World's Fair and unavailable for fun or even significant conversation. When Earl Miller arrived to spend a week with ER at Val-Kill and brought his splendid color films of the royal visit, ER was grateful for his company. His new camera provided the best coverage of the famous hot dog cookout. She enjoyed his visit, their hikes and horseback rides in the woods. He was, for the moment, her steadiest companion besides Tommy.

ER remained devoted to Esther Lape and Elizabeth Read, her great mentors and political allies. Although she and Esther regularly went to the theater and occasionally to the World's Fair together, Elizabeth was not well and spent most of her time at Salt Meadow, their country estate in Westbrook, Connecticut. The community of intimate friends that ER, Nancy Cook, Marion Dickerman, and Caroline O'Day had created at Val-Kill no longer existed. Tommy wrote Esther and Elizabeth regularly that the air at Val-Kill had soured, peppering her letters with unkind observations about "the Cook and the Dickerman," the two most egregious "chiselers" in ER's orbit. Except for Esther and Elizabeth, Tommy did not much like any of ER's friends: "I can't for the life of me understand why such a fine person as she is has so many chiselers around her. . . . I do say sincerely 'Thank God for Esther and Elizabeth.' You save her faith in human nature."

Nancy Cook did nothing but sulk, Tommy complained, and pretend to be "very ill." Because she and Cook shared a physician, Tommy had learned that there was "not one thing wrong with her except that she was getting old terribly fast." As for "chiseler" Dickerman, Tommy thought she had very bad timing and appalling manners. Val-Kill had become a center of cold discontent and bitter resentments.

The political stalemate in Washington groaned on, with no movement by Congress to advance any of FDR's goals. FDR had threatened to stay in overheated Washington until Congress acted—throughout the summer if necessary. At Val-Kill, increasingly agitated, ER began to write a book on democracy, which she envisioned as a companion to her 1938 book, *This Troubled World*. She also wrote an essay on religious freedom in which she stressed the importance of civil liberties and the needs of youth in crisis, to counter a growing evangelical crusade to "keep America Christian." She emphasized the importance of spirituality and responsibility—in accord with Christ's own commitment to love all humanity, especially those in need and in want.

As ER prepared for her summer 1939 appearance at the NAACP convention, the conservative forces in Congress regrouped with stunning ferocity to battle the New Deal and all liberal advances. She was outraged by congressional inaction on lifting the arms embargo and by the raging right-wing crusade against the National Youth Administration and the Works Progress Administration—youth and the poor. An astonishing movement to criminalize poverty was under way—to regulate, fingerprint, and even disenfranchise the unemployed, especially WPA workers and relief recipients. New York congressman Vito Marcantonio (who switched from the Republican Party to the American Labor Party) deplored that Congress was "playing politics" with the suffering of millions of Americans.

The Dies Committee sought to defund and destroy all New Deal arts projects. After a year of assault, on 15 June 1939, the House passed a devastating bill that discontinued payment of relief workers at "prevailing wages"; demanded the dismissal of WPA personnel after eighteen months; ordered a loyalty oath for new workers; and continued the Writers', Music, Art projects "only if locally sponsored."

It defunded the Federal Theatre Project entirely. Ten thousand theater workers were to be dismissed. Popular and meaningful, entertaining and provocative, the Federal Theatre presented plays, circuses, operas, vaudeville, dance theater, and children's theater events in public parks, schools and colleges, community centers and hospitals. Under its auspices, new regional theaters were built throughout the country. From Boston to Los Angeles, Chicago to Iowa City, in Dallas, Tampa, and Birmingham, twelve regional theater centers hosted resident and touring companies. In every region of the country, in America's cities and hamlets, mountains and deltas, the Federal's many projects had thrilled vast audiences, drawing in over forty million Americans, most of whom had never been to a play or live performance before. It thus created an entirely new generation of theatergoers. From a theatrical perspective, the pioneering, innovative Federal Theatre was an astonishing success.*

That was, of course, the problem. Conservatives in Congress condemned federal support for creativity—music, art, and puppet shows—since it increased political awareness and contributed to fun. Every aspect of the Federal Theatre Project was deemed suspect, un-American, subversive. After all, it challenged the old order in thrilling, enduring terms.

Hallie Flanagan, director of the Federal Theatre, received the news after seeing *An Enemy of the People* in a high school auditorium. One "of our ticket men, looking white and sick, handed me a newspaper" that headlined a "specific ban against the use of federal money for theatre projects." Flanagan called Washington, only to be told that WPA would not fight to save one of its most successful ventures. She resolved to fight and organized a national protest of critics, performers, and stars. And she called ER.

ER had long been impressed by Flanagan's creative scholarship and her experimental theater at Vassar. For four years she had championed the Federal Theatre Project in her columns and on the air. Profoundly disheartened by its defunding, and outraged by congressional belligerence and its campaign of lies and calumny, ER began a campaign to oppose the defunding. On 20 June she wrote in her column, "I confess that I am just as concerned as [Flanagan] is about the proposed ending of the Federal Theatre Projects. There seems to be nothing I can do to help. Apparently the House of Representatives has decided that it doesn't

---

*According to T. H. Watkins, fifty-eight "traveling troupes carried shows to the wilderness camps of the Civilian Conservation Corps." Watkins, *Righteous Pilgrim*. In addition, the Federal Theatre of the Air produced three thousand radio shows a year. There were French, German, Italian, Spanish, and Yiddish language companies. There were African-American theater companies in major cities, north and south; in New York and Chicago, Birmingham, Atlanta, Raleigh, and Greensboro. Chicago's Negro Unit produced *The Swing Mikado*, a vastly popular "jazzy window-rattling" Gilbert and Sullivan adaptation—it ran for five months. When it moved to New York, ER and Mayor La Guardia were among the enthusiastic dignitaries at the opening night gala.

matter what happens to people who have definite talents" in the theater arts: stagehands, set designers, lighting designers, puppeteers, actors, writers, and directors. They "can starve, go on local relief, or dig ditches, if they can find ditches to dig." She was uncommonly irate:

> I know that this project is considered dangerous because it may harbor some Communists, but I wonder if Communists occupied in producing plays are not safer than Communists starving to death. I have always felt that whatever your beliefs might be, if you could earn enough to keep body and soul together and had to be pretty busy doing that, you would not be very apt to have time to plot the overthrow of any existing government.

She concluded with the hope that the Senate might agree with those who believed "this is an era of civilization," recognize that this theater might "serve as an instrument to that end," and reconsider.

ER also defended the Federal Theatre's work in a national broadcast: "Somehow we must build throughout this country a background of culture. No nation grows up until that has been accomplished, and I know of no way which will reach more of our people than the great plays of the past and of the present-day authors."

The war over the Federal Theatre reminded ER of the controversy that erupted over the dramatization of Sinclair Lewis's 1935 novel *It Can't Happen Here*. The play warned that dictatorship can arrive not only "by way of military invasion" but also by "a sudden silencing of free voices." ER never doubted that it could happen here, especially if certain congressional committees were fully empowered, but she trusted in the future of dissent and the activism of youth. "I must say that talking to young people gives me great hope. There is a willingness among them to think along cooperative lines, and a desire to act unselfishly," which was for her the most "heartening" fact during these weeks of assault.

Her friends in Congress, notably Caroline O'Day, also vigorously defended the theater, arguing that ideas and creativity involved controversy and disagreement. Less than 2 percent of the plays produced were by contemporary writers, she noted—classics from Shakespeare, Molière, Aristophanes, and Chekhov dominated the scene. Yet their timeless works were relevant to "modern social problems."

In the final days of the debate, the House branded certain Federal Theatre plays lewd and "salacious." To some members of Congress, practically everything with love in the title seemed "Red" propaganda, including classics like Sheridan's *School for Scandal* and Molière's *School for Wives*; modern plays like Susan Glaspell's *Suppressed Desires*; and newer titles like *Love 'Em and Leave 'Em*, *Up in Mabel's Room*, and *A New Kind of Love*.

On 30 June 1939, by a vote of 321 to 23, the Emergency Relief Appropriations Act for 1940 was passed. The WPA lost $125 million in funding, and all workers on the payroll for over eighteen months were dismissed. A loyalty oath was now to be required of WPA workers. The Federal Art and Music projects would require state sponsorship to continue. And the Federal Theatre Project was terminated, effective midnight the very next day. FDR could not veto the legislation, since it involved the entire relief budget for the next fiscal year—the relief expenditures for over two and a half million people.

Final curtains came down all over America. The theater's production of Marc Blitzstein's opera *The Cradle Will Rock*, which dramatized union activism, was canceled.* At the last performance of *Pinocchio*, at New York's Ritz Theatre, the cast and crew changed the play's happy ending: Pinocchio "having conquered selfishness and greed, did not become a living boy. Instead he was turned back into a puppet," as the cast mourned: "So let the bells proclaim our grief that his small life was all too brief."

---

*It was produced by John Houseman and directed by Orson Welles. After weeks of rehearsal, the production was canceled before it opened. Considered "dangerous" in Washington, *The Cradle Will Rock* dramatized a steel strike and featured "bloated capitalists," "heroic union organizers," prostitutes, and molls. But it was not merely leftist propaganda. According to Aaron Copland, it was a musical drama of such power and achievement, inspiring an entirely new generation of American opera. In any case, Welles and Houseman resolved to open the production independently. After last-minute frantic negotiations, Welles rented another theater and moved the entire production uptown along with the opening night audience of six hundred. The twenty-block walk, and the magnificent evening, made theater history and underscored the pending war between politicians and performers. Blitzstein played the score on an old upright piano, center stage. The cast, placed throughout the audience, burst into song from where they were, so as not to violate Equity union rules against performing in "an unauthorized production." See Tim Robbins and Susan Sarandon's 1999 film *Cradle Will Rock*.

Stagehands then knocked down the sets and laid the puppet in a pine box with a boldly printed epitaph: "Born 23 December 1938; Killed by Act of Congress, 30 June 1939."

The Congress that killed Pinocchio was also determined to strangle the New Deal. Congress killed FDR's housing bill, which would have given Wagner's housing act the money to build needed affordable housing nationwide; and it rejected FDR's spend-lend bill, which would have made it easier for hardworking people to get credit. Having destroyed the Wagner-Rogers children's refugee bill, and having sent the *St. Louis* away without comment, Congress seemed to give Hitler a clear signal: *Do as you like—the United States is determined to do nothing at all.*

ER and FDR were both distraught when Caroline O'Day voted to retain the 1935 Neutrality Act's arms embargo. A pacifist but never an isolationist, and an antiwar activist since World War I, O'Day was closely associated with the Women's International League for Peace and Freedom (WILPF). Carrie Chapman Catt, Jane Addams, and Lillian Wald were mentors to both ER and O'Day among peace activists. In the 1920s and 1930s ER and O'Day and their allies had supported U.S. adherence to the World Court and Senator Gerald Nye's (R-ND) campaign to remove profits from war industries.

Jane Addams had donated her Nobel Peace Prize money to the WILPF when she died in 1935. In January of that year, on the occasion of Catt's birthday, ER delivered a speech calling for an end to the "absolute waste" of war. "The more we see of the munitions business, of the use of chemicals, of the traffic in other goods [needed for war]," she said, "the more we realize that human cupidity is as universal as human heroism. If we are to do away with the war idea, one of the first steps will be to do away with all the possibility of private profit." She contributed the speech as an essay, "Because the War Idea Is Obsolete," to Catt's collection *Why Wars Must Cease.*

ER and O'Day had also campaigned for democratic control over international relations. They were together during a spring 1937 meeting of the Emergency Peace Campaign, when ER spoke ardently for peace through justice: "We must find a way whereby the grievances of nations, their necessities, their desires can be heard by other nations and passed upon without recourse to force." She concluded, "We have found a way to do away with dueling in settling differences between individuals"; now law must replace force.

During the Spanish Civil War, O'Day had sought to lift the arms embargo, correctly arguing that it supported fascist aggression. She signed a February 1937 congressional protest against the embargo along with thirty-one members of Congress. And ER, in her 1938 book *This Troubled World*, had agreed. Back then, FDR had opposed all congressional efforts to lift the embargo. Not until Franco's triumph did he permit arms sales to Spain. ER had found this policy incomprehensible.

Now, with Nazi aggression on the rise, FDR had changed his position, advocating repeal of the arms embargo because it helped the aggressors and weakened their victims. ER welcomed the change; she thought FDR had stood by the embargo far too long. Now O'Day's vote to retain the embargo was incomprehensible. When she cast that vote, FDR wrote her a frank and bitter letter:

> I think it may interest you to tell you in great confidence that two of our Embassies abroad tell us this afternoon that the action of the House last night has caused dismay in democratic, peaceful circles. The anti-war nations believe that a definite stimulus has been given to Hitler . . . and that if war breaks out in Europe, because of further seeking of territory by Hitler and Mussolini, an important part of the responsibility will rest on last night's action.
>
> I know you always want me to be frank with you and I honestly believe that the vote last night was a stimulus to war and that if the result had been different it would have been a definite encouragement to peace.

For several months after O'Day's vote, she and ER did not speak; a blast of cold transformed their friendship.

O'Day was part of Congress's isolationist group, representing the pacifist, liberal wing. Her fellow members there, like Oswald Garrison Villard, were veterans of the peace movement—civil libertarians, dedicated progressives, antifascist pacifists. They deplored war, because they believed that it was merely destructive. The new warfare of unlimited aerial bombardment against open cities, as in Barcelona and Madrid, left only rubble and agony. War destroyed democracy and civilization: it created only victims, never victors. O'Day supported the Ludlow Amendment, which called for amending the Constitution to require a national referendum before Congress could declare war.

Other isolationists, however, had very different politics. "America Firsters" supported Nazi efforts to rid the world of Communism—Hitler's publicly stated goal. Some publicly supported Hitler's messianic call for a final war of good against evil, defining evil as Bolshevik-Jewish democracies. Some, with no consideration for human rights violations against Hitler's subject peoples, generally despised liberal, "Communist," and Jewish efforts to rally interventionism or protest against Nazism.

Although ER shared many of O'Day's convictions about the costs of war, she rejected the proposed Ludlow Amendment as a dangerous restriction that threatened America's security. Finally she rejected neutrality and asked again, as she often had in the past: "I wonder whether we have decided to hide behind neutrality? It is safe, perhaps, but I am not sure that it is always right to be safe." In February 1939, when Carrie Chapman Catt called for increased military appropriation, ER defended her. A peace ally, Elizabeth Baker, associated with Catt's National Committee on the Cause and Cure of War, protested to ER:

> Protect our Mrs. Catt from this spectacle. A dear sweet faced old lady internationally known as a worker for peace, now at eighty, begging for guns with which to kill other mothers' sons. Preserve her past testimony against all wars and killings. Save her international friendships and prestige.

ER replied, "I am sorry that I cannot agree with you. Mrs. Catt's attitude is based on years of study and is correct."

While FDR remained in Washington to negotiate urgent Senate support to lift the arms embargo, ER left to attend the thirtieth anniversary of the NAACP in Richmond, Virginia. On her journey she considered the dire international situation. What would be the impact of continued U.S. silence on the new refugees streaming out of Jozef Tiso's fascist Slovakia, as well as Romania and Hungary? Poland was pro-Nazi, but Poland was a diverse country, with millions of democrats, antifascists, and Jews. Global war seemed imminent, and Hitler had spies everywhere, even in

U.S. pressrooms and throughout the country. She very much hoped that FDR's urgent lobbying with the senators to repeal the arms embargo succeeded.

Her talk at the convention, which included her presentation of the Spingarn Medal to Marian Anderson, was scheduled for the closing gala on 2 July. NAACP president Walter White had arranged live national radio coverage of her speech as well as Anderson's response and performance.

As ER stood before the huge crowd, formally dressed for the splendid occasion, she remained silent for a moment, reviewing the situation: African-Americans were segregated or restricted from full citizenship by poll taxes and literacy tests, which deprived them of suffrage, and by limited job and educational opportunities. Fully aware that the congressional revolt against New Deal promises was aimed in part at her audience, and knowing her words would be broadcast nationwide, she launched into a powerful speech regarding America's future.

ER focused on education. Educational reforms were needed to ensure a well-educated citizenry and should emphasize the study of history and politics, music, art, dance, theater—precisely those programs Congress so meanly targeted: "The danger of people who cannot understand the problems before their government is a real danger for us, because Congress represents the people. . . . It goes back to the people every time in a democracy and therefore it does not matter whether you belong to one race or one group. All races and all groups must see today that we as a whole, as a people, are able to understand the problems before us."

This could happen only in the right "environment," one that allowed "good citizens" to flourish. America can no longer turn its back upon the needs of the people for health care, housing, the special needs of young people: "We have to have healthy citizens. Physical health affects the mind, affects the spirit. But you cannot have physical health, mental development, spiritual happiness" without the proper environment. "Now, this may require sacrifice from the nation as a whole. Very well. Then the sacrifice" must be made. Making these changes will involve "all of us, if we care about America—and we do." But these things "mean a future for the nation or decay."

ER then presented the Spingarn Medal, awarded annually to a person who had overcome great obstacles on the path to significant achievement. Marian Anderson, she noted, had

the courage to meet many difficulties. She has always had great dignity; and her modesty and her dignity together with her great gift have
gained for her wide recognition. . . . I am glad to have been chosen to
give you this medal, Miss Anderson, for your achievement far transcends any question of race. It is an achievement in the field of art, and
this medal is given to you in recognition of the perfection of your art.
My thanks and good wishes go with you, Miss Anderson, for you
bring to this country as a whole not only enjoyment but much beauty.

Anderson thanked ER, saying, "I feel it a signal honor to have received
the medal from the hands of our First Lady who is not a first lady in
name only but in her every deed." She then asked the assembly to join her
in singing "We Are Climbing Jacob's Ladder."

ER's appearance at the NAACP convention received recognition in
the black press for months. The *Chicago Defender* celebrated her commitment to democracy:

Speaking in the very stronghold of southern reactionary groups, she
made no attempt to compromise with southern traditions. She stated
in clear, definite language the problems of a democracy and the tasks
of its citizens, in the presence of those stalwart sons of Virginia—
Senators Byrd and Glass—who have opposed every major liberal legislation of the New Deal.

Only a woman of great courage and of unusual foresight could
have registered her convictions with such force and persuasion. It was
a great speech, a great occasion, surpassed only by the greatness of
Mrs. Roosevelt.

ER returned to Washington that night. The next morning she flew to
New York City to attend the annual conference of the American Youth
Congress (AYC). Always inspired by young people, a rainbow of race and
politics, she listened to their earnest speeches, as they explained their
activism, and watched a colorful pageant. They fortified her hopes for a
democratic future.*

*This July 1939 AYC congress, still influenced by united front politics, was demo-
cratic, pro–New Deal, and pro-Roosevelt. ER was particularly drawn to specific
leaders, including Joseph Cadden, who accompanied her throughout the event;

In her evening keynote address to over five thousand delegates, ER hailed especially the group's democratic creed, which condemned dictatorships, while insisting on absolute free speech for all: "Nothing finer could come out of any organization of youths. Some people are afraid to see youth come together for discussions. They should not be afraid after reading the creed you have just adopted." She urged all members of the AYC to research conditions in their own communities, and report them to the nation: "There are many things happening in the country today which would not be happening if the people of the country knew about them. . . . It is almost impossible sometimes to find a way of informing the nation." People were suffering and actually starving from lack of work, and programs were being cut that had formerly ensured people jobs. It was up to every member of the AYC, ER advised them, to rededicate themselves with courage and fortitude to the ideals the nation would celebrate the next day, Independence Day.

As the war clouds descended, ER assumed the United States would be completely involved and determined that her role would be to encourage her allies to become more active in movements for democracy's survival. For months she spoke to large political groups to urge specific actions.

Before a large gathering of the Women's International League for Peace and Freedom, she emphasized the need for freedom of the press, deploring propaganda and government control of information. Americans had a right to "guard against" government's "undue influence" over the press, radio, or movies. "All points of view have the right of expression," and "real freedom, not sham freedom of the press," meant independence and controversy. Everywhere she went, she celebrated democracy as the alternative to "fascism and communism," which at a minimum required "economic freedom." People who "did not know where their next meal was coming from" could not possibly make "good citizens." In a democracy, "we must think of the greatest good for the greatest number."

In the face of growing assaults on democracy by Communist and

---

Mary Jeanne McKay, president of the National Student Federation; Frances Williams, student director of the Foreign Policy Association; Harriet Pickens of the Business and Professional Girls Committee, YWCA; Molly Yard, chair of the American Student Union; Robert Spivack, secretary of the International Students Service; Ephraim Kahn, of the American Medical Students Association; and Joseph Lash, executive secretary of the American Student Union.

fascist movements around the world, ER insisted that Americans must "hold firmly to our intellectual freedom." No democracy could survive "where schools and universities are not free" or where religious freedom was curtailed. She courageously highlighted racial injustice and said, "It is not a true democracy as long as some citizens cannot vote, and there are parts of this country where some citizens cannot do so; it is not a true democracy . . . when everyone does not feel free in every way."

She never deviated from her belief that what was good for the United States was, ultimately, good for the world. All spring in speeches and broadcasts she urged her audiences to confront "the root problem"—which was an "economic one," and a "world problem," and "none of us knows the answer." "We have bought ourselves time to think." But not much time: "We cannot establish peace when the underlying reasons for unhappiness and discontent remain the same the world over. . . . It is all very well to try to do things which will keep us safe," but we must see "the things which will keep us safe have to do also with keeping the rest of the world safe."

On 15 June 1939, ER launched her first 1940 campaign speech in an address to the northeast regional conference of Democratic women. ER's friend, the popular novelist Fannie Hurst, introduced the first lady as "the torchbearer of today" who lights up hope for tomorrow. To that audience, ER stressed the need for partisan activity: "Democracy must have from every citizen the kind of service which gives without seeking." Her husband had said it best regarding 1940: "We will have a liberal democracy, or we will return to the Dark Ages!"

Increasingly the New Deal was called the "Jew Deal," and increasingly the Roosevelts were called Communists and Jews. The New Deal did endanger absolute privileges long held by white planters and industrialists who had never needed to consider labor costs or labor relations. More democracy did mean the end of white power monopoly in southern states. In Virginia, for example, only 12 percent of the population voted. Because of the poll tax, wives did not vote; nor did the poor. Black people, no matter how educated, were not allowed to pass the discriminatory literacy tests required to register. Only more intense political activism would ensure democracy's survival.

ER did not underestimate the widespread bigotry that flourished in America. Even her closest friends made the most appalling remarks. Hick, for example, made disparaging remarks about Jews and blacks.

When ER asked the Federal Theatre people to find a job for Hick's brother-in-law Julian, Hick launched one of her furious tirades at how he was treated, but this one was unusual even for her. She reserved her particular wrath for Paul Edwards—that "damned kike coward" who had interviewed and insulted Julian. After the Federal Theatre hired Julian, Hick's gratitude to ER did not entail an apology: "I suppose I should say I'm sorry I wrote you that blast . . . , but I'm not."

There is no evidence that ER ever chided Hick, or anyone else in her circle, for prejudiced comments. Instead, she increasingly invited her Jewish friends to accompany her to public events, wrote more fully about them in her columns, and called for greater interfaith amity. She delivered a Fourth of July appeal to the National Conference of Christians and Jews: "If anything is evident today, it is the need of all groups of Americans to cooperate. . . . Mutual respect . . . and the promotion of better understanding among Protestants, Catholics and Jews in America is truly one of the most necessary tasks confronting us."

On Independence Day, encouraged by the public protests against the New York State Assembly's plans to cut teachers' salaries and vacation time, ER noted that children's education was America's first line of defense: limiting "educational opportunities is not wise economy, nor should the salaries of teachers be lowered. . . . We should stress better teachers and higher salaries and economize in other ways."

Fortified, ER journeyed to Hyde Park for the family's annual Fourth of July Picnic. Alone on the train, she contemplated the changes in her life—her new alliances and urgent efforts, and her old friends, so uninterested in and critical of her new friends. For the first time, Nancy Cook and Marion Dickerman would not even be at the picnic. Nor would Hick, although Earl Miller might appear.

ER and FDR had one day together only at Hyde Park; the congressional rancor demanded the president's return to Washington that very night. After their traditional picnic with family and friends including the Morgenthaus, FDR called an "impromptu press conference." He was told that Senate isolationists were "prepared to filibuster" through September. Filibuster was their right, he said, but he too was prepared to remain in session all summer, until the Senate reversed the House's failure to lift the arms embargo. It was the only thing to do to prevent war. That evening ER wrote that "we all dined with my mother-in-law" at a gala farewell party, because SDR was soon to sail for Europe. Immediately thereafter FDR boarded his special train to the capital.

ER remained at Val-Kill. She rode in the cool of the morning; later with Tommy, Aunt Maude, and her husband, Uncle David Gray (on a brief visit from his post as ambassador to Ireland). She paid a nostalgic visit to Grandmother Hall's "old house" at Tivoli. Early the next morning "I left in my own car for New York City and went straight to my mother-in-law's [Sixty-fifth Street] house to go with her to the steamer. I always like to go on board and see where my family is going to be ensconced . . . but I never like to stay to see the steamer actually leave. Even when people are going for pleasure . . . the actual moment of parting is never very pleasant."

Meanwhile in the capital FDR was urgently lobbying his allies to remain in the city. He wrote, for example, to Senator Pat Harrison (D-MS), "Pat, old dear: What is this I hear about your going home ahead of time? Do please don't! I need you here on lots of things, including the next big thing on the calendar—the Neutrality Bill."

ER rarely wrote about pending legislation, but she devoted an entire column to the Neutrality Act of 1939, which would end the arms embargo. Every U.S. citizen "ought to understand clearly what we mean by a desire for neutrality. We have certainly not been neutral under the present neutrality bill." To be neutral meant to have no power at all in world events. If "we exert no influence to prevent war until it has begun," it would be too late. If war broke out, even if the United States remained neutral, it would have an impact on American "social and economic life." ER was asking Americans to consider the true meaning of neutrality. Not being involved also meant not having the power to influence events and thereby to control their impact on our society. Congress shared "the burden of declaring war," of course. But the only hope for "real neutrality" was to permit the chief executive and the State Department to consider "each case on its merits."

On 11 July the Senate Foreign Relations Committee voted, 12 to 11, to postpone consideration of the neutrality bill until the next session of Congress. FDR appealed to the entire Senate to reconsider, and ER wrote archly: "These gentlemen must go on the theory that if you delay making up your mind long enough, perhaps you may never have to. . . . My own experience is that the things you refuse to meet today always come back at you later on, usually under circumstances which make the decision twice as difficult."

Daily, ER read disturbing accounts of thousands of refugees in desperate search for shelter. In the spring Hitler's newest territories, Slovakia and Hungary, had issued a variety of anti-Jewish laws; Jehovah's Witnesses were being arrested throughout Germany; and two thousand Gypsies (Roma) from Austria were removed to German camps. By June, there were over 300,000 "political prisoners" in concentration camps.

The situation in China was equally alarming, after three years of the calamitous Sino-Japanese War. ER received a bulletin from the Federal Council of Churches: "The amount they say will feed a Chinese child for a year seems unbelievably small. When war is going on . . . the women and children . . . suffer the most." ER called for a movement to build support for innocent civilians: "Those of us who are at peace, should do what we can to alleviate the suffering of those who do not fight, but who nevertheless reap the results of war."

On 6 July, U.S. ambassador Nelson T. Johnson had reported from Chungking that Japan had bombed the city, narrowly missing his residence and the U.S. gunboat *Tutuila*. FDR requested that Secretary of State Hull send Japan a presidential protest against "indiscriminate bombing." For several weeks fighting raged along the borderlands between Russia and China, with Soviet Mongolian troops battling the Japanese. The Soviet ambassador to the United States, Konstantin Oumansky, told Harold Ickes and others that the Soviet leadership was predicting a long, intense war. Now that England and France had sacrificed Spain, Austria, and Czechoslovakia to German perfidy, the Russians saw no reason to trust Great Britain. If Hitler were to attack the Soviet Union, the Kremlin believed the British would continue to support him.

Ickes agreed with Oumansky's assessment. An "illuminating and forceful" book, Frederick Schumann's *Europe on the Eve*, had convinced him that British and French appeasers were "willing to sacrifice all their European neighbors if only they can persuade Hitler to turn his attention to the East." Ickes believed that FDR's State Department was dominated by men who shared those views and worked for that outcome.*

*Oumansky reported to Ickes that destroyers that Russia had ordered from U.S. shipbuilders, and that had been agreed to by FDR and Hull almost two years before, were still not delivered—even though the Soviet Union had agreed "to accept the ships without any armament" and to every other "consideration imposed." State Department protocol, and the very same people who now agitated

While blood still flowed through the streets of Spain, a loan to Franco was unacceptable to ER and administration liberals—who believed that some of the responsibility for Spanish policy belonged to Ambassador Joseph P. Kennedy. Ickes showed FDR a copy of the *Week*, Claude Cockburn's radical London paper, which reported that "carried away by his pro-Franco sentiments, Mr. Kennedy, an ardent Catholic, ... goes so far as to insinuate that the democratic policy of the United States is a Jewish production." Kennedy, Ickes recorded, paraphrasing the paper, "was privately telling his English friends in the Cliveden set that the Jews were running the United States."*

FDR, Ickes noted, acknowledged Kennedy's well-known behavior. Ickes thought it was grounds for the ambassador's recall, but FDR was determined, for the moment, to ignore the unpleasant situation. Still, the president continued to support a loan to Franco.

In that tense and fractious atmosphere, FDR found it unacceptable that Hitler believed that "because of its neutrality laws, America is not dangerous to us." He made a last-ditch effort to end the arms embargo by calling Senate leaders, State Department officials, and other cabinet members to the Oval Office on the evening of 18 July. ER, having spoken to FDR earlier in the day, wrote, "he sounded very cheerful," and she hoped clear thinking would prevail that evening.

---

for a loan to Franco, had held up the deal. Ickes was appalled. Morgenthau told him that he had "held out" against the State Department—but then FDR said he wanted to make that loan. Subsequently, Ickes noted, Morgenthau "imposed conditions" on Franco's loan, which had not yet been met. Morgenthau also wanted to impose duties on imports from Italy, but the State Department absolutely refused. It all made Ickes want to write an article about the "State Department and its tender consideration of the dictatorships while pretending to serve the cause of democracy." Ickes, *Secret Diary*, pp. 2:669, 670, 677.

*Claud Cockburn's controversial left-wing paper was read both by business leaders and by radicals. MI5 kept an amazing file on Cockburn, while the Soviet Comintern criticized him as too close to bankers and the "bourgeois camp." Married three times to journalists, he is best known today as the father of journalists Alexander, Andrew, and Patrick Cockburn and as the grandfather of Laura Flanders. See Patrick Cockburn, *The Broken Boy* (New York: Vintage, 2006), for details on Claud Cockburn's MI5 file. See also Hope Hale Davis, *Great Day Coming* (Hanover, NH: Steerforth Press, 1994).

FDR began the meeting in his most cheerful manner. After many friendly glasses of wine, whiskey, gin, and bourbon, the discussion began shortly after nine o'clock. It might be appropriate, the president said, "to open this meeting with a prayer, for our decision may affect the destiny . . . of all the peoples of the world." As Nazi-fascist aggressions were bringing Europe to the brink of war, he once more asked the senators who were present to lift the arms embargo. "I've fired my last shot. I think I ought to have another round." He then turned the meeting over to Secretary of State Hull, whose position had changed and who now wanted the arms embargo repealed. FDR added that the "extreme isolationism of Senator Nye" endangered the future.*

Senator William Borah (R-ID), another leading isolationist, inter-rupted FDR to observe that Nye did not stand alone.† Borah rejected everything FDR and Hull said and insisted this current war "hysteria is manufactured and artificial." There would not be "any war in Europe." Hull invited Borah to his office to read incoming cables. Borah contemp-tuously countered that he had his "own sources" of information, and they were far "more reliable than those of the State Department." Hull was silenced and reportedly close to tears.

Of the Republicans present, only Warren Austin (R-VT) agreed that it was time "to repeal this impossible act." Toward midnight Vice President Garner sought a sense of the meeting and reported, "Well, captain, we

---

*Senator Gerald Nye (R-ND) was particularly bitter toward FDR, in part because of the president's incomprehensible insistence on maintaining the embargo against democratic Spain. On 2 May 1938 Senator Nye had introduced a resolution to raise the embargo on the lawful government of Spain and maintain it against the fascist insurgents; all shipments were to be sent to Spain on a "cash and carry basis." Nye's commitment to democratic Spain was courageous in an election year, since so many of his North Dakota constituents were German Catholics. Had the resolution had FDR's support, it would have passed easily, according to FDR biog-rapher Ken Davis. Instead, the president endorsed the evasive policy of Cordell Hull, preferring scrupulous noninterference and the avoidance of all possible "com-plications" in such a complex situation. After that, Nye was convinced that FDR's policy was shaped by Britain and was dangerous, dishonest, and unjust. See Davis, *FDR: Into the Storm*, pp. 398–99.

†Borah, the "Lion of Idaho," was known in family circles as Alice Roosevelt Long-worth's lover and as the father of her daughter Paulina. See Felsenthal, *Alice Roo-sevelt Longworth*, chaps. 8 and 9.

might as well face the facts. You haven't got the votes and that's all there is to it." FDR could not bring the bill to the Senate floor. The meeting was over.

ER read the details of her husband's failure to budge the senators, even as they faced tragedy, and wrote an irate column judging the senators harshly. We put our trust in these veteran legislators, and on their decision, "perhaps, hangs the fate of the world. And how much do the rest of us know about it?" We cannot go on as citizens "so complacently," leaving the most dire "burdens on the shoulders" of tired, disgruntled, overworked men.

Deeply disappointed, FDR nonetheless continued to fight. ER pressed him to take executive action. He asked Attorney General Frank Murphy, "How far do you think I can go in ignoring the existing [Neutrality] act—even though I did sign it?!" For six months, Congress had refused to take action, and now it had opted to wait a further six months.

ER awaited his return to Hyde Park. "I finished the mail just in time . . . to get over to the big house and be on the doorstep when my husband arrived from the station. My mother-in-law is always there to greet any of the family who come, so when she is away I should feel very guilty not to be on hand." The weekend was packed and delightful, with relatives and ten children romping and playing and eating all the time: "It is fun to see children enjoy themselves." Alexander Woollcott, a good friend and forever "the Man Who Came to Dinner," was superbly entertaining. "His fund of tales is endless, always varied and interesting." ER enjoyed the relief from war tensions and delighted in the Morgenthaus' "annual clambake," attended by all her weekend guests. The entertainment featured songs led by a "colored" trio, and everybody sang around the bonfire. The evening ended in the house for a dance party. ER, who loved to dance, was exhilarated by the Virginia reel, which "seems to have become popular and we had a roomful doing it in a most enthusiastic fashion."

ER again proved herself an expert negotiator and strategist, one who knew how to harness her husband's strengths in the pursuit of vital support within the Democratic Party. FDR was to meet with James "Jim" Farley, long the boss of the Democratic Party. ER was closely allied with Farley (who still served as postmaster general), and trusted him completely, but tensions between Farley and her husband ran high. The brilliant New Dealers led by Tom Corcoran and Ben Cohen, who had helped create so many progressive programs, sharply attacked Farley on every issue. Farley endured their rudeness in silence. After "violent" months of personal bitterness, nobody was certain where Farley stood.

Seeking to restore peace among Democratic leaders, ER and Anna teamed up with young Norman Littell, one of Farley's most ardent supporters and a leader of the young western liberals organizing for 1940. Farley explained that "the Senators were 'sore' at not being consulted by the Executive" and resented especially FDR's "deference to the Corcoran group." Farley acknowledged their splendid service, but "they are splitting the party wide apart and we can't win without the party."

Littell was close to Ben Cohen and considered himself a member of the liberal Corcoran group, but he knew that Farley's support was essential. Moreover, Farley spoke urgently about the need for party reconciliation and national unity and said he wanted "the most liberal administration in the history of the country to be preserved." Much to Littell's relief, Farley told him the "liberal vote is the vote which will turn the election. . . . The party never wins with a conservative or middle-of-the-road candidate."

Littell was moved and prepared a nine-page letter in which he listed all of FDR's mistakes in his dealings with Farley. He addressed it to Anna: "Your father's amazing success in the political history of this country is based upon leadership. . . . And your father cannot be alienated from that vast network of party relationships which Farley represents. He forms a personal link with a great mass of party workers who can only think in terms of personal loyalties." Littell concluded, "I willingly accept the leadership of young liberals to whom the President has given his confidence. . . . Therefore I reach my own conclusion that Farley is essential to 1940."

Before lunch on Sunday, ER met with Littell, and the two spent significant time in intense conversation. He gave her the letter. Then she went to confer with FDR, to prepare him for his meeting with Farley. Benefiting from Littell's efforts, and from Anna and ER's intervention, FDR gratefully acknowledged Farley's many contributions to his career for over twenty years. Regarding 1940, FDR was evasive. He was not a candidate, but if there were a war, "all bets will be off."

After Farley's meeting with FDR, there was a family lunch with John and Anne Roosevelt, who were about to sail on the *Manhattan* with Farley. ER, although pleased that her son and daughter-in-law would be spending some time with their grandmother and great-aunt Dora Forbes in Paris, was uneasy that so many people she loved were off in Europe at such a threatening time. She wondered about their journeys, after having dramatically recalled ER II less than a year before.

ER wrote Anna that Farley had left, optimistic and sanguine. With her daughter's assistance, the boss of the Democratic Party had reunited with the most significant players. Pleased that their teamwork had succeeded, she wrote Anna that Norman Littell's letter "was very useful in making Pa's conference with Jim really good. I don't think there will be any break, and Jim left on the boat today really happy."

After FDR returned to Washington, ER drove to New York for one of her whirligig days: errands and chores in the morning; the World's Fair in the afternoon; and a preview of *They Shall Have Music*, a film featuring the violinist Jascha Heifetz, to benefit the Greenwich Settlement House Music School and the High School of Music and Art. The entire audience "was moved" by the celebration of a "great artist" and by the several fine orchestras that "played so beautifully with him. I enjoyed it very much and hope that many people will see it and be led to support music schools for poor children of talent."

On 29 July, ER and Tommy drove to Esther and Elizabeth's Connecticut home for an overnight visit. Their property, Salt Meadow, extensively damaged by the hurricane of 1938, had recovered. The entire day was pleasant and relaxing, but "I suppose I had better make a confession. I was stopped by a highway patrol officer yesterday. My boys have always said that it would give them great satisfaction if I would be arrested [presumably, for speeding]. . . . I had been talking and apparently not watching my speedometer. . . . I was most humble about it, for when you are in the wrong you might as well own up. . . . I was sent on my way a much chastened and more careful individual, by a very polite but firm gentleman."

Two days later ER reported in her column that she had received a telegram—evidence that "someone reads my column." It included a verse.

> Your car was stopped.
> Oh shame, oh shame
> You'll never live it down.
> That cop should be the next President,
> The vigilantic hound.

Much amused, she considered this "rather severe punishment."

ER's attention was also on racial and religious bigotry. "Instead of acting with kindness, we seem to do the very things which promote intolerance and hatred among races and religious groups, to say nothing of the way we treat each other when we happen to be labeled workers or employers. This is happening in the United States where there is really an opportunity for leadership to create better understanding and more kindly feeling between different types of peoples."

ER refused to believe that the senators would continue to ignore the rolling thunder of impending war. She appealed to her former allies of 1935:

> It is wearisome to read of the balance of power. I would like to see somebody write about a balance of trade and of food for the world and the possibilities of so organizing our joint economic systems that all of us could go to work and produce at maximum capacity. . . .
>
> It may be somewhat impertinent for a mere, unimportant citizen, and a woman at that, to have the presumption to suggest that we are not moving forward toward the fundamental solutions at the present time. . . . Let's ask our leaders not to weaken their stand against war, but to tell us what more could be done for permanent peace.

But it was hot in Washington. Everyone wanted to return home. There was no further international policy debate. Congressional business was limited to spiteful rejections of FDR's domestic policies. For example, the House resolved to investigate the National Labor Relations Board; and the Senate refused to reinstate money for Wagner's housing bill. The president endured the final insults of the 76th Congress with equanimity.

Congress also passed the Hatch Act, which prohibited civil servants—WPA and other federal workers—from participating in campaign and political activity. It was specifically aimed at New Deal liberals, who were increasingly labeled "subversive." Corcoran and Cohen advised FDR to veto it, as did Ickes. Cohen wrote a suggested veto message that demanded that the "power of money" be removed altogether from politics and that urged congressional appropriation for all campaign expenses for all political parties: "No other contribution would be allowed."

But instead of vetoing the Hatch Act, FDR signed it into law. No

liberal in his circle understood why, as it opened the door to dismissal for
political beliefs, prohibited an unknown range of activity, specifically discriminated against federal workers, and established the principle of political "freedom with limits."

During the last days of the 76th Congress, administration liberals
were in disarray. Harry Hopkins was unwell, recently diagnosed with
stomach cancer and mostly absent from Washington. Ickes felt particularly aggrieved, since he lost several programs that he ran well and had
enjoyed creating—most notably the Public Works Administration: "I am
sore and bruised of spirit . . . and have a feeling of resentment against the
President."

On 5 August, ER, in a most uncharacteristic letter to "Dearest Franklin," asked him to invite Hopkins and Diana to Hyde Park, so that Harry
could meet a highly recommended physician for a second opinion. Then
she lobbied her husband to create a new federal post for her friend Josephine Roche—Vassar-educated, coal mine owner and administrator,
Denver policewoman, and a former assistant secretary of the Treasury.
Roche and ER had been allies on many projects over the decades. She had
recently resigned from Treasury "to put her business in order" but now
wanted to return to government. She hoped that FDR might find her a
suitable position.

After several other requests, ER concluded her long letter, "Some of
the Negro leaders feel that the Administration is losing ground. Would
there be any chance of putting T. Arnold Hill on the Maritime Commission? It sounds impossible to me but I do think that some attention should
be given to this Negro situation."

The day before FDR left Washington, ER wrote a blunt column blast-
ing the legislators for the new avalanche of suffering they created. The previous spring, when they cut funding for the WPA, they had boasted that
people would find jobs; that it would be cheaper to give "straight relief"
than coddle workers on the WPA; and that business would "take up the
slack, if it feels that Congress is not subservient to the President." But
instead, the cuts had caused real harm. "I wish the Congressmen who
enacted the bill . . . would answer some of the questions which come to
me," ER wrote, then detailed heart-wrenching appeals that she had received
from the public. One family of six had no money to buy food or to send
their children to school. Women and children were abandoned; many

families were literally starving. A hardworking veteran wrote to her, "I am a veteran of the last war, my father, his father, and his father before him fought in the wars and I think that I am a loyal and true American, yet I am not sure that I wouldn't rather have a full stomach and shelter under some other regime than to be hungry and homeless under the present one."

ER concluded, "This is not an academic discussion, this is actually what happens to human beings. Mr. Legislators, what are your answers?"

As she assessed "the last few weeks," she was certain that what the Republican minority, and the conservative Democratic minority, exhibited was "their sporting disposition." This new majority "have made two bets with the public. One is that there will be no war in Europe until they return in January. . . . The other bet is with business. . . . By next spring business will put three million people to work or the bet will be lost. Let's hope they win both bets and let's wish them all, majority and minorities, a happy holiday."

These trying months had sharpened ER as she engaged both her husband and Congress on issues that caused economic strife and political divisions. FDR continued delicate negotiations with his adversaries, while she was free to write and speak more directly. Yet perhaps the one good thing about the 76th Congress was that its sorry record had drawn the first couple closer together than they had been in years. She had revived his trust and confidence.

At Hyde Park that week the Roosevelts appeared as a team as they had never done before. FDR "let his wife join in at his regular press conference," *Time* reported, and "he openly adopted her ideas and figures of speech." He invited her opinions, and she answered with vigor. He adopted her "two enormous bets" phrase for his own and added that in the relief gamble Congress endangered 20 million Americans; in the war gamble they involved "one billion 500 million world inhabitants." ER said that the "sudden cut-off in Government spending was like pushing the country off a precipice." She was reminded of her uncle, Theodore Roosevelt, who used to make herself and other young Roosevelts jump off sand cliffs at Oyster Bay, to teach them how far you slide going downhill and how hard it is to climb back up. "Precisely," chimed in her husband; his latest lending program had been devised "to create a gentle gradient instead of a cruel precipice."

Neither Roosevelt was much damaged by Congress's "smacking

around," reporters concluded. Rather, they were determined "to fight a whole lot more." After that extraordinary press conference, FDR left early the next morning, 12 August, for his ten-day cruise aboard the *Tuscaloosa*, headed for cool northern waters.

ER was uncommonly nostalgic after his departure. The Big House became "a silent, empty place. There is one guard at the gate and one by the house. Outside of that there is no life anywhere. I left promptly for the cottage where by 1:00 o'clock, a very pleasant group of people gathered." The rest of her day ER, Tommy, and several guests swam and "spent a quiet evening reading and writing." Later, she began her Christmas list: Tommy compiled lists of things to order and those "I must buy personally."

The guests were interesting but thoughts of her loved ones plunged her into a bone-cracking gloom she had not felt for years. So many members of her family and her closest friends were abroad, and she never liked to be home while people she cared about were away. Moreover every broadcast brought news of impending war, secret meetings, and bitter deals.

She tried to work on her new book, *The Moral Basis of Democracy*, a call for the kind of activist citizenship she believed essential to the survival of democracy. But she was unsettled, impatient, and introspective.

The last thing she did before bed was to listen to the eleven o'clock radio news. "I can't say that the foreign news sounded very encouraging. How different our situation is when the man at the head of the government can leave on a vacation." She found it unbearable that the "fate of the world seems to lie in the hands of one man," meaning Hitler, ensconced "on a mountain top," giving orders. Everybody agreed that "war would leave no victors" and would only postpone "necessary economic changes which will eventually have to be made. . . . And yet we do nothing."

On the night of 14 August, forty-five years earlier, ten-year-old Eleanor had learned that her beloved father had died. Ever since, she had experienced a mid-August melancholy. That evening she wrote an unusually personal column:

> I lay the other night and watched one particularly bright planet shining in the sky above me. All the little stars around twinkled with more or less brilliance. That particular bright point, however, seemed to be the only thing that really shone out of the sky and for the time it seemed to shine for me alone in all the world. It was curiously like

the human relationships we sometimes allow ourselves when one particular person outshines all others. A balanced impartiality is supposed to be the ideal in family relations, and yet perhaps it is good for every individual to feel occasionally that he [or she] is the one bright star in the heavens.

With her father, and then for a time with FDR, ER had felt secure in that feeling. There had been other relationships, notably with Hick and Earl, and her feelings of love, longing, and loss continued to swirl around her. She had been reading an informative book filled with good advice, *Counseling Young Workers*, by Jane F. Culbert and Helen R. Smith. "I wonder if they would agree with me that every one of these youngsters who come to be counseled should have back of them the feeling that they are the bright star on whom someone is counting? That, it seems to me, is the greatest incentive to real success." That was how her beloved teacher Marie Souvestre had made her feel at Allenswood. Now it was how she tried to be in relation to the young people she so admired in her family, and among the activist leaders of the American Youth Congress, whose profound convictions regarding freedom and democracy impressed her.

She had spent the day with Joe Alsop, her young cousin, who was closely connected to her Allenswood years, which triggered her ruminations and his column. At Allenswood Eleanor had been a "plain, insecure, lonely little girl," a family orphan malnourished on "meager, weary, leftover love." The witty, brilliant, enchanting Marie Souvestre had not only mentored her but had chosen her as her "supreme favorite."

After ER left Allenswood, Corinne Robinson, who had arrived during Eleanor's last year there, became the recipient of this same "intoxicating honor." Souvestre would read aloud to Corinne, but even so she frequently stopped to "exclaim how much she missed her *chère Tottie*, the wonderful Eleanor who was so courageous and intelligent and good. Then her hands would go up in the air and fall into her lap as she sighed, 'Mais pas gaie— pas gaie.'" Corinne believed Eleanor's childhood of tears and longing "helped forge the iron in her soul that the world came to appreciate."

Years later Corinne told these stories to her son Joseph Alsop. Now a journalist, Alsop had always found ER warm, charming, generous— indeed, he compared her to his great-aunt Bye Roosevelt Cowles, who had been another guide and lifeline for ER: "Auntie Bye had a tongue that could take the paint off a barn, while sounding unusually syrupy and cooing. The harsher the sentiment, the sweeter the tone seemed to be her recipe, which was regularly borrowed by her niece Eleanor Roosevelt, whom she helped to bring up."

Now Alsop had requested an interview with ER for a "light, cheerful sort of piece" in *Life* and asked if he might drop by Hyde Park: "I know you well enough to know that you will tell me frankly whether or not you want to see me, and whatever your answer, I shall be wholly satisfied." ER had said she would be "delighted" to see him and invited him for the night "or for any length of time you can stay."

In her column, she wrote, "I enjoy all the younger generation in the family very much, but especially the ones who are at work. . . . I had the pleasure of having one young cousin with me, who seems to be doing more and more interesting work and to be constantly developing himself." Her letter to FDR explained, "Joe Alsop was here . . . and I like him better and better. He is doing a piece for *Life* called the President's Family Album which ought to be very nice." The result was indeed a "glowing" family profile, published shortly before the election of 1940.

Nancy Cook and Marion Dickerman continued to stay on at Val-Kill. Tommy Thompson continued to report to Esther Lape that their intrusive presence ranged from dreary to "poisonous," but ER never mentioned the frosty tensions between them. In one column, however, she sounded almost wistful as she explicitly announced their breakup:

> When I was connected with Miss Dickerman in the Todhunter School, I always admired her extraordinary ability to combine the old with the new and to give each child under her care the type of training that child needed. I was always interested in watching her work with the young people and in the contacts which I had with the young people myself. In resigning from the school, I miss not being able to be in such close contact with an expert in handling youngsters.

She wrote their mutual friend Mary Dreier, in Maine, "I do not understand Nancy any more than you do. She has been here most of the summer. . . . Perhaps you are correct that she has had a nervous breakdown." ER's ability to tolerate her ever-complaining former friends continued for years. They refused to depart Val-Kill until 1947.

On Tuesday, 15 August, ER left to do a radio broadcast in New York and visit her brother Hall on Long Island. Hall had rented a "little cottage" on a wildlife preserve in Sayville. With a party of his friends, they ferried "to the beach on Fire Island and the water was perfect in temperature and not too rough. Even a smooth water swimmer like myself could enjoy it. There is nothing quite like lying on a sandy beach in the sun for complete relaxation. We had the best possible picnic." ER's hours were entirely filled, but she felt "a little guilty" that she had been in New York "without going to the World's Fair" to see Hick.

It is unclear what ER learned on her trip to New York, or what letter she received in the mail, or who arrived to change her mood. But on her return to Hyde Park, her tone of melancholy was replaced with a new verve and more familiar bold purpose. Perhaps it was that her brother was momentarily in a good situation.

Or perhaps she had had news of her traveling family, and her mother-in-law's doings in London and Paris. That August SDR and her great friend Grace Vanderbilt were being escorted around London by Grace's son Cornelius "Neil" Vanderbilt Jr., who provided ER with the fullest details.

"Mother and Mrs. Roosevelt beat me to London by about six hours," he wrote. They were much excited because they were to have tea with Grace's "dear friend, Queen Mary." Their "thirty or forty years" of correspondence had even survived Grace's nine-page letter urging the queen not to be so harsh and unfair to the Duke of Windsor. Now Neil escorted them to "Buck House," as his mother called it—and observed that the gatekeepers and guards recognized her as she presented "the mother of my President."

"That night at dinner, Mother and Mrs. Roosevelt regaled me with an account of their afternoon. They were so proud of themselves and so very happy and gay; they had a sense of accomplishment." They were convinced they had forestalled the coming of "another world war." Neil himself predicted war was imminent, "certainly not later than this fall, but perhaps as soon as next week." But both women abhorred war and thought themselves supremely influential: "We went over to talk to Queen Mary and tell her that we three people were not going to permit another world war to come to civilization.

"And Mother truly believed that because Mrs. Roosevelt, the mother of the President of the United States, and Queen Mary, the mother of the King of England, and she herself, a powerful person in financial circles" on two continents, had gotten together and agreed, the war would be prevented. They were perhaps among the last to insist that relations were more tidy, and everything was safer so long as the cousins ruled the world.

For the next several days, as Neil took them about London, they saw dramatic preparations for war everywhere. The streets were "torn up," electric wiring for new communications was being strung, trenches were being dug, anti-aircraft installations were being created. It reminded Neil of the war preparations he had seen in Danzig weeks before. ER, upon receiving Neil's news, was filled with dread.

After Grace returned to the United States, SDR, now accompanied by her grandchildren John and Anne, journeyed on to Paris, where Neil met up with her again at Ambassador William Bullitt's Chantilly residence. "The President's mother, is in grand form," reported Bullitt's executive secretary, Carmel Offie.

At dinner Bullitt introduced SDR and explained that the United States under her son was not a monarchy, a dictatorship, or a socialist state—it was a "matriarchy under her." Dinner was interrupted by ominous international phone calls, and a surprise visit from French president Albert Lebrun: "I have come to tell the United States, and the very charming mother of the President, that the French Republic is mobilizing. . . . Good night my friends, and may God bless us all."

After a round of liqueurs and brandy in the library, Bullitt drove his guests to a village fair in Chantilly. Beyond the sideshows and carousels, an elaborate shooting range had been set up for serious competition. SDR picked up a rifle, and in "no time at all, she shot the bowls off the pipes, hit many of the little ducks and other moving animals, and before we knew what happened, she won the first prize"—an elaborate gingerbread pig, to be personalized with her name. The entire party spelled the name slowly for the attendant, who replied, *"Oh, comme le président."* Yes, they acknowledged. Asked what she would do with her prize, SDR said she intended to give it to her son. Bullitt asked, "Do you think he will understand?" "Yes, my son understands everything his mother does, although he often does not agree with her. . . . You know, when Frank was a little boy he was pretty much of a piggy-wiggy, and sometimes he still is."

Chapter Five

"If They Perish, We Perish Sooner or Later"

In August 1939 anyone privileged to read diplomatic dispatches, listen to shortwave radio, or garner clear signals from abroad in any other way, knew that war was imminent. Although it is uncertain what messages ER received while her husband was on the cruiser *Tuscaloosa*, fishing for salmon off the Newfoundland coast, she was aware that momentous events were under way. Congress was in recess, Parliament had adjourned "angry and anxious," and last-minute efforts to forestall Danzig's absorption by Germany failed.

For years, Russia had appealed to Western countries to form a united front against Hitler. Maxim Litvinov had long tried to achieve such an alliance, and his successor as Soviet foreign minister, Vyacheslav Molotov, who was married to a Jewish woman, had continued that quest. Working together in an alliance, Russia, England, France, and Czechoslovakia—with its vast Skoda works, and its military and chemical industries—could have defeated the fascists and prevented war. But British prime minister Neville Chamberlain had allowed Russian negotiations to languish. Worse, he had sent to Moscow low-level negotiators without proper credentials and instructed them to move slowly, vaguely. They were discourteous.

Stalin was insulted, as he was meant to be. On 15 August Molotov announced that Stalin believed that Britain actually sought war in the East, from Poland to Russia, and that Chamberlain preferred to see the Soviet Union crushed. The Soviet leadership no longer had any reason to pursue an alliance with Britain against Hitler.

Instead, Stalin now sought an economic agreement and nonaggression pact with Germany itself. Hitler, ecstatic, responded immediately. On 17 August a Russo-German trade agreement was signed, and by 19 August a nonaggression pact was drafted. German foreign minister Joachim von Ribbentrop traveled to Moscow, and on 23 August he and

Molotov signed the Nazi-Soviet Pact. By its terms, Hitler and Stalin divided up the Baltic States—Lithuania would be in Germany's sphere of influence, while Latvia, Estonia, and Finland were in the Soviet sphere—and they agreed to partition Poland.

When the pact was publicly announced on 24 August, it stunned the world. Anglo-American leaders cut their vacations short. "All talk of appeasement is now stilled," Harold Nicolson wrote. For Communists like the Paris-based Russian journalist Ilya Ehrenburg, the pact, a treaty of "friendship cemented with blood," was "blasphemy." It was literally sickening—he took to his bed and could not eat regularly for eight months.

Churchill—who wondered which of the two enemies, Hitler or Stalin, "loathed [the pact] most"—returned to London. He had been in France touring the defenses along the Maginot Line with grave misgivings; he found France's "defense" line to be illusionary, offering no protection, since Germany was on the march in every direction.

FDR cut short his Newfoundland fishing cruise. Jettisoning his plan to sail to Annapolis, on the morning of 24 August he anchored at Sandy Hook, New Jersey, from where he left at once for Washington by special train. Cordell Hull, having returned from a vacation in Virginia, met the president at the dock. The president appeared "grim and preoccupied," the *New York Times* reported, as he debarked to make his "dramatic dash back to the capital."

The details of the Nazi-Soviet Pact were still secret, but during a series of urgent meetings that week FDR and his cabinet correctly surmised them. The pact "probably means a partition of Poland," Ickes wrote in his diary, and the Soviet Union "will not have to worry about the Ukraine, and her annexation of Bessarabia." Germany would likely take over Romania and Hungary. Yugoslavia "will either fall to Italy or be divided." The Balkans would remain "buffer states between Germany and Russia but more . . . under Russian influence." In sum, the pact undid the geographic changes made between the Baltic and the Black Sea by the Treaty of Versailles. Germany would then turn to the West, and the war would affect the world on every continent. It was "terrible" on every level. Ickes, like Churchill, did not blame Russia for the disaster. Rather, "Chamberlain alone is to blame," he said.

The discussions at cabinet meetings were wide-ranging. FDR specifically rejected any settlement that would be reminiscent of the Munich

Agreement, which had devoured Czechoslovakia's national independence and integrity. Unlike Czechoslovakia, Poland would not be sacrificed to Nazi aggression: "Parliament has been recalled," noted FDR, "and war powers granted. . . . Chamberlain's stiffer attitude is resulting in cheers when he appears on the street and soldiers in uniform are also being cheered."

After the first day of meetings with his top advisers, including Hull, Undersecretary of State Sumner Welles, and Assistant Secretary of War Louis Johnson, FDR acted, noted the *Times*, "under the greatest urgency and in the belief that war was merely a matter of hours, unless some extraordinary effort was made to avoid it." He "dispatched three appeals for the preservation of world peace," addressed to Hitler, Poland's president Ignacy Mościcki, and Italy's King Victor Emmanuel III, urging each to "accord complete respect to the independence and territorial integrity of the other." In April he had sought a pledge of territorial integrity from Hitler and Mussolini, he recalled, to be followed by a "conference of world powers on disarmament and economic problems." Now, he insisted, if there were no settlement, wanton aggression would result; brutal "efforts by the strong to dominate the weak" would lead only to endless war.

France and Poland had mobilized, and German troops were on the march from East Prussia and the Slovakian border. FDR instructed the War and Navy departments "to raise no question" regarding the shipment of planes and matériel to be delivered to England and France "on pending orders."

FDR had warned Stalin that Hitler would turn on the Soviet Union eventually, but his warning went unheeded and "meant nothing in the context" of FDR's explicit rejection of all responsibility up to that point. For months, the U.S. ambassadorship to Moscow had been vacant. Lawrence Steinhardt was appointed in March 1939, but he did not arrive in Moscow until August. By then it was too late—Stalin had already embarked upon the Nazi-Soviet Pact.

Stalin's pact with Hitler forestalled not only a Nazi attack on Russia but also a Russian war with Japan. Japan had been moving along the Siberian border, specifically encroaching beyond Manchuria through Outer Mongolia. Now Japan, aware that its 1936 Berlin-Tokyo Anti-Comintern Pact had been trumped by the Nazi-Soviet Pact, turned in momentary panic to FDR for an agreement "to go into Siberia and take it away from the Russians." This strange appeal to block Russia's flow of supplies to China and "stabilize" Asia was quickly withdrawn after late August conversations between Hull and Japan's ambassador to Washington revealed that the U.S. government actually intended to increase its aid to China. Indeed, by summer's end FDR instructed Henry Morgenthau "to do everything we can that we can get away with" to help China repel Japan.

ER was pleased by FDR's decision. She detested most of her husband's State Department and deplored his policies of inaction. She never doubted the essential connectedness of all nations and all peoples, and had consistently campaigned for collective security, for a united front against fascism. She considered Hull spineless and useless as each outrage by Hitler and Mussolini unfolded; she particularly disliked Joseph Grew, FDR's Groton and Harvard chum, who rejected economic pressures against Japan and equated sanctions with acts of war. In *This Troubled World*, her 1938 book, she had been critical of FDR's failure to block German and Japanese trade. But if she regarded her husband's inaction impatiently, she appreciated his sincere, patient commitment to the democratic process.

Above all, FDR was concerned about the forty thousand Americans still abroad—including his eighty-four-year-old mother, his youngest son, John, and his daughter-in-law Anne. They were not expected to sail until 1 September, but unknown to him, they had booked immediate passage out of Paris and were already aboard the *George Washington*. SDR and her grandchildren had departed right away "in order not unnecessarily to add to my son's worries." She added, "I have every faith that my son will do everything he can to save peace for the sake of liberty and democracy."

ER was vastly relieved that her mother-in-law and children were homeward bound, but she worried about SDR's ninety-year-old sister Dora Delano Forbes, "who stays on in Paris with absolute calm." ER had deep respect for Aunt Dora, who "is so interested in everything going on in the world. I know it is not indifference which makes her calmly stay on in her Paris home." During the first war Aunt Dora had taken ER to a Paris hospital to bring the wounded "comforts and pleasures." ER was always impressed by her large and generous heart, but the new war was escalating at such a fast pace, ER worried that her aunt might not fully appreciate the dangers.

ER did not refer immediately to the shocking Nazi-Soviet Pact but expressed revulsion that "one man may decide to plunge Europe into war. . . . Every citizen in a democracy [must be appalled] that this important decision rests with one man." She absolutely resolved to continue her work, even though "the newspapers these days are most depressing to read. I hardly dare think of the implications both for Europe and for ourselves of the last few days' occurrences."

In times of crisis and war, she knew that her job was to bang the drums, rattle the pots, and help develop the needed climate for change. To do so, she relied on her established network of women activists and increasingly on the younger people associated with the National Youth Administration (NYA) and the American Youth Congress (AYC). She was pleased, as summer ended, to spend time with "quite a number of young people these past few days," notably NYA administrators Aubrey Williams and Mark McCloskey and their families. And when Senator Robert Wagner, South African writer Sarah Gertrude Millin, and Commander Flanagan visited, she took them for a tour of Dutchess County's NYA projects: the Hudson River State Hospital in Poughkeepsie, which trained young workers for jobs in health care; an abandoned trade school transformed into an exciting NYA program for carpentry and wooden crafts; and a work center in Newburgh, where girls studied home economics and treated the visitors to an "excellent lunch." At the trail museum in Bear Mountain Park, many youngsters were performing splendid services. Every program they visited boasted many graduates who had gone on to real and rewarding jobs.

Savoring life's natural course even amid tensions, ER ended her column of 25 August with a reflective rhapsody:

> I sank into bed last night with a feeling of great luxury. The city had been hot and not very attractive, so [to] lie with the moon shining down on my porch and find two blankets a pleasant covering, seemed good beyond measure. Our purple loose-strife is almost gone, but it is fading very beautifully, giving the green grass across our little pond a lovely rosy tinge. We humans should take lessons from nature and fade as gracefully. Perhaps we cling too much to the years of full bloom. If you fade gracefully, you may be just as attractive. Our loose-strife certainly is.

On Friday, she confessed that she had created something of a scene when she asked her husband when he would return to Hyde Park:

> I talked to the President in Washington last night and, I suppose, like all women who like to keep the daily happenings on as even a keel as possible, I casually inquired the hour of his arrival Monday night, only to be told firmly that . . . arrivals and departures are of no importance now. In fact, nothing individual counts, perhaps the fate of civilization hangs in the balance. What does it matter whether we eat or sleep or do any of the things which we thought important yesterday? My heart sank, for that was the old 1914 psychology. It is rather horrible to have a past experience of this kind to check against the present.

She applauded her husband's work, however:

> Both the Pope and the President have issued pleas in the attempt to preserve European peace. Negotiation, mediation or arbitration are just words, but any one of them if put into practice now by people who really want to keep peace, might mean life instead of death. . . . It is not only the young men whom we need to consider, for when the first airplane flies over a foreign country and drops its bombs, then all women, children and men are in equal danger.

For almost a week, daily news of war flooded every radio, every newspaper. Letters detailed war preparations across Europe. Vita Sackville-West at Sissinghurst wrote her husband, Harold Nicolson, in London while waiting for Parliament to act:

> What ghastly hours. If only you were not in London. It makes me physically sick to think of air-raids. I was rung up in the middle of my luncheon and asked if the Buick would take an eight-foot stretcher or "only sitting-cases and corpses." I feel sick with apprehension, but I find that I get braver as the day goes on, a curious psychological working which I wish I could analyse.

On 30 August, ER described the gloom and dread of each suspenseful morning:

> I feel that every day that bombs do not actually burst and guns go off, we have gained an advantage. . . . One trembles to think of the

number of human beings who stand opposite each other armed to the teeth. . . .

Everyone's ear is glued to the radio. . . . I feel sorry for the German people, waiting for hours while their fate is being decided upon by one man. They are no more anxious for war, I am sure, than the people of Poland.

ER's conviction that the people of Germany opposed war was influenced by the stunning radio broadcasts out of Berlin and London by William Shirer and Edward R. Murrow, two journalists she particularly admired. For much of August, Shirer reported on the "lies and invented incidents" that Joseph Goebbels, Hitler's propaganda minister, inserted into broadsides and newspapers throughout Poland and Germany. Goebbels, the "master of the twisted word," had created a new level of propaganda: Poland wanted war, it was reported; Poland butchered German families; Poland was a land of maniacs and monsters. People were either convinced or confused, while others decided that nothing was as it was reported.

Every German citizen Shirer spoke with—in the streets, "riding around on the subway, street-cars and buses"—opposed war, he reported. They protested the absence of real news, the disaster of false news. It was hot, and most Berliners "betook themselves to the lakes around the city, oblivious to the threat of war." But even as Hitler added to his demands for the return of all that Germany had lost at Versailles, he imposed "ration cards for food, soap, shoes, textiles, and coal," on his people. The mood was becoming somber and fearful.

ER felt fortunate to have at this moment as guests her aunt Maude Gray and her lifelong friend Alice Huntington, who shared her enthusiasm for young people and democracy. On 30 August they motored to a nearby summer school and work camp for college students from all across America and for refugee scholars, "boys and girls, Jews, Catholics and liberal Germans." Some had advanced college degrees, while others were high school students; some spoke English, while others had yet to learn the language. For seven weeks, on scholarship from "various universities," these students studied "democracy theoretically and practically" by working and playing together. They read, argued, and debated as they improved roads, painted houses, and built badminton courts and a swimming pool: "The girls work as hard as the boys at every kind of work." They studied "economics . . . as a basis for a better understanding of democracy . . . and they have turned out a set of maps and charts which are extremely interesting and informative." ER enjoyed her time with this "varied and stimulating group," and was certain their mutual concern and shared experiences would make them "wiser in democratic ways."

The next day, the last day of peace in Europe, ER, Tommy, Alice Huntington, and Maude Gray drove to the World's Fair. They collected Hick at her office, and she escorted them to Finland's exhibit. ER was impressed by its glass and pottery, and the "moccasins made me think . . . of our own Indians' work." They toured the Italian building and the Federal building, then lunched at the Danish pavilion, where they enjoyed the extraordinary smorgasbord table. At the Greek building, "the glass, pottery and furniture all were very lovely and bore witness to the fact that the glory of Greek genius is not a thing of the past."

Returning to Hyde Park, ER reflected upon the many contributions of refugee groups. Her mail was filled with urgent appeals and dreadful details of refugees everywhere on the run. She was bewildered that such human suffering was met by routine silence and official disregard.

On the morning of 1 September 1939, she was awakened at five o'clock, when FDR telephoned from Washington to tell her that "Germany had invaded Poland and . . . her planes were bombing Polish cities. He told me that Hitler was about to address the Reichstag." FDR had been roused two hours earlier by Ambassador Bullitt in Paris. The U.S. ambassador in Warsaw, Anthony J. Drexel Biddle, had been unable to get through to Washington and had called Bullitt and told him that "several German divisions are deep in Polish territory, and fighting is heavy." There were bombers over the city, "then he was cut off." FDR replied, "Well Bill, it's come at last. God help us all."

Immediately FDR called Cordell Hull and Sumner Welles at State; Secretary of War Harry Woodring; Charles Edison, the acting secretary of the navy; and William Haslett, acting press secretary. ER was evidently the last person FDR called that morning, with the specific request that she listen to Hitler's broadcast. The president had made certain the lights were lit throughout the administration. By three-thirty Hull was in his office, making the necessary international calls.

Accompanied by Tommy and Alice Huntington, ER listened to Hitler's broadcast with a "sense of impending disaster":

The thing we had feared had finally come, and we seemed to know that sooner or later we would be dragged into the vortex. . . . I do not think Franklin ever felt that war was inevitable, and he always said he hoped we could avoid it, but I had a feeling that once the war started, there was not much chance for any part of the world to escape it.

That day an eight-page letter had arrived for ER ("My dear Totty") from Carola von Schaeffer-Bernstein, a classmate at Allenswood, her British boarding school. ER had maintained a correspondence with Carola over the years, despite Carola's commitment to Nazism, which she considered Christ's answer to Bolshevism. Now her German friend wrote that "when hate was rampant in the world, it was easy to believe harm of any nation" and insisted that "all the nations believed things that were not true about Germany." She begged ER "to see Germany's point of view and not to judge her harshly." When ER wrote her column, she recounted the incident:

> As I listened to Hitler's speech, this letter kept returning to my mind. How can you feel kindly toward a man who tells you that German minorities have been brutally treated, first in Czechoslovakia and then in Danzig, but that never can Germany be accused of being unfair to a minority? I have seen evidence with my own eyes of what [Hitler] has done to people belonging to a minority group—not only Jews, but Christians, who have long been German citizens.
>
> Can one help but question his integrity? . . . How can you say that you do not intend to make war on women and children and then send planes to bomb cities?
>
> No, I feel no bitterness against the German people. I am deeply sorry for them, as I am for the people of all other European nations facing this horrible crisis.

ER did not answer Carola for a week. Instead she and her friends discussed the range of Nazi atrocities and considered Hitler's unique evil. All that day she remembered details of diplomacy, the missed opportunities as well as the positive achievements, such as the triumphant visit of Britain's royals. "I could not help remembering the good-bye to the king and queen," she mused, "and the lump that had come into my throat as they stood on the back platform of their departing train. Now their people faced the final hour of decision."

His Majesty's Government decided to evacuate children, old people, and the infirm from London, a move that filled her with dread and wonder. "It was the greatest mass movement of population" in British history. "From London, Birmingham, Manchester, Liverpool, Edinburgh, Glasgow and twenty-three other cities the greatest exodus is going on. . . . The numbers are stupendous. More than 3,000,000 of these helpless human beings are being taken out of danger of German bombs."

In Washington, FDR discussed Hitler's maniacal methods, his barking and screeching, his bizarre lies and uncivil behavior with his companions. Reports from London confirmed the most grievous observations about Hitler's character. According to Ivone Kirkpatrick, first secretary at Britain's embassy in Berlin, Hitler emitted "such a sense of evil arrogance that one is almost nauseated." Harold Nicolson noted, "Even the highest Nazis are amazingly disloyal to Hitler at times," and many heard associates whisper, "For God's sake don't let him get away with it." Whether or not Hitler was "a nut," he was ready to destroy civilization. On Saturday night, 2 September, FDR hosted five intimates—Harold Ickes, Solicitor General Robert Jackson, his military aide Edwin "Pa" Watson, his physician Ross McIntire, and his press secretary Steve Early—for a stag dinner and poker party. Their wide-ranging conversation was interrupted by several news bulletins. At eleven, FDR read a dispatch handed him and said, "War will be declared by noon tomorrow." That news ended the suspense. The appeasers had been overruled.

After the poker party broke up at one a.m., FDR studied a memo from Navy secretary Charles Edison. News of war returned him in mind and spirit to those wartime events when, as assistant navy secretary, emergency calls awakened him to disasters all through the night. But the parallels between "then and now" must not be repeated. Above all, FDR had said on 1 September 1939, the disaster and "frenzy" of "excessive prices, profits, and costs must be avoided." We know from that bitter experience that "excessive profits and sky-rocketing prices for materials and labor are paid for out of human misery. . . . Our defense, geographically and in a military sense, and particularly in a financial and economic sense, remains adequate only to the degree that we soberly and earnestly refuse to be drawn into the byways of profiteering and speculation." Our defenses will be strong and adequate, and it will not be necessary to invoke "the drastic powers of wartime to maintain our economic structure," but only if "our business men, our manufacturers and our labor leaders exert their great influence . . . and succeed in restraining the cupidity of those jackals of war, the profiteers."

FDR's warning to "Wall Streeters and economic royalists," already broadcast in Washington to the great distress of such administration stalwarts as Ickes, Perkins, Corcoran, and Cohen, was indeed a highlight of FDR's Sunday evening Fireside Chat, which covered many issues. Since Americans received news "through your radios and your newspapers at every hour," and were "the best informed people in all the world at this moment," FDR cautioned against rumors and propaganda. "You are subjected to no censorship of news, and I want to add that your government has no information which it withholds or which it has any thought of withholding from you."

But FDR urged his listeners to discriminate carefully: "Do not believe . . . everything you hear or read. . . . When peace has been broken anywhere, the peace of all countries everywhere is in danger."

As far removed as America was from the fields of battle, nobody, he said, could remain detached. Every word spoken, every ship afloat, every battle fought "does affect the American future." Therefore "let no man or woman thoughtlessly or falsely talk of America sending its armies to European fields. At this moment there is being prepared a proclamation of American neutrality. . . . And I trust that in the days to come our neutrality can be made a true neutrality." That was the president's only reference to his intention to repeal the embargo clause in the 1935 Neutrality Act. The jackals of war, although unnamed, were specifically addressed:

> I cannot prophesy the immediate economic effect of this new war on our nation, but I do say that no American has the moral right to profiteer at the expense either of his fellow citizens or of the men, the women, and the children who are living and dying in the midst of war in Europe.
>
> Some things we do know. Most of us in the United States believe in spiritual values. Most of us, regardless of what church we belong to, believe in the spirit of the New Testament—a great teaching which opposes itself to the use of force, of armed force, of marching armies and falling bombs. The overwhelming masses of our people seek peace—peace at home, and the kind of peace in other lands which will not jeopardize our peace at home. . . .

This nation will remain a neutral nation, but I cannot ask that every American remain neutral in thought as well. Even a neutral has a right to take account of facts. Even a neutral cannot be asked to close his mind or close his conscience.

I have said . . . many times, that I have seen war and that I hate war. I say that again and again. I hope the United States will keep out of this war. I believe that it will. And . . . every effort of your government will be directed toward that end.

FDR's "neutrality proclamation," broadcast internationally, offered slight comfort. Harold Nicolson considered it "a bad proclamation from our point of view. He says that nothing on earth will induce the Americans to send forces to Europe. But he also says that no man can remain neutral in mind and that he knows where the right lies."

ER never overtly opposed her husband's policies on important issues, but a close reader of her columns would have noted divergences. After listening to her husband's words from her sanctuary at Val-Kill, she wrote:

It is curious when great tragedies occur, how suddenly the minor inconveniences and sorrows of life, even personal things which seemed important, become overshadowed by the general weight of world conditions. . . .

I hope that, in spite of the contagion of war, we can keep out of it, but I hope that we will decide on what we believe and . . . I hope that we will throw our weight . . . toward a speedy termination of the war, for when there is war no one is safe and the economic consequences . . . are serious [for all]. . . . Let us do all we can for those who suffer.

If ER was distraught that years of appeasement and international decisions she abhorred had led to this, she was perhaps gratified that her husband was finally adopting policies she had championed since 1935, when she opposed the embargo and supported the Nye Committee's proposals to remove profits from war and nationalize war industries.

Amid all the horror, there were also diversions. On 1 September she left Hyde Park at dawn and drove herself to New York Harbor, where she "met the steamer 'George Washington'" and escorted her mother-in-law, Johnny, and Anne off the boat." Then at 9:15 a.m. she flew to Newport

News, Virginia, to christen the SS *America*, scheduled for 11:49. ER proudly noted in her column, "We reached there in ample time and the ceremonies went off without a hitch. I read a letter from the President to Admiral Land, for I represented him." The ship was duly launched amid whistles and pomp, "and in spite of my usual anxiety I broke the bottle without any difficulty, so the 'America' began her career under auspicious circumstances." From Newport News she entrained to Washington, where she "spent an hour and a half with my husband and reached Hyde Park again at 7:45 for dinner with my guests. Quite a full day."

In her daily life, ER was increasingly her husband's stand-in. While he prepared his message to the nation that Sunday, she attended the annual FDR Home Club party in Hyde Park, accompanied by SDR, John and Anne, and, surprisingly, given the pervasive tensions between them, Nancy Cook and Marion Dickerman. The president "always enjoys" this "opportunity to see and talk with his neighbors," ER noted, but today she conveyed his message of regret and stood in for him to discuss three new schools and the details of a proposed Hyde Park post office.

The next day John and Anne drove to Boston, and Jimmy left for California. ER sensed in all her children "a feeling of uncertainty," a sense of urgency, for tomorrow all might be disrupted—hurtled into the dreadful unknown.

We were discussing the 1914 psychology of today and I think people are much more aware of what war will mean from the economic standpoint as well as the military. We have had a good many years of preparation watching Spain and China and the radio is a more vivid medium of information than the newspapers were in 1914. I think it has made us more realistic, more reluctant to see war anywhere in the world, but I also think it is making us feel the necessity of knowing the facts and thinking out for ourselves what the position of our country should be.

On 6 September ER finally answered her former friend Carola von Schaeffer-Bernstein's letter, with its defense of Nazism. In a long and rambling response, she directly questioned Carola's effort to maintain her Christian precepts alongside her Nazi enthusiasms. But her letter contains one of history's most curious anomalies, namely the antithetical approach adopted by even the most humane, where hatred of Hitler and the need to curb the "ascendancy of the Jewish people" continued along parallel paths:

> I cannot say that I feel the present situation had a parallel in 1914. All of us, of course, are appalled at plunging the European continent into war, but I do not think there is any bitterness toward the German people in this country. There is an inability to understand how people of spirit can be terrified by one man and his storm troops to the point of countenancing the kind of horrors which seem to have come on in Germany, not only where the Jews are concerned, but as in the case of the Catholics and some of the liberal German Protestants.
>
> I say this with knowledge, because I have actually seen many of the people who have reached this country from concentration camps. I realize quite well that there may be a need for curtailing the ascendency of the Jewish people, but it seems to me it might have been done in a more humane way by a ruler who had intelligence and decency. . . .
>
> You are wrong if you think the people of this country hate Germany . . . but they do hate Hitler and Nazism because of the evidences that have been placed before them. . . .
>
> You who believe in God must find it very difficult to follow a man who apparently thinks he is as great as any god. I hope that we are not facing another four years of struggle and I hope that our country will not have to go to war, but no country can exist free and unoppressed while a man like Hitler remains in power.

The "Jewish people" had, of course, been at the center of discussions about the war, about America's role, and about what should be done to help them out of their plight. But the issue was always weighted for Eleanor, for many of her friends were anti-Semitic and did not hesitate to air their opinions. ER, ever the peacemaker, juggled between her own beliefs and those of her friends. It is impossible to know whether her contemptuous reference to Jews was intended to offset her harsh letter, or whether it actually represented a lingering feeling she worked throughout her life to uproot.

ER was distressed that somebody she cared about, who was above all a fervent Christian, could at the same time condone cruel acts of bigotry. Indeed, she had focused on this peculiar mix of Christian righteousness and prejudice in her first public consideration of the "present catastrophe for Jew and Gentile." Written on 25 November 1938 for the journalist Fulton Oursler, called in typescript "On Jews," ER criticized an article by H. G. Wells in which he blamed Jews for their plight because they were "always conscious of their race." ER blamed a long history of restriction, segregation, and hostility. From the Middle Ages forward, their ghettos and economic limitations walled them into confined spaces, narrow opportunities. When restrictions were lifted, steps toward assimilation began. And then the road toward integration was blocked, "and today we are seeing in some countries a return to the attitude of the Middle Ages."

ER was blunt: This was not solely about what the Jews had done. If they "always remain a nation within a nation," Christians needed to accept their role in keeping them apart, then criticizing them if they become "too ostentatiously patriotic" in their efforts to assimilate as nationals. "The blame it seems to me cannot be entirely shrugged off the shoulders of the Gentile." Perhaps "the Jewish people haven't scattered themselves sufficiently through a wide area where they could be less concentrated in a racial group." Perhaps they had not sufficiently diversified "their occupations," and were too concentrated "in certain professions which leads inevitably to resentment." But why should this resentment lead to "hate and persecution"? Was it, ER wondered, because of a "secret fear that the Jewish people are stronger or more able"? She reluctantly concluded that while the Jewish people might

> be in part responsible for the present situation, they are not as responsible as the other races who need to examine themselves and grapple with their own fears. I think we, and by we I mean the people of Europe as well as the people of the United States, have pushed the Jewish race into Zionism and Palestine, and into their nationalistic attitude. Having that great responsibility upon us, I think it lies with us to free ourselves of our fears. . . .
>
> Suppose that the people of a given state decided that one of their cities had become [dominated] by politicians of one racial group [and represented therefore a government of another country and were] a menace to the state. Would we go forth and slay the foreign citizens? By so doing it seems to me that we would arouse the compatriots living in other countries or in other parts of our own country to defend their racial brethren. . . . A little imagination would scatter and change this population without resorting to tyranny.

ER's discussion of what Gentiles feared about the Jews involved all the stereotypes of the moment. But her essay was meant to warn against stereotypes and violent prejudice. ER concluded:

> If tyranny and fear triumph in us we will bring out in the persecuted foreigner, greed and cunning and egotism for self-protection, and we are increasing the emphasis on religious and racial hatred.
>
> In view of what is confronting us, the Jew is almost powerless today. The future depends entirely on the course the Gentiles choose to pursue. It can be cooperative, mutual assistance, gradual slow assimilation with justice and fair-mindedness towards all the racial groups living together in different countries—or it can be injustice, hatred and death.
>
> It looks to me as though the future of the Jews were tied up as it has always been with the future of all the races of the world. If they perish, we perish sooner or later.

ER's personal commitment to her Jewish friends and her commitment to end bigotry evolved slowly but were absolute. On 9 September Elinor Morgenthau was to arrive in New York from Europe, with her children, Henry (twenty-two) and Joan (sixteen), aboard a Norwegian steamer. ER drove to be at the dock to meet her: "This will be a happy day of reunion for them and I shall certainly be glad to have all these dear friends safely home."

ER was probably thinking of the recent sinking of the *Athenia*, a Canadian vessel carrying fourteen hundred passengers to North America. On 3 September a German U-boat had torpedoed it off the coast of Scotland, and 112 lives had been lost. "We awoke," ER wrote, "to the news of the tragedy. . . . We must all try to remain calm. . . . I shall be thankful when all of my family and friends are safely back in this country." ER's primary concerns were for Aunt Tissie in Scotland, Uncle David Gray in Dublin, and Aunt Dora in Paris. She was relieved to learn that the Morgenthaus' voyage across the war-infested Atlantic had been stalled only once, by a British ship.

During the first months of the war, ER concentrated on issues of bigotry and rescue. With Esther Lape and Elisabeth Read, she reconsidered what was ultimately needed to end the scourge of war. Her allies in the World Court fight and great guides in the political realm had spent hours

together discussing how to reorganize the world "to plan a more permanent way of peace." Lape and Read remained ER's most intimate confidantes as the world around them plunged into bitter disarray. That week
ER and Tommy had "the most beautiful drive over to Westbrook, Conn."
Autumnal colors heightened the spectacular journey. But the enchant-
ment of the afternoon involved their earnest, galvanizing conversation.
They agreed, above all, not to give in to a defeatist war mentality concerning domestic issues: the goal was to "continue our own recovery . . . and
still be of use to the people of the world."

Her friends' way of life appealed to ER, and she devoted a column to
describing their sanctuary.

> We cooked our lunch and ate it in the woods overlooking the marshes
> which run in front of the Sound. . . . A solitary figure could be seen
> poling a flat bottomed boat along the channels which run through
> the salt meadows. In front of us was a most beautiful old oak tree
> which had withstood the ravages of last year's storm. . . . The sun
> flickered through and it was a most peaceful and restful interlude.
> When we walked up through the woods after lunch to the higher
> ground, we had a view of the blue water with the dancing sunlight
> on it. . . . We will look back happily on one of our last days of sum-
> mer freedom.

She devoted a subsequent column to their conversation. During the
last war, she said, we lost "sight of domestic problems, [and shoved] aside
things which were really vitally important to peace, because we were at
war. We must not do that again." Courage and foresight were essential
"to plan a more permanent way of peace." People would dismiss this
intent as an impossible "pipe dream," ER asserted. "Well, I for one, want
to try and I hope there will be many other people who feel as I do." She
hoped an international group would begin to meet now to plan continu-
ously "for future peace." She wanted internationalist thinkers and young
people determined to "aid humanity and civil populations everywhere,"
to meet and build an "awareness of what war means to the lives of all
people" and consider the ways that this "world shall be organized for
peace in the future."

On Friday night, 9 September, FDR arrived in Hyde Park for the last
weekend of summer and his mother's birthday. ER had returned from her

travels and chores "in time to greet the President. . . . In spite of the fact that he needed badly to make up sleep, we talked until late that night." On Sunday evening, ER closed the cottage at Val-Kill for the season. Alone, she wound up "all the little tag ends which need to be done in a house at the end of the season. . . . We boarded the train at about 11:00 o'clock and we were all sorry to leave the country." She returned to a vigorous lecture schedule, which would take her south, and many immediate meetings to prepare Democratic women for the upcoming campaign season.

Chapter Six

"We Have to Fight with Our Minds"

World War I, the "war to end all wars," fought "to make the world safe for democracy," had concluded with a hard, vengeful, unforgiving peace that wantonly reordered national boundaries and communities. Now there were new victims and conquerors, treacherous and confused alliances, silent or careless bystanders, appeasement and collusion. The map of the world created at Versailles was being burned to ash, drenched in blood. All geographic borders and imperial designs were to be reordered. Hitler had moved slowly, step by step. He paused and waited after every victory. Hearing no protest, seeing no opposition, he had moved on, from the Rhineland in 1936 to Spain, Austria, and Czechoslovakia in 1938.

Now Warsaw had been bombed. ER, involved with planning the 1940 campaign season for the Women's National Democratic Club with its leaders, Dorothy McAllister and Mary Thompson Evans, could not help but be affected by news of Poland's invasion. Under other circumstances, she might have felt invigorated by making plans with spirited Democratic women. But part of her heart remained each day with the people in the bombed-out villages of Poland. With every newspaper report, her mind followed the agony of women and children fleeing their burned homes, past fields of dead soldiers, who had ridden horses and farm animals to slaughter by German trucks and tanks. There was no escape from the relentless, mechanized *Blitzkrieg*.

The Democratic women had planned a broadcast for the next week to be held at the White House and feature the president. But FDR told his wife that "in the present crisis he must only speak as the President of all the people, and not as the representative of a particular party." ER agreed to speak in his stead, and the unprecedented radio event was moved to the club's headquarters.

The war news caused her to reflect upon her years in school in England during the Boer War. En route to Sweetwater, Tennessee, she wrote her column in the dining car behind a Roanoke newspaper, which provided a good shield behind which I could observe my neighbors. The train was filled with young girls, all pretty and full of life, evidently returning to school or college. One of them wore a thin gold chain with a cross on it around her neck. It took me back to my childhood when my grandmother gave me a similar one, and I thought of the people who lovingly bestow such a gift, with a prayer in their hearts that it may protect the child. Well, youngsters are going to need those prayers, for they are facing a troubled world.

The carnage in Poland raised essential questions about U.S. priorities and ended fantasies about isolation: "We must not forget that what we do at home has an effect on the world situation." The New Deal must be expanded, and Nazism must be defeated.

ER's mid-September trip coincided with an "orgy of massacre" against Polish civilians. Old people and children, infants in houses, priests and intellectuals were entrapped and burned; prisoners of war were ordered to dig mass graves and were machine-gunned into them; pillage and rape abounded as Nazi killer units, the SS *Einsatzgruppen*, stormed through Polish towns and villages. There were three million Jews in Poland; in many towns they were herded into synagogues, to be incinerated. The bombing of Warsaw, which continued for weeks, was reportedly most severe on 14 September, coinciding with the Jewish New Year: in Nalewki, the Jewish quarter of Warsaw, "the synagogues were filled."

Months before the war erupted, in February 1939, Hitler had declared that war would have one result: "the annihilation of the Jewish race in Europe." By mid-September, the SS was calling the program of "racial extermination" a process of "cleansing and security measures," and it resulted in the slaughter of Poles, Catholics, Jews, and all "suspicious elements."

Admiral Wilhelm Canaris, Germany's chief of military intelligence, and General Johannes Blaskowitz, commander of the German army in Poland, witnessed conditions at the front with horror. These "old school" officers felt disgraced by the wanton brutality and by the unlawful mass civilian executions. Blaskowitz wrote to Berlin that widespread abominable acts threatened the morale of his troops: "Every soldier feels disgusted by these crimes committed in Poland." But such crimes reflected the new order, and Blaskowitz was soon relieved of his command. No further military complaints followed.

ER's columns for that week focused on her speaking tour in the South, where she had good audiences. In Gadsden, Alabama, she was impressed by a library for cotton mill workers, a trade school for poor white boys, a nursery school staffed by NYA girls, and other NYA projects for hundreds of formerly neglected young people that now promised meaningful work. Aware of her duties as the election season loomed, ER found time for a cordial lunch with Senator Lister Hill (D-AL) and other politicians.

She and Tommy then toured the Tuskegee Institute, founded by Booker T. Washington in 1881. At Tuskegee's impressive teaching hospital, ER met the physician in charge "of the infantile paralysis work and attended a little ceremony in the chapel. Everyone present carried away the choir's singing in their hearts. The work done here for young colored people is outstanding in the South." They also visited a "gout hospital for colored veterans, a really fine institution, which, however, is already filled to capacity," and the new parole board, which boasted for the first time "a woman member."

After her lecture, sponsored by the Parent Teachers Association, she boarded a train to her next lecture in Danville, Virginia. Then she and Tommy continued to Washington for one overnight. ER was touched to be met at Union Station by her brother Hall and several of his friends. Their breakfast on the White House porch was "a very pleasant beginning to a busy day."

But her mood was blighted when her husband told her at dinner that the Soviets had entered Poland at six o'clock that morning, 17 September. Those who recalled ex–foreign minister Maxim Litvinov's six-year effort to forge a united front against Nazi aggression were stunned by Russia's perfidy. In addition to the Nazi-Soviet Pact, Russia had had a nonaggression pact with Poland. Now, William Shirer wrote, "Soviet Russia stabs Poland in the back, and the Red army joins the Nazi army in overrunning Poland."

ER wrote to Aunt Maude Gray, "The attack on Poland by Russia has depressed FDR. He feels we are drawing nearer to that old decision, 'Can we afford to let Germany win?' Stalin and Hitler are much alike, aren't they?"

On 24 August, Anna Louise Strong had written to ER, "I think this [Nazi-Soviet] pact may have saved peace for the time in Europe and without the sacrifice of Poland." An outspoken journalist and activist, Strong had always had ER's respect. A minister's daughter from Nebraska who earned a PhD from the University of Chicago, she devoted her life to feeding hungry children and supporting radical unionists. ER admired her robust manner and mountain-climbing escapades as well as her political enthusiasms. After going with the AFSC's 1917 famine relief mission to postwar Europe, she worked to build support for the Soviet Union, and ER had been impressed by her reports from Spain. Strong was now married to Joel Shubin, a Soviet official.

Now ER, in her column, rebutted her: "A curious way to aid the cause of peace!" A month later she answered Strong's letter point by point:

> I know that you know Mr. Stalin and I do not know him, and you know the Polish situation far better than I do. I cannot help, however, being distressed at another army on the march, nor can I quite bring myself to trust a man who, as part of a government, wipes out a people's religion, no matter how the church may have deserved correction, and it seems to me also that wholesale killings are hardly a help to civilization. . . .
>
> Even if [Russia] could [not] conclude a trade treaty with Great Britain and France, did she have to sign up with Germany . . . ? It seems to me that it gave Hitler just the strength he needed to plunge Europe into this horrible war. Hitler might have done it anyway, but one cannot help wondering if these two men might not believe in some of the same things.

ER received war information from many sources, and all the news was ghastly. From Paris, Carmel Offie, Ambassador Bullitt's assistant, sent a running river of gossip and military updates. He sent Missy LeHand, personal secretary to the president, a "piece of anti-aircraft shell which fell on the terrace outside the Ambassador's office during our first air-raid." Offie was amazed by the attitude of calm that seemed to blanket Paris: "Actually, this whole war seems absolutely pointless. I wouldn't give Martha's Vineyard for the whole of Europe but the fact is that a mad dog is loose on the Continent, so what is to be done about it?" He hoped Congress would immediately lift the embargo, since France had virtually nothing to fight with.

On 18 September, ER wrote Mary Dreier, "The war continues to be too awful." But her focus now returned to domestic issues. That day she wrote her column in Clarksburg, West Virginia, where she was appalled by the most distressed mining conditions. As her train journeyed through "beautiful country," where agriculture and industry converged, she was reminded that "a great nation at peace still has many problems to solve." The coal mines were now closed in an area where "the extremes of wealth and poverty shook hands" even before these dreadful conditions emerged. For ER, war had only exacerbated the plight of the miners. As the gap between rich and poor widened, she wanted to see these matters addressed with "a sense of urgency."

The Nazi-Soviet Pact had thrown U.S. Communists into disarray. For weeks, the *Daily Worker* failed to publish the facts of the pact and minimized international coverage. The Soviet newspaper *Pravda* had announced that Poland was in a state of collapse and chaos: the air force was destroyed, the army was rendered useless, industrial centers had been lost, the government had disappeared. It ignored all Polish resistance and the ongoing defense of Warsaw. According to *Pravda*, without "any effective help" from Britain and France, Russia was left to liberate and protect the "eleven million Ukrainians and Belorussians" who have lived under Polish rule "in a state of national oppression." There were "happy days in the liberated villages," *Pravda* noted, and the Soviet occupiers were "heartily welcomed" by "jubilant crowds." In addition to what journalist Alexander Werth called Russia's "orgy of rapturous articles," the Russian law enforcement agency (NKVD) deported to the East hundreds of thousands of "hostile or disloyal" Poles, as well as 68,000 Polish officers—additional seeds of future wars.

But Anne O'Hare McCormick's regular columns in the *New York Times*, vivid and prescient, stirred ER. The military "monster" that had shattered Polish cities was also terrorizing Romania and Hungary "into a useless stupor." "Human life has been uprooted and blown about like dust in a pounding wind." Europe was "crumbling." "What chance of survival," McCormick asked, has this new "prison house of conquered nations," defined by massacres and plunder, hatred and unlimited destruction? "Hitler has let loose a war to begin all wars." ER agreed with McCormick—"a wise observer of European affairs"—and journalist Dorothy Thompson that "in this war the seeds of other wars are being sown." There seemed to be no end to the misery human beings were capable of inflicting on one another.

The West sent no aid in any form to Poland, even as the siege of

Warsaw intensified. Since the declaration of war, Britain had dropped several million anti-Nazi leaflets over Germany and pursued German merchant ships, but without much success. There were no significant troop movements, no real action, no effort even to distract Germany from its relentless assault on Poland. Indeed, according to the *New York Times*, "to maintain a fighting front," Polish troops had gone east on the assumption that Germany would "become fully engaged by the British and French on the west." But, as Hitler gloated, "not a shot had been fired on the western front."

British and French inaction in these months seemed like betrayal and appeasement. Anti-appeasers were in despair. In London, Harold Nicolson confided details of his "appalling depression" to his diary: "The whole world is either paralysed or against us. These are the darkest hours we have ever endured." Britain, he discovered, was entirely unprepared for war. At dinner with several friends, he learned that every military branch was "frightfully short of ammunition. . . . [We] have in fact no Army, Navy or Air Force." Winston Churchill—now restored to his old post as Britain's First Lord of the Admiralty—was making elaborate remilitarization plans for a long war, but nothing could be ready until the spring of 1940.

ER now considered those who continued to clamor for "America's splendid isolationism" fools or cowards. The era of neutrality was over, at least ideologically. "I hope and pray that we will not have to fight with armed forces in this war, but we do have to fight with our minds, for this is as much a war for the control of ideas as for control of material resources. If certain ideas triumph, then what our forefathers founded in this nation in the way of ideas and ideals would receive a very serious blow." Everywhere she went, she appealed to her audiences to pressure Congress to revise the Neutrality Act in order to get needed supplies to the United Kingdom and France.

On 19 September, Hitler marched into and "liberated" Danzig, which had been ripped from Germany at Versailles. Crowds greeted him so "hysterical with joy" that it recalled his entry into Vienna, where he had been showered with cheers and flowers; the reception convinced him that "Almighty God has now given our arms his blessing."

The next day Hitler chose the nearby resort town of Zoppot to finalize his eugenics, or medical-cleansing, program. On 21 September, surrounded by his personal physician and the chief medical officers of the Reich, he decided to secure the "purity of German blood" through the elimination of all medically impaired and mentally deranged patients deemed incurable. Painless gas was the preferred means of "euthanasia." This program, centered at a clinic in Berlin at 4 Tiergartenstrasse, known therefore as Operation T4, was headed by a professor of neurology and psychiatry at the University of Würzburg, Werner Heyde. Soon seven euthanasia centers were built, for the elimination of imperfect newborns and young children and "feebleminded and asocial" adults.

On 8 September FDR issued a proclamation of "limited national emergency." He asked for no new legislation, no new executive authority. But then by executive order he authorized increases in the army, navy, Marine Corps, and Coast Guard; earmarked a considerable sum "for the reparation of Americans caught in the war zone"; and added 150 officers to the Department of Justice "to be used in the protection of the United States against subversive foreign activities within our borders." Then he called Congress back into session to reconsider the embargo provisions of the Neutrality Act of 1935.

On 21 September, FDR appealed to Congress, saying there was no exclusive "peace bloc." During the 1920s and 1930s the United States had led many peace efforts because it understood that "any war anywhere necessarily hurts American security and American prosperity." But the Neutrality Act, he said, had been a deviation from established principles of "neutrality . . . and peace through international law. . . . I regret [that the Congress passed] that act. I regret equally that I signed that act." He requested from Congress a new policy, called cash-and-carry, by which the United States would sell arms to Britain in exchange for cash; Britain would provide the transportation: "All purchases [will] be made in cash, and all cargoes [will] be carried in the purchasers' own ships, at the pur-chasers' own risk." This cash-and-carry policy, he said, could avoid a repeat of such incidents as the 1917 sinking of the *Lusitania*.

Finally, he urged Congress to repeal the arms embargo in the Neutral-ity Act of 1935.

"Darker periods may lie ahead," he warned. "The disaster is not of our making; no act of ours engendered the forces which assault the founda-tions of our civilization. Yet we find ourselves affected to the core; our currents of commerce are changing, our minds are filled with new problems, our position in world affairs has already been altered." In such circumstances, it was vital to protect American interests.

> Rightly considered, this interest is not selfish. The peace, the integrity, and the safety of the Americas—these must be kept firm and serene.
>
> In a period when it is sometimes said that free discussion is no longer compatible with national safety, may you by your deeds show the world that we of the United States are one people, of one mind, one spirit, one clear resolution, walking before God in the light of the living.

But the House declined to repeal the arms embargo, by only two votes, 159 to 157.

ER and Tommy had listened to FDR's address to Congress on the radio while traveling to Illinois. Afterward ER wrote her husband, "Your message was grand and came over very well, even on the train."

She had hoped to be sent to Europe for the Red Cross to create a refugee relief effort. Because of the atrocities associated with Hitler's *Blitzkrieg*, Secretary of State Hull and Red Cross head Norman Davis had vetoed ER's plan to go to war zones for purposes of rescue and refuge.

During her first press conference of the fall, on 27 September, ER stressed that hemispheric peace and U.S. security depended on the repeal of the "dangerous" embargo clause. For Americans to believe they can "go scot-free," she told the press conference, was to fail to appreciate "the responsibility that lies on us as one great nation at peace. That responsibility is to be thinking seriously of what we can do to alleviate suffering for civilian populations. . . . The only nation that can think of what to do for a future peace is the U.S., so . . . we have a so much greater responsibility than just to think of how we can keep out of war." During her travels, she said, many people "come up to me and say, 'Oh, let them stew in their own juice. It's none of our concern, as long as we can stay out of it.' That always gives me a horrible, sinking feeling, because you can't help but suffer when all the rest of the world is suffering." She had not met one person in the country who did not want to keep out of war, but she insisted

Americans must "lead"—be imaginative in thought and action, to work for a lasting peace.

Asked if she was still a pacifist, she replied, "I have never been a pacifist in the sense that I don't believe in defending this country, but I am most anxious to do everything possible to prevent war wherever one possibly can." What had she meant when she said during her tour that "one should not think only of one's own skin and one's own pocket book"? "In the end," she replied, "if the skins of the rest of the world are removed and the pockets of the rest of the world are empty, we will grow thin and lean."

Did "the foreign situation" ensure her husband's third term? ER demurred, suggesting the reporter consult the president. Had the president ever criticized her columns? someone asked. The first lady laughed: he "never said a word about a thing [I] wrote. . . . We are very careful about not trying to influence each other." What about their frequent use of the same expressions? ER replied that it was "natural," since they "were enormously interested in the same things. We do talk things over in a general way. We argue about everything in the world." After all, "we do not just sit at meals and look at each other." But while they talked about everything, she "never tried to influence the President in anything he did and . . . he had not tried to influence her." They took it for granted that they would each do what they "considered the right thing." Their marriage represented the best possible alliance of independence and deep connectedness. They both grew within it, while drawing closer and farther apart.

On 28 September Warsaw fell to the Nazis. German troops did not immediately occupy the Polish capital, but they took prisoner 140,000 Polish soldiers and massacred Warsaw's civilian leadership, rounding up over 10,000 teachers, doctors, librarians, priests, journalists, writers, business leaders, and landowners for slaughter.

From the U.S. embassy in Paris, Carmel Offie sent details to the White House. American ambassador to Warsaw, Anthony "Tony" Biddle, and his wife had arrived on 24 September and "are now living at the Embassy Residence." Bullitt was trying to restore their spirits: "The stories they tell are, to say the least, gruesome." John Cudahy, who had been U.S. ambassador to Poland from 1933 to 1937, told Missy LeHand, "If you feel sad think of me. . . . No trace can be found of my former secretary, or her mother. And a family I knew best of all has vanished without a trace. Everyone in the Eastern half of Poland have lost every stick of their possessions, and I suppose with the few exceptions of Pro-Germans, everyone in German occupied Poland is little better off."

Twenty-two million Poles were now under Nazi rule. Two days later *Pravda* published a photograph of Molotov and Ribbentrop signing the "German-Soviet Boundary and Friendship Treaty." Poland, the borderland of rolling plains and industrial resources, was dismantled and partitioned again, for the fifth time in history. In exchange for including Lvov and its nearby oilfields on the Soviet side of the new border, Russia promised to supply Germany 300,000 tons of oil a year.

ER wrote nothing about these specific events, but every morning she read several newspapers and enjoyed columns by journalists such as Anne O'Hare McCormick, who railed against Soviet expansion and was particularly disturbed about Lvov. McCormick considered the fate of that town, formerly Lemberg in the Hapsburg Empire and the center of the Ukrainian independence movement, "even sadder" than the fate of Warsaw. The specter of Communism throughout Eastern Europe, the reason so many appeasers preferred Hitler to a treaty with Russia, was for McCormick the primary fear: "Hitler has released forces he is powerless to control." The weak Central European states, like Romania, "are more vulnerable to Soviet than to Nazi penetration. . . . The Nazi-Soviet alliance is a merger of the forces of destruction." They are united in "revolt against European civilization."

Britain did not believe the Nazi-Soviet alliance would last, and most of Britain's leadership, as well as public opinion, preferred war to a servile peace with Hitler. But U.S. ambassador to Britain Joseph Kennedy counseled FDR to avoid providing any support for the doomed nations. The Soviets were prepared to take over the Balkans and the Baltic States, and the Nazis were ready to move on Belgium and Holland. Kennedy was certain there was nothing to be done. He believed Churchill would do anything to get the United States into the war, but Britain would "go down fighting"—it could not possibly win.

Some argued that the German people were prepared to remove Hitler, Kennedy wrote to FDR, but that could result in chaos, and Germany could turn Communist. Then this nation of eighty million hungry people would be an even greater "menace to Europe." Surely the United States did not "want any part of this mess."

He urged FDR to reconsider his commitment to the putative democracies. The coming war would not be "a holy war." After all, Kennedy insisted, democracy in France and England hardly existed: England was not a democracy "in our sense of the word," having always been ruled by its "governing class." And "France is ruled by a dictatorship which has just this week made illegal one of the largest Parliamentary parties," the Communist Party, and expelled elected Communist members from Parliament.

The United States had nothing to gain, Kennedy advised, nothing to win, and no reason to support "a hopeless struggle" that could only end in "the complete collapse of everything we hope and live for," no matter who won. Therefore "we should curb our sentiments and sentimentality and look to our own vital interests," which lay in the western hemisphere. "It may not be convenient for us to face a world without a strong British Empire. But . . . we shall have to face it . . . and the leadership of the English-speaking world will, willy-nilly, be ours."

Kennedy visited his friend Nancy Astor, finding her fully committed to Britain's war effort and vigorously allied with Stella Reading, ER's great friend who founded the Women's Voluntary Service in 1938. They "wanted to know when America was coming in and of course I told them we weren't coming," he wrote his wife, Rose. "So perhaps, dear, you went home [to the United States] at the height of your husband's popularity."

ER disagreed entirely with Kennedy's defeatist isolationism. His willingness to sacrifice Britain rendered him a pariah, even in FDR's eyes. To an antiwar correspondent who believed that one "who goes to war for an ideal sacrifices his ideals," she replied, "I agree with you in theory but I would rather die than submit to rule by Hitler or Stalin, would not you?"

During her autumn tour, most of ER's columns dealt with the people she met, the books she read, and her observations. She kept busy lest she plunge into one of her "Griselda moods," never far from her heart these bitter days. As she worked to fortify the people who benefited from and worked for New Deal agencies, she fortified herself. She believed fervently that war and civil war arose when countries neglected the real needs of the people.

She was disheartened to see, firsthand, how economically depressed parts of the country remained. The New Deal had achieved much in housing, employment, and hope, but as she traveled through West Virginia, its failures and limitations were apparent.

> We passed first through a coal-mining section . . . with bad housing and underfed children. Then, for a time, a rather fertile farming country. Later, some small oil and natural gas wells. Just before we reached Glenville, some badly eroded hillsides. . . . They have been denuded of trees and are now being used as pastures or cornfields. But shortly there will be no soil on which anything can grow. Strange that people will not realize that lack of soil conservation eventually means not only loss in land productivity but deterioration in human beings.

In Carbondale, Illinois, "two very kind and enthusiastic young men" working for the NYA gave her a tour. Although Illinois had "risen to fifth place among oil-producing states," it was still one of America's most depressed regions, much to her grief. The farming and mining populations were both "at a very low ebb," and "one of the counties near Carbondale has the greatest number of people on relief in any one county in the U.S." But there were also hopeful signs of community renewal: the region's flourishing NYA project not only employed but educated "boys who never had an opportunity for acquiring any work skill or getting any job" beyond that of "temporary day-laborer." In addition to programs for gardening and "subsistence farming" skills, the boys were being trained "in auto-mechanics, electrical wiring, woodworking and iron work. They have the advantage of being near a State Teachers' College which is cooperating in every way." There were also wonderful "monuments to WPA work—a paved and widened main street, a fine armory, other lasting improvements."

On a return swing through West Virginia, ER visited the Red House, a resettlement community built under the auspices of the Farm Security Administration. She believed in the value of these projects, like Arthurdale, that were new communities of comfort and dignity. She was pleased that the Charleston Business and Professional Women's Club sponsored a handicrafts project for local women to learn "various handicrafts" for home consumption and sale. As she set out all the changes under way, ER made a compelling plea to her readers: "I wish more people . . . would take an interest in their government homestead, for there is so much that can be done for these communities if people nearby lend a hand. I have never felt that the government should be expected to carry the burden alone."

Also in West Virginia, she visited a WPA project that included a Crippled Children's Hospital, with a pool to benefit all the children of the region: "The pool is one of the most delightful I have ever seen."

After that, she returned to Washington for a brief visit. She dashed in to see her husband in his office on 28 September but wrote nothing of their conversation. Most of her time "was spent in a truly feminine and frivolous matter—getting my hair done." In her lightning stopover, ER was happy to see that young Diana Hopkins and her ailing father, Harry, were "in such good spirits. Diana is evidently a good companion."

After the Washington stopover, ER resumed her tour, reaching Wilmington, Delaware, and Reading, Pennsylvania. The new public address systems now found in most halls helped keep her "voice on its natural pitch. This is to me a great relief!"

Finally she reached New York City, where she visited art galleries, attended a reception for women sculptors and painters, and visited the World's Fair twice in three days. Although she did not mention Hick, those two visits were in part to see her great friend. Hick's work at the fair so absorbed her that she was in an uncommonly good mood. Between the fair and her weekend place on Long Island, she seemed uncomplaining and satisfied.

At the General Motors pavilion, ER found the recent discoveries in science on display to be "the most encouraging thing I have seen." In a world only recently introduced to electricity and telephones, the rapid changes in transportation and communication would open vast opportunities for employment and comfort "if our scientists are able to delve further into the mysteries which lie all about us in the universe."

Friday night she saw Philip Barry's new play, *The Philadelphia Story*, advising her readers that "[Katharine] Hepburn and all the cast do so well that this play deserves its great success." Saturday evening she and her unnamed company (presumably including Aunt Maude Gray) returned to the World's Fair to see Billy Rose's Aquacade, an extravaganza with music, dance, and swimming: "It is so delightful that it should not be missed by anyone."

ER then set off for Seattle, for a long-planned visit with daughter Anna and her family. She was "thrilled" that Anna had encouraged the visit, as she was eager to see her grandchildren: Sistie, Buzzy, and six-month-old John. "People ask me about them everywhere! I am dying to see 'little' John who must be a monster!"

To be with Anna's children and see how quickly they grew seemed to ER the perfect antidote to the world at large: "It certainly is fun to visit one's children. I found myself marveling at the strength of my youngest grandchild. He is the most friendly, happy baby. . . . The older children are fascinated by him and when he grows up I suppose it will be hard to keep them from spoiling him." ER also enjoyed a walk with Anna, Sistie, and their two Irish setters. "'Jack' never forgets me and greeted me warmly, but 'Jill' is a fickle lady and took very little interest in my arrival, but she has no objection to be petted, which some will say is a woman's trait."

On the flight from Seattle to San Francisco, ER read the October issue of the *Survey Graphic*, devoted to "the schools of our country." Thirty-one educators and experts had been asked about the most basic questions of democracy "with which we are all concerned":

1. What are the goals of our schools? Are they meeting the tests of American education in the American way?
2. Are our children learning how to think for themselves as citizens of a democracy, or are they likely to fall in line behind a rabble rouser?
3. Can we cut across economic and racial barriers and really provide equal opportunities?

ER considered these questions fundamental to democracy's survival, yet over 800,000 children "did not attend school last year." Either there was no school in their neighborhood because the community was too poor, or the family was too poor to provide books, shoes, clothes, or the means to send them to school. In addition, because of economic demands, in "certain parts of our country, the school year has been curtailed." Although "some great men succeeded without schooling," most came under the influence of "a great teacher who pointed out the way whereby they might educate themselves." In her own life, Marie Souvestre at Allenswood had inspired vision, commitment, and deep learning. Today, in too many places, "we are giving little thought to the development of

great teachers," ER lamented. "We think more about curtailing their salaries than we do about improving their qualifications. A really good
teacher can never be [sufficiently] paid, and they do not develop well on
starvation wages."

In San Francisco, ER spent most of her time with her dancer friend
Mayris "Tiny" Chaney, whom she had met through Earl Miller. They
went to the West Coast World's Fair, which was spectacular. The grounds
were filled with exotic, wild, colorful flowers and extraordinary plants;
the art exhibit featured a great range of contemporary artists and old
masters; and the Asian and Pacific Island exhibits were unique. The next
day ER visited Tiny's new hat shop and "bought for myself two winter
hats." Then they went off to Chinatown and Gump's "to see the miniature silver display."

In San Francisco the Western Union strike hampered ER's ability to
file her column. "How can we ever hope that different races will sit down
and in a spirit of justice and goodwill consider [their] difficulties . . . if
we in our own country cannot even persuade groups with different interests to meet and arbitrate their difficulties?" To ER, the surest way "to
prevent war," a question she was asked over and over again by women
particularly, was to "desire justice and goodwill at home. We cannot have
peace unless we begin with the individual and we must build up machinery to bring this peace about. . . . There must be representatives of varying points of view. There must be disinterested people who listen and
patiently try to solve the difficulties. There must be a place for discussion.
This is true at home and true in international affairs." ER wanted all the
human stories behind the picket lines told, to give "management a better
understanding of the actual human needs." Until we understood and
respected each other and our differences, there was little hope for peace.

Her son James flew up from Los Angeles with several friends to have
lunch and tour with his mother. They returned together to Los Angeles,
where James now worked for Hollywood producer Samuel Goldwyn. In
September, he had separated from his wife, Betsey. Everyone feared
impending divorce, and Sara Delano Roosevelt had taken the news very
hard. ER was glad that FDR had gone to Hyde Park to be with his
mother.

After her time in California, ER flew to Fort Worth, Texas, to visit
her son Elliott and her "very attractive" grandchildren. "I am always

fascinated when I hear Tony, aged three, solemnly address me as 'Grandmother Roosevelt.'" ER went with Elliott's wife, Ruth, to listen to FDR's radio broadcast, then flew home for her birthday week.

On 7 October her daughter-in-law Betsey's father, Dr. Harvey Cushing, first Sterling Professor of Neurology at Yale University, suddenly died. ER flew to New York, where she met SDR to take the noon train to New Haven for the funeral. "It seems to me that the unexpected is always happening in life. One never knows from day to day what fate may have in store."

Surrounded by work and grief, ER was uplifted by art exhibitions and an exciting new musical organization called the Little Symphony Society of Philadelphia. Directed by Esther Lape's friend Leopold Stokowski, this orchestra was to provide accompaniment for emerging soloists "in a great music center" and offer guest conductors opportunities to premiere new works. It meant "an opportunity for young musicians to be heard, which has been difficult," and ER considered it a thrilling development.

The eleventh of October 1939 was ER's fifty-fifth birthday. She reflected on her life as the world she loved plunged once again into the madness of war. Twenty-one years earlier the Great War had ended with her marriage in disarray because FDR loved another woman. ER had been in a crisis of gloom, unable to eat, lonely, and afraid. But new friendships, new interests, new work, and bold political activity had helped her out of her despair. She had created a new life within the hearth of her old one. Her travels and contacts enabled her to ward off her "Griselda moods," and the good work she was able to do in partnership with her husband advanced the best of their shared vision.

ER had a full and happy birthday. Bernard Baruch sent an admiring birthday telegram: "May you be spared many years to bring happiness comfort and courage to those who are privileged to call you friend and to those countless thousands who are bettered by what you say and do and stand for." She received a mountain of cards, letters, and more telegrams filled with good wishes, so many that she thanked her friends in her column. She "deeply appreciated" their kind thoughts, although so many of her correspondents asked her "actually to do something definite" that she would not be able to respond personally. In "a very busy day, all these good wishes were a very pleasant background to many activities."

Actually, ER was happiest when she was busiest, especially when she felt needed. On her birthday she met with Frances Perkins at the Department of Labor about jobs and training for youth and had an informative lunch. Perkins seemed "very jittery about 'reds,'" due to the continual assaults on her and her department by the Dies Committee—it was "getting on all their nerves," ER observed. Throughout October, the House Committee Investigating Un-American Activities, chaired by Martin Dies (D-TX), was railing against liberal Democrats and administration officials. The "Committee has been running hog-wild lately and has become a danger of the first magnitude," remarked Harold Ickes. Recently in Washington and Chicago, it had raided various organizational headquarters "under the pretense of serving subpoenas . . . and then simply walked out with all written records and lists." Ickes compared Dies to A. Mitchell Palmer, who had committed the Red Scare outrages at the end of the last war. Dies was now "an actual menace" who threatened "to give out names of prominent New Dealers in the Administration connecting them with communistic activities. I know perfectly well that he will try to smear me." That very week Dies investigated the Spanish Refugee League Campaign Committee, which Ickes chaired. Furious, Ickes noted that he knew no Communists and had never read Karl Marx. He had every right to help collect money for "Spanish refugees who are miserably circumstanced in France." That week ER wrote about the need to send relief to Chinese and Spanish civilians.

Her sons Jimmy and Elliott, her brother Hall, and several other guests were at the White House for ER's "pleasant" birthday party. Her husband gave her a check, with a note on which he had scrawled in a bold large hand, "E.R.: Many Happy Returns! With this goes the necessary for a good 'Green'"—a reference to the new lawn around the swimming pool at Val-Kill. FDR's abrupt scribble, lacking their customary salutation of love, is a curious anomaly in their correspondence. Had he made a more loving toast? Had he even attended her birthday dinner? There is no evidence of his presence or any other exchange that day.

FDR spent part of that afternoon in a momentous meeting with Dr. Alexander Sachs, who appealed for government support for new experiments in atomic physics. A Wall Street economist and director of the Lehman Corporation, the Russian-born Sachs had impressed FDR in the past with his economic advice. Now Sachs appeared on a different mission. He had been trying to arrange a meeting with the president since

2 August, when Albert Einstein agreed with Leo Szilard and Enrico Fermi that the United States needed to be prepared to face specific challenges from Nazi laboratories, based on research they had once all done together.* That same day, Einstein had written in a letter to FDR:

*The atomic age arrived slowly, and every scientific step was published and celebrated globally, until 1939. Many of the German physicists were Jewish and were expelled in 1933. Some emigrated to the United States, including Hungarian-born Leo Szilard, Edward Teller, Eugene Wigner, and John von Neumann. Enrico Fermi had emigrated when Mussolini's anti-Jewish laws threatened his wife, Laura, and his two Jewish children. In December 1938, Fermi was awarded a Nobel Prize for his neutron-bombardment experiments; he and his family left Stockholm for New York, where he joined Columbia University's faculty. Austrian physicist Lisa Meitner also fled Germany but joined Niels Bohr's laboratory in Sweden. Meitner's physicist nephew Otto Frisch, who worked with Bohr in Copenhagen, joined her in Sweden for the holidays. Together they used Einstein's equation to calculate "the energy release per split atom" of the chemical observations made by Hahn and Strassmann. Their paper on "the atom-splitting process called nuclear fission" was published in London's *Nature*, a journal read by scientists worldwide. Armed with the details of the Meitner-Frisch research, Bohr sailed for a term's collaboration with Einstein at Princeton and with Fermi at Columbia—where in Pupin Hall a second experiment succeeded on 26 January 1939. That week America's leading physicists met at George Washington University to hear Bohr and Fermi. Their words and equations "created a sensation." Some scientists left abruptly to phone their home institutions or flee to their laboratories. The energy released from one chain reaction might equal hundreds of pounds of explosives. Within weeks the process of uranium fission was confirmed by studies at Johns Hopkins University, Carnegie Institute in Washington, and the University of California at Berkeley. While Szilard and Walter Zinn worked at Columbia, and the Joliot-Curies worked in Paris, Hahn and Strassmann—along with Max Planck, Werner Heisenberg, and many others—continued to work in Germany. Moreover, Carl von Weizsäcker, one of the best young physicists, was the son of Baron Ernst von Weizsäcker, Ribbentrop's close associate.

When the militarized use of their nuclear researches was confirmed, Fermi and others resolved to speak with U.S. military and naval officers. His appointment with a navy research scientist, 17 March, coincided with Hitler's occupation of all Czechoslovakia, the only site of Europe's uranium deposits. But the admiral he intended to see was too busy, and he was greeted by junior officers, who infuriated him by their contemptuous, ignorant lack of interest. For months, the émigré scientists received reports that all research was now "concentrated in the Kaiser-Wilhelm Institute," where they worked on uranium.

The letter was hand-delivered to FDR by Dr. Alexander Sachs on 11 October 1939; Sachs had been introduced to Szilard by former Reichstag member Gustav Stolper. According to Martin Gilbert, on 26 September Berlin scientists met in

In the course of the last four months it has been made probable—through the work of Joliot in France as well as Szilard and Fermi in America—that it may become possible to set up nuclear chain reactions in a large mass of uranium, by which vast amounts of power and large quantities of new radium-like elements would be generated. . . .

This new phenomenon would also lead to the construction of bombs and it is conceivable—though much less certain—that extremely powerful bombs of a new type may thus be constructed. . . .

You may think it desirable to have some permanent contact between the administration and the group of physicists now working on chain reaction in America. . . .

I understand that Germany has actually stopped the sale of uranium from the Czechoslovakian mines. . . . That [Germany] should have taken such early action might be understood on the ground that the son of the German Undersecretary of State, von Weizsacker, is attached to the Kaiser Wilhelm Institute in Berlin, where some of the American work on uranium is now being repeated.

In addition to Einstein's letter, Sachs gave FDR a memo written by Szilard and a letter of explanation and urgency he wrote himself. Nobody else was in the room, and there is no record of the discussion. But as soon as Sachs left, FDR summoned his senior aide Edwin "Pa" Watson, handed him the three documents, and said, "Pa, this requires action!"

Action was taken slowly over time, but for several years little was done with the support of U.S. military assistance. Meanwhile misery, suicide, and death prevailed in Poland and all Nazi-occupied territories. As the numbers of the dead, wounded, plundered and dislocated rose, Hitler called it the *Sitzkrieg*, while Senator William Borah called it "the phony war."

---

secret to discuss their work on nuclear fission. The German War Office agreed to spend whatever was necessary for the new secret weapon. Hitler was exultant. It is very likely that the émigré community learned of this meeting. Davis, *FDR: Into the Storm*, pp. 471–85, 509–12; Gilbert, p. 14; Jungk, *Brighter Than a Thousand*.

Engorged by his victories, Hitler issued a series of horrific edicts. He signed an amnesty order to release all SS officers who had been arrested by army authorities on charges of depraved brutality against civilians and mass executions of old people and children. Warsaw was designated Poland's "General-Government," with Cracow the new capital. It would be ruled by Hans Frank, a vicious Nazi who initiated an "Extraordinary Pacification Program" whereby thousands of leaders, teachers and intellectuals, priests and potential "subversives" were summarily executed. Frank also instituted a "Housecleaning Plan" specifically to remove Jews. Ordinary Poles were systematically forced from their homes, farms, and businesses. Unable to take their possessions, they were purposefully rendered destitute—"so poor the Poles would want to work in Germany."

The "methods employed" during the forced removals, General Field Marshal W. Keitel noted, were "irreconcilable with all our [German] existing principles." While Germanic Poles were removed to German provinces, special Jewish "reservations" were created where Jews deported from Vienna, Czechoslovakia, Baltic ports, and western Poland were to be dumped, along with groups of stray Jews, some of whom had been captured in Hamburg as they waited to board ships for the United States.

Many Jews fled eastward, across the River Bug, to the Soviet side—and were surprised to see Jews fleeing west, imagining that Nazi rule might be "less burdensome" than Communist rule. Throughout occupied Poland the "New Order" meant Nazi work camps for all Jewish males, aged fourteen to sixty. By December 1939 there were twenty-eight labor camps in the Lublin area, fourteen near Warsaw, twelve near Cracow, and dozens more scattered across the plains. In Lodz, where 200,000 Jews lived, Goebbels announced the "surgical task" of removal and slaughter. The insane nightmare had begun. Evidence was sent to ER and FDR through many sources, including photographs and newspaper cuttings.

On 11 October, ER's great friend Caroline Astor Drayton Phillips (Helen Astor Roosevelt Robinson's cousin, FDR's second cousin), a member of ER's World War I–era biweekly Sunday dinner "club," left for Rome to join her husband, the U.S. ambassador to Italy, William Phillips. She wrote in her diary, "I go, not without fear and dread, into the black cauldron of war, which is Europe, glad to be going to my dear William, but in every other way, most unwillingly."

Within weeks Caroline Phillips's diary was filled with details out of

Poland: "Dreadful reprisals by the Germans. . . . The Polish Ambassador told William about an old Polish Countess in Danzig, aged seventy, who was taken out and shot for having burned a table [for warmth and fuel] in her own house. Everything is considered to be German property now. They are trying . . . to kill off as many Poles as possible. There are now 30,000 Polish refugees in Hungary and 10,000 in Romania."

On 22 November she recorded the account of trusted visitors; airplanes were bombing "peasants working in the fields," "women and children fleeing from Warsaw":

> The Germans kill everyone, far more than the Russians do. The Russians confiscate all the estates of the nobles but only rarely shoot them, but the Germans shoot them and take the property and shoot and loot the peasants also. They said the Bolshevik soldiers were more humane than the German ones. They also told us that the Polish doctors attending wounded German airplane pilots found they had all been drugged with morphine and other drugs and that it is well known that they send them up with very heavy drinks as otherwise they could hardly stand all the killing they have to do.

For all the reported agony, the "phony" war continued for almost eight months. The British called it the "the Bore War"—a "bloody bore" of waiting, tension, and discomfort. Churchill called it "the Sinister Trance."

ER, silenced by her husband's political needs and his own secrecy regarding refugee negotiations with international and business leaders, avoided public discussion of the situation. In early October FDR wrote to Secretary of State Hull with his "original" observation that as the war continued "there will be, in all probability, more Christian refugees than Jewish refugees." Since so many "of them will be Catholics, the Vatican itself may [decide] to take an active interest." He wanted discussions with American Christian organizations, as well as European groups. Moreover, he envisioned sending a "special Minister or Ambassador" directly to the Vatican, in order to put "the whole refugee problem on a broad religious basis, thereby making it possible to gain the kind of world-wide support that a mere Jewish relief set-up would not evoke."

Then on 17 October FDR held a White House Conference on Political Refugees. The president addressed the delegates with a sense of urgency: there would be between ten and twenty million refugees "before the European war was over." Places of "permanent settlement" would be needed. That was now to be the immediate task of an Inter-Governmental Committee on Refugees, under the direction of Paul van Zeeland, Belgium's former premier.

FDR considered this resettlement program an enormous challenge. It was too late "to speak of small settlements. . . . The picture should be in terms of a million square miles occupied by a coordinated self-sustaining civilization." FDR had a long-range fantasy of postwar resettlement that required unlimited investments—from governments and business leaders. He believed it could be done, at least partly, on a profitable basis: "It is my judgment that 50 percent of the cost can properly be financed on a business basis but that the other 50 percent would have to be given—not loaned—in the form of gifts from governments and individuals."

The president understood Britain's opposition to continued large-scale resettlement in Palestine, and at this conference Britain withdrew its offer of British Guiana as a potential homeland for European Jews. FDR had no intention of changing America's own restrictive immigration laws and sought a "supplemental national home" in one of the many unpopulated or "vacant spaces" on earth. His rhetoric aggravated American Jews, who favored Palestine.

While Britain and France now intended to consider refugees from Germany "enemy aliens," Germany was building its own "resettlement" camps in Poland. Despite FDR's rhetorical conclusion, imploring leaders to "lift a lamp beside new golden doors and build new refuges for the tired, for the poor, for the huddled masses yearning to be free," the conference was futile. With no consideration for the immediate crises, the delegates left in despair and sorrow.

At her press conference, ER avoided mentioning her husband's conference on refugees, or that on 13 October she had attended a B'nai B'rith luncheon to celebrate the Washington chapter. Nor did the journalists who covered the first lady bring up the subject. However, when asked how she felt about being called a "warmonger," she replied fully that it was now clearly a matter of "self-defense" to be "concerned about what is happening . . . in the rest of the world." The past taught that "a breach of the peace anywhere is a menace to peace everywhere." She hoped "we never will have to go to war," but she was not "a prophet." The time to have worked against war was before the war broke out, through an international peace organization. Implying that it was too late, she said, "You must look to the future now." But it was urgent for everybody to take a real interest in their own community and broaden democracy, "to make democracy work" by their own active participation. Disarmament, for example, would work only if "all nations cooperate." Therefore all questions of war and peace and of this war's impact on American democracy were connected.

One immediate threat to democracy was the burgeoning Red Scare, unleashed by the Nazi-Soviet Pact. While no significant antifascist or anti-Nazi movement was under way, ER and her young friends became primary targets of the new crusade.

On 6 September 1939, FDR told his cabinet that "someone who knew Goebbels well" had just reported that the Nazi chief of propaganda believed Germany would destroy Poland "within a very few days and [would] then quickly smash both France and England, largely from the air." When FDR's informant asked Goebbels "What next?" he replied, "You know what is next, the United States." To the suggestion that 3,500 miles of distance made that boast absurd, Goebbels retorted, "It will come from the inside."

On 6 September 1939, FDR had issued an executive order that empowered the FBI to monitor all dangers, subversion, and rumors of subversion—to check "espionage and subversive propaganda" and block "sabotage." For that purpose the FBI staff was to be increased "by 150 operatives," and all "local officials throughout the country" were ordered "to cooperate in this campaign." The Attorney General asked all citizens to report any information they may gather on such activities to the nearest FBI. Clearly, the order was intended to target those allied with both Nazis and Communists. But only Communists and "fellow travelers" interested FBI director J. Edgar Hoover and Martin Dies.

The Dies Committee led the crusade, accusing ER of hosting a "Red Tea" at the White House for young Communists, meaning the American Youth Congress and its leaders. ER, their friend and advocate, publicly acknowledged that she supported the AYC and participated in their conferences at Vassar and other places. But she was convinced that her young friends, whom she knew "as individuals," were not Communists. There was nothing "reprehensible" or disagreeable about their meetings, where controversial issues were fully and frankly discussed.

Then on 27 September rumors that FDR had ordered a "Red purge" rocked Washington. Allegedly he sought to "purge the Federal payroll of Communists" and sent the Department of Justice an order to begin the process. Dies considered it a victory for his committee and leaked the story, but Justice Department officials refused to comment. ER dismissed it as a publicity stunt, and nothing immediately happened.

But throughout the autumn of 1939 attacks against her became more insidious. For weeks, she was asked about the expansion of "subversive groups." She had seen "no evidence of un-American activities in her travels about the country," she replied. There was "little to fear" from Communist groups, so long as "all of us make an effort to live our democracy day to day." Moreover, she said, the United States needed to do more to improve the conditions "of migratory workers," help them to organize, see to their needs during harvest season, and provide necessary "mobile schools and better camp" facilities.

In France, the first months of the war seemed to be fought not against Nazis but exclusively against Communists. On 27 September the French government outlawed the Communist Party along with "hundreds of societies, unions, leagues suspected of Communist sympathies. Mass arrests began." Communist deputies were dismissed from parliament and prosecuted. Leftist journals and newspapers, including *L'Humanité* and *Ce Soir*, were closed down. Freedom of the press disappeared. But no similar action was taken against fascists.

For ER, France—the home of Marie Souvestre, the Enlightenment, and modern democracy—seemed doomed. The country had waited too long, she wrote, to address the crying needs of the people—poverty, dislocation, confusion. It had instituted no New Deal–like measures, and so the people turned to Communism—or fascism. And now even the Communists were under Hitler's thumb. ER hoped that continued and extended New Deal reforms would block such a situation from developing in America.

But in this new era of raids and the Red Scare, begun in 1939 and supported by FDR, the president's wife was to become, and remain, a primary suspect and target, even as she became increasingly anti-Communist.

Chapter Seven

Red Scare, Refugees, and Racism

Wherever ER went that autumn, three issues dominated her thoughts: the unprecedented human suffering in Hitler-occupied Europe, the need to combat racial injustice throughout the United States, and the domestic Red Scare. She considered it a profoundly dangerous time that required continual learning and activity to confront these threats to democracy.

Since the early 1930s her friend Clarence Pickett, head of the American Friends Service Committee (AFSC), and his wife, Lilly, had been ER's chief informants about conditions in Europe. Their travels in Germany and their Quaker colleagues provided firsthand reports and analyses that she used to guide her contributions and private efforts.

In 1934 Pickett had visited a celebration in Worms to mark the synagogue's nine hundredth year of service. He observed, "Jews were in Germany before Christ's time. They love Germany. Most Jews will remain in Germany . . . driven in on themselves, but they will suffer through." Later from Vienna he had reported on pitiable scenes of humiliation and weeks of reported suicides. When Kristallnacht took place in November 1938 he told her about brutality and destruction throughout Germany, when twenty thousand German Jews were rounded up and sent to camps.

Hitler's race laws transformed the meaning of citizenship, religion, and being German. A Jew, Hitler declared, was not a follower of a religion or faith but a member of a pestilent race. One drop of Jewish blood poisoned the bloodstream; one Jewish gene polluted the pool. Only "Aryans" could be German citizens. Studies were undertaken to find "hidden" Jews, families who were secular, Unitarian, Catholic, or Quaker, who had for generations been German, assimilated or converted, or of mixed marriages and parentage. *Mischlingen* and intermarrieds were no longer safe, no longer citizens. It was no longer possible to convert or assimilate. For ER, all hope expired in Poland, when countless Jews were herded into synagogues, set aflame, and burned to ash.

From September to December 1939, as the Nazis massacred fifty thousand civilians and rendered millions more homeless refugees, the world looked on, whispering concerns but unready, unable, or unwilling to respond to the victims of atrocity. In the United States, the prevailing fervently anti-interventionist isolationists roared any public sympathy into silence and indeed fueled a crusade against "un-Americanism" that targeted trade unionists, New Dealers, and young people. ER herself, still restrained by FDR's slowly evolving international policies, wrote little about refugees, the slaughter of civilians, or the suffering of war.

The unfolding European tragedy was met in the United States by growing anti-Jewish, anti-Communist fervor. Nazi sympathizers were gaining momentum. Father Coughlin's popular radio program had an audience of over a million Catholics and pro-fascists each week. Congressmen made hysterical speeches against "refugee hordes" who sought to undermine and overthrow America on behalf of Jews and Communists. When Nazis occupied new territory and Hitler's race laws were imposed, domestic fascists celebrated—on the radio, in Congress, at mass rallies. ER found it upsetting and frightful.

Moreover, Hitler's laws cast a harsh light on America's own pattern of discrimination. Who was a full citizen? Who could vote? Who was "Negro"? Who was American? What did it mean to be "white," Jewish, Christian, Communist, or un-American? ER considered the range and shades of her friends and allies in the NAACP, from Mary McLeod Bethune to Walter White. Sometimes her head swirled with the insanity of it all.

ER believed that fulfilling the promise of America's democracy required enlarging it so that it embraced everyone. And she never wavered in her conviction that to resist fascism and Communism, it was essential to save and expand the New Deal, to end racial violence, bigotry, and discrimination, and to support youth and the youth movement. While increasingly shrill voices equated calls for racial justice with Communism, her friends in the youth movement were trying to fulfill the American promise. They were radical, but they considered themselves American activists for democracy.

They opposed bigotry, segregation, the poll tax, and all racial divides. They proved, both in their spirited meetings and in their daily lives, that it was possible to respect one another, work closely together, and form friendships across racial and religious boundaries. Their fresh intensity stirred her. Many AYC leaders were Jewish or of Jewish descent. Some were religious and belonged to Young Judea, which sought a Jewish homeland in Palestine; others were secular, agnostic, or spiritual. And by 1939 they were all being reviled as Communist Jew traitors.

From September on, ER publicly condemned Communists whose deeds proved they were not loyal to the United States. For instance, Earl Browder, head of the Communist Party of the United States, had openly avowed that his "first allegiance is to Russia"—for which she criticized him. It was "impossible to remain neutral," she wrote repeatedly to correspondents. "Hitler and Stalin combined are a very great danger to us. It is not just a question of boundaries, population, or raw materials. . . . You cannot insulate yourself from ideas. . . . In the end I prefer to die fighting for freedom than to live under a Nazi or Communist regime."

But she also believed that civil liberties applied to all political parties, and that the right to speak and dissent, to march and rally, were sacrosanct. She accepted the AYC's right to have Communist members, since to limit the rights of any one group was to endanger the rights of all. And she was convinced that her AYC friends were not in fact Communists, and that the AYC was not Communist-dominated. She had personally asked J. Edgar Hoover whether there was any hard evidence that her friends were Communists, and he told her there was nothing specific. Then she met with her friends privately to ask them to explain their political views.

> I told them that since I was actively helping them, I must know exactly where they stood politically. I knew well that the accusations might be false, since all liberals are likely to be labeled with the current catchword. . . . In every case they said they had no connection with the communists, had never belonged to any communist organizations, and had no interest in communist ideas. I decided to accept their word, realizing that sooner or later the truth would come out.

ER's great friend and benefactor Bernard Baruch was a secular Jewish-American and a southern patriot. He had long supported various programs now condemned as "Communist"—most notably, the schools and health centers at Arthurdale, and refugees from the Spanish Civil War, as well as the AYC. And he too had long been assailed by American bigots. In 1919 Henry Ford's *Dearborn Independent* had assailed him specifically

as the leader of an "international Jewish conspiracy." Throughout the
1930s those charges were renewed by the KKK, Father Charles Coughlin, Gerald L. K. Smith, Dudley Pelley, and various leaders of fascist
groups in the United States. Now a primary target, viciously slandered as
a predator-Jew-capitalist, Baruch wrote:

> These attacks never hurt me as much as did the discriminations my
> children suffered. My two daughters were brought up in the Episco-
> palian faith of their mother. Yet they were refused admission to the
> same dancing school their mother had attended. Even when the pas-
> tor of their church intervened, they were denied admission to several
> private schools for girls.
>
> It was not easy to explain to my children why they were suffering
> such senseless discriminations. Instead of allowing these things to
> embitter and frustrate them, I told them to take these discrimina-
> tions as spurs to more strenuous achievement—which is how I myself
> have met the problem of prejudice.

ER believed Baruch would understand the AYC's politics and appreciate its goals. So when it was attacked, she turned to him for advice and
support. Although he did not particularly approve of its style and disliked
some of its members personally, he never refused her requests. After 1938
ER was not merely a casual friend of the AYC—she was its most generous
supporter. With funds derived from Baruch, as well as from her broadcast
and lecture fees, she helped finance its operations—mostly anonymously,
through the AFSC.

During the last week of October, the Dies Committee viciously attacked
ER's closest allies in various New Deal agencies. Dies insisted there were
more than 569 Communists on the government payroll, and that they
aimed to destroy America. Federal employees with radical sympathies
had no protection or privacy. Dies's agents raided the Washington office
of the American League for Peace and Democracy, claiming it was a
Communist front. The committee then released a list of hundreds of
federal workers who were members, and in late October the *New York
Times* published their names, positions, and salaries. Included on this list

was Oscar Chapman, who had helped organize the Marian Anderson concert on 9 April 1939.

The night the story hit the press, ER was participating in a panel on "The Challenge to Civilization" at Helen Rogers Reid's *Herald Tribune* Forum, whose purpose was to oppose fears of Communist-Nazi-Fascist "Termites" who bored from within. One panelist, FBI director J. Edgar Hoover, told the audience of more than five thousand that he wanted to receive reports of "sabotage, espionage, or neutrality violation," but he urged Americans to avoid "a witch hunt." Poet Edna St. Vincent Millay wondered what was unneutral about "repeal of the embargo." While Harvard University president James Conant emphasized "academic and political freedom of the mind," he cautioned against "becoming more intensely class conscious" and suggested a return to the promise of universal education and "social mobility."

ER told the crowd she was not afraid to meet or speak with Communists, so long as she remained free to speak about democracy. In her talk, "Humanistic Democracy—The American Ideal," she articulated the distance between our national facts and American rhetoric. Everyone should be able "to come into the world healthy and strong," but "too many mothers were without adequate food or medical care." Every child should have the opportunity to be educated, she said, and "to earn a living under decent working conditions," but we "fall far short of that ideal." Until these basic democratic rights were made real, the threats of Communism and fascism would persist. Yet we could not suppress adherents of these *isms*, their right to speak or organize, without suppressing "our own freedoms." "It is not enough to say we believe in the Sermon on the Mount," she concluded, "without trying to live up to it."

She worried that FDR was too engrossed in the war at the expense of domestic issues. "Pa agrees wholeheartedly when you say we must not neglect domestic affairs," she wrote Anna, "but he is so full of the war. . . . Perhaps when [repeal of the embargo] is out of the way he will be freer in mind."

When ER resumed her autumn tour, she used it partly to emphasize those New Deal issues that seemed no longer to interest her husband. In Texas she spoke to the Altrusa Club, a women's group that she belonged to that provided job training and support for young girls and older women—including counseling and comfort "in a home for unmarried mothers."

She met with representatives of the Works Progress Administration, the National Youth Administration, and the Civilian Conservation Corps. She visited a CCC camp where seven hundred Indian boys were trained to do soil conservation work, and Indian girls were taught to revive traditional Indian crafts and beadwork. She was given a belt of "exquisite workmanship" that celebrated the skills of "our native Indian groups."

At the Texas State College for Women in Denton, she dedicated "a little chapel in the woods" with magnificent stained glass windows. More than ninety local "NYA boys" and the college's art students had built it to illustrate the many services "performed by women," from motherhood to industry. She took the opportunity to caution her audience of four thousand that such monuments to art and the spirit were endangered, and she told them that the future depended on their vision and actions. It was, she said, up to each individual to show the world that "a democracy can work when the day of peace comes." Her address, called "A Typical Day in the White House," was broadcast across the Southwest.

ER celebrated the creativity and excellence of individuals whose talents were discovered by and trained in the arts programs the New Deal funded. Such individuals needed a well-rounded education. Both sports and the arts were vital to society, since they not only provided opportunities for talented individuals but also helped build community. Nurturing the arts required local, state, national, and individual support. A homesteaders' group in Tennessee supported mountaineers whose craft and folk-music festivals inspired the young; the Florida State Music Teachers Association formed a club of twenty thousand professional musicians to benefit music education, orchestral opportunities, and a "congenial home for retired musicians."

Although signs of distress and poverty in Missouri and Nebraska were disturbing, ER was heartened by NYA programs that trained white and colored youth in stonework, which had resulted in an "epidemic" of new stone houses. Several judges in the Ozarks sponsored this project, with the result that "delinquency has been cut down 65%." Too often homeless, orphaned, abused children were designated "delinquents," but ER was adamant: across the country, we must care for our hurt, abandoned, needful children.

During her tour, on 27 October, the Senate finally voted 63 to 30 to repeal the arms embargo. ER wired her husband, "Delighted all went well in the Senate, Much Love." Several days later another moment of private jubilation came when the House passed the 1939 Neutrality Act and FDR signed the legislation, which at long last lifted the embargo. Now the United States would be able to sell desperately needed supplies to Great Britain and France. FDR considered the law a triumph. ER was relieved by the victory, but to her great dismay, her friend Caroline O'Day had again voted against it. An absolute pacifist, O'Day agreed with those World War I antimilitarists like Oswald Garrison Villard and Norman Thomas who were allied with isolationists like Senator Arthur Vandenberg, who declared that repeal and cash-and-carry "would suck the war right into our front yard."

ER returned to Hyde Park to vote in the November election, and conferred with her husband. He still wanted her to write nothing about conditions in conquered Europe, or about the secret negotiations and private conversations regarding long-range but vague plans for potential havens. But she was now free to write about the refugee situation. In her column, she compared the urgent appeals from "war refugees in different parts of the world" to the good work done in each locality by community chest drives:

> I wish very much that we could have some central organization, now coordinating civilian relief, make the contacts necessary . . . for adequate care of refugees in our own country and help other nations whose refugee loads are far greater than ours. . . . Think of sixty million Chinese war refugees! "Bowl of Rice" parties held all over the United States under the auspices of the United Council for Civilian Relief in China.

Such efforts could be coordinated "for the Chinese, Spanish, Polish, Czecho-Slovakian and German refugees."

An American journalist in Bucharest, Romania, wrote a long letter to ER that detailed "the deplorable conditions" faced by refugees in Eastern Europe. Ann Cardwell, wife of Paul Super, national secretary of the Polish YMCA, had been residents of Poland for over seventeen years. While she and her husband were safe in Romania, they had witnessed firsthand the deplorable plight of the refugees:

> It is of these Poles I want to write you. From the hour we left Warsaw we have been traveling with crowds of them. The roads have been full of trucks, cars, wagons, motorcycles, bicycles, . . . people afoot.

There were no rest rooms, flies swarmed. . . . It was extremely difficult to prepare food for babies and young children and no place to bathe or rest but in the homes of kindly people. Nowhere would Poles take money from us, American guests, though we were abundantly able to pay. But a word more about the children. We do not see how half of them could survive this awful retreat. Then there were the old and the ill, who could endure it no better. It was dreadful to see the wan, worn faces.

Cardwell warned of the winter to come and the impossibility of survival.

In addition to the unsanitary conditions of such life, there was constant danger from bombs and machine guns. Since coming here we have talked with a young doctor who was in charge of a train load of women, children and wounded soldiers being taken out of Krakow before the city fell. And he told of how . . . they had to stop [repeatedly] to take out the dead—8, 10, 12 at a time. The German planes continually bombed the train though it was evident that it was filled with people being evacuated. . . .

How many Poles have escaped from Poland nobody knows. None has come because he was a coward. They have come as did we, to avoid falling into German or Russian hands. . . . Every person I meet among the refugees tells me a tale of tragedy. . . . More, these people are stunned by the passing [of Poland], even though it will be but temporary, of the state their ancestors and they fought through 150 years to restore and rebuild on the basis of respect for personality and human rights. The material and social advance accomplished in the 20 years of freedom was little short of marvelous.

My husband and I will stay here and do everything we can, he as head of the Polish YMCA and director of the American Y relief work for Poles, I to help wherever I can, chiefly . . . by writing. We have little more than the clothes we have on, having had to leave everything in our beautiful Warsaw house, now without doubt a mass of ruins. . . . But these people must have money or die. . . . Romania, it seems, will let them stay here. . . .

And so, Mrs. Roosevelt, in the name of humanity, I appeal to you to do what you can for these people who have been robbed of their all and driven from their home. Russia, I know has urged all Poles to return, saying that Russia will take care of them. The Poles know the Bolsheviks well, and . . . cannot trust themselves to Russia. It is to

England, France, and America they must look for help. If England and France give their sons and share their sufferings and loss of war, surely America will come forward with relief funds. I am not addressing you . . . as the wife of the President, but as a woman deeply interested in human decency.

The next week in her 14 November column, ER celebrated the creation of a new Polish relief organization: "I was very glad to see this morning that a committee had been set up again, with Dr. Henry MacCracken as chairman, which will undertake relief work for the Poles. I hope that everyone who can, will help this committee."

While cautious discussions about refugees and safe havens continued, FDR offered refuge to several European leaders: "The United States would be glad to receive former [Polish] President Mościcki if he cares to visit this country." Since Hitler's next targets would be Holland and Belgium, FDR personally invited King Leopold of Belgium and Queen Wilhelmina of the Netherlands. He wrote Cordell Hull, "In view of the fact that Leopold is an old friend of mine and that I have ancestral Dutch connections it would be a decent thing to do." FDR assured the monarchs that "Mrs. Roosevelt and I would gladly look after their safety and well-being and . . . we would regard them as members of our own family."

Rumors of impending attacks accelerated so furiously that even Dora Forbes, SDR's ninety-three-year-old sister, reluctantly agreed to leave her Paris home. Carmel Offie wrote Missy LeHand, "We were very glad Mrs. Forbes left. She looked very well," and her behavior was "magnificent." Offie "could have died laughing when the night before she left she asked the Ambassador whether he would not lend her $100 and a portable radio; otherwise she would not leave. . . . She was very nice indeed to both of us, and especially the Chief" and evidently left Bullitt and Offie with treasured tokens from her beloved home and "many kindnesses."

Avenues of safety, access to escape, were rapidly closing. On 15 November, ER wondered if "we will ever return to the day . . . when little was thought of passports." On 19 November Hans Frank, the Nazi governor-general of occupied Poland, announced that "the Jewish ghetto in Warsaw must be shut off from the rest of the capital." It would be barricaded and walled off, since Jews carried "diseases and germs." William Shirer was told by a friend just returned from Warsaw that "Nazi policy is simply to exterminate the Polish Jews." They were herded in massive numbers to eastern Poland, along with "several thousand Jews from the Reich," without access to food, shelter, or warmth, sent there simply "to die."

Safe now in Paris, America's ambassador to Poland, Tony Biddle, and his wife, Margaret, worked closely with the Polish government in exile and performed vital relief services for refugees from everywhere. For over a year, Biddle had reported the daily horrors of "unchecked Nazism." Shortly after Kristallnacht, he had cabled Cordell Hull that almost half a million Jews in Hungary were subjected to various new laws of cruelty, 900,000 Jews of Romania faced "increasing pressure . . . as its Fascist government mimicked Nazi measures." In Poland, 3.5 million Jews were in desperation.

Tony Biddle, a staunch humanitarian in the State Department, represented a distinct minority. His warnings had gone unheeded in 1938, and his reports were ignored in 1939. Privately, he and his wife did as much as they could. "Margaret has been [wonderful] with the Polish refugees," Offie wrote, "and also for French refugee children who have been evacuated from the large cities. She [donated] blankets, medicines, tobacco, etc. to the Poles." Margaret also sent the French prime minister Édouard Daladier a check for a million francs "to give a little happiness to some of the soldiers for Christmas. And she does it all anonymously."

Given the isolationist, antiwar fervor that dominated U.S. politics during a critical election year, private efforts may have been the only efforts possible. Throughout the autumn, ER's audiences everywhere asked one question: could the United States "stay out" of Europe's wars and Europe's miseries? Her answer was always the same: the United States was connected to Europe's wars and miseries in myriad ways. The only way to "stay out" was "to protect and enlarge our own democracy . . . from assault both within and from afar."

The United States, still "on the outside" of war, was in a position to evaluate the situation created in part by "patriotic" lies. We should, ER wrote, notice "how many people are being taken in, and try to study how a method can be evolved whereby in the future leaders cannot fool their people. . . . Will we ever learn to use reason instead of force in the world, and will people ever be wise enough to refuse to follow bad leaders or to take away the freedom of other people?"

In her effort to stem the rising tide of bigotry and anti-Communism within the United States, ER answered the many letters sent to her in the hope that her words would contribute to activist democracy, which she considered essential for humanity's survival. In November 1938 a Yale University instructor, William Mulvey, wrote that he deeply appreciated her "poise and patience during this period of turmoil and tribulation." But he had been profoundly shocked to hear her say, concerning "the Jewish situation," that she hoped we "'will remain as free of prejudice and tolerant as we have been.' Have you unwittingly disregarded the present deplorable status of the Negro in the United States? Or, have you completely given up the whole problem?" He could not believe either could be true, but her "broad statement must surely have caused despair and derision in the hearts of twelve million beleaguered colored folk." He considered "our prevailing attitude of passive indifference even more deadly than the old active antagonism."

ER replied:

I think we are in grave danger in this country of being swept away by a fear of communism, which has been inculcated by various groups . . . into a panic which will bring us greater prejudice and intolerance. We have been making some progress even in the South as regards the Negro, but at the moment there is a general attitude of fear which will affect every solution which I had in mind. . . . That is why I have reiterated on every occasion that we have to live up to the traditions of our country as expressed in the Bill of Rights, in the Constitution and the Declaration of Independence even though I know in many cases we have fallen short. . . . I am far from giving up the problems of the Negro situation or any other. I am too old not to realize that lost causes usually are won in the end.

In September 1939 Mulvey wrote again, this time to ask if, in this new era dominated by "the brawls of busy little men abroad," something more significant could not be done to alleviate the suffering and neglect that still dominated America's "Negro problem." In this more rambling letter, which in part seemed to blame the victims for their own inaction, he suggested the "modern weapon" of propaganda: "Prejudices are built up by propaganda. Why can't they be torn down with the same agent?"

In reply, ER disagreed that Negroes were inactive:

Most of the educated ones I know are interested in bettering the lives
of their people and are leading them in a kindly and sane manner. A
few, of course, are fanatical but we white people have fanatics too.

It is a long process of education for both white and colored. They
should have better pay for their work and an equal chance at education before the law. The white man especially in the South must learn
that keeping the Negro at a low economic level keeps him down
too. . . .

I agree we must keep hate out of our thinking—both white and
colored and remain sane as only by keeping our democracy at peace
can we have a real influence toward a permanent peace. We can all
help by maintaining a fair and honest and unprejudiced attitude.

Convinced that the United States could have no influence on democracy abroad while lynching and bigotry at home continued, ER agitated
publicly and privately to end inequality in all its forms. When Walter
White told her about a campaign to keep Negro workers out of new ship-
building jobs, she asked Admiral E. S. Land of the Maritime Commission to do something "to make the labor unions take a little better attitude
[regarding] an even break to the workers of different races" and perhaps
"insist on fairness both for skilled and unskilled laborers."

She encouraged Walter White and the NAACP to revive the anti-
lynching law effort and supported his resolution. White wrote:

It is our conviction that before the US sets forth again, directly or
indirectly, to preserve democracy beyond the borders of the US it
must wipe out such undemocratic practices as lynching. . . . Negroes,
who are the chief sufferers from lynching, will be among those
American citizens called upon once again to fight for democracy.
Congress must see to it that there is no repetition of what took place
during the first world war when relatives of Negro soldiers, fighting
in France for democracy, were seized by mobs in the US and lynched,
some of them being burned at the stake.

Many letters ER received were filled, to her dismay, with contempt
and disdain for various minorities. Congressional Democrats were still
dominated by the "solid South," which demanded political silence regarding racial justice. Indeed, attempts to improve the lot of the Negroes,

Dixiecrats claimed, would destroy New Deal programs and Democratic unity. Nevertheless, ER kept issues of race and New Deal progress at the forefront of her considerations. She was disappointed that these issues were no longer visible on her husband's agenda while he focused on aid to Britain, military rearmament, and his new library.

ER and her husband were increasingly at odds as she was more routinely kept out of political conversations and denied access to international deliberations. While the couple rarely confronted their differences on race and refugees, tensions between them escalated. ER understood that her primary purpose was to accommodate and facilitate her husband's preferences, which she made every effort to do. Still, their political distance amplified their private grievances.

The week before Thanksgiving the Roosevelt family turned its attention to plans for the FDR presidential archive. The cornerstone was laid at Hyde Park on 19 November. ER's column devoted to this occasion was circumspect, as the lunch at the dedication of the library revealed a growing separation between her court and the president's. She was specifically hurt by his cavalier dismissal of her performance as official hostess, though the "very simple" ceremonies had rather pleased her. Before the event, however, she had heard a resounding "crash and discovered that one of the card tables around which some people were sitting, had collapsed and all the china had fallen to the floor! It was too bad to break the china, but I had to laugh, remembering the table which collapsed when the King and Queen were with us."

ER wrote nothing of her own feelings, but Tommy sent Anna the full story:

> We had a funny time on Sunday—funny now. . . . Your father and the [library's fundraising] committee made up the lists of people to be invited, etc. Missy and Tully apparently had a hand in it—neither [Edith] Helm nor I were invited to anything. No one asked our advice and the lists were given to our social bureau to send out. . . . Your mother asked how many for lunch and was told it was a selected few. . . . Your grandmother added a few of her pets. I was to have lunch at the cottage for some of our pets. Your mother asked your father who was quite calm and said the people would not expect lunch and when asked what they were supposed to do between 1:30 and 3, he said blandly: "Oh, they can just wander around."

November in the country! [Everyone arrived] cold and hungry. They were given sandwiches and coffee, ice cream and doughnuts. . . . Your mother said she deliberately kept out of the dining room so she wouldn't have to be embarrassed. The selected few, of course, had a good lunch which your grandmother had planned. I never saw your mother so mad!

Riled, ER mounted her horse for a long afternoon ride.

Tommy concluded by mentioning the strains on the once great Val-Kill friendship among ER, "the Cook and the Dickerman," as Tommy referred to Nancy Cook and Marion Dickerman. While emotionally their friendship had dissolved by 1938, politically they were still connected. Personally, at Val-Kill, Tommy explained to Anna, they "leave us very much alone," but Marion Dickerman still expected every convenience when she stayed at the White House, which she did for the labor hearings. "I urged your mother to say the house was being cleaned, or any excuse . . . but your mother didn't think she could do that, so Dickerman . . . ordered cars and generally made herself at home. I don't see how anyone could have such thick hide. Your mother has certainly made it unmistakably plain that she doesn't want anything to do with them."

Now the toxic dynamic threatened to poison ER's planning for the 1940 election season. "Your mother and her friends Agnes Brown Leach and Dorothy Schiff Backer," Tommy wrote, "are keen to start 'state operations.'" But Leach and Backer refused to work under Nancy Cook. Backer, a generous funder, said she would give much less than before since "nothing is done" under Nancy's direction. ER and her allies wanted Nancy removed.

Whatever her private feelings and disappointments, from Warm Springs ER listed her reasons for gratitude on Thanksgiving:

I am thankful that I live in a democracy and that it is in the United States of America. I am thankful we are not at war. I am thankful that more of our citizens are thinking about their government today and are realizing their obligations to that government.

I am thankful that I can think as I please, and write as I please and act as I please. . . . I am thankful that in this country, courage can still dominate fear. I am thankful for the answering smile of the passer-by, and the laughter of children in our streets.

Even here in Warm Springs, where many people are facing handicaps which must give them moments of stark terror when they are alone, they can still manage to meet the world with a smile and give one the feeling of a marching army with banners flying.

Thanksgiving revitalized ER's spirits. Whenever she felt wounded by her husband's thoughtlessness, or became impatient or distrustful of his political strategies, she considered his heroic determination, his steadfast vision, and his unwavering pleasure in so many things despite his great physical limitations. She loved to watch him in the pool, where his strong arms and torso muscles camouflaged his useless legs, and where he shouted and played with children and adults at various levels of impairment, his own merriment and spirit always in the lead.

Still, race remained an immediate issue of concern for ER during this Thanksgiving visit. Earlier that year FDR had built a new school and infirmary in Warm Springs, "where the patients needing hospital care are housed," but they were to be segregated. ER decided to build a similar brick school for the area's many children of color. The Thanksgiving dinner entertainment was integrated and included a chorus from Tuskegee Institute, which was "enjoyed by all."

Recently, in New York, ER had met with the white Quaker educator Rachel Davis DuBois and been excited by the vision and the pioneering multicultural work of this lifelong activist for peace, women's rights, and racial harmony. DuBois's work, inspired by their mutual friend Jane Addams, seemed to ER immediately essential. As a high school teacher in New Jersey, she had been alarmed when her students used racial and religious differences to attack one another. So she decided to create a program "to introduce practical steps . . . for teaching children tolerance and democracy." She created a Service Bureau for Intercultural Education to show how all groups contributed to America's power. New York City's board of education had recently adopted her program.

DuBois's work, ER wrote with enthusiasm, would benefit "school systems throughout the country. . . . The first step, of course, is to reach the teachers and through them to capture the children's imagination. To do that, all modern progressive methods are being used. Radio scripts and dramatic episodes are being published . . . and even television will soon be called upon to contribute." The U.S. Department of Education sponsored and broadcast one of DuBois's radio series called "Americans All, Immigrants All," which won the annual award of the Women's National Radio Committee as the most original program for 1938–39.

During this election season, ER was the only person close to the administration who was determined to discuss hatred and bigotry and their corrosive effect on democracy. But making progress required a movement, and she was relieved that bold visionaries like DuBois worked with Quakers, the NAACP, and WILPF to strengthen that movement. Upon returning to Washington after Thanksgiving, ER had a new demand when she met with various political groups: youth must be added to leadership positions in each organization. If that did not happen, the movement for change and betterment would atrophy and fail.

ER did not criticize her husband's failure to promote these issues. Instead, she sought to work with him to elect a liberal Democrat as the next president. Although not for publication, she bluntly told anyone who asked that she opposed a third term for him. At the time, she believed he preferred not to run again and that he looked forward to new work in retirement.

After Thanksgiving, ER turned her attention to the needs of refugees. She invited refugee singers and musicians to play at the White House and met regularly with refugee artists and scholars. As she became increasingly active with émigré organizations, she urged her column readers to contemplate "the refugee problem from the point of view of gain to us in the long run," not just the momentary cost of accommodating their needs, and she advocated a welcoming attitude toward them. Impressive studies showed that "the volume of refugees entering this country to take up permanent citizenship under the quotas was [generally] balanced by the number of foreign people departing from our shores." Moreover, while "in the old days, a vast majority of people coming in were in the unskilled labor group," that had changed: "at present it is the educated, highly skilled in both professional and technical work" who arrived in the United States. They brought the skills and means to start businesses, which could "employ some of our own unemployed citizens. It is not, therefore, as one-sided a business as we think. People are not throwing Americans out of work to employ refugees."

ER's column on refugees was blasted by those who claimed refugees were agents of Communism, anarchism, and un-Americanism, while others said too many of the refugees were Jews. Bigotry was as epidemic in the United States as it was in the heart of once-enlightened Europe—now dominated by Nazi parties. But ER persevered in her effort to extend her network of activist allies.

More than a thousand activists and educators celebrated her at New York's Hotel Astor, for the 135th anniversary dinner of *The Churchman*, a journal of religious activism that was also being honored that night for its campaign against anti-Semitism. Dr. Henry Leiper said that those clerics who employed Nazi propaganda were a "disgrace to their calling." The great danger to democracy, in his view, came not from enemies within or without but from its friends' "indifference and blindness."

Most of the evening was dedicated to ER. Dr. Frank Kingdon, president of the University of New Brunswick (now Rutgers University) said she was "the kindliest of American women, who occupies so unique a place in American life that no other individual can be compared to her." The journalist Dorothy Thompson said, "Few people received universal admiration, and virtually nobody universal affection. . . . I doubt if any woman in the whole wide world is so beloved."

The bestowal of the award, noted the *New York Times*, was "a condensation of the praise" that had been showered on the first lady at the dinner: "To Eleanor Roosevelt, apostle of good-will, for her achievement in abolishing time and space in the pursuit of happiness for all, for her understanding and love of people, and her daring to believe in the potentialities of their best."

Receiving all these compliments, in addition to the award, felt "somehow a bit unreal," ER said afterward. "When you sit and hear people whom you admire and respect, say things [you feel] cannot apply to you, and find that you have to get up and accept all this—well, it is disconcerting." The praise songs that accompanied her award genuinely "bewildered" her.

Speaking to those assembled, ER said she wanted to make it clear that she did nothing extraordinary, just what came to hand. She answered letters, calls, and appeals. She went out and met the people who made up America, to see what they needed and wanted. "Anyone would have done what [I] had done, given the opportunity." Her goal was simply to promote "better understanding among neighbors."

Though she remained self-deprecating, this public recognition of and praise for her efforts, in the name of the principles and causes closest to her heart, was a proud and gratifying moment. It also fueled her energies for the battles ahead, giving her "courage to keep on trying to be more worthy of all that has been said," as she acknowledged in her column.

ER would need that courage.

On the railroad platform that night, while she was waiting for the midnight train to Washington, she encountered some of the AYC leaders who were her friends. They had been summoned to appear the next day before the Dies Committee, which continued to scrutinize allies of the New Deal for links to un-American activities.

The Nazi-Soviet Pact had created tensions and disarray within the AYC and other leftist organizations. Some members remained committed to the Communist dream, believing that the pact had bought Stalin time to build Soviet defenses. In their view, the West had refused all Soviet efforts to form a united front against fascism because it preferred a German-Russian bloodbath, the better to preside over an extended imperial future. Others were horrified by the pact and felt personally betrayed by Stalin's new partnership with Hitler, who promised annihilation for their families, their parents, and themselves.

This internal conflict served the Dies Committee's purposes, as former Communists volunteered to ruin, often with lies and exaggerated calumnies, those who remained in the party's thrall.

In its new round of hearings, the Dies Committee proceedings appalled her, violating her sense of American justice and fair play. That it could get at the "truth" seemed doubtful, since its smear campaign had splattered virtually every decent philanthropist and liberal in Washington. A confidential list of individuals who were allegedly "communist or subversive or un-American," prepared by the FBI for the committee, amused both ER and FDR. It contained the names of every notable New Dealer and included future secretary of war Henry Stimson, the 1936 Republican nominee for vice president; Secretary of the Navy Frank Knox; and the president's own mother. "Franklin and I got particular amusement out of the inclusion of her name," ER recalled. They could picture SDR's "horror if she were told that the five or ten dollars she had given to a seemingly innocent relief organization put her among those whom the Dies Committee could easily call before it as belonging to subversive organizations." FDR was repelled not only by the publication of government employees' names but by the methods employed to obtain them, including break-ins and records thefts. He "denounced the committee's methods as sordid."

Moreover, when the committee investigated people who were without "influence or backing," its "questions were so hostile as to give the impression that the witness had been hailed before a court and prejudged a criminal." It resembled "intimidation," and "Gestapo methods." That show trials had found a happy home in America was not something ER could accept silently. Such tactics never harmed "the really powerful, but they do harm many innocent people who are unable to defend themselves."

On Wednesday morning, 30 November 1939, the Dies Committee was to question ER's young friends in the AYC leadership. Summoned to appear within twenty-four hours, they were allowed no time to prepare. ER had decided, with FDR's approval, to show up and provide moral support for them. Unaccompanied and unannounced, she entered the committee room. "Mrs. Roosevelt appeared at the hearing . . . at about 11:15 A.M., [and] looked around for a seat," the *Times* reported. "She wore a stunning dark-green silk dress with matching woolen coat, gloves and felt hat. Her coat and hat were trimmed with Persian lamb."

Joseph Starnes of Alabama, presiding over the committee in Dies's absence, noticed her and stopped the testimony: "The chair takes note of the presence of the First Lady of the Land and invites her to come up here and sit with us."

"Oh, no thank you," she replied. "I just came to listen." She found a seat between William Hinckley and Jack McMichael, the current and former chairs of the AYC, who along with Joseph Cadden, the executive secretary, were waiting to be called.

After Starnes's initial courtesy, the committee ignored her, although as the morning session ended, Jerry Voorhis, of California, a representative sympathetic to the New Deal, asked her if she wished to testify. She replied, "It's just a question if I can contribute anything to you."

Then Starnes announced a lunch break until three in the afternoon. ER invited the AYC delegation to lunch at the White House.

Finally at four p.m. the committee called the AYC witnesses. Hinck-ley, Cadden, and McMichael defended their movement and attacked the committee's witch-hunt procedures. After the intense questioning, which all observers believed went as well as could be expected, Hinckley was given permission to read the AYC's petition to discontinue the Dies Com-mittee immediately.

When the long day was over, ER invited the AYC delegation to dine at the White House and stay the night. Joseph Lash of the American Stu-dent Union (ASU), who was to testify the next day, was among the group. At the dinner, he later recalled, "in addition to the 'gutter-snipes,' as someone had dubbed us," Hollywood stars Melvyn Douglas and his wife, Helen Gahagan, were present, as were the progressive assistant attorney general Norman Littell and his wife, Katherine; Aubrey Williams, "the embattled head of the NYA who was having almost as much trouble with Mr. Dies as we were"; and Williams's boss, Colonel Francis Harrington, head of the WPA.

FDR was eager to hear about their experiences and listened pensively to their accounts. He "chuckled, roared," and suggested he might "be slipped into the hearings under a sheet." Melvyn Douglas replied that he would be most welcome "as a Ku Kluxer."

For ER, that dinner party was a "pleasant interlude," but all was not celebratory that night. On 30 November the Soviets invaded Finland with twenty-six divisions and over 465,000 troops and bombarded Helsinki, the recently redesigned capital city of glass and hope. Unlike the Nazi air raids on Poland, the Soviet attack on Finland was met with significant international protest. Photographs of the damage to Helsinki were pub-lished worldwide, accompanied by the details of hospitals overwhelmed by civilian casualties: "One girl, Dolores Sundberg, twelve years old, had both her legs smashed to ragged stumps, and died on the operating table."

At the White House, FDR said the Soviets had done "a terrible thing." Lash "shared that view," but his AYC colleagues were silent. Some clam-ored to have the U.S. ambassador recalled from Moscow, but FDR opposed that, saying that to sever diplomatic ties with the Soviet Union would make it impossible "to play a constructive role" in whatever peace efforts might emerge. On that point the AYC members agreed with him.

After FDR withdrew, the party moved upstairs to discuss the plight of liberals, who were without leadership on domestic issues now that the war dominated FDR's concerns. Aubrey Williams, Helen Gahagan, and Melvyn Douglas sought to reforge a popular liberal movement to win the fall election and save the New Deal. Lash found ER "down to earth and practical" as she considered measures "to pull liberals together" for 1940.

Before they left, filled with gratitude for ER's support, Aubrey Williams looked hard at the youth leaders, and said: "Don't let her down; it will break her heart!"

When the party finally broke up, ER went to her desk, "piled high with mail." Late that night Bernard Baruch called from South Carolina to say if she "needed help he would come right up." At breakfast, ER told her AYC friends that Baruch had offered his home if the "youngsters needed a rest" and said if "there were any expenses, he would be glad to cover them."

That morning, as the Dies Committee hearings resumed, ER sat with Lash "and spoke with him confidentially" until he was called. According to the *Times*, "newsreel agencies had cameras, sound equipment and special lights ready for the possibility" that ER would testify, but instead "the elaborate equipment was used to record bits of Lash's testimony." ER's "costume today was all black except for a vivid red scarf."

For two hours Lash was interrogated by J. B. Matthews, a former Communist now on the Dies Committee staff. Lash and Matthews had actually worked together as Young Socialists, and Lash knew him well. "All of us on the left had gone through many changes," Lash later reflected, and Matthews "was now on his final journey to the far right."

Lash had gone to the hearings "with a divided soul," he subsequently wrote. The ASU had been organized at Columbia University during Christmas 1935 and included the Student League for Industrial Democracy, a Socialist Party organization allied with Norman Thomas; the National Student League, an arm of the Communist Party; and a number of unaffiliated liberal clubs and student societies organized on college campuses throughout America, such as the Harvard Peace Society. Among the original officers were Lash; James Wechsler, director of publications; and Molly Yard, treasurer.

Matthews noted that Communist Party chair Earl Browder had called the ASU a "transmission belt" for the party. Lash insisted it was not. There were Communists in the ASU, he acknowledged, but they did not dominate.

Congressman Jerry Voorhis pressed Lash: why did the ASU allow Communist participation? The ASU was democratic and always supported majority decisions, Lash said. It was concerned with civil liberties, academic freedom, basic and real human needs, peace, and culture. It did not care "what students think," it cared only that "they should think" and be actively concerned about "social problems." And it would be "unfair" to "sacrifice the Communists to the lions right now," when everything was in flux.

Voorhis said Communist policy was unpredictable. Lash replied, "Well, they can't predict what I'll think either." To which a *Daily Worker* reporter called out, "Hear! Hear!"

At a moment when the questioning became harsh, even vitriolic, ER stood and moved from the back of the room to the press table. "I took a pencil and a piece of paper, and the tone of the questions changed immediately," she later wrote. "Just what the questioner thought I was going to do, I do not know, but my action had the effect I desired."

Fearlessly, Lash submitted a chronology of his life thus far. In 1929 he had joined Norman Thomas's Socialist Party. Then he had gone to Spain to fight for the Loyalists—and resigned from the Socialist Party because of all he had witnessed there. Yes, he still blamed the "profit system" for many domestic problems and did not consider it "disloyal" to favor changes in an unjust economic system.

Someone on the committee accused Lash of having been a poor soldier during the Spanish Civil War because he could not sing in tune or keep in step. Resentful, Lash burst into song with gusto:

If you see an un-American lurking
    far or near,
Just alkalize with Martin Dies and
    he will disappear.

The *New York Times* summed up the scene: "The Dies committee heard words and music today, while Mrs. Franklin D. Roosevelt looked on with manifest amusement as Joseph Lash warbled."

As she listened to Lash's spirited testimony, ER was impressed by his directness and interested in his occasional discomfort; she felt her faith in the young man was vindicated.

ER's young friends had been subjected to contemptuous vitriol by congressmen and reporters and had done well. But her commitment to youth, and her personal admiration, were now focused upon Lash, who seemed such a needful, earnest, and genuinely good young man. In fact, their meeting during the Dies Committee hearings marked the beginning of one of the most important friendships in her life.

On 6 December Lash wrote to thank ER for "your great kindness to me last week. I know that you have not wanted to stir up another hornets nest by befriending the ASU. And so I am all the more grateful for your appearance . . . when I testified. I regret that I did not do a better job. When one's political opinions are in a violent state of flux, one should go to a hermitage rather than before a Congressional Committee with its thousand tongues."

ER replied, "I appreciate your note very much and was very glad to go to the Dies Committee hearing when you testified. I had a feeling that your political opinions were not completely clarified, but I think on the whole you did a pretty good job. If you ever feel that you would like to see me and talk over things, either in New York or here [Washington], I shall be glad to have you come either alone or bring any one you want with you."

Perhaps it was Lash's integrity—his concern for his former friends, now his opponents, as well as for the future—that stirred ER deeply. Perhaps it was simply that they agreed profoundly on issues, while so many other young people she had trusted, daughters and sons of friends, and other AYC members, now disappointed her. He had renewed her faith in youth and in its potential both to spark change and to stay committed to one's ideals.

After the Dies Committee hearings, various politicians who agreed with its approach attacked ER personally for her appearance at the hearing. A group of Republican women assailed her presence as "horrifying" and "indecent." The borough president of Queens, George Harvey, declared that AYC members should be sent to concentration camps, yet the first lady had had them for tea at the White House. Harvey said he did not believe in "free speech for Reds" because they stood for "sedition, treason, rebellion." He would not let a Red speak anywhere in Queens, and he was relieved that many of the city colleges and universities now banned them as well.

But others applauded ER's determination to defend America's civil liberties during the growing witch-hunt atmosphere. In 1939 America's political climate was as discordant and divided as any in Europe, becoming ever more accusatory and dangerous, filled with wild, threatening rhetoric and laced with occasional acts of random, sickening racial and labor violence. In that atmosphere, ER's support for her much-maligned friends seemed to many a reflection of her valor and steadfast decency. She called for calm, discernment, and especially the survival of democratic values. Civil liberties meant very little unless they prevailed during moments of war and tension, when disagreements were most sharply revealed.

The Nazi-Soviet Pact was a double-edged sword. It cut liberal-left united front alliances to shreds. New Deal liberals were stunned to see their former radical allies fall supine before Soviet aggression in Poland and Finland. The pact drove Communists into a new and strange union with isolationists, Nazi sympathizers, and anti–New Deal Republicans. Communists could now be attacked as Red Nazis.

As the 1940 presidential race neared, the New Deal agenda hung suspended by the twisted cross of the Nazi-Soviet Pact. FDR initiated a bipartisan campaign for war preparation, emphasizing a massive air and fleet buildup that required industry's cooperation and participation, but he turned away from efforts to further the New Deal. Liberals were on the defensive, and activist New Dealers were confused, able only to wait for him to renew his commitment to their primary goals of job security, housing, education, and public health. Moreover, when FDR's Justice Department began to compete with the Dies Committee in its crusade against Communists, the civil liberties record of the Roosevelt administration went virtually to smash. Loyalty oaths for federal workers were introduced in the Relief Act of 1939.

For months after the Dies Committee hearings, ER defended the AYC in speeches, in columns, and in replies to citizens' critical letters. Her most earnest letters went to her closest friends, who were concerned about her reputation and worried about her judgment.

On 2 December she appealed to Baruch for a long-range financial aid package for the AYC. Baruch still disliked the tone used by the AYC leadership, regretted many of its actions, and never believed it was all that the first lady thought it was. And he defended the Dies Committee, saying, "no harm comes from these investigations if we get the truth." He would not give the AYC a long-term commitment, but he gave it the money she requested to pay its rent and other bills, and he assured ER in a handwritten postscript to his letter of firm disagreement: "Please always be frank with me. We shall always be friends—as I have enlisted with you."

In Philadelphia on 4 December, ER accepted the AFSC Humanitarian Award, presented by Curtis Bok, before an audience of more than a thousand Quakers, philanthropists, and citizens. Referring to the Dies Committee, she said that America owed to "all groups trying to solve their problems our sympathetic interest and attention. I doubt if putting them in a category, and trying to decide if this or that group is dangerous, will help solve their problems." To the Quakers, she expressed her gratitude for the teaching she had received from them over the years: "It is an education to work with people who have ideals and live up to them, but are practical enough to make their ideals become realities."

During these weeks of turmoil, ER hosted an evening of frolic and fun at the annual Gridiron Widows Party at the White House. She was particularly pleased that her great friends Esther Lape and Elizabeth Read would join her for the event and spend the night. Lape and a group of physicians had been campaigning for a national health care program, initially to have been part of the 1935 Social Security Act. Lape had asked ER to arrange a meeting with FDR, and after several postponements, ER wrote Lape that FDR "says that he does not want to get into any difficulty with the American Medical Association just now when he has so much to contend with." Lape tore the letter in half and crumpled it. ER was relieved that Lape came to the White House party anyway. She and Lape were both determined to keep agitating for a national health care program.

Lape and Read thoroughly enjoyed themselves that evening, especially during ER's star performance in an off-the-record skit, accompanied by Elinor Morgenthau, Bess Furman, Tommy, and Edith Helm. The theme of the evening was a Wild West "whoopee 1940 roundup," filled with journalistas strutting their stuff for the first lady. According to press reports, all the skits, songs, and supper speeches were amusing. A jolly array of potential presidential wives were serenaded. The ER character was given the first and last song. The message of the first was that the Roosevelts were on their way out:

I'm waiting for the '40 roundup.
Gonna saddle old Frank for the last time.
So long, old gals. I'll ride in on
"My Day". . . .
Git along, little Frankie, git along.

But in the "grand finale," the situation changed: the Roosevelts were here
to stay.

Oh, give me my home,
Where the New Dealers roam,
And the Congressmen vote as they may.
Where never is heard an encouraging word.
And the press keeps on printing "My Day."

"We all had a pleasant time," ER noted, "laughed at our own pecu-
liarities as shown in the skits," and thoroughly enjoyed the monologues.
The next day she and her guests were entertained by a repeat performance
of the Gridiron Clubists. "They were so proud of their songs, they invited
their excluded wives and women colleagues." The men, aided by show
business professionals Moss Hart and Max Gordon, addressed a giant
sphinx with FDR's face and cigarette holder, with "Is He or Ain't He?"

Will you run?
Or are you done?
Will you be eternally the one?

Music was a great solace for ER. Planning the Christmas festivities,
she included many concert artists from Europe and noted that "we have
developed a little in the past 25 years." We no longer banish, as we did
during the Great War, "music by composers who happened to be of this
or that nationality. . . . The one thing which is above war, is art. We can
still enjoy music and pictures and theatres and books, no matter what the
nationality of the artist may be."

In mid-December ER devoted a column to the 148th anniversary of
the Bill of Rights: "I hope that every citizen in this country will read over
those first ten amendments to the Constitution and keep them constantly

in mind, particularly Articles IV, V, and VI." Article VI guarantees criminals being prosecuted

> certain rights. I am wondering if in the present day these rights should not be observed for all people, whether accused in a criminal case or whether merely accused through the public press. It seems to me that "the right to be informed of the nature and cause of the accusation; to be confronted with the witnesses against him; to have compulsory process for obtaining witnesses in his favor, and to have the assistance of counsel for his defense," would be a safeguard to a great many people today who find themselves suddenly held up as dangerous citizens when they have not had an opportunity to be heard.
>
> If you are not accused of being a Communist these days, you may be a Communist front and now you may be a Communist transmission belt. . . . I do not question that all three . . . exist, but I begin to wonder whether some perfectly innocent people may not be suffering because of the fears which are being aroused.

That same month, J. B. Matthews issued a blast against several consumer groups that ER had long been part of, including the League of Women Shoppers and the National Consumers League. Created to protect the health and safety of citizens, to keep poisons out of food and drugs, these groups were charged now by Matthews with being Communist "transmission belts."

At a press conference, FDR censured the committee's procedures, and ER "joined the President today in criticizing" the report. In its coverage, the *New York Times* quoted most of her Bill of Rights column. An illustrious group of educators, scientists, writers, and artists, including the novelists Dashiell Hammett and Theodore Dreiser and the anthropologist Franz Boas, joined ER to defend the Bill of Rights. The notables spoke with alarm of a "growing witch hunt" in the Dies Committee's efforts to suppress dissident groups. "We have before us the example of many European countries where suppression of the Communist Party was but a beginning, followed by a campaign against trade unions, cultural groups, Jews, Catholics, Masons, and ending with the destruction of all freedom."

Matthews's attack on consumer groups was followed by his promise to investigate the influence of "Reds" in schools and teachers' unions, then move on to "the domination of un-Americanism in Hollywood." ER considered his Gestapo-like assaults to be the real menace. She was outraged that Congress emphasized the Dies investigations instead of examining the causes of poverty and unemployment. The real problem that faced America, she insisted, was that four million young people were out of school and out of work. Until something was done to find them jobs, they would be "a potential menace to their communities." Work, she emphasized, was "the number one problem confronting youth." Many colleges and high schools failed to prepare their students for meaningful work. She received countless letters from graduates who wrote, "We have nothing to sell. We are not [trained] to do a single thing. Please, Mrs. Roosevelt, what shall we do?" ER called for a business-industrial-educational alliance that would actually serve the needs of the nation, and the community.

Many Americans who had found gainful employment in the WPA had recently been laid off because of new regulations that severely limited the best training and job projects. A woman who had been with WPA for four years, but was now back on relief, wrote to ER of the loss of "personal pride and self esteem sacred to the individual." Mindful of the outbreak of war in Europe, she concluded, "The long-time tragedies of peace may be more devastating, if allowed to continue, than those of war. . . . Until democratic society can find a dignified use for all the individuals who comprise it, there can be no peace." ER agreed completely: "In a really successful democracy, those who want work should find work."

In New York City to deliver a town hall lecture, "On the Problems of American Youth," ER met with Joe Lash at her Eleventh Street apartment. They had corresponded since the Dies Committee hearings, and she sensed that he was "in trouble." She had invited him to visit and discuss his difficulties in the ASU. Lash explained that the Communists now dominated and that he and his allies, including Molly Yard (the ASU's "independent-minded chair"), Agnes Reynolds, and Jimmy Wechsler, were in the minority.

ER replied that he was "not the only one having troubles with Communists" and showed him a recent *Daily Worker* attack on her: "Mrs. Roosevelt has it down to a science. She manages to 'defend' such progressive organizations as the American Youth Congress and to slap the Dies Committee, and at the same time to rail against Communists as 'foreign agents' . . . [She] is playing a very sinister and crafty game [and her aim is to] make it easier for the administration to sneak America into war."

Lash replied, "The Communists know that you rather than the Dies Committee are their most dangerous foe."

During this early meeting in their burgeoning friendship, Joe Lash took notes, as he would always do. When Lash said he and Molly Yard intended to leave the ASU, ER was concerned. She wondered about his future, suggested they meet again, and invited him to use her place at Hyde Park to rest, reflect, and restore his energies. Their relationship, defined by their shared quest for a better future, was launched.

After her town hall lecture, which was attended by over two thousand young people, ER left for Hyde Park for the holiday season. The next day Anna and her family arrived by train from Seattle, and ER noted their relaxed manner. "I think my daughter must have done a very remarkable piece of work," ER told her readers, "for everybody including the father . . . and the baby looked well and cheerful. My recollection of traveling with babies is a succession of difficulties. The food was never right, they wouldn't sleep when they should and altogether a twenty-four hour trip seemed endless. This family, after four days of travel, seemed rested and well and, wonder of wonders, entirely good humored. It is evident to me that each generation improves upon the last!"

ER's holiday was festive and prayerful. Social events, films and escapades, and snow-filled frolics with four generations of family filled her days. From Hyde Park to the White House, it was a time of harmony. Private moments in New York City and quiet dinners with special friends—including ER's annual holiday dinner with Hick—brought respite from her busy social calendar.

ER and Hick had not spent significant time together in recent months. Although they wrote and called regularly, Hick missed her exclusive time with ER. One morning she was relieved to hear ER's voice: "I needed reassurance! I had wakened at 6, moaning and covered with a cold perspiration, dreaming you had died! . . . It would be so much better, wouldn't it, if I didn't love you so much! It makes it trying for you. You are very sweet to me always." Still, Hick wrote to congratulate ER for an award as "leading statesman of the week" and for "standing by the AYC. . . . I'm darned proud of you." She recalled their time alone in the country as "two perfect weeks. . . . I cant remember having had a happier time on a vacation—except that time you and I drove around the Gaspe Peninsula. We DID have a good time on that trip, didn't we?" Hick let ER know that if she could not be alone with ER, she preferred to be alone.

She had even refused to attend the Gridiron Widows Party. "It's sweet of you to invite me down," she wrote, "but I think I'd better sit tight financially." It was not only travel expenses, "but I'd have to get my evening things out, have them pressed, etc." Yet in the same letter she described all she purchased with "the money you gave me for my vacation." In addition to paying many bills, she had bought "new corduroy breeches and hunting boots" and felt "all dressed up" as she wrote her letter: "Gee I love clothes like these." ER, always conscious that her schedule and obligations kept her from spending time with Hick, compensated by being sympathetic and as loving as possible. Their ongoing correspondence shows their continued affection for and trust in each other.

ER hated to be alone and was happiest when she was busy and her homes were filled, especially with young people. Soon after the Dies Committee hearings, when she hosted the AYC delegation, she wrote Hick that it seemed "funny not to have the house full of young people!"

ER's commitment to her new young friends coincided with her growing disappointment over some decisions made by her son Elliott. In an October radio address, he had "lauded" the Dies Committee, saying it "has done more for the United States in the last two years than many able and sincere statesmen achieve in a lifetime. If it has done nothing else, it has made the people conscious of the fact that in their midst, perhaps in their own circle of friends, are men and women who despise everything this Government stands for." And now he was campaigning for politicians who aggravated her husband, such as Vice President John Nance Garner. ER understood that all children have to rebel in their own way, and often in strange ways. She and FDR never publicly criticized their own children.

ER's holiday was also marked by personal sadness—the sudden death of Heywood Broun, president of the Newspaper Guild. In a column, she expressed her "deep respect and genuine affection" for the controversial journalist: "he set us all a high standard in that he wrote what he really believed. . . . No writing has any real value which is not the expression of genuine thought and feeling. He was critical sometimes, but almost always there was something constructive about his criticisms."

Her 1939 Christmas message was in part a tribute to Broun's advice, "Drink ye all of it." She concluded, "This is the season for forgiveness and self-searching." She urged everybody to "do something a bit unusual," to go beyond "customary gifts" to families, friends, charities—and provide "unexpected pleasure."

Her article of "inspiration especially for the children and youth of our time" was featured for Christmas Eve in the *New York Times*:

> "Peace on earth, good-will toward men!" . . . He came into this world as a defenseless, helpless Baby, born in a stable and laid in a manger, because the world of His day had no room for the poor and He belonged to a group which was oppressed and harassed.
>
> In the year 1939 the angels' song will be repeated in homes and in churches throughout the world, perhaps even in forts and in trenches where men lie in wait to kill each other.
>
> After all these years the world is still the same, a world in which groups of people are harassed and oppressed. A world in which there is danger, just as there used to be—danger even to the lives of little children.

Just as "the kings of old knew that their material power would not save them," it was clear today that "comfort and ease" guaranteed nothing. Young people especially had that "vision of Christ in their hearts" and acted generously for good—"full of enthusiasm and bent on seeing happiness reign in the world." But "Peace on earth, good-will toward men" would occur only when "this song in our hearts [entered] into our daily way of life." Only then would the world become "a place of joy and peace!"

ER's Christmas season was full, with tree-lighting ceremonies, children's parties, church services, her columns, and a broadcast "right in the middle of dinner, but . . . I was back before the next course was served." Stockings filled by Santa caused much excitement and merriment, a reading of Dickens's *A Christmas Carol* edited by granddaughter Sistie and FDR. There was an afternoon ride in the park with family friend Harry Hooker, and an unusual newsworthy reality: "We tried very hard at dinner to make the President enter into a real, old-fashioned, family argument. But he said the Christmas spirit was upon him and he was not going to argue with anyone!"

During the week there were films, including *Gone with the Wind*, which dazzled everybody. Even critical SDR "sat through" the entire four-hour film—which ended at two a.m.! There were also meetings on youth and conferences on a new Institute on Human Relations sponsored by the National Council of Christians and Jews.

As the New Year approached, ER was surprised to be invited to succeed Heywood Broun as president of the Newspaper Guild. On 30 December she sent a telegram to decline: "Absolutely impossible for me to take full-time job so could not even consider the position." She was also asked to consider the presidency of Bryn Mawr. She and Helen Taft Manning, President Taft's daughter and the college's dean since 1925, seemed to be serious contenders. Appropriately, Manning was named Bryn Mawr's president.

On New Year's Eve, ER wished everyone would make the effort in every locality to "meet the needs of the people," so that "when peace comes again to the world, we may have a concrete contribution to make in proof that through democratic methods a great nation has been able to face its own problems, and at least attempt to solve them." To match her wish, ER's last act of the year was to give significant "financial and moral support" to launch Rachel Davis DuBois's experiment in multicultural education in five New York high schools. ER believed this would aid boys and girls of different groups to respect and enjoy one another: "Fun and hard work would be combined."

Chapter Eight

The Politician and the Agitator: New Beginnings

ER's first column for 1940 contained a simple yet vastly portentous phrase: "The New Year is a time for new beginnings." Politically, she agreed with Harold Nicolson, who wrote in his diary, "The old year is foul and the new year is terrifying."

Throughout the holidays, highlighted by family and grandchildren, both ER and FDR were deeply disturbed by the information they received from their closest, most trusted sources. Letters and reports from friends posted abroad enabled the first couple, separately and together, to face the mounting challenges of the world at war with clarity and determination.

Those countries not yet at war with Nazi Germany were under immediate threat. ER's friend Caroline Drayton Phillips, wife of the U.S. ambassador to Italy, recorded her vivid impressions as various refugees and notables visited the U.S. embassy in Rome. With Russia's invasion of Finland, a wanton effort "to destroy a free and peaceful country," the continual unfolding "of horror in the world" reached a new level of "cruelty and destruction, tales of which come to us from every side."

Martha Gellhorn, in Finland on assignment for *Collier's* magazine, sent ER extraordinary eyewitness accounts. ER had promised Edna Gellhorn to look into her daughter's whereabouts, and a week later Edna wrote: "Praise be, and thanks to you! The enclosed message has this moment come to my door. . . . She was in Helsinki at the very moment the war started." ER replied, "I am delighted that Martha Gellhorn was back in touch again [but] I do wish she were safely back here."

Most of Martha's letters—those sent to her husband, Ernest Hemingway, and those to her mother—were forwarded to ER. Gellhorn's reports showed ER clearly the oppressions and sufferings of the Soviet invasion. The day it began, 30 November 1939, Gellhorn had written to Hemingway, there was an air raid in the morning, but the Soviet bombers only "dropped propaganda leaflets [that said] 'You know we have bread, why do you starve?'" Since it was well known that Finland was a rare nation in which nobody

starved, she considered the Russian effort ridiculous. Then they bombed the
people, farms, workplaces, and houses all over Helsinki. The bombers

> came in unseen, dived to 200 metres (imagine) and dumped the
> stuff. From the sound and results they must have been 500 kilo
> bombs, and they dumped thermite as well. I never felt such explo-
> sions. . . . [I saw] three colossal fires, four big apartment houses—
> just plain people's homes—burning like tissue paper. Glass was
> shattered for six and seven blocks. . . . A burning bus lying beside it,
> and a man shapeless and headless. . . . The people are marvelous,
> with a kind of pale frozen fortitude. They do not cry and they do not
> run; they watch with loathing but without fear this nasty sudden
> business which they did nothing to bring on themselves.

By the time Gellhorn wrote again, a week later, she had received two
cables from Hemingway as well as a letter from FDR that gave her the
sole "privilege" to go to the front. "War in the arctic is a very remarkable
business," she observed. "The climate is the best protection as are the forests. . . . It snows and we are not bombed." The Finns fought on bicycles
and on skis, and everybody hid in the forests at night. Their "pilots are
wonderful. And they can't be starved like our beloved Spaniards; they
already produce 90% of their own food." Gasoline and munitions were
the major problems, but Gellhorn would bet "on 3 million Finns against
180 million Russkis. After all, they are fighting for their lives and their
homes and God alone knows why the Russians are fighting."

In fact, the Russians wanted the port of Hango and about two thousand square miles of Finnish territory along the Gulf of Finland, to protect and enhance Leningrad's access to the sea. They had offered payment
and territory farther north. But after two months of negotiations, the
Finns refused, and the Soviet forces invaded. For a country that was min-
imally militarized, Finland fought with valor and vigor and held the Red
Army off through the long winter of 1940–41.

The Finns also introduced a new hand-thrown weapon they named a
"Molotov cocktail"—because Russia said it dropped bread, not bombs.

In the United States there was tremendous bipartisan support for Finland, but ER's sympathy embraced all the refugees, including the Poles.

From the American embassy in Rome, Caroline Phillips wrote that at Cracow University, the Germans had ordered the faculty to attend a conference by a German professor. When they arrived, they discovered a Gestapo officer, who announced that since the university was known "to be anti-German, the professors were to be arrested and sent to Germany and their wives and children turned out of their homes, which was forthwith done."

Some good news arrived from Italy. Foreign Minister Galeazzo Ciano told Ambassador William Phillips that "Mussolini had reversed his order for expelling the 3500 German Jewish refugees from Italy into a concentration camp in German Poland" and would allow them to remain. He also rescinded an order to expel an American journalist, at Phillips's request. Caroline proudly told ER that her husband's "efforts have saved many people from misery."

On 20 October 1939, Pope Pius XII had issued a remarkable encyclical condemning racism and urging Poland's restoration. *Summi Pontificatus*, "On the Unity of Humanity"—often referred to as "Darkness Over the Whole Earth"—was an extraordinary declaration. In 117 paragraphs the pope established his creed for his followers and announced his vision for a postwar future of love and inclusion across all religious and national boundaries: the restoration of God's mandate to all his children everywhere to respect and love one another.

The goal of his office and his church, the pope announced, was to "restore and ennoble all human society and to promote its true welfare." Christ's teachings were not limited to the members of His Church but extended "to a world in all too dire need of help and guidance."

Germany's abandonment "of the noble kingdom of law" for the unlimited ruthless "rule of force" now threatened the "unity of the human race." "Our paternal heart is torn by anguish as We look ahead to all that will yet come forth from the baneful seed of violence and of hatred for which the sword today ploughs the blood-drenched furrow. . . .

"Can there be . . . a greater or more urgent duty" than to resist the falsehoods of this bitter moment? "What heart is not inflamed . . . at the sight of so many brothers and sisters who, misled by error, passion, temptation and prejudice," have "wantonly" broken all ethical precepts from "the Tablets of God's Commandments" to "the spirit of the Sermon on the Mount"? To abandon the law of truth and the law of love is to travel

a road that leads to "spiritual and moral bankruptcy" and returns the
world to chaos.

Therefore humanity must remember: as "God's children," we are the
"culmination of His creative work, made . . . in His Own image," however scattered and diverse, always and everywhere united by His Love.
We are kin in "one great family," and no matter the differences of speech
or national origin, "principles of equality" prevail. "In the midst of the
disruptive contrasts which divide the human family," we return to the
unity of bonds that unite us, where "there is neither Gentile nor Jew, cir-
cumcision nor uncircumcision, barbarian nor Scythian, bond nor free."

Appealing directly to "the rulers of the peoples," he wrote:

> Venerable Brethren, the hour when this Our first Encyclical reaches
> you is in many respects a real "Hour of Darkness" . . . in which the
> spirit of violence and of discord brings indescribable suffering. . . .
> The blood of countless human beings . . . raises a piteous dirge over a
> nation such as Our dear Poland, which . . . has a right to the gener-
> ous and brotherly sympathy of the whole world, while it awaits, rely-
> ing on the powerful intercession of Mary . . . the hour of a resurrection
> in harmony with . . . justice and true peace. . . .
>
> Pray then, . . . pray without ceasing . . . that all may be one.

Many warned that this stirring message was merely a subterfuge, but
we may only assume that when ER and FDR read it, they expected that
in the coming days of unfolding dread, Pope Pius XII would turn out to
be an ally. Its message caused ER to imagine new cooperative efforts for
sanctuary and refuge.

FDR and the pope had met on 6 November 1936 when, as secretary of
state for Pope Pius XI, Cardinal Eugenio Pacelli had traveled to Hyde
Park. Now, since so many European refugees were Catholic, FDR hoped
that the Vatican might become a stirring voice of moral authority for rescue and sanctuary and might galvanize Latin American nations to greater
activity. Over 70 percent of Americans wanted no change in the U.S.
quota system—and FDR saw no reason to waste any of his political capital
on fighting to raise the quotas. But over time papal support would make it
easier for him to cast the growing refugee crisis as a universal issue.

FDR responded to the pope in a letter:

Your Holiness: Because, at this Christmas time, the world is in sorrow, it is especially fitting that I send you a message of greeting and of faith.

The world has created for itself a civilization capable of giving to mankind security and peace firmly set in the foundations of religious teachings. Yet, though it has conquered the earth, the sea, and even the air, civilization today passes through war and travail. . . .

Because the people of this nation have come to a realization that time and distance no longer exist in the older sense, they understand that that which harms one segment of humanity harms all the rest. They know that only by friendly association between the seekers of light and the seekers of peace everywhere can the forces of evil be overcome.

In these present moments, no spiritual leader, no civil leader can move forward . . . to terminate destruction and build anew. Yet the time for that will surely come.

It is, therefore, my thought . . . that we encourage a closer association between those in every part of the world—those in religion and those in government—who have a common purpose.

I am, therefore, suggesting to Your Holiness that it would give me great satisfaction to send to You my personal representative in order that our parallel endeavors for peace and the alleviation of suffering may be assisted.

When the time shall come for the re-establishment of world peace . . . great problems of practical import will face us all. Millions of people of all races, all nationalities and all religions may seek new lives by migration to other lands or by re-establishment of old homes. Here, too, common ideals call for parallel action.

I trust, therefore, that all of the churches of the world which believe in a common God will throw the great weight of their influence into this great cause.

In retrospect, FDR's conviction that no national or religious leader could more vigorously oppose the cascading horrors remains inexplicable. However, his letter to the pope was neither cynical, spontaneous, nor casual. Its terms were so clear that ER, who rarely commented on her husband's diplomacy, fervently believed that FDR's decision to write the pope—controversial at the time—was wise and significant.

Both Caroline and William Phillips were tremendously enthusiastic about FDR's "very fine letter" and William read it to their luncheon guests on 24 December. It gave everybody there hope that a new alliance would result.

On 23 December FDR announced that the industrialist Myron Taylor would be U.S. ambassador to the Vatican but made no mention of aiding refugees. Rather, in his discussions with the pope, Taylor was to follow specific guidelines: to prevent the war from spreading, and to establish common ground upon which to build a structure for permanent peace. He told Taylor to emphasize four points: "freedom of religion; freedom of communication, news and knowledge; reduction of armament, and freedom of trade."

On 7 January 1940, FDR received a long letter of gratitude from the pope, who looked forward to receiving Taylor, well known as a man of peace.

As supportive as ER was of FDR's efforts concerning the Vatican, she wanted him to do more for refugees. The situation in Europe had become dire. The longtime pacifist Oswald Garrison Villard filed a report for the *Nation* stating that buried, actually covered up, in the "flood of war news" was the latest development in Hitler's crusade against the Jews. The Nazis were deporting Jews from Austria, Moravia, and elsewhere in an effort "to jam them all into a small piece of Polish territory which is to be called a 'Jewish state,' but which is to be nothing else than a huge concentration camp and charnel house."

This issue of the resettlement of the Jews would turn out to be not only the most controversial situation ER would have to tend to but also an emotionally wrenching one. She had characterized FDR as "the politician" and herself as "the agitator." The world needed both, she had said. But anti-Semitism in America would prove to be a stronger foe than she had expected.

Hitler, Villard continued, seemed "obsessed with the idea of moving minorities" and was determined to "dump all the Jews possible into a territory at present described as 'from Nisko on the River San to a point southwest of Lublin.'" All Jews were to leave without their belongings, thus to be stripped of their possessions and "robbed of all their wealth." Lacking supplies, tools, or money, they would be unable to till the soil or do any business. They were not expected to survive.

An "Aryan German from a town in Moravia," Villard reported, had sent a letter "to an American official begging him to get the American government to intervene."

He said that he was a loyal German but that he could no longer remain silent. He declared that a train of cattle cars—the Jews are allowed no others—has stood for twelve hours in the station of his town. The weather was cold, and there was no heat. There were no toilet facilities. No food or water was provided. He said that the moans and groans of the older people could be heard blocks away. German laws forbid such treatment of cows or swine or dogs.

Villard ended his report with some cold, harsh details: "In Vienna, the Dutch papers report, eighty-two Jews, thirty-six of them women, have committed suicide in the last two weeks." He believed a great wave of protest from non-Jews—for example, from American Quakers—"might help, because the Germans are particularly anxious just now not to draw America into the war."

ER, who routinely read the *Nation*, would have seen Villard's stunning article. That same week, her great friend and first biographer, journalist Ruby Black, sent another article. "Just in case you missed seeing it," Black wrote, "I'm enclosing a clipping from the *Washington Star* of 16 December, written . . . by W. L. White, son of William Allen White." William Allen White, editor of the *Emporia Gazette* in Kansas, was one of the most revered journalists of the day. His son's article, datelined Berlin, was the

story of a little man who cried. I met the little man going from counter to counter at the American Embassy. He spoke almost no English and he carried the passport of a Balkan country, and there was no reason why he should come to our Embassy except that little people who have heard that America is big and powerful and generous and kindly somehow do go there to tell their little stories and plead for a little help when the rest of the world is too cynical or calloused or realistic to listen.

And this was the story of the little man who cried as he told it to me in the big high-ceilinged room of the Embassy, only at first he did not cry, but spoke only with a polite and desperate earnestness.

He said he himself was not Polish, but his relatives came from a little village in what was once Czechoslovakia and then for a while was Poland and is now German.

One morning, the SS announced that all the Jewish men "between 14 and 70" would in six days be sent to a labor camp. . . . So, not knowing quite why, the doctors took their instrument cases and the workers their spades or saws or picks. What has become of them is known in the village only through several post cards passed along from town to town, and always by hand, for they were not allowed to use the mails. . . . But they were not taken to a labor camp. They were put into railway freight cars and for many days were shunted about the country. . . . Sometimes when the train stopped near a farm village the German guards let them buy food from the farmers. Then when there was no more money, the farmers would sometimes give them food, for the farmers were Polish, not German.

The Jewish men were careful to write on the cards that the German guards were very kind to them, and that they were all well and warm and happy. The little man who showed me the cards and explained this did not cry at that point. The cards said that for six of the many days they were kept locked in the freight cars, but the German guards passed in to them warm water, with a little tea in it.

Then, no one yet knows why, they were taken out of the freight cars and put into another train which had only open cars, such as are used for hauling coal.

Then one day the train stopped and half the men were told to get out and to walk east, where they would come to a river, and over the river was that part of Poland "which now belongs to Russia, and maybe the Russians would take them in." White continued:

Then the train went on, leaving the Jewish men standing in an open field . . . no one knows if they got there, . . . for nothing else has been heard of them. . . . The men still on the train were taken to a village near Lublin . . . where the Germans . . . set up a Jewish reservation. Here they were told to build barracks for themselves and their families. Then the women and children left in the original village [were] told they must be ready to leave in four days, and this is why the shabby little man who cried made the desperate trip to Berlin where the foreign embassies are.

He did not ask that these Jews be allowed to come to America, for he knows that cannot be. . . . He was only sent to ask that the women and children be given more time . . . Nobody can do anything and the little man who cried has gone back to the village.

In mid-December, perhaps because of White Jr.'s reports, FDR asked William Allen White to meet with him "to spend the night at the White House and let me sit you on the sofa after supper and talk over small matters like the world's problems." ER hoped that White's interest would induce her husband to form a new committee for refugees, but FDR's agenda was not yet so broad. The great journalist from America's heartland had worked avidly to mobilize public opinion to lift the arms embargo and accept the idea of cash-and-carry to convey needed supplies to England and France. FDR now wanted "a few helpful thoughts from the philosopher of Emporia."

FDR reviewed the "several schools of thought" about the Nazi-Soviet Pact.

One thinks that Germany took hold of the Bear's tail in order to keep England and France out of the war and that Germany today is much concerned over Russia's unexpected policy of action—Eastern Poland, Finland . . . [the future] of Norway, Sweden, Rumania, Bulgaria, etc. The other school of thought, with equal reason, believes that there is fairly definite agreement . . . for the division of European control [extended to] Asia Minor, Persia, Africa and the various British, French, Dutch, Belgian, etc., colonies.

Since Hitler and Stalin both assumed they would be victorious, they were to divide the earth's resources. Concerned about German-Soviet domination in the world, FDR worried to White that if that geographic deal were true, and Germany and Russia were to win, our civilization

is indeed in peril. Our world trade would be at [their] mercy . . . and our increasingly better relations with our twenty neighbors to the south would end—unless we were willing to go to war. . . . Things move with such terrific speed, these days, that it really is essential to us to think in broader terms and, in effect, to warn the American people that they, too, should think of possible ultimate results in Europe and the Far East.

Therefore, my sage old friend, my problem is to get the American people to think of conceivable consequences without scaring the American people into thinking that they are going to be dragged into this war.

White's subsequent visit resulted in a significant new offer to mobilize a movement to defend America by aiding the Allies.

While ER was generally impressed by FDR's geopolitical vision, his 3 January State of the Union message, which promised budget cuts for everything except defense, was a disappointment. She attended with "rather a large family party" that included SDR, Sistie, and Buzzy. "I enjoy going up to Congress largely because I like to watch the reaction of the 'floor,'" she wrote in her column. She did not criticize the president directly but commented on the partisan nature of congressional applause. Even when FDR referred to bipartisan issues agreed upon by all, Republicans sat motionless while Democrats applauded. "When the President announced, however, that except for national defense, all other items of the budget would show a decrease, the Republican side . . . applauded vigorously." She asked with uncharacteristic candor whether the Republicans meant by this that "issues of health, unemployment, the preservation of people's morale . . . are apparently party matters not matters of national interest, and have no part in the national defense. What is this? Blindness? Ignorance? Indifference or partisanship?"

With the future of America imperiled, and the world at risk, ER considered it her primary job to build or revive support for her husband's best policies. She could only hope that Congress would transcend its partisan limits and reach "national unity on questions of national importance."

On domestic issues, she still considered her closest allies the activists of the AYC, but this alliance was now frayed and in disarray. In the wake of the Nazi-Soviet Pact, their onetime antifascist idealism had yielded to reactionary "anti-imperialism." They attacked Britain and France and showed a surprising unconcern regarding the hideous torment of European Jews.

By contrast, her new friend Joe Lash shared her concern for Europe's agony, the plight of Jews, and the needs of refugees. Lash, earnest and sincere, thoughtful and brash, increasingly fascinated her, lifted her spirits, dominated her thoughts, and enchanted her heart. After the Dies Committee hearings, she had noticed his disgust and confusion at the new positions adopted by his mostly former friends, and she had only sympathy for him: "I have rarely seen anyone more unhappy." But he despised rats, and with absolute integrity he told ER that he would not name those among her AYC friends who were Communists, and he hoped she would understand. Of course she did, and she respected him for it. At an ASU convention in Madison, Wisconsin, the delegates had refused to condemn Russia's invasion of Finland, by a vote of 322 to 49. He told ER he had been prepared "for defeat but not quite for the clobbering." He and Molly Yard resigned from the ASU immediately.

His contemplative and inquiring mind impressed her. Some considered him brooding, but ER was drawn to his serious manner and his deep consideration for others. She invited him to dinner at the White House, with her cousin Forbes Morgan; Charlotte Kraus, a Viennese singer; and Abbott Simon of the AYC. Simon's views, wrote Lash, continued to influence ER, who was beginning to believe the student movement was Communist-dominated. They all went for a swim before dinner, in the White House pool, and Lash witnessed the first lady diving. It was rather a "breathtaking affair, a sheer triumph of will," followed by an extraordinary "splash." She then swam about, "got under the diving board, and chinned up several times."

At dinner, there was a discussion of the recent novel *Address Unknown* by Kathrine Taylor. Written in the form of an exchange of letters between an American Jewish art dealer in California and his former friend and partner who "returned to the fatherland" to surrender to Nazi pressures, it is a story of "craven betrayal." Both FDR and ER found it impressive and provocative, Lash observed:

Mrs. Roosevelt wondered whether she would not have acted in the same cowardly way in the same circumstances. "I really am a coward," she added. [But] the President wouldn't hear of this. He was absolutely sure she would have done the right thing whatever the consequences. It was a theme to which she would revert frequently. Was she standing up firmly enough for what she believed in, she would ask. How would she behave if put to the test of torture and death for her convictions?

Subsequently, she explained, the question was more general: Why had the German people "gone along with the policies of their leaders"? Could such docility occur anywhere? Would Americans do the same, "or were the Germans as a people more submissive?"

There were of course many "resisters" in Germany, Lash reminded the first lady. "The concentration camps were full of them." In fact his friend Karl Frank, an underground leader whom ER had agreed to see the next day, was one of them.

Karl Frank was the German socialist leader of the underground movement Neu Beginnen, then based in London. A psychoanalyst and political agitator, he dedicated himself to bringing about Hitler's demise and became leader of the German Social Democratic Party in Prague. He assumed the name Paul Hagen, to protect his family still in Germany. He had visited New York in 1935, married "activist-heiress" Anna Caples, and forged the progressive American Friends of German Freedom, supported by Norman Thomas and chaired by Reinhold Niebuhr.

When the Hagens returned to New York in December 1939, Lash, who had known the dashing, charismatic leader for five years, was eager to arrange a meeting between him and ER. Lash believed Paul Hagen's work for refugees, his vast network of exiled Socialists from Lisbon to Stockholm, and his broadcasts and publications for German freedom would move her. She agreed, and the meeting had been scheduled for the following day.

Meanwhile dinner consisted of significant banter between the first couple concerning fair wages, money for extended benefits, and the prohibitive costs of the Youth Act. FDR supported his wife's efforts on behalf of the act but wondered where the money might come from. ER said youth wanted more money for training, jobs, and social services—and less for armaments. "At this," recounts Lash, "the President pushed back in his chair and said, 'All right. Let's accept the opinion of youth, but I want my protest recorded for history.'"

Abbott Simon suggested that the United States did not "need all these battleships," while ER expressed concern that the congressional pressure for 85,000-ton battleships was navy- or industry-inspired. The president "snapped, 'Utopianism.'" Ultimately, he feared a German-Russian victory in Europe throughout the Americas: "We had to be armed to prevent penetration of the continent and disruption of the hemispheric system."

Social services and armaments, the Youth Act and the navy, were all necessary, he agreed. But we had to arm first. He turned to Simon and said, "You will have to wait a year. You can wait a year."

ER offered Joe Lash her home at Val-Kill as "a haven for a few weeks." Lash returned the next day for lunch to learn more about Val-Kill and "where to find things"—notably "wine, skis, and cigarettes." And he brought Karl Frank with him.

Frank told ER detailed stories of the many German underground leaders in concentration camps, and the urgency for rescue and Hitler's defeat. Their compelling discussion of refugees caused ER to call Dorothy Detzer of the WILPF, who told her about a U.S. consul in Geneva, who was reputed to be "anti-Semitic and anti-Catholic" and who held up visas, even for those whose "number had been reached." More than one State Department official, it seemed, was determined to block refugees from entering the United States. With Frank and Lash present, ER called Assistant Secretary of State James Messersmith to protest. He could do nothing within the State Department and wondered if FDR knew about its inaction. ER was hopeful about Karl Frank's energetic movement to bypass and resist it.

By this time ER and FDR knew everything anybody would need to know to change the popular mood regarding rescue and sanctuary. They had personally received reports. Hitler's decrees had been published and disseminated widely as propaganda. On 5 December he had announced that some were to be sent to concentration camps to be enslaved; others were to be stamped "NN" for *Nacht und Nebel* (night and fog), marked for execution. Mass public executions of Jews and Poles were ongoing, as William Shirer reported in his amazing broadcasts from Berlin and Helsinki: Hitler was engaged in "a holy struggle against the Jews . . . an ideological struggle against world Jewry." According to Nazi propaganda, Shirer continued, England was "spiritually, politically, and economically at one with the Jews. . . . England and the Jews remain the common foe."

Moreover, on 22 January, Pope Pius XII used the Vatican Radio to denounce Nazi atrocities in Poland. "The horror and inexcusable excesses committed on a helpless and a homeless people have been established by the unimpeachable testimony of eye-witnesses." Fifteen thousand Poles had been executed since September. General Friedrich Mieth, chief of staff of the German First Army, deplored these executions "without proper trials," which "besmirched" the honor of the Germany army.

Yet the next day, 23 January, FDR promoted his friend Breckinridge Long to be assistant secretary of state and widened his portfolio at the State Department. Wealthy and well-connected, Long was dedicated to keeping America uncontaminated by un-Americans. ER was stunned—she had consistently protested Long's politics. Now, he would be in charge of all visa and refugee issues and supervise twenty-three of the forty-two divisions of the State Department, including the visa section, the legal division, and the Foreign Service Personnel Board. His hand would prevent the granting of visas even for those whose numbers had come through.

On a snowy day in January, Lash arrived at the Poughkeepsie station to take ER up on her offer to use the Val-Kill cottage as a haven while he decided what to do next. He was greeted by Earl Miller. It is not clear whether the first lady asked Miller to meet him or whether Miller, ever suspicious—and now her self-appointed protector—wanted to investigate the new kid in town.

Joe unpacked, went down to the kitchen for lunch, and "found he had company." Miller explained he liked to "keep an eye on the place." He was eating a simple ham and cheese sandwich, while Joe was served "three of the thickest chops I had ever seen." Joe's immediate offer to share the feast was "gratefully accepted," and the road to a tentative friendship unfolded. Miller introduced Joe to ER's favorite walks through the snow and ice. The time went by "placidly," surrounded by books, the deep quiet of Val-Kill, splendid food, and long walks with companionable if snarling dogs. During his last days there, the first family arrived with various guests, and conversations about the future continued.

At moments when they were alone that week, Lash asked ER probing, poignant, even impertinent questions. Had she read in the social sciences? Yes, she replied, and Ibsen too. While his blunt banter might have caused others to bristle, his awkward intensity amused her. She enjoyed his manner, his quest for the good, his deep sense of responsibility—a quality she considered spiritual. He was easy to talk to, interested in everything, witty, and generous. In a letter, he had compared FDR's leadership style to Abraham Lincoln's. He suggested the president's relationship to militant New Dealers was akin to Lincoln's relationship to "radical abolitionists." Both had to compromise with congressional reality and not abandon "basic purposes."

Lash's broad understanding pleased her. She explained that FDR was the politician, she the agitator, and the world needed both. The challenge, the two new friends agreed, was to find the dividing line between accept-able acts of power and needed compromises. ER told Lash that she "fre-quently disagreed with the President," while others—especially anti–New Dealers—believed he had gone too far too fast. Democratic decision-making depended on a free press, an opposition, and the electorate.

Lash left on a Sunday afternoon train with ER. Their friendship had solidified with his visit, and she offered to write letters of reference for him whether he applied for a job in journalism or to a university for graduate studies. He continued to ask brash questions. He had read that publisher Roy Howard censored her *My Day* column. Howard had accepted her "plea for funds for Finland" but had cut an appeal to aid Spanish refugees. Howard, she explained, had said he "employed her to write a diary, not to talk about the things that really mattered to her." Joe noted, "It was clear from the tone of her voice" that Howard's attitude "irked her."

They discussed the Soviet Union: "until the Nazi-Soviet Pact," she said, "she had looked upon Russia as a positive force in world affairs, a nation from whom we could learn much." Now Lash thought a second revolution was needed. But the purges, ER noted, had "so effectively decapitated" all potential opposition and leadership. Still, she was certain that the future belonged to those who learned, who read deeply and stud-ied and fought for their dreams. People like her new friend Joe Lash.

In New York, as she dashed for her connecting train to Washington, she urged him to return to Val-Kill that summer. In the meantime she would look forward to his February visit in Washington during the AYC meeting she was already helping to organize.

Chapter Nine

Radical Youth and Refugees:
Winter–Spring 1940

Shortly after the Dies Committee tried to disgrace the AYC in November 1939, ER agreed to write the foreword to a book celebrating the AYC written by one of its leaders, Leslie Gould. Bennett Cerf, president of Random House, had agreed to publish the book when it was discussed at a Val-Kill picnic on 7 December 1939.

In her foreword to *American Youth Today*, ER wrote:

> This is a book which I think it is high time to publish. . . . The author naturally sees it through sympathetic eyes, but he has, I think, given a picture which is historically correct. . . .
>
> He is a little too kind about me . . . and a little too unkind about the President. He forgets that in spite of the President's words on one occasion, he has given the young people real support and understanding many times, and that without his willingness to stand behind me, I would frequently be unable to do many of the things which I have done for them.
>
> As you read these pages, you will realize that youth is youth and cannot be expected to see things in the light of experience, or to act with the calmness of age. Youth's great contribution is its enthusiasm and its fire, and this contribution to the future should never be belittled. . . .
>
> I have no great illusions about the perfection of any organization or of any group. I do believe, however, that a group which is honestly trying to help young people in their own communities to get together and face such problems as unemployment, recreation and health, should receive cooperation and understanding.

ER's words were written after her most grueling and painful encounter with the AYC, during their much-heralded Citizenship Institute, which she did much to promote and enable.

· · · · · ·

More than five thousand young people from every state and many nations were expected to attend the Citizenship Institute, planned for Lincoln's Birthday weekend 1940. The four-day marathon was billed as "a monster lobby for jobs, peace, civil liberties, education and health." Specifically, the AYC would lobby for passage of the American Youth Act, which would earmark millions of dollars for jobs and vocational training for young people.

ER helped prepare by cajoling friends, associates, hotel owners, and the army to provide rooms, blankets, food, and general support. She imposed on every Washington hostess, every government official for housing, meeting rooms, and entertainment. She housed twenty delegates at the White House and persuaded cabinet and congressional wives to house many more. At her urging, the officers of Fort Meyer provided "cots for 150 boys." She was especially pleased to have gotten Colonel George S. Patton to put up many boys "in the riding hall," where she had recently visited the horse show.

She arranged for a fleet of buses to transport the delegates to meetings, helped get flags and costumes for their parade, and in every way looked after America's visiting youth. On Friday there was to be a rally at the Lincoln Memorial and a meeting in the auditorium of the Department of Labor. She secured public spaces and meeting rooms in federal buildings, arranged for private meetings, luncheons, teas, and dinners all over town, including at the White House.

The Republican National Committee chair refused to participate in the Citizenship Institute unless the AYC purged all its Communist representatives. ER chided him, considering the idea of "purging" young Communists an un-American ploy. Since democracy assured Communists the right to "believe in the communistic theory," no group had the right to expel them. Surely, ER said, "a youth organization must stand for the same tolerance and freedom of expression and representation that we as a nation have stood for under the Bill of Rights."

On Friday, 9 February, the institute opened, haunted by the increasingly dismal news from around the world. Fear ruled the day; betrayal and bombs, exile and rivers of blood set the tone. The Nazi-Soviet Pact heightened the impact of war, which was felt everywhere: Ethiopia, Spain, China, Vienna, Prague, Poland, Finland.

That Friday Jack McMichael, a southern divinity student, AYC national chair, and one of ER's closest AYC friends, gave the keynote address. He attacked FDR for neglecting domestic issues in favor of an enhanced military policy. America's liberal leadership had vanished. Instead of continuing the good fight, liberals now advocated "retrenchment" and had become "international messiahs" who would lead America's youth directly onto Europe's battlefields.

McMichael said he regretted the ongoing disenfranchisement of and violence against black citizens. In the South, African-Americans were still denied their legal rights: race terrorism continued unabated. The Dies Committee targeted students and union leaders, but the Ku Klux Klan went on its way unmolested.

Edward Strong of Alabama, chair of the Southern Negro Youth Congress, agreed with McMichael: the Department of Justice ignored the Klan's activities, and did nothing to protect black Americans from bodily harm or legal abuse.

AYC enemies had placed themselves strategically around the room: they included not only right-wingers but also New Deal supporters who were increasingly suspicious of the AYC leadership, and a group of self-styled youth patriots led by ER's own cousin Archibald Roosevelt, boxing hero Gene Tunney, and a pamphleteer named Murray Plavner.

After the opening remarks, these adversaries rose to introduce parliamentary ploys to derail the meeting. Someone introduced a resolution to condemn the Soviet invasion of Finland. A serious scuffle ensued. Finally, two of the leading antagonists were forcibly ejected, and Archibald Roosevelt walked out after "a brief wrestling match with Joseph Cadden."

The antagonists would continue to try to disrupt the meetings, interrupting with criticisms of FDR and creating disturbances. They were repeatedly ruled out of order. ER watched the tumult from the second row. Asked her opinion, she said, "My only comment is that this was a meeting with a pre-arranged program." The Finland resolution, intended to create mayhem, was also ruled out of order. But the issue was bitterly divisive and defined the weekend.

Despite her private feelings, she defended the AYC against its enemies—specifically the organized right led by Father Coughlinites, Silver Shirts, and anti-Semitic ruffians. They had, ER wrote, "served only a destructive purpose."

Nevertheless, the Friday meeting ended on a conciliatory and hopeful note, when recently appointed attorney general Robert Jackson responded to McMichael and Strong's criticisms of the administration. In a vigorous speech that was broadcast nationally, he surprised the audience with welcome news. "For more than a week," he said, "the Department of Justice has had an attorney in South Carolina gathering evidence [on Ku Klux Klan] activities. And less than a week ago the Department of Justice dismissed more than 100 indictments against WPA workers in Minnesota.* Perhaps the Department of Justice is not as heartless as you think."

Several New Dealers in FDR's inner circle, including Ben Cohen and Tom Corcoran, hoped that Jackson would run for president later that year. At the Citizenship Institute he read a prepared speech that opposed any retrenchment on New Deal policies and supported the Allies. FDR had wrought great changes, culminating, said Jackson, in fundamental governmental powers that never existed before: the ability "to govern the powerful, [and] protect the weak."

Jackson's speech also affirmed the rights of youth: this was the time to have "your dreams and your adventures." The correct role of elders was to provide "patient and understanding counsel." He dismissed those who saw youth's "spirit of social and political unconventionality" as some "terrifying" or "nightmarish plotting against government." Nonconformity was neither treasonous nor the work of "radicals and communists." At this moment, with depression ongoing and war raging, youth could hardly afford to be complacent. No "honest" observer should expect a "free and hopeful youth" to support the status quo when so much "involuntary unemployment," so much insecurity and dependency on the part of the aged, and "so many injustices" lay before us all. Youth faced "an indefensible legacy," Jackson said. But "before you look wistfully to any other form of government, let's see what we can do with this American Government with its powers thus restored." This democracy, enhanced by

---

*The WPA indictments, widely cast, with little evidence, and aimed at suspected Communists, had actually surprised Jackson. They had been initiated by his predecessor Robert Murphy, who was now a Supreme Court justice. Jackson considered them politically unwise, unconstitutional, and reprehensible.

the New Deal, was "a great system for changing the status quo by peaceful and orderly means."*

Pleased by Jackson's speech, ER noted that most of the audience received it with cheering enthusiasm. She was relieved especially since earlier that day Joseph Lash, while attempting to speak in favor of the administration's policies, had been persistently interrupted, actually "booed for fifteen minutes before he could continue his speech." ER, aghast, understood that this was no ordinary meeting of activist youth, and their friends and mentors in government.

On Saturday, 10 February, the air was heavy in Washington, frosty, wet. It rained, hard and cold and bitter. Fingers were numbed; feet were sodden. Some students danced; some painted signs; some stayed in bed and clung to each other. FDR was scheduled to address the young people at the White House that day.

In the morning a young woman on horseback, dressed as the Joan of Arc of 1940, led a parade of America's youth along Constitution Avenue. Almost six thousand young people marched: farmers and sharecroppers, workers and musicians, from high schools and colleges, black and white, Indians and Latinos, Christians and Jews, atheists and agnostics, freethinkers and dreamers, liberals and Communists. This extraordinary patchwork of American youth had arrived an hour early to hear the president. As they waited, they alternated between silence and song, as if in homage to the tensions behind the banners.

Banners for peace predominated: LOANS FOR FARMS, NOT ARMS. JOBS NOT GUNS. SCHOOLS NOT BATTLESHIPS. BURY THE SLUMS BEFORE THEY BURY US. HEED THE VOICE OF 20,000,000 / KEEP THE CCC CIVILIAN. ALL BOW DOWN TO MARTIN DIES, 57 KINDS OF LIES. ABOLISH THE POLL TAX. PASS THE AMERICAN YOUTH ACT. YES TO MORE SCHOOLS / NO TO WAR TOOLS. THE YANKS ARE NOT COMING.

---

*Robert Jackson's speech was written in part by Michael Straight, who had only recently departed from his own radical student days among the Communists at Cambridge in the UK. The son of ER's great friend Dorothy Payne Whitney Straight Elmhirst, Straight now worked for Ben Cohen.

Songs of protest filled the air. The students sang as they marched; they sang as they waited. Initially stirred by a sense of their own unity, the vigor of their banners, the certainty of their goals, and the wit of their parodies, they felt confident. For that moment, even in the rain, the future was theirs. But the rain was relentless, and the winds grew colder.

The White House lawn turned muddy. For over two hours, their banners still aloft but heavier and limp with rain, they waited patiently. FDR was to speak on a national radio hookup, and they were told there was an unfortunate delay. The mud grew softer and the rain came down harder. They sang more songs. ER wandered through the crowd, covered in rain cape and hood, giving warm words of greeting. She had persuaded FDR to speak, but now as the rain poured and the winds intensified, the mood changed from anticipation to anxiety. Finally Jack McMichael went to the microphone, set up on the South Portico, and led the crowd in "America the Beautiful," chants for the Youth Act, and words of introduction:

Deep in the dream of Americans is a picture of the land of the free and the home of the brave. A land free of the misery of war and oppression. . . .

Now, more than four million young citizens are without work. Now, the doors to industry, yes, and even the relief rolls, are closed to them. Are we to rear a generation in hopelessness and despair? Now war, which brings nothing but death and degradation to youth and profit and power to a few, reaches out for us. Are we to solve our youth problem by dressing it in uniform and shooting it full of holes?

America should welcome and should not fear a young generation aware of its own problems, active in advancing the interests of the entire nation. In this spirit, [thousands] . . . have streamed into Washington. . . . They are here to discuss their problems and to tell you, Mr. President, and the Congress, their needs and desires. . . . I am happy to present to you, Mr. President, these American youth.

Finally FDR appeared on the balcony—with ER now beside him, leaning against a White House column. He looked at the crowd below and smiled, with an expression nobody had ever seen before. The audience was hushed and silent. Jonathan Mitchell, standing in the crowd beside his friend Michael Straight, whispered, "He doesn't like the smell of the Albatross that his wife has hung around his neck."

And then he began. FDR stood before the Youth Congress not to praise America's young activists but to insult them, to administer not a blessing but "a spanking." Joseph Lash, standing with a small group of former ASU allies, recalled a "tough, uncompromising speech. Clearly we did not enchant him. . . . We were welcome, as were all citizens. It was 'grand' we were enough interested in government to come to Washington," where they had a guaranteed right to come and advocate change. In another country, under other governments, "this kind of meeting . . . could not take place."

Then came a set of dreary statistics, followed by a rehash of old achievements and a list of warnings: Do not expect Utopia; do not seek panacea, "handouts" to guarantee jobs or training. This administration could solve the nation's problems only "as fast as the people of the country as a whole will let us." The "final word of warning" seemed a specific insult, lodged in contemptuous tones: Do not deal with subjects "which you have not thought through and on which you cannot possibly have complete knowledge."

FDR defended his call for a loan to Finland and attacked those who opposed it—as New York's Youth Council had, on the grounds that it was an attempt to lead the United States into an "imperialistic war." FDR called that "unadulterated twaddle," based in small part on "sincerity" but also "on 90 percent ignorance."

Several people booed and hissed, while others hushed them.

FDR went on: 98 percent of the American people wanted to support Finland. To discuss a U.S.-Soviet war over Finland "is about the silliest thought that I have ever heard advanced in the fifty-eight years of my life." "All of you," he assured the crowd, "can smile with me on this." Nobody smiled. He then criticized the Soviet Union: whatever his former hopes had been for the future of "that experiment," it was today "a dictatorship as absolute as any other dictatorship in the world."

The boos began again.

Some in the AYC were called Communists, FDR noted. He acknowledged the right of Americans to advocate "ideals of theoretical communism," but they also had the "sacred duty" to confine their visions to our constitutional framework. He was sure they all agreed with him and would be at it long after "I am gone from the scene. . . . So I say to you, keep your ideals high, keep both feet on the ground, and keep everlastingly at it."

The crowd stood silently, stunned and disheartened; many were near tears.

FDR raised his hand in a flippant gesture, turned, and walked into the darkness of the White House on Pa Watson's arm. ER followed silently behind. For the student activists who had traveled so far, memories of that bitter day would never fade.

A great range of student and future leaders were in that crowd. My own friends, activists, and, notably, founders of Women Strike for Peace—Bella Abzug, Amy Swerdlow, Mim Kelber, and Victor Teisch—said they never forgot what seemed to them a blunt dismissal by a man they had so admired, who had turned so completely into a careless politician. According to Michael Straight, FDR had ignored the "hopeful and constructive" address that had been prepared for him. Education commissioner John Studebaker and Aubrey Williams had both drafted suggestions for the speech, but FDR had discarded them. Instead, he "scolded the delegates in a rebuke that extended beyond the Left to the liberals and to his own wife." Joe Lash considered the president's speech a specific rebuff to his wife: "The young people had begun to irritate him," and ER's efforts to defend them "irritated him even more." But he could not reproach her directly, Lash noted, and in a speech broadcast nationwide that he had written himself, he confronted the differences between them. It was the first time he publicly displayed his antagonism.

Woody Guthrie, who had "hoboed in from Galveston Texas" to Washington that day, was staggered when FDR called the students' "trip and the stuff that they stood for 'twaddle.' It come up a big soaking rain and he made the kids a 30-minute speech in it." On the spot, Guthrie wrote a song: "Why Do You Stand There in the Rain?"

> It was raining mighty hard in that old capitol yard
> When the young folks gathered at the White House gate. . . .
> While they butcher and they kill, Uncle Sam foots the bill
> With his own dear children standing in the rain.

ER admired Guthrie and evidently never objected when this song was sung in her presence. But one Guthrie song that members of the AYC repeatedly sang during the years of the Nazi-Soviet Pact really annoyed her:

Oh, Franklin Roosevelt told the people how he felt.
We damned near believed what he said.
He said, "I hate war and so does Eleanor,
But we won't be safe till everybody's dead."

People closest to FDR were deeply distressed by his performance. Anna wrote a letter to her mother, unusually dismayed by her father's words. ER replied:

I felt as you did about Pa's speech to the American Youth Congress, tho' I wish they had better manners about it! Many of the youngsters are inclined to believe well of Russia but that is because they are so afraid of all propaganda & feel Russia in Finland may be a victim of that. [Russia] helped Spain and they don't trust [Herbert] Hoover's efforts for Finland since he did nothing for Spain or Czechoslovakia or Poland or China. They think "well the Finnish government was fascist once we know." I found them *not* communist except for a few city groups, and not concerned about communism which was forced down their throats at every turn but deeply concerned about getting a job and finding out how they could help themselves and each other in their respective communities to do this. Pa lost their support and will have to win it back. I'd like to show Pa [your letter] but I wont for the sake of family peace!

ER wrote Anna nothing of her own ordeal during the Citizenship Institute. The afternoon FDR was booed, she attended a plenary session where John L. Lewis scorned FDR in general, and the paternalistic condescending tone of his address in particular:

FDR gave you statistics that indicate improvement. I reject such statistics, while 12 million Americans are still unemployed.
    FDR dismissed your views as "twaddle." Your resolution on Finland was substantially the same as the mineworkers' resolution. That is not twaddle; that is democracy.

Every sentence was greeted with gusts of approval, whistles, and cheers. In the end, Lewis urged America's youth to leave the cold embrace of the Democratic Party and join his Labor's Non-Partisan League.

ER's inner torment, both at her husband's humiliations and at the savaging of her own beliefs in such hostile fashion, can only be imagined. Yet while Lewis hurled contempt at her husband, ER sat passively knitting. On his way out, Lewis paused to greet her. He leaned over, hand extended. As they shook hands, there was a momentary intake of breath throughout the filled-to-capacity auditorium—a pause of courtesy on a bitter day.

As the afternoon proceeded, ER's hopes for the AYC were restored. Speeches by the young delegates themselves were important, fact-filled, and galvanizing. Harriet Pickens of the YWCA, daughter of NAACP officer William Pickens, spoke for civil rights and decried a Mississippi proposal for free but censored textbooks for grades one to eight. All references to "citizenship and voting rights" were to be deleted for Negro children. According to Lash, Harriet Pickens's "speech was a cry from the heart."

ER was particularly stirred by the vigor and eloquence of Dorothy Height. An NYU graduate, journalist, and social worker, Height represented the Christian Youth Council. "War is an outrage and a sin. It violates the very fundamentals of Christianity," Height said. "For Christian young people there is no alternative. We join with the young people of America and the world in working for . . . a true peace which transcends race, nation or class." An African-American student leader and YWCA officer, Height had worked closely with Mary McLeod Bethune since 1937 at the National Council of Negro Women and had been one of ten AYC leaders who worked with ER to make the Vassar World Youth Congress a success. ER admired her as an independent force within the AYC.

The first lady was also impressed by Louise Meyerovitz's vigorous words on behalf of Young Judaea:

Tactics of anti-Jewish persecution which proved so successful in Germany are being transplanted to the United States. One group has been used as an entering wedge. When that group is done away with, another group is selected until all the people who oppose the suppression of freedom are put off the map. The threat of war paves the way for dictatorship and rule by decree. It endangers the freedom of life of all the citizens, including American youth of Jewish faith.

Frances Williams's concluding presentation appealed to ER most of all. As AYC administrative secretary, she represented the leadership's vision, which gave ER abiding hope in the group. Williams's emphasis on civil liberties and full citizenship rights for all included fearful warnings about new anti-alien and sedition laws, the end of free speech, press, and assembly, and the march of repression in troubled times, which particularly targeted labor's rights through corruption, vigilantism, and terror. Democracy itself was in a state of siege, Williams warned, and academic freedom and all minority rights were imperiled. ER agreed with Williams, and with the AYC, on most issues.

But the meeting was entirely divided between those who wanted to support Britain and France and those who were so pro-Soviet that they declared Britain and France imperialist enemies. ER's close friend Abbott Simon, the legislative chair, recently returned from Europe, declared France to be "a semifascist state," where Spanish refugees lived in squalor and misery and were forced to repatriate to "the firing squads." An Indian student asserted: "We in India [see] no difference between German fascism and British or French imperialism." Several others gave speeches to make it clear that "the Yanks are not coming."

That was "the harsh setting" ER faced on Sunday night, Lash later noted, when she rose to address the final session, titled "How War Affects American Youth." For this most controversial session, ER had previously agreed to answer questions from the floor.

In the past she had entered AYC events accompanied by AYC leaders. That night she arrived on the arm of her son FDR Jr., with harsh lights of newsreel cameras upon her, in a long black evening dress, and a corsage of orchids given her by AYC leaders.

"When I rose to speak," she remembered, "I was greeted with boos, but that made no difference to me. I waited until I could be heard and then remarked that since they had asked me to speak and I had listened to all the other speakers, I thought in return they had an obligation to listen to me." According to Leslie Gould, newspaper accounts "made it a giant boo demonstration . . . of antagonism and disrespect to Mrs. Roosevelt." Actually, the response was aimed at the first question, "on the sore spot of Finland" asked by "one of the disturbers" who had wrangled with Joe Cadden the night before.

The audience of over two thousand remained politely quiet throughout, after she held up her hand to cut their initial reaction short: "I want you neither to clap nor hiss until I have finished and then you may do whichever you like."

She took the first question from her cousin Archibald Roosevelt: "Don't you think that a congress truly representative of American youth should be willing to pass a resolution condemning the Russian invasion of Finland?"

No. I don't think you should go on record for anything you don't believe in. . . . However, I think it is only fair to say that I do not think you fully understand some of the history underlying many situations. . . .

I agree with you that a stand should have been taken when Ethiopia was attacked. I agree with you in your sympathy for Spain; I agree with you in your sympathy for China and Czechoslovakia. I also have sympathy for Finland. Even though you may think that the government which came into Finland originally had certain fascist tendencies, I think it has been clearly proved that the government . . . is what the Finns want it to be. In all fairness, I think, however, it should be said that there is no excuse for a big nation invading a little nation which has not been attacked by that little nation. . . .

Therefore, our sympathy as a free people should be just as much with the Finnish people as it would be with any other small nation which is invaded.

ER answered every question put to her for over an hour—gravely, sincerely. She chose, above all, to defend her husband's remarks. She tried to explain the administration's failure to end unemployment: it "is a world question—a basic economic question. The administration does not know the answer. The administration program is to do what seems possible, do it fairly and continue to look for the answer." She agreed that all programs so far, the "increased social security legislation," the NYA and WPA efforts, were "a drop in the bucket." On the subject of economic retrenchment for social programs, she turned the question to a failure to organize public opinion. She called upon the audience to rally movements in their home to communicate "because Congress is responsive to you."

On the hope for continued neutrality and aid to belligerents, she was vigorous: "I do not want to see this country go to war again. . . . But domination of any great part of the world by any great nation is always a danger." She did not know what constituted "adequate defense." "I want to see war abolished," she declared. But when wars were being fought, defenses were needed. To a mounting rumble of protest, she continued:

> You never go to war unless the nation wants to go to war. You cannot because Congress is responsive to the nation. . . . You are not the only ones who don't want war. I don't think there are any older people in this country who want war, and certainly none of us who know what war is like. . . . Do you think that the President wants war? Then you forget that we have four sons who are just the age to go to war.

The United States, she said, was in no position to criticize struggling nations facing war "when we do so little." She wondered if Abbott Simon had been "fair to criticize France" when the Wagner-Rogers bill to bring in refugee children, "all of whom were to be paid for, the money had been acquired," had been defeated "because the people of this country would not back it." The United States, therefore, was in no position, she insisted, to sit in "harsh judgment on other nations."

In conclusion, ER thanked the AYC for its patience and courtesy. "I am very, very fond of many of your leaders," she said, "and I am sure I would like to know all of you personally."

It had been a frank, painful, courageous evening. There were no easy answers, no simple solutions. The audience gave her a standing ovation. All observers agreed that, both for ER and for America's youth, it had been an exhausting, extraordinary ordeal.

ER's feelings about the event ranged from depressed to philosophical. In the end, she confided to Hick, she answered their questions "in a way which was not too popular & there was considerable hissing. FDR made them very sore, more by the way he said things than by the things he said & it is especially hard to stand in the rain & 'take it' when you feel as sensitive as youth does." Then John L. Lewis "walked away with them," and "I brought them down to earth . . . which wasn't pleasant either. However, when all is said & done it was remarkable to have so many come & talk & listen & I think it was a great experience for them & I learned much myself."

Hick was unforgiving. Imagine! To hiss ER! All the Democratic leaders Hick met as she traveled for the party to build support for the 1940 election, and explore FDR's third-term possibilities, were wild with outrage. What nerve, Hick declared, "after all you have done for them! It does make them look sort of bad."

Dewey Fleming of the *Baltimore Sun* observed: "The nation probably has not seen in all of its history such a debate between a President's wife and a critical, not to say hostile, auditorium full of politically minded youths of all races and creeds."

Betty Lindley wrote to Anna: "I went to all the sessions of the American Youth Congress—and I'm still boiling mad. They were impudent, closed-minded and destructive. . . . And how they can talk! Your mother was magnificent Sunday evening when a bunch of rigged-up questions were handed to her to answer."

ER's closest friends were aghast throughout the weekend. The young people's rude behavior toward FDR made Tommy livid. At tea, immediately after that event, she confronted several AYC leaders: "How dare you insult the President of the United States?" Before dinner, FDR sent for Tommy. It was unusual for her to be summoned to his study. As she entered, he looked up from his papers and whispered intently, "Thank you, Tommy." While her outrage consoled FDR, he sought to comfort his wife. Later that evening, he leaned over to ER and with his most disarming smile said, "Our problem children are always unpredictable, aren't they!"

ER left almost immediately for an unprecedented vacation in Florida. She had never before departed just to get away, to heal her heart, and to assess her changing alliances and friendships. Safe and secluded at a beach house that Earl Miller had borrowed from a friend, with Tommy and her partner Henry Osthagen, ER did little but read, ruminate, and relax. She swam and wrote her columns, enjoyed the good cheer and playful games Earl invented, and filled her days with an abandon she had never before allowed herself.

For the next two weeks ER's columns were datelined "Golden Beach, Florida": "Here I am installed in a very comfortable house . . . and our holiday has already begun." She launched her time off with a visit to Mary McLeod Bethune's college in Daytona Beach. Until then, "I never

realized what a really dramatic achievement" Bethune-Cookman College
actually was. Founded in 1905, with five dollars, faith in the future, and
"five little girls" enrolled in what was then called the Literary and Industrial Training School for Negro Girls, the college now "ministers to the
needs of 100,000 Negroes from Daytona south, and it takes 250 students." Bethune-Cookman trained "leaders who will return to their communities and serve their people." Bethune's vision and achievement
profoundly moved ER, who alerted her readers that "like all other colleges, they still need a great deal—a library building, for instance, and
many more books . . . a substantial endowment fund," and new buildings
to keep up with its splendid growth. ER ignored the fact that her visit and
call for donations rankled Dixiecrats. Subsequently she would visit
Bethune-Cookman College many times and support it in various ways.

While on vacation, she told her readers that except for her columns,
she would have no social engagements "or duties of any kind" for the
duration. It "is really a very nice feeling, but not having experienced it
very often in my life, it makes me feel a bit guilty. . . . In any case, I am
going to enjoy every day as we live it." The next day she wrote her daughter, "I'm getting a good tan & doing nothing social. Henry [Osthagen] &
Earl are having some friends for cocktails today & yesterday Tommy,
Earl & I went to see 'Grapes of Wrath,' otherwise I've lived on the beach
in a bathing suit."

But in her columns, she ceaselessly struggled to work out her feelings
about the Citizenship Institute. She wrote about sitting on the beach with
nothing to do: "My husband likes the ocean from the deck of a ship, even
when the vessel rolls and pitches so much that most people retire to bed.
My own appreciation of the ocean is always enhanced by being on dry
land." Actually, she preferred to drive along the coast, "close to the beach,
or high above it." She never wrote that she hated the sand, which she did,
and besides, "it does not seem to me particularly warm here," but she was
assured it would get warmer. She enjoyed her days on the beach. "I should
record that during the past twenty-four hours I have spent many of them
lying in the sun and find it very pleasant." Moreover, such enforced relaxation heightened her interest in local conditions. Notably in segregated
Florida, she was drawn to issues of race. A local effort to introduce retrain-
ing schools for unemployed workers excited her imagination, and she suggested it for all communities.

The new Association for the Study of Negro Life and History seemed to her spectacular:

There is nothing which gives one so much pride as to be familiar with the achievements of one's own race. There is so much today in literature and art which can give the Negro people a sense of the genius and achievement of their race, but too often their history is forgotten. I think this association will promote goodwill and respect between neighbors of different races in our own country.

As always, human suffering and issues of respect for others dominated ER's thoughts. The film version of *The Grapes of Wrath* struck her as "well done," but she feared it did not convey the full reality of people's suffering. She was particularly moved by Mrs. Joad's question to Tommy when he returned from prison: whether he had "been hurt so much that he is just 'mean-mad.' I have felt people were 'mean-mad' at times and wondered if life were not treating them so harshly that they were unable to retain any of the qualities which make people lovable and that make life worth living."

During her vacation, "in the midst of a world which seems to provide one at every turn with new tales of horror and suffering, a story has come to me which has nothing to do with war." Korea was suffering due to "the mercilessness of nature." A protracted drought and heat wave had resulted in famine. Korea's chief winter food is rice and "'kimchi,' a kind of pick-led cabbage." Their cotton crop failed, and the people of Korea "are starv-ing, freezing and dying." ER again asked for donations. "Perhaps you will send an occasional check to . . . the world's suffering people." And she acknowledged, "It seems hard to sleep at night because the stress of home-less, hopeless people haunt one's dreams."

Several books lifted her spirits. Antoine de Saint-Exupéry's *Wind, Sand and Stars*, dedicated to airline pilots and "their dead," left her with an intensified understanding of real courage—which involved "a zest for life [no less than] contempt for death." Indeed, the book was not about contempt for death at all but about responsibility. Without responsibility, "contempt for death is the sign either of an impoverished soul or of youth-ful extravagance." ER agreed with Saint-Exupéry's definition of responsi-bility: "It is to feel shame at the sight of what seems to be unmerited misery. It is to take pride in a victory won by one's comrades. It is to feel, when setting one's stone, that one is contributing to the building of the world." His words caused her to observe "some of our young people today, who rather clumsily express their desire to keep this country at peace and continue . . . to make life more worth living." Their attitude stemmed from their sense of responsibility for world conditions. Their courage to accept that responsibility, she concluded, was probably the courage most needed today.

She exhorted her readers to consider the most needful issues before every community, recommending Elsie Clapp's new book, *Community Schools in Action*, and she wondered what might be done to improve the plight of handicapped children. The National Society for Crippled Children's Easter seal drive was on, and the need was more urgent than ever. Each state required significant federal aid for the care, education, and treatment of physically handicapped children. Almost two million children in the United States "needed special education, and less than ten percent" received it.

ER's Florida sojourn coincided with FDR's vacation cruise aboard the *Tuscaloosa* in the Caribbean and through the Panama Canal. As he neared Colón, Panama, to "inspect the Atlantic defenses and cross to the other side," he sent a cable addressed "Dear Babs." Concerned about her well-being after their public ordeal, he was unusually instructive: "I was glad to get your telegram. . . . Do get a real rest even if some of the mail gets 'acknowledged' instead of answered." He anticipated splendid fishing, "and I've already had lots of sleep and some sunlight."

Their vacations also coincided with Undersecretary of State Sumner Welles's mission to visit British prime minister Neville Chamberlain and French prime minister Édouard Daladier, as well as Mussolini and Hitler. As FDR's personal emissary, bypassing ordinary diplomatic channels, Welles undertook this desperate, controversial, fact-finding trip in an effort to forestall worldwide catastrophe, keep Italy neutral, and pursue every hope that might lead to negotiations for disarmament and a just and durable peace.

In Berlin, Hitler's swagger "horrified" Welles. The Nazis, in a triumphant and celebratory mode, greeted him with contempt and exhibited no interest in FDR's overture. Indeed, their manner toward Welles was "arrogant and brutal," Nicolson was told. As European antifascists prepared for Hitler's next step, Welles departed for England.

England's strategy was still uncertain. In London, U.S. ambassador Joseph Kennedy foretold defeat and disaster if America joined Europe's war. Harold Nicolson's parliamentary allies were horrified by Kennedy's evident willingness to accept a negotiated peace on Hitler's terms. "In this he will have the assistance of the old appeasers," the Communists who followed the meanderings of the Nazi-Soviet Pact, and "left-wing pacifists."

In France, a strange torpor, a brooding national fatigue, seemed to cloud political vision and sway public opinion. Communists and unionists were being arrested, hounded, and isolated, while fascist fifth columnists were ignored. Ambassador Bullitt's assistant Robert Murphy said the Communists were the primary appeasers. The fifty Communist deputies in Parliament, before being jailed the previous September, had "faithfully followed Moscow's lead" and opposed France's preparations for war. In Paris, Ilya Ehrenburg was more agitated by France's continuous disregard for Nazi atrocities: the only outrages it seemed to notice were those committed by Russia in the Soviet-Finnish War. Those who proclaimed it useless to "die for Danzig" now proclaimed it "necessary to die for Helsinki." Those who considered it impossible to fight on the Rhine now considered it possible to fight for Vyborg. Yet nothing was done; no troops marched; no tanks moved; no planes flew overhead. French generals opined that France was safe, protected and forever secured by the Maginot line.

When Welles returned to Washington, he pleaded for more military and economic aid for France. His plea bitterly exacerbated State Department rivalries. William Bullitt, who considered himself FDR's primary European adviser, was aghast at Welles's assignment, taking it as a slap in his face, undermining all his efforts for more aid to France. His resentment of Welles grew into a destructive hatred that permanently affected U.S. policy.

The diplomatic community now had no doubt that Hitler's goal was world conquest. The democracies would need to do far more in unity and with vigor to block his next moves. ER was keenly aware of that; at the AYC, she had rejected Abbott Simon's criticisms of France. We were, she said, all responsible for this situation: how can we criticize others when we ourselves have done so little?

It was at the bleakest point of her Florida vacation that she received a cable from Stockholm signed by twenty-four international women's organizations, representing "various ideals and political views." It was "addressed through me to all American women." The organizations agreed on a resolution calling upon all women everywhere to focus on "the consequences of a total war in all its inhumanity." Given current conditions, "women of all countries" must unite "to stop the process of devastation and prevent the impending catastrophe which threatens humanity."

In February 1940, public opinion polls revealed overwhelming opposition to U.S. involvement in the European war. A Gallup poll showed that 85 percent of America wanted to stay out. When asked, if Germany appeared to be "defeating England, should the United States declare war on Germany?" 71 percent answered no. *Fortune*'s poll found that while 85 percent thought America might be drawn into the war, 38 percent believed it would be because of "business interests" or government manipulation; 14 percent because of Allied propaganda; and 34 percent because "we hated Hitler." Only 1.2 percent thought "we must help the democracies."

One point two percent—the figure staggered ER. In that bitter context, she spent her last evenings in Florida in the company of Martha Gellhorn, who flew over from Cuba. Gellhorn updated ER about Finland and gave her a copy of her new novel, *A Stricken Field*, a collection of stories about Czechoslovakia that were rooted also in Gellhorn's feelings about Spain. She was, ER rhapsodized, one of America's best foreign correspondents and "an exciting person. . . . She has seen so much in Europe and felt it as only a really good writer can. I enjoyed every minute of our talk."

Gellhorn, like ER and Joe Lash, regarded Spain as the moral compass. It was where antifascist people of courage turned for hope. An entire generation of activists, writers, and artists had met there and boldly fought dreadful evil. Ilya Ehrenburg explained Spain's moral impact on the world.

It was difficult to breathe in the disturbed and humiliated Europe of the thirties. Fascism was advancing, and advancing unhindered. Every country, and even every man, hoped to save themselves singly, save themselves at all costs, achieve safety by silence, buy themselves off. . . . And then suddenly, a people arose that accepted battle. It did not save itself, nor did it save Europe, but if . . . there still remains any meaning in the words "human dignity," it is thanks to Spain. Spain became the air that allowed people to breathe.

Only Spain and Finland, Gellhorn felt, had stood up against evil and fought back. After she left Finland, she had stopped in Paris because she had learned that France had arrested some of Spain's most intrepid heroes, including Germany's bold antifascist writer and Spanish Civil War hero Gustav Regler. Gellhorn had pleaded for his release from a French detention center for enemy aliens, without success. Perhaps ER could do something? she now asked. ER would, of course, do her utmost. Ultimately Regler was released and found sanctuary in Mexico.

As ER considered the herculean tasks that faced contemporary youth, her thoughts turned to great teachers and to her own great teacher, Marie Souvestre. ER's love for literature, history, geography, music, and the arts had all been enhanced by Madame Souvestre, whose love of learning and of life had inspired her students with a passion for life's enchantments. As she ruminated and read on vacation in Florida, she recalled all those maps she was meant to memorize—the geography lessons and history lessons, the wars without end that humanity has endured. Friends from her student days were now endangered as Europe entered a state of siege. She quoted at length Mary Ellen Chase's celebration of great teachers, *A Goodly Fellowship*, because Chase's "conception of the good teacher agrees with my own."

For ER, "teaching and being taught are always inextricably woven together, for there is really no better way of learning," and good teachers, who "must really love" their subjects, were in a perpetual state of learning. Chase referred to a great teacher, whom ER knew and admired—William Allan Neilson, a Shakespearean scholar and president emeritus of Smith College. ER thought "all of us will do well to remember" Neilson's farewell address to the students of Smith, because he named the enemy—the elusive enemy, he who always puts the body before the spirit, the dead before the living; who makes things only to sell them; who has forgotten that there is such a thing as truth, and [who] measures the words by advertisement or by money; who daily defiles the beauty that surrounds him and makes vulgar the tragedy. . . . The Philistine, the vulgarian, the great sophist, all the greedy, selfish, egocentric manipulators [with] outposts inside us persecuting our peace, spoiling our sight, confusing our values . . .

A certain very popular educator, an "enchanting classicist," had recently been in urgent need of help. The extraordinary Dr. Vera Lachmann was the headmistress of an academy in Berlin-Grunewald "for half-Aryan and Jewish boys and girls." She had founded the school in April 1933 and maintained it despite "mounting difficulties," until the Nazi government ordered it closed on 1 January 1939. After that, she gave private lessons, volunteered with Kate Rosenheim and other concerned Germans who worked to secure shelter for Jewish children abroad; in the spring she gave a lecture series on Rilke. Her sister Nina took the last scheduled flight out of Berlin to London in July, but Vera explained to her worried friends that she intended to remain in Berlin so long as she might be useful to others.

Amid mounting rumors that Jewish scholars, attorneys, and physicians had been rounded up by the Nazis and had subsequently disappeared, Dr. Lachmann's German friends and colleagues persuaded her to try to leave. U.S. friends organized to rescue her and petitioned the U.S. consul in Berlin for an "ex-quota visa." But such visas were limited to university faculty, and despite appeals from many scholars and from Vassar College's president H. N. MacCracken, who offered Lachmann a "generous contract" to teach at Vassar, the State Department was unwilling to grant her a visa.

After months of delay, her friends turned to ER. President MacCracken explained the situation in detail: "Dr. Lachmann, who is a cousin of Erich Warburg of New York, was deprived of her position owing to her race, and since 1933 has conducted an advanced school for Jewish students driven from universities and gymnasia in Germany." But the U.S. consul refused to consider her school "an academy, seminary, college, or university." Vassar's president included a letter from Radcliffe dean W. K. Jordan, assuring the State Department that "the academic board of

Radcliffe College considered the instruction to be equivalent to that offered students regularly enrolled in an American college." Her school was equivalent to a gymnasium, and Erika Weigand, a Radcliffe student who studied at Dr. Lachmann's school from 1933 to 1935, had received college credits for her work. MacCracken assured ER that Dr. Lachmann was an esteemed scholar of "published works and recognized ability, and in every way the equal of other members of the Vassar faculty."

Erika's parents, Frances Rhoades Weigand and Dr. Hermann Weigand, chair of Yale's department of Germanic languages, sent personal letters to ER. "Vera Lachmann is not only our dearest friend," Frances Weigand wrote, "but a person we dare not let the world lose." Hermann Weigand added, "I believe Dr. Lachmann to be one of the most valuable people alive in the world today." He thanked President MacCracken for "whatever you may be able to do to secure for this life the possibility of continued existence and a sphere of usefulness."

ER was moved by these many appeals. This profoundly learned classicist had graduated magna cum laude in German literature and Greek philosophy from the University of Berlin in 1931. She was also a poet, whose splendid dissertation was a study of the Eddas, Icelandic political verse of the Middle Ages, which involved translation from Old Norse. In addition to her work as headmistress, she taught Greek, Latin, German, French, Hebrew, ancient history, and the Bible. ER sent her entire file to Sumner Welles, her only State Department friend, and promised Dr. MacCracken that she would ask them "to do all they can to help her." ER's last note on the subject, dated 11 September 1939, contained one sentence: "Dear Sumner: Thank you so much for what you are doing to help Dr. Vera Lachmann."

That same day ER wrote her daughter, "I feel sick about the war & want so much to do something that looks beyond toward building a better peace. We can't go on with ever recurring wars in a modern world." She wanted especially to go to Europe to build a significant "refugee relief effort," but all her suggestions were rejected.

Dr. Lachmann—a great and beloved teacher, an inspiration for so many, the Marie Souvestre of Berlin—was one life endangered in a world of lives in jeopardy. ER did what she could, one life at a time. In this case her effort was successful. The visa was granted, and on 16 November 1939 Vera Lachmann left Germany for New York, via Denmark and Sweden, where she boarded the *Gripsholm* for a twelve-day journey to her new life. ER could not foresee that over time Vera Lachmann would become a legendary American classicist, charismatic and inspirational, or that students around the country would sing her praises long after her death in 1985.*

ER prepared for the end of her beach vacation in a serene and contented mood. She wondered where the next battle would occur, and when it would begin; and she wondered how long it would take for Americans to heed the crisis. But her grand vacation had gone a long way to restoring her spirits: "Another heavenly day and I grieve my time here draws to an end." On one of her last evenings, she enjoyed a perfectly frivolous Florida adventure, going off, with unnamed others, to the Royal Palm Club. "It is very attractive and there is excellent food and one of the best floor shows." Tony Martin sang, the ladies of the chorus were most charming and "graceful and wear attractive costumes." Martin was introduced to her, and wanted his picture taken "with our group." ER entirely enjoyed the "spirit of carefree gaiety here which is contagious."

Finally "the day has come to leave Florida and I am afraid this lazy life is going to be hard to shake off. I have discovered that there is much in a change of atmosphere. I imagine that the President most reluctantly neared his home port." But he had already picked up the "threads of all state affairs," and she was certain that when she flew into Washington "this evening I shall forget in the twinkling of an eye that there are such things as days which are not scheduled and hours when one can lie in the sun or sit and read a book. It has been a delightful holiday and I feel a deep sense of gratitude to the kindly people who were so considerate and allowed me such freedom."

*Vera Lachmann taught first at Vassar, 1940–41; then at Brearley; then in the German departments at Salem College in North Carolina, Bryn Mawr, and Yale. In 1948 she moved to New York, where she taught classics at Brooklyn College until her retirement. From 1944 to 1970, she ran Camp Catawba, a summer camp for boys in the Blue Ridge Mountains of North Carolina. There she and her life partner, Tui St. George Tucker, a composer, flutist, and recorder teacher, inspired generations of classicists, musicians, artists, dramatists, poets, and writers. See Miller, *Catawba Assembly*, and Miller, ed., *Homer's Sun Still Shines*, a collection of Vera Lachmann's works.

As she considered her return to state affairs, ER made two suggestions to her readers. Former president Herbert Hoover had proposed that the U.S. government donate $20 million for Polish relief, because when the war was over, all Europe "will be starving." She agreed and wrote, "Unfortunately, it is always the little people who starve. They are starving now," if not in Finland, where food was bountiful, certainly in Poland and probably in Germany, Spain, and Italy, and to some degree "even in France and England." She urged her readers to heed Hoover's appeal and also to support Dorothy Canfield Fisher's crusade to encourage school-children in every state "to share what they can with the children who are in want in other countries."

Tommy had arranged for ER to stop in and visit Lape and Read in Connecticut—"so you can see for yourself that she is brown and rested," she explained to Lape—but ER insisted upon being on "a very strenuous diet and I hope she wont stay on it too long because she works too hard." Few of ER's friends satisfied Tommy, a fierce mother-bear protector. Critical and acerbic, she distrusted almost everybody ER befriended and felt close only to Esther and Elizabeth. Regarding their time in Florida, she had mixed emotions:

> I would not have had any personal satisfaction . . . if I were in her place, but then we are all constituted differently. Such unadulterated selfishness as I observed could hardly be matched, and an equal amount of what I would call unkindness and thoughtlessness, if not worse. I had a certain amount of rest—that is I worked every morning and loafed in the afternoons and evenings. However, it was not my idea of a vacation.

Tommy's reference was to Earl Miller, who was unexpectedly accompanied by his new lady friend Simone von Haver.

ER returned to the White House in time to greet special guests who had converged for the anniversary of FDR's inauguration. She enjoyed a breakfast reunion with the first family's most steadfast friends, including Grace Howe, Louis Howe's widow; Groton's headmaster, Endicott Peabody, and his wife; and FDR's mother. To celebrate, they attended a service at St. John's Church, where a prayer impressed ER so deeply, she printed it in full in her column:

Our Father, who hast set a restlessness in our hearts, and made us all seekers after that which we can never fully find; forbid us to be satisfied with what we make of life. Draw us from base content, and set our eyes on far-off goals. Keep us at tasks too hard for us, that we may be driven to Thee for strength. Deliver us from fretfulness and self-pity; make us sure of the goal we cannot see, and of the hidden good in the world. Open our eyes to simple beauty all around us, and our hearts to the loveliness men hide from us because we do not try enough to understand them. Save us from ourselves, and show us a vision of a world made new. May Thy spirit of peace and illumination so enlighten our minds that all life shall glow with new meaning and new purpose; through Jesus Christ Our Lord.

ER carried that prayer with her and made copies for her friends. Her quest for "the hidden good in the world" on the road to "a world made new" would fortify her every day as she confronted a springtime of horror, one lonely step at a time.

Chapter Ten

"When You Go to War, You Cease to Solve the Problems of Peace": March–June 1940

World events moved with staggering speed after ER's return. As the Soviet-Finnish Winter War continued, Hitler warned that any Scandinavian support for Finland would result in immediate Nazi invasion, so Norway and Sweden maintained neutrality. They refused British and French troops cross-border access and blocked the transport of supplies into Finland. On 12 March, Finland, exhausted and unsupported, surrendered. The treaty was harsh, requiring Finland to transfer Karelia and Vyborg—a large city, all of whose inhabitants fled—and other essential territories between Lake Ladoga and the Gulf of Finland. It ended the slaughter of the Winter War but left a bitter legacy.

Soviet foreign minister Molotov estimated that Finland's earlier failure to agree to the "small frontier rectification" that he had proposed had cost Finland 60,000 dead and 250,000 wounded; Russia 49,000 and 158,000 wounded. Most accounts, however, estimated Russian deaths at over 200,000, and it was considered a terrible price to pay for the illusion of Soviet security.

Nobody knew where the next battles would be fought, but everybody knew they were imminent. In these tense months, ER determined to spend more time with her grandchildren and her friends. Being with those near and dear to her had always mattered, but now she began setting aside even more evenings for attending the theatre, concerts, and films. She needed to nourish her heart. Her sense of well-being would enable her to be of greater service and help save her sanity.

Her columns became more political, more direct. Two short films shown at the White House, she wrote, should have wide commercial distribution. They described efforts in the windswept prairies and across mining regions not only to conserve nature but to protect mine workers and their families "from the dust which eventually give them silicosis and a predisposition to tuberculosis, from which they die at an early age." People who "live in the shadow of great piles of waste which disintegrates and blows around in dust, so that the children are affected in precisely the same way as the workers in the mines," require protection. "There must be ways of discovering methods of keeping this dust down in the mines. The living quarters of those families should be moved from the dangerous area." ER wanted these films shown widely, to arouse public interest and "make it easier for the unions to obtain proper working and living conditions."

In another column, ER reported on the work of Leopold Stokowski, who had assembled a splendid orchestra comprised of NYA youth. Before he departed on a national tour, the great conductor said it represented "a musical awakening for the United States, and an international force for goodwill throughout the world."

Also during this spring of gloom, ER challenged herself by taking longer hikes and exercising more strenuously, and she agreed to engage in more controversial debates, write longer articles, and attend countless political meetings. Ilya Ehrenberg understood during his prolonged exile, as ships were sunk and cities bombed, that when one is happy, idle hours are tolerable, "but in misfortune, action, however futile, is a necessity."

In early March four hundred seniors at Fordham College, a Jesuit school, named Pope Pius XII the most popular man in the world and ER the most popular woman. "No other President's wife has been so much a topic of conversation," the *New York Times* noted. Since the AYC controversy, ER had risen in the public's estimation: 68 percent approved of her activities, while 32 percent disapproved. Most Americans, regardless of party or class, agreed that the first lady "is a great lady doing good work" and sets "a good example for American women." In fact, her approval rating was 4 percent higher than the president's.

At Easter, the paper of record rhapsodized about the first lady's blue ensembles for the holiday, saying her outfits "not only gladden the hearts of all women, but in an entirely nonpartisan way harmonize with the spirit of our democracy." The *Times* went on to explain that which ensemble she wore on Easter Sunday

matters, one guesses, because the wife of an American President is not royalty and does not pretend to be; because she maintains her dignity without losing the common touch; because she seems to have established a sympathetic relationship not only with fashionable ladies who are to be seen on Fifth Avenue but with motherly persons in Middle Western kitchens wearing aprons [and] young wives in the Southern States, New England and the Pacific Coast.

The *Times* praised her work as well as her choice of ensemble. Her "sympathies, basic attitudes, manners and interests" added "prestige" and bolstered "the institution of the President's wife."

Inspired by such words, ER set off for a lengthy tour determined to speak bluntly about the need to confront the growing humanitarian crises worldwide. In the absence of government action, she urged private citizens to follow her activist example. In Philadelphia's Kensington Nursery School, where toddlers would starve if their parents on relief did not get additional funds, she sponsored a foster care program. She helped to organize the Foster Parents Plan for War Children, which sent thousands of dollars to needy refugee children from Poland and Germany who were now in France. With the American Friends Service Committee, Clarence Pickett, Marshall Field, Caroline O'Day, and others, she helped organize a Non-Sectarian Foundation for Refugee Children, to place such children in American homes upon their arrival in the United States. The group, noted the *Times*, would cooperate "with Catholic, Protestant and Jewish refugee agencies [and] care for children eligible to enter under existing quota laws, but separated from their parents by reason of death, concentration camps or war conditions."

During the hectic six-week tour, ER and Tommy made stops throughout the Midwest, from St. Louis and Chicago to East Lansing and Kokomo. They visited college campuses, viewed NYA and WPA projects, lectured, and conferred with students, faculty, politicians, and activists. She was especially impressed with Michigan State College, which had taken full advantage of New Deal opportunities to build dormitories and impressive centers for music and sports.

ER enjoyed much of her time away, she told her readers. As soon as she arrived at her hotel in Chicago, she got a call from her son Jimmy, who was in "on business" from Los Angeles, and so he "dined with us last night and breakfasted with us this morning. . . . This was a real joy."

ER's commitment to the AYC continued to be tested. Although most of her friends, such as Aubrey Williams, no longer trusted the AYC leadership and advised her to end her support for its projects, she insisted they did valuable work, and she still cared about their causes. ER was "undaunted" by all the criticism she received about the AYC, according to Tommy: while many people in ER's circle "are convinced that these youth leaders are really communists," ER "intends going on with them." In Chicago, ER met with Frances Williams, executive secretary of the AYC, which only fortified her unswerving support for its activities. Williams's group, ER noted in her column, was doing splendid work: "These youngsters work hard trying to build a worthwhile program . . . and I have a great respect for the unselfishness with which their work is done."

On 14 March ER delivered a major speech on civil liberties to the Chicago Civil Liberties Committee at the city's opera house. It was part of a program to honor courageous journalists, sponsored by Chicago's WPA writers, the American Civil Liberties Union, and the *Chicago Tribune*. Nothing was more significant, ER emphasized, than the protection of civil liberties—freedom of speech, press, religion, conscience. These freedoms, "which emphasize the liberty of the individual," needed to be protected at all times, particularly when people were in such profound disagreement. In this troubled world, nations at war could lose their freedoms quickly.

Speaking personally and from the heart, she noted that her travels across America had given her the opportunity "to meet people and see things that have happened to little people," which highlight our obligations in each community. Poor people, noncitizens, and minorities did not benefit from many aspects of the U.S. Constitution. It was up to individuals in every community to work for "the full observance for all our people of their civil liberties."

To dramatize the need, ER related a "story" concerning her visits to Arthurdale. "I happen to go every now and then to a certain mining community [where] there are a number of people who came to this country many years ago. They have been here so many years that they have no other country. This is their country. Their children have been born here. They work here. They have created great wealth for this country." But they had no opportunity to learn the language or find out how to become citizens. Some time earlier ER had met a family headed by a woman who had been here over thirty-five years, a meeting she considered most important:

I was standing with a group of people, and a young girl with arms full of packages came along the road. She stopped . . . and said, "Why, you are Mrs. Roosevelt. My mama say, 'She is happy if you come to her house.'" [ER agreed to visit.] When I got to the house a Polish woman was sitting at the table. The girl walked in and said, "Mama, this is Mrs. Roosevelt," and the woman got up and threw both arms around me, and I was kissed on both cheeks. She told me she had been expecting me to come for a long time. She wanted me to come because she wanted me to see how really nice her house was, and we went through the four rooms and it was nice. She had made crochet pieces which decorated every table. The bedspreads were [quilts] of real beauty. We admired everything together . . . [and] she wouldn't let me leave without eating something.

When ER returned six months later, she said, everything had changed. The home was dark and glum. The mine had closed down, and there was no work. The man worked for a time "on WPA . . . and then they tell me I no citizen. Mrs. Roosevelt, I vote. I vote often. Why I no citizen?" In the community, there was nobody he could ask for advice, no place to "find out what his rights were, or what he should do." His children were citizens, but he was not. They were destitute and survived because the county allowed them to take in four old men.

To ER it was simply unacceptable: "It hurt you. Something was wrong with the spirit of America that an injustice like that could happen to a man who, after all, worked hard and contributed to the wealth of the country. It should have been somebody's business . . . to see that he learned the English language well enough to find things out for himself." ER hoped to see a civil liberties committee in every community, a "group of people who really care when things go wrong and do something when there is an infringement of the individual's rights."

The need to defend aliens was as great as the need to defend dissenters. Freedom of expression must apply to all. Americans had to be "willing to listen" and to speak with one another, to argue and debate. They had to trust one another in the process of democracy and majority rule. "Of course, that means that we have to have a real belief that people have intelligence enough to live in a democracy. And that is something which we are really testing out . . . because . . . we are the only great democracy that is at peace and [able to continue] a normal and free way of life. It is only here that people do not have to tremble when they say what they think."

She recommended Martha Gellhorn's *A Stricken Field*, a "vivid picture of the kind of fear that has gradually come to all the people of Europe." The novel depicts the horror that came to Czechoslovakia when anti-Nazi citizens were labeled dangerous and forced "underground," to live "in hiding, afraid to speak to each other, afraid to recognize each other on the streets, for fear they would be tortured to death." The message for ER was profound and urgent: "Only great fear could bring people to treat other people like that." We must take heed that we do not follow such a path, and become "dominated by fear so that we curtail civil liberties."

She attacked "the growth of religious prejudice and race prejudice. [They] are a great menace because we find that in countries where civil liberties have been lost, religious and race prejudice have been rampant." Some of the literature of hate and prejudice printed by "various denominations" had stunned her. Religious persecution and bigotry challenged our constitutional rights, she said. The core principle of religious freedom, that lay at the heart of the vision of our forefathers and was ratified by our Constitution, was the "right of all people to worship God as they saw fit, and if they do not wish to worship they were not forced to worship. That is a fundamental liberty." We have people here from many nations, and "proof that people can understand each other and can live together amicably, and that races can live on an equal basis, even though they may be very different in background. . . . Above all, there should never be race prejudice" here; "there should never be a feeling that one strain is better than another." After all, Indians are the only nonimmigrant inhabitants of the country "who have a right to say that they own this country."

She urged Americans to "have courage" and "not succumb to fears"— to be "a united country," strongly committed to equality, civil liberties, and justice. Her faith in the younger generation was stronger than ever and she was especially grateful that we could "trust the youth of the nation to herald the real principles of democracy."

ER's Chicago address, the keynote of her tour, was received with great enthusiasm. She went on to visit several schools and was particularly pleased to speak at the Teachers State College at Terre Haute, Indiana. Reflecting on the enthusiasm and dedication she encountered, she wrote: "No real teacher can ever stop learning. The only way that one can inspire youth is to keep on being enthusiastic and eager to learn also. That can only be done if one touches new subjects constantly and opens new windows of the mind and heart that give one a zest for living and keep one eternally young." ER had loved her own teaching days at the Todhunter School. She was energized by her students, and they were inspired by her. She understood that teachers had the gift to transform young lives, and she always credited Marie Souvestre as the great guiding light in her life.

Back in Washington, having witnessed successful schools on her tour, she was dismayed the next day when she visited the city's underfunded public schools with a delegation of congressional wives. Even the school closest to the White House was unsanitary and heartbreaking: Children played "in a damp and fairly dark cellar room. . . . Even the tiniest tots have to go down into the cellar to reach the toilets. There is no auditorium, no gymnasium and in spite of years of [teachers' efforts], a modern curriculum has not yet been adopted."

Moreover, health care across the country, she observed, was in crisis. Medical procedures and medicines to prevent deaths, which were particularly high among the poor, were not widely available. While in Chicago, she had been taken to a "small hospital on the lake where children with heart ailments are cared for. They have the capacity for one hundred children. . . . If they are given proper care, they almost always get well. If not, they die." Everything about the place was exemplary: nutrition, care, management. "As I looked at those youngsters, I felt grateful that so many people in Chicago had been moved to give them a chance to live useful and happy lives." But the pediatrician in charge told her, "We can take a hundred, and we are the only institution caring for this type of case. There are approximately 10,000 children in Chicago needing this care." ER was anguished that medical attention and treatments were limited to those who could afford them. In her columns she continually raised the issue: health care should be available to all.

She planned to celebrate her thirty-fifth wedding anniversary with FDR on 17 March. "For the first time in some years [we are both] at home for our wedding anniversary," she noted. "There is no special celebration, for we are rather an ancient married couple, but the President is going to see *Gone with the Wind*, which ought to be enough entertainment for any day in the year!"

Alas, FDR was sick in bed and missed their anniversary movie date. Initially disappointed, even irate, ER soon appreciated that FDR's nasty flu was serious. It was "swamp fever" or "jungle fever," he told her and several journalists. He stayed in his room for almost ten days and failed to greet even visiting international dignitaries. When the president-elect of Costa Rica, Rafael Calderón Guardia, and his wife arrived for a formal tea, ER "greeted them under the front portico alone, for the President did not think it wise to go out of doors on the first day he has been out of his room." She was "so sorry that the President had to disappoint the Easter Monday crowds on the lawn by not giving his usual few words of greeting over the radio from the South Portico."

It is unclear whether ER failed to realize how sick he was, or felt he unnecessarily pampered himself, or thought he should perform his tasks no matter his miseries. Since many of her notes to him end with advice that he get more rest and take good care of himself, several curious columns on FDR's malaise seem uncommonly chiding. They are more reminiscent of her much earlier advice to a visiting grandson: if you have to cry, do so in the bathtub, with the door closed. Clearly she was in a dismal state of mind. In one column she noted that upon her return from New York, she walked into her sitting room to be greeted by "a huge vase of daffodils . . . and I felt my spirit, which had been somewhat low, rise like a rocket." That afternoon, "I looked in on my husband [and] he looked really better . . . so that raised my spirits one point and the yellow daffodils did the rest."

Still, during this Easter season, family disasters seemed only to annoy her—and her judgments were harsh. When her daughter-in-law Ethel, Franklin Jr.'s wife, had a hunting accident, ER virtually blamed the victim and launched into a public lecture. The accident "upset us all considerably," she wrote, and we are "grateful that she was not killed. I suppose one cannot blame the horse, for the ground was still somewhat slippery. . . . I suppose it is a great deal to ask, but I wish that all young married people with children would give up hunting. I know how much fun it must be for them and that they never expect any accident to happen, but to an old and timid person like myself to take risks seems unnecessary."

Ethel du Pont Roosevelt's hunting accident surely must have evoked for ER the 1934 tragedy that took Mary Harriman Rumsey's life—which orphaned her children and deprived ER of her great friend and closest

Washington confidante. Still, ER gave structure to her grief in the form of a scolding:

> I suppose weeks in bed give us an opportunity for inner growth which nothing else might achieve and so, perhaps, this is one of the ways in which the Lord educates His children. When I was a child, we had an old nurse who used to say whenever anything particularly unfortunate happened to us: "Whom the Lord loveth, He chasteneth." Perhaps it is comforting to feel that whatever happens to us is probably intended to give us a chance for spiritual development.

Neglecting to follow her own advice, ER rode her new horse in Rock Creek Park, despite the fact that it was stormy and "the coldest" Easter week since 1890. She recommended the new film *Rebecca*, based on Daphne du Maurier's best-selling novel and starring Judith Anderson. It was "excellent," the cast "charming and convincing," and the subject was close to home—everybody's home. "They were wise to end the picture so that you can imagine the future will be happier and that Rebecca's evil influence will finally pass away," ER concluded on a philosophical note. "Evil influences have a dreadful way, however, of sticking around and one disagreeable person in a family can shadow the present and the future for a long time."

The subject of ER's reference is unknown, but it was not her mother-in-law. By this time, SDR was ER's most abiding ally on issues closest to her heart—racial justice, education, housing, and health care reform. Increasingly, ER admired her intrepid, courageous, hearty way of being. In New York, en route to the second round of her western lecture tour—which would include a stopover to visit Anna and her family in Seattle—ER's plane was delayed by a storm. She used the extra time to visit SDR, who had also been sick for a week but was "up at last." As ER arrived, the doctor was telling SDR to rest much more. Her solemn reply was "Why, I do nothing but give up things I want to do!" ER wrote, "Let us hope we all keep that amount of enthusiasm for doing things, it gives zest to life."

At this time, ER was preoccupied by the problems refugees faced. "These homeless people," she insisted, "must find shelter somewhere." The

Dominican Republic announced it was considering taking in sixteen hundred Polish refugees.* But the United States was not a welcoming nation. Indeed, senior State Department officials actually sought to dismantle FDR's Intergovernmental Committee on Refugees, which FDR angrily resisted. Still, his vision for long-range plans and solutions after the war did not involve action during the war.

ER continued to urge public activity for sanctuary, and during these tense days family visits comforted her. In Seattle, Anna and her grandchildren Eleanor (Sistie), Curtis (Buzzy), and one-year-old Johnny were a source of delight. There was a birthday party and a walk in the woods with Tommy and Anna, featuring new spring flowers along the path. Across the lake stood white-capped mountains. Seattle was a beautiful and serene place, and ER felt refreshed to return to her lecture tour.

Traveling south, ER stayed in her son Jimmy's Beverly Hills apartment, although he was away on film business. While in California, she asked Tommy to arrange a visit with Mayris "Tiny" Chaney, the dancer whose company ER enjoyed. But Tommy did not approve of Tiny and dreaded ER's time with her, "with the press stalking her every move." Tommy could not understand the friendship and wrote to Esther Lape, "I can't imagine there could be any kind of conversation, except when Tiny unburdens her troubles and Mrs. R seems to have a yen for listening to people's troubles. . . . If she were my friend, I know Mrs. R would raise her eyebrows at my choice."

In the same letter Tommy ripped into Hick, who now worked for the Democratic National Committee and lived most of the time in the White

---

*Shortly after the 1938 Evian Conference, General Rafael Trujillo offered the Dominican Republic as a haven for up to 100,000 refugees, partly in order to whiten his island country; see Edward Paulino, "Forgotten Atrocities: The 1937 Genocidal Haitian Massacre in the Dominican Republic," in Smith, *Genocide Essays*, pp. 79–99. Paulino also discusses the U.S. rejection of Haiti's offer for haven. Trujillo contributed an estate on the island's north shore, called Sosúa, with timberland, agricultural land, a deep harbor, and "buildings enough for 200 people," with an eye toward fostering agricultural development. See Wyman, *Paper Walls,* pp. 60–63; Smith, *American Empire,* pp. 299, 513n18; and "First 37 for Sosúa Settlement Reach Dominican Land of Refuge," *New York Times,* 9 May 1940. But wartime conditions limited refugees' movements, and by May 1940 only thirty-seven Jews had arrived. In the end no more than five hundred refugees disembarked in the Dominican Republic.

House: "Our friend, Hick, is still holed in her room here and I imagine it will take dynamite to blast her out. . . . How does she make a sinecure out of every job she has? How does she convince Mrs. R that she is killing herself with work?"

Tommy's protective impatience with ER's deep need to help people she cared about was an ongoing source of static between Tommy and ER's "pets," as she called them. While Tommy criticized almost every one of ER's friends (except Lape and Read), she had become ER's sole companion during most of her travels.

The political highlight of ER's California trip was a tour of migrant camps and quarters with Melvyn and Helen Gahagan Douglas. Hollywood stars and activists for justice, the Douglases were ardent New Dealers outraged by the desperate conditions endured by farm families who had been "tractored out" by mechanization or who had migrated from the dust bowls of Texas, Oklahoma, Arkansas, and Missouri. During the mid-1930s an estimated six thousand Okies poured into California each month, to be met with indifference or contempt.

Their plight was described in John Steinbeck's powerful novel *The Grapes of Wrath*, a feat of emotional reportage that stirred people to action. The Steinbeck Committee to Aid Agricultural Organization was formed to press for decent living conditions, expanded Farm Security Administration (FSA) camps, and the creation of a farmworkers' union to provide migrants with better working conditions and a fair wage. Members of the Steinbeck Committee included Paul Schuster Taylor, a social scientist; his wife, photographer Dorothea Lange; and the great civil libertarian Alexander Meiklejohn and his wife, economist Helen Everett. The chairperson was Helen Gahagan Douglas. The committee worked with Laurence Hewes, regional FSA head, to improve housing and work conditions everywhere. Meanwhile the growers and their allies, Helen Douglas observed, had nothing but hostility and contempt for the "ragged starving people" in their midst. They were very bitter against the New Deal and ER personally.

"DEAR YOU MUST READ GRAPES OF WRATH," Hick wrote to ER, who did so and joined the movement, supporting all the Steinbeck Committee's efforts. On the morning of 3 April, ER and the Douglases arrived at the Bakersfield airport, where Laurence Hewes met them, and they set off in two cars for a tour that would permanently influence the first lady's work. When she "spotted a cluster of makeshift shacks constructed of old boards, tarpaper and tin cans," she demanded that the driver stop the car, and she walked across the field. Helen Douglas "followed at a trot," amazed that one of the "bent figures . . . recognized [ER] at once. He greeted her with hand outstretched and a beam on his face. 'Oh, Mrs. Roosevelt, you've come to see us.'" When ER headed toward his shack, he "tried to stop her. 'Please don't go in there. . . . My wife and children are sick with the raisins.'" According to Douglas, "migrants called all skin rashes 'raisins,'" but this was chicken pox. ER insisted that it did not matter, "and in she went."

The migrant farm families' homes ranged from unbearable to hopeful. "Squatters pay no rent," ER wrote, "and may be moved at any time. Private camps are large pieces of land leased by an individual, who then re-leases it into lots about big enough to hold a tent and a car." Three families who had been driven out of a squatters' camp into a private camp "all came from Oklahoma and before that . . . a New England village. There were young women with their children and women who looked old before their time." Yet she also noticed "a universal effort to make life as decent as possible under appallingly difficult circumstances." For example, in a "narrow strip beside one of the tents, I spied a small flower garden which was evidently tended with loving care. Even the children playing about it [were careful not to harm] this one little effort to bring beauty into drab surroundings."

ER detailed the costs and the difficulties the migrants faced: a family paid five dollars a month for a lot, got "an electric light in your tent; without it you pay only three dollars. . . . There are two outside toilets for the use of fifty or more families. There are some hydrants from which you may draw water." *The Grapes of Wrath*, she told a reporter firmly, had not exaggerated the living and working conditions of the migrant workers.

At the Kern County camp, "the county authorities take some responsibility. The land is free, they put in water and electricity and people are given sites on which to pitch their tents." But in wet weather, the tents were "deep in mud. Several people yesterday had to change their sites because they were flooded out. Their pitiful belongings were stacked up waiting to be moved. In hot weather, all these camps must be well nigh unbearable. This county camp . . . is better, but even here living conditions are hardly what we call decent."

Finally, ER visited FSA camps at Shafter and Visalia that offered the possibility of new "standards for decent existence"—including a nursery school, playgrounds, health clinics, and a cooperative store. "They are run by the people themselves so that democracy may be seen in action." California, ER wrote, "must be proud of this effort to find a way to meet the problem of the migratory worker, who must always be with us because he is needed to follow the crops" around the nation. But for the uprooted, the real solution was land redistribution, getting these people onto land that they owned. "Above everything else, I carried away from my day in the migratory camps an admiration for the indomitable courage which can continue to have faith in the future when present conditions seem almost unbearable."

Subsequently ER would write Helen Douglas, "I know the President will be enormously interested in what I have to tell him" about her trip to the San Joaquin Valley. ER's memories and descriptions of her trips provided context for FDR's efforts on behalf of the farmers.

When they returned to Los Angeles, the Douglases hosted a concert for ER, performed by the National Youth Administration orchestra on their patio. Then they attended her lecture at Long Beach. They were "filled with apprehension," because early "that evening we heard rumors that an attempt would be made on her life." In the end, there was no violence. The "huge crowd" that gathered to hear the first lady was polite, although the auditorium was filled with "hostile" opponents who asked rude questions.

The next day ER and Tommy flew to San Francisco, where ER finally had her long-planned private time with Tiny Chaney. The first lady relaxed in Tiny's company and trusted her completely. Soon after Earl Miller introduced ER and the dancer in 1932, their intimate talks over late-night sherry while all the household slept, had resulted in shared confidences and painful memories, in both cases, of a childhood defined by a beloved alcoholic father.

Born on 7 April 1902 in San Francisco, Mayris Chaney had vowed never to marry and never to share a home with any man. Earl understood that, although he always loved Tiny. All her dependent and faithful dance partners understood it. As soon as any man got possessive, she fled. The reason, she explained to ER, was simple: her father, a loving, brilliant engineer, drank. Her mother, born in London, had been a beautiful woman, with pretensions and debtor's disease. He drank and drank; she spent and spent. Her childhood home, not unlike ER's, was filled with alcoholic rage, regret, and cold empty spaces. She and her sister were somewhat protected by good schools, music, and dance lessons. Books and dance became Tiny's life. In her teens she fled San Francisco for a successful career that took her around the dance floors of the world, to countless clubs and cabarets. Ambitious and enterprising, she established several businesses. But her affections, like ER's, were for neglected, hurt people.

Vital and beautiful, with penetrating, luminous eyes, Tiny, at five foot two and 108 pounds, was indeed tiny. For extra height she wore her long blond hair piled high atop her head and the highest heels she could find. Quick-witted and charming, flirtatious and popular, she was widely regarded as a "show-girl"—which caused some with money and power to wonder why the first lady preferred her company to theirs. When ER decided to stay at her home, Tiny got used to being asked, "Miss Chaney, just *who* are you?" Tiny replied, "I am nobody, just ER's friend." A true friend, opinionated and honest—and alert to ER's needs—Tiny gave her the luxury to be herself and to bring down, if only for a short while, the "protective wall" she had built around her emotions.

Tiny also advanced ER's performance skills. Before each public appearance, she said, remind yourself: "I must lower my voice." Tiny recommended a voice coach for ER's lectures, then another for the radio. Because they shared a childhood of sorrow, they shared a need to help, to contribute, and to laugh at the foibles around them and deep within.

ER's California lecture tour ended on 5 April. Tommy wrote Lape that the speeches were everywhere successful, with "good audiences and full houses," and that both Los Angeles and San Francisco signed up for next year.

Their hard work was rewarded when Chief Ranger Forrest Townsley arrived at their hotel to drive ER and Tommy to Yosemite National Park. ER was happy to see Townsley—he had been one of their guides when she and Hick visited Yosemite in 1934. ER had a magnificent weekend. "The waterfalls are beautiful, and the blue sky made our day in the open a great joy. Mariposa Grove, with its giant sequoia trees, was even more impressive than I remembered it." She attended the seventh-anniversary celebration of the founding of the CCC camps in Yosemite and was impressed with the vast work done.

At some point during these two days at Yosemite, Tiny called ER to alert her to a barrage of newspaper stories that followed her purchase of a kimono in a Japanese shop on Laguna Street near Tiny's Nob Hill home. According to the *New York Times*, the Japanese community of San Francisco was "'tickled' by the spectacle" of ER making such a purchase "after leading the boycott on Japanese silks." ER, reached at Yosemite, "laughed over the telephone, and denied that she had ever aided a Japanese boycott," adding, "This country is not at war with Japan and the Government has not boycotted Japanese goods. . . . Neither as the wife of a Government official nor as an individual do I believe in boycotting the goods of any nation with which this Nation is at peace. We should preserve good will if we possibly can. I have many Japanese friends and many Chinese friends. Any report I ever led a boycott on Japanese silk is erroneous."

Grim news arrived as they drove to Reno: the Nazis had bombed and invaded Norway and Denmark. Denmark would succumb to Hitler's *Blitzkrieg* within hours, while Norway put up a fierce resistance. But on 10 April, once the Nazis captured Oslo and four key seaports, Major Vidkun Quisling declared his pro-Nazi government in the capital, while King Haakon and his cabinet set up a resistance movement in the northern mountains.

ER's scenic drive through the high country contrasted with brutal international events: in this world of "emerald green, merging into a deep purple and blue," across the snow-covered range, the beauty of nature fortified "the soul against the ugliness of much that is going on in the world today."

ER wrote FDR to commiserate over the news from Europe: "It is all horrible & goes deep in our theories of civilization for if this is done then only force counts, & our concepts that right & wrong had to be considered all go by the board." No longer in her peevish March mood, she concluded, "Much love & try to take some rest & relaxation even in this crisis!" She may have felt apologetic, since FDR's fever and flu had lasted for over three weeks—and his lingering discomfort worried her.

For the final phase of her lecture tour, she and Tommy enjoyed the leisure of a cross-country train. One afternoon ER was amused to read *Time* magazine's mockery of her upcoming radio series. Midafternoon, each Tuesday and Thursday for many weeks, "Sweetheart Toilet Soap" would present ER "over NBC's Network." ER, "in her seventh paid radio job," noted *Time*, "will broadcast for a soap company." For each fifteen-minute broadcast, she would reportedly receive "her standard rate: $3000." Since 1932, according to *Time*, ER had received that fee from Simmons (Beautyrest) mattresses, Johns-Manville building materials, Selby shoes, and Pond's cold cream, among others. "An indignant citizen" once protested that nobody was worth $500 a minute of airtime. ER agreed but pointed out that she gave most of it away, to taxes and the AFSC, which would also receive the net proceeds of her upcoming series.

In between her lectures as she proceeded east, ER read newspapers, wrote letters, drafted her address for the Southern Conference for Human Welfare (SCHW) meeting in Chattanooga, and gazed out the window. The comfortable train ride through such a beautiful place was a momentary balm—since nobody could "think of anything but the war news." Even when people made polite conversation, "you soon find out that it is the one thing they are thinking about. No wonder, for what is a world going to be like which is ruled entirely by force?"

In Battle Creek, Michigan, ER said the United States "must keep out of war, so that we may be the one torch of hope in the world. . . . When you go to war you cease to solve the problems of peace. This nation has a responsibility to go on to solve the world's problems."

Throughout this leg of the tour, ER fielded ignorant and rude questions about her husband's disability. Generally, their enemies continued to ask whether FDR's handicap affected his mental capacity. She always answered that the president's condition strengthened his concern for all people. While Hitler rampaged against "lives not worth living" and targeted infirm and handicapped men, women, and children for elimination, ER was met at stations all across the country by groups of handicapped children.

At Joplin, Missouri, for instance, a "group from the crippled children's school" greeted her train. They were accompanied by railroad officials who cared "for these youngsters" and were taking them "for treatment to Kansas City and St. Louis."

In Kansas City, ER met a young girl who had been a patient at Warm Springs. "She is very much upset," the first lady reported, "because she has not been able to find a college within her means where it would be possible for a crippled youngster on crutches to . . . get the proper assistance." The solution is not to establish "a special college for crippled children" but rather to install useful facilities in all "state universities, so that handicapped young people may obtain college educations at the least possible expense in normal surroundings."

As her train turned southward, ER looked forward to spending time at the SCHW conference with activists who shared her sense of urgency about racial justice and democracy's future. She was particularly eager to resume her conversations with her ally Dr. Will Alexander. A Methodist minister and southern race radical disturbed by the resurgence of the Ku Klux Klan after World War I, Alexander had founded, with other white southern liberals, the Commission on Interracial Cooperation (CIC) to oppose lynching and race violence. During the 1920s and 1930s the Atlanta-based CIC was the only interracial grassroots coalition across the old Confederacy. It grew and flourished—but so did the Ku Klux Klan.

During the 1930s, as chair of the Farm Security Administration, Alexander had been ER's primary adviser and supporter on the Arthurdale project. His work and vision continued to inform and fortify her efforts. Now ER was delighted that the SCHW was to honor him with the Thomas Jefferson Award for Vision, Service, and Leadership.

In Chattanooga on 15 April, ER joined her many activist friends and allies who worked to move America forward. Unlike the 1938 meeting in Birmingham, where Sheriff Bull Connor had insisted on segregated seating, these proceedings took place in a largely calm and fully integrated environment. Among the delegates were iconic leaders of the twentieth-century civil rights movement: Frank Porter Graham, Virginia Durr, Mary McLeod Bethune, Lillian Smith, Joseph Gelders, Maury Maverick, Lucy Randolph Mason, Clark Foreman, Walter White, and Judge Louise Charlton. ER was close to them and also to Myles Horton and James Dombrowski, who ran the Highlander Folk School in

Monteagle, Tennessee, which ER supported and the Dies Committee attacked; and southern youth leaders Helen Fuller and Howard Lee, who now served as SCHW chair. Howard Lee denied that he was a Communist, but ER no longer trusted him completely. Still, she believed it was important to continue to fight together on urgent issues for youth, for the South, and for America. She did trust Frank Graham, president of the University of North Carolina, who had assured her that she would be surrounded by friends and there would be no "untoward happenings," and thanked her for supporting the SCHW "personally, financially, and spiritually."

ER spoke on a panel, "The Children of the South," with Georgia educator Horace Mann Bond and executive director of the National Negro Congress John P. Davis. She also presented a keynote address, calling for federal aid to education, so that every child in every region would be guaranteed "an equal opportunity" to develop all their talents for the best interests of the nation. Education must become a national responsibility, "if we care anything at all about democracy."

For three days the delegates met in harmony. There were no agitators or divisive upheavals. But one moment of tension arose when a delegate introduced a resolution to condemn "Communist aggression in Europe." A bitter debate ensued, but Frank Graham saved the day with a substitute resolution to condemn "the violation of human rights and democratic liberties . . . by all Fascist, Nazi, Communist, and Imperialist powers alike." Graham's resolution "was overwhelmingly approved."

ER attended a panel on "The Industrial South" with Judge Louise Charlton, who spoke about the important advances, in both industry and agriculture, made possible by the Tennessee Valley Authority (TVA). Indeed, the rural electrification project had improved the lives of all people in the region. Despite difficulties faced by organized labor in the South, rural residents now had refrigerators, electric lights, flush toilets, and more. Meanwhile, ER noted in her column, the utility companies had benefited with a mighty "rise in net profits."

ER returned to Washington energized and active. She conveyed to the Justice Department a message from Judge Charlton concerning violations of civil liberties and union rights in Alabama and Tennessee, which she hoped Attorney General Robert Jackson would investigate. She sent a sizable check to the Highlander Folk School in Tennessee, which she considered a splendid training center for labor leaders and southern activists. Since the Dies Committee had attacked the school's leaders, her friends Horton and Dumbrowski, as Communists, she intended to show her support publicly.

Her tour had crystallized her main theme: Americans must remain free to speak with, disagree with, and know one another. While on tour, she had revised and edited a long article for *Liberty* magazine, "Why I Still Believe in the Youth Congress," which appeared on 20 April, the day she returned to the White House. Her defense of the AYC dismayed many of her friends, but it was what she believed most profoundly. Because the millions of unemployed young people in the United States represented half of those out of work, she stressed, the government had a responsibility regarding job training and new jobs. It was good that youth congresses and other forums existed where younger citizens could share their experiences, air their grievances, and seek guidance.

Regrettably, members of the AYC had exhibited "bad manners" on the White House lawn in February, but "it was raining and it was cold." Four to five million young people out of work and suffering were "good material for Communists," she wrote. "Of course we have Communists in this country, and of course they appeal to youth. The Communist Party leaders are giving youth training. . . . They are giving them a feeling that they are important in the world." She warned of the dangers of ostracism and appealed for understanding, respect, and cooperation across the generations. "We have gone about obtaining this cooperation most stupidly. . . . We certainly cannot help [youth-led organizations] by attacking them, or by refusing to cooperate when we are asked for financial assistance or for speakers to attend their meetings. . . . We must go and deal with them as equals, and we must have both courage and integrity if we expect respect and cooperation."

ER's ability to express such controversial positions depended largely on her husband's consent. In areas where he asked her to be silent, she was silent. In others, he trusted her understanding and political efforts. Her defense of the AYC, despite its radical elements, appeared to be an example of the latter.

She was rarely entirely silent, and her newspaper column provided her

with a large audience for many of her ideas and beliefs, some of which
FDR's government rejected and key members of the Senate vehemently
opposed. ER knew her boundaries, since she knew FDR so well. But she
pushed against those boundaries as hard as she could, never actively going
against her husband but making her case as vociferously as possible.

In the first *My Day* column written upon her return, ER expressed her
gratification at FDR's welcome: "It is nice to be home again! From the
cheerful sound of my husband's voice when he greeted me, the pleasant
smile on everybody's face, I enjoyed the happy feeling of welcome." She
concluded with a moment of reflection about "the pleasure of a dinner at
home with a talk about all the happenings of the world. I think this is one
of the things I miss most when I am away, the evening opportunity of
discussing with the President the events of the day."

The war in Europe remained "disheartening in the extreme." A letter
from her uncle David Gray, posted from Dublin on 16 April, was
alarming:

> The news from Norway and Denmark has shocked people here in a
> way hardly realizable to you at home. The unexpressed feeling is that
> if the British fleet goes we [in Ireland] are next. Thoughtful people
> feel that if that fleet goes, European civilization goes with it. A wave
> of barbarism will spread over the continent. . . . There is great grati-
> tude to the President for his clear thinking and courageous speaking
> on this question. But they wonder what he can do about the peace, if
> England is beaten. It will be, they say, a German peace and the US
> will have to prepare alone for the great struggle for existence that
> must ensue.

Uncle David's letter compounded ER's distress regarding Nazi barbarism.
For several months she had received almost daily letters of vivid detail,
including an appeal from a group of Polish women who had escaped to
Paris:

> In the very heart of Europe, Poland has become a great prison, a
> place of torture. Polish mothers implore American women to help us.
> Germans kill our children and mishandle our women. Our beautiful
> capital is ruined; its defenders starve in German prisons. Our houses
> are demolished, our families ruthlessly ejected from their home. We

ask the women of the U.S., with whom we worked for principles of civilization and culture. Help us in the name of liberty and common ideals.

ER's immediate response continued to be endless work. She could not sleep at night, could do nothing really to relieve the Hitlerian horrors. But she would work every day for a bolder, better America. The United States, she was convinced, needed to step up its own defenses, which she defined broadly to include decent jobs, education, and housing. Efforts to stifle dissent, outlaw free speech, and criminalize Communism not only would be counterproductive but would also lead to the erosion of "our basic liberties." In the United States as in France, the Nazi-Soviet Pact had resulted not in an effort to stifle fascism but rather in a drive against Communists and labor unionists. The Quislings, the traitors who devoured from within, had shown American constitutional precepts to be fragile. Many other countries, "in their fear of ideas, of people and of groups, resorted to restrictive measures which resulted in the loss of liberty for all." She cautioned the press and the public to beware "of the jitters."

Subsequently, she expanded on that theme. Before Americans demanded new laws to limit freedom, we should review how our "regularly constituted government agencies" functioned. It was to the courts that government agents must bring "any accused person and present proof of guilt. This necessity of proving any suspicions should never be relaxed for a minute, because if we once begin to neglect any of our carefully built-up protections, we are leaning toward the solution arrived at by dictatorships to protect the dictator and not the public. Here, in the United States, we are interested in protecting the public."

ER's whirlwind of Washington activity exhausted Tommy and surprised even the first lady. She met with social workers, with the prison reformer Dr. Miriam Van Waters, and with unemployment and worker activists who complained that there was no labor department in the District, where occupational diseases were rampant and industrial safety measures were "sadly needed." ER agreed to put the issue on her national agenda.* At a luncheon "with the ladies of the 75th Congress," she

---

*The Occupational Safety and Health Administration (OSHA) was not founded within the Department of Labor until 28 April 1971. .

emphasized the need for more education and funding to stamp out venereal disease. Congressional funding was "still inadequate," although the
public health battle for the treatment and prevention of venereal disease
was a priority.

One afternoon ER consulted a speech teacher to improve the place-
ment of her voice during public lectures. The teacher "believes she can tell
a great deal about a person's make-up from the voice and she proceeded
to tell me that I was extremely nervous and excitable. This shows, I am
afraid, that my voice is not well coordinated with the rest of my body and
character, for I think that everyone around me will bear witness to the
fact that I am neither excitable nor nervous!" ER was insulted not to be
seen as calm and steady or alternatively, if her voice did betray her innermost feelings, as intense and passionate. However calm and steady, ER
acknowledged that she had been living life so rapidly, she had "forgotten
to mention the riot of daffodils" and magnolia trees in spectacular blos-
som throughout the White House gardens.

Within the next few days, ER commuted between Washington, New
York, and Hyde Park, amid rain and even snow, for dinners and meetings. Every hour was filled with urgent issues. Still, she had moments of
relaxation and joy. The New York Metropolitan Opera Guild was having
a fundraising drive, leading her to observe that "if you have enjoyed [the
opera] radio broadcasts as I have, you will perhaps feel as I do that . . .
everybody in the country has a stake" in their continuance. Now, "when
it is so hard to think of things which draw us together instead of splitting
us apart, music and art" are vital to our well-being and represent "a world
interest." She was also glad to be of use to Dr. John Rothstein, director of
London's Tate Gallery, who toured Canada and the United States to find
safe places for great works of art. Tommy wrote Esther:

Such a week as we have put in! Even Mrs. R said she was ashamed
to tell anyone about all the things she did because it seemed so ridiculous to have planned so much for one short week. She spent her
time dashing from one thing to another and going back and
forth. . . . [And] all the people who had existed somehow while she
was away, were panting for appointments—the Aubrey Williams
type, plus the women of the Democratic National Committee!

Then ER left for the southern phase of her speaking tour. She spoke in Miami and then visited the Everglades "to see some of the Farm Security work." Not yet a national park, the Everglades were "miles and miles of flat, rich soil, beginning with muck" from one to six feet deep. "This is probably the biggest acreage of undeveloped farm land we have left" in the United States. Its "fields of beans, celery, tomatoes, cabbage and sugar cane" covered more than 100,000 acres. But with absentee landowners and a mix of tenant farmers and farmworkers housed in tiny shacks jammed close together, the conditions were "deplorable." ER hoped that the "new Farm Security Camps being established for both white and colored labor will set a new standard of decency" for employers to follow.

From Florida, ER journeyed by train to the Carolinas for more lectures and visits to NYA and WPA camps and projects, which she championed but which faced congressional budget cuts. The decision to cut off truly needy WPA workers from all support bewildered her. Unemployment, mounting hardships, and familial crises were spiraling out of control. "What is going to happen to them?" she angrily asked her readers, referring to the hungry and afflicted. "How would you meet their situation?"

On 1 May 1940, the *Nation* magazine honored her with its "first annual award for distinguished service in the cause of American social progress." More than a thousand political leaders and professional luminaries gathered at New York's Hotel Astor for the magazine's seventy-fifth anniversary dinner.

William Allen White, who now ran a committee to keep the United States out of war by aiding the Allies, gave a witty speech about partisan confusions, then turned to ER and said, "My dear, I don't care if he runs for the third or fourth term as long as he lets you run the bases, keep score and win the game." Frank Kingdon, who worked with ER on international aid and refugee issues, said she had "a remarkable revenge upon the Presidency since the time when another President Roosevelt stole the show on her wedding day. . . . She has demonstrated that while the Presidency could overshadow the bride it has not been able to eclipse the woman. Few will dispute the statement that today she is the most widely beloved person in our whole national life."

When Freda Kirchwey presented the award, ER used her acceptance speech to emphasize the responsibility of every individual to make "democracy a reality to more people." The stories of refugees, she said, had shocked her to a new level of recognition about our task: it is not for ourselves but "for all people" that we must fight to create a "life worth living." We now fight to keep a flame of "hope for the rest of the world," and we must work so that in some future time, we may be able "to offer" that hope. As for the *Nation*, it "has stood for freedom of thought and expression, and has often voiced the defense of ideas which could have had a hearing nowhere else."

To be recognized by people she admired, and by a journal she respected, which routinely called her "The First Lady of American Liberalism," was important to ER when she was under increasingly shrill attack.

That May she was in Washington at the National Institute of Government conference sponsored by the Women's Division of the Democratic National Committee. Her old allies surrounded her, including Molly Dewson, Dorothy McAllister, Josephine Roche, May Evans, Helen Gahagan Douglas, and Lorena Hickok. Hick, Dewson, and Douglas were her houseguests. The meeting, which also included representatives of the NAACP, Young Democrats, and other groups, heralded what was yet to come.

In March, ER had told her husband to be prepared for a gathering of one hundred women, eager to meet with him, with legislators, and with their Democratic allies. Now five thousand women converged for what *Time* called the dream program of "solid, tweedy, 65-year old Mary Williams (Molly) Dewson, ex-director of the Women's Division of the Democratic National Committee." At a lawn party at the White House, the large crowd of delegates surged so vigorously toward the first lady to greet her that their enthusiasm "tore a ribbon from her hat."

The National Institute was a stirring, stimulating event. In part a tribute to Dewson, its key visionary, the event was unusually integrated. Many states sent biracial delegations, and Bethune chaired "a committee of Negro women who will welcome to Washington the Colored Delegates." At all luncheons and dinners, "the delegations were seated by states and included the Colored Women." Careful planning resulted in a harmonious event, with nobody insulted or excluded.

ER had a grand time, and the event did much to ready policy for the

party's 1940 election platform. In the final session, the delegates named
peace and jobs as their priorities. When ER took the podium, she cautioned the women to consider their resolutions carefully. "What will keep
peace, what will serve the cause of more permanent peace?" Merely to
"have peace tomorrow as we had it in 1918 will simply mean again a
pause in preparation for another war." Without economic security for
everyone in every nation, more world trade, and "international law and
order," peace would remain an ideal far from reality.

She suggested a three-point platform: peace, jobs, and health. Peace
was "a beautiful idea," to be vigorously "worked for." Unemployment was
a scourge that had to end, one that required the cooperation of business
leaders and government. Public health was essential, as people suffered
and died for lack of "a better health program . . . which shall be of value
both to the medical profession and the people who at present are deprived
of medical care."

The National Institute demonstrated ER's conviction that change
with respect and justice was possible. America's official policies took no
account of racial injustice, brutality toward the disenfranchised, and
economic disparity, therefore she increasingly publicized the SCHW's
campaign to end the poll tax, an unjust tax levy that systematically disenfranchised black, poor, and women voters. In the South, she reminded
her readers, only one-third of the electorate voted.

In a Q&A column in the *Democratic Digest*, she featured her friend
Virginia Durr's question from Birmingham, Alabama: "Do you think the
poll tax prevents the working of democracy?" ER replied, "I think the
poll tax anywhere is apt to discourage participation in government of
men and women with small means and when any of our citizens do not
fulfill their obligations by voting, they are apt to neglect their obligation
to study candidates and policies. . . . This is very serious because it puts
the government of the country in the hands of a few instead of the hands
of the people as a whole."

Often now in her daily column she referred to racial issues. "I would
like to tell you about Karamu House in Cleveland, Ohio, founded 25
years ago by Russell and Rowena Jelliffe. . . . Their objective is to further
'the more complete functioning of the American Negro in the democratic
life of the community and the nation [particularly] through the field of
the arts.'" Karamu House included "the most outstanding Negro little

theatre in the country," having produced over 160 plays. The work of its artists and craftsmen was widely seen in museums and galleries.

On 7 May, Hitler issued an ultimatum to the Netherlands and Belgium that caused FDR's cabinet to expect war within hours. "One cannot help but have an anxious feeling about Holland," ER wrote in her column:

> Last evening, at our table, there was much talk of old wars and new wars, history already written and history in the waiting. When all is said and done, and statesmen discuss the future . . . the fact remains that the people fight these wars. I wonder that the time does not come, when young men facing each other with intent to kill, do not suddenly think of their homes and loved ones and, realizing that those on the other side must have the same thoughts, throw away their weapons of mass murder.

In Britain, members of Parliament were demanding that Neville Chamberlain resign as prime minister. Why had England failed to bomb known German munitions plants in the Ruhr and the Schwarzwald? they asked. The call went up: *Go! Go! Go!* On 7 May one of Chamberlain's closest friends, Leo Amery, a staunch Conservative ally for over twenty years, delivered a "terrific attack," which he concluded by quoting Oliver Cromwell's 1653 words to the Long Parliament: "You have sat too long for any good you have been doing. Depart, I say, and let us have done with you. In the name of God, go!" That evening Chamberlain announced his resignation. An all-party unity government was formed, led by Winston Churchill, who was now both prime minister and minister of defense.

On 8 May, the Nazi invasion imminent, FDR reiterated his offer of refuge for the royal families of Belgium, the Netherlands, and Luxembourg. At dawn on Friday, 10 May, the Nazis bombed airfields in Belgium, Holland, Luxembourg, and France. They quickly occupied Luxembourg, and German forces parachuted into the Netherlands: Rotterdam, Leiden, and The Hague. They bombed Brussels and the nearby French city of Nancy. In Norway, Britain continued to hold Narvik, and the Royal Navy sank eight German destroyers, but it was no match for Nazi air power.

ER, while driving to the Choate School to address an assembly, listened on the radio as news of the Nazi invasions of Holland and Belgium was broadcast, with rumors of bombings of Lyons, Orleans, even Paris and towns in Switzerland. At noon she faced the young Choate boys in the chapel and wondered somberly about, "All these young things, knowing so little of life and so little of what the future might hold!" Youth faced a "cruel world," filled with uncertainty and terror.

"Altogether," ER wrote, "my mail these days is pretty heartrending." In her column, she gave examples of the many urgent requests she received. A family of Ukrainian-Americans could neither find nor reach refugees from "what was once their country." Hyde Park neighbors sought information "about their closest relatives in Norway, from whom they heard nothing since the war engulfed their country."

In early May ER had suggested to FDR that British, French, and Dutch Guiana be developed as havens for refugees. FDR replied that the climate and topography of these South American colonies were "so vile that it would cost huge sums to make life there inhabitable for white people." He was willing to study some kind of "Pan American trusteeship" in the "remote possibility that the American Republics may be forced to do something about European possession in this Hemisphere. I think it is best not to discuss this out loud, however."

ER longed to do "something worthwhile," she wrote to Hick on 11 May, and particularly hoped to travel to war-ravaged cities to work with refugees. She had spoken to FDR about her wish and scheduled a meeting with Red Cross director Norman Davis for the next day. She and Davis joined the president for lunch aboard the *Potomac*. FDR, the first lady noted in her column, wanted to discuss the Red Cross's nationwide appeal to "alleviate human suffering . . . throughout the world." She hoped every American would respond "to the extent of their ability."

She continued to seek out like-minded individuals and gather them around her. Her friendship with Lash intensified at this time in part because he and his friends supported the victims of Nazi atrocities, organized rescue missions for refugees, and defended civil liberties in wartime. As the situation in Europe worsened, Lash and his circle became increasingly important to her.

In mid-May, Frank Kingdon's Save the Children Federation received a radiogram to help 200,000 Belgian and Dutch refugee children find homes in France and Britain. ER was a sponsor of Kingdon's International Child Service Committee and also a vice president of the Non-Sectarian Foundation for Refugee Children, which had sought since 1938 to find shelter in American homes. Now a reported five million refugees from Belgium, Holland, and Luxembourg were on the roads into France.

ER also worked closely on refugee matters with writer Dorothy Canfield Fisher, who had founded the Children's Crusade for Children, which asked schoolchildren to collect pennies for children in China, Poland, Spain, Czechoslovakia, Finland, and Norway. By May 1940 there were Children's Crusade drives in 250,000 U.S. schools. According to *Time*, 150 "moppets" in the Bronx Orphanage for Colored Children contributed a penny for each year of their age, from five to sixteen. ER agreed to chair the Children's Crusade, and FDR said, "Every child in America ought to feel vividly the suffering and loneliness experienced by the children who are victims of racial and religious intolerance."

While there was much dismay, there were also rays of hope. She had received a book of poetry by H. Nelson Hooven, called *The Laughing One*. One poem pleased her, and she wondered if her readers would agree that the poet was correct: "Darkness is only a shadow on the ground. / Behind us lie the things we have fashioned. / Before us, ever, an invitation to beauty."

Chapter Eleven

"If Democracy Is to Survive, It Must Be Because It Meets the Needs of the People"

On 13 May, Winston Churchill addressed Parliament to announce the policy of his new government: "I have nothing to offer but blood, toil, tears and sweat." Our intention "is to wage war, by sea, land and air, with all our might and with all the strength that God can give us; to wage war against a monstrous tyranny, never surpassed in the dark, lamentable catalogue of human crime."

The next day Hitler ordered a massive bombing of Rotterdam to break Holland's unexpected resistance. The Luftwaffe dropped thousands of 2,200-pound bombs on the Dutch seaport, gutted the city center, destroyed bridges, and rendered eighty thousand people homeless. As civilian deaths mounted, the carnage and destruction were compared to that of Guernica and Madrid in the Spanish Civil War.

On 15 May, as Nazi forces continued to smash through Belgium and Holland, ER spoke at City College, New York's first free public university, founded in 1847. She invited Joe Lash to accompany her, since it was his alma mater. "It must be a most exhilarating thing to teach in a college of this kind," she wrote, pleased by her enthusiastic and diverse audience. "One of the faculty told me that there never was any dearth of conversation. I can well imagine that, for I am sure that every type of thinking is present because every type of background is there."

As she left the campus, a group of students at the gates shouted at her, "The Yanks are not coming!" Mystified by their ignorance of world danger, she replied, "But what if the Nazis are?" In her column, she noted, "My heart sank. Poor youngsters, they have the same desire we all have to live in a civilized world and yet are obliged to face, as we all must, the impact of [those determined] to wipe out what we have called civilization."

Churchill, in his first telegram to FDR as prime minister, explained, "The small countries are simply smashed up, one by one, like matchwood." Britain fully expected "to be attacked . . . in the near future," he said, not only by Germany but by Italy, as Mussolini was eager "to share the loot of civilization." For its very survival, he said, Britain needed "40 or 50 of your older destroyers . . . several hundred of the latest type of aircraft . . . anti-aircraft equipment and ammunition . . . [iron] ore and steel." Finally, he noted, "I am looking to you to keep that Japanese dog quiet in the Pacific, using Singapore in any way convenient."

By the time FDR cabled his reply, the Netherlands had surrendered to the Nazis. The president advised Churchill that destroyers were impossible because a loan or gift would require congressional authorization. However, he was making every effort to speed up production of the latest aircraft and other military essentials. Regarding Japan, the U.S. fleet would remain "concentrated" in Hawaii "for the time being."

On 16 May, FDR addressed a joint session of Congress to describe the crisis and detail the needs of the nation and the Allies. He requested appropriations to increase production of new aircraft from six thousand to fifty thousand a year. All military equipment for land, sea, and air would be upgraded and modernized. Harold Ickes and other liberals in his cabinet worried about war profiteering, and the return of corporate greed and control to American political life, but the enthusiastic congressional reception to FDR's speech came as a relief. The president's "magnificent" address, Ickes said, "had the finest reception" from the bitterly divided Congress in "five or six years."

ER, proud of her husband's vigorous presentation, fully supported his purpose. She had spent the day at the Madeira School in Virginia, where the girls asked "far more personal questions" than had the boys at Choate. But the questions all reflected the issue "in all our minds today, namely, personal responsibility in a democracy." Americans who read the news must realize "this is a crucial moment for the world." The president's request for "a great increase in our national defenses" was vital to America's survival.

Still, for ER, national defense went beyond modern weapons: America's future depended on fortified and expanded New Deal efforts. "If democracy is to survive," she wrote, "it must be because it meets the needs of the people." So long as so many people live in poverty and distress, the survival of one form of government is "immaterial." For the survival of democracy, "we need a united front regarding economic betterment, as well as the more tangible front of creating war materials. It requires greater cooperation and it will require greater self-sacrifice really to make democracy something for which every citizen will feel" ready to fight, and to die for—the survival of "economic as well as intellectual freedom."

Urging Congress to authorize the defense funds the president sought, she argued that "a nation of healthy, strong, well-fed people who are decently sheltered, clothed and educated" would strengthen the national defense. Surgeon General Thomas Parran had said America's health system should be considered "part of our national defense." Unless they had good health care, Americans could not possess the necessary "toughness of moral and physical fibre." After all, "the one-third of the nation, ill-fed, ill-housed and ill-clothed, is the most fertile ground for the seeds of dissension strewn so ably today by some of the world's enemies." Those denied "the decencies of life may be as serious a menace as a foreign invasion."

ER's ongoing commitment to work across political differences in "united front" efforts set her apart from many New Deal liberals. Youth's dissent, its interest in socialism and Communism, did not disturb her as much as the growth of "Gestapo methods," alarmist calls for mass firings, roundups of "aliens" and refugees, renewed efforts at censorship and conformity, and threats to civil liberties and dissent. Indeed, she was among the last to accept the bitter reality that the Nazi-Soviet Pact had destroyed progressive alliances for education, racial justice, housing, health, and human betterment. Convinced that the pact could not possibly serve the Soviet Union and could not possibly last, she could not believe that her young friends refused to acknowledge that Nazism had to be resisted and military preparedness was essential. Americans were "facing a sinister power with no scruples," she told a Washington church meeting on unemployment and relief. "Every time we are not united, every time word goes back to Germany that we do not mean what we say, we are nailing one more nail in our coffin," for Germany has contempt "for diplomacy, and unresolve."

She was vigorous in support of her husband's emergency defense program, devoting two columns that week to his speech. Yes, many protests and petitions from youth groups demanded jobs, "not wars for death." But "one cannot live in a Utopia which prays for different conditions and ignores those which exist."

While U.S. factories increased military production, and planes and matériel were designated for England and France, Europe continued to crumble town by town under Hitler's rolling tanks and relentless aerial bombardments. On 20 May German forces were triumphant on the Channel coast, capturing critical ports. Panic spread throughout France, Belgium, and Luxembourg. An estimated five million families fled the besieged areas with whatever they could carry on their backs, in their cars and trucks, or atop their wagons.

From Paris, Ambassador William Bullitt cabled FDR, asking him to get Congress to vote $20 million "for the succor of these refugees." It was urgent; people were dying every hour of neglect. They needed bandages and iodine, wounds were open, children were crying. For many days, Bullitt cabled in a frenzy: please send help immediately.

The Nazis took Boulogne and Calais by 26 May. Rumors spread that England was to be attacked; Kent and Sussex evacuated. In France, Paul Reynaud's government rounded up Communists; the vigorous group of French appeasers spread wild rumors about a Communist takeover of Paris. The propertied classes had long preferred Hitler to their own social-ist "popular front" governments and had previously rallied against "the Jew Prime Minister" Léon Blum with cries of "Better Hitler than Blum"; now they suspected a "compromise peace" with Nazi Germany would be preferable to a new Bolshevik menace. At the U.S. embassy, Robert Mur-phy and Ambassador Bullitt agreed and blamed all France's troubles on the Communists.

On 26 May, in a major radio address that went far beyond a Fireside Chat, FDR transported millions of Americans to the battlefields and vil-lages of a hurt and wounded, utterly transformed reality. "My friends . . . Tonight over the once peaceful roads of Belgium and France millions are now moving, running from their homes to escape bombs and shells and fire and machine gunning, without shelter, and almost wholly without food. They stumble on, knowing not where the end of the road will be." Every American family listening could help. The American Red Cross stood ready to rush food, clothing, and medical supplies to "these desti-tute civilian millions. Please—I beg you—please give according to your means to your nearest Red Cross chapter. . . . I ask this in the name of our common humanity. . . .

"Together . . . you and I," he continued, must "consider our own pressing problems. . . . There are many among us who in the past closed their eyes . . . to events abroad." Some believed events in Europe were "none of our business." Others believed the "many hundreds of miles of salt water made the American Hemisphere so remote" that we might continue undisturbed "in the midst of [our] vast resources without reference to, or danger from, the other continents of the world." But all those who have "closed their eyes" or turned away from the "approaching storm" for whatever reason have now been awakened by the shattering events of the past two weeks. "I did not share those illusions," FDR reassured his listeners. "I do not share these fears."

Let us calmly consider all that has been done, he said, and what needs to be done. The United States now has "the largest, the best-equipped, and the best-trained peacetime military establishment in the whole history of this country." From 1933 to 1940 the country spent almost $1.5 billion on the navy and had 215 new ships, including twelve cruisers, sixty-three destroyers, twenty-six submarines, three aircraft carriers, eight new battleships, and many more smaller craft. Modern aircraft, almost six thousand "long-range bombers and fast pursuit planes," had been purchased; thousands of modern anti-aircraft guns, armored cars, and heavier tanks had been built. "Within the past year the productive capacity of the aviation industry . . . has been tremendously increased." Congress and the chief executive, the military and industry, are ready to

> work in harmony, as a team. . . . I will not hesitate to ask for additional funds when they are required. In this era of swift, mechanized warfare, . . . what is modern today and up-to-date, what is efficient and practical, becomes obsolete and outworn tomorrow. . . . We are constantly improving and redesigning, testing new weapons. . . . The government of the United States itself manufactures few of the implements of war. Private industry will continue to be the source of this matériel; and private industry will have to be speeded up to produce it at the rate and efficiency called for by the needs of the times.

But the required expansion of factories and additional personnel was beyond the scope of most private businesses.

> Therefore, the government of the United States stands ready to advance the necessary money for . . . new plants, the employment of thousands of necessary workers, the development of new sources of supply for the hundreds of raw materials required. . . . We are calling

on men now engaged in private industry to help us. . . . Patriotic Americans of proven merit, of unquestioned ability in their special fields, are coming to Washington to help.

There was to be no profiteering, price gouging, or new military-industrial pyramids by opportunists or fiscal tricksters. "No new group of war millionaires shall come into being in this nation as a result of the struggles abroad. The American people will not relish the idea of any American citizen growing rich and fat in an emergency of blood and slaughter and human suffering." It was crucial to sustain "the spirit and morale of a free people." There would "be no breakdown or cancellation of any of the great social gains which we have made. . . . We have carried on an offensive on a broad front against social and economic inequalities, against abuses which had made our society weak."

Those gains, FDR now pledged, would continue—and expand. He foresaw a situation where those presently unemployed would find employment. He promised that minimum wages would not be reduced, nor would old-age pensions or unemployment insurance be affected. He pledged to continue conservation of natural resources and consumer protection programs.

Another challenge to American security, he said, was saboteurs, spies, traitors, Trojan horses, and fifth columnists determined to betray, weaken, and disrupt the nation. They would be exposed and "vigorously" handled. Groups dedicated to racial, political, or sectional discord, who sowed confusion and panic, would be disarmed. "Fortunately, American men and women are not easy dupes. Campaigns of group hatred or class struggle have never made much headway among us." But the fraudulent propagandists who spewed their "undiluted poison" among us could not "be allowed." Defeating these people required individual vigilance in every community, among every American, for the sake of our future, our survival.

This passage seemed to many, including ER, a nod to the "anti-alien" hostility to immigrants and refugees demanded by Martin Dies and his supporters. But FDR added a note of disapproval to their call to round up and deport all recent arrivals and noncitizens: "For more than three centuries we Americans have been building on this continent a free society, a society in which the promise of the human spirit may find fulfillment.

Commingled here are the blood and genius of all the peoples of the world. . . . We have built well," and now we must defend our creation—not only for ourselves but for the future. "Ours is a high duty, a noble task."

FDR ended his speech in prayer that all the "suffering and starving, death and destruction may end—and that peace may return to the world. In common affection for all mankind, your prayers join with mine—that God will heal the wounds and the hearts of humanity."

That Sunday ER was in New York to address the closing session of the New York Congress of the AYC at the Mecca Temple in Harlem. She told the delegates that their continued opposition to America's defense efforts was a "tragic mistake." "You don't want to go to war. . . . I don't want to go to war. But war may come to us." Moreover she found the slogan "The Yanks are not coming" to be insulting. It slurred the brave volunteers who "went overseas" to do "for the world what you think you are doing." The United States now faced a stark reality. The war would end with "a Nazi-dominated Europe or . . . with exhaustion of all nations involved, France and England worst of all. Whatever the outcome, the US will be affected seriously. . . . We tried to prevent this situation from arising, but now that it is here, we must admit it and do what is best."

The congress received her words politely, with applause and without boos. But the "temper of the delegates" was revealed by the wild cheers with which they greeted Mike Quill, head of the Transport Workers Union (TWU), who said, "The war in Europe is a war between two thieves," and New York congressman Vito Marcantonio, who had cast the sole vote in the House against FDR's defense appropriation. ER left before Marcantonio's remarks because, the *New York Times* reported, she "wanted to listen to the President's radio address."

That evening AYC leader Joseph Cadden told the Massachusetts chapter's congress that the war "served no democratic interests" and only engorged the real "fifth column"—led by "anti-unionists, the Associated Farmers, vigilantes and the Ku Klux Klan." Repeatedly, Cadden and other AYC leaders insisted that "we are not threatened by invasion and this is not a war for democracy."

Since the AYC's position seemed increasingly at odds with ER's, her closest friends wondered why she continued to speak at its meetings. Indeed, she had her own doubts about whether her ongoing involvement had any influence, and Joe Lash thought "her sensible words" no longer "convinced anyone" in that group. But she would not give up. It was her responsibility to teach and to try, especially when her husband rejected her entreaties to help refugees.

Her efforts to raise awareness aroused a storm of abuse in *Time*, which editorialized that she had "addressed the brattish assembly, with kindly reproof." Such "coddling" of the "Communist-saturated" AYC seemed "sentimental" and "extraordinary." But she ignored it all and continued to support her AYC friends—especially Cadden and his fiancée, Vivian Liebman. Indeed, she planned and hosted their June wedding reception— which Vivian remembered as the last "united front" party.

The news from Europe worsened daily. Hitler's triumphs across Europe were simply astonishing. It had taken only twenty-eight days for Poland to collapse in September 1939. When he mobilized after the "phony war," or *Sitzkrieg*, in April 1940, nations crumbled or succumbed within hours. Luxembourg was crushed in a day, the Netherlands in five. Calais fell on 26 May, cutting Britain off from the Continent.

On 28 May, Belgium's King Leopold, without consulting his government, "quit" the Allies and personally surrendered to the Nazis, shocking his nation. The Belgian government repudiated the king's decision, but it was already in exile in Paris, and the Belgian army, which had resisted relentless tank and plane bombardments for eighteen days, "no longer existed; it had been broken to pieces," in the words of historian Martin Gilbert. Entire towns and villages were destroyed, with countless civilian casualties. The king's decision stunned ER: "It seems incredible to hear of the surrender of the Belgian King. Yet, I suppose there comes a point where human endurance can bear up no longer. One more country is now officially under Nazi domination."

On every front German planes and tanks continued almost unimpeded. Between 27 May and 3 June, British, French, and other troops evacuated the blood-soaked beaches of Dunkirk, including Polish and Czech troops who had been eager to fight Hitler. "The miracle of

Dunkirk" was a cooperative cross-Channel success that involved naval vessels, passenger ships and destroyers, and every kind of civilian carrier—even private yachts and fishing boats. The great historian Marc Bloch was transported to Dover with sixteen hundred of his French compatriots aboard a ferry steamer wondrously named the *Royal Daffodil*, "which came from an Indian fairy tale."

But, as Churchill noted, an evacuation is not a victory. That tormented spring, Clare Boothe Luce, who witnessed the bombing of Belgium, was aghast at Europe's unpreparedness for Hitler's sweep through Western civilization.

As the battle for France intensified, Bullitt cabled FDR that the French had nothing to fight with "but their courage. In all forms of matériel they were now desperately outclassed." The president promised Prime Ministers Reynaud and Churchill that substantial American assistance was on the way. The British purchased matériel to replace equipment lost at Dunkirk. That week 105 U.S. Army and Navy planes were flown to Quebec, where they were immediately transferred to a French aircraft carrier.

A certainty of doom defined most White House conversations, and ER was gloomy. "What a life I have been leading!" she wrote to Anna on 17 May 1940. "It really isn't decent to work so hard but the civilized world is crumbling round one so it is well to be busy! . . . Pa is gloom personified about Europe. . . . Hitler says he will win in 7 days and Pa murmurs 30 days!" There were no conversations about peace goals, and no reason for discussion since "I don't think there will be anyone left in Europe by way of a government with whom to cooperate. Just the US & Hitler!"

In these weeks of torment, ER sought to arouse public opinion to the plight of dying Europe. On 26 May, in an impassioned radio address, she joined an all-star Red Cross gala to benefit war refugees. The stars broadcasting from New York and Hollywood included Jack Benny, Eddie Cantor, Bob Hope, Laurence Olivier and Vivien Leigh, Jimmy Durante, Gertrude Lawrence, Judy Garland, and Alfred Lunt and Lynn Fontanne. In her speech, ER described the unbearable impact of war on the devastated cities Hitler attacked. Millions of people were in flight, she said in an emotional call for aid: "Today there are more people suffering and homeless and in need of the care which only the Red Cross can give . . . than in any other period of recent history." She concluded, "If we turn away from the needs of others we align ourselves with those forces which are bringing about this suffering."

The next day her friend and ally Hamilton Fish Armstrong, the respected editor of *Foreign Affairs*, filed a dispatch in the *New York Times* from Paris. There was nothing to analyze, he wrote; there were only immediate needs for "Planes, Food, Medicine." Five million refugees were fleeing the Nazis, he estimated, and civilians were "flooding down across the country, making every crossroads, every village and every railway junction a station of misery." The Red Cross was doing what it could, but food, medicine, and blankets were desperately needed.

He appealed to the generosity of his countrymen. "If there is a single reserve American Army plane to be spared, it ought to be flown or shipped across the Atlantic tomorrow." And as American ships sailed to Europe to bring home Americans, he wanted those vessels packed with lifesaving supplies.

ER was profoundly moved by Armstrong's eloquence and resolved to assist in every way she could and also to help FDR focus on the humanitarian needs of the war and on the young, whose future seemed increasingly bleak.

In early June at the World's Fair in New York, she was surrounded by friends and in that celebratory atmosphere, felt hope for the future. She opened the Fashion Building, celebrating women's works and costumes. She dedicated the "People's Common," a new meeting square and band shell, pronouncing it a symbol of American respect and tolerance. It would feature international music, folk dances, pageantry: "the common," she said, was to celebrate the gifts "all people in this country had in common." After the first lady's dedication speech, young girls from the Hudson Guild Neighborhood House, representing more than forty nationalities, filed past her to shake her hand and drop flowers into a basket held by Tachawin Seymour, granddaughter of Chief Yellow Robe of the Sioux nation. ER was deeply moved by the ceremony of "little girls of all nationalities which make up our great country." Brilliantly costumed, nation by nation, they placed flowers in the basket of an Indian girl, "acknowledging thereby that she was the one whose race originally owned this country."

From the fair, ER returned to Manhattan to attend an exhibit of Persian art, which she urged her readers to see "at once." Every room was spectacular, filled with "an art which has survived through 6,000 years of invasion, war, tyranny, prosperity and power. Here is the real proof that the spirit as expressed through the arts transcends all material things. These priceless treasures from the Iranian civilization are gathered from collections all over . . . and may never again be seen by the public, so do not miss this opportunity."

Afterward ER met with a group who worked to find jobs for youth released from New York State reformatories. This pioneering reentry program, to help young boys "get a new start in life," was precisely the kind of project that guaranteed hope needed across the nation. ER ended her day with an "experience I shall never forget": she attended a play that dramatized the impact of the Soviet invasion of Finland. Robert Sherwood's *There Shall Be No Night*, starring Alfred Lunt and Lynn Fontanne, transported her "through every experience in that Finnish family's existence, which tragically enough, is now part of the life of so many other people."

The next day, with Tommy and Joe Lash, ER returned to the fair to celebrate the fortieth anniversary of the International Ladies' Garment Workers' Union. Senator Robert Wagner gave a speech to the crowd of 75,000 gathered in the Court of Peace, appealing to them to keep FDR's great leadership talents in office until "we have absolute assurances that *Mein Kampf* will never be rewritten to include American continents." But labor unionists had a responsibility as well, Wagner said. To face Hitler and the domestic "shock troops of reaction," workers must unite and "halt the war" between the AFL and the CIO.

ER praised Wagner's "grand speech." In her column, she expressed gratitude to labor leaders who had taught her so much:

> Some of us forget occasionally that this cooperation for the good of all of us is the basis of our strength. A meeting such as [this] reminds us how great is our power when we work together. Our citizens come from many lands where sacrifice and oppression and resistance are nothing new. They have met these conditions with determination through generations, and this generation will find strength to meet whatever comes to us. I get such a sense of power and solidarity from a meeting like yesterday's that I can face the uncertainty of the future with far more strength and courage.

This was a special day for her friendship with Joe Lash. Europe was never for her an abstraction, a remote or distant shore "over there." Much of her life, much of her heart, was built, shaped, healed, and restored by her experiences in Paris, London, Edinburgh, Rome, Venice, Florence, Berlin, and Vienna. That day at the fair, she confided to Joe the story of her childhood, and her endless inner struggle to feel secure, even worthy.

Germany, Austria, Italy, and France, she told him, were places where her beloved father, Elliott, had sought relief from his advanced alcoholism. He had gone from spa to spa, with his hopeful wife and sorrowful daughter, on an endless quest for a cure. Wherever they went, his daughter was tutored and spoke German and French quite fluently. In Paris in 1891, ER was sent to a convent school while her parents searched for a cure in Neuilly. But six-year-old Eleanor, sullen and rebellious, was expelled for tantrums and lies, disgracing her mother. That summer her father was left alone in Paris, institutionalized and isolated. Part of her heart remained always with him, in exile.

Forever hurt by her mother's cold disdain, Eleanor's spirits were uplifted by memories of happy days she had shared with her father. One enchanted day in Venice, on the beach at the Lido and on the canals, Elliott had acted as a gondolier and sung "with the other boatmen, to my intense joy." She loved her father's voice and "the way he treated me. He called me 'Little Nell' . . . and I never doubted that I stood first in his heart."

ER told Lash that her "very miserable childhood" determined her reaction to the many people who showered her with appreciation and love. Meanwhile everywhere they went, Joe noted, crowds surrounded her, hugged her, and took photographs with her, and she "responded to this loving acclaim with obvious warmth and affection." She "did not wish to disappoint and hurt people by not acknowledging their love," she told him, but also "drew strength, sustenance, and satisfaction from it even as she protested that it had nothing to do with her personally. In her childhood she had been given the feeling of being the unwanted, the ugly duckling." That feeling prevented her from ever believing she was really loved for herself. Yet "I wanted to be loved so badly," she told him, "and most of all I wanted to be loved by my father." Now, she never quite believed that the public "outpourings of affectionate homage were for

Eleanor Roosevelt, the person, rather than for Mrs. Franklin D. Roosevelt, the wife of the President."

ER told the story of her childhood to all her close friends, and Joe Lash was her newest best friend. Not only was she pleased to spend more time with him, but she increasingly trusted his vision, enjoyed his conversation, and looked forward to his surprising connections. Lash and his friend Agnes Reynolds would be her guests at the White House later in the week, when FDR was scheduled to meet with fifty youth leaders from across the country. In fact, the first lady invited him to spend as much time as he liked at the White House and at Hyde Park.

One reason for this invitation may have been the fact that Harry Hopkins had moved into the White House on 10 May 1940. After months of postsurgery recovery for stomach cancer, Hopkins had tried to return to work, collapsed, and could not return to his home. FDR, often lonely and always delighted by Hopkins's wit, invited him to stay—which made sense, since ER had virtually adopted his daughter, Diana.*

At first, ER imagined Hopkins would fill the role Louis Howe had once played and serve as a bridge between the first couple's frequently competing courts. After all, she had championed Hopkins's social justice activities and advanced his WPA efforts. They had once been close. But now he seemed more a turncoat than a friend. He was no longer interested in social reform and was critical of, even hostile to, her young friends. The issues that most engaged her now seemed of little or no importance to him. She distrusted him, disliked his new social friends, and deplored his lack of respect and consideration for such hardworking party leaders as Jim Farley. Moreover, as a key player in FDR's court, he rudely excluded her from most urgent conversations about the war. FDR, Hopkins, and Missy LeHand conferred behind closed doors, leaving ER on the outside. Hopkins's presence, unlike Howe's, unsettled the competing Roosevelt courts, and actually exacerbated tensions between the president and the first lady.

---

*When Hopkins's second wife, Barbara Duncan, died of cancer in 1937, Diana was not yet five. ER offered to be her guardian if Harry were to die, and she spent as much time as possible with the little girl. See Sherwood, *Roosevelt and Hopkins*, pp. 35–37, 106–7.

Upon her return to the capital from New York, ER was eager finally
to ride her new horse, Charley. She hosted a reception for the Daughters
of the Confederacy, had many meetings, and wrote a long letter to Anna:

> You are right that the world makes personal things seem unimport-
> ant. I think we must continue our normal lives, doing what we can as
> well as we can & preparing ourselves to face whatever the future
> holds. . . . Living here is very oppressive because Pa visualizes all the
> possibilities, as of course he must & you feel very impotent to help.
> What you think or feel seems of no use or value so I'd rather be away
> & let the important people make their plans & someday I suppose
> they will get around to telling us plain citizens if they want us to do
> anything. . . .
>
> Pa is working very hard, is worried and short-tempered but I
> think remarkably well all considered.
>
> I'm having a lot of young people (Youth Congress & other) to
> talk with Pa, Harry Hopkins & Sidney Hillman (CIO) so they will
> feel they have some share in knowledge of conditions & defense
> plans. They may not believe it is for defense but I think they should
> be given a chance to hear.

Despite ER's irritation about being excluded, her views were heeded more
than she knew. FDR had agreed to meet informally with a group of
young people on 5 June, and to prepare for it, she had a long conversation
with him about how young people might consider the future. They
wanted jobs and faced not only insecurity and unemployment but
discrimination. She worried about freedom of speech and freedom to protest. Why should young people rally to war? What was worth fighting
for? ER asked. And what would it take to end the scourge of war?

FDR was moved by his wife's questions. They kept him up much of
the night, he confided the next morning.

On 5 June, the president, the first lady, their son Elliott, and Harry
Hopkins greeted more than fifty young people who gathered in the State
Dining Room. According to Lash, FDR took every question they asked,
no matter how nasty. The questions focused largely on domestic issues,
civil liberties, "Negro" voting rights, cuts in New Deal programs, the
future of education, the WPA, and farmers. Some made speeches; others

chided him as a new reactionary who "no longer cared" about progressive causes.

FDR replied to each question with courtesy and interest. The State Dining Room "sparkled and danced with the President's replies," Lash recounted, impressed, but he wondered why the president bothered. He concluded that FDR liked young people and cared profoundly about their well-being. Like ER, the president was an educator who sought to persuade. It disturbed him that so many young people distrusted him and considered the New Deal over. It "grieved and worried" him that his call for fifty thousand planes and a policy of national defense had resulted in "an avalanche of telegrams," mostly oppositional, from young people.

The president explained that he was "conducting a two-front war—against Hitler and the dictators abroad and the reactionaries at home." He found the young people's dedication to "isolationism" mysterious. How could they fail to appreciate Europe's slaughter and suffering? How could they remain aloof from America's need to defend against "possible aggression"? He made it clear that he wanted their support.

He was fighting "the evils of appeasement," he explained, a pattern that had been long and wrong. The Japanese invasion of Manchuria in 1931 and the Italian invasion of Ethiopia in 1935 were two cases when the international community had rejected sanctions. It continued with Austria, Czechoslovakia, Poland—"anything to avoid a war." It had taken over a year for the Senate Foreign Relations Committee to acknowledge the dangers of the Neutrality Act. Even FDR's "most ardent champions," he said, had opposed his refusal to sell arms to Spain.

The young people stared at him, unmoved and mostly unimpressed.

He continued, "The Spanish War—where Congress acted not on the desire or policy of the administration, but because the League of Nations was afraid, afraid of war, a general European war."

The Communist students had been appalled by his inaction then but favored inaction now. ER might have winced at her husband's wobbly rhetoric. But no one said anything.

Unchallenged, FDR assured his audience that he had recited this "grim inventory" not "to assess blame" but to address the future. Young people faced a dreadful choice, and he was certain that if he were young himself, he would not care to live under Nazism or under Fascism. But the Allies would seek to create and ensure a world based on the Four Freedoms, "the indispensable pillars of peace—freedom of religion, freedom of speech, freedom from an arms race (that is disarmament), and freedom for commercial and cultural interchange."

For another two hours, he sought to impress his audience. They said he had failed to do enough about health, jobs, education, civil rights, and housing. The president agreed with their domestic concerns but countered that he could do only what Congress and U.S. public opinion allowed him to do. "Remember this always," he said: "85 per cent of the papers of the US are opposed to this administration—84 per cent because they regard the administration as being too damned radical, and 1 percent because . . . [it is] too conservative."

ER interjected that the young people failed to appreciate the need to build support for each issue, as well as the role played in a real democracy by public opinion. The president's efforts were limited by people who had very different priorities and interests "as represented by Congress."

After almost three hours, FDR explained that he had to leave for a telephone conference with Secretary of State Hull, and he called on Harry Hopkins to answer "any more questions you have in mind." It had been "a grand evening," and FDR was rolled out to a standing ovation.

Hopkins stressed that FDR had led the fight on progressive issues for seven years but understood the need for democratic support. ER interrupted to point out that FDR had been trying to persuade members of Congress for two years that urgent military defenses were needed. They had rejected his advice and laughed at his fears of impending war. Only now, after the Nazi assaults, did they "run to him" because the facts of world horror finally "have hit them in the face." It was the same thing with other issues: only when the comfortable were pressed by a movement for change would they agree actually to make change.

Harry Hopkins asked bluntly, "Don't you people ever want to go home?" ER, irritated, announced she had to leave to catch a train. Somebody thanked the first lady for "this opportunity," which she brushed aside. "The President was very much interested by you or he never would have stayed so long. You made your own opportunity."

Absorbed by the unfolding calamities of *Blitzkrieg* and destruction, ER feared the agonies of the war would create discontent and confusion.

"Every patriotic citizen is anxious to do something these days," she observed in her column. "It is desperately hard to wait in inactivity," she acknowledged, "when a battle costing thousands of human lives is going on across the sea and when things of great moment to the human race are hanging in the balance." Mix philosophical perspective and action, she advised. Every citizen must decide "where we stand and what we are willing to do for our own country and other countries. These decisions are always hard." She counseled: "Probably the best thing we can do is to go about our regular jobs, doing them as well as we can, improving them where we can, keeping as calm as possible and waiting until some definite plans are evolved where we can be of real value."

She took her own advice: she slept less and did more; she worked longer hours and took longer rides on her new horse. Mary McLeod Bethune, back at work in the National Youth Administration after eight weeks in the hospital, appealed to ER to consider "where the Negro people could function" best to help "the unfortunates in other countries" and take "a real part in national defense."

She visited a new craft center near Quantico, Virginia, with Elinor Morgenthau, where she saw splendid woven blankets and "some rather nice pieces of pottery." A woman who demonstrated her spinning wheel told ER "she had carded and spun thousands of pounds of wool," but since she "no longer had her own sheep the wool was not as good." That amused ER, "for it sounded like my mother-in-law, who believes that only when a thing is produced on her own farm is it really good."

ER and Tommy motored to Connecticut to visit Esther Lape and Elizabeth Read at Salt Meadow, then to Boston to visit Anne and John and to meet her newest grandson, "always an exciting experience." Her tenth grandchild, Haven Clark Roosevelt, had been named for his maternal grandfather.

On 10 June, ER returned to Washington to hear that in France "the only reality is dead and dying human beings." Overwhelming Nazi forces now surrounded France. The French argued about whether to fight or surrender, with Prime Minister Reynaud and Deputy Prime Minister Henri-Philippe Pétain on opposite sides.

Italy had declared war on France and Britain, which particularly upset both ER and FDR. The president had been working behind the scenes to try to prevent Mussolini from entering the war, but all the messages that U.S. ambassador William Phillips conveyed to Il Duce had been to no avail.

Italy's entrance into the war changed FDR's mood and strategies. The next day he was to give a commencement speech at the University of Virginia Law School, where their son Franklin Jr. was among the graduates. The speech would be resolutely anti-isolationist. Secretary of State Hull tried to persuade him to soften the tone, to omit a "stab in the back" reference to Italy. But ER agreed with FDR and approved of the speech—it represented both what he believed and what needed to be said. The first couple discussed it on the train to Charlottesville. "The times were fraught with promise of evil," ER later reflected. "Franklin's address was not just a commencement address; it was a speech to the nation on an event that had brought us one step nearer to total war." It was broadcast live at six o'clock nationwide.

Addressing the isolationists directly, FDR said it was a delusion to believe that the United States could be "a lone island in a world dominated by the philosophy of force. . . . Such an island represents to me and to the overwhelming majority of Americans today a helpless nightmare of a people without freedom, the nightmare of a people lodged in prison, handcuffed, hungry, and fed through the bars from day to day by the contemptuous, unpitying masters of other continents."

In ten paragraphs, he detailed earnest negotiations between Italy and the United States to keep the "hostilities now raging in Europe" from spreading. Mussolini's decision to fulfill his "promises to Germany" plunged Italy into "the suffering and devastation of war. . . . On this 10th day of June 1940, the hand that held the dagger has struck it into the back of its neighbor."

Stressing that U.S. material support abroad would be bolstered by a strengthening economy at home, he said, "We need not and we will not, in any way, abandon our continuing effort to make democracy work within our borders. We still insist on the need for vast improvements in our own social and economic life. But that is a component part of national defense itself." In conclusion, he called for "effort, courage, sacrifice, devotion. Granting the love of freedom, all of these are possible."

FDR's words were greeted by "the wildest applause, cheers and rebel yells." The faculty on the dais, the 497 graduates and their families,

"The First Lady of Radio": Listeners all over America and the world heard Eleanor Roosevelt's voice regularly throughout the war.

ER's constituency took in all ages.

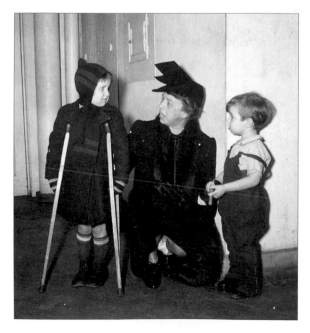

A harmonious four-generation family moment at Hyde Park,
with SDR in the center.

ER and Queen Elizabeth in an automobile as they leave the station for the White House in 1939.

ER with boys from the Wiltwyck School at Val-Kill.

Journalist Lorena Hickok was among ER's closest friends and confidantes.

ER presenting Marian Anderson with the Springarn medal from the NAACP in 1939. The medal is awarded for outstanding achievement.

ER with Director of the Office of Civil Defense Fiorello LaGuardia (center) and Assistant Director James M. Landis (right) in 1942.

The folk singer Pete Seeger entertaining ER, honored guest at a Valentine's Day party to mark the opening of the racially integrated United Federal Labor Canteen in Washington in 1944.

ER with King George VI and
Queen Elizabeth.

ER with students of a motor pool
school during her trip to England
in 1942.

ER talking with a woman machinist
during her goodwill tour of Great
Britain in 1942.

ER with Tuskegee Airmen pilots.

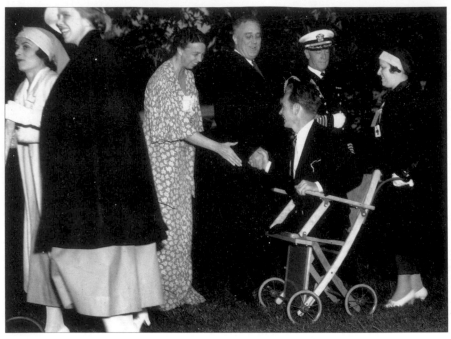

FDR and ER greet war wounded at the White House.

ER smilingly chats with an injured naval man.

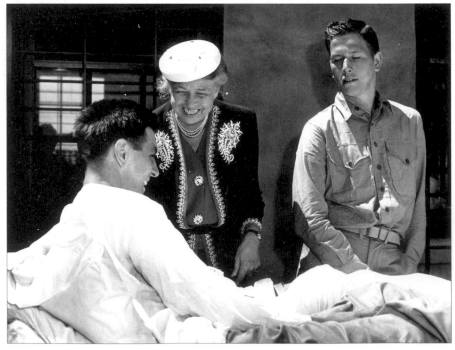

ER on a trip to Central and South America.

ER visits an injured soldier in a South Pacific hospital.

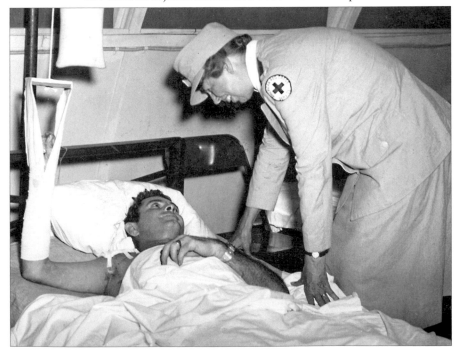

Bernard Baruch and ER, 1949.

ER with Esther Lape.

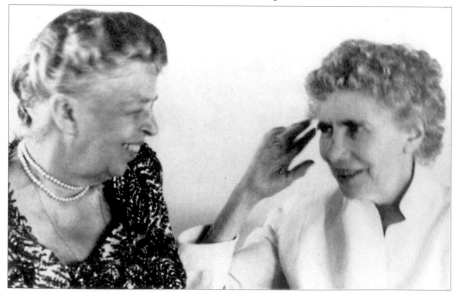

ER arrives at the opening of the Washington Labor Canteen, sponsored by the United Federal Workers of America, Congress of Industrial Organizations (CIO) in 1944.

ER continued to appear at community events long after leaving the White House.

ER as a UN delegate.

Madame Vijayalakshmi
Pandit (right) with
Vera Brittain.

ER holds up the Universal Declaration of Human Rights, 10 December, 1948.

ER at the Metropolitan Duane United Methodist Church, New York City, 3 November, 1949.

ER with JFK and other politicians in the 1960s.

ER with her friend Mayris "Tiny" Chaney, the dancer.

ER being garlanded by Princess Te-Ata at the launching of a wooden barge at "Pine Tree."

Future congresswoman Bella Savitsky Abzug on the dais with ER and Hunter president George Shuster, at ER's first speaking engagement at Hunter, February 1941.

Eleanor Roosevelt, 1884–1962.

"forgot academic decorum in spontaneous enthusiasm" for every reference FDR made to sympathy and support for Britain and France.

ER devoted her column to her husband's speech and its implications. "When the soldiers at Valley Forge wanted to go home, it was not only loyalty to George Washington which kept them suffering in the snow." Rather, "deep down in their hearts they knew they could not live as free men unless they stuck it out, just as we will today if the need arises."

FDR's speech made it clear that the era of neutrality was over. ER also understood that day that her husband would run for a third term, if nominated. Immediately after the speech, the Roosevelt party left for Washington, and ER went on to New York.

As German forces marched toward Paris, the city's residents fled. Prime Minister Reynaud telephoned Ambassador Bullitt with an urgent message for the president. France would continue to fight, but a public pledge that the United States "will give the Allies aid and material support by all means 'short of an expeditionary force' would mean a lot"—as would the actual delivery of such aid. Reynaud left this message, then he and his government fled Paris.

On 11 June, Bullitt cabled FDR in a rare fury. Due to the evacuation of the city, France now had more than six million refugees, "whose lives can be saved only by American aid." Three weeks earlier, the ambassador reminded FDR, he had promised to ask Congress for $20 million in aid. Then the Red Cross had held a drive and pledged to launch a ship filled with Red Cross supplies "within three days." However, that promised ship had not yet left U.S. waters and was not expected to arrive in Europe until 30 June. Bullitt suggested that FDR find alternative aid structures or appoint a U.S. Navy admiral to the Red Cross. FDR replied simply that he was doing "everything possible" about the Red Cross shipment.

That month Senator Edward R. Burke (D-NE) and Representative James W. Wadsworth (R-NY) introduced legislation calling for a compulsory draft. The Burke-Wadsworth bill would conscript young men between twenty-one and thirty-five. The debate over conscription would rage throughout the summer of 1940. FDR at first distanced himself from the bill: with his eye on the election, he was wary of moving beyond public opinion. Ever the pragmatist, he nevertheless encouraged congressional testimony in favor of the legislation by Secretary of War Stimson and by Army Chief of Staff General George Marshall to rebut the isolationists and noninterventionists.

ER, for her part, opposed compulsory military training. The nation was not yet ready for a military draft, she believed, and the creation of a large military force immediately suggested aggression and empire building: "We have never thought of ourselves as having frontiers to defend." War, she still believed, "was the most stupid thing on earth," the "worst of all ways" to adjust differences.

But there were situations you could not live with: "Personally, I would rather be killed than submit . . . to certain types of restraints. I would resist and die rather than live under conditions which would be to me intolerable." And national defense was built on many factors: learning, physical stamina, health education—all advantageous in both peace and war.

Instead of a military draft as such, she proposed the creation of a universal draft of all Americans for community service. Young and old, males and females, should be trained not only in military defense but for service, public health and education, social work, farmwork, and forestry. Drafted women would be trained in areas useful for peace and war, both at home and in jobs. All citizens would contribute: "A national mobilization of all of us which gives all of us something to do, trains us so we fit, according to our capacity, into a [useful] place. It will make us better citizens and . . . our communities better places in which to live." An expanded CCC and NYA would result in full employment and universal education. This "national muster" for unity and democracy would give everyone a job, so that "burdens and sacrifice would be equally shared . . . a mobilization of spirit and faith in democracy's future."

With this proposal she sought to infuse the nation with a new "sense of national purpose" and end poverty. The country would benefit in many ways from attention to "self-discipline," the "build up" and maintenance "of a good, strong physique," the ability to "do things with our hands and to live and work with other people." "We must consider the education and training of our youth an immediate goal. Until the need for universal military service was agreed upon," she would "advocate universal training and [general] service to the country."

Least of all did she support limiting compulsory service to "the jobless and needy." It would be "all wrong" to place "the needy in a class by themselves" and regard them "in any way different from . . . other citizens of the Republic." It would be cruel and punitive, the establishment of a new "class" servitude: "any plan of national training should be for all or none."

When a New Jersey relief director issued an order to deny assistance "to unmarried men of military age in order to force them into the Army," ER condemned it as a "class ruling" that connected "poverty with military service." It was "arbitrary, undemocratic and coercive." It had nothing to do with the fair universal service that she supported.

France had been the refuge and hope of those in flight from Nazi rule in the rest of Europe: political activists and Jews, antifascist artists, poets, scholars, scientists, attorneys, workers, and farmers. In May a shocking decree had ordered "all foreigners living in France" to be interned in detention camps. Then on 14 June Nazi troops marched into Paris. That evening ER "sat out on the south porch" of the White House with Martha Gellhorn. Their eyes fixed on the Washington Monument, the two friends spoke "as everybody else does today of the world in which we find ourselves." Gellhorn, like other writers the first lady knew, seemed to appreciate the ambivalent feelings of America's youth. Adults continued to hope that youth "will always feel that war is a horrible thing," but in the current situation in Europe, one had to "accept force as a weapon," unless one surrendered to brutality.

Alone that night, ER read every word of every newspaper and bulletin in the White House. Chaos and carnage threatened Paris, a city she particularly loved and associated with carefree splendid moments: her happiest days with Marie Souvestre; alone sightseeing as an adolescent; with FDR after the first war's end; the places they went to heal the hardest days of their love-torn marriage. She longed to be among those about to sail to support the refugees and the children. Unknown to her, Reynaud's government had agreed to declare Paris "an open city," not to be bombed and destroyed—but emptied and occupied. ER agreed with Anne O'Hare McCormick in the *Times*:

It isn't only the shock of the fall of Paris you feel in the marrow of your bones. . . . It is Europe cracking—and cracking over the head of the United States of America. Nowhere outside the war zone does the disaster cause such a jolt . . . , and no place in this country is so shaken as Washington.

The spectacle of the "world's best army" in forced retreat, with the industrial areas of France in the hands of the enemy, comes as a startling demonstration not of German strength but of Allied weakness. . . . The heroic fighting men of France fall back for lack of planes and tanks and guns. . . . As for us, it is literally true that at the moment the US can do no more in response to Reynaud's desperate appeal—France's cry of agony—than the President has ordered done. Like the Allies' own effort . . . it is too little too late.

Throughout Paris the tricolor was replaced by the swastika—atop public buildings, churches, the Louvre, the Opéra, Notre Dame, down the boulevards. The largest of all was strung across the Arc de Triomphe—where the flame for the Tomb of the Unknown Soldier continued to burn.

On 15 June the Maginot Line was broken to bits, and the French government left Tours in haste—for Bordeaux. On 16 June, Prime Minister Reynaud resigned and turned the government over to Marshal Henri-Philippe Pétain, who within a week signed an armistice with Hitler. The settlement Hitler imposed on France was harsh. ER was outraged: "The Germans have learned only bitterness and no wisdom from past history. They are exacting even more severe terms from their conquered enemies than were exacted of them." To destroy another nation to ensure the ascendancy of one's own, she thought, was "a hopeless attitude if you have any faith" in the possibility of amity between nations, which in the end was the only "protection against future war."

All those who had previously fled Berlin, Vienna, and Prague for Paris were once again dislocated. Now there were fourteen million refugees on France's roads. ER received appeals "from the women of France . . . begging the women of America to do all they can to assist them." Their pleas were "heartrending when one can do so little. It must be stark anguish when these women receive the refugees from other places, knowing that their own fate may be similar in the course of the next few days, and realizing that their men may never return."

As she read the letters and news accounts, she considered what role she, the first lady of the only powerful democracy left in the world, might now play in a world everywhere endangered and clearly deranged. Above all, she wanted to be part of an aid operation. She envied Clare Boothe Luce, who had been in Europe, interviewed many, and seen for herself what was needed. Then she had written articles and a book to detail the truth.

ER wanted to do all that and more. Since May she had been lobbying FDR and Norman Davis to permit her to join a rescue or refuge team. Surely her talents, her fluency in French, German, and Italian, her international friendships, and her administrative abilities would be useful. But FDR insisted it was impossible. She was too well known; she could be kidnapped, tortured, or killed. Moreover, he did not want her to go—she was needed at home.

ER was disappointed and bitter. On 18 June, she wrote Esther Lape and Elizabeth Read, "I'm not going abroad, nor am I going to do anything else except to hold people's hands now and then. Well, I'm probably good at that!"

Tommy worried about ER's unusual discontent: "She has wanted desperately to be given something really concrete and worthwhile to do in the emergency and no one has found anything for her," she wrote to Anna confidentially.

They are all afraid of political implications, etc., and I think she is discouraged and a bit annoyed. . . . She works like Hell all the time and we are busier than ever, but I know you can understand that she wants to feel she is doing something worthwhile and it makes me mad, because she has so much organizing and executive ability she could do a swell job on anything she undertook.

I would never dream of speaking to your father about her being discouraged because I have never done anything like that and I would hate to bother him when he has so much on his mind, and I would not trust Harry Hopkins . . . because he might let her know that I had done so, and that would upset her. [Harry and Missy were allied on] the other side of the house. It makes me mad and ready to smack him because your mother was so darn faithful about going to see him when he was sick, agreeing to take Diana, etc.

Tommy appealed to Anna to invite ER to Seattle during the summer. "She would probably dismember me if she knew I wrote this to you, but I know you are about the only one to whom I could write." Tommy hated to see ER so upset "and I feel powerless to do anything about it."

Never one to cave in to depression, ER persevered and kept herself engaged. She traveled between New York and Washington, cared for her aging relatives, went to meetings, wrote her columns, and called for action.

She and the novelist Pearl S. Buck opened a drive for medical aid to China. The press reported that, "dressed in a pink-and-black print jacket dress and a black baku hat with pink flowers," ER spoke in tribute to the women of China for "their bravery, courage and perseverance through three long years of invasion." In her column, she pointed out that "women in every country are being forced to show qualities of heroism and endurance which in recent years of civilization they have hardly been called upon to develop."

But this war had just begun, and the suffering continued to mount.

Chapter Twelve

"The World Rightly Belongs to Those Who Really Care": The Convention of 1940

FDR felt the tragedy of France's collapse to the Nazis to the very core of her being. The "debacle," as the French called it, challenged her precepts. What would become of all the people fleeing from so many places on the road to somewhere? What would happen to the world of travel, freedom, and culture that Aunt Dora and the entire family had known and loved? Dora Forbes, who had left her beloved home in Paris so reluctantly in November, took to her bed after France signed the vicious armistice with Germany. How long would it be before Hitler attacked again?

More than ten thousand French women and children were sent to camps like Gurs in the Pyrenees, including Hannah Arendt, the painter Charlotte Salomon, and Gerda Lerner's artist mother, Ili Kronstein. Camps that had initially been opened for Spanish Civil War refugees and still housed 150,000 veterans were now further filled with people in flight from Berlin, Vienna, and all the fallen nations. With the City of Lights occupied by the Nazis, there was too much to do simply to mourn, yet mourning was in order.

The president's failure to confront the isolationists in his own cabinet, and his refusal to further extend and protect the New Deal, had left some leading liberals like Interior Secretary Ickes in despair: "I have been tired and nervous before but never have I been so close to the verge of a breakdown," he wrote in his diary on 12 June. "It looks to me as if the President were throwing away everything that we have gained during the past seven years." Moreover, FDR seemed contemptuous of his closest advisers: "At the White House comment is being made upon the bad state of his temper . . . and those closest to him, including 'Missy,' do not know what is running in his mind. . . . Apparently he is taking absolutely nobody into his confidence. He has promised a dozen people that he would get rid of [Secretary of War Harry] Woodring, but he makes no move."*

---

*In addition, Ickes worried profoundly about the return of industrial profiteers to Washington. He disapproved of FDR's apparent willingness to create a

But after the fall of France, FDR, who hated to confront anybody, purged his cabinet of those who refused to aid Britain. Colonel Frank Knox, Alf Landon's running mate in 1936 and the much-admired publisher of the *Chicago Daily News*, would replace Charles Edison as secretary of the navy. And Henry Stimson, a Republican internationalist who had been Herbert Hoover's secretary of state, would succeed Woodring as secretary of war. In recent weeks, Knox and Stimson had both called for resumption of a draft, providing "unstinting aid" to Britain, and repealing the Neutrality Act. In step with rapidly changing public opinion, their commitment to national defense and U.S. military support against Hitler had a powerful influence on the presidential race of 1940.

FDR announced the two replacements, on behalf of bipartisan unity, as Republicans gathered to nominate a presidential candidate in Philadelphia on June 24. His timing not only upstaged the convention but actually isolated the isolationists. Congressional pacifists and isolationists immediately attacked the appointments of Knox and Stimson and decried FDR's new "war cabinet." But Ickes hailed FDR's appointments as a great victory for sanity. Even though he had a secret ambition to become secretary of war, he recognized the excellent wisdom of the Stimson appointment. "As to Frank Knox, I had suggested him originally [and] at once wired the President to say that he could not have selected two better men." FDR's reshuffling of his cabinet relieved ER, who shared Ickes's enthusiasm for FDR's renewed fighting mood.

With most of the European continent tethered to Nazi rule, the Reich announced plans for a "new order": Britain would be blockaded and destroyed. The "new Europe," as Nazi advances continued, "would be Judenrein, Jew free."

Paul Reynaud, Édouard Daladier, and thirty parliamentarians who had left France to fight from North Africa were arrested in Casablanca. Vichy was now fully allied with Hitler. In fact, Pétain's government pronounced Britain the primary enemy. Britain was preparing for an

---

"super-government" led by William Knudson of General Motors and Edward Stettinius of U.S. Steel. While FDR spoke about the need for an excess profits tax on industry's naval contracts and plant expansions, nothing was done to protect workers, or limit greed.

imminent Nazi attack. The only hope left was immediate U.S. intervention of some kind. How long could the British survive without it?

Neither Churchill nor FDR wanted to see France's powerful fleet fall into Nazi hands. In late June Churchill and his cabinet formulated Operation Catapult. In Oran, Algeria, and in other Mediterranean ports, Churchill presented the French fleet commanders with stark alternatives: they could bring the ships to British harbors; demilitarize or sink them; sail them to the United States; or do nothing, and the Royal Navy would destroy them. FDR supported this plan.

Negotiations proved futile, and on 3 July heavy British bombardment destroyed most of the French fleet. Nazi propagandists called Churchill "the greatest criminal in history," and condemned the attack as a "most disgraceful act." The next day Churchill addressed Parliament to explain why he could not have allowed the French fleet to pass into Hitler's hands and inflict "mortal injury" upon Britain. His short speech was much needed, since the bombardment had killed more than a thousand French sailors, to Britain's shock and grief. "We may find ourselves actually at war with France," Harold Nicolson wrote, "which would almost break my heart. The House is at first saddened by this odious attack but is fortified by Winston's speech. [It ended] in an ovation, with Winston sitting there with tears pouring down his cheeks." Britain was ready and resolute. There would be no surrender. It would be a long war.

An extraordinary wave of anti-Communist and anti-alien bigotry and violence emerged in the United States in the spring of 1940. The Dies Committee's attack on Communist and left-leaning groups had resulted in Red Squad raids on Communist Party headquarters in Pittsburgh, Philadelphia, Detroit, Milwaukee, and Baltimore. Many condemned the predawn raids and seizure of files and papers as a "conspiracy to violate the Bill of Rights." Photographs of a Milwaukee raid showing over a dozen "Spanish Civil War vets and their supporters handcuffed and in chains" were published to much outrage.

The bigotry culminated in passage of the Alien Registration Act. This notorious sedition law, popularly known as the Smith Act, ended civil liberties, including freedom of speech, press, and assembly, for aliens and dissenters. It required all aliens—adult noncitizen residents—to register

and be fingerprinted by the federal government, or face deportation. Anyone who had ever belonged to any organization that advocated "the violent overthrow of the government" could now be deported. It imposed a
$10,000 fine and ten years in prison for anyone convicted of "attempting
to undermine the morale of the armed forces," or anyone who "advocates,
abets, advises, or teaches" the violent overthrow of the government,
including anyone who joined or was associated with a group that did so, or
published or distributed printed matter to advocate that overthrow.

The bill had been introduced by Congressman Howard Smith (D-VA),
the powerful chair of the House Rules Committee who in 1939 had
launched an anti-labor investigation of the National Labor Relations
Board (NLRB) and a general assault on Communist influence—although
fascist and Nazi groups seemed not to disturb him. His bill passed the
Senate by voice vote on 15 June, and the House on 22 June, by a vote of
382 to 4. FDR signed it into law on 28 June.

Sweeping and incoherent, dangerous and un-American, the Smith Act
appalled ER. Representing the virulent march of hatred and hysteria, it
threatened the right to disagree—the very essence of American democracy. She wrote a column of protest, to be published on the day FDR
signed the law: "Something curious is happening to us in this country
and I think it is time we stopped and took stock of ourselves. Are we
going to be swept away from our traditional attitude toward civil liberties by hysteria about 'Fifth Columnists'?" She agreed with the attorney
general that the Smith Act was "dangerous" and extreme, an "historic
departure" from America's best practices and traditions.

Even more extreme, ER wrote, "a leader of great prominence in Catholic Youth, Boy Scouts and Boys Club of America" advocated immediate
suspension of all civil liberties for Communists, and especially the Communist elements of the AYC. Roundups and imprisonment were in order
for "these birds [who are all] saboteurs."

In the wake of the passage of the Smith Act, anti-Red hysteria
mounted. Fifteen states, including New York, ruled the Communist
Party off the ballot. Local vigilantes and police harassed petitioners going
door to door to collect signatures for party nominees. More than three
hundred electoral canvassers were arrested and charged with various
crimes, including "criminal syndicalism in Illinois and Oklahoma," and
"robbery, assault, housebreaking, and disturbing the peace" elsewhere,

according to historian Ellen Schrecker. Fines were exorbitant, "and most of the defendants were convicted" and imprisoned.

Very soon after the Smith Act was passed, the Supreme Court heard the case of two Pennsylvania schoolchildren who were Jehovah's Witnesses: they had refused to salute the flag, because their religious group regarded it as an act of idolatry and a violation of their religious freedom. The Court's majority issued a decision requiring that all schoolchildren be compelled to pledge allegiance to the flag. The Supreme Court thereby supported a ritual of state against religious liberty. "We live by symbols," it read. "The flag is the symbol of our national unity, transcending all internal differences."

The decision bewildered and dismayed liberals in FDR's cabinet. "And to think," Harold Ickes wrote in his diary, "Felix Frankfurter wrote that opinion!" But their bewilderment turned to outrage as the decision unleashed a wave of violence against Jehovah's Witnesses. Throughout the country, from Maine to California, communities rioted against people who refused to salute the flag for religious reasons. In Maine, a child was wounded in a riot after a group of Jehovah's Witnesses refused to salute the flag, and the governor threatened to call out the National Guard. In Wyoming, crowds forced Jehovah's Witnesses to march with the flag. Six people "were dragged from their homes and forced to pledge allegiance." In Illinois sixty-one Jehovah's Witnesses were jailed for "safekeeping" when their neighbors attacked them and burned their cars.

Attorney General Jackson told Ickes, "People are breaking into other people's houses and confronting them with a flag demanding that they salute it." Both men were astonished by "the hysteria that is sweeping the country against aliens and fifth columnists" in response to the decision. Frankfurter's former friends called it "Felix's Fall of France Opinion."

ER simply could not comprehend how the man who had written to her husband in April, "Fear is the child of ignorance and the parent of intolerance," could have written such a decision. Aggrieved, she complained to FDR, but much to her astonishment he rejected her criticism. Indeed, in conversation with Frankfurter at Hyde Park, the president supported his onetime mentor. But others never forgave Frankfurter. Yes, he hated Hitler; yes, he was an American patriot. But in the name of patriotism for democracy, he had "ordered the children to 'Heil.'" ACLU cofounder Roger Baldwin and other civil libertarians ended their long alliances with the justice: no decision "dismayed us more than his labored defence of compulsory flag saluting." Baldwin said he hoped never to see his old friend again.

The first couple spent the weekend of 21–23 June together at Hyde Park, driving around their woods of elm, cypress, and oak. "We have been remarkably fortunate in having sunny, beautiful weather while the President has been here," ER wrote in her column for the weekend. "Friday afternoon, we spent an hour driving up to his cottage and looking at a number of plantings of small trees. They were not visible until you gazed into the tangle of grass and weeds for a long time, but my husband said by winter we would discover quite a forest growing up. Yesterday morning, we visited the new school which has been given his name and is just back of our cottages." All that weekend, they went back and forth between the Big House, Val-Kill, and FDR's new Top Cottage. They visited with SDR and consoled Aunt Dora; they spent many hours alone in conversation.

News of the war preoccupied them. They listened to William Shirer's broadcasts from Berlin and read aloud C. Brooks Peters's vivid reports from the German capital in the *New York Times*. In the past, the first couple had disagreed about priorities and strategies. They had argued about the World Court, Ethiopia, and Spain; but now they were often in agreement. It was a time to bolster their common interests and their shared visions for the future, both in America and abroad.

The president's long periods of inaction often exasperated ER, even though she knew they were part of the careful process of a politician biding his time in order to outwit his opponents. She was generally impatient for him to get to the point of action after a long period of hesitation and juggling.

He did not consult her about his plans for the presidential election of 1940. "I never asked my husband what he really wanted to do," she wrote in her memoir. She knew he preferred to retire, which was also her wish, and she had long believed he would not run for a third term. For one thing, she worried about his health, especially after his much-witnessed "faint" during a festive dinner in May. He was rumored to have had a heart attack, and the episode was even reported as such in *Time* magazine. Another concern was his shifting team of advisers, especially Harry Hopkins's disturbing new prominence. But she never said a word publicly about FDR's health or his advisers. Finally, ER was dismayed by his consistently indirect political strategy. Even as her own efforts and writings were becoming ever more direct, he seemed more inclined to dissemble and prevaricate.

But his 10 June "stab in the back" commencement speech against Mussolini's treachery persuaded ER that he would run again. And she was now convinced that he was the only man in America fully able to lead a united democratic struggle against the forces of totalitarianism, which were now triumphant in Europe and Asia. His new cabinet appointments confirmed her certainty that he would run again, but true to form, he kept his thoughts to himself. This time the man who often said he never let his right hand know what his left hand was doing annoyed her.

On Sunday evening ER went down to the station to see "the President and his party off for Washington with much regret, for the country is very lovely and it is possible to forget for a little while how horrible conditions are in much of the rest of the world.

> I drove through the woods just as the sun was setting last night, a most mysterious magic hour. There was a soft light on the deep green leaves. A fat woodchuck scuttled across the road ahead of me. A little white-tailed rabbit ran along the road, too frightened to get out of the way, until I stopped the car and let him run to cover.
>
> How can one think of these woods converted into a battlefield? Peace seems to be in the heart of them and yet, I remember some just like them outside of Paris and in the forests of Germany and England.

While ER was at Hyde Park, Joe Lash stopped by with three friends en route to an AYC convention in Lake Geneva, Wisconsin (for which ER had raised funds). The owner of the car was Trude Pratt, a brilliant and generous activist whom ER was delighted to meet.

Born Gertrude von Adam Wenzel in Freiburg, Germany, on 13 June 1908, she was the eldest of five children. Independent and rebellious, she had been expelled from a convent school (as had ER), then studied in Paris and at the University of Heidelberg. She taught school and studied journalism in Berlin, then she worked for a PhD in literature at the University of Freiburg in 1930. Her dissertation, "The Baroque Style of John

Donne," was highly regarded, and she was awarded a fellowship to teach at Hunter College in New York. She worked with the International Student Service (ISS), an organization founded to support students who had been displaced by war.

At an ISS meeting in Manhattan in 1931, she met and fell in love with Eliot Pratt, the philanthropic son of an oil-rich family who shared her views. In 1932 she returned to Germany to work as a reporter for an anti-Nazi paper, infiltrating Nazi meetings for the ISS. Pratt joined her in Berlin, and they married. After Hitler came to power in January 1933, Nazis plundered and ransacked her office. Trude and Eliot returned to New York in February. In 1936 they journeyed to Germany during the Olympics to establish a rescue network. The Nazi propaganda effort to appear democratic during the international games enabled the Pratts to help many of their Jewish and political friends escape. Their rescue network brought six of Trude's friends out in 1936 and expanded during the war.

When Joe met Trude at an ISS meeting in 1938, she was the very busy mother of three young children and a dedicated antifascist activist. Now in 1940 ER saw that Joe was "more than casually attracted to Trude." She was immediately impressed by her and wrote Joe a letter to tell him so. It was the beginning of a long and deep relationship among the three of them, a bond that grew over the years and brought ER much joy.

John Gilbert Winant was a man of legendary stature in ER's circle and was especially close to Esther Lape and Elizabeth Read. In the 1930s, although he was an independent progressive Republican, he had also been a New Deal idealist and labor rights advocate during his tenure as governor of New Hampshire. FDR was so impressed by his integrity and vision, he appointed him first chair of the Social Security Board.

In 1940 he became director of the International Labor Office (ILO), based in Geneva. At the time FDR applauded the choice as a chance to demonstrate that "Washington had moved away from isolation." Winant's first speech to the ILO was generative: "Everything that is in me . . . is dedicated to the service before me. . . . The world rightly belongs to those who really care."

But on 15 June 1940 the world of hope and amity in Geneva fell into immediate danger as the Nazis overran France. Winant appealed for sanctuary to save his staff, the ILO library and papers. He feared that "twenty-four of the best members of his staff" faced "liquidation" if they did not get out. They all had "unquestioned loyalty to democratic principles" and deserved visas. He turned to Frances Perkins and Cordell Hull for help in obtaining refuge for the ILO in the United States.

According to Winant's biographer, during an evening meeting on 17 June, Perkins "convinced" FDR to approve Winant's request. But FDR subsequently retracted his invitation, explaining to Perkins that while he had formerly agreed to "harbor" the League of Nations at Princeton, he did not want to upset Congress any more than necessary during his efforts to bolster aid to Britain. In the end, the State Department offered the ILO staff transit visas if they would proceed to another country. Happily, Winant had a good friend at McGill University in Montreal, which offered the ILO "a home for the duration." The ILO could continue its work safely in Canada. Winant decided to spend much of his time in Washington, to work with Nebraska's Senator George W. Norris and other independents for FDR's election.

ER never understood FDR's State Department. She was bewildered by its seeming indifference to the plight of refugees and its adamant refusal to help them in any way. What did State officials think of the bitter and ongoing human tragedies her allies and friends related? Every day brought news of further outrages, horror stories of refugees rounded up. FDR's refusal to stand up to the department's intransigence dismayed her, although she believed he would ultimately do the right thing and bypass State.

Meanwhile she would continue to work to change public opinion regarding the plight of European refugees as well as the need for aid to Britain. She determined to write more bluntly and vividly, devoting a column to her visit to Congress House. This refugee home in Manhattan had been established by Louise Wise, wife of Rabbi Stephen Wise, and the women's division of the American Jewish Congress. "The three houses she has taken over," ER wrote, "must indeed seem a cheerful haven to strangers landing on our shores. I wish we could receive everyone who comes to this country with the same spirit which [Louise Wise] and her colleagues have been able to create in these houses." She made it clear that "not only Jewish, but Catholic and liberal Protestant refugees from Germany have found a haven here." In a short time, Congress House, "a

Shelter for the Homeless" on Sixty-eighth Street near Central Park, would welcome over four thousand European refugees.

As the swastika unfurled all across Europe, ER wrote and spoke almost daily about refugees. She was determined to assist them before all the doors out of Europe's inferno slammed shut. She worked to organize *Kindertransporten* so that vulnerable children could find havens in Britain and North America. For the moment, FDR seemed to support her, although he grew annoyed when she broached this subject.

In New York on 25 June ER met with several individual philanthropists and representatives from the AFSC, as well as Catholic, Jewish, and nonsectarian relief groups, to organize a new Committee for the Care of European Children. "I am thankful beyond words," she wrote, "that it is going to be possible to do something for these European children, but my heart is heavy when I think of the tragedies which haunt the lives of many grown people." She persuaded Chicago philanthropist Marshall Field to serve as the committee's director, and she agreed to serve as honorary chair. From that moment on, the battle for refugee children would be in very good hands.

That same evening, 25 June, Joe Lash brought Trude Pratt and Karl Frank to ER's Eleventh Street apartment for dinner. Also present was Joseph Buttinger, head of Austria's underground socialist movement. Frank explained that in its armistice with the Nazis, the Vichy government had agreed to "surrender on demand" anyone on French soil who was of interest to the Reich. That meant antifascist activists in France were trapped, within reach of the Gestapo. Political and labor leaders were immediately endangered, as were artists, writers, academics, and intellectuals who had in any way opposed Hitler.

That night the five dinner companions—Lash, Pratt, Frank, Buttinger, and ER—created the Emergency Rescue Committee (ERC), to save these refugees. The first step was to compile lists of the people who were in immediate danger. A number of lists had already been compiled, and Frank and Buttinger gave them to ER.*

---

*Among those who compiled lists were Thomas Mann, the French theologian Jacques Maritain, Max Ascoli, Jan Masaryk, Alvarez del Vayo, and Joseph

ER then picked up the phone and called the president to ask him to help these refugees. According to Lash, FDR received the request somewhat impatiently, stressing that everything that could be done was being done. ER was persistent and responded to each of FDR's reasons with a counterargument. When he mentioned that Spain refused to admit even American refugees, she reminded him that he "always said it was possible to bribe Spanish and Portuguese officials." Then he said, "Congress would not let them in." She wondered what had "happened to us. . . . We had been the traditional land of asylum and now we're unwilling to admit political refugees." She was tenacious, and the president grew annoyed. Their long conversation that night was only the first of many on the subject.

In the end, ER took Frank and Buttinger's lists and promised to see that they were sent to American consulates throughout Europe. With the creation of the ERC, ER had work to do, the kind she most wanted. It would become one of her most enduring contributions to rescue efforts.

Her fellow ERC cofounders soon introduced her to Varian Fry, the key figure in the group. A scholarly journalist whose life had formerly been devoted to learning and literature, Fry had been a classics major at Harvard, then studied international relations at Columbia. While on assignment in Germany in 1935, he had witnessed outrages against Jews in Berlin, which changed his life. Upon his return to New York, he raised money for anti-Nazi groups and worked closely with Karl Frank's American Friends of German Freedom, led by such luminaries as Reinhold Niebuhr, head of Union Theological Seminary, and ER's friend the educator Dr. Frank Kingdon.

Then Fry made a fateful decision: as he told ER on 27 June, he would go to Marseilles, lists in hand, to help these endangered people personally. By obtaining emergency visas, he believed he might be able to rescue them all within a month. He gave ER a letter for the president, asking him to appeal to Latin American governments for asylum. On 8 July ER wrote Fry, "The President has seen your letter. . . . He will try to get the cooperation of the South American countries."

Buttinger, who identified endangered Italians, French, Czechs, Spaniards, Austrians, and Germans. Alvin Johnson of the New School for Social Research and Alfred Barr of the Museum of Modern Art sent names of condemned artists whose books and works had already been banned or burned.

Between the ERC and the U.S. Committee for the Care of European Children, refugees would be high on ER's agenda for the foreseeable future. Her deep depression, her recurring "Griselda mood," was over. Tommy noticed that she was "happier now that she has so much to do for this child refugee committee." As honorary chair of the U.S. Committee, she actively sought to protect refugee children. In her column, she described what the U.S. Committee was doing and how refugees could help the war effort:

> Under the quota we have received a number of German, Austrian, Italian and Spanish refugees. People who have been marked people in their own countries because of their active opposition to Fascist or Nazi regimes. They have left behind them, however, in France, Sweden and England members of their families, intimate friends, beloved political leaders and now cannot rest in safety because of the dangers which surround their loved ones. Most of these people could help us greatly in the next few weeks or months, for they know how Communists, Nazis and Fascists work.

Her work on refugees would keep her increasingly in New York, although the Washington summer was cool so far, and, she wrote to Anna, "I love my porch at night." In New York, she met with members of the U.S. Committee's fundraising subcommittee, notably Marshall Field and Frank Kingdon. She was grateful that Drew Pearson and Robert S. Allen gave her ample time on their *Washington Merry-Go-Round* broadcast program personally to launch the campaign for refugee children. She was rarely so insistent about the need for donations, but the need was urgent, and she intended to be increasingly blunt.

As the threat of a German invasion of Great Britain loomed, the first ship, with thousands of refugee children from Britain and the Continent, was scheduled to leave Britain for North America. The children, out of harm's way, should be admitted as guests, not as refugees, ER argued. In a national broadcast over the CBS network, she declared: "The children are temporary visitors, not immigrants." Applying current State Department regulations on immigration would strangle the chances of the children sent "to this country to escape the war. . . . Red tape must not be used to trip up little children on their way to safety."

Emphasizing interfaith efforts, she hosted a picnic and concert for the

Christian Action Committee for Scandinavian Relief to aid Finland and Norway. She met regularly with the Paderewski Fund for Polish Relief, served as vice-chair, and called repeatedly upon Americans to work to "break down the wall of indifference" and realize that "anything any American can do to help is a contribution to the effort to return the world to sanity."

Still, across the country a spirit of unwelcome toward refugees continued. Perhaps "the years of depression have made us less sure of ourselves, oversuspicious and overcautious," she wrote at Hyde Park during a pounding thunderstorm. "Take, for example, our attitude toward the acceptance of any foreign political refugees. . . . These people love liberty and value it [and] have had experiences which may be of value to us in recognizing the propaganda methods used by totalitarian dictators. We must, of course, use caution, but we need not be cautious to the point of going back entirely on our traditional hospitality to political refugees."

In the political surprise of 1940, the Republican Party at its convention nominated Wendell Willkie as its candidate for president. Up to that point the isolationists of the GOP, led by Senator Robert A. Taft (R-OH), Senator Arthur Vandenberg (R-MI), and New York district attorney Thomas Dewey, had been the front-runners. Willkie, an internationalist, had formerly campaigned for America's entrance into the World Court and was now running as an interventionist. Handsome, tall, and hulking, the "huggy-bear" of American politics triumphed on the sixth ballot over the isolationists.

Willkie, a former New Deal Democrat, was a genuine progressive and civil libertarian, as well as an attorney and business magnate. A director of the Morgan Bank, he was a leader of the water power industry and president of Commonwealth and Southern Corporation. He had campaigned against the creation of the Tennessee Valley Authority, but that seemed his only difference with FDR—until he decided the president had retreated from his most significant liberal commitments. Now Willkie favored national health care, absolute racial equality, and an extension of all social and economic benefits. He opposed engorged bureaucracy and feared dictatorship. He suspected FDR and the "third term-ites."

Many of ER's friends, including Helen Rogers Reid, Isabella Greenway,

and evidently Esther Lape, supported Willkie. So did many NAACP leaders, the boxing champion Joe Louis, and every Republican internationalist, led by Henry and Clare Boothe Luce and their publishing empire.
Thousands of We Want Willkie clubs emerged from nowhere. Many
believed he represented a new movement, like populism in the nineteenth
century.

But ER was unimpressed. She found his platform devoid of specifics.
"Sometimes I wonder if we will ever grow up in our politics and say definite things which mean something," implying that this was no time to
support an unknown. There is something unreal, she wrote, "about all
this political activity when the world seems toppling into chaos."

From her perch in the Democratic Party offices, Hick offered her
impressions of Willkie: "I don't care for the crowd that is backing him.
And he is too darned plausible—*too* simple, etc. . . . I don't know whether
Willkie is a fascist or not, but I certainly *do* suspect the crowd behind
him. By his charm and his smooth talk, he may win over a lot of women,
young people, and even liberals." From February to May, Hick had been
on the road to assess and build public opinion for the party. She made a
decent salary, all her expenses were paid, and she wrote splendid speeches
for state and local politicians. She loved her new job, and she fully enjoyed
the game. "This job is such fun dear. . . . I am having the time of my life."
Democratic Party chairman Jim Farley and the party's publicity director,
Charles Michelson, were pleased with her work.

FDR, for his part, was relieved by Willkie's nomination. Since he was
an interventionist, it removed from the race the question of support for
Britain. The Democrats soon decided upon a campaign strategy. Willkie
represented "corporate, entrenched wealth, against the great mass of the
people," as Ickes put it. He and other Democratic leaders believed that on
this issue "we can win . . . and [then] go far toward correcting some of
the economic and social abuses that still exist in this country."

Only days before the Democratic National Convention was to open
on 15 July in Chicago, nobody in FDR's inner circle knew what he
intended to do about a third term. His refusal to participate—to name
floor leaders or to contribute platform positions—as well as his ongoing
duplicity and coyness regarding his intentions, appalled and enraged his
oldest friends and most ardent champions.

Meanwhile at Hyde Park, ER and FDR were celebrating the Fourth of

July with a group of family and friends. The president read the Declaration of Independence aloud with gusto, and ER in her column stirringly affirmed American values:

> I personally want to continue to live in a country where I can think as I please, go to any church I please, or to none if that is my desire; say what I please, and within the limits of any free society, do what I please. . . .
>
> I want to have within my own hands the choice of my leaders, and if the majority of opinion is against me at any time, I want the right to differ, while recognizing the necessity of cooperation . . . in order to prove fairly whether the majority opinion is right or not.

Accompanied by Tommy, ER spoke at several political meetings in New York State. One of her destinations was a town on the Finger Lakes, and "my husband had a grand time asking everyone where Odessa was." When the reply "In Russia and on the Black Sea" came, "he would gleefully remark: 'My wife is going there on Friday and will be back Saturday night.'"

FDR told ER he had decided to stay in Washington, so there was no need for her to go to Chicago. She counseled the party leaders to emphasize Willkie's "essential indifference to labor." She wrote Hick, "Don't get tired & don't get a defeatist attitude. Willkie can be beaten. The strategy must be good and the campaign well planned. But he isn't so hard to beat—Of that I am sure." Then she and Tommy went to Val-Kill for the week. They invited Tommy's companion Henry Osthagen, Earl Miller, Earl's fiancée Simone von Haver, and Joe Lash.

As the obligations of politics were altered by war and carnage, ER sought to build an alternative network for action, comfort, and hope. Tommy, Earl Miller, Alice Huntington, Esther Lape and Elizabeth Read, Bernard Baruch, Isabella Greenway, and Elinor Morgenthau remained intimates she could rely on—they shared her evolving vision and priorities. Hick, politically engaged and always informative, retained a special place in ER's heart. But she was not much interested in refugees, and was occasionally bigoted. Increasingly, ER's quest for deep friendships that embraced personal and political interests was satisfied by Joe Lash and his vigorous circle of international activists.

At Val-Kill, much of their conversation concerned the rifts among the convention delegates. Beyond the political commentary, it was a relaxing, easy week at Val-Kill, and they "had a gay time." They swam and frolicked in the pool, and played ring tennis. ER and Earl defeated Joe and Simone, although, as Joe noted, "we had youth on our side." They all enjoyed walks in the woods, despite the swarms of mosquitoes, and grilled picnics on the porch.

In a private conversation one evening at dusk, ER was surprised to learn that Joe had lost his father when he was nine. Sharing their childhood griefs strengthened the growing bond between them.

Then Joe also asked whether he could invite Trude Pratt to join them. She "was in trouble and might be helped" by a conversation, he explained. ER was eager to be useful. When she was young, she "never had anyone to whom she could go and talk," and it was so important to be able to discuss things. But she warned Joe that "she never imposed advice."

When Trude arrived, she "turned shy" and avoided "talk about her personal affairs." Instead, they spoke about politics, and how Trude might volunteer and work in some useful way during the campaign. They also spoke about her determination to help her friends in the German and Austrian underground, now stranded in Marseilles, flee to England, Sweden, or any open port of hope. ER was moved by Trude's wide-ranging knowledge and charmed by her great wit and fun-loving nature.

ER felt sure Joe and Trude were in the early stages of something serious, even though Trude was still married with three small children. When she asked Joe bluntly about his love life, she discovered that it was "in a mess." Joe admitted he "was taken with Trude" but planned to marry Agnes Reynolds, yet he was not yet legally divorced from Nancy, his first wife. Married in 1935, they "had separated amicably in 1937." ER offered to loan him any money he needed for Reno, where one could get a divorce easily after a six-week residency. "The more troubles I had, the more she insisted on helping me," he wrote.

While no one could doubt the immense respect and affection FDR felt for his wife, in her closest relationships ER revealed her own longings and desires and spoke about her own flaws. Joe felt that the first lady's own marital realities and romantic longings were much on her mind as they talked. Her husband was often aloof and inapproachable, and perhaps most keenly she felt her limitations and failures as a mother. To Joe,

she confided that she was making "every effort to improve her relationship with her children, and she was certain now that providing unconditional love and understanding was essential. She also filled Joe in on her
past problems with her mother-in-law. "She was in rebellion against her
mother-in-law but kept it bottled up," he wrote, "[since] she had been
taught to defer to the views of older people."

With Joe and Trude, ER felt a new level of hope as they negotiated
complicated issues of love and loyalty, immediate questions of rescue and
survival as the vicious war unfolded. They pondered short- and long-term
political needs to strengthen democracy, and dreamed of a truly just and
humane future.

On 16 July ER and Tommy took SDR and Betty Roosevelt (Rosy
Roosevelt's widow) to dinner with Joe and Trude at Norrie Point, a Scandinavian restaurant on the Hudson shore. Joe finally met the formidable
mother-in-law ER had told him so much about. At eighty-five, SDR was
impressive—in his words, "spry" and "ever-curious," even "adventurous."
SDR reminded Joe of the president, with familiar hand gestures and facial
expressions. When Betty Roosevelt referred to the vice president, SDR
snapped, "Oh, Garner! A stupid man." Altogether it was quite a "spree."

Afterward they hurried home: FDR had told them that the one convention
moment they should not miss was Kentucky senator Alben Barkley's address
late that first evening. Barkley's nationally broadcast keynote included a
message from FDR: "The President has never had, and has not today, any
desire or purpose to continue in the office . . . , to be a candidate . . . , or to
be nominated by the convention for that office. He wishes . . . to make it
clear that all of the delegates . . . are free to vote for any candidate."

At first the delegates were silent, then bedlam erupted. From every
loudspeaker throughout the convention hall, a powerful voice boomed:
"We want Roosevelt!" The ensuing demonstration included music,
marching bands, and shouts of "The world needs Roosevelt!" Every state
delegation and all police and fire units present marched and sang "Happy
Days Are Here Again!" Joe noted that when the demonstration began,
ER "shook her head resignedly" and timed all fifty-three minutes of it.

Harold Ickes, who had initiated the third-term movement in 1938
and "led the procession," was furious to be bypassed by Harry Hopkins

in Chicago. But he was even more furious when he saw that the impact of FDR's strategy on the convention was to make it "dead and cold. Everything was dull and bogged down." Many friends, legislators, and journalists including Herbert Agar and Ulric Bell begged Ickes to call the president: if FDR had "any hope of saving the international situation," he needed to fly to Chicago "and lift the convention out of the gutter."

Eventually, Ickes sent a cable, an eloquent plea for FDR to attend: "this convention is bleeding to death," and your "reputation and prestige may bleed to death with it. Prompt and heart-stirring action is necessary. A world revolution is beating against the final ramparts of democracy in Europe." He assured FDR he was the only man to lead the country. The delegates in Chicago were "milling about," anxious and leaderless, "waiting for the inspiration . . . that only you can give them."

If FDR were to remain silent, Ickes feared that "men who are determined to destroy you at any cost" would appropriate the convention. "It is the strangest sight in American politics to see a convention dominated by men who are bent upon betraying their leader, their party, and their country." He referred to the party's isolationist wing, led by Burton Wheeler, but he feared that Jim Farley and "the Farley coalition" would join them. To "clear away the sordid atmosphere," Ickes appealed to FDR to fly to the convention and to send immediately his platform for democracy's international and domestic future. If he did not, "a ticket will emerge that will assure the election of Willkie, and Willkie means fascism and appeasement." FDR did not answer Ickes's cable.

Then Frances Perkins called him, frantic. The situation was out of control. He must come. But it was impossible, he told her: people would "get promises out of me. . . . If I don't make promises, I will make new enemies. If I do make promises, they'll be mistakes. . . . It is better not to go."

What was there to do? He told Perkins to ask Eleanor. That would be an "excellent" contribution, he said. As always, she was his beacon in a storm. At times, she was also his canary sent out to gauge the public mood, at others the voice of reason that he could count on to prevail above all others. Throughout his presidency, FDR never lost his faith in her. She "always makes people feel right," he told Perkins. "She has a fine way with her. . . . Telephone her. I'll speak to her too, but you tell her so that she will know I am not sending her on my own hunch, but that some of the rest of you want her." He advised Perkins to speak to several of ER's friends before she called.

A call from Frances Perkins interrupted their dinner. ER at first hesitated, but Perkins was insistent: the party, and the future, absolutely required her presence.

ER called her husband, who said it would be grand if she went. But how would Jim Farley feel about it? she worried. "I certainly am not going out there unless he invites me." FDR encouraged her to call Farley, since "she could say things to Jim Farley he could not."

ER's consideration for Jim Farley was genuine. During his years as the Democrats' party chairman, his dedication to the party had been steadfast, and his leadership had been effective and far-seeing. Now he was actually being "frozen out" by Harry Hopkins, who had no official role except as FDR's personal surrogate. Hopkins was rude and self-centered and barked orders to Farley, disregarding his advice. It was wrong, and ER was incensed at Hopkins for it.

When she called Farley for his advice that night, he was "overcome with emotion" and could not continue the conversation. Hick and her boss, publicity director Charles Michelson, happened to walk into the room and heard Farley say agitatedly into the phone, "But I do mean it! You have got to come. We need you—badly." In tears, he could not continue. He saw Hick, said she would call her right back, and hung up. Then he grabbed Hick's arm: "Call her back and tell her I meant every word . . . and wasn't just being polite. . . . And tell her I'll get up a committee of delegates to meet her."

Hick called ER and was adamant: the future of the Democratic Party— of everything they cared about—depended on her presence at the convention. FDR would be nominated, but he had chosen Secretary of Agriculture Henry Wallace for his running mate—and the stadium had exploded in opposition. But FDR said that if he could not have Wallace, he would not run. The convention would hold off on the vice-presidential roll-call vote until after ER arrived and spoke, Hick said. Persuaded that "Jim Farley really wanted me," ER agreed to fly to Chicago the next morning: "Tell Jim to meet me at the airport, alone. No delegation."

That night at Val-Kill ER's party stayed up until three a.m. "We sat thru the nominating speeches," Lash wrote in his journal. "I tallied votes, while ER sewed initials on sheets and Tommy knitted. Henry made us scotches. Mrs. R was unhappy when Sen [Carter] Glass did not do a good job of nominating Farley. [But] the convention sang 'When Irish Eyes Are Smiling'" in Farley's honor, and ER "sang along in a low voice."

The final vote was overwhelming: FDR, 946 votes; Farley, 72; Vice President Garner, 61; Maryland's Senator Millard Tydings, 9; Cordell Hull, 5. After the votes were announced, Farley moved that FDR be nominated by acclamation.

But there was nothing unanimous about the battle that brewed over FDR's decision on Wallace as his candidate for vice president. Hopkins urged the boss to go with Supreme Court Justice William O. Douglas. House Speaker William Bankhead believed he was FDR's choice, and so did Indiana's former governor Paul McNutt, business leader Jesse Jones, South Carolina's Jimmy Byrnes, Alben Barkley, Cordell Hull, Harold Ickes, Sam Rayburn. Actually more than seventeen men believed they were in line, or even preferred.

Diving into that maelstrom, ER's friend C. R. Smith of American Airlines sent a Piper Cub to Wappingers Falls for her trip to New York City. Smith's pilot, she noted, "allowed me to fly the plane for a while, following the Hudson River, which gave me a real sense of exhilaration." In New York, Smith met her and flew her to Chicago.

At sunset she stepped off the plane in Chicago, to be greeted by the women's press corps. Farley insisted she speak with them, and the first question was: "'Are you happy about the nomination?' 'Happy!'" she exclaimed, without a trace of a smile, her demeanor reflecting "an unusual gravity." "'I don't know how anyone could be happy [about this nomination] . . . in the present state of the world.'" Why, ER wondered, "would anyone want to carry such a burden" of responsibility—not only for our people but to preserve the nation's "place among the peoples of the world"? Told that her own name had been placed in nomination for vice president that afternoon, "she laughed heartily." I can "imagine nothing more foolish or less wanted."

Jim Farley drove her from the airfield to the hotel for dinner. She was surprised to learn that "Franklin had not talked to him since the convention opened and had never told him . . . his choice for vice-president. I was horrified to realize that things had come to this . . . because I always had a feeling of real friendship for Jim Farley."

ER persuaded Jim to talk with FDR. They called from the hotel, and the two men had a tense conversation. FDR said that only Wallace would do as his running mate, since he cared both about the New Deal and about the international situation. "It must be Wallace," because he "could be trusted to carry out our policies." Farley said, "You are the boss. If you say so I will do all I can . . . but I will have to work fast." With that, the first lady and Farley left immediately for the convention hall, "and I could see Jim was much disturbed." Farley handed ER over to Perkins and Hick, and left immediately.

According to Frances Perkins, ER's very presence "sweetened the convention." Even before her speech, "she made friends, shook hands with thousands of people," and began to warm up the entirely divided room. Hick's observation differed: "The Stadium was packed to the rafters . . . half the state of Indiana had moved into the galleries to root for McNutt. . . . [Every] mention of Wallace started a roar of boos and catcalls. . . . The convention was out of control. In the uproar hardly anyone was aware of Mrs. Roosevelt's presence."

At ten-thirty p.m., as "the State delegations were still at fever heat," Jim Farley escorted ER to the podium, and the entire convention— delegates, spectators, reporters—rose to its feet. She "moved forward," Hick wrote, "through the haze of dust and tobacco smoke under the glaring lights to the speakers' stand—tall and proudly erect, her head held high. For a split second the crowd stared at her in astonishment. Abruptly the boos and catcalls stopped. In dead silence she started to speak."

Her "obvious affection" for Farley, wrote Hick, had "a healing effect," as the bitterness on the floor subsided with her first words. "For many years I have worked under Jim Farley and with Jim Farley, and I think nobody can appreciate more what he has done for the party, what he has given in work and loyalty. And I want to give him here my thanks and devotion." Then she addressed the devastating moment that framed this convention: "I know and you know that any man [in office today] faces a heavier responsibility, perhaps, than any man has ever faced before in this country. Therefore, to be a candidate of either political party is a very serious and very solemn thing. You cannot treat it as you would an ordinary nomination in an ordinary time. We people in the US have got to realize . . . that we face a grave and serious situation."

A candidate who was also a sitting president could not run an ordinary campaign.

He must be on the job. So each and every one of you . . . assume for yourselves a very grave responsibility because you will have to make the campaign. You will have to rise above considerations which are narrow and partisan. . . . No man . . . can carry this situation alone. This is only carried by a united people who love their country and who will live for it to the fullest . . . with the highest ideals, with a determination that their party shall be absolutely devoted to the good of the nation . . . and to doing what this country can do to bring the world to a safer and happier condition.

ER's brief presentation, with its "impressively delivered appeal for a united country," was initially greeted by "sustained silence," noted *Times* reporter Kathleen McLaughlin. "It was striking after the pandemonium," ER would recall. As she returned to her seat, the organist broke into "God Bless America," and the hall burst into tumultuous applause. ER's appearance was unprecedented. She was, as McLaughlin noted, "the first wife of a President or nominee to address a major political party."

Farley was pleased—she had saved the convention for the president. With Jimmy Byrnes and others, he had lobbied the delegates in favor of the president's preference. Byrnes had repeatedly asked, "For God's sake, do you want a president or a vice president?" In the end, Wallace was nominated, but it was close. Of 1,100 votes, 627 went to Wallace, 327 to Speaker Bankhead, and 83 to others, many of whom had withdrawn on FDR's behest—including McNutt, Rayburn, and Farley.

Back on the tarmac, as ER was about to take off, her plane was flagged to a halt. There was an urgent message from the president—FDR wanted to thank her and said she "had done a very good job." Harry Hopkins, on another phone, also thanked ER. You young people know nothing about politics, she told him. "Then I dashed back to the plane and we took off."

In addition to the enthusiastic press coverage, she was most pleased by Senator George W. Norris's letter of gratitude. Independent and progressive, a great American maverick, Norris had been allied with ER and Esther Lape since their 1923 campaign for the World Court and a democratized League of Nations. He also supported the best of the New Deal. Both FDR and ER considered him, as a leader and a visionary, "the perfect, gentle knight of American progressive ideals."

The day after her speech, Norris sent ER a long typed letter. As a lifelong crossover Republican who considered issues before party and championed government responsibility for all its citizens, he was appalled by the opposition to Wallace, and by the convention's failure to court the independent vote. Above all, he was committed to Roosevelt and opposed to Willkie—who had been a lifelong Democrat, until his virulent opposition to the TVA:

> I listened over the radio to the proceedings . . . and for a while it looked to me as though the convention was going to "blow up." At this stage of the proceedings, when it seemed to me all of the good work President Roosevelt had done, all of his great accomplishments, all his ability to continue his work in the future, were about to be overthrown and cast aside, at this juncture, when it seemed the battle for righteousness was about to be lost, you came on the scene, and what you said in that short speech caused men of sense and honor to stop and think before they plunged. Like Sheridan in the Shenandoah, you stopped the fleeing warriors; you renewed the faltering courage of those who believed in righteousness, who for the moment had been stampeded. You turned a rout into victory. You were the Sheridan of that convention. Perhaps you do not realize it now. It may be that you never will, but I am convinced . . . that the country owes you a debt of gratitude it can never repay and which it does not now fully comprehend.
>
> As a humble citizen, with no personal ambition of my own . . . representing as I believe I do millions of progressive, patriotic citizens throughout the country, I thank you and I congratulate you.

The victory, Norris concluded, was entirely due to ER: her presence and her words "made you heroic, and unknown and unseen, citizens all over our land are today thanking God that you were there at the right time, to say the right thing in the right place."

ER treasured that letter and on the back wrote: "File carefully, in file of always to keep!"

The FDR-Wallace ticket remained embattled, and the convention created a disturbing international legacy. According to the Democratic platform, "We will not participate in foreign wars, and we will not send our army or navy or air force to fight in foreign lands outside of the

Americas." Promoted by Burton Wheeler's group of isolationists but supported widely, the plank was unacceptable to FDR—who had insisted they add "except in case of attack."

From as far away as Australia, the press protested America's ongoing failure to grasp realities. The Democratic platform seemed a "retreat" into isolationism, commented the *Sydney Herald*, after FDR's promises of aid to "sorely beset Britain." But perhaps there was hope, editorialized the *Melbourne Herald*: FDR was, after all, "ahead of his party," and his renomination might be evidence that public opinion was more with him than with his isolationist opponents. Both papers reported that ER's speech was "broadcast throughout Australia."

Back at Val-Kill, ER was satisfied with her efforts but distraught by the stunning opposition to FDR and his policies. She worried about her husband's health, the fate of the New Deal, and the ongoing refusal of so many Democrats to consider Europe's woes as America's concern. The catastrophic fall of France and the bitter Democratic convention had stirred her deeply. Her thoughts returned to the book she had been unable to write all year. Now she was prepared to focus on *The Moral Basis of Democracy*.

Chapter Thirteen

War and *The Moral Basis of Democracy*

After Chicago, ER had a renewed understanding that her words mattered, and with the world in a state of siege, there was no time to waste. Every column, every radio program, every letter might make a difference. She confronted crises, traveled nonstop, supported rescue efforts—and worked to complete her remarkable meditation upon democracy.

The process of writing *The Moral Basis of Democracy* helped her to hone her own vision. What defines individual responsibility, ethical commitment, and moral vision in brutal, chaotic times? ER hoped her words might "stimulate the thoughts of many people so that they will force themselves to decide what Democracy means." Can they "believe in it as fervently as they can in their personal religion?" Is it worth "a sacrifice"? Her first paragraph defined the urgency of her quest: "At a time when the whole world is in turmoil and thousands of people are homeless and hungry, it behooves all of us to reconsider our political and religious beliefs . . . to clarify in our minds the standards by which we live."

As totalitarian dictators stormed the globe, ER considered democracy's roots in religion and the evolution of "the right to any religion, or to no religion." The principle of individual "responsibility . . . for the well-being of his neighbors," and the precept "Love thy neighbor as thyself," remained the root of "the Democratic ideal." Today, as dictators crushed individual liberty and rights beneath the boots of state power and terror, democracies depended on freedom of expression, the rule of the majority in an environment of cooperation, and service. For democracy to survive, ER wrote, we must "live cooperatively" and serve the community. For our "own success to be real, [we must] contribute to the success of others."

ER's second chapter detailed the history of democratic theory from the Magna Carta of 1215, which ensured certain basic individual rights and freedoms: "No taxes shall be imposed except by common counsel. No man shall be imprisoned, exiled or destroyed except by the lawful judgment of his peers or by the law of the land. To no one is right or justice sold or refused." Then came religious freedom for dissenters and freethinkers, Pilgrims, Puritans, Catholics, and Quakers. As democratic theory unfolded, William Penn, Thomas Paine, and "radicals" prepared for the American Revolution. Paine's *Common Sense* (1776) and *The Rights of Man* (1791) codified "the fundamental principles for representative" government and made Paine "the leader of the republicans in France and the radicals in England."

ER's journey through the American Revolution from Patrick Henry to Benjamin Franklin and Thomas Jefferson—from the Declaration of Independence to the Constitution to the Bill of Rights—was, she wrote, a study in cooperation. In the politically diverse world, "we must all compromise when we come together to formulate plans for the public good." Progress toward "the rights of the individual had to be obtained by continuous vigilance in those days just as the rights can only be maintained today."

She reviewed these rights: The right to freedom and equality and political liberty; the rights and responsibilities of all citizens; the right of habeas corpus; the right to hold opinions without fear of molestation; the right to freedom of expression ("one of the most precious"); the right to demand accountability of public service agents—each of these rights, as she saw it, contributed to the dignity of the individual and helped citizens to live full and unoppressed lives.

Through the eighteenth century, as democracy was codified and limited, Thomas Jefferson represented a visionary departure from tradition, she affirmed. He "believed in the education of all classes" and called for an end to slavery. Although a slave owner, "he realized that slavery was the denial of the equality of man." To deny man's equality was to lose "the basis of Democracy." While the "ideal of Democracy" persisted, if "we are honest with ourselves . . . we will acknowledge that we have not carried it out, and in our lack of faith we have debased the human being." We still have slavery, in different forms among different groups, she emphasized, and we have yet to "accept the brotherhood of man as a basic truth."

The 130 million people who make up our great nation come "from every nation" on the globe. Asians, Africans, Europeans, and Latin Americans truly make us "the melting pot of the world." We now face "almost an entire continent of vast resources." But "we have allowed a situation to arise where many people are debased by poverty or the accident of race in our own country, and therefore have no stake in democracy; while others appeal to this old rule of the sacredness of property rights to retain in the hands of a limited number the fruits of the labor of many." Today issues of economic opportunity and security define our problems. "It is often said that we are free, and then sneeringly . . . 'free to starve.'" That is not an amusement. Nobody can say the "Indians or Negroes of this country are free." Racial prejudice enslaves, and "poverty enslaves." Other "racial and religious groups . . . labor under [other] discriminations."

"Some of us have too much of this world's goods," she wrote, and we "are thereby separated too widely from each other" to appreciate daily hardships and suffering others endure. Clearly, "we do not completely practice the Democratic way of life," especially "in our relationship to submerged people." We must consider what has become of our "sense of obligation" regarding our community and "the welfare of our neighbors," which is essential to democracy's success.

Political democracy requires economic democracy, while greed debases it: "either we must make our economic system work to the satisfaction of all our people," or we will lose the competition, the war already under way. The New Deal introduced a "type of revolution," and we now recognize that government is responsible for social conditions. But there "is still much to be done." A minimum standard of security, and "equality of opportunity," are required for every child. We must achieve "an economic level below which no one is permitted to fall." But we have not yet discovered the economic secrets of full employment, and far too many "are left with nothing to do, and therefore without the wherewithal for living."

Yet the questions of democracy are not merely economic. Our failure to expand democracy at home and "to spread [democratic] values throughout the world" is rooted in our failure to appreciate "the spiritual concepts" that define democracy. We have been too devoted to "the gods of Mammon." Humanity must "rise above purely selfish interest" and take responsibility for one another. Democracy "necessarily involves the spirit of social cooperation."

In this era of catastrophe and danger, ER continued, instituting change requires having a bold new vision for the future that will transform "our whole attitude toward life and civilization" and motivate us to seek "an exciting new world," steeped in principles of democracy and

justice. We must build "a social conscience and a sense of responsibility."
We need a new national purpose that guarantees "each individual" a
secure and meaningful life, setting new standards "for good health, equal
education and equal opportunity to achieve success according to each
individual's powers." These opportunities involve every "line of work,
either of hand or head," and mean for everyone a share of "full responsibility" for the well-being of "the whole people."

To be sure, those with affluence and leisure build great galleries and
museums, fund science and research projects, and support learning and
recreation. Foundations and charities are worthy, but "it is time to take a
new step in the progress of humanity." The education and enlightenment
of people "for the benefit of our country as a whole is a concern of the
whole country." Public support for the arts and sciences needs to be developed everywhere, with opportunities for engagement for everyone. It will
occur slowly, when we have a "better understanding of people of different
races and creeds." But it will occur, and the United States will be a model
of such understanding for the world.

Some say that "human nature cannot change," but change is under
way. Look at the changes wrought "by Nazi and Fascist dictators." Life is
never static. Education, "moral and physical training," affects all of us. "If
human beings can be changed to fit a Nazi . . . or a Communist pattern,
certainly we should not lose heart at the thought of changing human
nature to fit a Democratic way of life."

Religious leaders must address social questions, for "religion [is] a way
of life which develops the spirit." Too often churches have failed to provide spiritual haven in troubled times. Too often they limit their efforts to
ensuring their own survival and no longer consider humanity's needs.
But "if human beings can be trained for cruelty and greed and a belief in
power which comes through hate and fear and force, certainly we can
train equally well for gentleness and mercy and the power of love which
comes because of the strength of the good qualities to be found in the
soul of every individual human being." ER called for a new "spiritual,
moral awakening" that depended on no specific church or religion. We
must seek "the spiritual force which the life of Christ exemplifies . . . [or]
the life of Buddha," specifically the tangible ideals of love and compassion
"for our neighbors."

Taking our "democratic experiment" forward to "its fullest development" will require a great amount of "individual responsibility," not only in our leaders "but in the people as a whole." ER called upon leaders to proclaim these aspirations for democracy in "clear words" for all the people to heed. Here she was making a call, though coded and indirect, for her husband to move democracy forward with a bold statement of intention.

Ultimately, ER believed, we will change our definition and "standards of success" to celebrate those who create "a place in the community through service to the community," those who contribute to others more than those who benefit themselves alone. For too long, democracy has failed to challenge traditional "selfishness." For democracy to go forward, we must ask, "What are we prepared to sacrifice?" Might we imagine "the fruits of our labors" not exclusively our own but as "a trusteeship" for "the greatest number of people"?

With such participatory democracy, we will "know what we believe in, how we intend to live, and what we are doing for our neighbors." Our neighbors are not limited to our families down the road but consist of "all those who live anywhere within range of our knowledge. That means an obligation to the coal miners and share-croppers, the migratory workers, the tenement-house dwellers and farmers who cannot make a living." ER's radical definition of *democracy* was service for all, and her definition of *neighbor* was global: We are many; we are everywhere; we are all.

Ultimately there was nothing modest about ER's proposal. For democracy to work, every individual needed to participate in the government. For the government to work, it must be responsive to the people:

> We must make that will and desire of the people the result of adequate education and adequate material security. We must maintain a standard of living which makes it possible for the people really to want justice for all, rather than to harbor a secret hope for privileges because they cannot hope for justice.
>
> If we accomplish this, we have paved the way for the first hope for real peace the world has ever known. All people desire peace, but they are led to war because what is offered . . . seems to be unjust, and they are constantly seeking a way to right that injustice.

After all, life's great appeal is the ongoing "adventure" and "excitement" in pursuit of a better, more humane world. When democracy works as it should, there is "a sense of brotherhood" and inspired leadership. She hoped her spiritual quest would lead to the ever-rising "living standard of all people."

ER wrote her "little book" at night, alone in her room—whatever room she happened to be in during that hectic campaign season—regularly interrupted by political crises and family woes. *The Moral Basis of Democracy* was an eloquent articulation of her goals for the future: to ensure the survival of the liberal New Deal and to meet the challenges of the unfolding world war. It elaborated her essential creed and would guide her efforts to the end of her life.

From her "little cottage," she sought to introduce Secretary Wallace to her readers. He would surely "strengthen the ticket," she wrote. "I have always felt in him a certain shyness and that has kept him aloof from some Democrats, but now that he will be in close touch with so many . . . I am sure they will find in him much to admire and love."

Back in 1933, she had deplored Wallace's programs. He had executed the Agricultural Adjustment Act so as to benefit only large plantation and farm owners, leading to human misery and accelerating the "great migration" from the rural South. His disregard for conditions faced by farmworkers and sharecroppers seemed to her cruel. Her many protests over the waste of cotton, grain, and livestock resulted in the Federal Surplus Commodities Corporation, through which Harry Hopkins's Federal Emergency Relief Administration purchased farm surpluses and donated them to relief agencies.

By 1936, his views changed. Surprised by the dire poverty he witnessed during a fact-finding southern tour, he was eager to make amends for the damage done by his AAA crop reduction programs, and he supported the demands of the Southern Tenant Farmers Union. But ER's contempt for Wallace's early policies lingered, and she was impatient with his statistical, scholarly approach to economic and human problems. She never referred to his progressive 1938 book *Paths to Plenty*, which heralded an era of "general welfare" defined by "democratic faith and universal social justice."

But in 1940 Wallace's goals were entirely in accord with her own. He too now called for an end to greed and selfish materialism and for economic democracy so that "all humanity might partake of the earth's abundance." He too now believed a global change in attitude required a spiritual and personal shift in belief, a revitalized "democratic faith" that placed human dignity and welfare above individual rapacity. In *Paths to Plenty*, he specifically criticized Social Darwinism, the regnant American ethic that merged Protestant fundamentalism to laissez-faire economics to justify rule by corporate capitalism, the "businessman's religion."

After the Chicago convention, ER and Wallace became great allies in the effort to enhance democratic movements and build upon the New Deal to create a world order to "humanize capitalism" for the general good. ER thought it would "take many years," and Wallace thought it might take "one hundred years" or more, but they both believed it necessary, even inevitable.

In her first postconvention column, ER ignored the rancor of Chicago to celebrate an imagined harmony: "To me there is something very contagious about the friendly atmosphere brought about by meeting old friends. I was so glad to see them from all parts of the country. . . . We may think differently on certain subjects but, taken by and large, there is a bond of real friendliness." She minimized the party's leadership battles. Farley had resigned as party chairman, and she considered his successor Ed Flynn, the "boss of the Bronx," a dependable ally. During the campaign, she would spend most of her time working behind the scenes, in league with her great friends of the Democratic Party's Women's Division, as she had done since 1920.

At Val-Kill, ER returned to the outdoors. A family of robins outside her bedroom window gratified her love of nature. Providing her readers with updates, she watched "with the keenest interest the growth of three little robins. I never knew diminutive objects could eat so much and grow so fast. The nest seems much too small for them." And then came the first hesitant effort at flight: "It reminds me of myself going off the diving board. I long to be able to communicate in some bird language that, if he just has self-confidence, it will be all right." Finally on 19 July: "My little birds have flown this morning out into a strange world all by themselves. I hope they lead happy bird lives and are preserved from the many dangers they must meet, long enough, at least, to give them a few months of whatever constitutes happy bird life!"

On 21 July, the week after the convention, family life at Hyde Park was saddened by the death of Aunt Dora. Surrounded by her family, Dora Delano Forbes died at ninety-two, devastated by the fall of France. She had always been in remarkably good health, and always "so young in spirit," ER observed, noting that Aunt Dora had been "a symbol of how to grow old gracefully." She mourned her and was always grateful for their marvelous and inspiring times together in Paris. After the Great War, Dora had introduced ER to hospital work among wounded veterans, and to the Lighthouse, which Aunt Dora had founded to assist French soldiers blinded in battle.

During these sorrowful days, FDR III's second birthday arrived, a joyous occasion highlighted by a party and his first horseback ride, "on the saddle in front of his father." Happy, on "the little walk" atop the "big hunter," little Frank repeated "'Again! Again,' and seemed disgusted that there was no further ride. . . . I was amused, for when we tried to put him on the pony by himself, he refused to have anything to do with riding!" ER's grandchildren added joy to her days. These challenging times, she noted, required each of us to discover and create new resources for strength and learning, so that we might "find somewhere within ourselves, the qualities and the intelligence to encounter whatever the future may hold in store."

But as Tommy wrote to Anna on 12 July, ER "is always happier when she feels she is doing something constructive." In the movement for racial justice, she worked closely with Mary McLeod Bethune, director of Negro Affairs at the National Youth Administration, to end wage differentials and intolerable conditions faced by women and black workers in defense plants. Back in 1938 ER and Bethune had sought to ensure that the NYA's Civilian Pilot Training Program include a Negro section. ER worked with the Rosenwald Fund and other agencies to establish flight schools on the campuses of historically black colleges, including Tuskegee Institute, Howard University, and Hampton Institute. Tuskegee's program had begun in October 1939.

Now she supported NAACP protests against degrading Jim Crow policies throughout the military, and she advocated expanding rights and opportunities for women and blacks throughout the armed forces. Secretary of War Stimson denounced her "intrusive and impulsive folly," but ER was convinced that the struggle against fascism required equal opportunity and respect to replace bigotry and violence in the United States;

otherwise democracy would remain an empty promise. Early in the presidential campaign, Wendell Willkie had put issues of race on the agenda. In September, before a black crowd of eight thousand in the Negro Leagues' Chicago American Giants baseball park, he announced his intention "to eliminate racial discrimination, abolish Jim Crow laws, [and achieve] an anti-lynching statute." FDR's southern strategy notwithstanding, ER shared these goals and remained steadfast in her pursuit of them.

Equally urgent for ER were efforts to rescue Europe's endangered people. She attended Hadassah meetings with Tamar de Sola Pool and supported a children's village in Palestine sponsored by the Young Women's Zionist Organization. She spoke and agitated for Jewish relief. And she continued her work with the U.S. Committee for the Care of European Children. She deplored "the horrid legal details" that hampered efforts to get British children to safety. In July several thousand children were ready for passage, but U.S. ships were allegedly not available. The United States had a responsibility to do everything possible to "facilitate their coming," the first lady wrote. She was "very impatient" with the "slowness, almost stubbornness" of career State Department officials involved and implored the president to hasten the process. "Time is so important," she wrote. "It seems incredible that anyone would let red tape and regulations slow up the process."

After an intense conversation, FDR, who had been unsupportive, agreed to establish an Emergency Visitors Visa Program to rescue "persons of exceptional merit, those of superior intellectual attainment." On 15 August, Karl Frank of the ERC wrote a letter of gratitude to ER: "I know it is due to your interest. You will certainly know that many hundreds of people have been granted visitors' visas." Now the task would be to get exit permits from Vichy for the notables and find safe havens for them. Young (thirty-two), dapper, and fearless, Varian Fry left for France in August, with lists of names and $3,000 strapped to his thigh.

Even as he departed, the SS *Quanza* set sail from Lisbon with 317 passengers—mostly European refugees—aboard. When the ship arrived in New York on 19 August, 196 people were permitted to disembark, including 130 Europeans, who presumably had acceptable visas. But the visas of 121 other passengers—affluent refugees, mostly Jews—were rejected.

The *Quanza* proceeded to Mexico, where another thirty-five passengers were allowed to disembark, then to Virginia, to take on coal for its return trip to Lisbon. While en route to Norfolk, Captain Alberto Harberts announced that nobody would be allowed to leave the ship there. On 10 September someone—it is unclear who—contacted ER about the plight of the remaining eighty-six passengers. Unwilling to see the tragedy of the *St. Louis* repeated, she insisted they be given shelter and called upon all her allies, notably Patrick Malin of the President's Advisory Committee on Political Refugees (PACPR), who went to Norfolk to try to arrange for their admission. The PACPR was a group that coordinated admission of refugees with the State and Justice departments.

Meanwhile several attorneys had filed habeas corpus petitions for various passengers, including Elisabeth Cartier, a wealthy Swiss citizen who had been living in France. And the Wolf and Moritz Rand family, who were also passengers, contacted via intermediaries a highly regarded admiralty attorney. Jacob L. Morewitz brought a $100,000 lawsuit on behalf of the Rand family, arguing that because the *Quanza* did not allow the family to disembark, it was in breach of contract with them. According to Morewitz's son, the goal was "to tie up the ship in court long enough for refugee leaders in Washington" to pressure FDR on behalf of the refugees.

Since the ship was to leave within twenty-four hours, the strategy worked. The U.S. District Court in Norfolk granted an injunction to hold the ship in federal custody, giving ER's allies time to act decisively.* FDR called upon James McDonald, PACPR chair; Patrick Malin, his assistant; Marshall Field, chair of the U.S. Committee for the Care of European Children; and Breckinridge Long, assistant secretary of state, to evaluate the immigration status of each passenger.

Long, the State Department official ER most despised, opposed admitting refugees in general, and in this case he acknowledged that the

---

*While some of the *Quanza* passengers who gained a haven within the United States remembered ER's offer to take them in as her personal guests, and gave her substantial credit for their safety, the efforts of Morewitz and others were critical.

claims of only eight of the passengers were valid. He was therefore astonished on 14 September when Patrick Malin and other PACPR officials granted permits for all eighty-six passengers to disembark. Malin had outmaneuvered Long, and the immediate press response was favorable.

But while the *Quanza* episode resulted in triumph, it generated a vicious backlash from the State Department (which may be why ER never mentioned it). Long vehemently protested granting the passengers asylum. Every refugee was a potential Nazi or Communist, he insisted. The United States had been "very generous in offering hospitality" to those in danger from the Nazis, but he insisted that eligibility for asylum now be closed for good. He demanded all authority to grant visas be placed in American consulates, where he could control the process. FDR complied with Long's demand, putting him in charge of all consulates and exit visas.

As always, during periods of high stress and distress, ER turned to her tried and tested remedies. Nature, exercise, music, friends, and work revived her spirits and restored her "vigor." Sports programs were key, for wherever they thrived, youth were empowered. On 20 September she attended a daylong Washington conference on sports education, and saw it as a sign of national maturity that the United States was expanding its recreation programs for "young and old." They were essential to the development of a healthy citizenry that could fight to defend the country. Now, she urged, we need "to go one step further" and integrate sports and recreation facilities through public and private agencies "for the good of the people."

Music education was equally essential. She applauded Leopold Stokowski's American Youth Orchestra, a group of public school boys and girls on tour in South America, for enhancing the Good Neighbor policy. Before the musicians embarked, they had studied Spanish, and they were evidently to study Portuguese on the way to Brazil. Acknowledging that "music is a universal language," ER hoped U.S. schools would adopt the study of Spanish. So thrilled was ER by the Youth Orchestra, she met their ship when they returned from their Latin American tour, which had been a resounding success. "Their performances," ER was delighted to note, "have made a vast difference in the way that people feel about the

United States in many South American countries." Moreover the "sixteen girls in the orchestra have created so much comment that they say the position of women in orchestras will be changed for all time."

Throughout the summer the Battle of Britain escalated, and the Blitz intensified. From 9 July, when dockyards in South Wales were bombed and almost one hundred civilians were killed, rarely a day went by without terror and carnage. On 11 August, British fighters shot down 62 German raiders but lost 25 planes. On 15 August, 100 German bombers struck docks, factories, airfields throughout the northeast, and 800 bombers attacked the south. Britain's fighters shot down 30 planes in the northeast, and only two British pilots were injured; in the south, 46 German aircraft were shot down, and 24 British fighters were lost, with 8 pilots dead. On 16 August, Prime Minister Churchill witnessed a ferocious air battle from an operations center in Uxbridge. The air war victories resulted in his 20 August words to Parliament, broadcast internationally: "Never in the field of human conflict has so much been owed by so many to so few."

On 14 August, the anniversary of ER's father's death, as fresh news of the war dead filtered in, she wrote:

> I looked at the moon last night . . . [and] could not help thinking of what its beauty means to us, and in contrast what horror its bright light means for England. [As news came in about] constantly renewed flights over various parts of England, we can only hope that bad weather will envelop the British Isles and those traditional fogs will be worse than they ever have been before. They are perhaps the best protection that Great Britain can have outside of her fighting air force which seems to be acquitting itself extremely well.
>
> I cannot help but think of ruined houses and countryside in terms of people whom I know. Having members of your family and friends in various parts of England, Scotland and Ireland makes bombing raids which victimize civilians a much more personal thing.

On 24 August German bombs hit central London. The next day Britain bombed Berlin. For almost a fortnight hundreds of German bombers struck British cities and coastal villages. Hundreds were killed each day, every night. On 7 September, three hundred Londoners died, forty in one air raid shelter alone. The Blitz continued nightly, and London's death toll escalated to one thousand in a week.

On that day, ER concluded her column with an unusual expression of her deepest feelings about the Blitz. "The horror grows worse and the feeling that you never know quite what is happening, or may happen, is very hard to bear. The weight of suffering in the world is so great one cannot be happy these days." But from Americans' current position of safety, it was "incumbent upon all of us to be grateful . . . and show it by as much cheerfulness and willingness to give to others, as we possibly can."

By September's end, 6,954 British civilians were dead. On 11 September, Churchill spoke to an international audience over radio. Hitler's "cruel, wanton, indiscriminate bombings of London," he said in his stunning broadcast, reflected his insane hope that the death of "large numbers of civilians and women and children [would] terrorize and cow the people of this mighty imperial city." He said:

> Little does he know the spirit of the British [people], or the tough fibre of the Londoners . . . who have been bred to value freedom far above their lives.
>
> This wicked man, the repository and embodiment of many forms of soul-destroying hatreds, this monstrous product of former wrongs and shame, has now resolved to try to break our famous Island race by a process of indiscriminate slaughter and destruction. What he has done is to kindle a fire in British hearts . . . a fire which will burn with a steady and consuming flame until the last vestiges of Nazi tyranny have been burnt out of Europe, and until the Old World— and the New—can join hands to rebuild the temples of man's freedom and man's honour.

ER was deeply stirred by the speech, with its "calmness and great fortitude." Churchill's words "seemed a challenge to every individual" to contribute whatever was needed to fight the madness and "made one feel that it would be impossible to do anything but endure." But she had an editorial addition: Churchill had emphasized the duty of "every man"; she would add "every woman" and all children. Indeed, the night of his speech, ER read a letter from "a little boy in a refugee camp in England" who casually "passed off the fires and the bombs," noting "they were so frequent now that he really could not take the time to tell about them."

Her efforts to save British children intensified. On 17 September a German U-boat torpedoed *The City of Benares*, embarked for Montreal and Quebec. Of the 406 passengers and crew, 248 were lost, including 77 children who had been headed for safety. The first lady spent much of that week meeting with various children's committees. Besides her work for the U.S. Committee for the Care of European Children, she was also active with the Foster Parents Plan for War Children, which raised money for the education and shelter of more than 32,000 refugee children currently at a large estate outside London, where they awaited transport to North America. And she worked with the Women's Committee for Mercy Ships, which advocated legislation, sponsored by Senator Carter Glass (D-VA), that would enable U.S.-registered ships to go to Britain to bring refugee children directly to the United States. There were reportedly 200,000 children who awaited refuge in North America. ER's committee made it clear that their work was not limited to British children: "We want American ships to rescue children who are in danger, without regard for race, creed, or nationality." Moreover, for those who managed to arrive in the United States, it would "give every possible aid."*

In Philadelphia on 20 September she attended a ceremony for FDR, who received an honorary degree from the University of Pennsylvania. She lunched with his party, which included her grandson Bill (Elliott's son), former daughter-in-law Betty Donner, Curtin Winsor, and William Bullitt, as well as Anthony Biddle, the American ambassador to Warsaw, and his wife, Margaret. Tony Biddle told ER about witnessing the carnage in Poland, and then France: "I used to pray every morning to be so busy . . . I could not stop to think. If you had nothing to do, the sights you saw were too overwhelming."

ER returned to New York for the opening of the film *Pastor Hall*, a British anti-Nazi film for which she had narrated the prologue. The film is based on Ernst Toller's last play, *Pastor Hall*,† which in turn was based

---

*Among them was ten-year-old Shirley Vivian Catlin who spent three years in Minnesota with WILPF activist Ruth Gage-Colby and her physician husband. Decades later, Shirley Catlin Williams, MP, the daughter of Vera Brittain and George Catlin, would be one of the founders of the Social Democratic Party.

†ER had met Toller and Klaus Mann on 11 May 1939, when she hosted a White House reception for the international writers' congress arranged by PEN in conjunction with the World's Fair. Mann and Toller "stuck together throughout the

on the real-life Reverend Martin Niemöller, who protested the mistreatment of Jews from his church pulpit and in 1937 was imprisoned in Dachau. He is best remembered for his words from Dachau:

First they came for the socialists, and I did not speak out—because I was not a socialist.

Then they came for the trade unionists, and I did not speak out—because I was not a trade unionist.

Then they came for the Jews, and I did not speak out—because I was not a Jew.

Then they came for me—and there was no one left to speak for me.

He spent over seven years in Dachau, Sachsenhausen, and Flossenburg concentration camps. He was liberated on 4 May 1945 when U.S. troops

---

whole festive, fatiguing day," when they were introduced to FDR in his study, and when they spoke at lunch with ER. That great lady, Mann wrote in his memoir, was always able to impart "a touch of intimacy" even in a large gathering. "A heartening appeal emanates from her smile and look. She seems particularly interested in the affairs and opinions of every individual with whom she just happens to chat. Only a woman of so aristocratic a background and with so democratic a heart can afford the exquisite simplicity typical of all her words and ways."

But, Mann wrote, it was the last time they saw each other. Ernst Toller committed suicide on 22 May 1939, in his New York City apartment, after he learned of the fall of Madrid. Poet, revolutionary, and dramatist, Toller had been one of Thomas Mann's most esteemed students, subsequently known as "the student prince" of Munich's unlikely, extraordinary "bloodless revolution." In 1918 writers and artists persuaded the army to declare "a democratic and socialist Bavaria." Their pacifist revolution was crushed in February 1919, when White Armies pronounced "a red terror" and slaughtered both partisans and bystanders. Toller escaped but was arrested and served five years in prison. When he emerged, he wrote *Hoppla, Wir Leben* (Hey, We're Alive)—selected by Erwin Piscator to open his new theater. It was a cry of agony against apathy and pretension, the lunatic nature of Weimar politics. People were crushed, and nobody noticed; everywhere "faces in the street" were blank disinterested "lumps of flesh . . . blown up with worry and conceit." One had only two choices now, Toller wrote in 1925: "to hang oneself or to change the world."

Toller left Hitler's Germany immediately. His last two major works were *No More Peace* and *Pastor Hall*. ER considered the decision to distribute Toller's film a tribute to his call for hope to change the world. See Klaus Mann, *Turning Point*, pp. 322–23; Friedrich, *Before the Deluge*, pp. 253–54; Heilbut, *Exiled in Paradise*, pp. 11, 271–72; and Heilbut, *Thomas Mann*, pp. 324, 530.

entered Flossenburg. He dedicated the rest of his life to German redemption, world peace, and nuclear disarmament.

The fictionalized version of Pastor Niemöller in the film, named Pastor Hall, suffers cruel torture until his escape and return to his church. According to Bosley Crowther's *New York Times* review, actor Wilfrid Lawson "achieves a moment of ascendant emotion when he exhorts his congregation to put on 'the whole armor of God' to fight the anti-Christ." After this last sermon, he is shot by waiting storm troopers and dies on the steps of his church.

ER previously had seen the vivid and controversial film at a private and secret viewing and felt inspired by Niemöller's courage. After leading Hollywood studios refused to distribute the film in the United States, James Roosevelt consulted his mother as to whether she thought he should do so. She encouraged him and volunteered to do anything to help get the film widely seen throughout the country. To that end, she had recorded a prologue to the film, in which she said:

> I am glad to introduce this motion picture because I believe it tells a story of most vital importance to all of us. It is a story that is true— tragically true—a story of the insidious growth of the spirit of hatred, intolerance and suppression of liberty which is now sweeping over the face of this earth. The leading character . . . is a simple man of God, . . . the same kind of minister that you and I have known and loved . . . in every community . . . where men and women are free to worship God in their own way. To me this picture carries a message of inspiring truth. It is deeply encouraging.

The film's opening in New York was a notable event. "Not even the oldest Broadwayite," the *Sunday Mirror* noted, "could remember a premiere like that in the Globe Theatre last night. . . . Chief among those in the distinguished audience" was the first lady, who "entered the theatre on the arm of her producer son Jimmy." ER was also accompanied by Tommy, Joe Lash, his friend Agnes Reynolds, and Harry Hooker.

ER was proud of her son's determination to bring this film to the United States and happy to be part of his act of courage and defiance. Still, "it seemed strange to see my son's name" on the marquee, and "even stranger to see myself announced at the beginning of a feature picture. I can't say that I like myself on the screen, but I do hope people will go to see the picture and remember the lesson it carries. Hate and force cannot be abroad in such a great part of the world without having an effect on the rest of it. . . . It is important for us to see what a system can do to human beings when it brings out all that is worst in them."

Most New York reviews of *Pastor Hall* were positive, and when Sara Delano Roosevelt saw it, an unnamed *Times* reporter observed that she "applauded vigorously" after ER's prologue. The reporter watched her carefully: "During some of the concentration camp scenes, at which several women walked out, she [remained calm]." Subsequently SDR told the reporter she would not call the film "brutal" but rather "realistic." "Anti-Nazi movies have my approval because the truth must be shown now as never before. I hope to see it again soon and I think everyone should see it."

ER herself viewed *Pastor Hall* as a prayer for the future in the battle for humanity. She considered the film "extraordinary" and hoped it would jar her many friends in the youth movement who still opposed any support for Britain and objected to her appeals for a year of service, universal conscription, and military preparedness. She was stunned by their apathy as well as the general public's disregard for the world's suffering. She was outraged that the film was banned in several cities, including Chicago, "as propaganda and too shocking," and that there were widespread protests against the concentration camp scenes. ER relied on her own creed, *The Moral Basis of Democracy*: life is about the struggle, and we are all responsible.

Chapter Fourteen

"Defense Is Not a Matter of What You Get, But of What You Give"

ER did not underestimate the bitter political climate within the United States in 1940. While most polls indicated a growing revulsion among Americans against Hitlerism and fascism, a vast majority of the voting public (83 percent, according to published polls) opposed any increase in immigration quotas and rejected providing military aid to Britain. She understood and shared the abiding antiwar sentiment, but she could not understand this passivity in the face of human suffering. If Americans could name it and even despise it, why did they turn away from action and even demand that nothing be done?

ER had read *Mein Kampf* and Hitler's speeches in German. She frequently asked her isolationist or anti-interventionist correspondents if they too had read his words—and if so, how could they be so passive while his plans for slavery, tyranny, and horror marched triumphant? Hitler's frequent references to U.S. history sickened her: he invoked "Indian removal," the reservations and massacres, as well as the legal segregation and humiliation of African-Americans, with separate drinking fountains and park benches, separate schools and swimming pools, separate sections on buses and trains. He considered America his great ally when it came to "savages" and eugenics. Blood ruled.

To purify Germany and create the "master race," one of Hitler's first 1933 decrees ordered the forced sterilization of more than five hundred mixed-race or Afro-German teenagers, and many thousands of physical and mental "*Untermenschen*" with disabilities, as well as the blind and infirm. Wherever he ruled, he outlawed those without "pure" German blood or who had allegedly blood-destroying limitations: Jews, Gypsies, homosexuals, deviants, disabled and other "problem people," including "single infertile women" and "useless eaters," who drained the economy and whose "lives were not worth living." They were to be removed to "reservations" and quarantined.

For ER, Hitler cast a floodlight on America's unfinished agenda for democracy. In the South, a surprising level of bigotry against Jews, foreigners, outsiders, and "aliens" prevailed. Southern Democrats remained committed to their traditions of "race etiquette"—those features of white supremacy regnant in Hitler's crusade for the master race. Some U.S. congresspeople were willing to support increased defense expenditures and conscription, but they rejected any steps toward racial justice, including Willkie's, and sought to defund New Deal agencies. Standing up for liberty, freedom, and justice against Hitler, ER thought, would require another, albeit different, New Deal.

She was proud to be part of the progressive Southern Conference for Human Welfare and to work with friends and advisers such as Virginia Durr, Lucy Randolph Mason, and Ellen Woodward—staunch New Dealers and radical activists for race justice. Hailing from Alabama, Georgia, and Mississippi, they vigorously opposed segregation, discrimination, the poll tax, and lynching. They understood that immigrants, migrant farmworkers, and African-Americans must achieve full citizenship and respect—immediately. They represented a growing movement but had little support among southern leaders in Congress.

Significant communities of activists elsewhere in the country also supported Hitler. Besides the Nazi Bund, many Catholic, anti-British, Irish, and Italian groups were in league with the fascist radio priest Father Charles Coughlin. By 1940 more than 110 fascist organizations were on the scene, opposing all U.S. defense measures. In a galling alliance, isolationists, pacifists, and antiwar progressives—many of whom had been among ER's closest friends—joined them. She increasingly distrusted her embattled allies within the youth movement, concluding that their international views had been defined by the Nazi-Soviet Pact. She also deplored the punitive measures made possible by the Smith Act and all efforts to stifle free speech and debone the Bill of Rights.

The deep divisions within the nation reflected the turmoil within ER's own divided heart. Like her great friends who had led the peace and social justice movements—Jane Addams, Lillian Wald, Carrie Chapman Catt, Caroline O'Day, Clarence Pickett, and the Quakers—she believed profoundly that war destroyed democracy and devoured liberty. During the 1920s and 1930s she had worked with the War Resisters League, the Fellowship of Reconciliation, and the WILPF. She never doubted that the passions of militarism forged intolerance and repression, demanded conformity and silence. While she did not want the United States to be at war, she could not bear to imagine a future that was everywhere dominated and controlled by Hitler.

Lillian Wald died on 1 September 1940. The founder of the Henry Street Settlement, the Visiting Nurse Service, and the modern public health nursing movement, Wald was a founder of WILPF and the American Union Against Militarism, which had created the ACLU. She introduced "so many things which we accept today as a responsibility of government," ER noted—playgrounds, public health services, music, theater and dance in schools, community centers, and settlement houses. Wald once said she would die happy because all she had fought for was now the government's concern.

ER had kept in close touch with Wald during her years of retirement and illness at her House on the Pond in Westport, Connecticut. "I always fall under the spell of her personality," ER wrote after one visit, "and wonder what quality . . . makes an individual sway others by the sheer force of her own sympathy and understanding of human beings," their needs and their suffering. She was grateful for Wald's "lifelong influence" on her own vision: "I have long paid homage" to her "amazing vitality and love of people." Wald embodied ER's own creed, that she who works for "culture and justice represents an art of humanity."

ER sent an extraordinary "spray of white dahlias and purple chrysanthemums" to Wald's funeral service at the Neighborhood Playhouse along with a telegram of regret that she could not attend, "but my thoughts will be with all those who loved and honored this shining spirit."

For ER, both Lillian Wald and Jane Addams left enduring legacies for peace and freedom—which meant security and human rights for everyone everywhere. Now the WILPF existed to continue their work, but its members were themselves endangered and threatened. In June the WILPF's international headquarters, which had been in Geneva since 1919, was removed for safety, along with the ILO and the League of Nations. Gertrude Baer, director of the WILPF's international work, moved to New York and issued monthly bulletins of information and news about "the most alarming situation created by the presence of millions of war refugees in all territories where war is raging." WILPF members participated in "the sheltering and caring of these refugees."

As a member of WILPF, ER received Baer's extraordinary circular letters with their urgent discussions of strategies and principles. In "From Europe to Women in America," Lida Gustava Heymann presented the pacifist's dilemma. Heymann, a suffragist and trade union organizer from Bavaria, and her life partner, Dr. Anita Augspurg, Germany's first woman judge, were ardent WILPF workers; Heymann had been international vice president since 1919. Although they were Aryans of "pure blood," the Nazis deemed them political unacceptables. In early 1933, as Nazis were harassing and arresting peace advocates and WILPF members in Berlin and Breslau, the two women fled to Zurich, abandoning their belongings and leaving behind their "considerable wealth" to live in a friend's attic. But they never thought of themselves as "exiles." As "world citizens," they felt everywhere at home.

But now it was time for action. Heymann wrote:

American Women: Listen to us in this very last moment when the hands of the clock are almost on the point of closing time. . . .

Brute force is on the point of destroying the whole world . . . [and] we have come to see that *today it is no longer possible* to overcome the violent methods of Fascism and Nazism by pacifist means. . . .

A small barking dog cannot stop a dashing train. The reversion to barbarism after a period of humanism is catastrophic. But catastrophes take their inherent course. Fascism and national-socialism today can be destroyed only through means [able to impress] the brutal men.

Those words reflected ER's thoughts in 1940: the Nazis had to be resisted. She hoped that Heymann's wise analysis would influence those pacifists in the WILPF, the American Friends Service Committee, and others who continued to reject war and military involvement.

That summer debate raged over the Burke-Wadsworth bill, which proposed to institute a peacetime military draft. Many were opposed to it, ER noted. Some objected to the age range, others to compulsory registration. Still others criticized the bill's failure to protect conscientious objectors, and ER agreed that "conscientious objectors should be protected, but they should be required to work for the country's good in ways which do not conflict with their religious beliefs. . . . To put a man in jail, even when at war . . . seems to me one of the regrettable actions we ought to guard against."

Still others, her own pacifist friends and allies, objected to conscription as such. When the Socialist Party leader Norman Thomas spoke on the radio against the draft, she wrote: "No one hearing him could refrain from feeling that he was a most able and persuasive speaker. . . . I think all of us should listen to both sides," debate the issue, and trust in democracy. ER was heartened by the "full and free discussion" under way.

For her part, she felt that aspects of this particular conscription bill "may prove to be wrong, and . . . [we will] want them changed." But in general "I approve of the principle of a selective draft."

Still, she was annoyed that discussions around the bill failed to consider her proposal for a universal draft for community service, to which all citizens would contribute. She also missed any sign that lessons on the impact of greed had been learned from the last war. Profiteering had tarnished past war investments. Any new military draft, she argued, had to be connected to a draft for business and industrial interests, so that "business and government [will be] working together." For "it is one thing to draft young men to give their services to their country and another to draft such capital as may be lying idle for investment [in areas] necessary for defense and which may mean little or no return to the investor." ER softened this radical call with a disavowal: "I am no economist. I am not a public servant. I am a mother and a citizen in a democracy." She called upon "the best minds in the country" to consider "how it can be made equally certain that capital . . . is drafted for the use of the country in just the way that lives are drafted." Congress and "administrative circles" had a responsibility to reassure the people that this was "being considered and adequately safe-guarded."

Finally, ER reaffirmed that "national defense is a matter of spirit as well as of material things." She demanded some recognition that spirit mattered, that "spirit is the most important part of it." We will not be successful until "we realize that defense is not a matter of what you get, but of what you give." Her democratic and nondiscriminatory vision of universal community service stirred controversy even among her young AYC friends. They championed work, education, welfare, and civil liberties—the best of the New Deal—but they opposed any military buildup. Meanwhile many of her other friends were staunchly for defense but dismissed issues of full employment and "morale" as "Utopian, superfluous, or irrelevant." Her riding companion and occasional ally Major Henry Hooker, for one, dismissed most of her ideas as dreamy.

But ER lobbied for them wherever she went, especially with those involved in the defense effort, including Dr. Harriet Elliott, the only woman on the National Defense Advisory Commission. She met with Aubrey Williams and other NYA officials on the ongoing problem of unemployment and the impact of "idle young people" on national defense. She approved the NYA's "youth occupation trips" in which young people met with industrial and professional advisers and learned about opportunities in "electricity, baking, nursing and public health, printing, business machines, art and design, automobile mechanics, farming, aviation and needle trades." She also argued for expanded youth training. U.S. defense, she insisted, must involve everybody.

But after her last summer meeting with Williams and NYA officials, she concluded, "I have yet to see anywhere a program or a statement which fully satisfies my own sense of what national defense really means."

As the refugee tragedies mounted, ER's work with the U.S. Committee for the Care of European Children expanded. In August she met with a delegation led by novelist and activist Dorothy Canfield Fisher, whose Children's Crusade for Children had raised money for refugees through the work of U.S. schoolchildren. They raised "a considerable sum," and in a deeply moving ceremony, "each American child handed a foreign child a check for the work which will be done either in their own country or for their nationals who are refugees in other countries."

Hyde Park itself became a sanctuary for several families of royal refugees. On 20 August, Norway's Princess Martha and her family arrived. The princess gave a brave speech predicting Hitler's ultimate defeat. "Everyone who believes that our own philosophy is right," ER noted, "will echo her words."

Along with ER's "Norwegian guests," her cousin W. Forbes Morgan and three young nieces from Michigan arrived—Amy, Diana, and Janet Roosevelt; they were Hall's daughters from his second marriage, to educator and pianist Dorothy Kemp Roosevelt. "A particularly happy time" at Hyde Park "included seven children and twelve grown-ups." They hiked, rode horses, swam, went to a county fair and an amusement park.

ER's ability to combine work with contemplation and relaxation was extraordinary. In mid-August Val-Kill hosted a gathering for New York's upstate Democratic women. ER, Tommy, and Elinor Morgenthau expected four hundred, but twice as many arrived: "We could hardly be blamed for being a little appalled." However, they collected "everything from everywhere," and nobody went hungry. FDR and Henry Wallace turned up too, and ER concluded the countryside was "the proper setting" for them as well. They were both "more natural" and happier than she had seen them recently. "They went off with a party to picnic in a distant spot," while she took another party to picnic "at my old home," in Tivoli:

> The house looks very much neglected. . . . Still, as we sat and ate our picnic supper, watching the sun go down behind the Catskill Mountains, I could not help feeling a sense of beauty and peace. It may be sad to return to the scene of one's childhood and realize all the things that have happened in the intervening years to the people one loves; yet there is also something very sweet in remembering the good things which no sadness can wipe out.
>
> For instance, into this house of adolescent life, with young aunts and uncles enjoying to the full a gay and fairly undisciplined existence I came with my brother after my mother's death. It was natural for my grandmother . . . to take in her eldest daughter's children. As I grow older, however, I appreciate more and more the spirit which made those young aunts and uncles make us, as children feel that our home was with them; that we had as much right to be there as they. There never was a question of what was thine or mine among us. That is something which makes for a deeper belief in the good of human nature and helps one through the rough spots all the rest of one's life.

ER had been hurt in her life, but she had been saved by love—and the generosity of love. Now she identified with everyone who was hurt and endangered and sought to protect and comfort every suffering citizen of the world. A new spirit appeared to be rising to expand security, community, and democracy—a curious gift generated by the need to unite during tragic times. Several British leaders advocated more positive war aims. "When bombing begins on a large scale" and suffering mounts, Harold

Nicolson wrote, "people will ask, 'What are we fighting for?'" The answer was evident: Britain was fighting to avoid Hitler's slavery, and in the end "we must have Free Trade and pooled resources" internationally; "Socialism [and] equality of opportunity" domestically. Nicolson was certain that "the old order has collapsed" and that Britain must "put forward a positive and revolutionary aim." He even drafted a cabinet statement that called for the end of the empire, "a Federal structure for postwar Europe and increasingly Socialist measures at home."

Subsequently, Bishop Atwood sent ER a note "by a young Englishman" affirming that "the nation has changed permanently and . . . return to our old grooves of thought is no longer possible." There will be no "swing back to 'business as usual' . . . at the end of this war." Historically, the young man continued, "apathy is man's besetting sin and it was apathy—reluctance to change, etc.—which caused us to stray so far from the purposes of life" in recent years. He now believed we were approaching another "point in our evolution" where we can reconstruct the social order. ER agreed completely: new democratic steps were required everywhere.

One early September day the French journalist Geneviève Tabouis arrived for lunch and explained the fall of France to Americans. ER, impressed, conveyed her message:

> There were too many people who had either a little money or a great deal, who cared more about what they had than about France, and who believed the Hitler propaganda that communism was something imminent and threatening because of demands being made by the workers. They were therefore almost willing to invite Mr. Hitler to control their country, in the hope . . . they would continue to retain all that they had without making any concessions to the workers. They never realized that these workers . . . had a right to share some of the things controlled by the little and big employer in shop or factory, mine or field.

Tabouis dazzled everyone around the table with a story of a man who owned a relatively big business. His daughter "slept with her jewels under her pillow [in fear] the workers would come and burn the factory when they heard of the French army's collapse. The workers did nothing of the kind, but Mr. Hitler has taken over the factory." Now the factory was gone, "and her country is gone too," ER concluded:

There is a lesson for us in this tragedy. Our people must be one. On Labor Day we must remember that this nation is founded to do away with classes and special privilege; that employer and worker have the same interest, which is to see that everyone in this nation has a life worth living. Only thus can we be sure that Labor Day [and all other holidays] will continue to be celebrated.

Since the passage of the Smith Act in June 1940, the Red Scare had escalated, and anti-immigrant sentiment was on the rise. The act, which ER considered a dangerous threat to democracy, ordered "every non-citizen who is 14 years of age or older, and who has not been registered and finger-printed prior to his entry into the U.S., [to] report to the nearest post office or [other places] designated by the Commissioner of Immigration, to be fingerprinted and registered. The parents of noncitizen children under the age of 14 shall apply for . . . said children." By mid-August, thousands of immigrants were in a panic, fearing deportation, criminal charges, or a return to the land of their origins—many of which no longer existed, having been swallowed up by the Nazi Reich.

The Smith Act legitimated the kinds of once-discredited "anti-sedition" activities that had so blighted America's civil liberties record in previous eras. Although FDR said there was nothing new about tyranny, ER was horrified by the return of the Red Scare, and by the way its new incarnation had quickly become race-based. Even as divided France fell to the Nazis, white supremacists were committing outrages under the cloak of anti-Communism.

Three New York journalists, for example, had been touring the South to film a documentary on "Negro education," sponsored by "the Rockefeller-financed General Education Board."* Although they had done nothing more than interview several people, they were arrested and jailed in Memphis "on suspicion of 'fifth column' activities." The police chief, Will

---

*The three were Richard J. Morris Jr., the twenty-two-year-old cousin of Newbold Morris, head of the New York City Council; Roger Barlow, twenty-eight; and Henwar Rodakiewicz, thirty-seven. ER personally knew Rodakiewicz, who was married to Peggy Kiskadden, the mother of future Harvard president Derek Bok. Peggy remained close to Esther Lape and Elizabeth Read and saw ER often—at Salt Meadow and in New York at 20 East Eleventh Street.

Lee, was certain they were subversives: "Why, they are a Communist set-up. One of them told me himself a Negro was as good as a white man. They're down here stirring up the Negroes." A fourth member of the group wired friends and relatives in New York and Washington for help, and they were freed after three days.

On 18 June 1940 Jane Sommerich, a New York neighbor, sent ER a newspaper clipping about the incident along with an irate letter:

> At a time when the tragic fate of most of Continental Europe has shown the dangers that eat at democracy from within, we are being overtaken by thoughtless hysteria and bigotry in our own country. . . .
>
> Under the guise of prosecuting 'fifth columnists' . . . American racists, Fascist in their psychology as the movements they ostensibly condemn, will take away the fundamental liberties of those of us most truly bound to democratic ideals. Such attacks on the Bill of Rights and the 14th Amendment must be pointed out and condemned with unceasing vigor!
>
> Would you find space in your column and time on your broadcast to inveigh against the undemocratic and intolerant attitude expressed so bluntly by Chief Will Lee of the Memphis Police Department?

On 30 July New York congressman Vito Marcantonio denounced the Smith Act and its harassment of the foreign-born:

> It is estimated that 3,500,000 noncitizens will have to submit to fingerprinting and registration. . . . Over 3,000,000 of these have lived in the United States 10 years or more. Thus in free America we will witness the Hitler-imitating spectacle of 3,500,000 men, women, and children . . . loyal, hardworking people in all walks of life— priests, nuns, rabbis, ministers, bricklayers, carpenters, and clerks— all of whom have been making a contribution to the greatness of America, being subjected to the criminal-like treatment of registration and fingerprinting.

ER's mailbox was soon flooded by letters from longtime residents who were now "alien" noncitizens. She sought to calm their anguish and find help for those who asked for it, and she wrote many letters of advice.

Although she deplored the narrowing of democracy, she trusted Robert Jackson's Justice Department and had faith that her husband's intent in signing the bill had not been to torment innocent people.

She advised her correspondents to follow the Smith Act rules. In a column marked by an unusually condescending tone, she sought to calm nervous correspondents "who are panicky about things they do not understand." She had received an anonymous letter from a woman "who wanted some information, and who is evidently a badly frightened human being." ER had no way to answer her directly, so she used her column to ask this woman and others in her situation to register under the Smith Act.

> Several people have written me who have been here for a long time, have led good lives, and have become respected citizens in their communities. But, when they originally entered this country, they perhaps slipped up on some necessary observances for legal entry. Instead of being terrified now, it is better to go to the officials and tell the whole story. They are sure to have fair and understanding treatment. Their standing in the community will be in their favor, and they will certainly receive sympathetic assistance in straightening out their difficulties, whatever they may be.

The column was an anomaly. One can only conclude that her faith in FDR's Justice Department was absolute.

Nevertheless, as the renewed Red Scare intensified in September, she was increasingly attacked for supporting her friends in the AYC. She resolved not to waver, even though most of the critics were allies who feared that she was endangering her husband's reelection.

The fall of 1940 saw more dreadful bombing raids on London. From 7 September to 3 November, massive German bombardments blitzed the city. Bombs crashed relentlessly for 57 days and nights. The raids of 7 September dropped more than 335 tons, which blasted the docks and dockside communities. More than 448 Londoners died. The next day 200 bombers targeted London's electric power stations and railway lines. The East End was devastated. The air war intensified; more German planes were shot down than British assault planes. As the Blitz continued, docks in Liverpool, Swansea, and Bristol were smashed; the dead and wounded multiplied. While homes burned and the city was reduced to rubble, Hitler gloated, "If eight million [residents] go crazy . . . catastrophe" would be certain.

On 15 September, 230 bombers and 700 fighters blitzed London as well as Southampton, Bristol, Cardiff, Liverpool, and Manchester. Fifty-six German planes were shot down; Britain lost 23. "Through all the mayhem, suffering, and tragedy, Britons were steadfast."

Churchill desperately needed destroyers for the Royal Navy and asked the United States to supply them. In early September, on an inspection tour of a war plant in Charleston, West Virginia, FDR announced that he had agreed to provide Britain with fifty obsolete, rusty World War I–era destroyers. In exchange, Britain would grant the United States ninety-nine-year leases to eight of its bases in North America, mostly in the Caribbean. Churchill was delighted with this Destroyers for Bases agreement, seeing it as a turning point in Anglo-American relations. The two countries were now "mixed up together . . . for mutual and general advantage." It was an ongoing process, he exulted: "No one can stop it. Like the Mississippi, it just keeps rolling along. Let it roll. Let it roll on . . . inexorable, irresistible . . . to broader lands and better days."

On 27 September, Germany, Italy, and Japan concluded a tripartite pact, extending the Axis to Asia. A week later Britain announced that it would reopen the Burma Road to China. Britain had previously closed this overland route from its Burmese colony in order to avoid war with Japan. The United States also came to the aid of China, with a new loan to support the government of Chiang Kai-shek.

ER might have considered that news a particularly welcome birthday present. In the summer, she had devoted a column to the grievous situation China faced as a result of the closing of the Burma Road, its major conduit for matériel and other supplies since Japan had cut off its ports. Japan had done to China, she feared, what might someday be done to the United States. "It is hard even to imagine such a thing, but the Continent of Europe under one dictator" has enormous economic and military power, and his alliance with Japan might well give us "some concern . . . for we might find ourselves between two fairly strong pincers."

Prime Minister Churchill urged FDR to send a naval squadron to Singapore, thinking it might have a "deterrent effect upon a Japanese declaration of war upon us over the Burma Road opening." Meanwhile members of FDR's cabinet urged him to include oil and steel in the embargo against Japan, but the State Department opposed it.

The will of the American people was shifting rapidly. In July, 69 percent of the public had agreed that a military draft would ensure the nation's defense. On 17 August presidential candidate Wendell Willkie endorsed the Burke-Wadsworth conscription bill. As the German bombings of Britain accelerated, Congress passed the bill, and FDR signed the Selective Training and Service Act into law on 16 September 1940.

On 12 October, in Dayton, Ohio, the president announced, "Our course is clear. Our decision is made. We will continue to pile up our defense and our armaments. We will continue to help those who resist aggression, and who now hold the aggressors far from our shores." He hailed the bravery of British people, who "have shown how free people defend what they know to be right." Democracy, when tested, was made of stern, commendable stuff. For one example, one night the dressing rooms of a London theater company were bombed. It had just opened a repertoire production of Shakespeare scenes. The next day it opened for its second performance. Headlines announced "Shakespeare beats Hitler."

From eight o'clock on the evening of 15 October to five the next morning, German bombs pounded the city, starting 900 fires and killing more than 400 Londoners. The next week these air raids were compounded when Nazi submarines in "wolf packs" destroyed supply ships from Canada. One wolf pack attacked a convoy of 35 ships from Nova Scotia, sinking 20. The next day the same six submarines attacked a convoy of 49 ships from Halifax, sinking 12.

On 28 October Mussolini's army invaded Greece from Italian bases in Albania. On 30 October FDR repeated his campaign promise that even though draft registration was now compulsory, American "boys are not going to be sent into any foreign wars." He did not mention a secret Anglo-American agreement signed on 24 October to equip and maintain ten British divisions with combat-ready U.S.-manufactured weapons. This agreement, Churchill believed, would enable Britain to resist and fight to victory.

Worried about her British friends, ER spent endless nights, generally until three a.m., working on her columns and her other writings and campaigning for her husband's reelection.

Convinced that democracy's survival depended on it, she was determined to move forward on the racial divide. She refused to let Willkie keep the lead on race matters. While she understood the need for FDR's southern strategy, she believed he could do more to effect change. She routinely sent him bitter details of white supremacy, state by state, as NAACP president Walter White revealed them to her.

On 16 September she was the featured guest speaker at a banquet to honor the leaders of the Brotherhood of Sleeping Car Porters and its International Ladies Auxiliary in New York's Mecca Temple. To prepare, she read the union's vision statement and decided to focus on one section: "We believe in American democracy. We know it is not perfect, but we have the right and the job here to make it so."

Among the luminaries at the dinner were Brotherhood president A. Philip Randolph, Walter White, New York City mayor Fiorello La Guardia, and NYA head Aubrey Williams. Mary McLeod Bethune introduced ER, saying, "No problem has been too great or too small for her thoughtful, sympathetic consideration. No life has been too lofty or too low for her tender touch. . . . To know her is to love her."

ER thanked Dr. Bethune, who "served as an inspiration" to people of all races—as a teacher, a woman of service, "a leader among leaders." Then she turned to the subject of American democracy: "You know, better than any other people, that it is not perfect, but we all have that . . . great obligation to improve the democracy of the United States. Only in doing that can we possibly make this nation really safe."

She specifically emphasized the enormous contributions that blacks had made to "the great arts," emphasizing "how much America and all its citizens owe to the culture and gifts and skills that have come to this country . . . from every one of the minority groups that are the citizens of the United States."

James Weldon Johnson, she said, had once told her, "'You are making a mistake, the people of your race. . . . You don't recognize how much more my race has to contribute in many artistic ways, and you don't try to develop them.'" She and Johnson had "spent a very delightful evening" together, and "I never had a more charming escort." His words reverberated in all her efforts to be aware of and try "to further any opportunities" for the advancement of art, literature, music, "and many, many things which perhaps, before, many of us had not thought of. I think you should feel very proud, just as many other people who have come from other lands should feel very proud of the contribution they have made to the culture and life of the country."

Perhaps never before had the contributions of black Americans been so poignantly recognized by a first lady. But this was no time to rest, she said, "and you know how many difficulties there are that you have to overcome." Her hope for the future lay in active young people, "and because I know a good many of the young people of your race, I know how great are their difficulties, and I appreciate their leadership."

ER specifically praised Harriet Ida Pickens, daughter of William Pickens, the longtime field secretary of the NAACP who had worked closely with Joe Lash when he was still in the AYC and had made a rousing speech at the contentious February 1940 AYC meeting in Washington. "I have the greatest respect for [Harriet's] ability and her tact, devotion and courage," ER said, "in doing the things which she thinks are right." A Smith College honors graduate who majored in classics and chemistry, Pickens was the first African-American awarded Smith's S-pin for all-around excellence in academics and sports. A dedicated youth leader, she condemned the ever-growing power of segregationists and decried Mississippi's proposal to provide free textbooks to grades one to eight, with all references "to citizenship and voting rights" deleted in books for "Negro pupils."

ER considered Pickens's AYC speech a mandate for action and closed her address to the Brotherhood with a call for deliberate, courageous, sustained action.

[You have shown] great courage in the way you have carried on your Organization. But I want you to feel something which I feel very strongly now, that in the past few years, we have come in many ways far along the road to better understanding . . . [and also] to a greater appreciation of the dignity of human individuals, regardless of their race, or their creed, or their color. And a great many of us no longer think in little sections about people; we think of people as individuals and as contributors to a common cause. . . .

I would like to pledge to you my faith and my cooperation to make this a better country . . . for all of us to live in and to make you pledge in return, that as we move forward, we may feel that our country is safer because it is a better country to live in for everyone.

With those words, the entire audience of eight hundred stood to cheer: It was better for everyone when it was better for everyone.

Walter White then took his turn and angrily denounced racial discrimination in defense industries and the military:

It is particularly fortunate that you chose to hold your Convention at this crucial period in the world's history, when the white world and what we have called "civilization" is reeling under the impact of totalitarian Stukas and Messerchmitts. . . . An upper-crust blithely and smugly gorged itself on the fat of the land and, because it had the ships and guns and economic power to get away with it, believed that God or Gobineau, or both, intended non-white races to exist only to create wealth for the so-called white nations of the earth.

But even in the face of [Europe's tragedies], the majority of white Americans have not yet awakened to the precariousness of the situation here in its similarity to European countries which have fallen victim to the dictators. England would be safe today, instead of on the verge of [conquest], did she have the loyal support of Ireland, India, Africa, and the West Indies. She does not have that support, because for generations, she has exploited these people and denied them all but the most meager share of the wealth which they produced.

Here in our own country we continue practices against minorities—racial and religious—which are so vicious [they endanger] loyalty to the United States. While Congress appropriated millions of dollars for material defense, industrial plants and military arsenals deny employment to Negroes. Yet black workers will be taxed the same as their white counterparts to pay for the bill. How, then, could loyal support among the black citizenry be counted on?

Recently, I ran across a case in a New England industrial city where the leader of the local Nazi Bund was given employment in a plant making airplanes. . . . That same plant curtly told a young Negro, whose grades averaged 98.4 percent in a topnotch technical school, that there were no jobs . . . "for niggers." What happens when such a young man witnesses such a disgrace, a Nazi leader given a job while he washes automobiles in a garage . . . [and] his hard-earned training goes to waste?

This, White declared, was going on all over America, north and south, where unions and industrialists denied African-Americans access to employment. Most bitter to report was the ongoing terror of violence and lynching. "The mob still rides, aided and encouraged by a minority of the U.S. Senate, which has filibustered to death every attempt to secure federal legislation against lynching." And while both political parties ignored the subject, NAACP efforts to register voters were being met with violence.

A reputable Negro citizen . . . Elbert Williams lies in a Tennessee grave, killed by a mob at Brownsville in June. . . . A minister of the Gospel and several other reputable Negro citizens . . . have been driven out of the town and told they will be lynched if they return. What was their crime? They asked local officials for information as to what they should do to qualify to vote in the presidential election. . . . Though the names of thirteen members of the mob were supplied to the authorities a grand jury returned the usual verdict—Williams died at the hands of parties unknown. The Federal Department of Justice—apparently afraid of the [local political] machine—has been "investigating" . . . for nearly three months.

After dinner, ER and Bethune asked Walter White for the details of Elbert Williams's lynching. He was thirty-three, a founder of Browns-ville's NAACP branch, which at that time had only fifty-four members—"a tiny fraction" of the county's nineteen thousand blacks. Although blacks outnumbered whites three to one, blacks had not voted in Haywood County since 1884. On 6 May, Williams and several other branch members had tried to register to vote. Then on the night of 20 June, while he and his wife were listening to the Joe Louis–Arturo Godoy boxing match on the radio, a city policeman arrived at their door. He demanded

Williams go outside for a "discussion" and forced him into a waiting car. Three days later Williams's body was found in the Hatchie River. Elbert Williams was the first known NAACP official to be killed in the struggle for civil rights.

The previous week Elisha Davis, who had also tried to register to vote, had been tortured by a mob of sixty men who "forced him to reveal names of NAACP members, and promised to kill him if he remained in Brownsville," according to historian Patricia Sullivan. Davis escaped to Jackson and warned about the "reign of terror" in the county. NAACP branch president Reverend Buster Walker had also been forced from his home.

On 10 August 1940 the *Pittsburgh Courier* editorialized: "If Elbert Williams is not avenged, if Elisha Davis, Rev. Buster Walker, and other refugees dare not return home, just because they sought to exercise their right to vote, then democracy . . . is a grim and empty fiction." Walter White and NAACP lawyer Thurgood Marshall urged the Justice Department to conduct a federal investigation and appealed for an end to the silence of the white press and of FDR. The president's failure even to express sympathy to Williams's wife and family was noted.

White and Marshall went to Tennessee to investigate and were momentarily heartened to learn that U.S. attorneys and the Justice Department had obtained the names of police officer Tip Hunter and a mob of a dozen terrorists. The NAACP collected funds to reunite Davis with his wife and seven children, and they moved to Michigan. But the investigation languished in the hands of the FBI, and the Justice Department made no move to prosecute.*

ER did not understand FDR's continued silence in the face of such tragedy, as well as Wendell Willkie's growing popularity. Staunch labor leaders like John L. Lewis and many black leaders, including boxing

---

*The Justice Department stalled for two years; Thurgood Marshall subsequently learned that Hoover's FBI agents questioned witnesses in the presence of Tip Hunter. In January 1942 the Justice Department closed the case for insufficient evidence, despite the evidence White and Marshall had presented. White concluded that the power of Senator Kenneth McKellar (D-TN) and Memphis political boss Edward Crump were involved in the cover-up, even after NAACP member Francis Biddle became attorney general and pursued such cases in 1942. See Sullivan, *Lift Every Voice*, pp. 237–42.

champion Joe Louis, were active for Willkie. Black newspapers criticized
the president for being "as mum as the Sphinx" on all aspects of "the
Negro question," and their coverage was increasingly pro-Willkie. The
Baltimore Afro-American even wondered if there were more Nazis south
of Baltimore than west of Berlin.

ER returned to her Eleventh Street apartment and wrote an urgent
letter, based on all she had learned from Walter White. The time for
silence was over, she told her husband. It was time for a conference. Most
immediately "there is a growing feeling . . . [that blacks must] be allowed
to participate in any training that is going on in the aviation, army,
navy. . . . This is going to be very bad politically besides being intrinsi-
cally wrong and I think you should ask that a meeting be held."

The next day White wrote to thank ER: "Your speech is going to do a
lot of good." He sent her articles about military segregation, which now
absorbed "the Negro press."

> As you of course know, Negroes object to being the one group* so
> segregated not only on the basis of the principle involved but because
> such separation makes easier discrimination by hostile or prejudiced
> superiors. I wonder if the time isn't ripe for the experiment to be tried
> in a state like New York, for example, where Americans could serve
> their country in a regiment, or division, on the basis of physical con-
> dition, loyalty and ability rather than on race, or creed, or color.

All that summer, as the Burke-Wadsworth bill was debated, the NAACP
campaigned against racial discrimination in the bill. Senator Robert
Wagner introduced an amendment guaranteeing Americans the right to
volunteer for military service regardless of creed or color. And Hamilton
Fish—who had led a black infantry division during World War I and
was, according to historian Gail Buckley, "an ally of the NAACP"—
introduced an amendment to outlaw discrimination in military selection
and training.

*There were no plans to segregate other racial groups. Indeed, a particular effort to
recruit tribal leaders among Native Americans was under way. In 1940 Indians
were to be fully integrated, and designated "warriors"—while African-Americans
were to be segregated and designated servants. Alison Bernstein to author; see Bernstein, *American Indians and World War II.*

But the bill as passed in September stated that inductees would be limited to those individuals who were "acceptable" to the military and who met the needs of "adequate" military accommodations. Walter White and A. Philip Randolph protested this language, and asked to meet with FDR. Since 11 August ER had also urged FDR and Secretary Knox to meet with White and a delegation of race leaders to ensure Negro participation in the armed forces.

On 21 September, when the president finally agreed to the meeting, ER forwarded White's correspondence: "This is for your consideration before the meeting with the colored group." On 27 September FDR met with White, Randolph, T. Arnold Hill (formerly of the Urban League, now assistant to Dr. Bethune at the NYA), and members of his military team—navy secretary Frank Knox and Assistant Secretary of War Robert Patterson. The meeting lasted less than an hour (11:35 to 12:10). White sent ER a full account of the discussion: "The President opened the conference by stating that he had been pleasantly surprised" when War Department officials told him, "without solicitation on his part, that Negroes would be integrated into all branches of the armed service as well as service units."

White asked the president "if this applied to officers as well as enlisted men . . . , if this meant that Negroes would be continued to be used only in separate units and . . . if this open door policy applied to the Navy as well as to the Army."

Evidently it did apply to officers, and there were plans to call up "600 Negroes who were reserve officers," and to train additional officers as needed. But the military had apparently never "even thought of non-segregated units in the Army. The President, however, was immediately receptive," White noted, to his argument that while there might be difficulties in Mississippi or Georgia if white and black soldiers were together in regiments, "there was no reason to anticipate any difficulties . . . in states like New York, Massachusetts, Pennsylvania, and Illinois, where Negroes and whites attend the same schools, play on the same athletic teams, and live in the same neighborhoods without difficulty." White "emphasized that . . . an army fighting allegedly for democracy should be the last place [to find] undemocratic segregation."

FDR promised to investigate paths "to lessen, if not destroy, discrimination." He thought it possible to "put white and black regiments in the

North side by side," and then, as replacements were needed, "through this continuity of Negro and white regiments . . . the Army could 'back into' the formation of units without segregation."

Patterson considered it "an experiment worth trying." But Secretary Knox rejected it—"since [in the navy] men have to live together on ships," and there could not be "Southern ships and Northern ships." FDR pointed out that since the navy "was organizing [musical entertainments and] new bands for ships," these "Negro bands might help solve the problem [to] accustom white sailors to the presence of Negroes on ships." Knox "promised to look into" this idea.

There was some discussion of elimination of discrimination in employment at army arsenals, navy yards, and national defense industries. But "the shortness of time" for the meeting prevented any significant exchange. It ended when FDR, Knox, and Patterson agreed to study the detailed memorandum for a "Non-Jim Crow Program" prepared by Hill, Randolph, and White, with the assistance of Charles Houston, Judge William Hastie, and Robert Weaver. FDR gave them reason to believe there would be another meeting to discuss their memorandum and to integrate the Negro into all aspects of national defense.

But there was no subsequent meeting, nor even a phone call. Rather, on 9 October, FDR issued a press release announcing a new official policy of complete military segregation.

> The policy of the War Department is not to intermingle colored and white enlisted personnel. . . . This policy has been proven satisfactory . . . and to make changes would produce situations destructive to morale and detrimental to the preparation for national defense. [Therefore,] the department does not contemplate assigning colored reserve offices other than those of the Medical Corps and chaplains to existing Negro combat units.

The black leaders were stunned by the press release, furious that White House press secretary Steve Early implied that they themselves had approved the policy. On 10 October they sent a telegram to the White House to reject the president's assertion that the army's Jim Crow policies had "been proven satisfactory." They "repudiated and denounced" FDR's decision to approve "segregation for Negro units" in the armed forces. Rather, the leaders asserted:

> Segregation has been destructive of morale and has permitted preju- diced superiors to exercise their bigotry on defenseless Negro regi- ments. . . . We are inexpressibly shocked that a President of the United States at a time of national peril should surrender so com- pletely to enemies of Democracy who would destroy national unity by advocating segregation. Official approval by the Commander- in-Chief of the Army and Navy of such discrimination and segrega- tion is a stab in the back of Democracy.

They protested the abhorrent press "trick" that implied they had agreed to the segregationist policy in conference.

The NAACP initiated a letter-writing campaign throughout its six hundred branches, all youth councils, and college chapters to encourage protests before Election Day. *The Crisis* published every word of FDR's duplicitous statement that "it is the policy of the War Department that the services of Negroes will be utilized on a fair and equitable basis." There was nothing fair or equitable about it.

Clearly FDR and the War Department, White editorialized, intended "to have as few Negro officers as possible." Out of 230,000 servicemen in the peacetime military, there were only 5,000 blacks, and of those 5,000, only 5 were senior officers. Three were chaplains. Two were line officers: Colonel Benjamin O. Davis Sr., and his son, Captain Benjamin O. Davis Jr., the first black graduate of West Point since 1889. White's editorial was bitter: "The whole trend in the army is known to be against having any Negro officers." The War Department's "long-range plan" was unaccept- able: there were to be "no Negroes sent to West Point; no Negroes accepted in the citizens' military training camps; very little, if any, training for Negro reserve officers; restricted training for Negroes in the ROTC." "Immediate Action" was required.

ER had been surprised by FDR's 9 October statement. She too consid- ered it duplicitous and unnecessary. The thought that her husband was captive to bigots in the military, as he was to those ruling his State Department, was intolerable. She had not expected him to endorse Knox's miserable attitude that "one could not have [blacks] on the same boat with white men." The close election polls worried her as well. She feared Willkie's victory in the short run, and democracy's demise over time. She understood that her friend Walter White intended to support the candidate who opposed segregation, but she hoped the conservatives who surrounded Willkie, so many of whom were eager to destroy the New Deal, would give him pause.

Joe Lash asked Harriet Pickens to sponsor a youth meeting in Harlem, but she replied that she would not endorse FDR because of his "statement on Negroes in the Army." Point seven was particularly repugnant and "for the first time enunciated" military segregation as policy. Ever since Woodrow Wilson resegregated Washington in 1913, "It has always been practiced but never before proclaimed as policy."

Pickens's views mattered to many people. As a leader of the YWCA's National Business and Professional Council, as public health and tuberculosis administrator in Harlem, and as youth leader chair of the AYC's civil liberties program, she was a notable force. When Joe told ER about their conversation, ER went to her husband.

Although there is no record of their exchange, on 25 October, one week before the election, FDR acted significantly. He appointed Judge William H. Hastie civilian aide to the secretary of war; Major Campbell C. Johnson became assistant to Dr. Clarence Dykstra, administrator of the Selective Service Administration; and he promoted Colonel Benjamin O. Davis to the rank of brigadier general, the first African-American general in U.S. history. He detailed these appointments in an extraordinary letter to Walter White, A. Philip Randolph, and T. Arnold Hill:

> I regret that there has been so much misinterpretation . . . of the War Department policy issued from the White House. . . .
>
> The plan, as I understand it, on which we are all agreed is that Negroes will be put into all branches of the service, combatant as well as supply. Arrangements are now being made to give, without delay, training in aviation to Negroes. Negro reserve officers will be called to active service and given appropriate commands. Negroes will be given the same opportunity to qualify for officers' commissions as will be given to others.
>
> These measures represent a very substantial advance over what has been practiced in past years. You may rest assured that further

developments of policy will be forthcoming to insure that Negroes are given fair treatment on a non-discriminatory basis.

However annoyed or disappointed ER was by her husband's political maneuvers, or bewildered by his slow, sidestepping approach, she always believed he would eventually do the right thing—since basically they shared the same goals for justice and democracy.

Willkie was a robust phenomenon as a presidential candidate. His vigorous campaign and huggy-bear style endeared him to millions of Americans. Although his supporters included appeasers, isolationists, and fascists, he rejected their support. Close to FDR in vision and New Deal rhetoric, his appeal crossed all boundaries.

ER was deeply involved with FDR's reelection campaign. One week before the election, she tried to stop the drift of progressive race leaders toward Willkie by inviting Mary McLeod Bethune to host a White House reception for the National Council of Negro Women (NCNW), who were "mainly Republicans." Like Harry Hopkins, Will Alexander, Aubrey Williams, and others, ER was unconcerned about offending white supremacist newspapers and conservative party leaders. Defiantly, the lead sentence of her *My Day* column announced her 26 October reception for almost one thousand women: "Friday afternoon, at the White House, I received the National Council of Negro Women, who are holding their convention in the District of Columbia."

During the campaign's last weeks, she was "constantly around headquarters making peace among the various factions and personalities," Lash observed. "Everybody trusts and yields to her—hard-boiled politicians, idealistic women, careerists, publicity hounds and publicity people. . . . She holds things together. Her presence alone is an important contribution to the campaign, but she is also full of ideas."

She worked closely with Lash and with her son Franklin to build Youth for Roosevelt, which Franklin Jr. directed. She was in charge at the Democratic Party's Women's Division and often arrived with Elinor Morgenthau and Agnes Brown Leach. She persuaded party chair Ed Flynn that Lorena Hickok would make a splendid publicity director— and she turned out to be perfect for it. Hick wrote the impressive copy for fliers, bulletins, and newsletters. Although she could be snippy and impatient, she was also generous and concerned. Ever acerbic but witty, she loved her eleventh-floor office in the Beekman Tower and worked with dedicated verve.

The campaign team was also bolstered by the participation of Trude Pratt, who volunteered many hours, paid for several assistants, and directed the research division for women speakers. Moreover Pratt was among the "indefatigable women" who "took to the streets" during the last week of the campaign. Day and night they converged on the busiest New York street corners, from Wall Street to Times Square, atop cleverly adorned Roosevelt-Wallace cars and "bedecked" kitchen ladders with loudspeakers. They attracted fascinated though frequently hostile crowds and were variously booed and cheered.

ER traveled many miles as part of her campaign efforts, and visited friends and family. On 11 October she took a night flight to Los Angeles, where she watched James drill with his Marine Reserve battalion, hoping that "someday we will reach a state of civilization where we can find, as William James suggested so long ago, the 'moral equivalent for war.'" Until then, "all of us must prefer to see the young people we care about receive the training which cannot fail to be of use to them in everyday life because of the value of discipline . . . [which] helps us in every occupation." ER was proud of James and Franklin Jr., who enrolled in the ROTC.

The Selective Service Act had set 16 October as the day of compulsory draft registration, universal and democratic:

> "Once accepted to military service, each inductee will be intelligently led, comfortably clothed, well fed, and adequately armed and equipped for basic training. . . . In the military service, Americans from all walks of life, rich and poor, country-bred and city raised, farmer, student, manual laborer and white collar worker, will learn to live side by side to depend upon each other in military drills and maneuvers, and to appreciate each other's dignity as American citizens. Universal service will bring not only greater preparedness to meet the threat of war, but a wider distribution of tolerance and understanding to enjoy the blessings of peace.

That day more than sixteen million young men registered. The draft would "swell the ranks of the US Army to the unprecedented peacetime figure of one million men by January 1941," observed *Time* magazine. Except for a small minority of "religiously-minded conscientious objectors," the country greeted the peacetime draft with "good-natured" support.

ER had advocated a year of national service for all Americans, but she recognized the necessity of the draft, even in this limited form. Since September she had urged a racially nondiscriminatory registration policy, but on registration day thousands of black youth "flocked to recruitment centers" and were "turned away because the Army had too few segregated facilities."

Time magazine mocked her for turning "on her old friends, the American Youth Congress and the American Newspaper Guild, for their 'claptrap' talk decrying the draft.... As the nation went, so went Eleanor Roosevelt." Then *Time* turned to her children, noting that "son Elliott, who has a wife and three small children, had obtained a captain's commission in the Army Air Corps Specialists reserve." That accusation of special treatment deeply disturbed ER. She hated the attacks on Elliott, and defended his commission.

Upon her return from the West Coast, she was astonished by the many hate letters she had received and the many "We Don't Want Eleanor Either" buttons. Personally she was "unruffled" by it all: "If I ... worried about mud-slinging, I would have been dead long ago." But she was upset by the debris thrown at the Willkies—tomatoes, eggs, creamy pastries, telephone books, bottles—and disapproved of the violent rhetoric against all the campaigners.

ER tried to persuade her husband to enter the campaign directly, but he refused. Then on 16 October, Willkie launched a blistering attack on FDR's campaign silence. The New Deal president, he said, had refused to speak about ongoing unemployment and the continuous misery at home. Internationally, "he will not discuss the issues that trouble people: He says: Trust me. I can't explain it all to you. You wouldn't understand. ... You must believe I am indispensable." Willkie boasted that he would expand the stalled New Deal, providing Social Security for all, rural electrification in neglected areas, and a program to guarantee full employment.

Infuriated, ER wrote her husband that night. He owed it to America to end his silence: "The people have a right to hear your say in opposition to Willkie between now and election day." She knew he enjoyed a fight, and there was no time to lose. FDR agreed to make five campaign speeches—but not until the week before the election.

On 23 October in Philadelphia, he finally launched his formal campaign. Yes, he declared in fine form, he "loved a good fight." He derided Willkie's "tears, crocodile tears" for labor, youth, the elderly, and the unemployed—on behalf of Republicans who had fought every one of his New Deal efforts to improve life for labor, youth, the elderly, and the unemployed. FDR went further and now promised full employment. It was the government's responsibility to add "the right to work" to the rights already established—"the right to vote, the right to learn, the right to speak, the right to worship." Without mentioning Willkie by name, he called his opponent a liar for saying FDR would lead the country into the war: "We will not participate in any foreign wars, and we will not send our army, naval, or air forces to fight in foreign lands outside of the Americas except in the case of attack."

ER listened to FDR's speech on the radio with Tommy and Alice Huntington: "I hope that everyone throughout the nation spent their evening in exactly the same way. I felt it was profitable."

On 28 October—the day Mussolini invaded Greece—she joined FDR for a rally at Madison Square Garden, with a standing-room-only crowd of twenty thousand. At this stunning event, the president tore into Republicans who had obstructed efforts to build up the national defense and provide urgently needed aid to the Allies. In Congress, the main obstructors had been Representatives Joseph Martin (R-MA, House minority leader and now Willkie's campaign manager), Bruce Barton (R-NY, an advertising executive who represented New York's Upper East Side), and Hamilton Fish (R-NY). Who, FDR asked the crowd at intervals, were the main naysayers? "Martin, Barton, and Fish!" they roared back with enthusiasm. ER was delighted: "It seemed to us a very good meeting."

But the rally had a bitter aftermath. White House press secretary Steve Early was on the way to the president's train when black New York City policeman James Sloan, on duty to protect FDR, stopped him. Unwilling to be stopped by a race man, Early kicked him in the groin with such force that Officer Sloan was hospitalized. Republican newspapers and commentators went berserk. Race leaders demanded an apology and Early's resignation. He did apologize; it had been an accident, he said. No recriminations followed, but Early feared he had cost his boss the election. Sloan saved the day, issuing a press statement from his hospital bed: "If anybody thinks they can turn me against our great President who has done so much for our race because of this thing they are mistaken." ER did not absolve Early, who had been FDR's friend since 1912, but she implied that his hot temper was color-blind—and sought to protect her husband and his loyal, if bigoted, press secretary.

On 30 October in Boston, FDR pledged to keep America out of war: "I have said this before, but I shall say it again and again and again. Your boys are not going to be sent into any foreign wars. They are going into training to form a force so strong that, by its very existence, it will keep the threat of war away from our shores."

The president also welcomed home "my Ambassador" Joseph P. Kennedy, in words so warm that Kathleen Kennedy wrote her father: "The President really went to town for you tonight . . . amidst terrific cheers from the crowd [for] 'that Boston boy.'" FDR's generous words to him reflected a personal campaign victory.

Ambassador Kennedy was a fervent isolationist, close to Neville Chamberlain. In London he had been sidelined by FDR's personal emissaries. His role usurped by others, Kennedy felt useless and insisted on his right to return to the United States. He had reportedly said that once home he intended to "put 25 million Catholic votes behind Wendell Willkie."

When he landed in New York, he was handed an urgent message from FDR to proceed directly to Washington and the White House for dinner. At cocktails, he had a few minutes alone with FDR and Missy LeHand, and the president was "very gracious," he said. Then they were joined for dinner by James Byrnes, FDR's closest ally among Senate Democrats, and Kennedy's wife, Rose. During the meal Byrnes sought to persuade Kennedy to broadcast a pro-FDR campaign speech, while FDR "worked very hard on Rose."

Kennedy, who had wanted to speak with the president privately, finally exploded. He complained bitterly about the way he had been treated. He had been loyal and supportive but was never consulted or even informed.

All agreements had been negotiated by others. The State Department had marginalized him while emissaries dealt with the British. All this "harmed my influence."

FDR denied everything, saying he knew nothing about it. It was all State Department mismanagement. As the discussion went on and on, Rose suggested that long distances limited communication.

"Finally," Kennedy recalled, "I said I had a great sense of responsibility and obligation and would make a speech." On 29 October, he broadcast over 114 CBS network stations—sponsored by Rose Kennedy and their children. "It is true that there have been disagreements between the President and me. . . . However, these are times . . . which clamor for national unity." In that regard, the third term was not an issue, as there was no time to waste on a "newcomer." The world "is on the move at a speed never before witnessed. . . . It is later than you think. Denmark was conquered in a matter of hours; Norway in days; Belgium and Holland in weeks. . . . Proud and honorable France fell in a month. We do not have the time to train a green hand even though he comes to his task full of goodwill and general capacity."

He concluded, "My wife and I have given nine hostages to fortune. The kind of America that they and their children will inherit is of grave concern to us all. In the light of these considerations, I believe that Franklin D. Roosevelt should be re-elected President of the United States."

This powerful affirmation of a third term for the president shocked Republicans. FDR sent a telegram to his ambassador: "We have all just listened to a grand speech! Many thanks."

ER, who had just spoken at Colby College, listened to the speech in Limerick, Maine, with the John Cutters. Like many others, she wondered what magic FDR had wrought to elicit Joe Kennedy's tide-changing words.

Upon her return to Hyde Park, she wrote her first column about the campaign, designed in part to modify her husband's promise in Boston not to send U.S. soldiers into war: "Today no one can honestly promise you peace at home or abroad. All any human being can do is to promise that he will do his utmost to prevent this country from being involved in war. . . . The fact is before you that in a world of war we are still at peace."

For all the abuse, vitriol, and violence, the two campaigns followed a gentlemen's agreement to keep two explosive items out of the press.

Wendell Willkie had an ongoing relationship with journalist and power broker Irita Van Doren, book editor of the *New York Herald Tribune*. They had fallen in love shortly after the brilliant, beautiful, southern-born scholar divorced Carl Van Doren in 1935, after twenty-three years of marriage. The entire political world knew about their relationship, but Irita wanted Wendell Willkie to win, as did his wife, Billie (Edith Willkie). The women in his life remained silent and discreet (which Willkie rarely did), and no Democrat leaked the well-known details.

FDR was willing to remain silent about Willkie's domestic relations because his running mate Henry Wallace, a student of world philosophies, had written letters to Russian artist, pacifist, and visionary Nicholas Roerich in the highlands of Tibet and Mongolia. These "guru letters" were seen as ammunition for those ready to dismiss Wallace as a spiritualist, or a mystical nut.

The Republican National Committee had "obtained" Wallace's embarrassing correspondence to his "guru," while unnamed Democrats had "intercepted" Willkie's correspondence with Van Doren, which they branded "dolly letters." Both sides agreed to protect their private correspondence. Curiously, FDR's choice of Wallace had partly been a mystical decision. According to ER, her husband had been persuaded by astrologers and "soothsayers" that no president elected in 1940 would complete his term—"so he talks all the time of Wallace as successor."

ER returned to Hyde Park to prepare for the arrival of many guests, but her campaign chores were not over. On Saturday morning she drove to New York for three crowded events in the Bronx and Queens, then continued on to Manhattan, where six thousand women gathered at the Roosevelt Hotel. Everywhere ER called for national unity: "Let us show the free world that after Election Day we can come together as a free people able to govern ourselves and make life better and happier for all the people."

That same day in Cleveland FDR gave one of the most stirring speeches of his presidency, envisioning a new American future:

> It is the destiny of this American generation to point the road to the future for all the world to see. It is our prayer that all lovers of freedom may join us—the anguished common people of this earth for whom we seek to light the path.

I see an America where factory workers are not discarded after they reach their prime, where there is no endless chain of poverty from generation to generation, where impoverished farmers and farm hands do not become homeless wanderers, where monopoly does not make youth a beggar for a job.

I see an America whose rivers and valleys and lakes—hills and streams and plains—the mountains over our land and nature's wealth deep under the earth—are protected as the rightful heritage of the people.

I see an America where small business really has a chance to flourish and grow.

I see an America of great cultural and educational opportunity for all its people. . . .

I see an America with peace in the ranks of labor.

An America where the workers are really free. Where the dignity and security of the working man and woman are guaranteed by their own strength and fortified by the safeguards of law.

An America where those who have reached the evening of life shall live out their years in peace and security. Where pensions and insurance . . . shall be given as a matter of right.

Step by step, FDR's vision of a better America mesmerized his audience, including his wife, who wrote the speech, saying it "was grand and nothing that I've heard from Willkie can touch it."

Surely she was relieved by FDR's brief but hopeful nod to racial justice. "We in this Nation of many States," he said, "have found the way by which men of many racial origins may live together in peace. If the human race . . . is to survive . . . men and nations . . . cannot accept the doctrine that war must be forever a part of [humanity's] destiny."

Perhaps that speech inspired Walter White to write ER on 4 November: "I would be grateful if you would give the President the enclosed personal note of thanks for what he did in the matter of the integration of Negroes into the armed forces of the United States." He told ER he would vote for FDR, but he may never have told her that Willkie forces had courted him from the beginning. It was her friendship and vision that had decided his vote.

It was a tense weekend at Hyde Park. Nobody was certain of the outcome the following Tuesday. ER was pensive, and although surrounded by a large party on Sunday, she rode her horse into the woods alone. She and her friends dined with SDR at the Big House, after which they sat on the porch to gaze at the stars, which seemed "particularly bright . . . as they do on a Western prairie. One star was particularly brilliant, and I wished . . . I was more familiar with astronomy." That night, from her sleeping porch, she gazed upon it. "Through the bare branches of a tree. . . . It seemed to rest on the top branch and all the other smaller stars seemed to light up all the other branches."

At the Hyde Park polling place on 5 November, a neighborly crowd gathered for conversation and photographs. ER turned up wearing an amusing gift from a friend, a "comical silver donkey with extraordinary long ears, pinned to her left shoulder." While FDR voted, ER helped SDR sign in and escorted her to the booth. They were about to leave when FDR reminded his wife that she had forgotten to vote. "She hurried back for the routine checking and signature" and went into the poll booth, while her family waited in the car.

After lunch at the Big House, FDR joined a poker game with Harry Hopkins and other friends while ER and Joe Lash went for a long walk through the woods at Val-Kill. ER felt "confident of victory" and told Joe that she hoped the vote would be "a decisive mandate for liberal government," to end the "stalemate of the last four years."

At seven that evening ER hosted a buffet supper at Val-Kill. More than forty people gathered, including sons Franklin III and John and their wives, the Morgenthau family, Harry Hooker, Edith Helm, Earl Miller, and Henry Osthagen, along with assorted "younger ones." "Everyone except Granny and Pa and Missy came over," ER told Anna. In Tommy's kitchen, Earl and Henry were dispensing drinks. At nine-thirty they went over to the Big House. Uncertain of victory, FDR insisted on quiet, linked by one telephone to Ed Flynn at the Biltmore Hotel and by another to the White House. As the early results trickled in, the group was divided into clusters of telephone banks and radio talliers. In a "smoking room" corner off the dining room, the news services had teletype machines.

ER sat mostly tranquil, often knitting, at a radio, with SDR, Betty Roosevelt, Harry Hooker, Joe Lash, and others. Although she denied that she was excited, she wore a flamboyant "ensemble of flame-colored chiffon with a long-sleeved, gold-embroidered jacket." Elinor Morgenthau, Agnes Brown Leach, Edith Helm, Tommy, Dorothy Schiff Backer, and other political women clustered around another radio.

At eleven Ed Flynn claimed victory, and the *Kansas City Star* reported that Willkie had conceded. FDR thought the announcement premature, but the party gathered—and ER called forth the customary scrambled-egg election night service, for journalists and guests. At midnight the family went out to greet a torchlight parade and brass band from the village. "We are facing difficult days," FDR told his neighbors, "but I think you will find me in the future just the same Franklin Roosevelt you have known a great many years." There were shouts of "We want Eleanor." She waved but refused to speak, and the party went back inside. The large crowd lingered, and yet another contingent arrived. "Mother, they want you," said young Frank. "There are 700 people still standing out there in the dark, asking for you. You'll have to go to them." ER and FDR went back out to greet the crowd. Then they telephoned Anna in Seattle, Elliott in Texas, and Jimmy in Beverly Hills. They did not retire until after two-thirty.

Almost fifty million Americans had voted that day, the largest turnout to date. FDR received 27,263,448 votes to Willkie's 22,336,260. The president had retained the support of unionists and the white-solid South. Urban America, including blacks where they could vote, voted for FDR.

ER faced the third administration with determination and new alliances. Her core friendship network was expanded, and she felt strengthened for the ordeals ahead. "The returns seem to indicate a vote of real confidence," she told her column readers. "All of us, whatever our political party . . . must [now] work together. . . . In our hearts there must be gratitude that we live in a country where the will of the people can be expressed."

Chapter Fifteen

"Heroism Is Always a Thrilling Thing": The Politics of Race

Between the election and FDR's third inauguration on 20 January 1941, ER celebrated the publication of two of her own books. Advance copies of *The Moral Basis of Democracy* had arrived during election week. She wrote her daughter on 3 November that she would send her first copies to the family after the excitement subsided. The *New York Times* gave the book a glowing endorsement, calling it "one of the clearest and most sensible discussions of a subject too many people discuss without defining." A week later her Christmas book for children of all ages, well illustrated by Fritz Kredel, was delivered.*

Ruby Black's *Eleanor Roosevelt: A Biography* was published on 11 October, her fifty-sixth birthday. Although ER often said no biographies should appear in print until the subject was dead, she admired and trusted Black, a veteran United Press reporter who had accompanied her for seven years—on tour in Puerto Rico and the Virgin Islands, to West Virginia, and during many White House occasions. While they were good friends and Black was part of ER's circle of most favored journalists, they did not always agree. Black, the editor of *Equal Rights* magazine, was disappointed when ER urged women leaders at the 1940 Democratic convention to continue to oppose the Equal Rights Amendment, after Willkie and the Republicans endorsed it. Although ER's message to the convention called for "equal opportunity," it emphasized the need for full unionization before an ERA endorsement.

Black did not publicly criticize ER's position, but according to her daughter Cornelia Jane Strawser, she was always privately astounded by

---

*In *Christmas*, ER's tale of the Netherlands countryside, seven-year-old Marta and her mother wait for her father to return from the war. "Greed, personal ambition, and fear all were strong in the world fed by constant hate. In the howling of the wind . . . evil spirits . . . seemed to run wild, unleashed with no control." Would it ever end? ER's answer was only the glow of hope from the child's candle—to light the way to love.

ER's habit of addressing envelopes, even "in her own hand, to 'Mrs. Herbert Little,' a person that my mother claimed did not even exist." Ruby Black and Ruth Hale (Heywood Broun's wife) had made national headlines when they battled "the State Department to issue them passports in their own names."

ER, while eloquent on so many subjects, was nonetheless a private person, even shy when it came to her innermost feelings and thoughts, and being so exposed to the public through Black's biography aroused mixed feelings. While reading the "interesting" book, she recognized herself in the first part, the years of her childhood, but then as it proceeded felt as if she were being introduced to "someone I really did not know." The woman "I thought I knew," she wrote, "never seems to have any of the attributes so many kind people" had reported to Black: "I hope their estimate is correct," since she seems "like a nice person, though at times I think she is very trying."

ER did not refer to Black's final pages, the description and prophecy that really generated ER's stingy self-deprecating words:

> She walks as a queen is supposed to walk. Even in trailing evening dress and high-heeled slippers, she runs with startling grace. She waltzes with . . . sweeping rhythm. . . . Her blue eyes glow, or sparkle, or glimmer, as her feeling changes—and they sometimes shoot fire. . . . Much of her life is yet to be. . . . [After] she is liberated from the restrictions and the duties . . . she is likely to reveal sides of her nature and her ability which have been suppressed.

Since Ruby Black had intended only to honor ER, she was puzzled by her reaction. Then at the end of FDR's final pre-election press conference, "the President stopped me, and said, 'Ruby, I *like* your book.' I gasped, 'You don't mean to say you've had time to read it.' 'Yes,' he said, 'and it's a grand job.' I asked, 'Did you find any news in it?' 'Yes, I really did.' Then looking very solemn, he said, 'But the Missus did not like it.' . . . 'Then she's been deceiving me. Why didn't she like it?' [He] replied, 'She said you found out too much.' Wasn't that swell? Tell me, honestly, [Black asked ER,] *do* you object to it, in any way that does not arise from your inherent modesty?"

On 13 November ER reassured Black, "I felt you had done a remarkable job." But "I was rather shocked to find that so many people thought I was actually responsible for things which I believe were really more coincidences or largely done by other people." ER's perception of herself was often at odds with reality. She saw herself as a watchdog, a keen observer, and especially a helpmate. To have political influence directly attributed to her was unacceptable. Specifically, she saw the last chapters "as a challenge. I confess that sometimes I have a very great desire to become Whistler's Mother, sitting by the fires with a cap and my knitting, but you give me a feeling that as long as there is much that ought to be done, anyone who had any kind of capacity to be of use should keep our shoulders to the wheel." ER wrote that she was not in the least upset and especially appreciated her emphasis on how valuable her activism was to the campaign and would be to the future: "If anything particularly useful is chalked up to me in the next few years, I think you should rightly feel that you had a part in urging me on. Of course, I do not object to any part of the book."

ER tended to be publicly discreet, even silent, about certain issues. She underplayed her activism and often repeated, rather disingenuously, that she "never made speeches" and knew little about politics. But in an article in *Look* magazine toward the end of the campaign, Black credited ER's contributions:

> If *Wendell Willkie* is going to be elected . . . he has to beat not one Roosevelt—but two. And . . . [ER] may prove the more formidable. [While her] overt political acts . . . are few [and she may do no] actual campaigning, . . . she does most of her work quietly behind the scenes, and chiefly from altruistic motives in the interests of better government—[which] makes her all the more potent as a political force. Charlie Michelson, veteran Democratic publicity head who does not like women in politics, calls her the greatest politician in the world. Jim Farley says she is one of the few top politicians of either sex.

Black named specific "elements" of ER's power:

1. Her personality: Eleanor Roosevelt is probably the most popular person in the country. Millions follow her doings in her column. . . . Women who referred to her as "that awful woman" in 1933–34 are now devoted to her. Even Alice Roosevelt Longworth finds she no longer gets laughs by mimicking her cousin maliciously.

2. Her leadership among women: Not only at election time, . . . [and] since long before her husband was governor of New York she has worked tirelessly [to get] women interested in their government, then [gave] them tasks to do. Largely through her efforts the Democratic Women's Division has become a powerful body.

3. Her friendship for youth: Of all national leaders, ER has devoted most time and effort . . . to understand the problems of youth. Although she disapproved many actions of the Youth Congress, she has never faltered in her sympathies. . . .

4. As a political strategist: No national Democratic campaign for years has been planned without her counsel.

ER cringed at such fulsome direct praise, but Black's fully illustrated article went on to detail her personal and political history. ER was grateful for its potential electoral benefits.

Presumably she also consented to Black's subsequent *Democratic Digest* essay, which celebrated ER as her husband's partner and as an independent party leader. ER went around the country, Black wrote, asking people in every community what they thought and what they needed. "Anybody will tell Eleanor anything," FDR said proudly. Because people trusted her, the government understood what people thought and needed. Because she "never let up for an instant" traveling, questioning, and urging people in every community to work harder for their community, she became the very symbol of New Deal energy and its philosophy. But she was "more than a symbol," Black wrote. Loved and respected, her influence was "unique," and "her independence, her candor, her sincerity, her serenity have won even many of the bitterest critics of the New Deal."

Black also rejected criticisms of ER's work for pay, her columns, articles and public appearances:

> She slaves away at writing, lecturing, broadcasting because she wants the money to give to those less able to earn. A few of her public philanthropies are known. . . . She has given hundreds of thousands of dollars for projects to improve health, education, and working-capacity of people in depressed areas. . . . She supports homeless children of China, Spain, Poland, Czechoslovakia, Finland [among] other places—besides helping children of jobless Americans. It is not known, for she won't tell, how many people's hospital bills she has

herself paid; how many . . . eyeglasses or braces or wheel chairs she has bought.

ER ignored all the nasty charges that she was a profiteering "money grubber," and all the friendly advice that her work was "unseemly." She answered that the many people she helped "are more important than anybody's opinion of me." And so, Black concluded, ER was not only "benefactor" but today's "living working example of true democracy."

ER's failure to grasp the full significance of her power in American politics was not just due to her self-deprecating nature. It was also a symptom of the times, when powerful women in politics remained anathema. Well aware of the charges of "petticoat government" in the White House, she shied away from public acknowledgment of her contributions. But Black accorded ER the full praise she deserved for the success of many of FDR's most significant policies.

Politically, ER was disheartened that Jim Crow still prevailed with violence and disrespect in too many districts in too many states. In 1940 more than 200,000 new black voters were registered in the South Atlantic states, but white supremacists sought to block and disallow every black vote. Until Americans were no longer turned away by poll taxes and fraudulent literacy tests, ER would not rest. She worked ever more closely with her NAACP allies and increasingly relied on her friend Mary McLeod Bethune. Director of the NYA's Division of Negro Affairs and leader of FDR's ever-expanding Black Cabinet, Bethune built bridges through her activism and achieved results.

ER's friendship with Bethune itself made a public statement, especially when they walked into a meeting together or were photographed seated side by side. According to biographer Catherine Owens Peare, "they appeared so often on the same speakers' platform . . . many affectionately commented that America really had two first ladies: Lady Eleanor and Lady Mary." The black press noted their friendship: on one occasion, while ER was giving a speech, Bethune began to cough in the middle of it. ER "left her seat, poured a glass of water," crossed the stage, and stood over Bethune "while she drank it. Those who witnessed the scene never forgot that gesture of humility and service." The white press either ignored such events or ridiculed them.

Some White House staffers, like Steve Early, resented ER's friends and allies, her words and activities, on behalf of racial justice. But others noted the power of ER's simple acts of courtesy. Chief Usher J. B. West wrote that as soon as Bethune arrived at the White House, ER "always went running down the driveway to meet her, and they would walk arm in arm into the mansion. Few heads of state received such a welcome." While ER's behavior "aroused the wrath of [many in official] Washington, it raised the hopes of millions of Americans."

The U.S. war against fascism and ER and Bethune's war against white supremacy converged. In 1934, when U.S. educators unanimously passed the first school integration resolution, ER had said segregation must end: "We will all go ahead together, or we will all go down together." But then she had allowed political considerations to limit her work in this area. Now in the urgent fight for democracy, racial justice was at the core of her political efforts. Together, as war needs mounted, she and Bethune forged a campaign to include with respect trained nurses, black and white.

In light of Joseph Kennedy's warm campaign message and FDR's gracious acceptance of his resignation on 6 November, ER was astonished when, just after the election, Kennedy launched a new isolationist campaign. On 9 November, during an interview with three reporters at Boston's Ritz-Carlton Hotel, the former ambassador insulted Britain, offended Jews, and appalled antifascists. Boasting that he knew "more about the European situation than anybody else in Washington," he rejected all talk about democracy's survival and development and foresaw nothing but England's defeat. "I'm willing to spend all I've got left to keep us out of the war," he said. "There's no sense in our getting in." Perhaps he thought he was speaking off the record, but his call for appeasement was published in full on the front page of the Sunday *Boston Globe* and was widely reprinted throughout the English-speaking world.

The next week in Hollywood, at a luncheon at Warner Bros., Kennedy met with producers Harry Warner, Samuel Goldwyn, Louis B. Mayer, and others, to warn that Jews in peril should not make films to "alienate the Reich." Douglas Fairbanks, who was also present, sent FDR a report of the meeting, saying that Kennedy "threw the fear of God into many of our producers and executives by telling them that the Jews . . . should stop making anti-Nazi pictures or using the film medium to promote or show sympathy to the cause of the democracies versus the dictators." Because some of the producers believed Kennedy voiced "new Administration thoughts," Fairbanks felt obliged "to tattle" to FDR—since so many more of us "do not, cannot and will not believe that this is so." Ben Hecht, for example, always believed that Hollywood's subsequent opposition to his work to publicize the Holocaust originated with Kennedy's 1940 meetings with studio bosses at FDR's "bidding to ask them not to publicize the Nazi persecution of Jews lest the war in Europe be labeled a Jewish war."

From Los Angeles, Kennedy flew to William Randolph Hearst's retreat near San Francisco. By chance, Anna Roosevelt and her husband, John Boettiger, were visiting Hearst, who was their publisher, and were alarmed by Kennedy's appeasement rhetoric. John wrote his father-in-law that he and Anna were dismayed by what "we thought were Fascist leanings."

Although FDR did not publicly repudiate Kennedy, he reported to his cabinet that the former ambassador "is out to do whatever damage he can." Interior Secretary Ickes was reassured that "there was not a sign of any sentiment for appeasement at the Cabinet meeting, especially on the part of the President." Moreover, FDR's plans for a major radio address to the nation, to announce that America must become "the great arsenal of democracy," began to take shape.

ER confided to her great friend Alice Huntington that Kennedy "has always been a pessimist and always wrong, so I do not worry very much. I do, however, hate to see any American want to make peace with Hitler by being short-sighted enough to think Hitler would ever keep his word." Still, ER was hopeful, "because I think the majority of the people in this country are beginning to understand . . . that no matter what sacrifice they have to make, a democracy is better than slavery."

In her tour of the country after the election, ER was heartened by the spirit of cooperation she found everywhere—an encouraging, prayerful commitment to democracy as bitter war news mounted. Tommy sent the details to Anna:

> We have been on this trip . . . since a week ago yesterday with a lecture every night. In every place the audiences have been capacity . . . and the attention and interest excellent. There is no question that your mother is an idol to the people of this country. . . . Your mother looked over my shoulder at this and said . . . I should say "your mother isn't idle"!

Where were the twenty million voters for Willkie? Tommy wondered, and sought to understand the election's message for the future. Above all, the fear of Communism was stark, she wrote Anna:

> In New York City even Catholics like Eddie Flynn [chairman of the Democratic National Committee] admit that the local priests urged their people not to vote for your father because they are so terrified of communism, and they believe your mother is at least tainted because of the American Youth Congress, the Workers' Alliance, the Newspaper Guild, and because there [were] newspaper stories about the number of communists in key governmental positions. . . . I think your mother is pretty definitely convinced that the leaders are communist controlled, but she likes some of them as individuals and will not give them up entirely. [ER insisted on her right to] see some of them as personal friends. I can see her point and you and I know how loathe she is to go back on anyone.

ER was indeed loath to abandon old friends. But she welcomed the shake-up at the Women's Division of the Democratic National Committee. Nancy Cook simply had to go, Tommy wrote Anna, since "she fought with everyone and did no work." Caroline O'Day had been ill, she said, and "never went out once in the campaign." An ardent pacifist, O'Day now spoke only to oppose all defense measures and had mostly retired to her estate in Rye, and Tommy even wondered "why she wants to hold on to her seat in Congress since she can't be there." The real work upstate, Tommy concluded, was being done by Elinor Morgenthau, Agnes Brown Leach, and Trude Pratt.

The DNC's Women's Division, the *Democratic Digest*, and eighty thousand volunteers had ensured FDR's 1940 triumph with the largest electoral turnout in U.S. history, and the largest turnout by women ever. Nationally over half the votes cast were the votes of women.

After the election, Dorothy McAllister retired as director of the Women's Division. On 11 November, in Chicago, ER met with party leaders about a successor, and agreed that Gladys Avery Tillett should replace her. They thought ER should name Tillet "just the way the President chooses the man who is to be national chairman. Eddie Flynn" agreed, and so did ER.

The *Democratic Digest*, too, was currently without an editor, and as founder and first editor, ER wanted to see it survive and expand. Dorothy McAllister and Molly Dewson also suggested that Lorena Hickok take over as DNC executive secretary—in charge of all publications and publicity, from Washington, working under Tillett. "Eddie seemed to like the idea," ER told FDR, delighted. Hick needed a job, and with her as editor, what ER long regarded as her own journal would continue in familial hands.*

ER assured Dewson that Hick could "make a magnificent job" of the *Digest* and even "succeed in making the men consider it their publicity organ as well as ours," to transmit news about government agencies and party concerns. "If it could be done we would be set for all time." She assured Dewson that Hick would work with Trude Pratt and was keen on Gladys Tillett, and "I can work with Hick."

Dewson was relieved, and the transition was remarkably smooth. As soon as Tillett was named head of the Women's Division, she appointed Hick executive secretary. Tillett announced her admiration for Hick's twenty-year career as a journalist "with unusual and wide experience"— which would now be used to expand Democratic Party influence, with enhanced print and radio activities. As one of her "male contemporaries" had noted recently, Tillett wrote, Hick is "not only one of the best newspaperwomen in the country, but she is one of the two or three best newspapermen."

It was a grand partnership. Hick had long been fond of Tillett and told ER that she was a true "liberal Democrat," and that in North Carolina she and her husband were progressive activists.

---

*ER was editor of the monthly *Women's Democratic News*, which first appeared in May 1925. It became *Democratic Digest* in 1936.

The first lady was very pleased that Hick had a position of significant power and influence. It would enable ER to remain at the helm—or at least at the center. In 1928 she had written a bold essay calling for the creation of "women bosses," since party politics had always been in the hands of men. Since public men often disliked women in public life and refused to share "any actual control" or power, women needed to organize and select "women bosses who can talk as equals" and stand for urgent issues with the support of their own constituencies. By "boss" she did not mean a sleazy and easy-to-buy politician; she meant a "high-minded leader." This 1928 idea now came to the fore in 1940. ER had found her voice, her footing, and confidence in her mission. With Hick in charge of editorials, columns, and all publicity, ER would have a safe and agreeable base for work and new collaborations.

ER's relationship with Hick continued to be loving and candid. Hick still lived at the White House, and Tommy lobbied ER to "gently urge" Hick to rent an apartment in Washington now that she had a salaried position. As she told Anna, "I think it wears on your mother to have her constantly in the house because she [Hick] doesn't like people and if she has to entertain visiting Democrats, I don't think she should use the White House."

Tommy was also upset that Hick had told ER that she had "become a personage and is no longer a person. Your mother is still the same with many more interests and perhaps does too much work and so she has little time for a personal life, but I can detect no change."

Actually, Tommy misinterpreted Hick's remark. Hick had read Ruby Black's book and told ER it made her aware of the difference between the woman she knew and the public persona the first lady projected. "My trouble, I suspect, has always been that I've been so much more interested in the *person* than in the *personage*," Hick told ER. "I resented the personage and fought for years an anguished and losing fight against the development of the *person* into the *personage*. I still prefer the person, but I admire and respect the personage with all my heart!"

Almost as an afterthought, Hick added, "All this explains why I shall never write your biography. I can think of only one other person who undoubtedly felt about this as I have—or would have felt so, increasingly, had he lived, Louis Howe."

"You are wrong about Louis," ER replied.

He always wanted to make me President when FDR was thro' & insisted he could do it. You see he was interested in his power to create personages more than in a person, tho' I think he probably cared more for me as a person as much as he cared for anyone & more than anyone else ever has! Sheer need on his part I imagine! I used to laugh at him & tell him I had no interest in the job & I still think the personage is an accident & I only like the part of life in which I am a person!

ER never considered Tommy's advice to urge Hick to reside somewhere, anywhere, else and encouraged her to continue to live in the White House. ER felt about Hick much as she felt about Earl Miller: they were her trusted "steadies"—she enjoyed their company and reserved privileged space for them in her homes and in her heart. Earl continued regularly to monitor ER's bills and correspondence to be certain that nobody cheated his "Lady" and personally went after vendors he thought had done so. Although ER once resented his ongoing suspicions, she had grown to appreciate his trained, discerning eye. But neither Hick nor Earl was any longer a source or subject of romance.

Deep friendship with ER always had an element of romance and excitement. Some people wondered if Bernard Baruch's continual support for her interests had romantic implications. She had frequent, mostly unrecorded, meetings with Baruch. They danced together and enjoyed concerts together. Sometimes she sat with him on his park bench in Lafayette Park to discuss politics, defense needs, and refugee issues.

When ER became unusually insistent about defense plans and the need to stockpile military supplies and to embargo supplies to enemy nations, people wondered whether Baruch had influenced her. But her concerns about such issues, including her opposition to ongoing oil shipments to Japan, had nothing to do with Baruch. She protested scrap iron and oil shipments to Japan throughout the autumn of 1940. On 12 November, she asked FDR, "Now we've stopped scrap iron, what about oil?" She was satisfied by her husband's response: "The real answer which you cannot use is that if we forbid oil shipments to Japan, Japan will increase her purchases of Mexican oil and furthermore, may be driven by actual necessity to a descent on the Dutch East Indies."

Although the first lady's friendship with Baruch deepened over the years, she seems never to have been romantically attracted to him. She was actually a serial romantic. Dynamic men and women whose interests coincided with her own, and who had fresh thoughts about them, interested her. She was both nurturer and intellectual companion, a combination that made her company a delight for many.

She was currently focused on Joe Lash. Maternally, she sought to bolster his frequently depressed spirits. She understood his moods: although bold and determined in public, he was often uncertain, hesitant, and depressed in private. His frequent meetings with ER lifted his spirits. She encouraged him, and he adored her: her penetrating eyes, her genuine kindness, her surprising insights. And she had become deeply involved in the burgeoning romance between Joe and Trude Pratt.

After the successful meeting in Chicago, ER continued her tour in Detroit. There she was enchanted by hours of splendid music; had lunch with her niece and namesake, ER II; and dined with her sister-in-law Dorothy Kemp Roosevelt and Hall's daughters, Amy, Diana, and Janet. They all attended rehearsals for WPA music projects, where, ER wrote, she enjoyed "two of the pleasantest hours I have ever spent." A Gypsy band played dance music "to which it was almost impossible to sit still." The "delightful leader" played in the band and also narrated Gypsy stories for the children. Then a "full orchestra" presented a new symphony by Florence Price, one of the few women to write symphonic music. "She is a colored woman and a native of Chicago, who has certainly made a contribution to our music. The orchestra rendered her symphony beautifully."

There were "more treats in store for us," ER noted. The next day "in a Negro church we heard a group of spiritual singers who fairly carried us away from our everyday world." Their leader had been discovered while digging ditches. ER was so impressed by Detroit's Negro Spiritualist Singers she arranged with Florence Kerr, assistant commissioner of the WPA, to have them perform at the White House on New Year's Eve.

The snowstorms that raged throughout the Midwest during this phase of ER's tour did not diminish her enthusiastic audiences. En route she received a much-anticipated cable from Joe Lash. The International Student Service (ISS) board had appointed him general secretary, with a generous salary. ER was delighted: "You will do a fine constructive job and I hope you will make me useful." She would see him before and after his birthday on 2 December. "My heart is singing for you . . . and this opportunity to help youth. . . . Much love dear boy."

The last week of her November tour took her to Wisconsin, Ohio, Pennsylvania, North Carolina, and Virginia. Although her columns rarely included war news, she was relieved to note Greece's ongoing resistance to the Italian invasion: "Heroism is always a thrilling thing. . . . This little nation's defense . . . makes us proud of that quality [that enables] human beings to rise above all selfish fears and interest and do their duty in the face of danger and death."

ER returned to Washington, and for the first time in many years, she and FDR did not go to Warm Springs for Thanksgiving. Instead they headed to Hyde Park, since it was important to spend the holiday with SDR—who had celebrated her eighty-fifth birthday in September. "The family is so scattered now that we are a small party here," ER wrote, "but it is very pleasant to be at home and what we lack in numbers we shall make up in gaiety." The country had many reasons to be grateful: "Today as a nation, we give thanks first and foremost for the fact that we are at peace. All of life is a struggle; at least, it should be a constant and unending struggle to make the world a better place. . . . The struggle goes on constantly against our baser natures." In the world at war, so many are "weighed down by the knowledge that in order even to exist ourselves we must try to destroy our fellow human beings—people who live in some other bit of land and speak some other language . . . and yet who have the same needs and the same desires we have ourselves, and whom we could love and understand if it were not for this thing called war."

In that context, ER gave "national thanks" because:

> We are free to register our will politically, to worship God as we see fit, to insist that even those with whom we disagree shall have the right to express their opinions, and that all men shall come before the bar of justice with the presumption that they are innocent until they are proved guilty, and with the right to defend their beliefs and their actions.
>
> We are thankful for our natural resources, for the productivity of our land, for the resourcefulness and ingenuity of our people. . . .
>
> As an individual, I am grateful for health and strength, the love of family and friends, for the power to enjoy so many things, for the

ability to see the humor in life which softens the bitterness, and above all else for the ability and the opportunity to give a helping hand in one way or another.

On Saturday ER journeyed to New York to do a radio broadcast and meet with Joe Lash, who took her to see his new apartment. She then hosted a dinner party at Eleventh Street for Earl Miller and two of his friends, since Earl was to leave for a month of Naval Reserve duty the next morning.

While commuting to Washington ER read Ernest Hemingway's *For Whom the Bell Tolls*, which she recommended to her readers as "compelling" because the characters, "the everlasting mixture of good and bad, of coarseness and sensitiveness, of cruelty and gentleness, are real." Hemingway's experiences during the Spanish Civil War "taught him that people will fight for their liberties. Perhaps the most interesting part of the book is the evidence of the appeal which a fight for human rights calls forth from the fine people the world over."

Joe Lash, who had fought in Spain, was a significant part of ER's thoughts about the Spanish Civil War. He "brought back from Spain" a small bronze figure of a young "militiaman in coveralls . . . a symbol of the Republican cause." She cherished the "little bronze boy," which always sat before her "on my very crowded desk & is a joy."

Between Thanksgiving and Christmas ER's days were full, but she was eager to spend more time with Joe and Trude. For his birthday, on 2 December, she sent him a book of poetry as a gift and left a letter at his apartment, "the first birthday letter I have ever written you & yet I feel as though you were very close to me & your concerns were mine."

I think I knew we were going to be friends . . . when I looked across the table at you about a year ago! Anyway my dear boy we can count on a growing understanding . . . out of which enduring love & respect grow. . . . I sent you the *Home Book of Verse* because sometime if you like to read aloud perhaps you'll let me come over & read some of my favorites in front of your fire.

She had also sent him a little radio, a transistor shortwave, noting, "I get the news in the morning on mine & I never cease to marvel that something so small can bring you a voice from Europe!"

Joe felt it was "a wonderful birthday week—mainly because of the thoughtfulness and love of ER." She filled his apartment and his life with "magical influences." She had restored his sense of purpose and helped him recenter his heart. He thanked her for becoming "the most precious friend in the world who walks beside me . . . counseling me to be a better person, a kinder person, a happier person. . . . I only hope that in some way I am helping you."

At the time he had no idea how much he and Trude did in fact help ER. They shared her vision of a better, more expansive democracy. They worked to rescue targets of Hitler's violence. And they gave her daily hope for trusted companionship in a landscape that was otherwise often lonely for her. ER's friendship with Joe had expanded to include Trude, with deep independent roots, and became profound and lifelong. They too shared political goals and a range of emotional journeys that forged a unique bond.

Scholar, teacher, and activist, Trude had been educated as ER had always wanted to be. The first lady deeply admired Trude's learning, her love for languages, and her activism. Trude was thirty-four, with three toddlers—the same age as ER had been (though she was the mother of five) when she learned of FDR's affair with Lucy Mercer. Now the romance of Trude's relationship with Joe was beguiling to ER, and she wrote Trude a remarkable letter:

Ever since our talk . . . I have wished that I could help you. . . . Somewhere along the line of development we discover what we really are and then we make our real decision for which we are responsible. Make that decision primarily for yourself because you can never really live anyone else's life not even your child's. The influence you exert is through your own life and what you become yourself. . . . There was a time when I thought happiness did not matter, but I think differently today.

Trude and Joe had a "sense of being driven by fate," but she was still married. Eliot Pratt gave his wife "whatever freedom she wanted," and they seemed to have an amiable understanding. Hence she agonized at each step, and her decision to divorce him took years. ER evidently supported that decision with an enhanced commitment to personal happiness that fortified her own being in an entirely new way. When Joe first told her of Trude's decision to separate, marveling at the "immensity of the step" and the "prospect of happiness," ER embraced him.

More immediately, ER was eager to do all she could do to support the Varian Fry rescue operation under way in Marseilles: the Emergency Rescue Committee (ERC), for which he worked, succeeded in getting people out of France, as the last exits out of Europe's horror slammed shut. Fry's operation would eventually be responsible for the rescue of nearly two thousand notable refugees. Using the skills of forgers and mountain climbers, he and his team guided refugees including Thomas Mann and Lion Feuchtwanger across the Pyrenees and onto rescue boats that transported them to America. Trude Pratt's role in the ERC has never been fully acknowledged, but she was responsible for much of its initial success, having introduced ER to Karl Frank and Varian Fry. She never wanted to be credited for her role, but ultimately acknowledged,

> Of course I knew and much admired Varian Fry, and I helped him where I could (not enough), one of the ways was an introduction to Mrs. Roosevelt. She realized how difficult his work was and how important. . . . It is still hard to think back to those times. So much more could have been done by people of this country, who were slow to believe that the horrors were actually happening. Mrs. Roosevelt was certainly not one of them.

Although Gertrude Wenzel Pratt's name appears nowhere in the Varian Fry record, the rescue operation was launched because of ER's absolute trust in her and in her extended circle of activist allies in the German resistance community.

Chapter Sixteen

"Isolationism Is Impossible": The Politics of Rescue

Varian Fry arrived in Marseilles on 15 August 1940, carrying a short list of two hundred notable artists, writers, musicians, "immediately endangered political refugees" and prominent antifascist activists whom he was determined to rescue. Within days he expanded his initial goal: he would now work to save everyone stranded in the crowded seaport city of southern France, including the hundreds of thousands of foreign-born, now stateless Jews. From his suite in the Hotel Splendide, with the support of the ERC in New York, his indefatigable efforts ultimately produced significant results.

But Fry's heroic determination to save lives contradicted State Department policies as well as FDR's diplomatic priorities. Ever since ER's "interference" regarding the passengers on the SS *Quanza*, Breckinridge Long had been firmly in charge of refugee issues and consular decisions. Although FDR had agreed to grant visitors' visas to the most endangered and noteworthy refugees who were trapped in unoccupied France, Long's policy of "delay and delay" ruled the moment. On 30 August, Karl Frank wrote to ER that her friendly interest had resulted in "many hundreds" of visitors' visas, but "the problem of exit permits from France" endured, so that, of the 576 people whose names the President's Advisory Committee on Political Refugees had presented to the State Department for visas, the vast majority remained trapped. Actually fewer than fifty had the papers they needed. On 6 September, outraged by the many bureaucratic hurdles, ER wrote Sumner Welles, "Is there no way of getting our Consul in Marseilles to help . . . a few more of these poor people out?"

After a month of earnest activity in Marseilles and Lisbon, ERC chairman Frank Kingdon told ER that the situation remained dreadful. The Lisbon consul "is holding up many people who have taken the first great step in escaping from France, and whose departure from Lisbon should be expedited." Kingdon hoped she would find something to be done about "this unnecessary stoppage," which merely added "to the over-crowding of Lisbon and the suffering of the refugees."

Moved by the agony of so many people stranded in peril, ER acted upon every request made of her. She was particularly emphatic regarding writers like Lion Feuchtwanger, whose works she had read and admired.

She had enjoyed Feuchtwanger's company during his November 1932–January 1933 U.S. lecture tour. On 19 March 1933, only a week after FDR's inauguration, ER's friend Helen Rogers Reid had published Feuchtwanger's article "Hitler's War on Culture" in the Sunday *New York Herald Tribune Magazine*—the first alert to U.S. audiences of the bitter and dangerous reality that had so quickly and completely distorted the Germany of Lessing and Goethe into a land of brutality and fear, violence and hatred. After leaving Washington, the author had joined his wife, famed German gymnast and athlete Marta Loffler Feuchtwanger, in Austria, where she had been on a skiing holiday. Within months Hitler revoked the citizenship of those "disloyal to the Reich," and Feuchtwanger, now stateless, had joined the German exile community in the south of France.

Comfortably settled in Sanary, on the Mediterranean coast, Feuchtwanger wrote five novels over the next seven years and completed a trilogy, *The Day Will Come*, on the life and work of Flavius Josephus, ancient Rome's Jewish historian who sought to transcend confining nationalisms and limited identities to achieve world citizenship. But France's debacle in June 1940 changed everything. The armistice signed by the Nazis and the French included a "surrender on demand" clause requiring the Vichy government to turn over any German nationals, including refugees, that the Nazis demanded. Like all "enemy aliens" in the country, the Feuchtwangers were sent to internment camps—Marta to Gurs, and Lion first to Les Milles, then to St.-Nicola, near Nîmes.

ER's AFSC contacts reported that the French internment camps were overcrowded, filthy places of "squalor and disease." When ER was shown a photograph of the famed author, grim and gaunt behind barbed wire, taken during the summer of 1940, she did everything possible to get support for Varian Fry's work in Marseilles and achieve his rescue.

In the initial plan orchestrated by Fry, the Feuchtwangers were to have escaped together with Heinrich and Nelly Mann, Gottfried Mann

(Thomas's son, historian/journalist known as Golo), and Franz and Alma Mahler Werfel. But Spain was rumored to have closed its borders to "stateless" people, and Fry left the Feuchtwangers in Marseilles. ER then contacted the Sharps—activists in Marseilles—for help. The Reverend Waitstill Sharp, a former minister of the Unitarian church in Wellesley, Massachusetts, and his wife, social worker Martha Sharp, had traveled from Prague in their efforts to help refugees escape. Now they accompanied the Feuchtwangers over the Pyrenees and then by train across the Spanish-Portuguese border to Lisbon, where they boarded a U.S. ship, the export liner *Excalibur*. When it docked on 5 October in New Jersey, an eager press corps greeted the Feuchtwangers. Unfortunately, the excited author told the story of their escape in dramatic detail. Although he did not name names, the secrets of Fry's operation and the activities of Hiram Bingham, Fry's only ally in the U.S. consulate in Marseilles, were fully reported.

The next week the Manns and Franz Werfel, author of the best seller *The Forty Days of Musa Degh*, a vivid study of the 1915 Armenian slaughter, and his wife, Alma Mahler Werfel, arrived on American shores. They had left Marseilles with Varian Fry on 12 September, and after several delays in Madrid and Lisbon, they had been able to book passage on the Greek liner *Nea Helias*. Press reports were ecstatic: several most esteemed writers and artists were safe.

Now at the dock in Hoboken, Werfel, surrounded by the press, relatives, and old friends—including Thomas Mann, there to greet his son Golo and his often estranged, more radical brother Heinrich—refused to answer questions regarding their journey: "It would be very dangerous to speak of it. Many of my friends are still in concentration camps." During their protracted ordeal, Werfel had destroyed twenty manuscripts, he said, in case he was arrested. He hoped for time to write in peace and complete his *Song of Bernadette*—which while stranded and despondent in Lourdes, he had promised Saint Bernadette herself he would do were he to be blessed by the miracle of escape.*

---

*On 27 June 1940, after weeks of panicked flight, Alma and Franz Werfel reached Lourdes, in the foothills of the Pyrenees, close to a border crossing and the hope of survival. They found sanctuary with several families and were told the story of Bernadette Soubirous, a nineteenth-century miller's daughter whose conversation with a statue of the Virgin Mary come to life engendered the pilgrimage center

Reporters noted that Heinrich Mann, almost seventy, looked particularly exhausted. The former president of Prussia's Academy of the Arts, and one of Germany's earliest and most prophetic anti-Nazis, he was most famous in the United States for his historical novel *Young Henry of Navarre*, translated in 1937, and for *Professor Unrat*, the story of an esteemed academic destroyed by his obsession for a seductive cabaret singer, filmed in 1930 as *The Blue Angel*. The film, produced by Germany's UFA Studios, was released in December 1930 and launched a new era in film history.* But Heinrich Mann was not the star—Marlene Dietrich and director Josef von Sternberg were. Now Heinrich Mann faced an unknown future as Thomas Mann's less celebrated brother.

At the dock the press failed to interview the extraordinary Alma Mahler Gropius Werfel, who had carried a rucksack on her back across the Pyrenees and kept it by her side at all times, on train, plane, and ship. It was filled with manuscripts, including the scores of Anton Bruckner's *Third Symphony* and of all of Gustav Mahler's works, as well as seventeen of her own songs for voice and piano.

Many of the forty-three passengers on the *Nea Helias* had recently escaped detention and concentration camps and were on their way to the Dominican Republic. They had agreed to become "pioneers" at Sosúa, an experimental farm community for refugees, and looked forward to their new lives in a place they had never heard of, free at last from Nazi rule. Ecstatic upon landing in New Jersey, they were stunned to be rounded up by immigration officials and sent to Ellis Island, another prison, where they waited for transit visas and other requirements "under lock and key"—for Jewish immigrants in flight from Hitler were deemed security

---

dedicated to Our Lady of Lourdes. As he listened, his depression slowly lifted, and Werfel began research on the historic novel that would sing her song. For Werfel, the road to rescue began in Lourdes. See Marino, *Quiet American*, pp. 68–76. Monumentally popular, *The Song of Bernadette* was published in 1941 and became an Academy Award–winning film starring Jennifer Jones in 1943.

*In 1929, as a student in Berlin, Gertrud Wenzel supported herself in part by acting at UFA Studios "as an extra in the films of Marlene Dietrich"—precisely when *The Blue Angel* was in production. Jerry Tallmer, "At Home with Trude Lash," *New York Post*, 26 February 1972.

risks: they might be "fifth columnists" or Communist spies. After a week, they finally sailed for the Dominican Republic.

On 14 September, two days after Fry's trek across the Pyrenees with the Manns and Werfels, the Marseilles consular official Hiram Bingham received a State Department memo ordering him to cease all aid and support for the ERC. Frank Kingdon, chair of the ERC, "feared there would be only a few weeks more in which escapes could be made."

One searches in vain for ER's reaction to these events—her columns are filled with her love for music, her presence at many concerts, her special interest in Mahler. There is no evidence that ER knew about the treatment of the Sosúa refugees at Ellis Island, but she was clearly aware of every step the ERC took to rescue the many notables on the emergency visa list. She was informed of every detail involving the incoming refugees.

Yet she wrote not a word about the people she worked to rescue, or about Frank Kingdon's fear that the State Department and the Gestapo were about to cut off all remaining escape routes, thereby ending the ERC's work. As always, she walked a tight line between her roles as an activist first lady and as the president's wife, carefully choosing when to go public and when to keep silent and acting only when she knew she stood a chance.

Her public silence during the autumn of 1940 was mandated by the demands of her husband's reelection campaign. Public opinion polls indicated that over 80 percent of Americans wanted no change in U.S. immigration quotas.

Moreover, FDR's long-range diplomatic commitment to maintain "friendly relations" with Vichy France defined his international priorities—and fully enhanced Breckinridge Long's power. Long saw every successful rescue as a challenge to his absolute authority, and every life saved as diminishing that authority. FDR refused to place limits on Long's power and seemed to agree that the refugee community was riddled with dangerous elements. Long now wanted all lists of refugees terminated, except for the few that his consular officers might recognize. James G. MacDonald, of the President's Advisory Committee for Political Refugees, was outraged to have been bypassed.

Given this situation, ER understood that the success of the ERC depended on her public silence and FDR's willingness to let her continue the work. She could press him personally, as she did on 28 September when she urged him to meet with MacDonald to "get this cleared up quickly," since "these poor people . . . may die at any time and . . . are asking only to come here on transit visas." But at times FDR's priorities and urgencies seemed at cross-purposes with hers, even virtually opposed to them. While she fought to ease restrictions on incoming refugees, he sought to stanch the flow. With one eye on his electorate and another on his supporters in the administration, he often spoke in an anti-alien rhetoric that must have alarmed and distressed his wife. Yet the dreadful circumstances mandated their opposing views as well as their collaboration and cooperation.

Indeed, the situation of the refugees stranded in Marseilles was becoming ever more dire as Vichy France implemented Hitler's "surrender on demand" clause. On 27 September Vichy ordered all Jews in the occupied zone to register at French police stations, carry their identification cards everywhere, be subject to search at all times, and place signs in their windows if they owned a "Jewish business." On 3 October it imposed the Statut des Juifs, which curtailed the civil rights of French Jews in the unoccupied zone and regulated and restricted their participation in national life, the economy, and the professions. "At a stroke [Jews] were excluded from government, the military, the press, education, and cultural institutions" throughout France. On 4 October it authorized the surveillance and internment of foreign-born Jews. On 7 October it revoked the citizenship of Algerian Jews. These exclusionary laws of October 1940 rendered Hitlerian rules regarding Jews "official French policy."

Autumn 1940 was a bitter season for Jews in all the occupied areas. A new decree regarding "ownerless Jewish property" enabled Nazi troops to remove valuables—books, jewelry, furniture, and art—from Jewish homes, schools, businesses, and cultural centers in France, Belgium, and Holland. Nazi curator Alfred Rosenberg established a unit to transport significant "cultural objects" to Germany. More than five thousand works by eminent painters—Rembrandt, Rubens, Goya, Gainsborough, and many others—were removed from museums and residences, along with thousands of statues and all manner of antiquities. At the same time, in Frankfurt, Rosenberg introduced the concept of *Judenrein* as the goal of the new Institute for the Investigation of the Jewish Question: Germany would regard the "Jewish Question [as] solved" when "the last Jew has left the Greater German living space."

More ghastly events unfolded. On 3 October 150,000 Jewish residents of Greater Warsaw were ordered to move, bringing only their hand-held belongings, into the newly defined ghetto. Up to 400,000 Jews were to be walled off into an area built for 250,000 people, initiating a new terror. On 4 October Hitler met Mussolini at the Brenner Pass and announced, "The war is won!" From 5 October to 3 November, Nazi night raids against London remained relentless. On 5 November, Churchill told Parliament that 14,000 civilians had been killed in the Blitz. On 14 November, 500 German bombers targeted Coventry. A giant blaze leveled the city, destroying 60,000 buildings, including seven major war production plants, and killing almost 600 civilians. Raids on Birmingham and London followed.

On 27 October, Churchill cabled FDR: "The world Cause is in your hands." Britain would defend the realm, but the old destroyers were insufficient. The Royal Navy needed supplies as well as protection on the high seas against Nazi submarines, which had sunk scores of ships. And it was broke.

Since Britain's survival was essential, FDR reconsidered the policy of cash-and-carry. Now he would ask Congress for a new plan: lend-lease, or authorization to lease, sell, or transfer supplies to Allied nations without immediate payment. He introduced his idea at a White House press conference on 17 December: "Suppose my neighbor's home catches fire, and I have a length of garden hose [close by]. If he can take my garden hose, and connect it up with his hydrant, I may help him to put out his fire. His home would be saved, and so would mine. Do I charge for the hose, say Neighbor, pay me $15, which the hose cost. No! I don't want fifteen dollars. I want my garden hose back after the fire is over."

On Sunday, 20 December, in the company of ER, SDR, cabinet members, and movie stars Clark Gable and Carole Lombard, FDR addressed the nation in a radio broadcast that he considered the most important message since the great banking crisis of 1933. He proposed that the United States become "the great arsenal of democracy."

The Nazi masters of Germany have made it clear that they intend not only to dominate all life and thought in their own country, but also to enslave the whole of Europe, and then to use the resources of Europe to dominate the rest of the world.

Isolationists still believed the oceans were barriers to harm to the United States, but "we cannot escape danger by crawling into bed and pulling the covers over our heads." Spies, fifth-columnists, functionaries of deceit and violence, were present on U.S. shores:

> The evil forces which have crushed and undermined and corrupted so many others are already within our own gates. . . . Their secret emissaries are active in our own and in neighboring countries. They seek to stir up suspicion and dissension to cause internal strife. They try to turn capital against labor, and vice versa. They try to reawaken long slumbering racist and religious enmities which should have no place in this country. They are active in every group that promotes intolerance. . . . These trouble-breeders have but one purpose. It is to divide our people, . . . to destroy our unity and shatter our will to defend ourselves.
>
> There are also American citizens, many of them in high places, who . . . are aiding and abetting the work of these agents.

No appeasement was possible with Nazi Germany, he said, as the fate of eight European countries now occupied by the Nazis proved. Instead, the United States must help Britain defend democracy. Britain was not demanding American intervention, only support, rearmament, and rapidly enhanced military production. The U.S. labor force could "provide the human power that turns out the destroyers, and the planes and the tanks" to make the United States "the great arsenal of democracy."

ER was moved by her husband's words, relieved by his decision to create the "arsenal of democracy," and pleased by his criticism of the Americans "in high places" who aided the dictators' work. Some of his staff had wanted that implicit reference to members of his State Department removed, but ER was gratified that he had insisted on leaving it in. ER also appreciated his references to labor, which implied that he would not abandon union rights and so many of the other New Deal efforts about which they increasingly disagreed.

She particularly approved of his decision to send ILO hero John Winant to London, replacing Joseph Kennedy as ambassador. Esther Lape had initially recommended Winant, who served on her American Foundation board, as the profoundly humane man most needed in London now. ER and Frances Perkins supported the recommendation, and his appointment was a triumph for ER's circle. But she was distressed by FDR's decision to appoint Admiral William Leahy as ambassador to Vichy on 29 November; he would represent FDR's "Vichy gamble" of "friendly relations." To her dismay, Leahy refused to meet with Varian Fry.

Rescue remained a contentious subject for the first couple. Knowing that refugees awaited the paperwork necessary to leave, and that they lived in prolonged agony, ER prodded and cajoled FDR almost daily. It was "a running argument between them," Joe Lash noted.

Frank Kingdon of the ERC sent her a report that dramatized the emotional cost of the "paper walls" erected by Breckinridge Long's consulates: "As a human document and a detailed account of one family's experience, this paper will, I am sure . . . stir you." The case was that of a Czech writer and filmmaker, Hans (Bohumil) Lustig, who had typed a five-page lament to the ERC detailing the story of his "a war of nerves." To support his visa application, he said, he and his wife had provided U.S. consular officials with his forty-week contract with MGM, cables from eminent leaders, and visas for Costa Rica.

> The contract with MGM was of no interest to [a certain official] at all, not even when I told him that, according to my information, this contract has been approved by Washington. "Washington has no right at all to interfere with us in these cases," was his answer.
>
> With that, my wife and I were dismissed without another word.

Subsequently he was asked for a full account of his radio and film career: "I stressed the fact that as a democratic journalist, and author of anti-Nazi sketches for Radio Mondial (which were broadcast to America every Saturday in an English translation) and finally, as the author of an anti-Nazi motion picture, I am particularly endangered." Again the U.S. officials dismissed his plea.

"How can you help us?" he asked Kingdon in his report. Perhaps a cable from MGM would help, or another from a group at PEN, or from Thomas Mann and his friends?

ER, moved, forwarded Lustig's report to FDR, with a handwritten note: "FDR Can't they be helped? ER." The President passed the item on to Assistant Secretary of State Long.

Long replied by writing a memorandum to ER:

MEMORANDUM FOR MRS. ROOSEVELT:

These individual cases are distressing. One cannot read them without definite sentimental reaction.

It is particularly difficult in Washington to superimpose judgment upon that of the consul. Under the law the consul is vested
with an authority of which the executive officers of the Department
of State are unable to divest him.

General instructions have been sent consuls to regard generously
the preference lists which have been submitted by the president's
committee, Dr. Stephen Wise, Mr. William Green and several others. However, the instructions also contain injunctions to the consuls
that they must be satisfied that the character, reputation and intentions of the applicants are such that their presence in the United
States will not be detrimental to the interests of the United States.
This is understood to be that their intentions are not subversive and
that their characters and reputations are clean.

Long suggested that "MGM may itself have communicated to the
consul some information" that might have been detrimental and been
"the determinative factor in the formulation of the consul's judgment. . . .
It is impractical and would be in violation of law to order the consul
peremptorily to issue a visa." There was no hope.

At the bottom of Long's 11 October memo, ER wrote a note to
Tommy: "Send to Frank Kingdon and say I am sorry." On 22 October
1940, Tommy wrote to Kingdon, "Mrs. R is sorry that this reply to [the]
inquiry which she made on the case you sent to her . . . is not more
encouraging. However, she knows of nothing else which might be done
about it."

There was no further correspondence regarding this case in ER's refugee file. It was unclear whether the Lustigs got out until 1 September 1954,
when one Charlotte Lustig wrote to ER from Beverly Hills, California:

I am just reading Ben Hecht's book *A Child of a Century* and I
reach the chapter "FDR," on page 567. This and the following chapters deal with the horrifying slaughter of the European Jews by the
Nazis.

Mr. Hecht is trying to explain . . . that President Roosevelt refused to intervene in behalf of the European Jews, refused to lend a helping hand to those unfortunates by warning the world of the atrocities happening in Europe. . . .

Will you please allow me, dear Mrs. Roosevelt, to say some words about myself. I belong to the numerous Europeans who have worshiped President Roosevelt from the very minute he appeared on the political scene of the world. I am a German born Jew, my husband—a writer—comes from Czechoslovakia. We fled Germany in 1933, lived 7 years in Paris and fled France 2 days before the Germans took over.

Shortly after our arrival in Portugal, my husband together with 12 other writers, obtained an Emergency Visa to this country—through the Roosevelt Advisory Committee. Upon our arrival in New York, in December 1940, the head of the [ERC], a very distinguished gentleman, sent us a message to visit him. He received us with unforgettable kindness; welcomed us to this country, regretting the fact that we had to wait 5 months in Portugal, although the State Department had sent a cable to issue the visas already in June. I hope you will believe me, dear Mrs. Roosevelt, that our gratitude, admiration and worship belongs to the late President, now and forever. . . .

May I add, at the conclusion of this letter, that I have read your column for many years, and that I have always admired your courage and deep sense of justice and fairness.

In December Joseph Buttinger of the ERC sent a desperate appeal to ER—the State Department had promised to cable visas to Europe but then delayed them. ER begged her husband, "Can't something be done?" And she implored Undersecretary of State Sumner Welles, "Is there anything that you could do to hasten this process?" In December she asked Welles to explain "why so many of these people who actually have visas are finding so much difficulty. One fact is that they cannot get visas to go through Spain." Wasn't there a way, she asked, to expedite visas through the U.S. ambassador, Carleton J. H. Hayes?

As secretary of the interior, Harold Ickes was in charge of U.S. territories. On 12 November 1940, he ordered Lawrence W. Carter, then governor of the Virgin Islands, to admit refugees "on their appearance at the port of entry. After a short residence . . . they may proceed without visas or formalities to the United States."

On 9 December, Ickes spoke at a dinner to benefit the ERC at New York's Hotel Astor, sponsored by the *Nation* and the *New Republic*. He pleaded that the United States do "everything in its power" to rescue "the thousands of men and women of intellectual achievement and democratic thought who are now in danger of the firing squad." The Virgin Islands and Alaska were "ideal places of refuge for the stranded believers in democracy.

> It is a simple matter to bring these men and women across the ocean, to the various countries of the Western Hemisphere. It involves no more than a little money, visitors' permits, and a helpful attitude on the part of the government.
>
> We are urging that, under the proper safeguards, the Virgin Islands be made available to political refugees, without visas, without diplomatic formality. We are urging the hospitable reception of all for whom there may be room and that they be allowed to stay in the Virgin Islands as visitors until they are otherwise provided for.
>
> This would involve no competition either with American labor or business. Instead of a burden upon the economy of these islands, an economic benefit would flow from the visitors . . .
>
> Here are two small corners of the Western Hemisphere in which American freedom would mean life and liberty to fellow human beings as well as economic improvement for ourselves.

Ickes concluded by celebrating America's immigrant reality, the Statue of Liberty legacy of "our golden door" heritage. People from Ireland, Scotland, France, Germany, and Scandinavia no longer bear names considered "foreign." "In this generation," perhaps a man named "Tschaikowsky" might not be a presidential candidate, but he would be considered "a candidate for all-American football tackle . . . [and] his son might be elected President." During the 1940 campaign, European dictators had stirred anti-alien hysteria, seeking to increase "racial antagonisms." But "Americans of German descent proved themselves to be followers of Carl Schurz and not of Hitler, and Americans of Italian descent proved themselves to be followers of Garibaldi and not of Mussolini." With this legacy, Ickes insisted, our doors must remain open for rescue and the survival of democracy.

ER agreed completely, but Breckinridge Long was in full, even hysterical opposition. "There are 12,000 refugees in Portugal," he had said a few weeks earlier, and among them "are many German agents." Communists, subversives, undesirables—Long could not believe that this "pipe line to siphon refugees . . . into the United States" was being created "without the precautionary steps of investigation and checking." He complained to FDR, who told him to speak with Ickes.

On 27 November Long accused Ickes and his allies in the Justice Department of "working at cross purposes with the Administration. . . . They are radical and have peculiar ideas—at least their ideas to me are radical and some of them are inadmissible and unacceptable." FDR sent Ickes a memo that "rather slapped my ears back by telling me that refugee matters were for him and the State Department to decide."

But when they discussed the Virgin Islands as a haven, "he seemed open to suggestions" and was both "friendly" to and "impressed with" the details of Ickes's scheme. "He thought that if certain conditions were met, it might be all right to go ahead with the plan," and urged Ickes to take "the whole question" to the Justice Department. But FDR himself made no decision.

In December Varian Fry and members of his staff, including philanthropist Mary Jane Gold, were arrested and detained on a prison ship in the Marseilles harbor. ER wrote Sumner Welles that "Varian Fry's arrest . . . troubles me greatly." Surely "there must be something we can do about an American citizen, & I am sure that though he was helping refugees, he did nothing actually reprehensible."

Welles assured her that nobody was hurt and "no physical harm" had been done. He sent a telegram to Marseilles immediately "requesting consul be permitted to visit." The consular official, Hiram Bingham, arrived on the prison ship and "shook hands with us," Fry recalled—whereupon the captain immediately became "more cordial" and served the Americans cognac. Fry and Gold were released the day after Bingham's visit, on 9 December.

Once Fry was freed, State Department and Vichy officials increasingly harassed him and urged him to leave. But he was determined to stay, to try to save every life possible.

The tension between Long and Ickes simmered for months as both men pursued their respective programs while fearing that FDR intended to downsize their authority. Meanwhile ER and FDR argued about

Long's disastrous policies. During one of their sharpest arguments, New York City judge Justine Wise Polier happened to be at the White House and heard their conversation. At one point Breckinridge Long's name came up, and ER said, "Franklin, you know he's a fascist." FDR replied, "I've told you, Eleanor, you must not say that." To which she replied, "Well, maybe I shouldn't say it, but he is." She said it, and he listened, even if he chastised her for it: this pattern was at the core of their relationship.

ER fully understood the limits of their marital partnership, which was defined by love and respect, consideration and concern. Still, these were the months of their most profound disagreements, although moments of agreement and shared vision gave her hope. She appreciated the pressures her husband faced regarding refugees. But as Justine Wise Polier noted in her oral history, ER's reticence gave people the wrong impression about the real arrangement. ER believed she was the only person in FDR's circle willing to disagree with him, or push him when he needed to be pushed. They were keen to know each other's opinion, and when they disagreed, they did so with respect; they *always* listened to each other. When they were apart, FDR called every day, and he relied on ER's observations. She was his conscience; he was her barometer. She trusted his political instincts and the direction of his heart. And she was conscious of the enormity of the opposition even on issues that she considered essential, moderate, and bipartisan.

Occasionally when they disagreed, her view ultimately prevailed. Sometimes an idea rooted in her own statements and writings would appear in FDR's policies. But charges of "petticoat government" really annoyed her husband—which she attributed to his mother's lifelong interference and badgering. Therefore she never took credit, never referred to her influence on him, and never mentioned her occasionally successful efforts at persuasion. Nor did FDR credit his wife for many positions he gratefully accepted from her.

We have no record to tell us, for example, what ER thought when FDR introduced the "Four Freedoms" at the opening of the 77th Congress on 6 January 1941. But the ideas they embody would have been familiar to readers of her column and *The Moral Basis of Democracy*. The four essential freedoms were freedom of speech, freedom of religion, freedom from want, and freedom from fear. FDR did not mean them as some far-off fantasy but rather as the basis for "a kind of world attainable in our own time," throughout the world. He presented this "moral order" to counter the dictators' tyranny now astride the world. It was a promise to address human needs "without the concentration camp or the quick-lime in the ditch. The world order which we seek is the cooperation of free countries, working together in a friendly, civilized society."

FDR's speech stirred audiences internationally, although at home ER was "saddened to notice that the applause came almost entirely from the Democrats." She wrote in her column, "Surely all of us can be united in a foreign policy which seeks to aid those people who fight for freedom and, thereby, gives us the hope of present peace for ourselves and a future peace for the world founded on the four great principles enunciated today."

Shortly before FDR's third inauguration, ER's efforts on behalf of rescue were evidently enhanced by a weekend visit from Thomas Mann and his family at the White House. Mann and his wife, Katia, had previously been guests at the White House during their 1935 U.S. visit, when Mann and Albert Einstein were honored at Harvard. In 1940 Mann partici-pated in the ERC.

Mann's children, writers Erika and Klaus, had left Germany together in April 1933. Klaus arranged for his friend W. H. Auden to marry his sister, whereby she became a British citizen. Although Auden and Erika Mann had never met, they were married in a civil ceremony in London surrounded by friends on 15 March 1935. Grateful to Auden, and to Brit-ain, Erika spent much of the war as a journalist for the BBC. She and Klaus also embarked on a lecture tour throughout the United States, which featured conversations about her book of horrors regarding Nazi education, *School for Barbarians*, and her anti-Nazi cabaret *The Pepper Mill*. Their book *Escape to Life* was published at the time of ER's 11 May 1939 White House luncheon for PEN's international writers' congress. There ER met Klaus and his friend Ernst Toller, and Erika arrived from London to accompany her parents. Erika had influenced the ERC's founding—indeed, at the first meeting in June she had suggested having a rescue agent on site to represent the ERC's lists.

"The Thomas Manns have been here since Sunday," ER wrote Joe, "& I have enjoyed knowing them a little better." She was particularly glad to see Erika.

Within weeks of the Mann family's visit, Varian Fry reported a "sudden" and "enormous" change in the rescue process. He did not know the reason, but for the first time in five months, exit visas were available. All spring ships from Marseilles to the French colony of Martinique were filled with ERC clients. They carried notables such as Jacques Schiffrin, publisher of the Pléiade editions of the French classics, and many members of the German and Austrian underground. Fry noted it was "the busiest . . . most fruitful" time in ERC history. Katia Mann's brother, the physicist Peter Pringsheim, was among those suddenly allowed to leave France legally, as were the artists Marc Chagall, Jacques Lipchitz, and Max Ernst.

ER was inexplicably involved in the circumstances of the rescue of Max Ernst, who left France in the company of Peggy Guggenheim. Max's son Jimmy had left Berlin in 1933 and sailed for New York in 1938; he was now employed by the Museum of Modern Art (MoMA). On 12 November 1940, Alfred Barr of MoMA had sent the paperwork needed for visitors' visas for Max and his ex-wife Lou. They were in immediate and extreme danger, Barr explained, because Max Ernst "has made no secret" of his contempt for totalitarian governments, and the "unrealistic nature of his work is . . . most actively persecuted. . . . His wife is Jewish. His son, James, is steadily employed in the Museum of Modern Art." Lou—Dr. Luise Straus-Ernst, a scholar, journalist, author, and philosopher—did not travel with them: her son Jimmy always said that she had not been considered "important enough and fell through the cracks" of the paper mountain. She and Max had been separated for eighteen years, and perhaps for that reason she was unable to get an independent visa.

ER supported Max Ernst's exit visa and evidently suggested the couple reunite, but nobody ever understood her suggestion or even why she had been consulted. On 21 April 1941 Varian Fry cabled the ERC in New York: "Eleanor right about Lou Ernst unable to pose as still Max's wife." Fry asked Hiram Bingham to meet the Ernsts at the consulate. There Max Ernst suggested they get remarried, but Lou rejected his offer: "Max, you know this is nonsense. . . . Jimmy will get me out. . . . I don't like charades. . . . A life for a marriage license?" She thought it all unnecessary: "after all, I'm an optimist." Jimmy continued his efforts to rescue his mother, and at the end of June 1941 she was promised a visa, "pending a definite sailing date."

. . . . . .

Just before FDR's inaugural, the Roosevelts had a family reunion at Hyde Park. Happy to be with Anna and John, in from Seattle, as well as Franklin Jr. and Ethel and her grandchildren, ER rhapsodized, "It was wonderful to have two full days in the country. We walked and talked, ate too much, and slept too little; which is always the way of family reunions, for once conversation starts, time slips by unnoticed!"

There were also direct, even combative, political conversations. FDR had recently appointed Charles F. Palmer, an Atlanta real-estate man who had served as the defense commission's building adviser, as the defense housing coordinator. ER asked if he would "be sensitive to problems of low-cost housing, schools and the like in defense areas." Noted Lash:

> The President became impatient. ER persisted and said she had heard that Palmer was partial to real estate people. Clearly very annoyed the president said alright he would appoint someone with Palmer to watch for those things. ER stuck to her guns. 'Would he have any authority?'. . . Meanwhile, the president's mother, noting the president's mood, had gotten the butler to wheel up the president's chair to the table.

SDR then removed her son "from a discussion that she saw did not please him. ER actually had become angry because the president would not be pinned down. The family all congratulated her on having stuck to her guns."

All weekend ER continued to urge expanded efforts for affordable public housing for workers. As with her groundbreaking work for Arthurdale in 1934, her commitment to decent affordable housing was consistently on her agenda. FDR was so peeved by her insistence that he uncharacteristically told Harold Ickes about their ongoing spat:

> The Mrs. came into my room yesterday morning before I was out of bed. She said, "Franklin, I have had a talk with Mr. Straus." I queried her: "Which Mr. Straus?" She said, "Nathan Straus" [who told her] that in building his housing projects he never had any difficulty with labor because, before the contract was signed, he always required . . . an agreement with labor. He wanted to build the Army cantonments. "He said that he has not seen you for a month and his feelings are hurt. Can't you give him just five minutes?"

I pulled myself up in bed and said [speaking firmly]: "No, I will not see him. And as for building the Army cantonments, they are going to be built by the Army."

Straus, head of the Federal Housing Authority, was "the most unpopular man in the Administration," Ickes noted, and could get no money from Congress. FDR had suggested that he needed a lobbyist and a popular "ex-Congressman" to represent him on the Hill.

For some reason, FDR gave Palmer remarkable power. This virtually unknown new man in this new job now presided over all defense housing. He was actually uninterested in building decent affordable housing, desperately needed by workers in the burgeoning defense industries, and Straus was out of the picture. Within weeks, ER took her protest to the public.

On 25 January, she addressed a large gathering of labor and civic leaders at the tenth annual meeting of the National Public Housing Conference at New York's Hotel Roosevelt. Thousands of "industrial workers employed under the national defense program" required immediate support, ER insisted. Moreover "in the long run all housing is defense housing." Ultimately, "if we are willing to defend our country, it is because we feel that the life we live is worth defending." She was personally interested in "prefabricated housing," which can "be put up and taken down to move to the next place."

But the new emergency, ER explained, demanded more than housing: "schools and hospitals must be provided." In Bremerton, Washington, for example, 2,500 children were without schools, and there were no plans to provide them. Wherever people lived, we had to build communities where "children are going to be educated," and the needs of the "future . . . well-being of the people who are going to be doing the work" were recognized as "essential to our defense. We have no right to ask them to sacrifice their home life." To get these needs met, ER warned, "we are going to have to be a nuisance" and campaign for government and industry "to be fair to people all over the country."

Still, affordable housing for workers was the primary theme of the conference. Gerard Swope (chair of New York's Housing Authority), Lawrence Westbrook (of the Federal Works Administration), and Peter Flynn of the CIO called for new housing in every region to end the unacceptably long journeys workers had to make to newly opened plants, and all called for an end to demeaning slum conditions in industrial workplaces.

Time credited ER—"the Number 1 U.S. humanitarian"—for her clarity, which "put this [housing] bottleneck on this week's front pages." After all, the National Resources Planning Board estimated that the United States needed "2,500,000 new homes" across the country—even before the new defense plants are taken into account.

But FDR's new appointee Charles Palmer saw no reason to worry about new affordable housing, declaring that "sociology was no part of his job, that over-crowding would remain the private builders' opportunity." He sent his assistant, another realtor, to Seattle to make a speech that infuriated ER's allies: "There's no need for more Government building . . . we have found . . . that idle ships can sometimes be converted into dormitories for single men. Also usable are summer resort cabins that sometimes lie idle for months." And given high lumber prices, tents would cost less.

The argument between ER and FDR regarding Palmer actually represented an ongoing change in their partnership. In the past, she had gone to the public to argue on behalf of FDR's New Deal programs—and to build public support for things a reluctant and divided Congress tried to hobble. Now, as FDR turned aside New Deal perspectives, ER increasingly went to the public to argue for her own version of what was right and essential. Every day reinforced her conviction that "the struggle for freedom today is the struggle for economic security."

As FDR's third term began, the divided White House, with its clearly established borders between his court and hers, was refortified. FDR worked mostly in the company of Harry Hopkins, while ER spent most of her time with her steadies—Tommy, Hick, Earl, and increasingly Joe. Indeed, according to Chief Usher J. B. West, by 1941 Joe and Hick were permanent White House guests. Although he exaggerated when he wrote they "never went home," they had their own assigned rooms.

Usher Howell Crim thought Lash was the first lady's "closest confidant." He wrote, "The two would sit in his room talking until late at night; she'd step across the hall to say good morning before her breakfast, and to say good night after everyone had gone to bed. They often walked together around the sixteen acres of White House lawn, or down Washington streets."

On one occasion, while ER was in New York City, the staff moved Joe from his second-floor bedroom because "Crown Princess Martha of Norway and her gentleman-in-waiting had arrived." Joe moved up to the third floor so the gentleman might have his room. The next morning ER arrived on the overnight train at dawn. Nobody had told her of the changes, and her "first stop was . . . Joe's room. As she usually did, she gave a little rap on the door and walked right in." There, she shocked Princess Martha's gentleman, "totally undressed." ER was "mortified" and furious. She telephoned the usher's office and in "her iciest tones" instructed: "Never, never move or change a guest . . . without first contacting me. The telephone operators can reach me wherever I might be."

At first surprised by ER's independence, Crim grew to appreciate her dedication to good works and to FDR's needs. "In contrast to ER's close relationship with friends, and her husband's with his staff," he said, "we never saw Eleanor and Franklin in the same room alone together. They had the most separate relationship I have ever seen between man and wife. And the most equal." They met, "usually in the evenings," with their secretaries. ER "always brought him a sheaf of papers, a bundle of ideas." She campaigned "for her own projects and for liberal programs she favored," and his concerns. She was "perhaps his most trusted observer," and he routinely sent her out "to assess the feelings of the people on just about everything, including his own policy statements."

Joe and Trude's deepening love reignited and replenished her faith in the future. Together they planned an international student conference in July at Campobello, the Maine House that ER had agreed to sponsor. Joe and Trude also worked on their unfolding relationship, with ER's steady support. Trude was reluctant to divorce Eliot Pratt and at one point she decided not to see Joe anymore. As she contemplated her future and changed her mind, she confided in the first lady.

In March, Trude joined ER for a ten-day vacation in Florida, which Earl Miller had arranged. Joe joined them for three days, but for ER the week was dominated by Trude. They walked along the beach and plunged into the ocean. "It is wonderful to be with [ER]," Trude wrote Joe. "She is so incredibly patient and understanding, and every hour I get more devoted to her—if that is possible."

While in Florida, Tommy had a splendid time with her partner Henry Osthagen, but Earl was annoyed by ER's new friends. He simply "did not like either of our guests," Tommy observed. As always, ER chose to ignore the routine jealousies among her intimates. Her time at the beach with Trude and Earl reminded her of an earlier vacation with Earl and Hick. ER reminisced in a note to Hick: three-mile walks on the beach, deck tennis, good reading. Paderewski arrived for tea. "How old he has grown & how sad he is!"

But the global stage did not leave ER's attention for long. In May, the State Department's opposition to rescue efforts escalated. At the U.S. consulate, Hiram Bingham was replaced by an officer determined to block all visas. Then the State Department ordered Fry to leave. Eileen Fry appealed to ER, to no avail. "I am sorry that there is nothing I can do for your husband," the first lady replied. "I think he will have to come home because he has done things which the government does not feel it can stand behind." On 22 June 1941, the day Germany invaded the Soviet Union, the State Department issued new regulations that made it virtually impossible for refugees in Europe to get visas. All pending visas would expire on 1 July, and all U.S. consulates in German-occupied countries would be closed on 15 July. State warned Fry that he would be arrested if he did not leave.

He appealed for more time, but the consul explained that he had to go: Vichy officials and the State Department were united in agreement that he had provided "too much help to Jews and anti-Nazis." But he did not leave until September, and the ERC continued to save lives for another year.

Frank Kingdon and the ERC kept ER informed about the hardships these new rules caused. Kingdon was outraged that visas were revoked, and he worried that all those in danger could "simply break down" after waiting months and months; "suicides will increase greatly." Dr. Lou Straus-Ernst lost her visa, which Jimmy had worked so hard to secure. She fled to the mountains, where she would remain in hiding until 1944.

It was tragic. ER despised Breckinridge Long and could not understand her husband's role. Couldn't he have stopped Long? Why were her own allies defeated?

Meanwhile in London, despite Long's opposition to his efforts, John Winant was an immediate success as ambassador. In contrast to Joseph Kennedy's defeatist negativity, he and his staff were quickly perceived as friends of England, dedicated to the needs of the people, and Churchill trusted him.

Given this shift, ER resolved to be more involved in diplomatic efforts. In Washington she arranged a reception for Lord Halifax, a Conservative politician who had just been appointed ambassador to the United States. She invited Bernard Baruch, who had a long friendship with Churchill. At the reception he told amusing stories of Anglo-American relations during the first war; the stories, according to Joe Lash, delighted the "tall, grave, almost funereal-looking man, dignity incarnate." The evening was successful, launching a warm relationship between the Roosevelts and the new British ambassador and his wife.

In London, ER's friends were completely involved in helping the war effort. In 1938, Lady Stella Reading had founded the remarkable Women's Voluntary Service (WVS), now the Royal Voluntary Service (RVS), which set up emergency shelters and provided assistance to civilians in wartime. It was being built only slowly; Reading was finding it difficult to recruit volunteers. ER intended to change that, and "to stir the women as Lady Reading had done" and galvanize a movement immediately.

And her old Allenswood friends in London were taking in neighbors who were homeless from the Blitz. Lady Florence Willert told ER that her home "had been thrown open to all sorts of people," to create a splendid "mood of democratic fellowship."

ER's closest school chum, Marjorie Bennett (Mrs. Philip Vaughn), encouraged ER to try to get the United States more involved in the war. Her sons' lives depended "on America's choice between honour and national egoism." Bennett understood why a great democratic movement was under way, and that war produced "a totally different sense of values." The Blitz made it clear that the era of greed and unbridled "self-interest" was over. Bennett hoped that isolationist feelings in the United States would change. "If we could only combine individual freedom with a genuine sense of responsibility. . . . Isolationism is impossible."

One February day in FDR's study, Harry Hopkins was dozing on a couch. "Suddenly he opened one eye" and said to FDR, "You know, Winston is much more left than you." But the president and the prime minister were in agreement about war aims. Everyone in England was "convinced there is no turning back," Lash recorded. "Hitler must be defeated whatever the cost in privilege. The British do not feel this must be stated explicitly. It is a sort of tacit understanding."

In March, ER traveled south for a stay at Bernard Baruch's South Carolina estate, Hobcaw. "This is a beautiful place," she wrote: "Acres and acres of marvellous trees & so quiet. Not pretentious just very comfortable living." She did not refer to the nineteenth-century plantation life of Hobcaw, still steeped in lost-slave customs. She spent significant time with Baruch's daughter Belle, who hosted the visit. She praised Belle's skills with "her beautiful horses. She has schooled them herself and trained them so they obey her voice and are perfectly familiar with what she wishes them to do." The magnificent horses jumped, riderless, at her simple words, cavorted and pranced to demonstrate "pure joy of living," and "trotted up at the word of command" for their sugar reward. Belle "liked Eleanor Roosevelt and enjoyed her visit," but we have no written record of ER's reaction to the tall, intriguing lesbian baroness of Belle-field, as her property was known. Since ER would have no doubt been interested in Belle's many happy years as an expat in Paris, ER's silence about her is curious.

That spring Hitler's onslaught continued: Nazi troops occupied Belgrade, bringing on the collapse of Yugoslavia, and suppressed resistance in Greece. General Erwin Rommel was victorious in the Middle East and in Libya, and Nazi U-boat blasts in the Atlantic sank countless merchant ships laden with supplies. While Congress dithered and even opposed convoys to protect U.S. supplies, FDR's cabinet and associates urged decisive action. Belle Roosevelt, wife of FDR's cousin Kermit, demanded to know why the president was so reluctant to educate the people: "Why don't you tell [them] the facts, no matter how grim . . . ? Isn't it part of your job to teach us to face the truth?"

The unbearable events made ER more determined to help transform public opinion—but also to find happiness in daily events. She told Joe Lash we must "snatch at beauty & joy & hug them close for hovering so near was hatred & ugliness, death & destruction." She encouraged his romance with Trude and enjoyed their company, their letters, their phone calls. At one point, when she felt unsettled by tensions between them, she asked Trude if Joe was enough to fill her "empty heart." The question revealed a good deal about ER, who was never alone but was often lonely. The ideal companionship she sought, the love that would have made such a companionship possible, had eluded her. Joe and Trude did much to fill the empty spaces in her heart. She told him that she understood his "mood of lonely despair" perfectly.

> [You must] reach the point where you are sure of Trude. Time and trust in yourself is all that will bring that about. Sometime I am going to tell you just how lonely I can be in a crowd & it may help you to overcome the same type of thing which I've had to fight all my life. You don't believe in others because you don't believe in yourself. . . . We have to be preoccupied with "self" when we are young otherwise the world would come to an end! Every experience will help you & others.

Joe feared that he was a burden or a pest. Of course not, ER insisted: "Time with you is pure self-indulgence."

On 20 April 1941 ER and Joe went to see Lillian Hellman's *Watch on the Rhine*. The first lady's entrance was greeted with "great applause and everyone stood," Joe noted. They were both moved by Hellman's "forceful play." At one point the character Kurt, a German antifascist, decides to return to work in the anti-Hitler underground, and the Spanish Civil War's International Brigade song plays. ER "gripped my hand," Joe noted. Afterward they had a long conversation about courage and Joe wondered if it was "possible to have single minded devotion to a better world, like Kurt, outside of the CP." ER thought less about "ideology or theory" as the source of action than character and the human heart. Would she herself "be able to stand up when the going really got tough?" she wondered. "Could one reconcile oneself to death and go forth to meet it indifferently?" While Joe insisted class interests were paramount, ER insisted that unselfish revolutionary courage across all class lines was needed.

The intensity of Joe and Trude's difficulties occasionally distracted ER, while the bitter war escalated. The Luftwaffe bombed London relentlessly on 10 May 1941, the worst day of the Blitz, causing damage to most of London's landmarks, including the British Museum, Westminster Abbey, Big Ben, and the House of Commons. A total of 1,436 civilians were killed that one night, bringing the death toll of British civilians to 43,000.

In the spring of 1941, ER's "service plan"—for universal conscription for public service—received a great deal of new publicity, most of it hostile. She now championed Massachusetts representative Edith Nourse Rogers's bill to create a women's army auxiliary corps.

Isolationists opposed ER's call to service, as could have been expected, but ER was appalled by the vigorous protests that came from Joe and Vivian Cadden, two AYC leaders she differed with but had sought to remain personally close to. She had believed them when they denied having any Communist affiliations. But now, patently in thrall to the Nazi-Soviet Pact, they likened her call to service to "Fascist or Nazi" slave labor and said it would lead "straight to the system of German Work Camps." Joe Cadden even accused ER of being a "social fascist."

It was unforgivable. ER refused to let their twisted words and abusive allegations distress her. Instead she courteously and eloquently refuted them. But the friendship was over, and the episode engendered a level of mistrust that would mark all of ER's future dealings with Communists.

On 3 May 1941 Winston Churchill cabled the president, calling on him "immediately to range [the United States] with us as a belligerent power." The president responded by declaring a new state of "unlimited national emergency." On 27 May he addressed the nation, promising to provide for all "naval and military" needs and "give every possible assistance to Britain and to all who, with Britain, are resisting Hitlerism." He did not name the controversial convoys but insisted, "The delivery of needed supplies to Britain is imperative. This can be done; it must be done; it will be done." Although public opinion favored FDR's announcement, he subsequently told reporters the United States was not about to enter the war or change its Neutrality Law.

June brought, in addition to the worsening international situation, a wave of personal difficulties. ER's brother Hall's alcoholism was endangering his life, and when his physician counseled immediate hospitalization, he refused. SDR's health too was a concern: all spring she seemed listless and fatigued. ER thought she had had a stroke and offered to take her to Campobello in July.

FDR underwent a protracted bout of silence and inaccessibility both in the White House and at Hyde Park, caused not only by the international situation but also perhaps by his mother's worrisome condition. He was rarely in his office and preferred to be alone in his bedroom. On

4 June, walking with Joe, ER compared the president's odd mood to SDR's delicate Dresden china, which had to be handled with very great care. When Franklin Jr. joined them the next day, he was more blunt, referring to his father's "I am Jesus—handle me with care" moods. "None of us saw him," Joe observed. "But he needed the isolation." Although the reasons for FDR's period of withdrawal remain unclear, Missy LeHand believed the president was exasperated by everyone about everything.

Then on 21 June, Missy herself had a massive stroke that paralyzed her right side and left her unable to speak. FDR's closest companion for over twenty years, she had been his secretary, gatekeeper, dinner partner, party planner, and mainstay. ER regarded her as FDR's junior wife, always treated her with affection and respect, and seemed entirely grateful for Missy's devoted service to her husband and their shared interests. Esther Lape expressed surprise that ER remained so close to Missy, who, she believed, had replaced ER in basic ways on a daily basis. But after 1920 Missy's presence had actually freed ER to live her own life. Now, after spending several weeks in the hospital, she was sent to Warm Springs to recover.

ER told Joe that she only rarely worried about Missy's role as "gate-keeper." While Missy was courted by and attracted to various people who believed they were "indispensable" to FDR—including men she had dated, such as Tommy Corcoran and William Bullitt, and others like Felix Frankfurter—they would all "be surprised at their dispensability." FDR "uses what suits his purpose, makes up his own mind and discards people when they no longer fulfill a purpose of his." They all played up to Missy, but ER told Joe she generally trusted Missy's judgment.

Grace Tully took over many of Missy's tasks immediately, but she did not live in the White House. ER was concerned about FDR's comfort, given all the vital roles Missy had played in his life, yet she remained in Campobello with Joe and Trude, preparing for the ISS summer institute for student leaders, which Joe would conduct. She hoped the five-week session there would focus on a global and democratic future, turning the war into a crusade not for fascism or Communism but for "human free-dom and happiness."

On 28 June she departed with Tommy and Trude after spending their final afternoon with Joe "assigning students to rooms and groups."

The summer institute was marked by serious discussions, earnest efforts, brilliant exchanges, marvelous entertainment, and jolly times. Some of the students who participated had been recommended by their colleges, while others had participated in earlier ISS conferences. Among the notable speakers were Shakespearean scholar and former Smith College president William Allan Neilson and his best-selling author wife, Elisabeth Muser Neilson, whose recently published book *The House I Knew* described her girlhood in Germany. The Neilsons set a delightful pace, despite the adolescent pranks and late-night noise in very close quarters.

Archibald MacLeish read poetry, discussed literature, and hosted several evenings during which his wife, concert vocalist Ada Hitchcock, sang German *Lieder* and French ballads with Elisabeth Neilson. ACLU cofounder Roger Baldwin, Louis Fischer and his son George, journalist James Wechsler, William Agar, and many others spoke about politics, international relations, and the need to organize for peace and justice. Walter White of the NAACP "did most to fire the group with the need to 'do something.'" His descriptions of southern bigotry and "the discrimination and humiliation he encountered in the defense industries and in the armed services shocked and aroused the institute." The students vowed "to change the situation [he] so vividly and horrifyingly described." Petitions to Congress were only the beginning; the students intended to return to their campuses and clubs to make racial discrimination a focus of their efforts.

The ISS event was stellar. ER enjoyed the students and was impressed by the work and sincerity of the notables who volunteered their time to galvanize the youth movement.

SDR was also at Campobello, spending her vacation mostly in bed. She was attended by a companion/helper, Kathleen Crawford, a nurse, her sister Aunt Kassie, and various friends who did not mind this "*very quiet life*" as much as SDR did. ER left Campobello after the ISS institute ended, relieved above all that "Mama was really well & cheerful." FDR, delighted, wrote his mother on 2 August, "I'm so glad you really are feeling better, & that you like the nurse & that you do what she says! . . . We go on board the *Potomac* . . . and cruise away from all newspapermen & photographers & I hope to be gone ten days—There is I fear little chance of my getting to Campobello."

FDR was actually en route to meet the USS *Augusta* on 9 August at Placentia Bay in Newfoundland—to anchor the *Potomac* alongside HMS

Prince of Wales, for his first wartime meeting with Winston Churchill. It is unclear whether ER knew his true destination. "Early in August," she recalled in her memoir, "my husband, after many mysterious consultations, told me that he was going to take a little trip up through the Cape Cod Canal . . . to do some fishing. Then he smiled and I knew he was not telling me all that he was going to do."

She was ultimately fascinated by the details of this secret rendezvous. Not only FDR's senior military staff but also his sons Franklin Jr. and Elliott, already on active duty in the area, were ordered to Newfoundland. Both were initially disturbed by the sudden order, and when Franklin Jr. was told to report to the "commander in chief," he wondered what he had done wrong—then was ushered into his father's arms.

Churchill and Roosevelt's candid meeting resulted in a new friendship. They issued a joint declaration, known as the Atlantic Charter, listing eight "common principles" and democratic war aims "for a better future." A statement of hope, the charter promised nothing, but it aroused a movement for global justice that grew over time. Decades later Nelson Mandela, like many in Africa and Asia, credited the Atlantic Charter for its inspiration to fight tyranny and oppression, since it "reaffirmed faith in the dignity of each human being and propagated a host of democratic principles."

In the short run, however, the Atlantic meeting disappointed Churchill, who had expected a stronger alliance. He wanted FDR to join him in a declaration of opposition to Japan's continued aggression in the Pacific: it must stop or face war. But the president refused. Such an ultimatum, he argued, would only exacerbate the Japanese war party's nationalism. Moreover, isolationists still dominated Congress, and despite FDR's urgent appeals for continued military training during this moment of real emergency, the House had voted to extend the Selective Service Act by only one vote.

While FDR was away, ER visited her children in Cambridge and gave a lecture at Harvard; hosted the Hampton Institute quartet and spiritual chorus at Hyde Park; dedicated a new NYA center; spent some time in Washington; visited Alexander Woollcott, the critic and journalist; read government documents and Shirer's *Berlin Diary*; wrote columns; and returned to Campobello for the institute's closing on 30 August, visiting Trude en route.

Trude told her that her time in Maine with her therapist had clarified her thoughts and she had decided to return to Eliot Pratt. She had not "honestly faced my situation before," she wrote to Joe. She had been "afraid and weak and now these last months seem terribly wrong—like a life snatched from somebody else." She had "to go back."

> I can promise that I shall be honest—and I pray for courage and insight. . . . You believed that I was free to love you—when I said I was—and now you are involved in something that belongs to my past and you suffer. A thousand times these days I have prayed for some way to help you—but I can only try to be a better person. Your love is true and right—and strong. And because you love so much you have made it possible for me to believe again that I might become able to serve a belief I had long since given up.

Joe promised to do his best to respect her decision, and helped ER to close the Campobello house. Joe had agreed to spend his two-week holiday with ER at Hyde Park, and the two of them drove there with Tommy.

Upon their arrival, ER was shocked to see SDR looking dreadfully haggard and gaunt. During the next few days, SDR got weaker and more listless. On 5 September ER called FDR in Washington and urged him to get home the next morning. He did and spent the day with his mother in amiable conversation. That very Saturday ER learned that her brother's liver had stopped working. During the night Sara slipped into coma. ER and FDR were at her bedside all night and the next morning, and they were with her when she died on 7 September 1941. ER devoted her column in tribute to SDR:

> An anxious 24 hours culminated a little before noon today in the death of my husband's mother. Had she lived until the 21st of September she would have celebrated her 87th birthday. One can have none of the resentment which comes when death cuts short a young life, but she was a very vital person with a keen interest in living, and I think had she had a few more years . . . she would have lived them with keen avidity and enjoyment.
>
> She was born in the year 1854, brought up in a large family and endowed with the Delano beauty. She sailed to China on a clipper ship, as well as to Europe on the most modern of today's steamers. Her early experiences were picturesque and interesting.

I think her family . . . would say that her strongest trait was loyalty to the family. She had no hesitancy about telling her near and
dear ones their faults or criticizing their behavior, but if anyone else
in the world were to attack a member of her family she would rise in
their defense like a tigress. . . .

She would give away large sums of money and save small ones.
The President's mother always attributed her little economies, like
undoing string and folding wrapping paper for future use, to her
New England upbringing. She was not just sweetness and light, for
there was a streak of jealousy and possessiveness in her where her
own were concerned. But when others were bored she would be kind,
and had the gift of making all those around her feel that the word
"grand dame" was truly applicable to her.

She spoiled her grandchildren perhaps a little, but they had great
affection and respect for her. I think even some of her great grandchildren will remember her when they grow up as a very beautiful,
stately old lady who loved them and made them feel that Hyde Park
would be theirs as long as it was hers.

ER's words were heartfelt. She admired her mother-in-law and was
impressed by her ever-expanding political vision and public activism. In
the end, they shared a commitment to freedom and justice, respect across
racial and religious divides. Yet she soon wrote to Joe:

I looked at my mother-in-law's face after she was dead & understood
so many things I had never seen before. It is dreadful to have lived so
close to someone for 36 years and to feel no deep affection or sense of
loss. It's hard on Franklin however and the material details are
appalling & there of course I can be of some use.

ER left SDR's funeral in Hyde Park to return to Washington. She
accompanied her dying brother Hall to Walter Reed Hospital, where she
spent most of her days and nights for the next two weeks. She sat at Hall's
bedside with Zena Raset, his devoted companion. Daily, Tommy came by
with her mail, and they worked on her broadcasts and columns. She also
made calls, did chores, and wrote letters, especially to Joe. "With Hall I
have an odd mixture of feelings," she told him. "The next few months are
going to be a strain so I'm going to cling to all the hours I can steal to be
with you and people that I love! Just don't let me be too demanding!"

Hall's final agonies recalled her father's ordeal and unleashed memories of hurt and abandonment. A lifetime of petty cruelties and disregard surfaced to rekindle ER's wrath. During the long hours she sat with Hall, she recalled many bitter moments concerning her late mother-in-law. Sara had despised ER's father's weakness and expressed contempt for Hall. Once, when Hall's eldest daughter, little Ellie, then ten, visited the Big House and sat alone reading, SDR called her over. She twirled her around, studied her closely, and said coldly, "I see. So you are Hall's daughter!" Then she pushed her away without another word. ER never forgot that moment; nor did her niece.

Joe came to Washington and spent almost a week in the White House, where his presence was comforting to ER. After he left, she wrote:

My idea of hell, if I believed in it, would be to sit or stand & watch someone breathing hard, struggling for words when a gleam of consciousness returns & thinking "this was once the little boy I played with and scolded. He could have been so much and this is what he is." It is a bitter thing and in spite of everything I've loved Hall, perhaps somewhat remissedly of late, but he is part of me. I do have a quieting effect on him & so I stood by his bed and held his hand and stroked his forehead and Zena stood beside me for hours.

On 17 September, she wrote Anna, "It's such an unattractive death. He is mahogany color, all distended, out of his head most of the time. . . . It is really most distressing."

ER's son James and his new wife visited. Hick and Tommy were in and out. Joe called often, which she appreciated: "I love saying goodnight and because this is a hard time for me, it means a lot to talk to you." She appreciated his daily letters even more:

I should indeed feel shut away & buried in my present horror if you did not write about yourself. . . . Of course you can say anything to me—I want you to be as sure of me as my own children are. These days are hard because Hall was always a little my child and the waste of a life seems a bitter thing. This way of dying seems so unnecessarily hard and I am weary & heartsick for Zena. I'll tell you some of the things she said which make me want to weep but I shall not for I

cannot let go. . . . I feel sure this cannot last much longer. . . . I have
slept in my clothes. Tonight will be the third night but we both sleep
and dare not leave. He is quieter tho tonight which means weaker
I imagine.

At five in the morning on 25 September 1941, Gracie Hall Roosevelt
died. The funeral was held the next day at the White House, attended by
fifty relatives and close friends. The *New York Times* reported: "Pale, but
stately and grimly composed, [ER entered] after all the others were seated,
accompanied by the president." They sat beside two of Hall's five living
children, ER II and Henry P. Roosevelt.

In its obituary, the *Times* detailed his life. ER's "shy and brilliant
brother was little known to the American public partly because of his
own aversion to publicity, partly because he was overshadowed by his
famous relatives. . . . But even if he had not belonged to the nation's first
family, he could have been justly proud of his career as an electrical engineer, World War flier, banker, financier and municipal official."

Hall's now-divorced second wife, Dorothy Kemp Roosevelt, a concert
pianist and teacher, had written regularly to ER over the years, often to
complain about Hall in the years before they divorced. At first ER complimented Dorothy on her endurance: "Hall is strong and very hard to
help, but . . . you are infinitely more gifted than I am." But by 1935, the
marriage broken, ER wrote: "I am sorry you still feel so bitter about Hall.
I do not think anyone is entirely selfish . . . You may not always be able to
see or understand things that people do, but at least you can keep from
hurting yourself by being forgiving." Their intense correspondence
revealed a great deal about ER's own struggles with love, disappointment,
and forgiveness.

Neither Dorothy nor any of their three daughters, Diana, Amy, and
Janet, attended Hall's funeral. After the service, FDR canceled his weekend appointments to be with his wife. Hall was buried in Tivoli in the
family vault. James, who was with his parents during much of their
ordeal, had never seen them so close or so emotional. At one point, while
ER recounted memories of Hall, she was stricken midsentence by grief.
In a rare moment of intimacy, FDR "sank down beside her and hugged
her and kissed her and held her head on his chest." We have no accounts

of their private conversations during these weeks of mourning for the death of SDR and Hall and the loss of Missy.

After Missy's departure from FDR's life, new women friends appeared significantly and flirtatiously—most notably Crown Princess Martha of Norway and Dorothy Schiff Backer, as well as FDR's attentive and jolly cousins Laura Delano and Margaret (Daisy) Suckley. ER accepted their presence and made them comfortable. Lucy Mercer Rutherfurd also made return visits to FDR's hearth, always while ER was away. There is no evidence that ER knew about them. But she understood that while she was on the road, increasingly at her husband's behest to enhance America's international position and his political goals, there would be people about to entertain and amuse him. She believed that was necessary and was determined not to grow cold and bitter as her mother had.

While she was still in mourning, ER was thankful to be offered a high position in the Office of Civilian Defense (OCD), established to coordinate federal and state programs in case of war. New York City mayor Fiorello La Guardia had agreed to serve as director, and he needed an assistant director in charge of community services and volunteers. Anna Rosenberg and Harry Hopkins encouraged ER to take the position, as did her husband.

ER accepted, in part because she believed she could be of service to the nation. Particularly interested in promoting a greater role for women and youth, she asked Elinor Morgenthau to be her assistant and Joe Lash to participate in the youth campaign; Mary McLeod Bethune and Walter White would also serve in various ways. She intended to build the kind of health, recreation, family security, and educational program in every community that Lady Stella Reading had established in Britain. She thought she could work well with La Guardia. But his interests as director were limited to firefighting and setting up air raid precautions for civilian defense. ER subsequently noted that all the activities La Guardia "did not want" were "thrust into my division."

ER dreaded adverse publicity and respected FDR's disdain for "petticoat government," especially in regard to social and economic programs. However, regarding such urgent issues as rescue and civil liberties in wartime, she considered her active involvement her primary responsibility. And in the wake of her brother's death, she wanted above all to be occupied. "The loss of someone whom you love is hard to bear," she wrote in her memoir, "but when sorrow is mixed with regret and a consciousness of waste there is added a touch of bitterness which is even more difficult to carry day in and day out. I think it was in an attempt to numb this feeling that I worked so hard at the Office of Civilian Defense."

ER walked a mile each day to her new office and worked long hours. She was assigned staff there, so Tommy accommodated. "I will carry on here," ER told Anna, "do the columns, the broadcasts, etc. and help in any way I can, mostly by working at night on the writings." Tommy usually went home by midnight, but occasionally ER worked through the night. "One morning my husband said to me: 'What's this I hear? You didn't go to bed at all last night?' I had been working on my mail . . . when it began to get light, I decided it was not worth while going to bed." The night patrol "reported it to the household, and someone told my husband." Clearly, FDR was impressed—although, ER noted, "I did not do that very often."

In October, ER's fifty-seventh birthday was celebrated uniquely. Usually, she insisted on no party or presents. "Her friends and family have a terrible time," Joe Lash lamented. "She seems to need nothing, is annoyed at lavish gifts, makes life difficult for all of us wanting to celebrate her." But for the first time, ER agreed to her husband's suggestion of a river cruise on the presidential yacht *Potomac*. The party would include Joe, Jimmy and his new wife, Rommie, and Helen Gahagan Douglas.

That day ER worked on her mail for three hours, while the president worked on his stamps. The guests sat around and talked and played gin rummy until six-thirty, when cocktails were served. The abstemious ER drank an old-fashioned, considering it a "kind of fruit punch." Then followed a "sumptuous" champagne dinner, with presents and good cheer. "The President drank a toast pointing out this was the first time he had gotten [ER] on a naval vessel," Joe reported, "and that by next year at this time [they] would have met the Prime Minister of Japan on an island in the Pacific." ER laughed and said, "Not unless she could fly."

But shortly thereafter, ER plunged into a significant depression, an actual "Griselda mood." Anna and John arrived from Seattle to discuss SDR's estate and spent time alone with FDR. Before SDR died, ER had moved out of her New York City apartment on Eleventh Street to reclaim the Sixty-fifth Street town house. She planned to make significant changes in the Big House at Hyde Park—to make it in some part her own. FDR had not disagreed with her then. But now he told Anna and John he did not want any changes. When Anna told ER of her father's decision, she was devastated. She would not live there, then, except when FDR was in residence.

She grew cold and found life wearying. "I feel as you sometimes look," she wrote Hick. "You know how I get these moods, they pass but they are a nuisance." The next day she wrote, "I'm in a horrid frame of mind, but I think it will pass & I hope I don't show it." Hick reassured her, "Remember, even when you're feeling that way, you do a better job [at every task] than most people."

By mid-November, FDR and the War Department agreed that war was imminent. An order of high alert had been issued to all Pacific theater personnel. On 30 November Japan announced that it was determined to end all American and British influence in Asia "for the honor and pride of mankind," and Cordell Hull requested that FDR return from Warm Springs immediately. Negotiations continued that week between State Department officials and two envoys who represented Japan's moderate group. They were in conversation at the State Department on Sunday afternoon, 7 December 1941, when Japan bombed the airfields and naval base at Pearl Harbor.

FDR and Hopkins were alone, waiting to be updated, when they got the news. ER was entertaining guests at a large luncheon, including FDR's cousins Ellen Delano and Frederick B. Adams, and their children, who were disappointed by FDR's unexpected absence. ER did not learn what happened until midafternoon, "when one of the ushers told me." The White House immediately filled up with generals, admirals, and aides. Congressional leaders of both parties arrived. Cabinet officials arrived in the evening and remained until after midnight.

Horrified by the carnage, FDR nonetheless spoke to them with restraint, announcing that this was "the most serious situation that had confronted any Cabinet since 1861." Everybody seemed to agree. Well after midnight, before the president turned in, ER went into his room, and "my husband and I did have a chance to talk." She "thought that in spite of his anxiety Franklin was in a way more serene" and more clear and determined than he had been in many months. The "long uncertainty was over."

The next day ER and a large White House contingent accompanied FDR to a speech before a joint session of Congress. "Yesterday, December 7, 1941—a date which will live in infamy—the United States was suddenly and deliberately attacked," he said, and asked for a declaration of war. That day Montana representative Jeannette Rankin cast the sole vote against war. Caroline O'Day, too sick to attend, sent a cable: had she been there, she would have voted aye.

On 11 December, Germany and Italy declared war on the United States. The dreaded thing had happened: the U.S. joined the world at war.

Chapter Seventeen

"To Know Me Is a Terrible Thing": Friendship, Loyalties, and Alliances

On 8 December, during FDR's speech before Congress, ER sat beside Edith Wilson feeling "a curious sense of repetition" as the United States once again joined the world at war. Afterward, eager to embark on her war work with the Office of Civil Defense, she left for California, where she and Fiorello La Guardia would consider the West Coast's most urgent defense needs.

As Japanese victories in the Pacific mounted, fear of and prejudice toward Japanese-Americans had soared. Some Americans were agitating for their removal, while others were taking immediate reprisals against citizens and businesses. The U.S. Navy ordered all fishing boats owned by Japanese fishermen to be seized.

While ER was on the West Coast, she observed this disturbing "trend of thought." Yes, some German, Italian, and other Axis-allied agents were at work in the United States, and some Japanese too "are here to be helpful to their own nation and not to ours." Suspicious activities should be reported, and "these people are gradually being rounded up by the FBI and the Secret Service," she observed. "But the great mass of our people, stemming from these various national ties, must not feel that they have suddenly ceased to be Americans."

Nonetheless Japanese nationals were now considered "enemy aliens." When the Treasury Department froze their assets, ER protested that hardships would result for the families. In response, Treasury Secretary Henry Morgenthau agreed to release limited funds for living expenses and needs. "I do not know how the freezing of Japanese money has affected your two men. I know the situation on the west coast was very serious with the winter vegetable growers," Tommy explained to Esther Lape. "The crops were ready . . . they represented 75% of the total supply of winter vegetables for the whole country and no one had any money, not even enough to live on. However, the Treasury made a ruling that . . .

$100 a month could be paid to Japanese nationals so this gardening could go on."

"The greatest test this country has ever met," ER wrote in a prescient plea, was to face fear and propaganda with unity and respect. "Perhaps it is the test which is going to show whether the United States can furnish a pattern for the rest of the world for the future. Our citizens come from all the nations of the world. Some of us have said . . . we were the only proof that different nationalities could live together in peace and understanding." Passing this test was America's obligation in "the present chaos," she maintained.

> If we cannot meet the challenge of fairness to our citizens of every nationality, of really believing in the Bill of Rights and making it a reality for all loyal American citizens, regardless of race, creed or color; if we cannot keep in check anti-semitism, anti-racial feelings as well as anti-religious feelings, then we will have removed from the world, the one real hope for the future on which all humanity must now rely.

The 150th anniversary of the Bill of Rights fell on 15 December. Since Americans were frequently ignoring its precepts in these barbarous days, ER wrote, eternal vigilance was required "if we are going to keep our freedom." In the nation's capital, a staff member was denied housing when the landlord asked his "religious affiliation," and he replied "Jewish." Outraged, ER wrote, "I hope every person in this country will read the Bill of Rights again." She also recommended that Americans take two pledges: "to be a little thoughtful every day about the meaning of freedom" and to consider "how, in a time of national danger . . . [our] own rights as a citizen are entangled and interwoven with the rights of others and these rights always deserve a decent respect."

ER departed the West Coast sure that her presence had calmed and reassured the communities she visited. Although the trip had been "strenuous," she wrote Hick, it was "useful and I have learned a great deal. It seems like a completely changed world."

ER received "an amazing letter from Pearl Buck" in which the novelist warned that "more basic than Chinese antagonism to Japan was colored races' antagonism" to white supremacy. Anglo-American promises "to police the world," she wrote, contributed to Asian fears of "domination by the white man." Such rhetoric, Buck wrote, would create an Asian-Russian-Negro "combination to resist white domination." ER was upset, Tommy confided, and urged FDR to initiate an antidiscrimination policy. Most immediately, she sought to protect the civil and human rights of Japanese-American citizens and their families from wrathful propaganda. "ER said she was surprised by FDR's sympathetic appreciation of the problem," Tommy wrote. "He said we would have to compel England to give dominion status to India," and "to get more equal rights for Negroes here."

ER believed the OCD should build "comprehensive community programs" for defense. It should establish day care centers to relieve working mothers and fathers; nutrition, counseling, and community health services; and recreation and educational programs. She hoped that people would volunteer in each community to create these services and acknowledge such activity as part of America's first line of defense.

Many young men failed army recruitment standards, which moved ER to fight harder for an expanded national health program. She urged labor unions and employers to forge a new spirit of cooperation regarding health care and accident prevention, since "health is a stepping stone to all real welfare and security." In her view, "real defense begins in every home."

She called upon a range of allies to help build social justice programs and home defense, notably Bernard Baruch; Justine Wise Polier; Florence Kerr, who headed WPA Community Service Projects; her friend and radio agent Betty Lindley; Jane Seaver, who worked with Joe Lash to build a youth division; Mary Dublin, the research director of the National Consumers League; and Paul Kellogg, the great social worker, activist, and journalist. Almost immediately after she entered the OCD, she addressed seven hundred members of the National Council of Negro Women—representing forty states, Cuba, the West Indies, and the Virgin Islands—to announce that "in the operating policy of the civilian defense program" there would be no Jim Crow. All programs were to be integrated. She brought in Mary McLeod Bethune, Walter White, and her activist allies for a campaign against the poll tax. She believed she had her husband's support on issues where congressional opposition kept him silent.

She arranged unusual alliances, ran creative conferences, and achieved surprising victories. When Congress threatened to end the school lunch and food stamp programs, she was determined to fight for them through the OCD, with her staff and her friends. A conference on the wartime needs of children produced an interagency agreement for federally supported day care, with additional grants to states for "maternal, child health, and child welfare services." Kellogg considered ER "inspiring," and Leila Pinchot, who volunteered in the OCD's Washington office, was dazzled by the way "her passionate integrity" affected community leaders.

But Fiorello La Guardia disagreed with her conception of the OCD's mission. He held that it should be limited to providing civilians with physical protection against air raids, through military defense, air raid wardens, and police and fire departments. On her first day back from the West Coast, ER called a staff conference to deal with the division.

On 19 December the realities of war and sorrow engulfed her own heart and hearth when she and FDR "had a strictly family party" for Jimmy and Rommie. It was Jimmy's birthday, and he was about to leave for active duty with Major Evans Carlson's new Marine Raiders Battalion. Only days before, ER had learned from a newspaper account that her son Elliott had returned to active duty, assigned to a bomber squadron. All four of her sons were now in uniform, and so "there will be three boys whose whereabouts for us are wrapped in mystery."

That night she took the night train to New York, and she phoned Joe the next morning. "Her voice did not have the customary ring to it," he recalled, "so I asked her how she was. There was a period of silence. I thought perhaps she had not heard. We both mumbled something inconsequential and hung up. I sensed something was seriously the matter and though I had a staff meeting [left] without hat or coat, jumped into a taxi and went up to 65th Street." ER started "to scold me for having come" but then confessed she was upset "and burst into tears." He thought it was about OCD tensions, "which shows how little I understand her." Jimmy had been ordered to Hawaii, and Elliott was now with a bomber squadron. Franklin Jr. and John were in the navy. "She knew they had to do it, but it was hard. By the laws of chance not all four would return."

On 22 December ER returned to Washington to prepare for Christmas, and learned a secret guest was about to arrive: Winston Churchill. The household went into mayhem mode to ready the rooms for him and his staff and to provide sufficient gifts around the Christmas tree. The Monroe Room, where ER held her press conferences, would become the Map Room, creating an office for the British delegation.

ER originally arranged for Churchill to stay in the Lincoln Bedroom, "the favorite of most male guests," recalled J. B. West, the chief usher. But upon his arrival on 22 December, the prime minister rejected the bed, so he wandered the second floor, "tried out all the beds and finally selected the rose suite," where SDR and the queen had resided.

Churchill's pink-faced cherubic style and literary flair amused ER, as did his cigars and costumes, which ranged from a one-piece "jumpsuit" to casual nudity. His "most colorful . . . living habits" would remain the subject of staff gossip for years. But she was unsettled and even disturbed by his rude presumptions, gruff behavior, and loud manner. Churchill, she was overheard to say, was unable to have real conversations. He made loud and abrupt speeches, during which he pronounced his verdict. He cared nothing about her opinion or anyone else's. Indeed, her most enduring worry about him was his disregard for public opinion and the people's right to know.

Churchill's incessant drinking also disturbed ER, who was still mourning for her brother and always in grief for her father. His frightful daily alcohol intake reminded her of their excesses. It began with a jigger of scotch when he awoke, and he appeared to continue with scotch all through the morning. He slept in the afternoon and drank champagne and wine at dinner. Then during late-night meetings he puffed on cigars, while FDR smoked cigarettes, and they drowned their differences and difficulties in buckets of brandy. His unrelenting schedule was exhausting to FDR, ER believed, and she grew concerned about her husband's health. When she approached him about Churchill's influence, however, he dismissed her nonchalantly: alcoholism was limited to ER's side of the family.

FDR had invited Bernard Baruch to the White House for the holiday as well, which pleased Churchill. Baruch believed that the prime minister's visit would galvanize U.S. public opinion. With the Pacific fleet in ruins, Wake Island fallen, Singapore besieged, and the Philippines invaded, Baruch considered Churchill "the best Christmas present" to restore heart and hope to the Allied world. "The pink-cheeked warrior in the air-raid suit" was the leading symbol of resistance to the Blitz: "Do your worst, we can stand it," his presence seemed to say. "We won't crack up."

On 26 December Churchill addressed the joint houses of Congress, invoking a vision of Allied cooperation to uphold the British Empire forever. That particularly disturbed ER, who found him to be a reactionary and an uncompromising imperialist. "I don't trust any of us with too much power," she wrote Anna, "& I want the other nations in too!" She had "talked much with the P.M.," she wrote Hick, "& he is a forceful personality but the stress on what the English speaking peoples can do in the future worries me." He was "loveable and emotional and very human," she told Anna, "but I don't want him to write the peace or carry it out."

Every day while Churchill was in residence, the White House was filled with dignitaries who concentrated on priorities and strategies for victory. Would this be an Asia-first war, or was the European theater still of primary concern? What about additional aid for besieged Russia? What of North Africa? They also discussed the postwar world. Since Churchill's arrival on 22 December, he and FDR had been working on a Joint Declaration of Unity and Purpose. They had each written an initial draft and then negotiated their differences.

ER wanted the discussions to take up what victory would mean for the suffering people of the world. On every issue she intruded the human factor: What was the right thing to do? What would be the human cost? How much would we regret this injustice? On occasion her husband listened to her views, but most of the discussions occurred after dinner, after the men had left the room to resume their negotiations. Increasingly, she was on her own—and she and a growing group of allies who insisted on real democratic change took their views to the public. She never knew which of her words her husband might accept and use.

On the morning of 29 December, FDR wheeled into Churchill's room to announce, "The United Nations—it would be a Declaration of the United Nations" rather than an alliance of "Associated Powers," as initially drafted. For a New Year's lunch, ER invited Joe Lash and seated him next to Churchill. "I did not open my mouth," Lash noted. "The language poured out of him . . . witty, poetic." There were political exchanges. Churchill "jested" FDR about his Vichy gamble: "You are being nice to Vichy. We are being nice to de Gaulle." When FDR replied it was best to leave the matter to Hull and Halifax, Churchill "muttered, 'Hell, Hull and Halifax.'"

At dinner that night, the discussion centered on the United Nations. Everybody present supported FDR's designation of a United Nations both as an ally for victory and as an institution to secure the Four Freedoms and human rights as detailed in the Atlantic Charter.

After dinner, Ambassador Maxim Litvinov and China's new ambassador, T. V. Soong (Madame Chiang Kai-shek's brother), arrived to sign the document. FDR had persuaded Litvinov that freedom of religion included all religions, as well as atheism or freedom from religion, and Stalin agreed to sign.

The Big Four, who would "police" the peace—the United States, Britain, the USSR, and China—were listed at the top of the declaration. Churchill had agreed after some argument, reluctantly, to include India among the other twenty-two signatories, listed in alphabetical order—rather than have the British Commonwealth as a unit atop, in dominance. In the wide-ranging discussion, Churchill said he hoped that a group of "other authorities," meaning Charles de Gaulle's Free French, might sign. FDR opposed that.

Then the difficulties of a genuine Soviet alliance were discussed. Harry Hopkins, recently returned from meetings with Stalin, urged greater support for Russia's war effort, more supplies, and Allied action to open a second front. Churchill recalled that in the war against the Bolsheviks in 1918–19, when he had served as Lloyd George's war secretary, he had "gotten as far as Tula, just south of Moscow. . . . Now he forgave the Russians in proportion to the number of Huns they killed."

Hopkins asked, "Do they forgive you?"

Churchill replied, "In proportion to the number of tanks I send."

FDR thought the Soviets did not forgive and did not trust—and that the future depended on policies that would change that. As the conversation wandered, Hopkins announced that Litvinov "was upstairs pacing . . . like a caged lion."

Shortly after ten, ER and her company were summoned to the Oval Office to witness the signing. She asked if the declaration might be read aloud. FDR "started to demur," but Churchill "said yes." Before he read it, he quoted from Byron's *Childe Harold's Pilgrimage*:

"Here, where the sword united nations drew,
Our countrymen were warring on that day!"
And this is much, and all which will not pass away.

FDR signed first, then Churchill, Litvinov, and Soong. Then Churchill
pranced about the room, exclaiming, "Four fifths of the human race" had
just sealed Hitler's doom. Playwright Robert Sherwood called it a "prelude to a new world symphony."

Bitter anti–New Dealers increasingly accused ER of socialism and
deplored her efforts to ensure racial peace. A group of corporatist promoters who supported the war effort sought to limit, even destroy, all progressive change. They wanted to end youth programs, curtail Social
Security, and terminate labor agreements. ER and her efforts at OCD
became one of their primary targets.

Newspaper columns and radio programs attacked her with vitriol.
Never before had she felt so alone. Previously her work had been to promote and popularize her husband's policies, or the ones with which she
agreed. Now his policies were cloaked in mystery and secrecy, and she
was uncertain about his priorities. After Churchill's arrival, his sensibilities seemed to change. Suddenly he seemed to disregard certain of the
courtesies and formalities she had come to depend on. He did not ask for
her thoughts and advice, and did not include her in discussions where her
input would have once been regarded as valuable.

To counter Churchill's influence on her husband, she was determined
to fortify democracy. Vigilant and anxious, she would go about the country to build community movements for wartime unity. She would use
every waking hour—on the radio, in her columns, at OCD headquarters—
to advance her vision.

During the Blitz, she learned, "group activities, especially dancing
and rhythmic exercises" had improved children's morale. Her friend
Mayris "Tiny" Chaney agreed to head a new OCD effort in which
children's exercise, especially physical education and dancing, would
become part of the program for defense and preparedness. Tiny moved
to Philadelphia and became director of children's activities under John

B. Kelly, an Olympic gold medalist in rowing and affluent Democrat, better known as the father of film star Grace Kelly, who ran the OCD's physical fitness department.

ER was so convinced that exercise and dance contributed to health that she encouraged her OCD staff to enjoy "physical exercise, dancing, and singing" during lunch hour. For weeks, they were seen dancing in the corridors or doing calisthenics on the roof.

She met with twenty-five representatives of the Save the Children Fund to discuss children's issues "largely in the mountain areas," especially the need for hot lunch programs; clothing and shoe distribution; and salvaging and woodworking projects. The fund provided desks for many schools that had never before had them. She continually argued for proper nutrition for children: "In one mountain county, I am told that 70 percent of the boys were rejected in the draft because of malnutrition. . . . Our interpretation of education must never be so narrow that we lose sight of the fact that learning to read on an empty stomach, or with eyes that are overstrained because of lack of proper eye-glasses, is not real education."

ER wanted race relations placed at the center of the nation's agenda. In January, the Fight for Freedom's stage, screen, and radio divisions presented a "Salute to Negro Troops." She commended this "most moving and thrilling . . . pageant on the contribution of the Negro people." Dedicated to "democracy and liberty," it reminded us, she wrote, of our national promise, "which we have never completely carried out."

Her friend Melvyn Douglas proposed the idea of a creative arts and performance agency for wartime "information and propaganda." The OCD's new director, Harvard Law School dean James Landis, approved and asked Douglas to head the Arts Council. Douglas was appointed on 4 February. ER looked forward to a close collaboration with him and with Helen Gahagan Douglas, and was startled when an avalanche of protest greeted the appointment. The most vicious and persistent attacks came from Congressman Leland Ford (R-CA), who chided Douglas for hiding his birth name, Hesselberg.

The Hearst press went berserk, and a startling range of Roosevelt haters joined the assault: ER was paying her "pink" pals—misfits, parasites, and fan dancers who "did the hoochee-koochee"—a huge sum of money that was needed for real defense.* The fact that ER's staff were mostly volunteers who worked only for their expenses was ignored in the deluge of meanness that flooded the airwaves and cascaded through the halls of Congress. Tiny Chaney was mortified, and Douglas was irate. "To know me is a terrible thing," ER lamented. The storm went on for weeks. As Congress debated appropriations for the OCD, ER offered to come in and testify on the work involved. Her offer was rejected.

ER spent much of January and February speaking to troops and to young people, to women's clubs and civic centers. In Texas and Tennessee, she had conversations with several pilots who had just "ferried planes to some place" and had flown for "a great many hours." Hailing from "all over the country," these young men had only a little free time to "sleep or see a show, or have a real meal at someone's home." On another flight she spoke to "Army boys" and sailors, including one who "must have added a few years to his age, for he looked fourteen." She felt it "curious" that so many Americans accepted the youthfulness of the military forces. "Every day that goes on, means more young men in every land are dying. I am confident that our cause is just, but I want to see youth free again to fight a different kind of war, a war to find a way by which we all live more decently and happily together." She never lost sight of the big picture and hoped that "in every factory today, and in every service camp," people would discuss "the kind of a world they intend to build" at war's end.

That new world, ER believed, must achieve political and economic "freedom for every individual regardless of race, creed or color," and her essential task at the OCD was to ensure that it did. She carried the message to North Carolina, Alabama, Florida, and Georgia, as well as to Arthurdale, West Virginia, the community she cared so much about and that had made much progress. ER encountered opposition to her racial views during her travels but wrote nothing about it. In Atlanta, she was told that no people of color were welcome in their civilian defense

*Chaney's program, in actuality, comprised Tot Lots (vacant lots to be rented and refurbished for playgrounds and after-school programs); nurseries for children of war workers; public facilities like settlement houses, schools, and parent-teacher cooperatives; emergency training programs; physical fitness and hygiene programs; and rehabilitation and juvenile delinquency prevention programs.

programs. But she met women of color who wanted to volunteer and "were anxious to do their part."

Working alongside ER were her ISS allies, as well as university and southern liberals—notably George Shuster, president of Hunter College; Frank Graham, president of the University of North Carolina at Chapel Hill; Harriet Elliott, a dean at North Carolina State Normal and Industrial College (now UNC Greensboro); and activists from the Southern Conference. But opposition forces grew stronger.

In mid-February, abuses were heaped upon her efforts at OCD. Certain members of Congress challenged Mayris Chaney's dance program, insisting that dance was "not quite moral," but ER defended it, and declared dance an art that belonged in OCD since many people "will not take other forms of exercise." When Director James Landis questioned whether John Kelly's physical fitness program really belonged in the OCD, she replied that it might go to a permanent agency, since nobody questioned the need "for young and old, rich and poor, in this country to be physically fit."

Finally, amid the unrelenting criticism, FDR encouraged his wife to resign. ER persuaded Tiny to step down at the same time, and they both submitted letters of resignation on 18 February 1942. Congress passed the OCD appropriations bill, which included an amendment prohibiting funds for physical fitness instruction, fan dancing, "frills and furbelows." Encouraged by ER to remain, Melvyn Douglas organized the Arts Division but would resign the following December to join the army.

ER's last day at OCD was 20 February 1942. Her entire staff resigned with her. Subsequently she wrote, "I do not think I was ever happier than when the weight of that office was removed from my shoulders." Her five-month ordeal serving as the target at which FDR's opponents vented their wrath "was one of the experiences I least regretted leaving behind me." In her column, she concluded her OCD journey with wartime advice from Calvin Coolidge about survival on slim means: "Eat it up. Wear it out. Make it do. Do without."

ER dismissed the countless editorials and snide letters. "I am not in the least disturbed," she wrote to Paul Kellogg. "It is purely political and made by the same people who have fought NYA, CCC, WPA, Farm Security, etc." As long as there was work to be done, she would not go quietly into obscurity. Walter Winchell, one of the journalists friendly to her cause, ended his weekly broadcast with the hope that the House of Representatives would reread their bill of 8 December and noted that "it was a Declaration of War on the Axis—not Mrs. Roosevelt!"

Tiny Chaney and Melvyn Douglas both appreciated ER's broadcast of 22 February, in which she berated the "small and very vocal group of unenlightened men" who renewed "the age-old fight of the privileged few against the good of the many." It was time, ER asserted that Sunday, to develop "a feeling of deep gratitude to the writers, actors, artists and musicians who always give so generously of their time and talents. . . . It is apparently alright for businessmen to come to Washington to give their services on an expense basis, but not for an actor. We should be grateful to these businessmen, and we should be equally grateful to men like Melvyn Douglas."

Although ER had lost her institutional base from which to build a "people's movement," she did not become depressed. Rather, her anger ignited a fighting spirit. Right away she demanded that army and navy officials give "more recognition" to Negroes in the armed forces. "She proposed a colored flying squadron and colored tank units." She also "aided various eligible Negroes" who sought to be admitted as navy officers "by communicating with Navy officials and the press." ER was part of the effort to honor the African-American hero Doris "Dorie" Miller, a U.S. Navy mess attendant third class, who on 7 December, during the bombardment of his ship at Pearl Harbor, manned a machine gun against Japanese planes.

One of the most remarkable aspects of ER's tenure as first lady was that the press gave her views a full airing, particularly in times of crisis. "What does Eleanor think?" was never far from the public's mind, and reporters were careful, solicitous even, to honor that and to ask ER for her opinion on political, cultural, and social developments. She never shied away from articulating people's fears and knew how to allay their deepest anxieties.

Her role was transformed by FDR's Executive Order 9066, dated 19 February 1942, by which Japanese-Americans—U.S.-born citizens and their parents—would be evacuated from their West Coast homes by military transport and confined in internment camps. Her husband's decision to issue it stunned her. She had long opposed Justice Department plans for the handling of Japanese-Americans in case of war. In November she had asked Attorney General Francis Biddle about them. On 4 December 1941 she had publicly broadcast her conviction that "no law-abiding aliens of any nationality would be discriminated against by the government." For months, her columns had emphasized civil liberties, the Bill of Rights, and due process. EO 9066 was a violation of everything she understood about her husband's commitment to law and justice, and everything she believed represented America.

FDR had never before indicated support for this idea. Rather, during Churchill's last White House dinner, on 13 January, the conversation involved the need to protect over one million "enemy aliens," longtime residents in the United States as well as refugees from Germany, Italy, and Japan. ER had urged FDR to "do something" to counter the discrimination and harassment they were already facing. Churchill had suggested the United States adopt Britain's policy of investigative "loyalty tribunals" to separate "the goats from the sheep." The British had "interned the goats and used the sheep," he proudly noted. ER rejected that idea, since, she insisted, it would increase unjustified suspicion and prejudice. There was enough bigotry already.

She had then turned to another dinner guest that night to ask for his view. She had invited the author Louis Adamic for dinner that night because she had been moved by his recent book on exporting American democracy to Europe, *Two-Way Passage*. At the dinner table the Slovenian-born Adamic suggested a government effort to counter the growing anti-alien hysteria, especially on the West Coast. FDR had seemed to agree. Adamic pointed out that the current political and press campaign to demonize aliens constituted an alliance between old-style bigots and California's agricultural interests, who saw an opportunity to end competition from Japanese farmers. The dinner guests seemed generally to agree that the FBI and military intelligence could handle any disloyal elements among the *Issei* (those born in Japan) and their *Nisei* children (born in the United States), and that the Justice Department and other federal authorities clearly realized that these two groups were loyal.

After the dinner, ER and her party attended a Philadelphia Orchestra concert conducted by Arturo Toscanini, which stimulated further conversation. Although the Japanese were the primary targets of the moment,

Italians and Germans were also suspect. Toscanini, himself an exile from Fascism, as he traveled around the country, endured the indignity of being stopped at every crossing to be "photographed and examined." "I must say this situation seems to me rather tragic," ER wrote. "There is an element of comedy, however, in suggesting that Arturo Toscanini needs thus to be classified."

Even Churchill, in their last White House conversation, had seemed to reject Britain's 1940 mass roundup of "enemy aliens," mostly refugees. Attorney General Biddle too had seemed determined "to avoid mass internment." Yet FDR signed the removal order in Biddle's presence: the attorney general had finally acquiesced to the president's argument that the decision was military, to be carried out by his military advisers.

ER was blindsided by EO 9066, which ended due process, derailed habeas corpus, and eliminated the most fundamental rights of Japanese-American citizens. In issuing it, FDR violated his own commitment to the Atlantic Charter and his own rhetoric regarding wartime aims. How had it happened? Why, despite assurances from a great range of advisers, had he caved to the brutal press diatribes and bluntly racist congressional campaign to remove all Japanese-American residents from the West Coast?

To head the War Relocation Authority, which would carry out EO 9066, the president appointed scholar and Department of Agriculture official Milton S. Eisenhower, the younger brother of General Dwight D. Eisenhower. Milton Eisenhower considered it the worst assignment of his life. Subsequently he wrote approvingly of ER's objection to internment: "I see absolutely no reason why anyone who has had a good record—that is, who has no criminal or anti-American record—should have any anxiety. . . . This is equally applicable to the Japanese who cannot become citizens but have lived here for 30 or 40 years and to those newcomers who have not yet had time to become citizens."

ER was never reconciled to EO 9066. To be sure, she understood the pressures her husband was under. Japan had overpowered Burma and Singapore and invaded the Philippines and New Guinea, and the Dutch East Indies, India, and even Australia were at risk. Still, this decision perplexed her. What was the message? Whose interests were served? If FDR could imprison Japanese-Americans by executive order, then why could he not designate sites for the rescue and safety of endangered Jews? And why could he not end segregation in the military and the defense industries? February 1942 marked a turning point in their relationship. She was appalled by his action, and by his refusal to listen to so many of the people he had once depended upon.

The vast majority of Japanese evacuated from their homes were American-born U.S. citizens, mostly under twenty. According to historian Greg Robinson, the others were "virtually all permanent residents, whose average age was over 50."

Only days after Pearl Harbor, Henry Morgenthau was pressured to seize "thousands of small businesses owned by Issei and Nisei" from California to Utah, but J. Edgar Hoover rejected the idea: now that Japanese-Americans were under surveillance, their phones were tapped, and monitors were in place, all that was necessary had been achieved. Morgenthau too rejected the proposal, as well as the campaign to remove countless Japanese-Americans to some remote place "behind barbed wire," as "hysterical," "impractical," and wrong. To the end of his life, for over thirty years, Milton Eisenhower "brooded about this whole episode," since it illustrated "how an entire society can somehow plunge off course":

> The evacuation of Japanese-Americans from their homes on the coast to hastily constructed assembly centers and then to inland relocation centers was an inhuman mistake. [Over 120,000] American citizens of Japanese ancestry were stripped of their rights and freedoms and treated almost like enemy prisoners of war. Many lost their homes, their businesses, their savings. . . . How could such a tragedy have occurred in a democratic society that prides itself on individual rights and freedoms? How could responsible leaders make such a fateful decision?

Federal and state officials disagreed among themselves. Two California military officials, General John DeWitt and Major Karl Bendetsen, were slow to call for mass arrests but supported alien registration and coastal evacuation. Congressman Leland Ford (R-CA), in conjunction with Hearst columnists, began the drum roll "for mass internments in concentration camps." Anti–New Deal journalist Westbrook Pegler insisted, "To hell with habeas corpus." California governor Culbert Olson and state attorney general Earl Warren agreed with the "best people" of

California, meaning the Native Sons of the Golden West and various agricultural associations: round up Japanese-Americans and send them away. General Mark Clark and Admiral Harold Stark, chief of U.S. naval operations, dismissed the idea that Japanese-Americans presented any danger, but bigotry grew shrill as southern congressional voices joined the removal chorus. "This is a race war," declared Mississippi congressman John Rankin. "Damn them!" Remove "Japanese barbarism" from the "white man's civilization."

ER met with Dr. Jerome Davis and Dr. Dri Davis, YMCA activists who investigated and sought to alleviate the miseries of the "appalling" number of "prisoners of war the world over." Prisoners suffered not only from food deprivation but from "barbed wire sickness," brought about by days with "nothing to do mentally or physically," while knowing that their friends and families were "anxious about them, and yet have no way of working towards [their] release." ER urged her readers to consider this "horrible situation" and realize that anything that might be done for "enemy prisoners" had a "double incentive," since our ability to help "Allied prisoners of war depends upon the work done with the enemy prisoners."

Milton Eisenhower too pondered FDR's decision, and the human tragedies it engendered. As head of the War Relocation Authority, he set out to evacuate and relocate the Japanese-American communities of California, Washington, and Oregon as "smoothly, quickly, and humanely as possible." Biddle urged him to establish relocation centers that included schools, work programs, courts, and all facilities for "self-governing."

Exhausted, ER flew to Seattle to be with Anna, who was to have surgery. From there she wrote to Elinor Morgenthau, who had served so well at the OCD and who, like ER, worried about her sons, somewhere in battle. The two army mothers, sharing the same fears and emotions, consoled each other. "I'm afraid no one can be very objective about the war," ER wrote, "and of course you worry about Henry and Bob and their friends and all young people now. It is just a horrible nightmare that has to be lived through and the only way is to live from day to day and not die a thousand deaths from apprehension if one can help it!"

In her column, she counseled, "These are days to store up memories which will see us through whatever may lie ahead." She concluded with her only public reference to Japanese removal: "I am very happy to see that there is established a War Relocation Authority, which will have charge of the program for relocation and employment of persons who must be moved out of military areas. Unfortunately, in a war, many innocent people must suffer hardships to safeguard the nation. One feels that a program which provides work is certainly better than having nothing to do." ER was hopeful that Eisenhower's alliance with Clarence Pickett of the AFSC would render aspects of the situation bearable.

Subsequently, ER visited several camps and helped young *Nisei* find work, attend college, and serve in the military. At one point she asked FDR if they might adopt a Japanese-American family, but he refused— the Secret Service would never allow it.

A new dimension of caution and emotional distance had entered the first couple's relationship. ER was no longer informed about her husband's priorities and could no longer understand many of his decisions. Henry Morgenthau, too, was puzzled by FDR's uncharacteristic dismissal of the human hardships his order entailed. He approached FDR hoping to develop a program to "secure fair prices, guarantee land values" for Japanese-Americans, and ensure the safety of their property left in storage, but FDR dismissed the idea: "I am not concerned about that." As a result, Japanese property losses were vast, estimated at $400 million in 1942 dollars, the equivalent of over $5 billion today.

Two months later Morgenthau met privately with FDR to discuss the Treasury Department's investigation of Argentine assets in the United States, and whether they might be seized as reprisal for Argentina's support of subversive Nazi efforts. Previously, they had agreed about the serious nature of Axis activity in Latin America, and FDR had supported Morgenthau against the State Department, which opposed his study. Then he seemed to change his mind. Morgenthau was confused by the president's "sudden shifts."

FDR explained his reversals in an extraordinary statement: "You know I am a juggler, and I never let my right hand know what my left hand does. . . . I may have one policy for Europe and one diametrically opposite for North and South America. I may be entirely inconsistent, and furthermore I am perfectly willing to mislead and tell untruths if it will help win the war." Perhaps that willingness to change his mind as the situation demanded gave him flexibility. But close friends and allies noted his cunning, his inability to be bound to agreed-on positions.

His new and differing stances on so many issues was emotionally difficult for ER. She countered the juggler with various strategies. She remained attentive to her roles as first wife and hostess and dutifully served as FDR's surrogate whenever he asked her to. After Anna recovered from her surgery, ER returned from Seattle refreshed. "It did your mother a world of good to see you and the family," Tommy wrote Anna. "She was in grand spirits when she returned and has been ever since."

The night of ER's arrival, Joe Lash joined her and Tommy for the drive to Hyde Park to spend the weekend with FDR. Despite some moments of tension, it was surprisingly agreeable. "Many times I wanted to disagree with the president," Joe noted in his diary, "but kept quiet because I felt he wanted a rest from incessant arguing and being on his guard." ER "goes after him because so few people disagree with him." She explained to Joe that she considered it "important that someone tell him how others are reacting" and deliver the opinions she gathered in her travels. "But even ER these days wonders whether she has a right to."

As always, FDR was able to separate his private and political lives. Around the fireside for drinks and then at dinner, there was much spoofing and banter. The serious conversation was limited to misinformation in the media. ER cooperated with the need for pleasantries. There were no disagreements, and after dinner around the fireplace Diana Hopkins, Harry's daughter, read a book, and everybody "chatted amiably"—ER with FDR, Joe with Harry Hopkins, and Tommy with Grace Tully. It was an unusually harmonious evening.

That Monday ER and Tommy went through SDR's Manhattan town house, with the aim of sorting through the family possessions and dispersing them among her children. ER was considerate of her family's feelings, promising Anna she would distribute "the linen and silver" when she visited the Big House.

She had chosen her new apartment at 29 Washington Square, in Greenwich Village, with the thought that she and FDR would share that fully accessible space. It was not only "very comfortable, there is light & sun & I hope air even in summer!" Tommy noted, "once we are settled, your mother hopes to stay put."

Joe helped ER to move into it, before leaving for the service. Upon his induction, he told reporters, "I just want to be the best soldier I can be." ER hosted a festive dinner and hoped that with his being a Spanish Civil War veteran, "they don't make things too hard for him but he seems resigned to anything."

But the first lady was unhappy with the ongoing tensions around the White House, which were now having an impact on their summer plans, Tommy noted. ER still felt responsible for Diana Hopkins and invited her with a friend to spend "the summer with us at the cottage." Since "Diana is no cherub," Tommy was pleased that Harry Hopkins agreed "to employ a maid to look after them," and everybody was relieved that Hall's friend Zena Raset was free and willing, since "she can swim, sew, etc."

Hick was still in residence, "to please your mother," Tommy told Anna. She wryly added, "It is so nice for her to find someone to welcome her when she returns. . . . You will gather that I am not in a sympathetic mood." Actually, Tommy continued to deplore ER's "satellites," including Joe Lash and Trude Pratt, although she was so polite to them they did not suspect the depth of her disapproval.

The next week "Elliott dropped from the sky," after a forty-five-hour trip from Liberia. "He has some kind of dysentery but they completed their mission." He was distressed by the imperial legacy, ER wrote Anna. "Africa was a shock to him, he can't get over the disease & filth & how the natives have been exploited. He brought back 18,000 plates & they photographed everything they went after." Although their "plane fell to pieces" and they almost crashed in the desert, he was home—and ER was profoundly grateful.

The White House was filled with notables: Crown Prince Olav of Norway and Princess Martha, who had become one of FDR's devoted companions; Peru's president Manuel Prado, "who is very charming"; and Philippine president Manuel Quezon. Quezon's family and war cabinet had been spirited away from Corregidor in a submarine by General Douglas MacArthur when Manila fell, and he was not only thankful but loyal. With most of the southwestern Pacific in Japanese hands, MacArthur had promised, "I shall return."

All the harrowing war news exacerbated ER's worries about her sons. Elliott and Franklin Jr. were recovering but would return to duty shortly. "Pa says Johnnie will get sea duty on a destroyer probably soon," she wrote

Anna. And James faced unknown service in the Pacific with his Marine battalion, the Carlson Raiders.

That spring ER wrote many articles demanding an end to bigotry and discrimination. In "Race, Religion and Prejudice" for the *New Republic*, she sought to convey the urgency of Madame Chiang Kai-shek's message that "this war [demands] we all face the question of race discrimination." The 1924 immigration law had blocked those "Chinese and Japanese who wished to enter our country," but after the war Americans would no longer be able to "differentiate between the peoples of Europe, the Near East, and the Far East." Since we were "fighting for freedom," we had to recognize that included "freedom from discrimination among the peoples of the world." This was, ER acknowledged, not the inclination of many Americans. But the "people of the world have suddenly begun to stir and they seem to feel that in the future we should look upon each other as fellow human beings, judged by our acts, by our abilities, by our development, and not by any less fundamental differences." So we must confront our "attitudes . . . our habits . . . our approach to the Jewish people, the Japanese and Chinese people, the Italian people, and above all, the Negro people in our midst." Since Negroes represented "our largest minority, our attitude towards them will have to be faced first of all."

For *This Is America*, a book of photographs by Frances Cooke Macgregor, ER wrote essays that boldly and forthrightly celebrated race and diversity during a time of conflict and danger.

The pictures in this book show you the length and breadth of the land . . . and the changes in climate, from such cold as has aided Russia today to stall the German war machine, to the balmy breezes of Southern California and Florida on the verge of the tropics. [Beyond the variety of landscapes] we are a land of people—people of various races, black, yellow, red, and white people. It is their combination which makes the United States. They represent innumerable differences of creed, occupation, education, taste, recreation, habits and custom. . . . When the present days are behind us, this may well be a universal condition, and if we play our part with courage and clear-sightedness, we may become the hope of the world. We may have here the example of what a family of nations can mean, since we in our nation are a family of varying races and religions.

ER's concluding essay, "The White Race in America," noted that many people from across Europe had emigrated to North America "fleeing from oppression and cruelties and abject poverty." Gradually they had awakened "to our responsibilities to and dependency on" African, Asian, and Native American peoples. "Now, Americans all," we must see that "after all, there is but one race—humanity."

In a radical and prescient essay in *American Magazine*, she heralded her vision for the future. Americans were fighting for a peace guaranteed by economic security: "Freedom to live under the government of our choice. Freedom from economic want. Freedom from racial and religious discrimination. A world economy guaranteeing all people free trade and access to raw materials." Since the last war, we had been "in a kind of revolution. It is a world-wide uprising of the people . . . [for] a better way of life." With the New Deal, democracy

> in its truest sense began to be fulfilled. We are fighting today to continue this democratic process. . . . Only if we recognize this general rising of the peoples of the world can we understand the real reason why we are in the war. . . . No future economic system will be satisfactory [unless] every man and woman [has opportunity, work, and adequate pay] not only for the decencies of life [but for a full life]. We will no longer cling to any type of economic system which leaves any human beings who are willing to work, without food and shelter and an opportunity for development.

ER wrote with excitement about the ongoing "revolution of people all over the world. We cannot stand still for the pleasure of a few. . . . We accept the will of the majority . . . the dream of a new world."

Written to inspire, ER's words galvanized the burgeoning civil rights movement and forged a new alliance with Vice President Henry Wallace. In May 1942 he gave a speech that introduced the concept of "the common man."

> Some have spoken of the "American Century." I say that the century on which we are entering . . . can be and must be the century of the common man. Everywhere the common man must learn to build his own industries. . . . No nations will have the God-given right to exploit other nations. Older nations will have the privilege to help

younger nations . . . but there must be neither military nor economic imperialism. The methods of the nineteenth century will not work in the people's century which is now about to begin. India, China, and Latin America have a tremendous stake in the people's century. As their masses learn to read and write, and as they become productive mechanics, the standard of living will double and treble. Modern science, when devoted wholeheartedly to the general welfare, has in it potentialities of which we do not yet dream.

Wallace's speech complemented ER's vision, and she never tired of quoting his words. She vigorously opposed Henry Luce's notion of an American Century and rejected completely his call for "the Americanization of the World."

Despite her many articles, her new alliances, and her daily column, ER had reasons for anguish during the spring of 1942. Her husband's refusal to create "a voluntary registration of women" for work and for the military left her outraged. His decision was, if nothing else, wasteful, since women's work would benefit the wartime economy. More than that, a voluntary registration would enable so many women currently unemployed and eager to work to have their wants and needs considered. FDR had also recommended budget cuts for NYA and government aid for college students, which she opposed.

She was continually disheartened by ongoing obstructions to limit, or even defeat, her work with the U.S. Committee for the Care of European Children. "We have a great many children under our care. We are bringing over 50 children on the [next] boat. They were to have come last month," but passport difficulties and full boats prevented that. A number would "come from concentration camps in France and others from Spain." The committee worked through social agencies, many families adopted the children, and "we watch over them." ER emphasized the difficulties of transporting them and mentioned the need "for State Department approval." Explaining the "dire" situation, she paraphrased Breckinridge Long's order to U.S. consuls in Spain and Portugal: "They have been delayed and delayed so often that they may be delayed again." It was time, she told her press conference, to consider new programs: "We should be at least studying ways in the future . . . to help the children in Europe."

ER did not specifically mention Jewish children, perhaps to avoid the well-established bigotry that surrounded every effort her committee made throughout the winter and spring of 1942. As Jews sought to flee from every port, the tragedies were numerous. On 12 December 1941, almost eight hundred Romanian Jews embarked on the *Struma*, an antique Danube steamer built in 1867 that they had chartered, and set out for Palestine. Off the coast of Istanbul, the vessel's engines failed, but Turkish authorities refused to allow the refugees to come ashore until Britain granted them permission to enter Palestine. Britain refused. The refugees remained aboard for weeks in wretched conditions, until Turkey towed the steamer to the Black Sea. On 24 February 1942 an explosion occurred, and the *Struma* sank with all 767 people aboard. After this tragedy, the British colonial office issued a new law against "illegal immigration to Palestine."

In March, Rabbi Stephen Wise wrote ER that the British colonial office was delaying ships full of Jewish children bound for Palestine. "This memo is perfectly shocking to me," ER wrote to Sumner Welles. "We have taken British children (as war refugees) and I think the British government ought to pay more attention to us in return. They have set a very low quota in Palestine and the Arabs have agreed. After all, these are anti-Axis refugees and they certainly will help us rather than the Axis and, from what I read in the papers, we may be needing some help in that part of the world before long."

Welles replied that he would do everything he could, but the British were adamant "for fear of Arab unrest."

ER suggested, "Why not try to give asylum and guarantee that such refugees will continue to Africa and South America? This British policy is so cruel that, if it were generally known in this country, it would increase the dislike of Great Britain which is already too prevalent."

Welles promised to refer the problem to the Intergovernmental Committee on Political Refugees, but there "were insurmountable" obstacles, such as a lack of ships available for refugee transport, and nations in Africa and South America were averse to further immigration. Moreover, there was nothing he could do since State Department policy was "bound to British policy in Palestine."

New legislation had established the Women's Army Corps (WAC), but at her 14 May press conference, ER deplored the fact that it did not contain an antidiscrimination clause. She was also surprised to learn that army nurses were "not allowed to marry while in the service," and that married nurses were barred from the military. Given the bloodshed and the need for nurses, ER thought a more sensible policy was required and that women must be given "the same privileges as men." Under the circumstances, ER was vastly relieved when Oveta Culp Hobby accepted her appointment as director of the Women's Army Corps (WAC) and Mary McLeod Bethune agreed to serve as her assistant. Not only was Colonel Hobby married (to former Texas governor William Pettus Hobby), she left her husband and two children (William, nine, and Jessica, five) at home to assume her new position. A journalist, literary editor, and publisher of the *Houston Post*, Hobby shared many of ER's views. Formerly president of Texas's League of Women Voters, she was a longtime member of the NAACP. She opposed discrimination against women and people of color, and as WAC director, she spoke and wrote on such topics as "The High Cost of Prejudice."

As war news worsened, with significant Allied defeats and Nazi horrors, ER asked FDR for a specific assignment. "I'm rather tired because I have nothing to do these days," she confided to Anna. But he had nothing to offer her, so she resolved to spend the summer in Hyde Park and "enjoy my leisure!"

She worried about her sons. James and the Carlson Raiders had been on Midway Island during the Japanese attack. Franklin Jr. had returned to his ship somewhere in England. ER wrote Esther Lape, "If only the war could end soon; people in Germany must be suffering terribly and the Chinese and the Japanese boys are dying too. It all seems so senseless and wicked." Sidelined and discontented, ER seemed oddly different to Tommy. "There is a great change in ER and I do not know whether it is anxiety . . . for the boys or what it is," Tommy wrote Lape. "We practically never have any conversation."

In July, Trude Pratt and her three children joined ER, Diana Hopkins, and assorted Roosevelt grandchildren at Hyde Park. ER filled her days entertaining guests, and together with Trude planned an exciting international conference for the ISS, to take place in September. But her grim mood continued.

Suddenly Harry Hopkins announced that he was engaged to marry the former journalist and glamorous society hostess Louise Macy—and that FDR had invited them to live in the White House. ER was flabbergasted. Had he "thought through what it would mean to have a married couple, plus Diana," in the White House? she asked him. And did he realize "what it would mean to them"? After all, "it seemed to me very hard . . . to be obliged to start their married life in someone else's house." In response, FDR insisted that "the most important thing in the world . . . was the conduct of the war and that it was absolutely necessary that Harry be in the house. That settled that."

Although profoundly angry, ER was publicly gracious. She told her press conference, "I am very glad [they] will be married in the White House" on 30 July and that to "carry on the work of the war better [they] will stay with us for a while."

After the wedding, Louise continued her war work as a hospital nurse's aide, "which meant she was out of the White House very early every morning, and returned late," ER noted. Despite Louise's schedule, "she managed to establish a close relationship" with her new stepdaughter, Diana, who benefited greatly from her presence. As it turned out, "Louise managed what must have been a difficult situation extraordinarily well."

But ER made no effort to become friendly with or even get to know Louise Macy. She interpreted FDR's decision to expand his court as a further effort to restrict and limit her own presence and influence. She was already cut out from wartime conferences; now her household had been invaded by one of the most dashing and esteemed hostesses of the international "smart set."

Louise Macy had been a fashion editor for *Harper's Bazaar*, based in Paris until the office closed on 10 May 1940. In the final weeks of peace, while everybody refused to believe disaster imminent, she had been at the center of farewell parties and merriment. According to Janet Flanner, the *New Yorker*'s Parisian columnist better known as Genet, Macy hosted the "best big party" of all. She "hired a long-disused historical mansion . . . , put in temporary furnishings and plumbing, a mobile kitchen, and several thousand candles, and requested her guests to wear diadems and decorations." Many considered it "the party of the year."

Upon her return to New York, Louise Macy incongruously continued to host stunning parties and was close to an eclectic circle of notables including Bette Davis, Bernard Baruch, and Jock Whitney, who married Betsey Cushing Roosevelt. The Whitneys remained close to FDR but visited only when ER was away—since Betsey never got over how meanly ER had treated her—and always thought of her (and SDR) as rigid "old drag-ons." ER had resented Betsey's role as FDR's hostess. Now she was faced with Betsey's replacement and felt her home again under siege.

Anna understood her mother's feelings. "Harry Hopkins and his bride give me a pain in the neck!" she wrote. "From what Tommy writes me he has the nerve of Balboa!" Anna's husband John had decided to join the military, as all the young men in the family had done. Given their three children—Sistie, Buzzy, and Johnny—it was "an awful dilemma for both of us." Anna wanted her mother's thoughts, while she sought to become "a stoic!"

ER also sought to become a stoic as new war agonies were revealed. That summer Varian Fry sent her urgent messages and a report dated 25 August 1942 by the Joint Distribution Committee and the Emergency Rescue Committee (ERC): "Vichy has agreed to deport 16,000 foreigners and French Jews from the occupied zone and 10,000 foreigners believed to be both Jewish and Gentile, but so far no French, from the unoccupied zone." On 16–17 July 1942, 13,152 Jewish men, women, and children were arrested from their Paris homes and taken to the Vélodrome d'Hiver, where parents and children were divided—to be sent in separate transports "to an unknown destination in east Europe." Subsequently, men, women, and children were arrested in the streets of Marseilles, Toulouse, Lyons, and other population centers. "All French exit permits have been stopped without distinction of race or nationality."

In response to Fry's information and breaking news, on 4 September ER wrote Norman Davis, chair of the U.S. Red Cross: "The U.S. Com-mittee for the Care of European Children is confronted with a problem. A thousand children may be evacuated from France, and we have to raise about one million dollars." ER's committee believed they could do it, but she and Marshall Field wondered "if the Red Cross would be willing to underwrite" their efforts. "It does seem that we should take these children who are in such dire straits and I hope the Red Cross will feel that they can do this."

In her column she appealed for funds:

> I was very sorry not to be able to get to NYC today to attend a meet-ing of the U.S. Committee for the Care of European Children. There is going to be an opportunity for us in this country to show our

concern for the suffering of children in Europe. It should be possible
to bring some children over here, whose parents are in concentration
camps, or who themselves have been interned. I think our committee should make every effort to raise the necessary money.

After ER's efforts, the State Department agreed to issue visas for five
thousand children who had been separated from their parents in France.
But despite vigorous work by the AFSC, the YMCA, and various aid
agencies to get the children to safety, Vichy France denied them all exit
visas. Pierre Laval's cruel obstructionist policies included a requirement
that they provide "proof" of orphanhood, which was impossible. On 9
November the Allies invaded French North Africa, and all rescue efforts
collapsed. Some 42,500 Jews were transported from France to Auschwitz-
Birkenau during 1942.

ER was furious about several other issues as well. On 22 June, Frank
Kingdon wrote her that over 100,000 people had signed a Union for Democratic Action petition requesting that the president end discrimination against
Negroes in the armed forces. A March on Washington and an NAACP conference were scheduled for 4 July, and Kingdon wanted to present the petition to FDR that day. He asked ER to help make it happen: "Naturally we
should get together a delegation of both white and Negro citizens of distinction." ER wrote her husband, "I hope you can receive Frank Kingdon's petition." He replied: "I am sorry but I cannot do this on July 4th!"

ER was undoubtedly stunned by FDR's rejection, since she had helped
launch Democracy in Action with a bold speech: "I am firmly of the
belief that the only basis for a permanent peace is one which recognizes
the necessity for cooperation among all peoples and domination by none."
ER increasingly worked with Democracy in Action, determined to end
"the deadly poisons of racialism."

As ER focused on civil rights and the need for "a new world order," it
was her burgeoning friendship with Pauli Murray that brightened her
days. ER's correspondence with Murray had begun in 1938 but increased
when the Hunter College graduate, WPA educator, and spirited NAACP
youth leader became active in the Odell Waller case. Waller was a Virginia sharecropper who had killed his landlord in self-defense and was
sentenced to death in 1940. Since the jury was limited to white men who
paid their poll taxes, the case became a national symbol of injustice for

nine million sharecroppers in the eight southern states denied all rights. Many Americans rallied for a stay of execution and an end to the poll tax, but on 4 May 1942 the Supreme Court refused to review the case. Virginia governor Colgate Darden issued six reprieves, then decided to end "the propaganda campaign" that only promoted "racial discord."

In June 1942 antidiscrimination activists, including ER, united to save Waller. Urgent petitions went to FDR for a presidential commission of inquiry, many demonstrated to save Waller, and on 16 June twenty thousand people participated in a rally at New York's Madison Square Garden.

A. Philip Randolph organized a delegation of race leaders to lobby in Washington on 1 July; they hoped to appeal directly to FDR. The group included such respected leaders as Mary McLeod Bethune and Anna Arnold Hedgeman, New York director of race relations at the OCD; Dr. Channing Tobias of the YMCA; and journalist Ted Poston, then with the Office of War Information (OWI). Pauli Murray, having completed her first year at Howard University Law School, and having been hired by the Workers Defense League (WDL), accompanied the group. They were shunted from office to office, and as Murray noted, even Henry Wallace "tried to evade us." Bethune, who knew the vice president well, "was compelled to run after him in order to be heard." He replied, "It is out of my jurisdiction." No one at the White House would see them.

The day before Waller was to be executed, Randolph put in many calls to ER, "our last resort," all day and was promised a return call that evening. At ten o'clock, ER telephoned him at NAACP headquarters, and other delegates listened in. She explained to Randolph, "in a voice that trembled and almost broke," that she had done everything she possibly could and even interrupted the president twice. FDR had said, "This is a matter of law and not of the heart." The case was in Governor Darden's jurisdiction, and the president said he had "no legal power to intervene. I am sorry, Mr. Randolph, I cannot do any more."

According to Harry Hopkins, ER called him "four or five times" that day. "She spoke and wrote to the Governor . . . and indeed, the President wrote a very long letter to request [life in prison]." After that FDR "felt he could not intervene again," but ER "would not take 'No' for an answer and the President finally got on the phone himself and told Mrs. Roosevelt that under no circumstances would he intervene . . . and urged very strongly that she say nothing about it."

Odell Waller was electrocuted on 2 July. At Randolph's request, Pauli Murray wrote an open letter to FDR, signed by members of the delegation, published in the Negro press, and nationally syndicated. The seven-page letter detailed the legal injustices and Jim Crow attitudes that hobbled well-trained attorneys when they sought to represent Negro clients in southern courts, and that caused the Odell Waller case to become a national symbol—which demonstrated how "the Government of the US has failed us."

This tragedy . . . comes at a time when the United Nations are desperately trying to hold back the Axis forces and when the eyes of the colored peoples of the globe are fixed upon the pattern of democracy which America sets for Negroes. . . .

Waller's execution has intensified a wave of determination for a show-down on the question of total democracy for the Negro which cannot long be held back by leaders who use the bargain and compromise method. It was the signal for the barbarous forces in this country to renew the unleashing of their hatred upon the Negro people. Within two weeks after Waller's execution, the press reported the lynching of Willie Vinson, 25 year old Negro youth in Texarkana, Texas, the lynching of Private Jessie Smith, 25 year old Negro soldier by a posse in Flagstaff, Arizona, and the brutal beating and jailing of the Negro tenor Roland Hayes and his wife in Rome, Georgia [after an argument with a clerk in a shoe store]. . . .

Negro citizens are demanding to know why Nazi saboteurs on trial are being given every opportunity to defend themselves, while American citizens are being hung to cotton gins and shot down like dogs. . . .

Don't you see, Mr. President . . . with the world in agony of a war for the survival of sheer human decency, the race issue in America is crucial to the whole struggle. If the Negro is not given full rights now, then the battle for Democracy is lost. . . . We call upon enlightened public opinion . . . to free you, our great President, and to free our country from a poll tax southern bloc which decided the fates of American citizens whom it does not represent.

Murray sent a second, personal letter to FDR. "If Japanese-Americans can be evacuated to prevent violence being perpetrated upon them," she wrote to the president, "then certainly you have the power to evacuate Negro citizens from 'lynching' areas." Moreover, Negro voters had noticed that Wendell Willkie was clear about the race question, while "you have never come out openly." She hoped that in the interest of the 1944 election, the president would take "a more forthright stand."

To Murray's astonishment, she received a stinging yet heartfelt response from ER, defending FDR in relation to Wendell Willkie: "I wonder if it ever occurred to you that Mr. Willkie has no responsibility whatsoever. He can say whatever he likes and do whatever he likes." If he had been elected president, he would have had to negotiate with congressional leaders "to pass vital legislation." The letter was the clearest statement of the limits ER endured:

> For one who must really have a knowledge of the workings of our kind of government, your letter seems to me one of the most thoughtless I have ever read. Of course I can say just how I feel, but I cannot say it with much sense of security unless the President were willing for me to do so. It is very easy for us as individuals to think of what we would do if we were in office, but we forget that with the election . . . go at the same time infinite restrictions.

During the summer of 1942 India was much in the news. Mahatma Gandhi, Jawaharlal Nehru, and the other Congress Party leaders were agitating for Indian independence from Great Britain, but Churchill was determined that the future of the British Empire would not be decided until the war was over. He would not offer India even dominion status until then. Nonetheless in March 1942 he sent the Christian Socialist leader Sir Stafford Cripps on a mission to negotiate with India's leaders.*

---

*A nephew of the Fabian socialist Beatrice Webb and son of Lord Parmoor, a Labour peer, Cripps in his twenties became "England's youngest King's counsel." Known as the "Red Squire," and living in a forty-room manor house, he was reportedly "one of the richest men at the bar" but gave most of his money to causes he believed in. Tall, underweight, and ascetic, he subsisted on a diet of raw vegetables. Churchill and others called him "Christ and Carrots Cripps." Always formal and distant, he had a socialist militancy and religious fervor that induced Churchill to remark, "There but for the grace of God goes God." Nevertheless, Churchill sent him to Russia as ambassador, then to India—despite his close alliances with Harold Laski and other leaders of the left wing of the Labour Party dedicated to the end of empire.

FDR supported imperial changes and hoped Cripps's mission would result in steps toward self-government, but Churchill was irate at this position. FDR agreed to remain publicly silent and abide by the prime minister's wishes. As for ER, she cared deeply about India because of her father's adventures there, as well as his travel journal and letters. Her heart belonged to the independence movement. She had not met Cripps but knew that Joe Lash and his friends held him in high regard.

In April, while the mission was under way, ER wrote a vigorous statement about race in her column: "Today what concerns us most deeply is the necessary change in attitude on the part of the white race. The psychology which believes that the white man, alone of all the races in the world, has something which must be imposed on all other races, must go."

The Cripps mission offered minor concessions, imposed strict limitations, and hence it failed—an outcome that seemed to many foreordained—and precisely what Churchill wanted. When he heard that the mission had come to nothing, Churchill reportedly "danced around the cabinet room." But ER was disappointed: "One cannot help hope that some new way will be worked out whereby the people of India may feel that the future belongs more surely to them in their own land."

A few months later, on 9 August 1942, certain that the United States would not interfere, Churchill publicly declared war on "the half naked fakir": he ordered the arrests of Gandhi, Nehru, and twenty other leaders of India's nationalist Congress Party. Widespread demonstrations erupted to protest the arrests and demand that the imperial government "Quit India!" When the demonstrations turned violent, ruthless military action followed. Neighborhoods were "machine-gunned" from planes overhead, killing a thousand Indians. British officials were assaulted, and more than fifty thousand demonstrators were arrested.

Ickes wanted FDR to pressure Churchill to free India, but even in the face of the arrests and violence, the president demanded silence from his cabinet and allies alike. "You are right about India," he told Ickes, "but it would be playing with fire if the British Empire were to tell me to mind my own business." FDR refused to challenge Churchill on India and repeatedly asked ER to remain silent as well. Despite her own convictions, ER honored FDR's request and urged her young allies to avoid the subject.

Intrigued by Pauli Murray's spirited brilliance, she invited the activist poet whom she called "the Firebrand" to her new Village apartment. On 27 August, Murray arrived, accompanied by her friend and mentor Anna Arnold Hedgeman. The first lady "met us at the door," Murray noted, "and disarmed me completely by throwing her arms about me and giving me an affectionate hug." The splendid meeting was the beginning of a lifelong friendship, defined by respect and trust, that kept ER informed about and connected to a new generation of race radicals.

All summer ER and Trude Pratt had been organizing an ISS conference, the objective of which was "to express unity of purpose" and build "mutual confidence" among the United Nations, as Murray, who represented Howard University Law School on the U.S. delegation, described it. The conference took place in Washington that September. Students from fifty-three nations participated, including exiles from Poland, Norway, Holland, Czechoslovakia, and Belgium, as well as young men and women in uniform from China, Britain, and the Soviet Union.

Murray's circle of friends proceeded to draft two resolutions. One demanded the release of India's imprisoned leaders as well as renewed negotiations between India and Britain to achieve the "political freedom" needed "to mobilize the Indian people for an all-out war effort [within] the United Nations." It also condemned "racial supremacy, renounced imperialism," and called for "independence for colonials." The other resolution condemned Russia's occupation of Lithuania. The resolutions' drafters—Louis Fischer, Lou Harris, and Bill Goldsmith, all known to ER—intended to present both to the conference's assembly for a vote.

During a break for a picnic on the White House lawn, ER "caught my hand, fixed her searching blue eyes upon me, and said 'Pauli, I want to talk to you later.'" Murray knew the subject and made every effort to hide, "but one simply did not evade" the determined first lady. "She found me in a far corner of the lawn" and argued that the two resolutions raised the "grave danger" that representatives from Russia and Britain "would walk out and leave the Assembly in disarray." We must not offend "our strongest allies," she implored.

Pauli found it difficult to resist ER but believed there was a difference between official U.S. policy and the independent views of young people. She agreed with the content of the two resolutions. When they were presented to the assembly, it rejected the one on Lithuania but accepted the one on India. To Pauli's relief, approval of the India resolution did not "split the Assembly." She was certain the goals it set were entirely in agreement with ER's personal views, which of course they were.

Given ER's views about race and empire, one must pause to consider her effort to censor the resolutions. She was clear about her own limitations: she might speak only when FDR agreed that she could speak. She never publicly countered his decisions and generally followed his instructions. Now FDR had requested silence about India—and she steadfastly accommodated that wish.

But many others who disagreed with FDR were also silenced by his requests. Increasingly she believed that she alone brought him face to face with political realities that he needed to address. Consequently, in private, she never gave up, going to him again and again. But the more insistent she became, the more impatient he grew. Tensions mounted, but she persisted because urgent issues of life and death were at stake.

India was an ongoing case in point. The NAACP and allied liberals were disgusted by the continued imprisonment of Gandhi, Nehru, and so many Congress leaders, and protests mounted. Former Pennsylvania governor Gifford Pinchot and his wife, Cornelia Bryce Pinchot, organized a meeting to demand that Britain "resume negotiations with India" and were eager for Vice President Wallace to speak. On 8 September ER asked FDR to see them. The president repeated his position: although he agreed in principle with their and ER's concerns, he would not pressure Churchill on India.

She championed other issues, too, that he did not seriously consider. Respectful access to military training for women, especially women pilots, was high on her list of things to be done. She was pleased that her early support for pilot training at the Tuskegee Institute was bearing fruit. In March 1941 she spent an hour in the air seated behind pilot C. Alfred Anderson, the chief flight instructor at Tuskegee. A photographer snapped her great smile upon landing. It hit the national press, announcing that black aviators were in flight and ready. Finally in July 1941 the fighting 99th Pursuit Squadron was created. ER continued her crusade to ensure that black officers would be allowed to fight and be sent overseas, and would not be limited to menial jobs and support services. As Roscoe Brown, subsequently one of the most decorated Tuskegee Airmen, put it, "Fairness gives you a chance to be excellent." Ultimately, 992 pilots were trained at Tuskegee, and 450 flew in combat missions.

ER engendered even more controversy when she insisted that women aviators should be equally trained and their skills equally used. Her own desire to fly and her friendship with Amelia Earhart had persuaded her that women were already outstanding pilots. Willa Beatrice Brown, one of two women in the all-black Challenger Air Pilots Association, founded in 1935, became the first black woman to receive a commission as lieutenant in the U.S. Civil Air Patrol. On 1 September 1942, ER wrote the first of several columns to celebrate women in flight, saying, "Women pilots . . . are a weapon waiting to be used." With 3,500 trained women fliers, ER was encouraged that pilot Jacqueline Cochran had been appointed to direct women's air work, an effort that would eventually result in the formation of the Women's Auxiliary Army Corps and the Women's Airforce Service Pilots.

In mid-September, Nazi slaughters were ravaging Stalingrad. "We opened our papers this morning to find that Stalingrad is still holding," ER observed. "This is certainly going down in history as a valiant defense." Indeed, the Battle of Stalingrad, which lasted from 23 August 1942 to 2 February 1943, would become the war's longest, bloodiest, and most brutal standoff. ER believed "everyone in this country must want to express admiration for [the Soviets'] extraordinary ability to stand and take it." While the RAF and U.S. air raids on Germany continued, it was clear that "raids alone" would not resolve "the battle of Europe. All we can do is pray that [we] will really reach the point where decisive action can be taken."

In May 1942 Soviet foreign minister Vyacheslav Molotov had visited Washington, and since then ER had been under the impression that FDR and Churchill were planning to launch a second front in Europe. Unknown to her, however, they had decided between themselves to move instead on North Africa. On 9 October, she forwarded to FDR an article regarding the dreadful starvation conditions in Russia and attached a note: "FDR read. It is horrible. When can we move?"

Perhaps it was because he wanted to get ER out of his way as he planned the invasion of North Africa; or perhaps it was because he wanted to benefit from her personal diplomacy and observations, especially as friction with Britain because of India mounted. Perhaps, too, he was actually concerned about her needs and saw that she was often depressed without specific war work to do. For whatever reason, FDR decided to fulfill a longtime wish of ER and send her to London. It would be her first international assignment and would be important in countless ways.

Chapter Eighteen

"Golden Footprints": A Permanent Bond in War and Peace

On 9 October 1942 Wendell Willkie returned from a seven-week world tour. In deference to Churchill, India had been off-limits to him, but Willkie had not needed to go to India to see what was wrong with British policies. Everywhere he went, Willkie was disturbed by the poverty and disease that resulted from those policies and the indifference of colonial authorities. Widely published, Willkie's words describing poverty, neglect, and subjugation in the British Empire sent Churchill into a fury.

In the Soviet Union, he spent many hours with Molotov and Stalin, who detailed Russia's desperate situation: the loss of fertile farmlands, important industrial centers, and the great oil fields of the Caucasus. The Nazis had burned entire cities and villages to the ground and caused millions of casualties. Russians felt betrayed by FDR and Churchill, who had reneged on their promises. Willkie called for the immediate opening of a real second front.

It was in the context of Churchill's upset over Willkie's observations, Stalin's bitterness about the Soviet Union's grim situation, and rising anti-colonial fervor that FDR finally decided to ask ER to go to London. Part of her task would be to use her personal warmth and diplomatic magic to fortify the Anglo-American alliance, encourage troop morale, and keep the United Nations together.

She would be walking into an Anglo-American stir over race relations. In July 1942 General Dwight Eisenhower had arrived to command the Allies' European Theater forces, and he joined Ambassador John Winant's efforts to build a solid U.S.-British alliance. During the spring and summer, U.S. troops and military staffers had arrived in London as well. But they were supposed to remain entirely segregated, both at work and off duty. However white American soldiers regularly insulted their black compatriots. This racism shocked British sensibilities, and Britons generally welcomed black soldiers. After violent scuffles, many pubs displayed signs reading, "For British people and coloured Americans only."

Eisenhower and Winant agreed that this situation must change. Eisenhower ordered U.S. commanders not to restrict black soldiers' association with British civilians, and to end discriminatory practices. He could not end segregation, but he sought to establish harmony and end instances of abuse. As for Winant, he established a British-American Liaison Board to investigate and settle race problems, which philanthropist and journalist Janet Murrow (wife of war correspondent Edward R. Murrow) agreed to chair. Subsequently Winant also persuaded Roland Hayes, a black American tenor and composer, to stay in England after a concert, tour bases, and interview black servicemen. Winant's report went directly to Eleanor Roosevelt, who worked with Walter White and others to insist upon change.

ER had heard that officers from the American South were "very indignant to find that Negro soldiers were not looked upon with terror by the girls in England and Ireland and Scotland." To avoid Anglo-American tension and racial violence, she thought "we will have to do a little educating." Her pending visit to Britain alarmed Secretary of War Stimson, who wrote FDR to demand ER not speak about racism, and was pleased to find that FDR sympathized with "our attitude." If ER agreed not to write about race, she was determined to observe everything—and submit useful reports.

ER's trip was mostly arranged by Lady Stella Reading, founder of the Women's Voluntary Service (WVS) and by Ambassador Winant, who would serve as her primary hosts. On 21 October, adventurous and determined, she set off with Tommy for their first nonstop international flight, "across what has now become a very small pond indeed," into the unknown abyss of war. Women's Army Corps director Colonel Oveta Culp Hobby and her aide, Lieutenant Betty Bandel of Arizona, were part of her entourage.

Greeted in Bristol by Ambassador Winant, ER and her party boarded a special train to London. On the two-hour trip, Winant detailed their schedule, which had been approved "by the queen and Lady Stella Reading." Then he announced that after her stay at Buckingham Palace, ER and Tommy would have his apartment—with staff for all their needs, an arrangement for which ER was profoundly grateful.

ER asked Winant why they had not flown to London, and he told her that the king and queen never met anyone at the airport. As they approached London by train, ER "grew more and more nervous and wondered why on earth I had ever let myself be inveigled into coming on this trip . . . to be treated as a 'Very Important Person.' . . . Finally we pulled into the station. The red carpet was unrolled. . . . There stood the king and queen and all our high military officials," notably General Eisenhower and Admiral Howard Stark, as well as Foreign Secretary Anthony Eden and Lady Reading. Queen Elizabeth said, "We welcome you with all our hearts," which evoked ER's memories of the king and queen's departure from Hyde Park in June 1939. ER would have been less nervous if she had known how tense King George VI and Queen Elizabeth seemed to observant reporters—as they checked their watches and paced about Paddington Station while huge crowds thronged the streets to greet the first lady.

The next morning ER held a press conference at the U.S. embassy. She was startled by the size of the crowd and their blunt questions. Lunch, which King George VI and the queen hosted for the heads of "various women's services," was more agreeable. That afternoon, their majesties escorted ER through the devastation of the Blitz—"blocks upon blocks of rubble." Their first stop was St. Paul's Cathedral, to visit the faithful firefighters who had spent many nights sleeping in the crypt ready to spring into action whenever needed to save the damaged cathedral. The queen wanted ER to "stand on the steps and see what modern warfare could do to a great city." They then toured miles of devastated residential areas, from which most people were evacuated.

Although ER had seen photographs, she was "in no way prepared for the great area of destruction." In a shelter that had housed over twelve thousand people nightly, and where still some three hundred people bedded down every night, ER learned "something about fear, and the resistance to total destruction which exists in all human beings." Despite the crowding and danger, every night people retained "spirits of kindness and cheerfulness," while "those who had lost so much still managed to smile."

True to her diplomatic assignment, she sidestepped controversy, even regarding issues that most concerned her, including the future of India. She refused to meet with V. K. Krishna Menon, leader of the Indian League, and declined several invitations from groups dedicated to Indian self-rule. But she dined several times with Sir Stafford and his wife, Lady Isobel Cripps. Political activists long associated with Indian self-rule, they knew Joe Lash and still worked actively with the international student movement. On 29 October, ER wrote Lash, "Sir Stafford and Lady Cripps dined with us tonight. . . . He remembers & admires you. . . . We had a pleasant time & I liked them *both*." Tommy, however, disliked them both, writing to Lape, "Cripps seemed completely cold and tight-faced . . . and would not inspire me in spite of his brilliance. ER disagrees with me completely."

ER also dined with William Phillips, who was in London to help build Colonel William Donovan's Office of Strategic Services (OSS), the forerunner of the CIA. Until October 1941 Phillips had been ambassador to Italy, where his reputation as a bigot had been attenuated by his many good works. As the esteemed writer Iris Origo's godfather, he had helped many of her friends, including international art critic Bernard Berenson. But ER distrusted him, because of his reputation as a conservative force in Breckinridge Long's wing of the State Department, and she was no longer particularly close to his wife, Caroline Astor Drayton Phillips. They, in turn, worried about the Roosevelt partnership. After a visit to Washington in May, Phillips had observed, "At the White House Eleanor and Franklin are hardly on speaking terms. She criticizes his policies . . . and he snubs her whenever he can. It is all tragic."

A bonus of ER's weeks in England was her friendship with Clementine Churchill. Although ER never felt comfortable with Winston, she grew to admire his wife, with whom she had much in common. Far more radical than her husband, Clementine believed government had a responsibility to protect and ensure the well-being of all citizens, with a special obligation to those in need. A suffragist who believed in women's independence, she was, like ER, an enthusiastic student who had intended to go to college and always resented her mother's opposition. Opinionated and often angry, Clementine Churchill was an activist who got things done. During the Great War "she ran nine canteens for munitions workers" and fed more than five thousand people a day. During the Blitz, she successfully fought for government payments for volunteer civil defense workers, and she introduced hygiene and basic comforts to London's air raid shelters. When John Winant arrived in London, they became allies in all struggles for the greater good. To many observers, they were two of the loneliest people in London, who enjoyed, and needed, each other's company. Until Winant's arrival, Clementine had spent most of her days alone, and her children and various guests had worried about her well-being.

ER contributed to one notably stressful evening with the Churchills, at a small dinner with U.S. treasury secretary Henry Morgenthau and Lady Gertrude Denman, head of the Women's Land Army, among others. It began when Churchill asked Secretary Morgenthau if the United States was finally sending sufficient supplies to Spain. ER said that "it was a little too late" for that question, now that Franco was in control of Spain: we "should have done something to help the Loyalists during their civil war." Churchill and ER sparred. Churchill supported Franco, while ER opposed him and never doubted that the Spanish generalissimo and his people helped usher in the era of fascism in Europe. She considered the West's failure to support the Loyalists in the Spanish Civil War the great error in international politics.

Now Churchill argued heatedly that "you and I would have been the first to lose our heads if the Loyalists had won." ER replied that the loss of "my head was unimportant," whereupon he said: "'I don't want you to lose your head and neither do I want to lose mine.' Then Mrs. Churchill leaned across the table and said: 'I think perhaps Mrs. Roosevelt is right.'" Clementine's intervention sent her husband into a frenzy, and he shouted: "I have held certain beliefs for sixty years and I am not going to change now." Thereupon, Clementine rose to "signal that dinner was over." ER welcomed her support but she evidently disappeared for the remainder of that evening.

ER appreciated the many difficulties Clementine Churchill faced. "Mrs. Churchill is a very attractive, young-looking and charming person," she wrote. "One feels that, being in public life, she has had to assume a role . . . but one wonders what she is like underneath." During the many hours they spent together, "my admiration and affection for her have grown. She has had no easy role to play in life, but she has played it with dignity and charm."

ER met regularly with Lady Stella Reading, founder of the WVS, whose public service began during the 1920s when she served on Viceroy Rufus Isaacs's staff in Delhi; Isaacs was the first viceroy to champion independence, and they had married in 1931. ER was delighted that

WAC director Hobby had this opportunity to speak with Reading. For years ER had admired the WVS and sought to emulate it with her call for women volunteers, even a women's draft for national service and "a Women's Land Army." Now that the United States had entered the war, the need was great, and many women were eager to serve, yet little was done to make it possible. Only belatedly had the Women's Army Corps been created. In Britain ER and Hobby would have a chance to see all that Reading and her allies had accomplished, and learn how completely women were trained and how vigorously they worked—with respect and dignity—at their many tasks, in every service. The first lady hoped the United States might emulate Britain's approach to women in the military.

During her first week in London, ER was addressing the women of the Auxiliary Territorial Service (ATS) when air raid sirens sounded. Undoubtedly aware that the first lady was in London, Germany assaulted the city with a day of nuisance raids. Through the alarms she kept talking "without faltering," reported the *New York Times*, "thereby winning the admiration of several thousand girls who have acquired their nonchalance toward sirens" after three years of war. After her speech, the ATS women asked her how she had remained so sanguine. ER explained that she was "accustomed" to the frequent practice alarms in the United States. She told them how much she admired their work and hoped that all they had learned for wartime might one day be found useful in peacetime. When she left the camp, "1000 girls lined up along the driveway—they cheered and sang 'For She's A Jolly Good Fellow.'"

ER and her party were later driven to the largest ATS training center in Britain, where she toured a vast garage to meet the girls of the motor transport who trained as mechanics and drivers. She was impressed to see girls drive and repair "every type of army conveyance" and "change the enormous tires without too much exertion." Oveta Culp Hobby was equally impressed and commented on the "toilet kits" with combs, clothes, brushes, and other useful articles issued to the girls at the quartermaster's store. "Such kits were not issued to the WACs," she wrote, indicating it was a situation she intended to change.

When she returned to London, ER met with Margaret Biddle, who ran the American Red Cross Club for U.S. Army Nurses in Mayfair. ER found it "a delightful place" and was pleased to speak with "two Negro women Red Cross workers, recently arrived in Britain to work with Negro troops"—Gladys Martin, of Topeka, Kansas, and actress Ruth Attaway, whom ER had recently seen on the New York stage in *You Can't Take It with You.*

During her travels with Stella Reading and Clementine Churchill, visiting factory workers, carmakers, and shipbuilders, ER realized that British public opinion regarding class had changed dramatically. The rigid distinctions of her youth seemed tempered or gone—in dress, in work, in conversation. The shared agony seemed to have generated a new unity of respect and mutual concern. Women of different classes, who had never known each other, now worked "side by side, just as the men [fought] side by side. These British Isles, which we always regarded as . . . nearly frozen in their classes . . . became welded together by the war into a closely-knit community in which many of the old distinctions lost their point and from which new values emerged." During a lunch with several WVS women who daily fed dockworkers, she was told: "We used to look down on the dock-workers as the roughest element in our community. We were a little afraid of them; but now we have come to know them and will never feel that way again."

Still, life in London had a hothouse quality, and key players lived in close proximity. Randolph Churchill, Winston's only son and highly spoiled favorite child, was married to Pamela Churchill, the daughter of Lord Digby of Dorset. Their marriage was difficult, since Randolph was "a blustering bully whose drinking, gambling, and womanizing" continually embarrassed his parents and hurt Pamela. While he was away with his regiment in Egypt, Pamela worked with Stella Reading's WVS. Young and free and twenty-two, she fully enjoyed the "erotic frenzy of wartime London." She evidently met FDR's envoy W. Averell Harriman, age fifty-two, at a party in the Dorchester Hotel, where both were living, during a night of intense bombing when it seemed everybody escaped into a love affair. By the time ER arrived in 1942, their affair was well known.

ER and Tommy were staying in Winant's apartment, and Harriman lived in the same house, so ER certainly saw them together. But her only reference to Pamela, written on a slant, was about her little boy Winston, whom she saw at Chequers. "Randolph Churchill's little boy Winston," ER wrote, "is a sweet baby and exactly like the Prime Minister. They sat on the floor and played . . . and the resemblance is ridiculous."

Undoubtedly ER's observations regarding London's romances recalled FDR's recent flirtations with Norway's Princess Martha. At Hyde Park only weeks before she left, Trude Pratt had expressed shock at Princess Martha's cooing, giggly adolescent behavior, which FDR seemed to encourage. As they walked through the woods, ER explained to Trude that her husband always depended upon such Marthas for diversion and relaxation.

While ER and FDR's marital arrangement involved separate and still expanding romantic courts, ER's chosen task now was to clarify and support FDR's political goals. With her four sons deployed in different battlefields, she sought to do something decisive each day. Just before Elliott's division left for North Africa, she set out to visit him and meet his photo-reconnaissance unit. The rain poured, and her driver got lost. ER was code-named "Rover," and after several frantic calls to the embassy, with the message "Rover has lost her pup," she was taken to her destination—where Elliott's troops had been standing in the rain waiting for her, and were soaked.

Senior army officers noted that ER seemed entirely satisfied by all she saw. She did not publicly criticize the discrimination faced by black troops, least of all the menial service jobs that limited and restricted them, despite the range of their skills, training, and education.* Wherever she went, the press noted, she shook hands and spent significant time in conversation with Negro service members. In London, she was pleased when one white officer, the colonel in charge of "young colored trainees," told her "his men were the best in the Army." She determined to see Secretary of War Stimson upon her return regarding race issues. Almost daily throughout the war, she sent letters to Stimson—and to General Marshall—to relay complaints and demand needed improvements. General Marshall assigned two assistants to deal with ER's correspondence. But during her British trip, her public statements were limited to words of satisfaction.

At FDR's special request, she made an overnight visit to Queen Mary in Badminton. Mary had been most cordial to Sara Delano Roosevelt during her 1934 visit, and ER thought her husband considered her "in

---

*Before Pearl Harbor there were only 97,000 black troops; by December 1942, over 467,000; by 1945, over one million African-Americans were in uniform, almost half overseas, and all engaged in the "Double V" campaign—victory in war, and victory against racial hatred, discrimination, and injustice. Moore, *Black Soldiers*, pp. 29–30.

some ways rather like his mother." Her visit to Badminton House, where the Queen Mother spent the war years with her niece, the Duchess of Beaufort, was important to FDR.

Queen Mary met ER and Tommy at the door, and the evening was rewarding if cold and spare. Dinner was "not . . . hilarious," and their rooms were vast and frigid. Tommy retreated to her bed as quickly as possible, to get under the warm comforter. But ER spent a good hour in conversation with the Queen Mother and her niece and left with a feeling of "real affection" and complete admiration for Queen Mary, whose generosity and democratic instincts were manifest. For example, she told ER that one evening she had stopped her car to pick up an American GI. After a cordial conversation, she asked if he knew who was giving him the ride. He did not. She told him, "I am Queen Mary." He said, "I'm from Missouri and you'll have to show me." Evidently she gave him a token of her identity and later entirely enjoyed the story. She gave ER a photo of herself sawing a dead tree limb—to prove to FDR she cared about conservation quite as much as he did. No other present from her trip gave FDR "more pleasure than that photograph."

The Queen Mother was impressed with ER and wrote her brother, Lord Athlone, "I liked her very much. She is very intelligent and her grasp of what our women are doing here is splendid and she hopes to do much in the USA to wake up the women there to emulate our manifold activities. She is on the go from morning till night and I fear will kill her unfortunate secretary, Miss Thompson."

ER and Tommy left early the next morning for a tour of day care nurseries, run by the government for industrially employed mothers. ER hoped to emulate them since they solved "very much the same" problems faced by American women. The women's husbands were off to war, they required employment, the government sought their services, and their children required care.

Some great landed estates were being used for "country nurseries," where preschool children lived full-time. Other estates were used by the new Women's Land Army, where former typists or housewives now worked the land and herded cattle and sheep. These changes, in addition to all the water wagons and community shops established in bombed-out areas, enabled everybody to "get on with the war" in a "spirit of cheerfulness" that ER found "extraordinary."

Finally, on 8 November, good news arrived. Operation Torch, the Anglo-American landing in North Africa under General Eisenhower's command, had begun, giving "the British people a tremendous lift," ER wrote. Months of defeat, "disappointment and disaster" now gave way to feelings of vast relief that finally "we are fighting together." ER was moved by expressions of gratitude for the Americans' participation and hope for the invasion's success.

On 7 November FDR made a speech, broadcast in France and North Africa, in which he explained, "We come among you solely to defeat . . . your enemies. . . . We assure you that once the menace of Germany and Italy is removed . . . we shall quit your territory at once." ER noted in her 10 November column that "we assured that nation [France] that we had no desire to take over any of her territory [in Africa], and that at the end of the war whatever we were obliged to invade, we would return." The promise to restore French colonies, however, conflicted with the promise of the Atlantic Charter.

The massive Allied armada had landed in three task forces. The western task force, under General George Patton, landed in Morocco at Casablanca; the center force disembarked at the Algerian port of Oran; and the eastern task force landed in Algiers. On all fronts, news of the early-morning landings was broadcast in London with enthusiasm.

All these areas were under the rule of Vichy France. After the French debacle and the June 1940 armistice, FDR's administration had given Vichy France full diplomatic recognition, hoping to encourage the collaborators to work against the Nazis, in what has been called his "Vichy gamble." In preparation for the November 1942 Allied invasion, FDR's State Department representative in North Africa, arch-conservative Robert Murphy, had chosen Henri Giraud to order the Vichy French forces to cooperate. But they ignored him and mounted a fierce resistance. It was what FDR's Vichy gamble had hoped to forestall.

As the fighting intensified, Admiral François Darlan was unexpectedly in Algiers to visit his son Alain, who was hospitalized, stricken with polio. Darlan was Pétain's most senior deputy and commander in chief of Vichy France's armed forces. Eisenhower asked him, in that high-level capacity, to negotiate a deal for a cease-fire to end the resistance, in exchange for French control of North Africa. At first Darlan refused. But on 11 November Nazi troops occupied the rest of France, ending Germany's armistice with Vichy. Darlan thereupon ordered a cease-fire, and French resistance ended throughout Algeria and Morocco. Some 3,000 lives had already been lost on each side during this most complex landing in military history, and this agreement saved an estimated 55,000 lives.

From 11 to 13 November, Eisenhower negotiated the so-called Darlan Deal. In essence, Vichy representatives retained sovereignty in North Africa, and French military forces remained under Vichy command. There was no effort to repeal or modify Vichy's anti-Jewish laws or restrictions. Darlan became high commissioner of North Africa, in command of the French SS, which he had previously done much to create. Charles de Gaulle, leader of the Free French, was entirely excluded from the deal.

The Darlan Deal was a fascist victory that outraged Allied observers and frightened all governments in exile. British leaders of all parties were appalled. Journalist Edward R. Murrow angrily asked, "Are we fighting the Nazis or sleeping with them?" To play thus "with traitors" was no path to victory but moral loss. Wendell Willkie gloomily lamented that good people everywhere "felt betrayed and baffled." ER made every effort to avoid discussion of the Darlan Deal, which exploded during the most exhausting phase of her journey across the Midlands, followed by a flight to Belfast and a tour of Londonderry; then a flight to Scotland and full days in Glasgow and Edinburgh.

Instead, she chose to speak of Allied unity and the need to organize for peace while war raged. On 11 November, Armistice Day, 1918, she reflected on the "futility" of former peace plans, ignored and discarded. She now prayed that "we will accept reality and grasp the fact that we are part of a world which cannot be divided and treated in sections."

On her last day in Glasgow, ER embarked on an open steamer and boated down the Clyde. When they disembarked at Brown's yard, they were met by "a big gathering of workers"—who joined the vaudeville singer Sir Harry Lauder to sing "To the End of the Road." Tommy was told this was the first time work had been stopped since they were visited by the king and queen. As she departed, Sir Harry took ER's hand and sang "Will ye no' come back again?" ER was deeply moved, and said she hoped indeed to return.

Bearing gifts of heather and shortbread for FDR, ER and her party entrained for London. Returning to John Winant's apartment seemed like coming home, "and it was good to have a bath in a warm room."

During her final days in London, ER visited with relatives, allies, and old school chums. Her last London lunch was with thirty-five "very old Allenswood school friends." In her diary, ER confided, "I suppose I look as changed as they do, but I hardly recognized any of them." She took tea with the entire royal family and on 13 November "went to report on all I had seen to Her Majesty, Queen Elizabeth." They spent "two solid hours" alone. At Winant's she met with the Soviet ambassador and Madame Maisky, who urged her to visit Russia. A large farewell tea that afternoon was followed by an intimate dinner with her beloved aunt Maude and uncle David Gray, "a delightful evening talking of home people and happenings."

The trip concluded with a visit from Clementine Churchill, who arrived with a personal note from Winston: "You certainly have left golden footprints behind you." The journalist Chalmers Roberts agreed, reporting to his chief at the Office of War Information that ER "has done more to bring a real understanding of the spirit of the United States to the people of Britain than any other single American who has ever visited these islands."

ER and Tommy departed at night on a military transport with six ferry pilots who had just delivered a bomber. Churchill and Winant did not want to take any chances with her safety, and FDR agreed: "I don't care how you send her home. Just send her."

On 17 November at nine-thirty a.m., as her plane landed, ER was "surprised to see the Secret Service standing around several cars, which I knew meant the President was there to meet us." That day she had lunch with FDR "in his office, which is something I only do on very particular occasions." That evening "the President and I dined alone." ER's surprise at FDR's interest was revealed by a note she penned on the last page of her diary: "I really think Franklin was glad to see me back and at dinner I gave a detailed account of such things as I could tell quickly to answer his questions. I think he even read this diary & to my surprise he had also read my columns!"

ER felt acutely the ways the United States lagged behind Britain. There women and men worked together with shared dignity; troops of different races were not segregated; and everybody contributed all they could for community betterment. But in the United States, separate facilities, separate training, inferior equipment remained the rule. Routinely insulted, Black troops could not eat in post exchanges—they could only "buy refreshments" to take outside. Routine discrimination continued throughout the war in numerous and surprising ways: "In some Army camps, black soldiers were forced to sit behind German or Italian POWs for all entertainment," including films and USO shows.

ER made no public criticism, but she wondered what it meant to "fight for freedom" in a segregated military that discriminated in so many ways. She visited Norman Davis of the Red Cross, Secretary of War Henry Stimson, and General Hap Arnold—who was relieved that she seemed "very temperate" with words of praise for the work of black troops and their officers. Everybody understood there was more work to be done, but ultimately only minimal changes were made.

The Darlan Deal now required attention. Almost everybody she respected on her journey had expressed fury over U.S. support for Darlan, who was known as a violently anti-British warrior and as the person responsible for the anti-Jewish laws in all Vichy-controlled areas. Winant, who was personally close to de Gaulle, was stunned, although he urged momentary silence. He persuaded Harold Nicolson and other parliamentarians that the Darlan Deal was a temporary military measure. "I do not want us to abandon de Gaulle," Nicolson wrote in his diary. "But we had best keep silence over this disgraceful and most profitable episode." FDR's refusal to support de Gaulle, whom he despised, cooled U.S. relations with Britain, and it was in that context that Churchill delivered his emphatic speech on 10 November: "I have not become the King's First Minister in order to preside over the liquidation of the British Empire. . . . Here we are and here we stand, a veritable rock of salvation in this drifting world."

Treasury Secretary Henry Morgenthau confided to ER his upset over U.S. support for Darlan in North Africa. ER was his confidante for all personally upsetting issues, and he trusted her "more than anyone outside of his own family." ER not only admired Morgenthau, she also trusted and depended on both him and his wife, Elinor, with whom she shared intimacies and personal concerns that she shared with no one else.

Morgenthau had met de Gaulle in London and, like Winant, respected him. When he learned of de Gaulle's exclusion and the details of the Darlan Deal, he protested to the War Department. Secretary Henry Stimson met with him and defended Robert Murphy's vision. Morgenthau countered that Darlan "was a most ruthless person who sold many thousands of people into slavery, and . . . to use a man like that in these times" was to lose the war.

The next day Morgenthau called on FDR to speak about North Africa, "something that affects my soul." He insisted that the president make a public statement to assure Americans and the Allies that the United States did not support or condone fascism. FDR's closest advisers, including Hopkins, Rosenman, and Archibald MacLeish, now representing the Office of War Information (OWI) agreed.

On 17 November FDR issued a statement to the press, to the effect that General Eisenhower's "political arrangements" in northern and western Africa were temporary. "We are opposed to Frenchmen who support Hitler and the Axis. . . . I have requested the liberation of all persons in North Africa who have been imprisoned because they opposed the efforts of the Nazis to dominate the world, and I have asked for the abrogation of all laws and decrees inspired by Nazi governments or Nazi ideologists."

Then on Christmas Eve 1942, a twenty-year-old French youth shot Darlan as he entered his office in Algiers. Immediately apprehended, Bonnier de la Chapelle was condemned by a secret military tribunal and executed by firing squad on 26 December. History will always speculate about the real identity of the assassin who had declared that he hated Vichy, the enemy of France. Rumors of Anglo-American involvement would persist. But even after Darlan's assassination, Vichy remained in charge in North Africa, and its fascist repression continued. With their alliance in disarray, FDR and Churchill agreed to meet in Casablanca in January to negotiate workable compromises.

For the rest of December, ER turned her attention to the Nazi massacres of Jews. For months Nazi atrocities committed against Jews and Poles had been much in the news in Britain, with grim details of forced removals and massacres. Protest was vigorous: John Winant received more than two hundred petitions from British organizations demanding that the government take action to stop Nazi war crimes.

The massacre at Lidice, six miles northwest of Prague, on 10 June 1942 was widely reported, in great detail. Most of the residents were killed; the town's eighty-eight children and their remaining mothers were sent to concentration camps. The massacre was said to be in reprisal for the assassination of SS general Reinhard Heydrich, who had been shot in Prague by Czech patriots who allegedly hid in Lidice. The Nazis boasted that the village "was now forever erased from the map and the memory of the world." In response to the ghastly reports, in June Britain endorsed a fact-finding UN Commission on Atrocities.

ER devoted two columns to the destruction of Lidice, promising that "none of us will ever forget a little village named Lidice." Indeed, the eradication of the village had captured the imagination of American artists only two days after the news reached the United States, as the Writers' War Board, comprising thousands of U.S. writers, including ER, "resolved to do all in its power to make sure that Lidice . . . would never be forgotten." Edna St. Vincent Millay wrote *The Murder of Lidice*, a dramatic verse narrative that was initially broadcast on 19 October over NBC "with a distinguished cast," including ER's friend Alexander Woollcott. "It was also short-waved to England and other countries" and published proudly as "one of the finest pieces of true propaganda to come out of the war." ER, deeply moved by Millay's work, gave her book to many for Christmas 1942.

Other June 1942 news articles headlined Hitler's extermination policies: "1,000,000 Jews Slain by Nazis." A "vast slaughterhouse for Jews in Eastern Europe" condemned countless men, women, and children throughout German-occupied Europe. From September through November, details of the removal and slaughter of fifty thousand Jews from the Warsaw Ghetto were reported. Cattle cars removed millions to "annihilation centers" in the East, including Chełmno, Treblinka, Bełżec, Sobibór, and Auschwitz. There "gas chambers are used" in camps established to complete the "Final Solution."

Throughout the autumn, Winant and others pressured FDR to join Britain in making a public statement against Nazi atrocities. On 5 December ER wrote, "This morning I saw that, in Poland, it was reported that more than two-thirds of the Jewish population had been massacred. There seems to be little use in voicing a protest, but somehow one cannot keep still when such horrors are going on." Protests and prayers were needed, but ER also demanded action—and intensified her work with Quaker relief and rescue agencies.

In a subsequent column, ER wrote about the resistance by the women of Poland against the Nazis. The prime minister of Poland, while visiting the United States, gave her "a message transmitted from a secret radio station in Poland" to London in September. In the message, Polish women told how they were "enduring awful times. . . . The shadows of thousands tormented to death in concentration camps in Oswiecim [Auschwitz], Ravensbruck, Oranienburg and other places hover around us. . . . We Polish women have, therefore, all joined the ranks of subterranean struggling Poland, and together with our husbands, fathers, brothers, and sons we will fight to the end. . . . We are prepared either to win or perish." Even to send that message, ER explained, was an act of tremendous courage—since if discovered it meant death, "and ten efforts were made before it was finally transmitted."

Throughout the autumn Varian Fry, who had done so much to rescue almost two thousand of Hitler's intended victims, had sent ER the details he received—and they again worked together, specifically to assist children who had escaped to Spain and Portugal. She was horrified and galvanized by Fry's powerful "The Massacre of the Jews," published in December in the *New Republic*. It presented the bitter facts of the slaughter, the ongoing failure to confront them, and specific suggestions for immediate action:

> Letters, reports, cables . . . add up to the most appalling picture of mass murder in all human history. Nor is it only the Jews who are threatened. . . . The entire Polish people may be wiped out. . . . The decimation of the Greek people is a matter of record. . . . The Nazis are systematically destroying the potential leaders of democratic movements in all the countries they have overrun. We must face the terrible truth. . . .
>
> President Roosevelt could and should speak out against these monstrous events. . . . A similar warning from Churchill might help. . . . Tribunals should be set up now to begin to amass the facts.

Fry had been told of an OWI directive that banned "mention of the massacres," which he considered "sadly mistaken." He called for broadcasts in every language "day and night." There was nothing to achieve by "appeasing" the slaughterers.

Proof the Nazis feared "news of their crimes" was that the massacres did not occur in the West; the victims were transported to the East to be destroyed. "Finally, and it is a little thing, but . . . a big thing, we can offer asylum now, without delay or red tape, to those few fortunate enough to escape." Fry rejected State Department notions of a "security risk"—which had ended his own efforts—with a very simple suggestion: "we can intern the refugees on arrival, and examine them at leisure." If there was doubt, "we can keep them interned for the duration of the war." But it would be preferable to the current visa situation, which had condemned so many "stalwart democrats" to death.

Fry's article was widely circulated in December, but there were many others. Finally, on 17 December 1942 a United Nations Declaration on the Persecution of the Jews was issued simultaneously in London, Moscow, and Washington. FDR and Stalin had agreed in principle to join the War Crimes Commission. The declaration was presented formally to the House of Commons: Samuel Silverman, MP, asked Anthony Eden if he had "any statement to make regarding the plan of the German Government to deport all Jews from the occupied countries to Eastern Europe and there put them to death before the end of the year?"

Eden replied,

> Yes, Sir, I regret to have to inform the House that reliable reports have recently reached His Majesty's Government regarding the barbarous and inhuman treatment to which Jews are being subjected in German-occupied Europe.
>
> From all the occupied countries Jews are being transported, in conditions of appalling horror and brutality, to Eastern Europe. . . . The ghettoes . . . are being systematically emptied . . . . None of those taken away are ever heard of again. [The Allied governments] and the French National Committee condemn in the strongest possible terms this bestial policy of cold-blooded extermination. . . . They re-affirm their resolution to ensure that those responsible for these crimes shall not escape retribution.

After Eden's speech, all Members of Parliament arose for a moment of silence to honor the dead.

While no similar congressional event occurred, FDR publicly announced his decision to join the effort to create the UN War Crimes Commission and declared it "official U.S. policy to punish racial and political murder"—after the war ended. It was a first step, with no reference to rescue or specific plans for asylum.

On New Year's Eve, ER applauded FDR's action as "we gathered at midnight in the President's study and drank the usual toasts," adding to them the United Nations. She considered it "a very significant toast," heralding "a permanent bond . . . in war and peace" that will gradually extend to involve all nations "into a circle of friendship." According to Sam Rosenman, FDR made another, even more notable toast with words he had never used before: "To the person who makes it possible for the President to carry on." And he raised his glass to ER.

FDR's renewed interest in her work since her return from Britain, as well as this significant toast, marked a new stage in their relationship—one of mutual respect and shared commitments even if their goals were not always the same. She concluded her New Year's column with her own toast "to the women of the country, with whom I feel a very special bond. We have the same anxieties and the same sense of frustration very often, because we feel we cannot do enough in the great war effort."

ER wrote Anna about the grandchildren in and out for the holidays, "I'm sure the kids were happy, they don't anticipate disasters." As for herself, "I wake up in the night & imagine every horror & cannot go to sleep again." But her friends were a great comfort. Joe and Trude, Tommy and Hick, Elinor Morgenthau and Isabella Greenway, all kept her company and socially busy.

ER reserved special holiday evenings for Earl and for Hick, who continued to live in the White House. Although she no longer occupied the center of ER's heart, she remained a close confidante. Some of her happiest times were with Trude and Joe, whose very company lightened her burdens by bringing her joy.

> I don't know if I can put in words what I want to say of gratitude & love to you and to Trude. . . . I've come of late years to dread . . . the formal impersonal things I have to do. I'm always with so many people & always so alone inside except with a very few people, so—I thank you—both—for sharing precious hours with me & giving me so much happiness.

ER was devoted to Joe and Trude in part because of their shared political vision and activism. That they had transcended the limitations of ethnicity and religion gave her hope for the future.

ER and FDR continued to live in peace within their two distinct courts. The president never asked Hick to move out of the White House, and he continued to meet and welcome ER's friends and allies. Nevertheless, upon his return from the Casablanca Conference, ER and FDR would face a new difficulty in their relationship.

In preparation for the conference, FDR met with Milton Eisenhower, whom he had sent to North Africa in December to investigate the reasons for the political upheaval over the Darlan Deal. Eisenhower presented his full report to FDR regarding Algiers. They also discussed the need for a new propaganda offensive and the expansion of the work of the Office of War Information (OWI), which subsequently would be headed by C. D. Jackson, an expert on psychological warfare.

As Eisenhower rose to leave, FDR "motioned for me to sit down again. He was in a pensive mood." First he asked about agriculture in Algeria and Morocco, and they discussed the ravages of war on fertile lands "between the sea and the Atlas Mountains." In climate and topography, "the coastal region was similar to the San Joaquin, Sacramento, and Salinas valleys." Before the war, French North Africa exported surpluses of fruits, vegetables, wool, olive oil, and "very good wine" to most of Europe. Nazi seizures disrupted everything; now scarcity dominated.

"President Roosevelt was deeply interested. I knew from previous discussions . . . that he had an amazing knowledge of world food and fiber production. He seemed to know a great deal about every major river system and drainage basin in the world." Now he pondered the future: "You know, Milton, when the war is over it would be wonderful to go to North Africa and trap the waters that now flow from the Atlas Mountains into the ocean. We could build dams and create one of the finest irrigation systems in the world." Although Eisenhower agreed with FDR "on questions of human values and programs," he was a fiscal conservative who knew FDR was "needling" him when he added, "'Of course, it would cost a lot of money but who cares about cost?'" In the end "we enjoyed a good laugh together."

While Eisenhower was not disturbed by FDR's fantasies, others found FDR's attitude regarding North Africa—indeed the entire globe— imperial. His opposition to empire was well known, yet he often spoke as if he intended to dominate if not control the geopolitical future, as if he alone might make decisions. As journalist John Gunther observed, FDR spoke about "the French empire as if it were his personal possession and would say things like 'I haven't quite decided what to do about Tunis.'" And ER continually urged a democratic structure in which all nations participated.

British foreign secretary Anthony Eden wrote in his memoirs:

> Roosevelt was familiar with the history and geography of Europe . . . but the sweeping opinions which he built upon it were alarming in their cheerful fecklessness. He seemed to see himself disposing of the fate of many lands, allied no less than enemy. He did all this with so much grace that it was not easy to dissent. Yet it was too like a conjurer, skillfully juggling with balls of dynamite, whose nature he failed to understand.

On 9 January, as FDR departed for the Casablanca Conference to meet with Churchill, ER imagined that he would act on behalf of rescue and a humane geopolitical future. But in fact FDR's goal was to achieve Vichy and Free French cooperation in North Africa, as well as a new and expanded U.S. economic presence there. From 15 to 25 January FDR and Churchill tried to heal the Allied fright engendered by FDR's opposition to de Gaulle and his continued insistence on his preferred French general, Henri Giraud, in North Africa. They arranged a shotgun wedding between de Gaulle and Giraud, who shook hands and were photographed together. There was reason to believe they would work in harmony for a free France.

Then on 19 January Giraud announced the appointment of a Vichy administrator, Marcel Peyrouton, as governor general of Algeria on the grounds that he was "the only man" fully knowledgeable about Arab issues in French North Africa. His appointment sent shock waves through all Free French and progressive circles and was immediately opposed by liberals within FDR's own administration and throughout the United States.

FDR's sons Elliott and Frank were present, and when FDR discussed empire with him, Elliott took notes. Churchill supported de Gaulle, FDR said, because their colonial interests coincided. They "mean to maintain their hold on their colonies. . . . That's why Winston is so anxious to keep de Gaulle in his corner." And de Gaulle was as eager to maintain France's colonial empire. FDR believed de Gaulle sought "to achieve one-man government in France. I can't imagine a man I would distrust more." Although FDR did not confide his own commitment to replace Anglo-French interests in oil-rich territories, he concluded that the "colonial system means war. Exploit the resources of an India, a Burma, a Java; take all the wealth out of those countries, but never put anything back into them . . . education, decent standards of living, minimum health requirements—all you are doing is storing up the kind of trouble that leads to war." FDR told his sons that he and Churchill did not agree. India required a measure of freedom "at once." The United Nations at war's end would change the world. It was three-thirty in the morning when their discussion ended.

Also at Casablanca, FDR and Churchill agreed to postpone yet again the much-promised cross-Channel invasion. Instead, they would open the second front on Churchill's preferred target—Europe's "soft under-belly," across the Mediterranean into Sicily. Harry Hopkins, George Marshall, and General Eisenhower were surprised and disappointed.

FDR did refer to Jews at Casablanca, but not in a way that had anything to do with rescue. Secretly, and not for attribution, he proposed that North African resettlement projects restrict the number of Jews who were allowed to become professionals. Evidently in agreement with geographer Isaiah Bowman's fantastical M Project, to spread Jews as thinly as possible across the world, FDR proposed a quota system whereby Jews might still be attorneys and physicians but would no longer be permitted "to overcrowd the professions." It would ensure Jews "full rights" but eliminate "understandable complaints" such as Germans had towards Jews, "namely that while they represented a small part of the population, over 50% of the lawyers, doctors, schoolteachers, college professors, etc., in Germany were Jews."

When he returned home to Washington, ER was pleased to see her husband fully relaxed and asked him about the shotgun wedding. FDR explained that General de Gaulle, while a patriotic soldier, was also "a politician and a fanatic and there are, I think, in him almost the makings of a dictator." In her memoir, ER reported that her husband never "changed his mind" about de Gaulle, "and I do not think that between

them there was any real understanding." FDR insisted that under Vichy
rule in North Africa, "97% of the political prisoners are freed." Liberal
protest against the regime irritated FDR but otherwise failed to impress
him. "The President is so obviously annoyed at anyone who dares question the arrangements in Africa," Trude wrote Joe.

Although unable to understand her husband's intransigence, ER never
publicly criticized his position, nor did she refer to his misrepresentation
of facts about Vichy North Africa. Privately, however, she continued to
pressure him. In mid-February, Henry Morgenthau confirmed for her
that her "fears about North African civil affairs are justified," as she told
Lash, and asked her "to go on prodding FDR because he feels everyone
except myself will give up."

China was key to FDR's vision for a future of world peace—and despite
all rumblings of civil war tensions between the Communist movement
and reactionary warlords, ongoing since 1911, efforts to maintain a united
front alliance against the Japanese invaders continued. The three Soong
sisters, all in their forties, among themselves represented the forever tense
spectrum of China's politics and key to the future. Ching-ling was the
widow of Sun Yat-sen, the founder and first president of the Republic of
China. Ayling was married to H. H. Kung, the republic's finance minister. And Wellesley-educated Mayling was the wife of Chiang Kai-shek,
the republic's current Nationalist leader.

In 1941 Madame Chiang, as Mayling Soong Chiang was usually
known, had provided James Roosevelt with gracious hospitality when
FDR sent him, along with his military mentor Major Evans Carlson, to
"trouble spots." The trip had been "difficult" after recent ulcer surgery, and
"when he visited the Generalissimo and Madame Chiang . . . she immediately understood [James's needs] and with her own hands had prepared
the proper kind of food for him. . . . You can understand that from that
time on Madame Chiang had a special place in my heart," ER recalled.

In mid-November 1942 Madame Chiang traveled to New York to
demand more aid for China, and undergo ulcer surgery herself. In advance
she sent ER a magnificent tapestry as a gift with these words: "The world
of war and woe is but a passing thing, however necessary it may be. For
over the edge of the horizon lies a path leading to universal harmony and

world brotherhood." ER was charmed by her rhetoric. China scholar Owen Lattimore, whom FDR had appointed in October 1941 to be Chiang's adviser, was sympathetic to Madame Chiang. So was Major Carlson, who supported Chinese cooperatives and the end of racial bigotries, in accord with ER's beliefs. ER was therefore initially inclined to believe Chiang's democratic rhetoric.

When she met Madame Chiang, ER was moved: she "seemed so small and delicate as she lay in her hospital bed that I had a desire to help her and take care of her as I would have if she had been my own daughter." FDR had asked her to inform Madame Chiang that he and Churchill had agreed on additional aid for China. He knew she wanted more aid for China's war effort against Japan as well as Chinese equality in the United Nations.

When ER delivered the message, however, she witnessed another aspect of Mayling Soong Chiang. Furious to have been excluded from the decision-making Casablanca Conference, she held forth with a torrent of bitter resentment that "mingled fire and ice." China was one of the United Nations and considered itself one of the world's four primary nations. "Global strategy could only be made by all . . . and if nations did not cooperate as equals during the war, no good peace was possible. China subscribed to the Atlantic Charter and was fighting for the Four Freedoms, not for herself alone, but for all peoples."

According to Joe Lash, ER, who was always "sensitive to the global nature of 'white supremacy,'" listened to Madame's outburst "with sympathy." In fact she admired China's independent, eloquent first lady and invited her to Hyde Park to convalesce, then to stay at the White House for as long as she liked.

FDR continued to negotiate for significant military and financial support for China, and in preparation for the creation of the United Nations, he made plans to meet personally with Chiang Kai-shek and to formally recognize China as an equal among the four great powers. Churchill and Stalin strenuously objected, as did the president's own advisers, who considered Chiang's regime brutal and corrupt and resented his failure actually to fight the Japanese. But FDR agreed immediately to ER's invitation to host Madame Chiang at the White House. She arrived on 17 February 1943—with a complicated entourage, unexpected demands, and astonishing manners.

Of her traveling staff of forty, only two nurses and her two assistants—
a niece and nephew, the children of her sister Ailing—moved into the
White House. Madame's behavior to the staff was surly, marked by clap-
ping and barking for immediate attention; some were appalled, but ER
seemed mostly surprised and rather amused. Tommy was not at all
amused and wrote Lape, "I think she is able and very lovely to look at, but
she is a prima donna, temperamental and [considers] the Chinese people . . . superior to *all* other people. . . . I think they are decidedly rude."
Madame Chiang "has a niece with her who is a curious, rather neuter
gender person, dresses like a boy . . . very small, aged 23, and a nephew
who looks normal." But ER, Tommy noted, "is quite impressed with
[Madame Chiang] and argues against my opinion."

Initially, ER was persuaded that Madame Chiang supported democracy in China. On 18 February Madame Chiang delivered an hourlong
address to a joint session of Congress and received a standing ovation,
which filled ER with "a great feeling of pride" and seemed to her unprecedented. Their cheers, she wrote, "marked the recognition of a woman
who, through her own personality and her own service, has achieved a
place in the world, not merely as the wife of Generalissimo Chiang Kai-
shek, but as a representative of her people."

On 24 February, ER invited Madame Chiang to her press conference.
The wide-ranging session touched on the need for an equal rights amendment both in the United States and in China. Madame Chiang said, "I
feel strongly that since the men expect us to bear over half the responsibility it is up to them to give us equal privileges. I have never known
brains to have any sex." When asked how China had endured so long
under the dreadful siege, Madame Chiang replied, "I think we are a very
old nation and we realize that spiritual values are eternal." Individually,
we only live "but a few years . . . but the nation" endures.

But ER slowly recognized Madame Chiang's cruel, even ruthless,
aspects. At one dinner party, FDR asked her how she would deal with a
labor leader like John L. Lewis, who was about to call a miners' strike.
Gracefully, without a word spoken, her "beautiful small hand came
up . . . and slid across her throat. . . . Franklin looked across at me to
make sure I had seen." Presumably FDR told ER about Chiang's anti-
union atrocities, as well as the anti-student and anti-Communist slaugh-

ters, like the one on 7 January 1941, when Chiang's forces massacred nine thousand troops of Yan'an's Communist Fourth Army.*

The insult to democracy that definitively turned ER against her, however, occurred when Madame Chiang refused to speak at a program sponsored by the NAACP, even after ER had negotiated for them to appear together. She refused even to meet with Walter White. Since ER had once described her to FDR as "a sweet, gentle and pathetic figure," it gave FDR "keen pleasure to tease me about my lack of perception." By then he was eager for her to leave.

Madame Chiang left Washington for a national tour to raise money for United China Relief. She appeared at a Madison Square Garden rally chaired by Wendell Willkie and later at the Hollywood Bowl, with film stars and thirty thousand of their fans. Afterward hotel staff in Chicago and Los Angeles told Tommy outlandish stories of Madame Chiang's "extravagance and arrogance" during her visits, at which point ER finally understood the antipathy she aroused. Henry Morgenthau noted, "The President . . . is just crazy to get her out of the country" before her rude manners get discovered and "spoil her public image—and with it his policy."

Before Madame Chiang left the United States in June, she encouraged ER to consider making a lengthy visit to China. In a late-night conversation, FDR acknowledged to his wife that he recognized Madame Chiang's "brilliance." "F. said one most interesting thing," she told Lash, "namely that he looked for less trouble between us & Russia & China than between any of us & Great Britain." ER believed FDR's true anticolonial sentiments underlay those words.

In December 1942, FDR had dispatched diplomat William Phillips, his trusted friend, to New Delhi as his personal emissary to India. ER objected, assuming that Phillips would merely support Churchill's commitment to

---

*At this time the Communist and Nationalist troops were supposed to be allied to fight the invading Japanese. The nine thousand-strong Communist force consisted of three thousand political workers and students, four thousand troops, and two thousand medical personnel and their families. On 7 January 1941 at Maolin some fifty thousand Kuomintang troops surrounded and slaughtered them. U.S. and Allied reporters and diplomats protested, and FDR threatened to cut off aid to Chiang. See Suyin, *Eldest Son*, pp. 174–75; Suyin, *Morning Deluge*, pp. 371–76; and Smedley, *Great Road*, pp. 374–80.

the empire and urged FDR to send Winant instead. The leaders of the Quit India movement were still in prison during Phillips's tour (which lasted from 11 January to 25 April 1943). From his jail cell, Mahatma Gandhi held a protracted fast from 10 February to 2 March—which generated worldwide sympathy. George Bernard Shaw told the Tagore Society, "The imprisonment of Mohandas K. Gandhi is the stupidest blunder. . . . It and the unpardonable flogging business associated with it has wiped out our moral case against Hitler. The King should release Gandhi unconditionally as an act of grace . . . and apologize for the mental defectiveness of his cabinet. That would do what is possible to save the Indian situation."

Phillips was not allowed to visit either Gandhi or Congress Party leader Jawaharlal Nehru in prison. Arguing that his services as FDR's special envoy would be incomplete without a conversation with Congress Party leaders, he appealed to the British viceroy Lord Linlithgow, who responded by suggesting he go "on a tiger hunt." Churchill himself "had put Gandhi off-limits" to Phillips.

But Phillips wrote full reports for FDR, in which he favored India's immediate independence. There were twenty thousand Congress activists in prison, he reported, and "growing dislike of the British and disillusion with us." On 3 March, he reported that India was part of "the new idea which was sweeping over the world: freedom for oppressed peoples. This movement had been given great impetus by the Atlantic Charter." FDR was surprised. "Please read this from Bill Phillips," he wrote to Hopkins. "It is amazingly radical for a man like Bill, but he has been there fairly long now and has his feet on the ground." Decency demanded action.

ER concurred, relieved to have been wrong about Phillips. "To throw [the Congress activists] in jail where they can do nothing is absurd," she wrote Joe. Phillips thinks "the British viceroy is stupid & obstinate," and he had recommended to Churchill that negotiations among all the leaders should be initiated and a program to lead to India's freedom be "inaugurated at once."

When Phillips returned to Washington in May, FDR was "very complimentary" about his work. That week Phillips went to the State Department and met with Breckinridge Long, who was also surprised by his perspective, noting in his diary that Phillips "says the British are obdurate about Gandhi and about self-government. . . . Bill is highly critical of the

English. He was always an Anglophile. . . . To hear him now was . . . unexpected and strange."

Phillips then went to the British embassy, where he met with Churchill himself. The visit was unsettling: "the great man thumped the table and screamed at him a la Hitler," Phillips told his wife afterward. To the Roosevelts, he described his meeting with the prime minister as useless—Churchill was not interested. In the end Churchill's view prevailed, despite all the protests against Britain's brutality. FDR decided to step back and instead of returning Phillips to India sent him to London with the OSS. The future of India would have to await the war's end.*

Eager to be part of her husband's grand design for a secure and peaceful future, ER made plans to visit Russia and China. But to her dismay, FDR decided they were premature, since he planned to meet Chiang and Stalin first. He wanted ER to go to New Zealand, Australia, and the Pacific islands for at least a month. Although crestfallen, she did not protest.

During the spring and summer of 1943, the significant differences between the president and the first lady intensified. ER invited a delegation of eminent German refugees to the White House for dinner with FDR and Henry Wallace. Among the guests were Trude Pratt's friend Paul Hagen; Paul Tillich, of the Union Theological Seminary; Adolf Loewe and Hans Staudinger of the New School; and Friedrich Pollock of Columbia University. The economists "Loewe and Pollock are Jews," Wallace noted; Tillich "is a good friend of both Reinhold and Richard Niebuhr," and all were connected with Germany's "Christian Socialism" movement. At the dinner table ER requested they outline possible directions for postwar Europe. Their learned conversation did not engage FDR, who had no interest in their independent socialist views.

During this time FDR became increasingly distant from ER, and his good friend and cousin Daisy Suckley called him "the loneliest man in

---

*Gandhi's time in prison was an unmitigated disaster. In December 1943, his wife of sixty-two years—Kasturbai, called Ba, or Mother—died in his arms. Also in 1943 a famine in Bengal took the lives of almost two million Indians. Britain did not undertake emergency food measures until Lord Wavell became viceroy in October. Gandhi and his associates were released from prison on 6 May 1944.

the world." Suckley, who visited the White House frequently to keep FDR company, disapproved of ER's friends, particularly Pratt and Lash.

Suckley was not alone in her disapproval. The Secret Service considered Joe Lash, a Spanish Civil War veteran, and Trude Pratt, a scholar, philanthropist, and anti-Nazi activist, "questionable." As her friendship with Joe and Trude deepened, ER herself became suspect.

The FBI had earlier investigated her closest assistants Tommy Thompson and Edith Helm. When she learned of it, she had directly confronted Hoover and protested his "Gestapo tactics." Now she was outraged to learn she personally was a subject of "investigation."

In March ER and Tommy spent two days in Chicago with Joe, who was now serving in the U.S. Army Air Force and was posted nearby at Chanute Air Field. Upon leaving the Blackstone Hotel, they were told that "G-2 operatives had shadowed her" and "bugged their rooms." According to Tommy, "what the hotel people thought was an FBI agent asked all kinds of questions about ER's guests, particularly Joe Lash who spent Friday and Saturday night with us. . . . It turned out that the agent was Army Intelligence and they have been shadowing Joe Lash constantly. ER was furious."

Joe's Spanish Civil War service was the issue, they understood, and everyone who "went over to Spain with the Abraham Lincoln brigade" was "suspect and being watched." Joe told ER about the searches he had endured in his room at the base. He understood that he would always be a subject "of special scrutiny."

The Counter Intelligence Corps (CIC) probe, which was either independent of or in cooperation with Hoover's FBI, collected letters and information from bugs in the wall and clippings of newspaper articles by such "Reds" as Harold Laski. On 17 March 1943 the CIC concluded there was a "gigantic conspiracy participated in by Subject [Lash] and Trude Pratt but also by ER, Wallace, Morgenthau, etc." The conspiracy was supposedly initiated by their disapproval of FDR's ongoing "Vichy gamble," a conclusion reached in part from something Trude had written to Joe: "I spent a rather terrible hour reading [the documents about Allied policy in North Africa]. They apparently all came from the Vice President and ER seemed troubled because more and more often [Henry Wallace] gives her those things and never shows them to the President. She wonders why he does not feel he can." Some of the investigators' personal observations were equally twisted. For example, Joe had written to ER in gratitude for their Blackstone night together: "I'm sorry that I was such a drowsy soul after dinner, but it was nicer drowsing in the darkness with you stroking my forehead than playing gin rummy." From such words the CIC determined that ER and Lash were "intimate."*

ER was distraught both for them and for herself. She spoke with Harry Hopkins and General George Marshall to "insist that Army intelligence respect her privacy." Hopkins and Marshall assured her the surveillance would be stopped, but she suspected that it would not. Tommy thought, from subsequent conversations with ER, that either Hopkins "isn't playing straight with ER or else his information isn't very reliable."

The historical record has confirmed some things. We do know that FDR gave Hoover a free hand to wiretap at will—although it was entirely illegal. We know that FDR enjoyed Hoover's intimate gossip and loved reading his secret documents. We know that FDR told Henry Wallace, several times, and with a certain amusement, that the FBI's file on his wife "would make her appear to be the worst enemy of the United States."

But many questions about the surveillance involving ER remain: Did FDR know that his wife's letters were read and her conversations monitored? Did he order the coverage? Did he read their correspondence? Did they ever discuss the situation? And we will never know if ER—after she learned of the bugs and mail cover—continued, even intensified, her correspondence with Joe and Trude, more fully to communicate with her husband. We can only ponder the effect upon him when he read the letters that caused Hoover's agents to conclude the existence of a vast conspiracy involving Morgenthau and Wallace.

*When Lash received his full file in the 1970s, he learned that military agents not only knew about his time spent with ER and Trude; they actually intended to arrest him for "sexual intercourse" on "morals charges." He was to be arrested either without publicity or with "sufficient publicity that ER would not care to intervene in the matter." Theoharis, *Secret Files of Hoover*, pp. 59–65. Theoharis notes that General Marshall was so "disturbed" by the excesses of the Counter Intelligence Corps, he ordered it disbanded and its domestic files destroyed. Military Intelligence Division officials passed on their reports to FBI director Hoover. See also Wiener, *Enemies*, pp. 74–108 passim.

The Nazi defeat at Stalingrad on 2 February 1943 gave rise to a wave of protest against Hitler within Germany. Posters and leaflets saying "Freedom!" "Down with Hitler!" and "Restore Democracy!" appeared at the University of Munich and in many German and Austrian cities. The White Rose, a student group organized at the University of Munich in May 1942, issued leaflets that were a call to arms and were meant to fire up student protesters by informing them of the atrocities committed in their name:

> There is great ferment in the German nation. . . . Are we to sacrifice the rest of German youth to the basest power . . . ? Never again! The day of reckoning has come, the day when German youth must settle accounts with the most despicable tyranny our people have ever endured. . . . Freedom and honor! Bravely on, students! The beacons are aflame!

Members of the White Rose were anti-authoritarian. Their student organizers were Sophia Scholl, a biology and philosophy student; her brother Hans Scholl, a medical student and Stalingrad veteran; and their friend Christoph Probst, a medical student. Accused of sabotage and treason, they were beheaded on 22 February 1943. Of the initial White Rose students and faculty arrested, six were guillotined at Plotzensee in May, and sixteen more in August. From April to August many other students and faculty members who had created, financed, and distributed anti-Hitler leaflets were also tried for high treason.

News of the White Rose spread widely and inspired hope. Thomas Mann told the BBC world network on 27 June that the German *Volk* and the Nazis were no longer indistinguishable. "The world is deeply moved" by the anti-Nazi student demonstrations, he said, by those who "put their young heads on the block . . . for the honor of Germany. . . . Good, splendid young people! You shall not have died in vain; you shall not be forgotten."

In the United States, the American Friends of German Freedom expanded their activities, and ER and Trude became more involved. The group planned a political warfare campaign to include coordinated contact with emigrants and refugees, radio and leaflet propaganda, and direct aid to the many underground groups that continued to struggle despite bloody reprisals.

At the same time, in the spring and summer of 1943, newly elected members of Congress made their presence felt. A new cohort of southern Democrats and conservative Republicans engorged the ranks of those who supported the Dies Committee and boosted the already virulent right-wing movement. They attacked ER as she worked to rescue European Jews and other endangered victims from Hitler and fascist appeasers, extend Social Security to domestic workers and farm laborers, end discrimination in war plants and segregation in the military, and create a movement to secure a just and lasting peace. She was forever baffled by Dies and his supporters who pursued "Communists" rather than fascists, ignoring the horrendous slaughters.

At this time a new campaign arose to challenge Hitler's extermination of the Jews, end the protracted silence and the ongoing inaction, and actually save people. Playwright and Hollywood screenwriter Ben Hecht and a group of international and Palestinian Jewish activists led by Peter Bergson (aka Hillel Kook) conceived of the stirring pageant *We Will Never Die*. Hecht wrote the script and Kurt Weill composed the music; Moss Hart directed it, and Billy Rose produced the star-filled show, which featured Stella Adler, Paul Muni, Edward G. Robinson, Frank Sinatra, Sid Caesar, George Jessel, Jerry Lewis, Dean Martin, and Hazel Scott. First performed at Madison Square Garden, it was broadcast live and performed for audiences throughout the country. On 12 April ER attended the sold-out Washington performance in the company of six Supreme Court justices, cabinet members, various military officers, diplomatic representatives, and more than three hundred senators and members of Congress. ER applauded "the mass memorial in Constitution Hall dedicated to the two million Jewish dead of Europe. . . . Flags of all the nations occupied by Germany came on the stage. No one who heard each group come forward and give the story of what happened . . . at the hands of a ruthless German military, will ever forget those haunting words: 'Remember us.'"

On 13 April, at Trude's request, ER spoke at a dinner for the American Friends of German Freedom in Washington. She insisted that her column readers "do all we possibly can to recognize" antifascist groups in Germany and its captive lands "and to strengthen them." Since most of the Friends of German Freedom were democratic socialists, associated with New Beginning (Neu Beginnen), ER addressed them specifically: "There must be a partnership between those who work with their hands and those who work with their heads. They must all insist on their common interest because they are the workers of the world . . . who must control their governments in order to have a chance to build a better life throughout the world."

In August ER addressed a White Rose memorial at Hunter College. It was attended by Kurt R. Grossmann, who subsequently wrote Sophie Scholl's sister Inge about the "moving, exciting, unforgettable evening." "Hundreds and hundreds of New Yorkers" paid tribute to the martyred heroes who proved that "Hitler was not the master of all Germans." According to Grossmann, "two of the speakers were extraordinary personalities." ER's speech "was moving and of great political significance," and the "leading Negro" activist Anna Hedgeman "spoke in the name of all suppressed people."

On 11 May, ER celebrated the spirit of defiance and learning that informed the White Rose: "Today is the 10th anniversary of the very notorious day when Hitler . . . ordered the burning of all books by such authors as Pearl Buck, Albert Einstein, Sigmund Freud, Ernest Hemingway, Selma Lagerlof, Sinclair Lewis, Thomas Mann, Stephen Vincent Benet and Sigrid Undset." The best way to enslave a people, she wrote, was to deprive them of education "and thus make it impossible for them to understand what is going on in the world."

But Germany was "highly educated," and Hitler had had to return to "medieval days and burn the books whose philosophies were opposed to his." By controlling and suppressing all the "ways in which ideas are transmitted"—radio, newspapers, all "sources of information"—he continually sought to enslave his people. But now after ten years that situation seemed about to end. Daily, "the people whom Hitler has enslaved" were in contact "with the world of free expression and thought." There was now hope that soon "Hitler will have to face the judgment of his own people"—who once liberated would be greatly changed and rededicated to freedom.

ER's spring 1943 efforts on behalf of rescue and refugees coincided with the twelve-day Anglo-American Bermuda Conference, called presumably to reconsider havens for Europe's remaining Jews and bolster the Intergovernmental Committee on Refugees. Britain insisted on the conference, in response to parliamentary distress and church appeals to provide sanctuary and rescue those immediately endangered. But neither the State Department nor the Foreign Office wanted to deal with a flood of refugees—not in Palestine, North Africa, or the United States. FDR had nothing to say about it and was content to leave it all up to Breckinridge Long, who considered it nothing more than a public relations distraction.

If anything, Long claimed, helping Jews would increase anti-Jewish and anti-Roosevelt sentiment, which were already widespread throughout the United States. Consistently opposed to all rescue efforts, he was adamantly opposed to a recent British proposal to use "North African territory for an internment camp for German, Czech and stateless Jews now in Spain. To put them in Moslem countries raises political questions [of] paramount military importance—considering that of the population of 18 million behind our long lines 14 million are Mohamedans." Long feared a conflagration if "Jewish people [were located] in Moslem territory." Rumblings of danger had already appeared in Palestine, Syria, North Africa, Iraq, and Iran. "Altogether it is a bad tendency." Alternatively, Long suggested Ethiopia or Madagascar.

Long did not mention oil, but earlier he had confided to his journal shock and outrage at Britain's arrangements for future pipelines. It had secretly made plans to exploit its lend-lease acquisition of "hundreds of miles of pipe to pipe oil—*after the war*—from *yet untouched* and undeveloped oil fields south of the Caspian Sea—to Basra." On 29 January 1942 Long noted that Britain had entered a treaty with Russia and Iran for "title to the lines in the post war settlement.... And *we* who own the pipe, transport the pipe, and furnish the pipe—were not to be considered." He quickly set up an arrangement with Iran so that the United States would not become a subject of "derision." Fearful and prescient, Long undoubtedly influenced FDR's changing attitude toward Britain: "England's policy seems to emerge. Suck the United States dry. When the peace comes ally with Russia. Let Russia have Poland, Eastern Germany, Baltic States, Finland. Hold the Mediterranean; Turkey ... the Dardanelles. Hold Iraq and Iran and India." By following this policy, Britain would render the United States politically isolated and commercially strangled.

In this climate, the Bermuda Conference, held in secret beginning on 20 April, was doomed to failure. It accomplished nothing for rescue refugees. No changes were to be made in immigration laws or procedures. Although "scarce shipping" was given as a reason, transportation was never the real issue: cruise ships floated back and forth mostly empty; troop transports returned home mostly empty; and prisoners of war were transported on such luxury liners as the *Queen Mary*.

Indeed, on 11 May, Churchill himself arrived on the *Queen Mary* with his daughter Mary and a considerable staff. Belowdecks were more than ten thousand German POWs who had surrendered in defeats ranging from Algiers to Tunis. Somehow there was room for them. Ultimately over 400,000 German POWs would arrive in the United States and be settled thinly and in comfort. ER was among the first to ask why there was room aboard these ships for POWs but not refugees. There was no response.

In a bitter irony, the Bermuda Conference coincided with the uprising in—and destruction of—the Warsaw Ghetto. For four weeks, from 19 April to 16 May 1943, Jews armed with rifles and handmade explosives rose up against fully equipped Nazi troops. After protracted street fighting, three hundred Nazis and seven thousand Jews were dead. Another seven thousand were deported to Treblinka, and ten thousand found refuge in Christian areas. Two days into the resistance, a Polish radio transmission "flashed news of the ghetto battle . . . ending with the words 'Save us.'" According to historian David Wyman, the appeal was "radioed around the world" and reached New York and London. But no aid was dropped from the sky. On 16 May SS general Jürgen Stroop reported, "The Warsaw Ghetto is no longer in existence."

ER continued to insist on an end to white supremacy during this war against race slaughter, and several real changes resulted from her determined stand. Responsible in part for the training of the Tuskegee Airmen, she was stunned to learn that while the first group of black pilots had passed all their tests, they remained restricted to the Tuskegee base in Alabama for over a year. In March 1943 the situation at Tuskegee was appalling. Local white police officers harassed black MPs on Tuskegee property, and a black army nurse, Nora Greene, was beaten "in a bus incident." Tuskegee's director, Frederick Patterson, wrote ER: "Morale is disturbed by the fact that the 99th Pursuit Squadron . . . is still at Tuskegee and virtually idle." She forwarded his letter to Secretary of War Stimson: "This seems to me a really crucial situation."

Her lobbying resulted in real change. On 5 April 1943 "the 99th was off to North Africa." The 99th was the first unit of the 332nd Fighter Group of black combat pilots, called by some, with derision, "Eleanor's niggers." Known as "Redtails" for their planes' insignia, the pilots called themselves "the Lonely Eagles." The valiant Tuskegee airmen—all college graduates, defiant and fearless—would see action on many fronts from Tunisia to Berlin. Despite unrelieved segregation and routine insults from various officers, their steadfast heroism ensured amazing victories.

This degree of progress was not enough for Judge William Hastie, aide to Secretary of War Stimson. Within the rigid confines of segregation, he could not fulfill his assignment, to develop "fair and effective" policies for black troops. He resigned and in 1943 returned to Howard University to teach and initiate more public opposition to segregation, working primarily with Thurgood Marshall's NAACP Legal Defense and Education Fund. ER was committed to all their efforts. Ultimately, Marshall called ER "Lady Big Heart"—and dismissed FDR as a tool of southern segregationists who "never did a damn thing" for the Negro.

ER did not judge her husband so harshly, but she regretted that he ignored her warnings about impending race violence. For over a year NAACP friends had reported that Detroit was a "hotbed of racial hatred." In April 1943, some 26,000 white workers at Packard Motors stopped production on bombers and PT boat engines—to protest the employment of three black workers. The strike lasted almost a week, encouraged by the Ku Klux Klan. White workers were overheard to prefer victory for "Hitler and Hirohito [rather] than work beside a nigger on the assembly line." On 21 June 1943 the city exploded as whites reacted, allegedly, to the integration of a lakefront beach at Belle Isle. Cars were burned; homes and stores were destroyed; thirty-four people were killed, twenty-five of them black; and seven hundred were seriously hurt. FDR ordered martial law and warned his wife to stay away. She agreed in principle, but then journeyed to Detroit to keynote the NAACP's "huge Freedom Fund dinner." Thurgood Marshall was forever impressed: "*The president's wife* had the guts to speak [in Detroit] when racial hostilities were at their peak."

That summer, as FDR prepared for his autumnal conferences with Chiang Kai-shek and Stalin and his preliminary meetings with Churchill, he increasingly fled from ER's concerns and criticisms. They spent little time together. They agreed she might go on a protracted trip to the South Pacific in August. The more she disagreed with FDR, the more she turned to Joe and Trude for friendship and hope.

In mid-July ER joined Trude in residence for her divorce at the Tumbling DW Ranch in Nevada.* Suddenly ER enjoyed a week of rest and recreation. They hiked and rode horses, read and gardened. ER wrote, "Dearest Franklin, I've ridden twice and am I stiff!" They visited a fine Indian school that "gives sensible training to both boys and girls." The area was "beautiful with a blue lake near us and mountains rising all around. But, the news is scarce and I wish I knew more about what is going on in the world . . . [and] I know none of your plans. Perhaps you'll telephone me in San Francisco or at Anna's?"

She returned home to news that Franklin Jr.'s destroyer had been torpedoed in Sicilian waters. She sent Joe a rambling letter recording her anxieties about losing a dear son, though Frankie "is o.k., but [despondent] about the men." She awaited more information, to contact their families. She reiterated to Joe that he seemed "like one of my children," but more than that, "a child with whom one has a deep understanding & friendship & for whom one has a deep respect." She cherished her close relationships with Joe, Trude, and her daughter, Anna: "To have three young people one felt really deeply tied to, if they feel the same way, is really more than anyone should expect from life!"

She urged FDR to appoint women to the Bermuda Conference and to the UN conference 18 May–7 June 1943 in Hot Springs, Virginia, which would be attended by over thirty nations and created the Food and Agriculture Organization (FAO).

But the growing refugee problem had reached critical proportions. A startling *New York Times* ad—written by Peter Bergson, Ben Hecht, and their allies—condemned the Bermuda Conference as "a mockery and

---

*Also at the ranch was Dorothy Schiff Backer, whose 1938 affair with FDR was well known to all except ER. Trude worried about her presence. While their conversations were pleasant, ER confessed she was puzzled by how Dorothy knew so many details about the family. With gratitude to Julius CC. Edelstein. See also Nissenson, *Lady Upstairs*.

cruel jest." The Bergson Committee then organized an Emergency Conference to Save the Jewish People of Europe, to be held on 20–25 July, at New York's Hotel Commodore. Over fifteen hundred people attended, along with an amazing bipartisan range of luminaries: Henry Morgenthau, Harold Ickes, Wendell Willkie, Herbert Hoover, and William Randolph Hearst. Speakers Dorothy Parker and Mayor Fiorello La Guardia called for a new government agency to focus on rescue, food relief, sanctuaries, and havens in neutral and allied nations. Perhaps because she had been advised to refrain from attending, ER declined to participate but sent a message affirming her certainty that "the people of this country . . . will be more than glad to do all they can to alleviate the sufferings."

The conference achieved extensive radio and press coverage. *PM*'s Max Lerner asked, "What About the Jews, FDR?"—"The State Department and Downing Street avert their eyes. . . . You Mr. President must take the lead. . . . The methods are clear. . . . The time is now." ER joined the lobbying campaign and wrote the committee on 26 July, "I will be glad to say anything or help in any way." Peter Bergson sent her a copy of his *Findings and Recommendations of the Emergency Conference*, which proposed a government rescue agency. ER gave it to FDR, who responded a few weeks later, "I do not think this needs any answer at this time."

In August, the *New York Times* published a country-by-country "extermination list," and ER met with Peter Bergson. "I do not know what we can do to save the Jews in Europe and to find them homes," she wrote in her next column, "but I know that we will be the sufferers if we let great wrongs occur without exerting ourselves to correct them." That month Stella Reading sent an open letter to Churchill:

> You know better than any words of mine . . . the horrible plight of the Jews at the mercy of the Nazis. I have said to myself what can I do, who can help. And the answer is clear, only Mr. Churchill can help and I can at least write and beg him to do so. In other days I would have come to you in sackcloth and ashes to plead for my people; it is in that spirit I write. Some can still be saved, if the iron fetters of the red-tape can be burst asunder. . . . England cannot surely sink to such hypocrisy that her members of Parliament stand to show sympathy to the Jewish dead and meanwhile her officials are condemning those same Jews to die? You cannot know of such things. I

do not believe you would tolerate them. There are still some 40,000
certificates for Palestine even under the White Paper regulations. Mr.
Churchill, will you not say they are to be used now, for any who can
escape, man woman or child. Is it possible, is it really possible, to
refuse sanctuary in the Holy Land?

I am your very ardent admirer and most obedient servant.

Stella Reading represented Britain's WVS, was close to Clementine,
and worked with Eleanor Rathbone, an MP who chaired the National
Committee for Rescue from Nazi Terror. Yet to ER's disbelief, Churchill
ignored the letter. Like FDR's State Department, Churchill's Foreign
Office avoided planning any rescue and continued to insist that all such
questions must await the war's end. This was not acceptable to Reading or
Rathbone—who published a pamphlet, *Rescue the Perishing*, and sent it
to the Foreign Office.

On 25 July news arrived that Mussolini had resigned in the face of
mounting Italian opposition after the surrender of Sicily. "Like everybody
else in the U.S.," ER wrote, "we were excited by the news." She had breakfast with two people who had interviewed Italian prisoners, in the United
States and in Africa. They told her there was a vast democratic movement
among POWs and throughout Italy. She believed this movement was to
be nurtured, and "we can make real allies of the Italian people in the
cause of future peace. . . . Perhaps we can help build something really
dynamic . . . which will bring us closer together and keep us working for
an ideal in the future, that will preclude the rise of dictators" and future
wars.

Count Carlo Sforza, Italy's former foreign minister, sought to create a
liberation movement for a free Italian republic. Uniting behind him, Italians were writing their own future by overthrowing the thousand-year rule
of the House of Savoy. "Death stares them in the face every minute," ER
wrote, ". . . and yet they go about their daily business unconcerned, knowing that the slightest slip might mean detection. . . . They will have the
satisfaction of knowing when liberation comes that they are the ones who
have kept alive the will to freedom among their people."

Unlike ER, Churchill was alarmed by anti-Fascist demonstrations in
Italy, which "was turning red overnight," he cabled FDR from the *Queen
Mary*, en route for a visit to Hyde Park with his daughter Mary:

"Nothing stood between the patriots rallying around the King and 'rampant Bolshevism.'" Churchill called yet again for attacking Germany through the Balkans or Italy and postponing again the cross-Channel invasion. This time FDR's advisers opposed Churchill's "peripheralism" and "pin prick" strategy.

Completely absorbed by these political divides—so much in the news, and in everybody's hearts—ER anticipated serious illuminating discussions during Churchill's visit. As she prepared days of entertainment for the prime minister and his daughter, she looked forward to an exploration of the controversies Churchill had traveled so far to settle with her husband.

She was disappointed. Everybody made small talk. Nothing of substance was discussed in her presence. Mid-August at Hyde Park featured picnics, long swims, deck tennis, rides through the countryside, mint juleps at the Morgenthaus, and interesting guests, including cheerful children (ER's nieces and their friends), Harry Hopkins, and Daisy Suckley. Mary Churchill sat beside FDR at several meals and found him "delightful and enthralling." ER, Mary wrote, "was kindness itself and took personal trouble to see that I had a good time, notwithstanding her many preoccupations."

But there "was no interesting conversation," ER wrote Lape. Italy was not mentioned. Nobody referred to India, although that week a dreadful cyclone and floods had devastated Bengal, and two million Bengalis were starving. Calcutta officials had cabled FDR to appeal for immediate food aid, presumably stimulated by his eloquent speech that launched the FAO, wherein he had promised to end hunger at war's end. There is no evidence that he replied to Calcutta's plea.

Finally, there was no mention of refugees or rescue—not of her column, nor of Bergson's report. But two days earlier FDR made a speech that acknowledged much she had argued for. The fourteenth of August was the anniversary of her father's death, of the 1935 Social Security Act, and of the 1941 Atlantic Charter. This 14 August, seeming to return to their primary alliance, FDR called for an extension of Social Security and a national GI Bill of Rights. ER's column that day supported her husband's goal to eliminate "destitution" everywhere it lingered. If Social Security covered all those groups not covered, including agricultural workers, domestic workers, and the self-employed, and if health care were covered by Social Security taxes, Americans would have cradle-to-grave security.

Once again their paths came together, their goals shared. They went off on their separate journeys, once again a team. Tommy, ever observant, wrote Esther Lape that "the P was very sweet to her as she left."

Chapter Nineteen

"The White Heron of the One Flight": Travels in the Pacific and Beyond

On 17 August 1943, ER departed for a trip to the southwestern Pacific to confront the realities of war on her own. The dangerous twenty-five-thousand-mile journey would take her from Hawaii to New Zealand, Australia, and seventeen Pacific islands.* It was from these places that so many of the wounded and distressed whom she had met during her many tours of stateside hospitals had returned.

It would be her first international journey entirely alone, without Tommy to help write her column, keep notes, be the observant critic, do all the routine protective and political chores. "I hate to see her go," Tommy confessed to Lape.

> She said last night that she knew she would regret many times not having taken me, but thought it good discipline for her to do things for herself. . . . ER left yesterday on schedule . . . and I went to the airport with her. I was sad and I think she was . . . because she said good-bye rather hastily and walked to the plane and never looked back. . . . She left all her jewelry—engagement ring, pearls, etc. with instructions as to their disposal in case anything happened. . . . It gave me a queer feeling [since] she did not leave them home when she went to Great Britain.

Major George Durno, a former Washington reporter, was assigned to accompany ER throughout her six-week trip. He provided assurance, immediate comforts, advice, and a new friendship.

Between 17 August and 25 September, her columns carried datelines from the Pacific, explaining that she traveled as a "representative of the

*She journeyed to Hawaii, Christmas Island, Penrhyn Island, Bora Bora, Aitutaki, Tutuila, Samoa, the Fiji Islands; New Caledonia, Auckland, Wellington, and Rotorua in New Zealand; Sydney, Canberra, Melbourne, Rockhampton, Cairns, and Brisbane in Australia; and Efate, Espiritu Santo, Guadalcanal, Wallis, and Canton.

American Red Cross, paying her own expenses." She visited Rotorua, the home of the Maori, the indigenous people of New Zealand, where she greeted her guide Rangi the traditional way—nose to nose. Rangi, she wrote, "was a wonderful woman—brilliant and witty and dignified. The area, with its geysers and hot-water pools, is like a miniature Yellowstone Park." The Maori, who took to her, named her Kotoku, the "White Heron of the One Flight," which according to Maori tradition "is seen but once in a lifetime."

There and in Australia, ER spoke to vast audiences and, wearing a Red Cross uniform, visited hospitals, rest homes, and recreation centers. She comforted more than 400,000 servicemen and promised to contact their mothers and their loved ones. Everywhere she went, malaria was "as bad as bullets & caused more casualties!" She wrote Hick, "The people here [in Auckland] are kind & they like FDR & our marines have won all their hearts, so they are very nice to me. . . . These boys break your heart, but they're so young & so tired. . . . They are hardly out of hospitals before they are at Red Cross Clubs & dances & they laugh at everything. I take my hat off to this young generation & I hope we won't let them down." Major Durno wrote Tommy that in New Zealand ER "did a magnificent job, saying the right thing at the right time and doing a hundred and one little things that endeared her to the people."

To her great chagrin, she generally was chaperoned by officials and generals, who forbade her to visit danger zones. She protested and took to rising at dawn to breakfast with enlisted men and civilians. During her first night on Christmas Island, she endured her "first encounter with tropical bugs." When she entered her room after dinner, the floor was "completely covered with little red bugs," and "I nearly disgraced myself by screaming." But then she remembered that she "was the only woman on the island" and stamped her feet until "all the little bugs scurried down through the cracks in the floor." She had no personal confrontations with rats and snakes, the scourge of several nurses she interviewed.

ER often worked from dawn to midnight, and after she finished her official duties, she wrote her daily column. In Bora Bora and the Cook Islands, she noted, all the troops teamed up together, and there "seemed to be no trouble anywhere out here between Southern white and colored." The men and officers in Bora Bora welcomed her, but the army colonel in charge of Aitutaki greeted her coldly. A Massachusetts Republican, he seemed rather "snobby and not pleased to see me." He protested the lack of army nurses, since too many of his men wanted to marry Maori women.

The hospital in Samoa held seven hundred men and was well equipped, but the lack of beer and wine troubled ER, who wrote Tommy, "Last night four men died from drinking distilled shellac." She wanted Norman Davis and the Red Cross to be informed.

Admiral William Halsey, the hero of the South Pacific, initially "dreaded" ER's arrival but was ultimately moved by the strength and stamina with which she endured her punishing schedule, and by the impact her visits to navy hospitals had on the men. He became her great ally.

> When I say she inspected those hospitals, I don't mean that she shook hands with the chief medical officer, glanced into a sun parlor, and left. I mean that she went into every ward, stopped at every bed, and spoke to every patient: What was his name? How did he feel? Was there anything he needed? Could she take a message home for him? I marveled at her hardihood, both physical and mental; she walked for miles, and she saw patients who were grievously and gruesomely wounded. But I marveled most at their expressions as she leaned over them. It was a sight I will never forget.

In Australia, General Douglas MacArthur assigned his aide, Captain Robert M. White, to be her escort. At first resentful of her presence, in the end he was dazzled by her manner: wherever she went, "she wanted to see the things a mother would see. She looked at kitchens and saw how food was prepared. When she chatted with the men she said things mothers say, little things men never think of and couldn't put into words if they did." She left "many a tough battletorn GI" moved to tears of hope, restoration, and gratitude.

Private Calvin Thompson described ER's epochal visit to one Red Cross club. He had been seated in the Negro canteen eating an ice cream cone when a sudden great commotion at the door announced ER's arrival. She entered, shook hands, and spoke with each man. "When she came to me I was still eating my ice cream cone . . . and she looked straight into my eyes and said, 'May I have some of that ice cream?' . . . Very gently,

Mrs. Roosevelt took the cone out of my hand, took a big bite, and handed it back to me. 'You see,' she said and smiled real wide, 'that didn't hurt at all, did it?'"

Ultimately, she so impressed Admiral Halsey that he allowed her to go to Guadalcanal, the site of much carnage that was now a temporary home for wounded troops. In Guadalcanal, she reflected on war:

> The natives of Guadalcanal completed a week ago the chapel which stands near the graves and it is a labor of love. . . . We must build up the kind of world for which these men died. They may never have put it into words, but I think they wanted a world where no one is hungry or in want for the necessities of life. . . .
>
> Long ago [I learned] the big thing men got out of war was the sense of shared comradeship and loyalty. . . . Perhaps that is what we must develop at home to build the world for which our men are dying.

In Guadalcanal, she spent several hours with Joe Lash, who was stationed there. "I shall have much of interest to tell Trude," she noted in her diary. At dawn the next morning she left for Espiritu Santo, writing to Joe, "How I hated to have you leave last night. When the war is over I hope I never have to be long away from you. It was so wonderful to be with you, the whole trip now seems to me to be worthwhile. It is bad to be so personal but I care first for those people I love deeply."

Admiral Halsey came to wish her a bon voyage and said (as Joe, who was standing with her, recalled) that "it was impossible for him to express his appreciation for what she had done for his men." Later Halsey wrote, "I was ashamed of my original surliness. She alone had accomplished more good than any other person, or any group of civilians, who had passed through my area." But Halsey's fears about her safety, noted Joe, were warranted. Both the night before her arrival and the night after her departure, the Japanese bombed Guadalcanal.

ER's Pacific trip was the longest and most perilous of her career. It was a journey of revelation and self-discovery, a soul-changing experience. The photographs and newsreels show an animated, engaged, free-spirited woman. Protesting all the limitations imposed on her, she enjoyed the opportunity to do vital work on her own. Thereafter, she wrote, "hospitals and cemeteries" would forever be "closely tied together in my head and my heart."

During her return flights, she spent many hours writing recommendations for her husband as well as a nine-page memo about changes needed in the Red Cross. Above all, she wanted legislation to guarantee veterans jobs and education, modeled on GI bills that had already been passed in Australia and New Zealand, and she wanted certain attitudes revised: "Men not chief concern anywhere. Officers have too much men too little. . . . French natives poorly cared for."

On her stopover in San Francisco, she phoned Tommy, who phoned Hick, saying, "I talked to her. I was crying." Esther Lape wrote to ER that she supposed we all "seemed pretty feeble to you, to have suffered jitters until you landed. . . . We are weaker than you thought us!" She had a splendid reunion with her granddaughter Sistie, who was "happy" at her boarding school, and the "headmistress likes her."

On 25 September she joined FDR at the White House. "Pa asked me more questions than I expected," she wrote Anna, "& actually came over to lunch with me . . . & spent two hours!" She was pleased that Undersecretary of War Robert Patterson told Bernard Baruch that "I did a wonderful job & that will help" promote some of her recommendations.

Nevertheless, upon her return, she experienced "the onset of a depression severe enough to be evident to the people around her." Some considered it merely exhaustion, but her depression, as revealed in her letters to loved ones, resulted from several factors. Her bedside visits with grotesquely wounded and psychologically devastated combatants had been deeply disturbing. Her son Jimmy was planning to return to the Pacific for his next assignment, under Admiral Chester Nimitz. And FDR had decided to travel to his upcoming meetings in Cairo with Chiang Kai-shek and in Tehran with Churchill and Stalin—without ER. She had wanted to be close to the center of gravity, close to the dialogue that would be taking place among these world leaders, but FDR's decision made it clear that he thought her safer at a remove.

Her impressions of her trip to the Pacific may have influenced his decision. She told him about the miles of hospital wards where "the men had been mentally affected by the experiences they had been through." She told him of her "horror" and of how the war's human agony that had caused so many to be "broken mentally and emotionally made me lie awake nights." She gave him vivid accounts of troops' exhaustion and battle fatigue, resulting in the disturbances we now call PTSD.

FDR was so upset by her report that he urged the secretaries of war and the navy to make immediate changes: "I know that the Army and Navy are doing the best they can with the subject of fatigue and stress . . . but I wish that further special consideration be given in all combat services." All officers and men in "tropical commands" where "there has been much fighting and where malaria and other diseases are serious factors" must from now on be offered definite schedules of relief.

ER's good work should have given her a new level of influence, but any hopes for that were quickly dashed. In August, while she was away in the Pacific, Sumner Welles had left the State Department and been replaced as undersecretary by Edward Stettinius, leaving her without even a modest ally on refugee issues.* And that same month, during the Quebec Conference, FDR had agreed with Churchill not even to address rescue or Palestine until after the war.

On 6 October 1943 in Washington, four hundred Orthodox rabbis converged for a pilgrimage, organized by Peter Bergson, to call for rescue. Marching from Union Station to the Capitol, they carried a petition to FDR to create a rescue agency. For weeks in advance they had appealed to the president for a meeting with them, but he refused. On the day of their

---

*Sumner Welles was a family friend, her brother's Groton schoolmate, and a lifelong ally. His removal was orchestrated in part by his rivals, Secretary of State Cordell Hull and former ambassador William Bullitt. In September 1940, Welles attended the funeral of Senator William Bankhead, and on the return train, just before dawn, the undersecretary of state—evidently inebriated—propositioned a sleeping car porter. The porter reported the incident. The matter was kept quiet for three years. In the summer of 1943 William Bullitt, with Alice Roosevelt Longworth's connivance, threatened to publicize the story. Welles offered to resign, but FDR not only refused but banished Bullitt. He told his former ambassador that Welles had acknowledged "human error" and would be admitted into heaven, but Saint Peter would condemn Bullitt: "You have betrayed a fellow human being. You can go down there!" In August Welles had a heart attack, and FDR reluctantly accepted his resignation. ER referred to these controversial circumstances nowhere. Welles, *Sumner Welles*, pp. 343–45; Brands, *Traitor*, pp. 748–51; Burns, *Soldier of Freedom*, p. 350. To date, there is no biography of Bullitt to explain his combined attraction and hatred for such sexual outlaws as his former wife Louise Bryant, his former aide Carmel Offie (who was subsequently fired from the CIA for homosexuality), and Welles.

pilgrimage, he left for Bolling Field to dedicate four bombers. So instead the rabbis met with Vice President Wallace. They read the petition aloud in Hebrew and English—"some Rabbis sobbed audibly"—and handed it to him. They then marched to the Lincoln Memorial to pray. At the White House they were met by FDR's secretary Marvin McIntyre.

Among the rabbis was a contingent of young theologians—including Rabbi Abraham Joshua Heschel. Years later, during his classes at Jewish Theological and Union Theological seminaries, he would frequently repeat the most profound lesson he had learned from this bitter moment: "In a democracy, some are guilty—but all are responsible!" Unfortunately, we have no record of ER's feelings about this episode, but that sense of responsibility defined her spiritual convictions. Responsibility for war and peace belongs to everyone, she wrote repeatedly. When a Japanese-American soldier told a reporter that he was happy to serve his country anywhere, ER called his attitude "perfect," for it underscored the unity of America and its peoples: "You are an American whether your features are those of a Japanese, or whether you have Italian or German ancestry, are born or bred in this country, or are naturalized." Under "the Constitution and Bill of Rights . . . we are Americans all."

The week after the rabbis' march, ER fulfilled her promise to Peter Bergson to record a message of encouragement to the Jews of Europe for international broadcast by the Office of War Information.

But on the issue of rescue, ER remained basically silenced. One searches her writings and correspondence in vain for a single reference to Bergson's Emergency Committee to Save the Jews of Europe. Nor did she refer to Britain's Emergency Committee to Rescue the Perishing, vigorously led by Eleanor Rathbone, independent member of Parliament for the Combined English Universities. From 1942 until the war's end, Rathbone issued many pamphlets and made numerous speeches demanding that Britain help rescue European Jewry. ER's friend Lady Stella Reading and more than 277 members of Parliament supported her efforts. ER's neglect of Rathbone's work remains a historical mystery.

On the evening of 11 October 1943, ER's birthday, FDR presided over a surprisingly congenial Hyde Park gathering including Hick, Elinor and Henry Morgenthau, Tommy, Grace Tully, and Trude—who reported to Joe, "The Boss was very gay and almost raucous and [ER] in the end seemed to enjoy it too. She looked very slim and beautiful in a marvellous long black dress." But she and Tommy were worried about ER. Often when she wasn't working, speaking, or presiding, she would become strangely silent and remote. Trude attributed her withdrawal in part to the effects of her Pacific trip. "As long as she had to keep going," Trude wrote Joe, "—her iron will carried her through in spite of her deep horror at what she saw and the great sadness at the continuing bloodshed and dying. And the happenings here since her return have not contributed to make her feel that everything possible is being done." ER did not want to discuss her feelings, and "brushed aside" Trude's concern.

Joe replied that part of ER's "terrible sorrow, made more acute by what she saw in hospitals out there, [is her fear] that [progressives] may be losing the peace. But I think another and larger part of it has to do with a great inner loneliness." He believed that Trude might "help a great deal there . . . [and] help dispel that kind of loneliness . . . [since ER] loves you."

FDR was working on plans for peace in the Middle East, for economic development and oil pipelines, for rescue, and for Palestine. In October 1942, he had sent Colonel Harold B. Hoskins to Saudi Arabia to "find out whether the Jews and Arabs could reach a modus vivendi about Palestine." The son of American missionaries, Hoskins spoke Arabic fluently and had many friends in the region. He returned to advise that all discussion about Palestine should be suspended until after the war.

Then on 1 November the president appointed Isaiah Bowman to head the top-secret M Project, which would conduct a global survey of "waste spaces for waste people" and study the possibilities for relocating and resettling European Jews in thinly populated areas worldwide. A geographer and president of Johns Hopkins University, Bowman argued, as we have seen, that European Jews should be resettled as thinly as possible around the world.* He had already concluded that Palestine was an "arid land" and overpopulated. For this study, he had FDR's mandate to be compre-

---

*Johns Hopkins geographer Owen Lattimore served as an adviser to the M Project. He later told Bowman's biographer, Neil Smith, that "Bowman was *profoundly* anti-Semitic." According to Smith, Bowman's purpose—like Breckinridge Long's—was to stall, delay, obfuscate. Smith, *American Empire*, p. 309.

hensive and to also pursue the president's own hydrological fantasies of irrigation, waterways, dams, canals, and bridges.

Other experts disagreed. Walter Clay Lowdermilk, an agronomist with the Department of Agriculture's Soil Conservation Service, insisted to Vice President Wallace that it would be easy to bring water in "from the Mediterranean Sea by canal to the Jordan River, thus developing power." In addition to "all the streams running into the Jordan River for irrigation," he believed there were "great possibilities of mining magnesium, bromine, and potassium in the Dead Sea." Lowdermilk's article "The Absorptive Capacity of Palestine" proposed a TVA-like program to develop Palestine's water resources and turn the area into "another California," able to absorb "20 to 30 million people."* The Jews should be allowed to develop such irrigation projects in Palestine, he argued, and Jews and Arabs alike would benefit, living together in prosperity and in peace. Hadassah leader Rose Halprin sent the article to ER.

The first lady was impressed by Lowdermilk's democratic visions of peace and development. Through Marion Frankfurter, Justice Frankfurter's wife, ER met with Dr. Chaim Weizmann, the world's leading proponent for Jewish settlement in Palestine. That autumn she also had several conversations with Peter Bergson about his vision of a democratic Palestine, where members of all faiths would be equal citizens with equal rights. He told her about many changes already under way due to irrigation and forestation programs.†

She was eager for FDR to consider Lowdermilk's and Bergson's views, but the president insisted that there was nothing to discuss until war's end. For the time being, he suggested that ER meet with Bowman herself and bring her contrary information to him directly. She proceeded to

---

*Lowdermilk's argument, subsequently published as *Palestine: Land of Promise* (1944), finally persuaded FDR to announce, in October 1944, that he favored a Jewish homeland in Palestine.

†Even in the twenty-first century, various groups still condemn Hillel Kook, aka Peter Bergson, as a "right-wing Zionist." Actually, he believed Israel/Palestine would be a multinational democracy, and when Israel refused to consider a constitution and real democracy, he quit the Knesset. Opposed to the creation of "a ghetto with an army," he remained a maverick dissenter until his death in 2001. Becky Kook to author, with her father's speeches.

invite the geographer to tea. Aware of ER's public significance, Bowman knew he could not simply ignore her, but behind the scenes the patronizing university president expressed contempt for the first lady's interference in "questions beyond her understanding," and he was filled with "scorn" for this "mischievous" woman, whom several of his State Department colleagues called "a meddling pest."

For several weeks he delayed responding to her invitation, then finally accepted. Facing her in person, he politely, even patiently, detailed his geographical understanding, then concluded by posing a political question: Were not Zionist intentions to dispossess the Palestinians akin to the Nazis' goal to root out the Jews? The future he pictured was one of perpetual war, at great cost to the United States in lives and money.

At a White House luncheon on 22 May 1943, the president told his guests that he agreed with Bowman's idea. FDR claimed, that in the U.S., local communities would not object "if there were no more than four or five Jewish families at each place."

FDR insisted that ER and Wallace maintain a public silence about Palestine, and both acquiesced, turning down all requests to speak about it. They declined an invitation to speak on behalf of Jewish settlement in Palestine at a Carnegie Hall rally on 1 November. But both Willkie and Dewey accepted. That night Willkie called for the establishment of a Jewish state in Palestine, and Dewey called for opening Palestine to Jewish refugees from Europe. If FDR worried about the Jewish vote, it did not extend to allowing ER and Wallace to speak. The next week ER wrote Joe that her day had begun with upset when she rendered "some Zionist ladies . . . sad because I felt I could not take up the question of the future of Palestine."

In July 1943, Secretary Morgenthau proposed to save seventy thousand Romanian Jews, who were eager to be evacuated, in exchange for payment of $170,000. The World Jewish Congress in Switzerland, as well as Bergson's group, agitated in favor, and Rabbi Wise made a personal appeal to FDR. The president verbally agreed to Morgenthau's plan, although he wanted no public discussions of it until he returned from Cairo and Tehran.

But with amazing indifference, the State Department delayed for six months, blocking every effort to move forward on rescuing the Romanian Jews. On 26 November 1943, Breckinridge Long, testifying before the House Foreign Affairs Committee, denied that the need was urgent. His words were astonishing, given the situation, and considering that annual immigration amounted to less than 10 percent of the quotas.

That November, Morgenthau also tried to save more Jewish children in France. Four thousand had already been deported "to gas chambers, probably," as he noted, and another six thousand were in peril. The French police, under German orders, were conducting a "census" to pursue these children, who were mostly "hidden in private homes." Relief agencies, including the Quakers and the YMCA, needed funds but could do nothing until dollars were converted into francs. Morgenthau approved a plan for foreign exchange and involvement.

Once again the State Department stalled. In December, Morgenthau discovered that State had entirely obstructed the Romanian plan. He no longer trusted State and concluded that an independent agency was needed to conduct rescue efforts. To that end, he asked his three closest aides in Treasury—Josiah E. DuBois, General Counsel John Pehle, and the head of Foreign Funds Control, Randolph Paul—to prepare a report exposing the State Department's obstructionism. They went to work, researching and drafting vivid memos. "The British say condemn them to death," wrote DuBois, "and we say they should get out. . . . Their position is, 'What could we do with them if [they] get out.' . . . Amazing, most amazing." Paul wrote: "I don't know how we can blame the Germans. . . . The law calls [this] para-delicto, of equal guilt." Pehle observed that when the British turned away, the real "enormous issues [were finally] flushed out."

The issue of rescue kept ER up many nights. Aware of her discontent and anguish, FDR sought to reassure her, and with his charming mysterious smile, told her he had secret plans. More immediately, he surprised her by adopting her positions on several issues. In a 27 October message to Congress, he promised to guarantee education and training, job security and health care for returning veterans—which echoed her August columns about the democratic security that had been legislated in Australia and New Zealand. The plan would subsequently be known as the GI Bill of Rights.

Even more surprising, on 1 November 1943, FDR issued an important, and lengthy, message to Congress on agriculture. Feeding the troops and the hungry, maintaining food prices, and achieving a new level of farm production, he said, would require subsidies and price stabilization. The speech contained many of ER's precepts. Trude wrote Joe that the first lady was "very happy" to hear the president support ideas she had long advocated and had thought he "never . . . accepted."

A week later, on 9 November, representatives of forty-four of the United Nations, their illuminated flags behind them, agreed to feed, clothe, house, and "rehabilitate the world." This ceremony established the United Nations Relief and Rehabilitation Agreement (UNRRA): "Today in the East Room . . . we witnessed a very memorable occasion," an uplifted ER declared. Years earlier, on 19 November 1919, the U.S. Senate had rejected the League of Nations; now ER, mindful of the anniversary, "watched each man go up to represent his country" and was glad that this time, "before the end of the war, we have the vision" actually to prepare for peaceful cooperation. Since "80 percent of the population of the world was represented in that room," she believed UNRRA had a real chance of success. The speeches of FDR and the forty-four delegates, she wrote Joe, persuaded her that "something great may have begun today." And she was pleased that two women were appointed to UNRRA's delegation: her great activist allies Ellen Woodward and Elizabeth Conkey.

On 18 October 1943, Secretary of State Cordell Hull had traveled to Moscow for a meeting with Allied foreign ministers Eden and Molotov, and on 1 November 1943 they issued the Moscow Declaration. Written by Churchill, it promised that the Allies would take postwar retribution for all "abominable deeds" committed by Nazi war criminals. It listed more than sixty of them specifically* but omitted any mention of outrages suffered by Jewish communities. Jewish groups were horrified by the declaration, which implied that Churchill, Roosevelt, Stalin, and their foreign ministers considered their slaughter irrelevant.

On 9 November, Congressman Guy Gillette (D-IA), Will Rogers, and the esteemed liberal Joseph C. Baldwin (R-NY) introduced resolu-

---

*The Moscow meeting had been scheduled to discuss not war crimes but strategy, in preparation for FDR's meeting with Stalin and Churchill to set a specific date for the much-delayed second front. The meeting was tense, since Churchill still favored his "soft underbelly" Mediterranean and Balkan invasions, while FDR's military chiefs dismissed them as wasteful "pin-pricks." (Cordell Hull, see Notes.)

tions into both the Senate and the House urging the president to create a "commission of diplomatic, economic and military experts" to act immediately "to save the surviving Jewish people of Europe from extinction," and establish camps in neutral nations of Europe and North Africa, for subsequent settlement in Palestine or one of the United Nations.

On 12 November, FDR acted on ER's concern about the Moscow Declaration and told Hull to make amends to the outraged Jewish community. Hull's thirty-minute speech to Congress on 28 November included an additional sentence: "Bestial and abominable Nazi crimes" had been committed "against people of all races and religions, among whom Hitler has reserved for the Jews his most brutal wrath." These crimes, he said, would be punished.

The next day FDR, along with Harry Hopkins, General George Marshall, and others, boarded the USS *Iowa* for his six-week trip to Cairo and Tehran, for meetings with Stalin and Chiang Kai-shek. During ER's Pacific trip, the Russian and Chinese ambassadors had invited her to visit, and she had hoped and expected to accompany her husband to these most critical meetings. But FDR was firm: "no women" were welcome. Trude, from New York, wrote Joe that ER was both hurt and bewildered—especially after she discovered that Madame Chiang translated for her husband in Cairo, and that Churchill's daughter Sarah was present at both meetings. "I've been amused that Mme. Chiang and Sarah Churchill were in the party," ER wrote FDR. "I wish you had let me fly out! I'm sure I would have enjoyed Mme C more than you did, tho all the pictures show her in animated conversation with you [while Chiang] wears a rather puzzled look as Winston chews his cigar." FDR's correspondence during this long trip was full of personal endearments, but they did not mollify ER. She hated to be "sidelined" during important events, and FDR's rejection of her presence seemed a dismissal of her work.

With her husband away and all four of their sons in battle, along with more than thirteen million American troops in uniform, ER was home alone. The thought of FDR spending six weeks mostly with Churchill, with his heavy drinking, filled her with dread: she worried about the prime minister's influence on him in terms of policy as well. In India, Gandhi, Nehru, and other Congress Party leaders remained helpless in prison, yet Churchill refused to free them. Moreover the famine in Bengal threatened to doom an estimated 1.5 million Indians to death and the ravages of disease, but Churchill refused to provide aid.*

In Cairo, FDR persuaded a reluctant Churchill to open the Burma Road, liberate Burma, and deal with the crisis. But during the subsequent meetings in Tehran, Churchill reneged, whereupon FDR became "furious." FDR "feels badly" that Churchill "did not remember" his promise to the Chinese, ER wrote Joe, ". . . and went back on it. To my surprise, F seemed really annoyed."

ER was also concerned that the prime minister did not want to include China as a partner. And even after two years, through protests and procrastinations, he sought to delay opening a second front in Europe that would relieve the burden on the Red Army. As news of Russian casualties and India's suffering, including the Bengal famine, was reported, ER descended into despondency.

An almost frenzied level of work enabled her to overcome, or at least repress, her depression. She wrote ever more forcefully about the need to end bigotry, discrimination, and poverty. The FBI, she noted, had suddenly tightened its surveillance on communities of hope—on Communists and activists for racial justice—but not on Klanners or fascists.

In November came the dedication of Roosevelt House. Hunter College's Hillel Foundation had transformed the family's twin East Sixty-fifth Street town houses (originally purchased by SDR and long the site of ER's great discontent) into an interfaith center. In her column, ER fully credited SDR's antiracist, equalitarian views: a lifelong world traveler, from her childhood in China to her journeys across Europe, SDR had "had a liking for many different countries and their people. Though she had been brought up a Unitarian and became an Episcopalian after her marriage, she was very tolerant of all other religions." She wrote that FDR was "par-

---

*The horrendous Bengal famine, and the protracted imprisonment of the Congress leaders, from August 1942 to March 1945, ended any vestige of legitimacy for British rule. After the war, an official inquiry blamed Britain's protracted neglect of India, and Nehru referred to the Bengal famine as "the final judgment on British rule in India," its legacy of misery, degradation, and "accumulated sorrow." Nehru quoted Rabindranath Tagore's observation, "When the stream of their centuries' administration runs dry at last, what a waste of mud and filth they will leave behind." Recent research has put the famine death toll at over five million.

ticularly glad" that his mother's home was to become the center of so much that "she would have approved."

While he was away, ER visited her beloved friends Esther Lape and Elizabeth Reed in Connecticut. She was heartened by their intimate conversations, which she and Esther continued by mail. "I find it hard to know sometimes whether I am being honest with myself," ER wrote. "So much of life is play acting, it becomes too natural! . . . . There is no fundamental love to draw on," she continued sadly, referring to her life with FDR,

> just respect and affection. There is little or no surface friction. On my part there is often a great weariness & a sense of futility in life but a life long discipline in a sense of obligation & a healthy interest in people keeps [*sic*] me going. I guess that is plenty to go on for one's aging years! I'll be a fairly good handmaiden and with all the others to help I think FDR's sense of a place in history will keep him on a forward going path. He'll know it has to be that way and he is really very well I think. . . . Much much love, ER.

Her trusted, loving relationship with Elizabeth and Esther provided a rare outlet for such sustaining confidences. Many of her other friendships were "proprietary," with levels of jealousy and competition. Concerned about the people—all people—and with her heart dedicated to profound democratic change, she refused to acknowledge the jealousies that swirled about her. Actually, she seemed to enjoy her ability to bring the most diverse people together.

While FDR was in Tehran, however, Elizabeth Read died. Since the 1920s ER had worked closely with Read and Esther Lape for world cooperation and national health care. Throughout the dreadful "isolationist" years, when FDR had refused to consider their advice on the World Court or aid to Republican Spain because of political "realities," ER had depended on Lape and Read for comfort and alternative strategies. A Smith College graduate and an esteemed attorney, Read was also ER's personal financial adviser and tax accountant. Since her first stroke in March 1937, her health had been in serious decline.

Upon her death, ER wrote to Lape, "Life without Lizzie will be almost impossible to face. She loved you so dearly & you gave each other so much. . . . She's been part of my life so long that I'll never forget her & life

will always be richer because of her friendship. I want to do anything I can
to make life more bearable for you & if you can bear to be with people I
hope you will come to stay as long as you can as soon as you want. I love you
very much & I wish my arms could be around you. Devotedly Eleanor."

FDR's letters from Cairo and Tehran were vague but hopeful. Much
to ER's relief, Churchill finally agreed to a real schedule for the second
front. Operation Overlord, the cross-Channel invasion of France, would
happen during the spring of 1944, with General Eisenhower as supreme
commander of the Anglo-American force.

On 5 December, ER wrote her husband, "I am sorry things only went
pretty well with Chiang. I wonder if he, Mme or Winston made trouble.
The questions are so delicate that the Sphinx must be a relief." Evidently
the press was more forthcoming. "Day by day news comes in of the meetings," she noted: the United States, China, and Britain pledged to guarantee "the ultimate freedom of Korea . . . under the Japanese yoke . . . for
a great many years." ER hoped for sufficient "economic and agricultural
development" throughout the Pacific, to ensure decent standards of
living—and end the ongoing starvation.

She had long doubted FDR's commitment to the Four Freedoms, to
the goals of leading a people's war and constructing a people's peace. But
after his return, he made a Christmas Eve broadcast from the library at
Hyde Park, with a democratic emphasis that encouraged her. At their
summit meetings in Cairo and Tehran, he explained, the four allies—
Russia, Great Britain, China, and the United States—had agreed to band
together to keep the peace: "Those four powers must be united with and
cooperate with all the freedom-loving peoples of Europe, and Asia,
and Africa, and the Americas . . . The rights of every Nation, large or small,
must be respected and guarded as jealously as are the rights of every
individual within our own Republic. The doctrine that the strong shall
dominate the weak is the doctrine of our enemies—and we reject it."
FDR saluted the ten million Americans stationed around the globe to
fight the war and concluded with a fervent prayer for the embattled and
suffering, for faith and strength to rid the world of evil so that "all men
and women everywhere" would be free, return to the comfort of their
families and homes, and meet "a better day for humankind."

The holiday season for ER, surrounded by family and friends at Hyde

Park, was marked by a new surge of trust in her husband's vision. "Though two of our boys and our son-in-law were far away," daughter Anna, two sons, and seven grandchildren were present, "so we felt greatly blessed." There were carols and celebrations, lunch for the boys of the Wiltwyck School, and a party for servicemen and students at the military police school and their families. ER's thoughts inevitably turned to all those who were not home for Christmas—and to those who would never return.

Sadly, Franklin Jr. and Ethel were in marital difficulty. "I guess one of the sad things in life," a grieving ER confided to Joe, "is that rarely do a man & woman fall *equally* in love with each other & even more rarely do they so live their lives that they continue to be lovers . . . & still develop & enjoy the constant companionship of married life. I imagine that the really great number of men & women who are faithful to each other not only in deed but in thought are so more often because of a lack of opportunity for romance elsewhere rather than because they've learned the secret of 'the one & only great love.' A cynic you will say!" According to Joe, ER believed that "faithfulness was . . . achievable"—which was why the current "emotional difficulties" of her sons Elliott and Franklin depressed her.

At the White House for New Year's Eve, ER hosted a smaller party than usual. Two grandchildren, Sara and Kate Roosevelt, were "to be with us for the next few weeks . . . a good way to begin the New Year." Besides the grandchildren, only Tommy, Daisy Suckley, and Elinor and Henry Morgenthau were present to welcome 1944. FDR was unwell, with a "touch of the flu" and fever. He appeared "in a wrapper" to toast the nation, and the party broke up early. "I want to tell you again how much being close to you & Trude mean to me," ER wrote to Joe. ". . . I'm grateful beyond words that you are my friend & care for me." She wrote a similar letter to Trude, then a missive of advice to Joe. "There is one thing I've always wanted to say to you. When you do come home & get engulfed in work, will you stop long enough now and then even if Trude is working with you to make her feel she is *first* in your life and even more important than saving the world? Every woman wants to be first to someone sometime in her life & the desire is the explanation for many strange things women do, if only men understood it!"

FDR's illness lingered throughout January. He was so unwell on 11 January that an aide read his State of the Union address to Congress, although the president was able to broadcast it with verve that night. Considered by many, including historian James McGregor Burns, "the most radical speech of his life," it was also a tribute to ER's persistence and endorsed her views.

> We have come to a clear realization of the fact that true individual freedom cannot exist without economic security and independence. . . . People who are hungry and out of a job are the stuff of which dictatorships are made. [Therefore] we have accepted . . . a second Bill of Rights [to achieve] security and prosperity . . . for all—regardless of station, race, or creed. Among these are: . . .
>
> The right to earn enough to provide adequate food and clothing and recreation; . . . The right of every family to a decent home; . . . The right to adequate medical care; . . . The right to adequate protection from the economic fears of old age, sickness, accident, and unemployment; The right to a good education. . . . [And an end] to domination by monopolies at home or abroad.

FDR's vigorous rhetoric, however, did not satisfy ER, who wanted immediate action and actually wrote a column critical of the speech. She had listened to his broadcast in the company of "WAVES at their head-quarters in American University," where she had spoken that night, and where they had been entertained by a "glee club of WAVES who sing delightfully and I wish we could have listened to them for a long time." Evidently, they were interrupted by the president's message—which ER reread in the morning: "The more I go over it, the more I realize that [the Second Bill of Rights] is a restatement, in more concrete terms, of the objectives for . . . which we have been striving since 1933."

ER insistently detailed the many chores that had to be done immediately. The Social Security Board recommended an updated "complete, unified social insurance system," since because of the program's limitations more than "20 million workers are not yet covered." As passed in 1935, the Social Security Act exempted "farm workers and domestic workers, the self-employed, employees of federal, state and local government, employees of non-profit organizations, maritime workers, and many employees of small firms."

Nor had Social Security established—as was initially intended—national "social insurance measures to protect American families against disabilities and sickness." ER agreed with the Social Security Board's conclusion that "health and medical care have an important place in any comprehensive and adequate program," and that it should be implemented immediately. Across the country, especially in rural areas, "the draft showed us our failures where health is concerned. . . . Low income groups can neither afford medical care nor a proper diet." She was impatient with those who argued that wartime was not the moment to "assume greater social burdens." Unless they were assumed now, "the war will not seem to have brought many people much that is worth fighting for."

Throughout January 1944 ER seemed inclined toward radical change—if not social revolution. In Washington, D.C., discriminatory housing regulations and new zoning laws further restricted affordable housing for black residents, which she found outrageous. The new laws would push "the colored residents more and more into a segregated little city of their own. This area will be as far out as possible, where transportation and utilities will be less available. This proposal to herd our citizens according to race and religion has many serious disadvantages and should be fought." Recalling the Warsaw Ghetto battles, ER opposed this effort to ghettoize the U.S. capital.

Many young Americans were underprepared for citizenship, even actually illiterate. ER met with National Education Association representatives who urged a movement to "wipe out illiteracy" and ensure educational opportunity. Teachers should be honored, since they were entrusted with "the most important job of the community—the education of youth in a democracy. Since we decided long ago that democracy could not exist without education . . . teachers are essential to our development." But real education continues "throughout our lives," and adult education requires new consideration. Schools should be open at night and become community centers to "radiate" and motivate community ideas.

Personally, ER was fortified by the good works of Carrie Chapman Catt, New York's Women's City Club, the YWCA, the Women's Brigade of the ILGWU, and the many women organized to promote a national service act for both women and men. They called for wage and price stabilization and an end to selfish greed. ER noted that people wanted to contribute "to the limit of their abilities, because [they] have an interest in someone whose life is at stake every day that the war continues."

Meanwhile Henry Morgenthau's team worked on their report on State Department obstructionism. The treasury secretary requested specific cables, but State refused to provide them. Then Josiah DuBois asked Donald Hiss, of the department's Foreign Funds Control, to try to get them, and Hiss, at great risk to his career, agreed to search. On 18 December he called DuBois into his office and allowed him to copy two cables. One was Cable 482, which documented the 1943 terror in Poland, where 6,000 Jews were killed each day, and in Romania, where 130,000 Jews had been deported to Transnistria in Romanian-occupied Ukraine. The other was Cable 354, which urged silence about the ongoing slaughter. It was the State Department's order to "cease and desist" the transmission of all future information.

When the team showed Morgenthau the bitter evidence, he became "physically ill" but told Randolph E. Paul, his counsel, to go ahead and prepare the full report. Paul asked Joe DuBois to write it, with John Pehle. In January the team finished the stunning "Report to the Secretary on the Acquiescence of This Government in the Murder of the Jews," and they presented it to Morgenthau on 13 January. Morgenthau changed the title to *Personal Report to the President* and shortened its eighteen pages to nine. On Sunday morning, 16 January, he and John Pehle presented it to FDR at the White House. The three Christian attorneys had detailed State Department complicity in Hitler's effort to end Jewish life in Europe: "One of the greatest crimes in history, the slaughter of the Jewish people in Europe, is continuing unabated" and involved not only a willful failure but acts "to prevent the rescue of the Jews"—needless restrictions, subterfuges, and bold mendacity.

The report quoted Congressman Emanuel Celler (D-NY) naming Breckinridge Long as the primary State Department barrier to rescue and refugees: he was responsible for "the tragic bottleneck in the granting of visas. . . . It takes months and months to grant a visa, and then it usually applies to a corpse." Without making any changes to the 1924 Immigration Act, the United States could have admitted 150,000 immigrants annually. In the previous year, Celler noted, only 23,725 immigrants had arrived on these shores, which included "only 4,750 Jews fleeing Nazi persecution."

The Morgenthau team's report denounced not only Long but all responsible State Department officials who "failed to use the Governmental machinery at their disposal to rescue Jews from Hitler, but have even gone so far as to use this Governmental machinery to *prevent* the rescue of these Jews." They failed "to cooperate with private organizations" engaged in rescue and sought to suppress information, even "to stop the obtaining of information concerning the murder of the Jewish population of Europe." "They have tried to cover their guilt by . . . false and misleading explanations" of their failure to act, and regarding their alleged "actions taken to date."

The president "listened attentively," and although he was "disinclined to believe that Long wanted to stop effective action," he did agree that "it was possible to facilitate the rescue of Jews from Rumania and France to safety in Turkey, Switzerland, and Spain."

The team had also drafted an executive order to create an independent War Refugee Board (WRB), composed of Hull, Morgenthau, and Stimson. FDR urged Morgenthau and Pehle to consult with Undersecretary of State Edward Stettinius. Morgenthau approached Stettinius that very evening and declared the State Department's deliberate obstructionism had to end, so that the United States would not be "placed in the same position as Hitler and share the responsibility for exterminating all the Jews of Europe." FDR had cooled toward the man he had put in charge of "the Jewish problems" and who became the primary enemy of rescue.* Breckinridge Long finally departed on 27 November, when FDR appointed

---

*Long documented their protracted estrangement. He and FDR agreed about negotiations regarding the great Arabian oil deposits and the need to suspend congressional debate about Palestine, but for three years Long was not invited to confer with or even meet with a single head of state. When Long went to the White House as a member of the Dumbarton Oaks team, he saw the writing on the wall: "It was the first time I had seen the President face to face for three and a half years. . . . I was stunned. He must have lost 50 or 60 pounds. . . . I smiled—he smiled—we shook hands—and he said 'Mr. Long'—nothing else. . . . It is the only time . . . he has called me anything but 'Breck.'" Within minutes the meeting was over, and Long understood that he would soon resign. Breckinridge Long Diary, pp. 334–38, 365–66, 373–74, 386–91.

Stettinius as secretary of state. ER, who had always considered Long a fascist, was relieved.

Stettinius considered the draft for a WRB "wonderful" and Morgenthau left his meeting with Stettinius heartened. "Those terrible eighteen months had ended," though it was too late for too many. Morgenthau confided in his diary that the struggle was "long and heartbreaking. . . . The threat was . . . total obliteration" of all the Jews of Europe. Now there was "hope that rescue for the remnant would proceed."

On 22 January 1944, FDR issued the executive order establishing the War Refugee Board, for the "immediate rescue and relief of the Jews of Europe and other victims of enemy persecution." The WRB was to cooperate with international agencies, use "the facilities of the Treasury, War, and State Departments in furnishing aid to Axis victims, and to attempt to forestall the plot of the Nazis to exterminate Jews and other minorities." John Pehle was named director, and FDR announced that he expected "all members of the United Nations" to cooperate with the WRB.

Within days Pehle was hard at work, and rescue "was withdrawn from the sabotaging hands of Breckinridge Long." Journalist Ruth Gruber wrote: "Cables would no longer be suppressed. Ships would be leased in Sweden to smuggle refugees out of the Balkans. Ira Hirschmann, an executive of Bloomingdale's Department Store . . . would be sent to Istanbul to rescue, if he could, the sixty thousand still alive in the Romanian concentration camp in Transnistria. Raoul Wallenberg, a young Swede of a distinguished family, would be sent to Hungary."

Between July and December 1944 the courageous and determined Raoul Wallenberg—with support from the WRB and an international staff of 115—saved more than 100,000 Jews in Budapest. He created imaginative safe houses, issued Swedish identification papers—"Wallenberg passports"—and achieved amazing feats of rescue.*

But the WRB faced many obstacles. Churchill continued to show no interest in rescue, and the Foreign Office remained actively opposed. A dismayed ER understood that the reasons for England's position involved

---

*The first Nazi transports of Jews from Hungary began on 27 April 1944; by July, Adolf Eichmann had sent 520,000 east. Then Horthy arranged a cessation, which enabled Wallenberg and the WRB to work.

Palestine, oil futures, Arab alliances, and pipeline agreements, but she was mystified that so many underpopulated and resource-rich nations refused to provide havens, including most of Latin America. Moreover, nations that ER had visited and considered virtually empty—notably Australia, New Zealand, and Canada—bolted their doors and seemed to agree that "none is too many." Most disturbing of all, the United States failed to offer safe ports and establish havens, which it could have done at least to demonstrate that rescue was possible. On this issue, Morgenthau was alone.

In May, at a White House meeting with Pehle, FDR was "cordial" to the idea of opening an "emergency refugee shelter" in the United States—but only one, and it would hold no more than a thousand people. On 24 May 1944, Morgenthau presented FDR's one-camp proposal to the cabinet, for one thousand refugees to be brought from Italy. Only Harold Ickes "expressed complete support," and now as honorary chair of Bergson's Emergency Committee to Save the Jews of Europe, he promised an "active alliance."

On 6 June, D-Day, the invasion of Normandy opened the long-awaited second front. As victory in Europe seemed imminent, seven members of Congress introduced resolutions urging FDR to open "free ports."

FDR's health was one reason for the delay. Unwell since his return from Tehran, his Christmas–New Year's episode of "flu" had been compounded by fatigue, chest pains, stomach upsets, and assorted unnamed discomforts.

After the holidays, Anna agreed to live in the White House and serve as her father's hostess during her mother's many absences and prolonged travels. Missy LeHand's stroke, Harry Hopkins's departure, and ER's refusal to play the role of FDR's most intimate companion often left the president alone. ER was grateful that Anna took on the role of hostess. "Anna's presence was the greatest possible help to my husband," ER wrote. ". . . She saw and talked to people whom Franklin was too busy to see and then gave him a digest of the conversations. She also took over the supervision of his food." Anna "had her hands full keeping peace" between SDR's chef, Mary Campbell, and Henrietta Nesbitt, ER's friend, the head housekeeper. But her daughter "brought to all her contacts a gaiety and buoyance that made everybody feel just a little happier because she was around." Evidently, ER and her husband operated best as a team with a little distance between them.

For years, ER had been aware of FDR's flirtations and special friends. She appreciated and was actually grateful for the companionship and devotion rendered by Missy LeHand; the president's cousin Polly Delano—purple-haired, eccentric, and always critical of ER; another FDR cousin, Daisy Suckley, who was also critical but less mean; and the flirtatious Crown Princess Martha of Norway. These women were necessary to FDR's circle, and ER, recognizing that need, allowed him wide berth.

Initially ER seemed to have dismissed Anna's concerns about her father's health, telling her that his prolonged fatigue and frequent headaches resulted from anxiety and distress and could "be conquered by will and determination." But ER was in denial. During his White House birthday dinner, on 30 January, Daisy Suckley noticed that ER graciously "greeted [all the guests] as we came in" and spent much of the evening sitting apart with Henry Morgenthau, with whom she "spoke quietly . . . most of the time." Then, at ten ER left for her annual round of "Birthday balls, Anna and John took the Norwegian Royals upstairs, and FDR went off with his poker players & the rest of us dispersed."

Three days later, on 2 February, Anna and Daisy Suckley accompanied FDR to the naval hospital at Bethesda, where he had surgery to remove a "wen" or sebaceous cyst from the back of his neck. The procedure lasted less than an hour, and he emerged with a small bandage to cover eight stitches. In her column that day, ER did not refer to her husband's procedure. Instead she described a splendid event at the Corcoran Art Gallery, a tea at the White House, and a stirring Philadelphia Orchestra concert, conducted by Eugene Ormandy, featuring the *Symphony of the Four Freedoms* and Ravel's *Daphnis et Chloe*.

Congress was in rebellion, challenging FDR's influence as never before. In February it passed a tax bill that FDR vetoed because it provided aid and relief "not for the needy, but for the greedy." Congress overrode the veto. ER called FDR at Hyde Park and found him "quite calm" over the congressional upset and "more philosophical" though increasingly "weary." She added, "He is also fighting the British now at every turn."

Unwell and exhausted, FDR resisted her efforts to bring neglected issues to his attention. He went back on his promise to endorse a "fighting liberal" to administer the 1944 campaign for reelection. Instead, the new national chair of the Democratic Party would be Robert Hannegan, with whom the "conservative-minded" bosses were comfortable. Hannegan seemed to ER a "practical politician, but that may be necessary." Subsequently, she was disturbed that Hannegan rejected her invitations to discuss civil rights.

On another occasion, she entered FDR's cocktail reception loaded down with a high stack of papers. To Anna's horror, she said, "Now, Franklin, I want to talk to you about this." Anna thought, "'Oh, God, he's going to *blow*.' And sure enough, he blew his top. He took every single speck of that whole pile of papers, threw them across the desk at me and said, 'Sis, you handle these tomorrow morning.'" Anna was shaken, but her mother "was the most controlled person in the world." She simply "got up . . . stood there for a half second and said, 'I'm sorry.' Then she . . . walked toward somebody else and started talking. And he picked up his glass and started a story. And that was the end of it."

ER tried to withdraw and trusted in Anna's presence. Increasingly, she replied to questions of policy or program by saying, "Only Anna would know about that." However distant their relations became, ER continued to bring issues to her husband's attention. As Joe Lash later observed, "In continuing to serve him she walked a lonely path."

That winter ER spent considerable time with Elinor Morgenthau, and they enjoyed many concerts and plays: "What fun our spree was." But Elinor's health worried her: "I am anxious to hear about your cardiograph. You shouldn't be fainting on the roadside." She entrusted her confidences to Joe and Trude and indeed fantasized about working with them. "Trude and I talk about a research institute very often. Between you the job could be superbly set up and carried through."

On 4 March 1944, at FDR's insistence, ER embarked on a thirteen-thousand-mile journey to the Caribbean and South America, to visit military bases and diplomatic installations in areas where the troops "felt they were in a backwater." They longed to be sent to battle zones, where they might do "a more important job." FDR sent his wife to reassure them that they were "not forgotten," and that the president "knew and understood the whole picture and believed they were doing a still vitally necessary job."

But ER was uncertain about the true purpose of her mission: Had FDR simply found an excuse to remove her for several weeks? She was reluctant to go and dreaded the trip. Tommy, who was to be her companion and scribe, worried about her mood. There was "a real weariness on ER's part which was not apparent before and a pessimism about the future. . . . I thought she was anxious to go but she says she is only going at FDR's request and there is no enthusiasm."

ER and Tommy flew to Miami first, then went on to the Caribbean—to Cuba, Jamaica, Puerto Rico, the Virgin Islands, Antigua, St. Lucia, Trinidad, and Paramaribo. They then winged down the South American coast to Brazil, Costa Rica, the Panama Canal Zone, Salinas, Colombia, Ecuador, the Galápagos Islands, and Guatemala. The twenty-four-day trip was filled with diplomatic meetings, hospital and base camp visits, speeches, and ceremonies.

On 10 March, ER sent FDR greetings for their thirty-ninth wedding anniversary: "Many happy returns of the 17th dear. I'm sorry I won't be home but will you get something you want and let me pay for it on my return? I have $50 earmarked—and I'd like you to squander it!" On the seventeenth, "flying from Recife back to Belem," she noted: "Many thanks for your message which came before we left this morning." Her frequent letters generally repeated the theme that it was an easy trip, everyone was kind, and there was nothing to report—which was the key problem. There was little news, and the boys were bored; they all wanted to go home or into action. "I quite understand why everyone here gets a feeling of being out of things," she wrote FDR. But true to form, according to the *New York Times*, ER routinely "cheered the men . . . with her friendly interest," and all agreed that her visits to hospitals and camps raised spirits.

On 28 March, they returned home from Havana. "The trip did [ER] a lot of good," Tommy wrote to Lape, and the first lady was in "better spirits" than before she left.

But ER soon had to face her husband's poor health. Anna and Daisy had persuaded FDR to undergo a thorough physical examination. After tests and consultations at Bethesda Naval Hospital, the president was diagnosed with "hypertension, hypertensive heart disease, cardiac failure (left ventricular), and acute bronchitis." Rest and diet, fewer cigarettes and highballs, codeine for his cough, and digitalis for his blood flow were prescribed.

He decided to spend two weeks at Hobcaw, Bernard Baruch's plantation in South Carolina, for a complete rest, and ER agreed that his health required it. On 9 April, FDR left by train. Instead of the scheduled two weeks, he spent a month there, relaxing and recuperating, with interludes of fishing, yachting, and driving with dapper Bernie and his entertaining equestrian daughter Belle Baruch.

During the third week, ER and Anna flew down for a brief visit. "Hobcaw was just the right place for Franklin," ER noted, "who loved the country and the life there . . . and I [felt] it was the very best move Franklin could have made. I have always been grateful to Mr. Baruch for providing him with that holiday."

Subsequently rumors have persisted that FDR underwent surgery to remove his forehead blemish, thought by some to have been a melanoma. ER never referred to it, although in her memoir she wrote that the entire family and all his aides "knew that Franklin was far from well, but none of us ever said anything about it—I suppose because we felt that if he believed it was his duty to continue in office, there was nothing for us to do but make it as easy as possible for him."

Daisy Suckley, who spent considerable time with FDR, including several days at Hobcaw, believed the doctors did not know what was wrong with him, or if they did, they kept it a secret. "I am more worried than I let anyone know," she confided to her diary. ". . . I pray that it is not a bad type of disease."

Since ER had spent only one afternoon at Hobcaw, she seemed actually unaware of FDR's views. Close to the AFSC and previously outspoken against the 1942 carpet bombing of Cologne, ER now endorsed British and U.S. air raid massacres of major cities, including Hamburg, Nuremberg, Leipzig, and Berlin. The issue, generally ignored by the press, would become a major controversy in March 1944 when New York's Fellowship of Reconciliation published "Massacre by Bombing," sections of Vera Brittain's manuscript *Seed of Chaos: What Mass Bombing Really Means*. Brittain was appalled by the human devastation wrought by the

carpet bombings and never believed that they would, as the propagandists insisted, "shorten the war." The Blitz had demonstrated otherwise;
daily bombings only intensified England's fighting spirit. Now war by air
terror threatened the end of morality and civilization.

Brittain prophesied that "the callous cruelty which has caused us to
destroy innocent human life in Europe's most crowded cities, and the
vandalism which has obliterated historic treasures in some of her loveliest,
*will appear to future civilization as an extreme form of criminal lunacy with
which our political and military leaders deliberately allowed themselves to
become afflicted.*" Brittain's piece was published in *Fellowship*, along with
an "American Postscript" of support by twenty-eight noted writers and
Protestant leaders.*

Vera Brittain's words unleashed a storm of protest. FDR wrote an outraged rebuke in the *New York Herald Tribune*, insisting that "their facts
are wrong!" Moreover "you cannot talk conciliation. . . . You cannot
effect a compromise." There was nothing to negotiate between the German and Japanese forces of "world-wide death and destruction" and "the
philosophy of peace and . . . civilization."

FDR returned from Hobcaw, and ER reluctantly resolved to spend as
much time as necessary with her husband. For the five days after he
returned, in May, she stayed with him at Hyde Park. "I must really live in
the big house this year," she wrote Joe. ". . . I'll never like the big house
but suddenly F is more dependent, the children & grandchildren look
upon this as home & the cottage is just mine, so I must try to keep this
'lived in' & really pleasant! Never from choice would I live here however &
never alone."

Daisy was impressed: ER "is so fine, and so interesting. These are the
first two days they have been alone together for years." In her column, ER
rhapsodized about her time in the country. The beauty of spring's renewal
"gave me a particular thrill." She picked pansies "in my own little border

---

*Dr. John Nevin Sayre's postscript was a "call to repentance." The signatories included
Harry Emerson Fosdick of Riverside Church, Paul Scherer of Holy Trinity Church,
Georgia Harkness of the Garrett Biblical Institute, and the bishops of Western
Massachusetts and Arizona. Clarence Pickett of the AFSC supported Brittain, as
did WILPF leader Ruth Gage Colby. Dorothy Thompson, William Shirer, and
other journalists condemned the piece as sinister—even, wrote Shirer, "Nazi-
inspired." For the twenty-eight signers, see Grayling, *Dead Cities*, pp. 332, 334, 341.

around the cottage, and the lilies of the valley from the bed" planted by my "very dear friend" Esther Lape. "From the porch of my husband's little cottage and looking down at the country side below, with masses of rhododendron and azaleas in bloom all around, made me almost forget that the world is too sorrowful at present for life to have much zest."

ER and FDR had a busy and pleasant time together as they rearranged furniture and unpacked the Sixty-fifth Street items ER and Tommy had brought up the week before, including three Persian rugs, "very good orientals," that FDR wanted at his cottage and in the library. ER, the independent orphan girl, was eager for change, and FDR, the mama's boy, was eager to keep everything as it was. When FDR was alone with Daisy, he worried that ER intended to get rid of things he wanted. Daisy concluded: "ER would like to make more changes but I think the P wants to keep things as his mother had them, as far as possible."

From Hyde Park, ER visited Dean Mildred Thompson at Vassar College to hear about the London meeting to establish a United Nations organization for postwar education—ultimately called UNESCO. Chaired by Congressman William Fulbright (D-AR), America's delegation "was composed of very distinguished men and one woman!" Displeased by the token regard for women on important delegations, ER celebrated in her column the great contributions of women, notably Clara Barton and Florence Nightingale in the creation of the International Red Cross. The world would require women's vision and energies, and this new UN committee of education was of paramount importance: "we will now have to bend our energies to make education bring about peace."

With Daisy and Grace Tully, FDR returned to the White House, where he prepared for gallbladder tests. ER did not return with them, and Daisy noted that FDR was easier when she was away. When she was present, "more serious subjects come up . . . and then he gets tense and concentrated again." Evidently ER sensed FDR's tensions and spent the next two weeks away on speaking engagements, mostly in New York, Baltimore, and Arthurdale, West Virginia.

As a renewed Blitz rained down on London that spring, thousands of American troops in England prepared to embark upon the long-awaited second front. ER's thoughts on Memorial Day were solemn: "Was this a war for freedom? . . . Was this a war for justice? . . . Was this a war to bring us peace in the future? Then we must see to it that we learn to cooperate with all the peoples of the world. . . . We must see that justice is done" and not become "exploiters." "Since we must be strong and we must be free," ER concluded, "let us pray for wisdom and humility to use our freedom for the seed of humanity."

ER, FDR, Anna, and John Boettiger were together at the White House for FDR's 5 June broadcast when Rome fell to American and Allied troops. Citing Rome's ancient origins, "the foundations of our civilization," FDR assured the country that the pope and Vatican City were safe, their freedom "assured by the armies of the United Nations. It is also significant that Rome has been liberated by . . . many nations. The American and British armies" had allies at their side: "the gallant Canadians. The fighting New Zealanders . . . , the courageous French and the French Moroccans, the South Africans, the Poles, and the East Indians." Though victory still lay ahead, Italy would survive and continue "as a great mother Nation, contributing to the culture and the progress . . . of all peoples."

On 6 June General Eisenhower issued his order launching Operation Overlord, the Normandy landing: "Soldiers, sailors, and airmen of the Allied Expeditionary Force! You are about to embark upon the great crusade." According to Daisy, ER and FDR discussed General de Gaulle's intentions, then ER "went off with some friends, the Boettigers went to bed, and the P and I worked on some manuscripts . . . when E came in with some correspondence." Evidently there was little sleep that night. Shortly after midnight, radio broadcasts were interrupted: "The invasion has begun."

ER's D-Day column was filled with dread and hope: "So at last . . . all the preparation . . . the endless air raids, the constant practice" of the troops as they readied for landing, and for battle, was all over. It was a column written by a mother with four sons in uniform. With hope and fortitude, we "wait for victory."

It is hard to believe that the beaches of France, which we once knew, are now places from which . . . boys in hospitals . . . will tell us that they have returned. They may never go beyond the water or the beach, but all their lives . . . they will bear the marks of this day. At that, they will be fortunate, for many others won't return. This is the beginning of a long, hard fight. . . . Day by day, miles of country

must be taken, lost and retaken. . . . How can we hasten [victory]? . . .
We can help . . . by doing our jobs better than ever before.

That night, FDR read his D-Day prayer in a radio broadcast: "Last
night, when I spoke to you about Rome, I knew that our troops were
crossing the Channel in another and greater operation. . . . And so in this
poignant hour, I ask you to join with me in prayer:

With Thy Blessing, we shall prevail over the unholy forces of our
enemy. Help us to conquer the apostles of greed and racial arrogan-
cies. Lead us to the saving of our country, and with our sister nations
into a world unity that will spell a sure peace—a peace invulnerable to
the schemings of unworthy men. And a peace that will let all [human-
ity] live in freedom, reaping the just rewards of their honest toil.

ER considered it "a good prayer to read and reread in these coming days."
The next day she went to the Senate Office Building for a moving ceremony where *The Black Book of Polish Jewry*, a study of what happened to
the Jews of Poland, was presented to Senator Robert Wagner and members of Congress. "I hope that many people will see this book. The pictures speak more vividly than the written word. It is a horrible book, a
book which explains the terrible . . . martyrdom of the Jews in Warsaw,
and makes one ashamed that a civilized race anywhere in the world could
treat other human beings in such a manner."*

---

*Though the miseries of the 433,000 Jews locked behind the walls of the Warsaw
Ghetto had occasionally been reported in the Anglo-American press, the realities
were mostly unknown or denied. On 19 April 1943 the Jews of the ghetto rose up
against the Nazis, and in the ensuing battle three hundred Germans were killed
and scores of thousands of Jews were slaughtered. The ghetto was burned; 55,000
men, women, and children surrendered. Most were deported to Majdanek or Treblinka. An estimated 10,000 escaped, temporarily. Only after the destruction of
the ghetto, on 16 May, did its realities become more widely known. See Gilbert,
Auschwitz and Allies, pp. 131–35; Gilbert, *Second World War*, pp. 421, 428; Kushner, *Holocaust*, pp. 144, 315; Nicolson, *Diaries and Letters*, p. 266; Dallek, Robert, *FDR
and American Foreign Policy 1932–45* (Oxford University Press, 1979), pp. 450–57,
463ff, 503.

Finally on 12 June 1944, after weeks of lobbying by Henry Morgenthau and his team, the president signed his executive order to bring a thousand refugees from Italy to America's only refugee haven, the army camp in Oswego, New York. Since the Department of the Interior was in charge of the camp, Ickes appointed noted journalist Ruth Gruber to undertake the rescue. Promoted to a "simulated" general, she left for Italy on 15 July, then returned from Naples on the *Henry Gibbins* in August— with 982 Jewish and Christian refugees.

ER made every effort to persuade FDR to publicly support Henry Wallace to continue as vice president on the 1944 ticket. She understood from Hick that the new party leaders, led by city bosses, were eager to replace Wallace with contenders whom the two women regarded as centrists or worse. As early as March, Hick wrote of a great push for Senator Harry Truman (D-MO). He had worked as chair of the Senate special committee to investigate war industries, and to limit corruption and corporate greed. But he was associated with Thomas Pendergast's Kansas City machine, and others considered him a border state ally of Dixiecrat Democrats.

On 6 July, FDR told Henry Morgenthau that, "ER is trying to force him to insist on Wallace for Vice President." But FDR and Morgenthau agreed on an "open Convention" with the party leaders in charge and in "good humor."

With many decisions still to be made, FDR asked his wife to join him for the preconvention. As ER boarded the presidential special headed for San Diego, California, she harbored a lingering hope that FDR would endorse Wallace. She agreed with Trude's observation, "Labor is firmly for Wallace, so are the Negroes." Wallace, like ER, supported taking real steps toward racial justice. The NAACP's *Crisis* quoted him as saying: "The future belongs to those who go down the line unswervingly for the liberal principles. . . . There must be no inferior races. The poll tax must go. Equal educational opportunities must come. The future must bring equal wages for equal work regardless of sex or race."

Aboard the train, FDR's attitude disturbed and puzzled ER. She wrote a column to support Wallace, "but F says I must hold it till after the convention," she wrote to Joe. "I wish I were free." On 16 July in Chicago, Hannegan boarded the train seeking a written commitment from FDR for Truman or Douglas. FDR chose to meet with Hannegan alone, without ER. Annoyed, she wrote Hick, "Hannegan came to see F. at the Chicago station & I gathered after he left that a conservative would be the next VP. I'm sorry because I think it is bad politics not to stick to Wallace as well as disloyal but I never would be any good in politics!"

"I don't know that I'm being useful on this trip as there is nothing to do," she confessed to Trude. "FDR sleeps, eats, works & all I do is sit through long meals which are sometimes interesting & sometimes very dull." She and Tommy "played some gin rummy," and ER was proud to be "a bit ahead." But as always when ER was sidelined, she was bored, and angry. FDR wrote a public letter regarding Wallace and refused to show it to her. It was, she feared, merely tepid, as she told Joe: "I am no politician but I think he could have had Wallace & been as strong as he will be if they put a conservative on the ticket." After Hannegan left, she noted that "Jimmy Byrnes seemed to be gaining strength, which from my point of view is deplorable." Always the strategist, FDR did not tell his wife that he and Hannegan had agreed to support Truman, not Byrnes.

At the convention, race was an immediate issue because of the ongoing cruelties that segregated men and women of color in uniform faced. In the days just before the convention, a series of violent racial attacks occurred. On 8 July a white bus driver in Durham, North Carolina, "shot and killed a Negro soldier in cold blood." The NAACP believed that that shot for white supremacy might defeat FDR. For all his sonorous phrases, FDR "and his War Department have done absolutely nothing about the treatment of the Negro in uniform. It is a disgrace which stinks to heaven. . . . [People ask] 'What is a Commander-in-Chief good for if he cannot stop the humiliation and murder of soldiers in uniform by ignorant and prejudiced civilians"? Respect and safety must be ensured. "Segregation in the armed forces should be abolished forthwith."

Then, on 17 July, a hideous accident revealed the routinely dangerous and dreadful work that navy officers of color performed. At Port Chicago in San Francisco, hundreds of sailors performed the work of loading live ammunition onto warships and merchant ships bound for the Pacific theater. They were made to work countless hours, without protection or training, under the most dangerous conditions. On 17 July some of the munitions detonated, and the blast caused a chain reaction that killed

320 sailors and injured 390. "There has been a horrible explosion in San Francisco Bay," ER wrote Joe, "with hundreds of men killed."*

When the train reached San Diego, ER visited her son James, as well as her son John's wife, Anne, and their daughters, Haven and Nina. With James she toured the naval hospital and visited Colonel Evans Carlson, who was among the fifteen thousand dead or injured in the decisive U.S. victory at Saipan. ER spent several hours with her friend Tiny Chaney, who was "dancing in a little theatre in Hollywood." ER wrote Anna that she most looked forward to returning to Hyde Park, which "has spoiled me for these trips when I feel I'm not doing much good!"

The convention opened, and Wallace made a fighting speech to second FDR's nomination. ER hoped the enthusiastic rally that followed would result in a Wallace "miracle." But the bosses who controlled the convention demanded an immediate adjournment. By morning, the ballots were ready for Harry S. Truman as the candidate for vice president. At least, to ER's relief, it was not James Byrnes. The NAACP concluded, "Wallace did not lose at Chicago; the Democratic party and the plain Americans lost. The big machine bosses would not let the people have Wallace."

On 20 July, FDR broadcast his acceptance speech from his train, which was stationed at the San Diego naval base. He promised "progressive leadership" and specified plans for the future: "What is the job before us in 1944? First, to win the war. . . . Second, to form worldwide international organizations . . . to make another war impossible. . . . And third, to build an economy . . . which will provide . . . decent standards of living" for people "at home and abroad."

Pleased by her husband's words, ER resolved to concentrate on plans for the United Nations. The next day FDR sailed aboard the USS

---

*ER's friend the renowned Jamaican-American singer and activist Harry Belafonte, then a young sailor en route to San Francisco, recalled the "vast explosion." He noted that this dreadful situation was the outrageous fortune of black sailors deemed "the lowliest and most expendable in the U.S. Navy." The tragedy would concern ER far into the future. She protested the arrest and court-martial of the strike force and supported their postwar commutations. But the sailors remained dishonorably discharged and were barred from civil service employment. Port Chicago highlighted the profoundly cruel disgrace of military segregation. Belafonte always believed this tragic example of horror moved ER and other liberals to fight ever harder for change. Harry Belafonte to author, Belafonte, *My Song*, pp. 53–54.

Baltimore for a three-week trip to meet with Admirals William Halsey, William Leahy, and Chester Nimitz, and General Douglas MacArthur, in the Pacific. Just before he sailed, true to his pattern before undertaking a long journey, he wrote to ER an ameliorative note: "Dearest Babs . . . It was grand having you come out with me—and the slow speed was a good thing for us both. Lots of love—back soon. Devotedly F."

On 24 July ER published her long-delayed column on Henry Wallace. "There is integrity and pride" in Wallace's history and essence. He had learned Spanish to contribute to our Good Neighbor policy; spoke Russian in Siberia, and Chinese in China. The "people of the United States owe him our deepest gratitude" for his work which has "made it easier for us to build enduring friendships." FDR had promised Wallace any other job he wanted, and she hoped her column might be useful for the administration's most progressive liberal—after the election.

ER frequently declared that she was no politician, but she was determined to use her influence and power on behalf of her husband's reelection campaign against the Republican candidate, Governor Thomas Dewey. She did everything she could to advance his chances, traveling and substituting for him as needed.

On 10 August she wrote one of her most radical columns, counseling Americans to choose candidates "who think first of people, and only second of things." Big business and small businesses were important, she acknowledged. But greed and materialism had to be replaced by full employment, training, and planning to "advance the people's interests."

In several columns she emphasized the need to change the entire educational system to ensure not only literacy but popular empowerment. She called for a "year of extra training beyond high school" for skilled work to improve everybody's "standards of living." And why should higher education not be free? she asked. Why should girls not be included? Some protested that such plans were Communist or fascist or somehow un-American. ER considered "the shriek" against free education and universal training "incomprehensible" and undemocratic.

On 4 August she went to Boston for Missy LeHand's funeral. Her death, she wrote FDR, "was sad, but for her a release." Her column paid tribute to LeHand's "valiant and important job" and expressed admiration for "the way in which she bore the last few years of illness."

Above all, ER was hopeful about the 21 August opening of the

Dumbarton Oaks Conference in Georgetown, where U.S., British, and Soviet delegates—subsequently joined by China—met to plan the new world organization, the United Nations.* Governor Dewey protested that the Big Four intended to "subject the nations of the world, great and small, permanently to [their] coercive power." That would be, he insisted, "immoral and imperialistic." ER, dismayed, had warned her husband about Big Four dominance months before but now she urged him to counter Dewey's protest. FDR compromised, giving John Foster Dulles, Dewey's primary adviser, observer status, and thereby removed the controversy from the campaign.

The Big Four were divided profoundly over the UN and plans for peace, so a series of further meetings was arranged. The first one would be held in Quebec in September, with Churchill. This time FDR invited ER to join him. At first she was delighted, but was soon dismayed to realize that the women were sidelined, with nothing to do. Neither she nor Clementine Churchill was invited even to listen to the discussions. "The ladies have no duties," ER wrote Trude, "so I'm being lazy and luxurious. I have breakfast in bed but it does not appeal to me much except it is a good time to read!" She wrote Elinor Morgenthau: "It seems such a waste of time. The ladies' duties are all social & it would be boring except for the meals with a few people when the PM and F are entertaining."

In her memoir, ER wrote that she enjoyed walking around Quebec's old Citadel, "particularly along the ramparts" above the St. Lawrence River. Canada's governor general, Lord Athlone, and his wife, Princess Alice—Queen Victoria's granddaughter—"were kindness itself." There were several "entertainments," and one afternoon they took ER and Clementine Churchill "for a drive in the country and a picnic tea which I shall always remember with great pleasure."

ER returned to Hyde Park before the meetings ended—to get back to

---

*The Dumbarton Oaks Conference, from 21 August to 7 October 1944, agreed upon the UN's basic charter. Ultimately, ER worked vigorously for the Dumbarton Oaks proposals—with Woodrow Wilson's widow, Edith Wilson, and the Women's Division of the Democratic Party. Indeed, the creation of the UN became ER's central focus, and the Women's Division organized over eleven hundred Dumbarton Oaks meetings in forty-four states to prepare support for the future organization.

work and to prepare for a visit from the Churchills. ER wrote Hick: "I don't know what work goes on here but we talk much at meals. These people are all nice people & in some ways that is discouraging because they've not found the answers." So many urgent issues remained confused, or suspended.

In July, Soviet forces approached Warsaw, and when they were ten miles away, on 1 August, Polish insurgents in Warsaw rose up against the Nazis, expecting Soviet arms and support. But the Soviet troops ceased their advance, and Stalin refused to support the Poles—whom he considered allied with the anti-Communist Polish government in exile.* The revolt divided the Allies: Churchill wanted to support the determined warriors for Polish liberation, but Stalin considered them anti-Soviet, and FDR wavered. It would remain one of the war's most bitter controversies.

As Soviet troops stormed west, they encountered many horrors: Gestapo headquarters, mass graves and torture chambers in the former industrial center Minsk, and the vast extermination camp Majdanek (Maidanek) two miles beyond Lublin. The first Nazi death camp to be studied and photographed, Majdanek had seven gas chambers, where two million Poles, Soviet war prisoners, and Jews from many nations were slaughtered. Some U.S. journals, including *Time*, published reports and photographs, but the Western press largely ignored Majdanek. Even the BBC rejected Alexander Werth's August 1944 reports from Lublin as "a Russian propaganda stunt." The *New York Herald Tribune* wanted to await "further corroboration. . . . Even on top of all we have been taught of the maniacal Nazi ruthlessness, this example sounds inconceivable." Still, U.S. correspondents continued to send reports from Lublin, and the *Tribune* concluded that "if [they were] authentic the regime capable of such crimes deserves annihilation." Nevertheless, it was not until the western camps

---

*Warsaw's agony continued until 2 October 1944. With over 300,000 slaughtered, the Nazis crushed the uprising—and destroyed most of Warsaw. The Soviets did not enter Warsaw until January 1945. See Werth, *Russia at War*, pp. 869–83; Wallace, *Price of Vision*, p. 388. Harold Nicolson noted that members of Parliament were "really horrified" at Warsaw's collapse and believed Russia "behaved abominably." Nicolson concluded: "distrust of the Russians [was now] universal." *Diaries and Letters*, 4 October 1944, p. 2:404.

(Buchenwald, Dachau, Belsen) were liberated, noted Werth, that the press became "convinced that Maidanek and Auschwitz were also genuine." Whether these grim issues were discussed at Quebec is unclear, but ER nowhere referred to them.

In her 26 August column she celebrated the liberation of Paris. That "the French people themselves . . . freed Paris must be a source of great joy."

> Paris has always been a symbol, and now that it is again a city where [the people] are free . . . the whole nation must breathe a sigh of relief and hope. . . . We, in [the United States,] have always had an admiration and an affection for the French people and for their culture, and we wish them well. Their comeback will be a courageous one, and their eminence in the intellectual and artistic fields will, I am sure, rapidly reestablish itself.

Loyal to her husband's wishes, ER did not discuss de Gaulle or the political details of France's joyous liberation. But she was surprised at Quebec when FDR and Churchill agreed not to recognize de Gaulle's government—which General Eisenhower nevertheless did immediately.

After Quebec, ER enjoyed a weekend with Hick and Trude to speak about politics and romance. During a long walk "through the woods" Trude was filled with high hopes, since Joe would soon return home for officer candidate school. "We even planned the wedding," ER wrote to Joe. ". . . When you two are married I shall feel that one of my great desires has come to pass!"

But then the Churchills arrived, and there were many obligations. She wrote Joe, "My time slips away in such useless ways. Today . . . I've just been a glorified housekeeper! My household however changed every hour," and there were so many conflicting needs. "These are the days when the resentment at the tyranny of people & things grows on me until if I were not a well disciplined person I would go out and howl like a dog!"

To ER's annoyance, Churchill continued to chide her about Spain: they disagreed, but "he insists on bringing it up at every meal. He talks picturesquely but I am almost tempted to say stupidly at times." Table talk was generally "interesting," and there was good news: Allied "paratroops [had] landed in Holland."

The next day during a picnic, ER did not feel sidelined, and Clementine Churchill considered it "rather fun really." That day at lunch "Churchill and Eleanor Roosevelt debated long-run peace strategy." ER insisted the future depended on improved "living conditions throughout the world," while Churchill was convinced peace depended entirely on a fortified Anglo-American military agreement. During the two-hour lunch, the prime minister "twitted me about our differences of opinion on certain subjects. I assured him I had not changed, and neither had he, but we like each other, nevertheless." Ever political, ER concluded: "It is a good thing to reach a point in life where you can agree . . . [or] disagree," and still "like and admire" each other.

FDR silently watched while his wife and ally sparred. Admiral Leahy was riveted. Perhaps inspired by conversations with Trude about love across all divides, ER formulated her often quoted message: "We can establish no real trust between nations until we acknowledge the power of love above all other powers."

By this time it was known that in the dreadful Bengal famine, three to seven million people had died. ER was in close touch with Pearl Buck, Walter White, and other friends at the NAACP who were deeply concerned. And ER was increasingly supportive of the work of Nehru's sister Vijaya Lakshmi Pandit. But we have no evidence that ER confronted Churchill about India during this meeting. In the past, her differences with Churchill over India had so enraged the prime minister that FDR asked her to avoid the topic. She evidently consented.

That September, Madame Chiang Kai-shek returned to New York, again unwell, for treatment. Madame Chiang had persuaded Madame Pandit to send her daughters to Wellesley, and helped arrange her subsequent visit. ER, Pearl Buck, and Madame Chiang were the chief contributors to Madame Pandit's Save the Children chapter for the children of Bengal, where the famine still raged, and British silence ruled. Somehow, with the "direct aid of the Roosevelts," Madame Pandit arrived in New York aboard a U.S. military plane in December 1944.

It is also unclear if ER challenged Churchill's insistence on the creation of "spheres of influence." The notion of big power control over recently liberated nations appalled ER and was contrary to all of FDR's publicly announced plans. Nevertheless, at Quebec, FDR had agreed to a short "three month trial period." Based on that temporary agreement,

Churchill made plans to go to Moscow—to discuss Poland and spheres of influence.

There, on 9 October 1944, Churchill and Stalin divided the Balkans: Romania would have 90 percent Russian predominance; Greece, 90 percent British predominance; Bulgaria, 75 percent Russian interest, 25 percent British interest; Yugoslavia and Hungary, evenly divided, fifty-fifty. FDR had said, after all, that the United States wanted to be out of Europe within two years, and nothing was binding until the Big Three met again—after the election. Repeatedly, after Quebec—with Greece and Italy much on her mind—ER urged FDR to be stronger, more direct, and more forceful with Churchill regarding their profound and growing differences. More immediately, the U.S. election predominated.

Dewey was popular among NAACP activists, and ER worried that he might actually win the election. "Half my mail," she wrote Joe, concerned the "Negro situation" among military families. It was "bad," and changes would have to be made "everywhere when the war is over." Many shocking indignities occurred in 1944. More than 350,000 German prisoners of war were located at military bases around the country, where they were welcome to watch films and eat in dining areas from which U.S. servicemen and -women of color were excluded or segregated in remote sections. ER visited many of these bases, and FDR, unwilling to be distracted by issues of race, told ER to send her persistent correspondence directly to military authorities. She fully reported to General Marshall, Oveta Culp Hobby, and others. Although segregation remained the rule, some adjustments were made.

Impressed by Hobby's recruitment campaign, ER wondered if "colored WACs are going to get a chance to serve overseas. They are very anxious to go and I should think now they would be very useful in some of the places where there are colored troops." Hobby agreed with her, as she had earlier when ER protested to Assistant Secretary of War John J. McCloy about the treatment of colored WACs assigned to Camp Shelby at Hattiesburg, Mississippi. In response to her protest, Hobby determined to end such assignments until "local conditions both on the base and in the vicinity" were suitable "for WACS to serve."

On 1 December 1944, ER sent McCloy a blunt memo: "Why do Northern Negro WACs have to be sent south?" She also sent a "sample" of reports from Mary McLeod Bethune that detailed conditions at southern camps, "which I must say disturb me very much." At Lovell General Hospital, at Fort Devens, Massachusetts, on 7 March 1945, sixty WACs, trained as nurses and medical technicians, went on strike. The hospital's commander, Colonel Walter Crandell, ordered them to perform only menial tasks, to scrub floors and toilets. When they protested he declared they were "fit only to do the dirtiest type of work, because that's what Negro women are used to doing." Their walkout lasted several days, until they were ordered to return to work or face court-martial for disobedience. Four refused to return to work and were arrested, convicted, sentenced to a year at hard labor, and dishonorably discharged.

ER received many protests, including an appeal from Lillian Jackson, Baltimore's NAACP president:

> Our people are greatly incensed. . . . These young women enlisted of their own volition to help save the country. The discrimination generally practiced against colored men and women in the Armed Forces is a matter of public record. Knowing your genuine interest in the problems of all races, we are earnestly requesting that you use your influence on behalf of these WACS.

The case was sent to the War Department for review, and within a week "the Negro girls were exonerated and restored to duty; evidently there had been discrimination." While all charges against the health workers were dismissed, Colonel Crandell was neither removed nor investigated.

ER was less successful regarding the surviving victims of the Port Chicago explosion—who refused to return to work. In August 1944, 328 men—who had spent days clearing the docks and retrieving the body parts of their friends who had been blown to pieces—were ordered to resume the frightful task of loading munitions. The 258 who refused were arrested and court-martialed. After weeks of counseling, 50 of them still refused and received long sentences for "mutiny."

Despite Thurgood Marshall's powerful NAACP legal defense team, and his demonstrations of "rampant discrimination," they were all pronounced guilty on 24 October 1944, and sentenced to terms ranging from five to fifteen years at hard labor. ER appealed directly to Navy secretary James Forrestal, who was in charge of the review process, to take "special care in the case of these boys" and consider how they "suffer" various difficulties from childhood forward. Forrestal, always polite to ER, refused to comment but promised "a fair and impartial review." Thurgood Marshall kept her fully informed of his efforts and finally won their release in January 1946.*

The complexities of bigotry in the United States were illuminated for ER on 20 September 1944 when she and Elinor Morgenthau visited the refugee camp at Oswego, New York. The refugees, escorted by Ruth Gruber to the U.S.'s only "Haven," lived behind barbed wire and were not free to visit relatives or travel. "It was an interesting day, heartwarming because the people were so evidently happy to be free from fear but pathetic beyond words because they were such good people. Educated, professionals and merchants." They all seemed "exceptional." One of her guides, Dr. Ernst Wolff, was a screenwriter who had also written more than sixty novels. Of the 982 residents, "14 nationalities were represented and four religions—50 Catholics, 10 Greek Orthodox, 10 Protestant & the rest Jewish." ER noted the Oswego people had welcomed them and appreciated how much they had "to contribute to the community."

In her column, ER described conditions at the "refugee shelter" in the soldiers' barracks at Fort Ontario. "Partitions have been put up, affording them some privacy, but only the absolute necessities of life are being provided." There was limited food, iron cots, army blankets, stiff chairs, little comfort. "Restrictions are plentiful . . . but at least the menace of death is not ever-present."

ER was touched by the flowers and many handmade gifts given to her; and almost everyone enhanced their "temporary home" with impressive art and decorative work. Their efforts testified to all they endured and to their "character which has brought them through. Somehow you feel that if there is any compensation for suffering, it must someday bring them something beautiful in return for all they have lived through."

Eventually the children were allowed to go to the local schools and were popular among their new neighbors. ER's intervention enabled the college-age students to attend classes the very next semester. Her continuing

---

*The largest mass trial in navy history, the Port Chicago tragedy symbolized for many the fraud of this war for democracy and allegedly against race hate. President Bill Clinton pardoned the surviving three "mutineers" in December 1999.

involvement with the refugees at Oswego resulted in some improvements, including the right to travel into the town of Oswego and to visit relatives.

As news of Europe's liberation spread, bitter discontent among the residents deepened. There was depression and suicide. On 17 January 1945 news arrived that Zhukov's Red Army troops had entered Warsaw. That month in Oswego more than fifty inches of snow fell, and Ernst Wolff wrote an essay "Storm in the Shelter" to describe the agony there. "We thought," he wrote, "that we were to be guests; but we became prisoners behind barbed wire." He wrote of his soul at war; as the wind howled and the snows raged, he was grateful to be alive, "safe from [Europe's] chaos. . . . The catastrophe increasing day by day." But his heart was anguished by the absence of freedom.

He sent it to ER with a letter on 1 February to appeal to "your world-known humanity." He wanted her to understand the "melancholy" of the thousand people "you so honoured with your visit." To save our souls, "Give us our Freedom, give us back to the life! Be our lawyer . . . your voice will be heard. . . . Reborn us and [become] our mother!"

Dr. Ernst Wolff's cry for freedom profoundly moved ER. She sent it to Henry Morgenthau with the hope that he and his WRB would liberate the refugees at Oswego, who felt like imprisoned inmates. Morgenthau rejected her request that the refugees be allowed to leave the camp, which crushed ER. She turned to Ickes and Ruth Gruber, who also sought liberation for Haven's inmates.

The FBI investigators who routinely monitored ER concluded that her efforts would surely result in what they initially expected—a movement "to culminate in the admission for permanent residence of this unselected, unscreened group of aliens." The FBI was correct. While there was a great effort to return the thousand Oswego refugees to Europe immediately after the war, ER was prominent among those who fought for their freedom within the United States. Despite much opposition and even Morgenthau's refusal to intervene, on 22 December 1945 Truman would declare the Oswego refugees "admissible under the immigration laws."

In the context of the 1944 campaign, ER understood FDR's preference for silence on many bitter and controversial issues. While she trusted his political sagacity, her own need to speak out at least to him contributed to a new level of tension between them.

In 1944, ER focused her fantasies for a really liberal Democratic Party and movement on Henry Wallace, the NAACP, the AFSC (through which she continued to give all her contributions), and the labor PACs—since they especially called for full employment and enhanced New Deal reform and racial justice. FDR had urged Wendell Willkie to join him in a new movement and seemed pleased by Willkie's global vision across race, ethnic, and national divides. His views were heresy to current Republican leaders—Dewey, John Bricker, and Arthur Vandenberg, who hated Willkie as much as they despised FDR. In his last two articles for *Collier's*, Willkie argued that a truly liberal party would work to end "the Old World's colonial empires, and achieve real civil rights laws—including an anti-lynch law [and] repeal of the poll tax." He urged FDR immediately to issue an executive order to desegregate the military. But on 8 October, after a series of fourteen heart attacks, Wendell Willkie suddenly died. The fifty-two-year-old visionary who ate too much, drank too much, smoked too much, and loved too much was gone.

On 10 October ER attended Willkie's funeral. In her column, she celebrated his "great leadership qualities" that were too soon "removed from this troubled world. . . . His outspoken opinions on race relations were among his great contributions to the thinking of the world."

After the funeral, ER took the night train to Washington for the next day's press conference. It would be one of the largest, in celebration of her sixtieth birthday on 11 October. She was grateful for the outpouring of love and admiration for her work and for the notes from friends. Hick assured her, "You are still my favorite person in the world." Joe wrote a long praise-song about the woman who transformed "the ornamental office of First Lady into an expression of American democracy's concern with all the people [marked by] warm friendliness and hospitality." And she did "all these things not for political gain or prestige but because of . . . your great heart. . . . None of these things were done without a struggle." Joe admired that she had done it all "against tradition and custom, against family sometimes, and class." And he said that as the political passions of the times subsided, "you would loom ever larger in the hearts and imaginations of the American people and that your life would be held up as an example to all." ER replied to Joe's "birthday letter" with gratitude: even "if I don't deserve [all the nice things you say], I love you to think them."

Lady Stella Reading's birthday note, filled with admiration for ER, detailed the new Nazi V-1s, unmanned drone bombs that had devastated

London, day and night, throughout the summer of 1944. The "buzz bombs" had killed or injured more than 33,000 people and destroyed almost a million homes.* Frightened and exhausted, over half a million Londoners had evacuated to the countryside—and all now faced the winter with dread. The task of "re-homing people" would be "colossal" and tragic, Lady Reading said, since "the amount of pain . . . caused by robot bombing [meant] a severe test for everyone." Even in the context of this agony, Lady Reading was certain that ER had the "indomitable strength of mind and belief" to face the future: "I do wish you knew how all of us think of you and of the work you have done, and of the lead you have shown us, and how truly we admire not only the strong and purposeful way in which you have pursued the things you thought right, but the complete ignoring of self that you have shown."

That autumn ER worried that FDR's reelection efforts were sluggish, while Dewey was gaining support. She repeatedly urged FDR to speak out boldly. Although he resented her badgering, he eventually followed her advice. On 23 September he belatedly launched his campaign with his most memorable speech before an assemblage of Teamsters and other unionists, to counter Dewey's "dirty campaign" attacks of Communism and thievery:

> Republican leaders have not been content with attacks on me, or my wife, or on my sons. No, not content with that, they now include my little dog Fala. Well, of course, I don't resent attacks, and my family doesn't . . . but Fala does. [As soon as the Scottie heard the Republican fiction] that I had left him behind on an Aleutian Island and had sent a destroyer back to find him—at a cost to the taxpayers of two or three, or eight or twenty million dollars—his Scotch soul was furious. He has not been the same dog since.

FDR was in the fight. In a series of stunning speeches, he presented the reasons the future of democracy depended on his election—all of which resonated with ER's vision and emphasized issues she had

---

*In August Allied troops destroyed V-1 launching sites in France and Belgium, but on 8 September 1944, the Nazis unleashed even deadlier—and silent—V-2s. They traveled faster than sound, devastated entire neighborhoods, and killed over three thousand people. The attacks lasted until March 1945. Olson, *Citizens of London*, pp. 323–26.

repeatedly urged him to address. While he never credited her advice, she was gratified when he opposed the poll tax and championed universal suffrage: "The right to vote must be open to our citizens irrespective of race, color or creed—without tax or artificial restriction of any kind."

During that 5 October speech, nationally broadcast from the White House, FDR vigorously slammed "propagandists" and "politicians" who dragged "red herrings" into this election. There were "labor baiters and bigots" who "use the term 'communism' loosely, and apply it to every progressive social measure and to the views of every foreign-born citizen with whom they disagree. They forget that we in the United States are all descended from immigrants (all except the Indians); and there is no better proof of that fact than the heroic names on our casualty lists."

On 28 October in Chicago, before a jubilant crowd of 100,000, FDR detailed his vision of the "economic bill of rights" he had announced in January. Our men and women would return from war to "this land of unlimited opportunity . . . where all persons, regardless of race, and color, or creed or place of birth, can live in peace and honor and human dignity—free to speak, free to pray as they wish—free from want—and free from fear."

ER joined FDR for a rain-drenched tour in an open car through New York City. Despite the downpour, crowds greeted him in every borough, and FDR refused to shorten his planned route. They stopped several times in garages to "change into dry clothes," but at the end of the day, ER wrote, "he was drenched to the skin." That evening he was to address the mostly Republican members of the Foreign Policy Association at the Waldorf-Astoria. To rest beforehand he went with ER to the Washington Square apartment in Greenwich Village that she had rented for their retirement. ("He had told me to get an apartment . . . where he could work in peace and quiet, with no steps anywhere for," whenever he was in New York and not in Hyde Park or Warm Springs.) This bright, airy apartment, which faced the park, seemed to ER "ideal." She "had never had a chance to show it to him" and was pleased that he "said he liked it very much."

She was also impressed by her husband's stamina: "I was really worried about him that day, but instead of being completely exhausted he was exhilarated." Churchill wondered about FDR's "prudence" in riding in an open car in the "pouring rain with a temperature of 40 and clothes wet through." He asked for "reassurance," which FDR sent immediately: rain "does not hurt an old sailor. Thank you for your advice nevertheless. I am in top form."

ER and FDR thereafter campaigned separately, and she limited her words to those her husband endorsed. On Election Day, 7 November, the first couple converged on Hyde Park. The gathering was festive, with private moments divided between his court and hers. Daisy described several "very peaceful and restful" hours at FDR's Top Cottage with his circle, while ER walked with Joe, just returned from Guadalcanal, and Trude through the woods of Hyde Park. Joe wrote that the conversation, "the leaves crackling underfoot, gave life zest." Joe and Trude both argued that ER "had a responsibility" to assert "a more forthright position of leadership in the country. Millions of people were voting for her as well as for the President." ER was glad that Trude and Joe were reunited and with her. He was to begin officer training in Virginia, and they were to marry the next day.

The entire party assembled in the library for a high-spirited dinner. It was "an unusually nice party," Daisy wrote, with a few "'odd' elements," meaning Joe and Trude—who nevertheless were made to feel most welcome. Joe noted that the president toasted his and Trude's marriage. At midnight the traditional torchlight parade of Hyde Park neighbors, joined by three busloads of Vassar students, arrived to cheer. FDR made a short speech, ER invited the press in for snacks, and a team of FDR's "helpers" stayed up until three-fifteen a.m., when Dewey finally conceded. A closer contest than 1940, it was still a significant victory. Democratic majorities increased in the House and the Senate.

On 8 November, ER and Tommy attended Joe and Trude's wedding at her apartment in Manhattan. Joe's mother was there, as were Trude's children and several friends. Paul Tillich officiated. The next day ER and FDR returned to Washington, where ER told her press conference that she anticipated difficult years ahead in "winning the war, making the peace, rebuilding the world."

Before the election, ER had not wanted to add to FDR's burdens, and since they were called Communists whenever they spoke on behalf of unionists or civil rights, was restrained in her public statements. But now that the election was over, she wanted all "pussyfooting" political compromises to end. Of FDR, Harry Hopkins, and Bob Sherwood, she demanded action: why, after all, had FDR run again if not to advance his stated goals? she asked. Hopkins was impressed: she remained not only her husband's eyes and ears but also the true keeper of his conscience.

Although ER and FDR agreed on many issues, especially the importance of the UN and its new agencies, she wanted him to address race, rescue, and refugees before war's end. His promises for "full employment" must take effect, and efforts to ensure quality universal education across the color line must begin. Exhausted and unwell, however, the president sought rest—and escape from his wife's persistence. They were together only infrequently after the election, although they spent Thanksgiving at Hyde Park. One day, Daisy noted, ER and FDR "had their lunch alone— a remarkable occurrence." In the afternoons, ER read and FDR played solitaire.

On Saturday night they all entrained for Washington, and FDR departed on Monday for an extended healing trip to Warm Springs with Daisy, Polly Delano, and a full staff.

In her column of 4 December 1944, ER discussed Auschwitz— perhaps the first U.S. journalist to do so:

> I received yesterday from John Groth, an artist-correspondent just returned from overseas, a pamphlet "The Camp of Disappearing Men," for which he did the illustrations. It is a story of German atrocities in Oswiecim [Auschwitz], and is published by the Polish labor group. I do not know whether it is generally available to the public, but it should certainly be given wide distribution. The story is made vivid by the illustrations. It is a tale to fill you with horror, worse than almost anything your imagination can conjure up. And the end . . . leaves you with a determination that such cruelty and such treatment, with men turned into beasts, must never again be allowed to occur in this world. Any system which can train men through discipline to do the things which were done in [Auschwitz] must be so completely eradicated that there will never again be a resurrection of it.

Secretary of State Stettinius had recommended new appointments for the department, but ER feared they meant the State Department would once again sabotage the president's stated goals.* "It seems to me pretty poor administration," she protested to her husband, "to have a man in whom you know you cannot put any trust, to carry out" important policies. One of the nominees, James Dunne, had "backed Franco and his regime in Spain." Now he wanted "German industrialists to rehabilitate Germany . . . for the sake of business here." Given the combination of Dunne, Secretary Stettinius, Dean Acheson, and Will Clayton, "I can hardly see that the set-up will be very much different from what it might have been under Dewey. . . . I suppose I should trust blindly when I cannot know and be neither worried or scared and yet I am both." But FDR intended to remain in charge of his own diplomacy.

In December, Count Carlo Sforza, who had been a leading Italian anti-Fascist for years, returned to office as foreign minister in Italy's provisional government. He was anticlerical and antimonarchist, yet Churchill opposed him. On 3 December, unarmed Greek civilians demonstrated in Athens in support of anti-Fascist partisans. Perversely, Churchill ordered British troops to fire on them, calling them Communists and "treacherous aggressors." Twenty-eight civilians were killed and more wounded. His insistence on monarchy steered Greece toward civil war.

Labourites and U.S. liberals unanimously condemned Churchill's policies in both places. Stettinius's first action as secretary of state was to issue a press release endorsing democracy in Italy and tacitly rebuking Churchill: "The composition of the Italian government is purely an Italian affair [and] this policy would apply in an even more pronounced degree with regard to governments of the United Nations in their liberated territories." On 6 December, ER wrote FDR to applaud U.S. support for Sforza: "I like the statement on Sforza and our attitude toward the other governments very much indeed, but are we going to use any real pressure on Winston? I am afraid words will not have much effect." As ER feared,

---

*Morgenthau, Wallace, and other liberals shared ER's worries. Stettinius's group of six included Joseph Grew, Nelson Rockefeller for Latin America, Archibald MacLeish for public information, and General Julius Holmes—who was identified with Robert Murphy's Darlan Deal and "expedient collaboration with fascists." Only MacLeish was liberal. FDR once told Morgenthau that Clayton "was thoroughly reactionary" but subsequently told Wallace that Clayton "is not so bad and his wife is a dear."

however, FDR did not oppose Churchill's Greek policy, and the State Department made no further protest.

ER tried hard not to be a "pest" and sent good news to Warm Springs whenever possible. Although she remained "suspicious of this whole bunch" at State, she told FDR that she was pleased that liberal journalist Ernest Lindley "wrote a column completely upholding all your State Department. So!" But her husband, in the company of Daisy and Polly, with occasional visits from Lucy Mercer Rutherfurd and her daughter Barbara, sought rest and quiet. According to Daisy, ER's phone calls and letters distracted and upset him. ER regretted the need to trouble him, but she believed her perspective was vital for his impending summit meeting at Yalta.

FDR returned for a Christmas family reunion, enhanced by many grandchildren, at Hyde Park. The holiday was marked by a significant snowstorm and distress about the great military losses in the Ardennes forest during the Battle of the Bulge. ER had private Christmas dinners with Hick, Earl Miller and his wife, Simone, and Joe and Trude, and she spent special times with Tommy and Esther Lape. Elliott had a new wife, Faye Emerson, a Hollywood star whom ER found "pretty, quiet & hard. . . . She seems capable but I don't think she is more than a passing house guest! I hope I've behaved well!"

ER came back to Washington to prepare the White House for New Year's and the president's fourth inauguration. She accomplished her chores as hostess and first lady with her usual grace and generosity, and she especially enjoyed her grandchildren—all thirteen would converge for the first time.

On 20 January 1945, a raw, cloudy day, FDR, hatless and coatless, delivered his fourth inaugural address, from the South Portico, before thousands of people assembled on the snow-packed White House lawn.

> You will . . . I believe agree with my wish that . . . this inauguration be simple and . . . brief. . . .
>
> The great fact to remember is that the trend of civilization is forever upward. . . .
>
> Our Constitution of 1787 was not a perfect instrument; it is not perfect yet. But it provided a firm base upon which [we] . . . all races and colors and creeds, could build our solid structure of democracy.

And so today, in this year of war, 1945, we have learned lessons—at a fearful cost. . . .

We have learned that we cannot live alone, at peace; that our own well-being is dependent on the well-being of other Nations. . . .

We have learned to be citizens of the world, members of the human community.

We have learned the simple truth, as Emerson said: "The only way to have a friend is to be one."

We can gain no lasting peace if we approach it with suspicion and mistrust—or with fear.

The Almighty God has blessed our land in many ways . . . [and our faith] has become the hope of all peoples in an anguished world.

So we pray to Him now for the vision to see our way clearly, to see the way that leads to a better life for ourselves and for all our fellow men, to the achievement of His will to peace on earth.

The splendid speech profoundly moved ER.

One "evening when we were quiet," as she wrote Joe, she asked FDR about his State Department appointments. He explained they were compromises with competing interests, along "the line of least resistance." In this private moment, she asked about his plans for refugees, and he confided his "secret" intention to meet with Saudi king Ibn Saud after Yalta, for which he would leave two days later. Envisioning irrigation and forestation projects, he expected their meeting to advance prospects of settlement in Palestine.

But when she offered to accompany him to Yalta, he rejected the idea, which hurt her deeply. "I am tired & so very depressed tonight," she wrote Joe on 21 January. "The next years seem impossible to live through. . . . FDR & Anna go tomorrow night & I'm not really happy about this trip but one can't live in fear, can one?" She wrote a revealing note to her Allenswood chum, Lady Florence Willert: "Franklin felt that if I went it would only add to the difficulties as everyone would feel they had to pay attention to me, but since Sarah Churchill was going, Franklin thought Anna would be a help and a comfort and I am sure she will be."

Clearly, FDR did not want his wife's advice; she was not a comfort, and he wanted no competition. Once he and Anna departed into the unknown across most dangerous waters, ER plunged into many activities.

At the Yalta Conference, in preparation for the UN's founding meeting in San Francisco, the issue of "territorial trusteeships and dependent areas" was raised. Churchill "exploded." Never, he "declared hotly, would he ever consent to the fumbling fingers of forty or sixty nations prying into the life's existence of the British Empire. As long as he was Prime Minister . . . he would never yield one scrap of Britain's heritage." Even when informed that the foreign ministers at San Francisco would initially limit their concern to enemy-controlled areas and League of Nations mandates, "he continued to mutter: 'Never. Never. Never.'" At this conference, then, promises to preserve Churchill's sacrosanct empire was key to achieving compromises.

The conference ended on 11 February, and the results were quickly publicized. ER sent her congratulations: "We seem to be almost united as a country in approval. I think you must be very well satisfied and your diplomatic abilities [were surely] colossal! . . . All the world looks smiling! I think having the first UN meeting in San Francisco is a stroke of genius."

After Yalta, FDR continued his journey aboard the USS *Quincy* to Egypt. On 14 February, while docked at Great Bitter Lake in Egyptian waters, he met for five hours with King Abdul Aziz Al Saud, called Ibn Saud. After the two leaders exchanged warm greetings, "the King spoke of being the 'twin' brother of the President, in years, in responsibility as Chief of State, and in physical disability." Thereupon FDR gifted the infirm warrior king—who had been wounded nine times—with his "twin" wheelchair, which was much appreciated, and a DC-3 plane complete with crew. The two leaders enjoyed congenial conversations and soon established "a very friendly relationship."

FDR asked Ibn Saud "for his advice regarding the problem of Jewish refugees driven from their homes in Europe." His Majesty replied that they "should return to live in the lands from which they were driven." FDR remarked that "Poland might be considered a case in point. The Germans appear to have killed three million Polish Jews, [so therefore] there should be space in Poland for the resettlement of many homeless Jews."

Ibn Saud "then expounded the case of the Arabs and their legitimate rights in their lands and stated that the Arabs and the Jews could never cooperate," neither in Palestine nor anywhere else. Jews had purchased large tracts of land due to their increased "immigration" and now threatened a "crisis" in Palestine. "The Arabs," the king said, "would choose to die rather than yield their lands to the Jews."

Ibn Saud concluded that the Jews' only hope resided in "the well-known love of justice of the United States, and upon the expectation that the United States will support them." FDR assured the king that he would "do nothing to assist the Jews against the Arabs and would make no move hostile to the Arab people." He pointed out that he had no control over congressional resolutions, and that Americans enjoyed freedom of speech and press. They agreed that "an Arab mission to America and England" to end rampant misinformation about Arab sentiment would be "a very good idea."

After lunch their conversation turned to oil and investment plans for the postwar world. In March 1938 the Standard Oil Company of California (renamed Aramco in 1944) had discovered vast oil deposits in Saudi Arabia. Thereafter competition among oil interests had intensified, and Britain had achieved a regnant position, with dominant interests in Saudi Arabia, Iran, Iraq, Kuwait, and Bahrain. At the 1944 meeting Ibn Saud seemed to have bluntly asked FDR, "What am I to believe when the British tell me that my future is with them and not with America?" FDR replied that he envisioned the end of traditional colonialism and the creation of "spheres of influence in favor of the Open Door." He hoped "the door of Saudi Arabia will be open . . . with no monopoly by anyone; for only by free exchange of goods, services and opportunities can prosperity circulate to the advantage of free peoples." Ibn Saud agreed and hoped the United States would consider providing "material substance . . . for long range economic and political accords with Saudi Arabia to open up the Open Door."

The next day Ibn Saud met with Churchill. Where FDR had honored the king's Wahhabi religious beliefs and neither smoked nor drank alcohol in his presence, Churchill puffed in Ibn Saud's face and generally insulted him. "I have never met the equal of the President in character, wisdom and gentility," the king subsequently confided to Colonel William Eddy. ". . . The contrast between the President and Mr. Churchill is very great. Churchill speaks deviously, evades understanding, changes the subject to avoid commitment. . . . The President seeks understanding . . . ; his effort is to make two minds meet; to dispel darkness and shed light." Ibn Saud told many that his meeting with FDR was "the high point of my entire life."

Within months of FDR's five-hour meeting with Ibn Saud, the United States replaced Britain as Saudi Arabia's favored trading partner. The king affirmed the United States' exclusive oil production rights and authorized Aramco to build a pipeline from Dhahran to the Mediterranean coast; he agreed to permit the U.S. Air Force to operate the air base it had built at Dhahran; and in 1946 he even accepted a U.S. Geological Survey team to search the desert for water and minerals.

Churchill was furious that Britain's oil arena no longer included Saudi Arabia. In his report to ER, FDR discussed his sense of victory over the prime minister. But he told her that "his one complete failure" concerned Palestine—which had been, ER believed, the initial reason for their visit. FDR imagined it would be easier to deal with the son, who succeeded him. But among his many wives were at least forty-nine sons. In the meantime, to avoid bloodshed, FDR decided to rethink U.S. policy concerning Palestine. His agreements with Ibn Saud regarding oil, military bases, pipelines, and Palestine were long-lasting and remained mostly unknown for decades.

After FDR's meetings with Ibn Saud, ER's columns included many more references to B'nai B'rith, the National Conference of Christians and Jews, and Hadassah. On 26 February she eulogized Henrietta Szold, the founder of Hadassah, who had died in Palestine on 13 February. ER, who had met with her several times, wrote: "Many people in this country loved and admired her, and through her leadership . . . 12,000 Jewish children have been rescued in Europe and given asylum in Palestine." Her contributions would "live long into the future."

On 20 February, FDR's journey home was rendered tragic when, Pa Watson died at sea of a cerebral hemorrhage. General Edwin Watson had been FDR's closest military aide and companion. ER felt a great "personal loss" but also "a great anxiety about the effect [his death] would have on Franklin." Daisy noted that "Franklin feels his death very much & will miss him dreadfully. He always leaned on him, both figuratively and physically. 'Pa' was a Rock, the only one of his aides who gave a feeling of security to FDR. . . . Always cheerful, ready with a joke, and completely and unselfishly devoted to FDR." Everybody grieved for his widow, Frances Watson—"they were a very happy couple." Pa's death, followed by Harry Hopkins's sudden departure from Algiers by plane due to his own illness, affected FDR badly, and put him in a somber mood.

Upon his return to Washington on 28 February, FDR said he wanted to move on to big issues. He invited ER to join him in April in San Francisco to open the UN conference, which reflected her vision for world democracy. In his 1 March 1945 address to Congress, he affirmed:

> I come from the Crimean Conference with a firm belief that we have made a good start on the road to a world of peace. . . . The Conference . . . was a turning point in our history. . . . We shall have to take the responsibility for world collaboration, or we shall have to bear the responsibility for another world conflict. . . . [But] the three leading nations [at Yalta found] a common ground for peace. It spells the end of the system of unilateral action and exclusive alliances and spheres of influence and balances of power and all the other expedients which have been tried for centuries—and have always failed. We propose to substitute for all these, a universal organization in which all peace-loving Nations will finally have a chance to join . . . [to discuss, debate and build a] better world.*

ER was persuaded of FDR's vision by the power of his rhetoric—and she was persuaded of his continuing good health by the power of denial. Almost everyone around FDR except ER worried about his health. Her husband seemed rested, she wrote to Joe, and looked ruddy. "He says he felt well all the time & he feels evidently that all went well" at Yalta. At the White House, ER's friend Margaret Fayerweather asked ER about his "thin and worn and gray" appearance and his uncontrollably shaking hands. ER acknowledged that he wanted her to drive at Hyde Park, "which he never did before," and that he "let her mix cocktails" when John Boettiger was out. But while she contemplated retirement, he said:

---

*FDR's long speech, the first he gave seated, was filled with personal asides, and details of difficulties still to be addressed. These included ongoing tensions over Greece, Yugoslavia, and Romania, as well as Poland's government and borders, all of which intensified despite Russia's agreement to enter the war against Japan, and the Anglo-American agreement to bomb strategic targets "in direct support of Soviet armies, as well as in support of our own in the Western Front." Most immediately, this referred to the firebombing of Dresden, launched on 13 February. The historic city of Dresden was obliterated. Because over 650,000 incendiaries (subsequently called napalm bombs) were employed, the death toll was incalculable; estimates ranged widely—from 25,000 to over 300,000.

"You know, Eleanor, I've seen so much now of the Near East and Ibn Saud and all of them, when we get through here . . . I'd like to go and live there. I feel quite an expert, I believe [with various irrigation and forestation projects] I could help to straighten out the Near East." "Can't you think of something harder to do?" I asked. "Well yes . . . it is going to be awfully hard to straighten out Asia, what with India and China and Thailand and Indo-China. I'd like to get into that." Does *that* sound tired to you, Margaret?

Slowly, reluctantly, ER faced the truth—he was exhausted and spent. "I found him less and less willing to see people," and he had no patience for argument or debate: "For the first time I was beginning to realize that he could no longer bear to have a real discussion, such as we had always had." One afternoon, during an argument with Harry Hooker, ER suddenly realized her husband was "upset" and "stopped at once." It was a defining moment: FDR "was no longer the calm and imperturbable person who . . . had always goaded me on to vehement arguments" over policy and politics. She at last understood she had to face "the change which we were all so unwilling to acknowledge."

She was glad when he decided to spend April in Warm Springs, the place he always went to heal, with Polly Delano and Daisy Suckley, since "they would not bother him as I should have by discussing questions of state." On 1 April, when she telephoned her husband, FDR seemed "settled in Warm Springs & the rest will do him good," she told her aunt Maude Gray. "He should gain weight but he hates his food. I say a prayer daily that he may be able to carry on till we have peace and our feet are set in the right direction." From Europe, Elliott cabled that Germany's end seemed imminent, but her three boys in the Pacific were "not so optimistic." ER worried about them all.

She put her faith in the 25 April San Francisco meeting, which FDR had done so much to prepare for. At her press conference on 2 April, she confided that she was more excited and enthusiastic about the "great meeting at San Francisco to draft the UN Charter" than by "anything since early New Deal days." Even Republican members of the Dumbarton Oaks Conference, including Senator Arthur Vandenberg, known to hate FDR, were supportive. Of course, ER asserted, there are many differences around the world, which is why there are conferences and negotiations. "We are now talking about the world. Why should we all agree?" She wanted to see unions and corporations consider "world use, not world markets." She wanted the needs of all people served, rather than limiting consideration to profits. The push to remove women from the workplace after the war outraged ER. Women were not only needed; they had rights. While they also required protection, she was now "in perfect sympathy" with the National Woman's Party demand for equality and the Equal Rights Amendment.

To promote the UN conference, ER traveled widely and spoke frequently. From Vermont and New Hampshire to North Carolina, on high school and college campuses, in community centers and before women's groups, she championed the idea of world citizenship. She was particularly pleased to participate at a forum at New York's Henry Street Settlement with Paul Kellogg and other veteran peace activists—where, she noted, the spirit of Lillian Wald continued. She held weekly meetings, dinners, and teas with wounded veterans from military posts like Forest Glen, Washington's Rehabilitation Center, and she continued to protest discrimination in the military. She worked ever more intensely with Mary McLeod Bethune and the National Council of Negro Women, with Walter White and the NAACP.

At Warm Springs, FDR decided to push for the end of colonialism, despite Churchill's certain objection. He decided to liberate the Philippines. On 4 April, ER learned that her husband would meet the next day with Philippine president Sergio Osmeña to embark upon the path of immediate independence. She worried, since that was the one subject FDR had so often insisted she avoid, given the depths of Churchill's wrath.

Madame Pandit, Nehru's sister, was increasingly popular with ER as well as her closest allies in the NAACP and among political women. Her brave and bold words were generating a movement to support independence and freedom for India. ER admired and agreed with her. They had first lunched together on 27 January, while FDR was en route to Yalta: ER wrote her husband that Madame Pandit was wise and did not agree with Churchill. All of Madame Pandit's subsequent speeches and public events were stirring and important.

On 1 March *America's Town Meeting of the Air* hosted a nationally broadcast debate on "whether colonial empires were a threat to world

peace." Madame Pandit was allied with Owen Lattimore against the eminent British imperialists Robert Boothby and John W. Vandercook. Town
Hall was packed, and millions of Americans listened by radio as Madame
Pandit affirmed, "The postwar world cannot be built on old and rotten
foundations. There must be a new concept in which all people can share."
A new world of peace would require the end of empire and a new world
order to ensure "the progress of humanity." The event stimulated anti-
imperialist and antiracist meetings throughout the United States—
Madame Pandit in specific partnership with the NAACP.

Freedom for India had long been on ER's agenda, and she supported
the new alliance, but on 4 April she wrote Stettinius that she feared that
Madame Pandit's plans for San Francisco might enrage Churchill enough
to endanger the UN conference. To protect and support her husband's
vision, she wondered if Madame Pandit and her delegation might somehow be stopped "so as not to stir up feelings against Great Britain."

Surely ER was relieved when on 7 April Stettinius rejected her idea,
since the United States believed in freedom of speech, and his colleagues
in the British Foreign Office were less disturbed. But her letter is a measure of how far she might juggle to support her husband's priorities if the
master juggler was unwell and unavailable.*

While FDR was in Warm Springs, Elinor Morgenthau had a serious
heart attack; ER's three sons at sea in the Pacific had not written; and
plans for San Francisco were still unfolding. On 8 April, after a pleasant
late-night conversation, she wrote FDR, "Dearest Franklin, I was so
weary last night . . . when you got me it was 10 our time & I was half
asleep!" She and Tommy had spent two days at Hyde Park—repacking
barrels of SDR's crystal, china, silver, and family treasures to distribute to
the children. "We ache from our unwonted exercise but we've had fun
too! . . . Give my love to Laura & Margaret & I'm glad they will be along
on the trip to San Francisco. Much love to you dear. . . . You sounded
cheerful for the first time last night & I hope you'll weigh 170 pounds

*I am grateful to my colleague Manu Bhagavan for this correspondence. ER and
Madame Pandit remained allies and friends. Their "close friendship" deepened
after Madame Pandit became ambassador to the United States (1949–52); in 1952
she arranged and hosted much of ER's trip to India; and in 1953 Madame Pandit
became the first woman elected president of the UN General Assembly. ER considered her one of the world's "most remarkable" women.

when you return." She did not know that those would be her last words to him.

Comforted by Stettinius's note, and eager to advance FDR's commitment to colonial liberation and Philippine independence, ER wrote a vivid column to honor General Carlos Romulo. The International Board of the YMCA invited her to New York's Cosmopolitan Club to hear General Romulo, resident commissioner of the Philippines, who had just returned from Manila and presented "perhaps one of the most interesting speeches on race relations that I have ever heard." On this Bataan Day, 9 April, he praised American teachers as unique and "beloved." U.S. policies enabled "75,000 Filipino soldiers [to fight] side by side with 9,000 American soldiers, and 18 million Filipino civilians were able to withstand Japanese propaganda and remain loyal to the United States and to their own freedom." For three years, his wife and three sons had fled the Japanese invaders, moving around over miles of mountains and shoreline almost every day. He spoke of "a blond boy from Texas, fighting in the same foxhole with a dark-haired, brown-skinned Filipino. Both were killed by [a] Japanese bomb, and their life blood mingled together as it ebbed away."

On 11 April FDR worked on his Jefferson Day speech; it is unclear whether he read ER's column, or whether ER knew that Henry Morgenthau visited Warm Springs that night. Morgenthau was "terribly shocked" by FDR's "haggard" appearance but evidently was not surprised by Lucy Mercer's presence at dinner, with her Russian artists friend Elizabeth Shoumatoff, who was there to do a second portrait of FDR. Dinner with the four ladies was pleasant, although Morgenthau was bothered by FDR's memory loss, "and he was constantly confusing names." They discussed Morgenthau's plans to write a book about Germany after V-E Day, which FDR considered "a grand idea," and he promised to contribute to it. Morgenthau argued that postwar Germany should be weak and pastoral. FDR was initially evasive but ultimately said, "Henry, I am with you 100 percent." Polly Delano ordered them to desist their meeting in five minutes, whereupon "the four ladies" entered. When Morgenthau said good-bye, "they were sitting around laughing and chatting, and I must say the President seemed to be happy and enjoying himself."

Curiously, FDR and Morgenthau did not discuss the WRB's rescue efforts. On 8 December, Soviet troops had entered Budapest, and they finally took the city on 13 February 1945. Thereafter Raoul Wallenberg, having heroically saved the lives of more than 100,000 Budapest Jews with the WRB, disappeared into the Soviet gulag, mysteriously taken prisoner by Soviet authorities. The Swedish legation in Budapest investigated his abduction, and Morgenthau joined the WRB/State Department effort. FDR was not involved or perhaps not even informed.*

On the morning of 12 April ER's press conference focused on plans for the UN and her thoughts about the controversies regarding Germany and V-E Day, since victory in Europe seemed imminent. She explained that once "real knowledge" of conditions in Germany was obtained, and a United Nations Organization was formed, all forty-four nations would participate in decisions: "We have to get over [our] habit to consider only what we will do. . . . We will have the United Nations Organization so all the world's opinion" would be considered.

Not for some time would ER learn the conditions that U.S. troops discovered when they liberated the death camps at Nordhausen, Ohrdruf, and Buchenwald. On the same day as ER's press conference, General Eisenhower toured Ohrdruf and Buchenwald with Generals Omar Bradley and George Patton. On 15 April, the British reached Bergen-Belsen, and within days the United States entered Dachau, ten miles from Munich. Never again, ER wrote, could the world live on an island of contentment "in a sea of misery." Our consciences against moral wrongs would have to be aroused to activism before it was too late. In this case, we did not stand up "against something we knew was wrong. We have [to] avenge it—but we did nothing to prevent it."

After her press conference, ER met briefly at the White House with

---

*The WRB and the State Department wrote memos about Wallenberg's disappearance between March and November 1945. WRB officer General O'Dwyer and State's George Warren, Dean Acheson, George F. Kennan, and Albert Szent-Györgyi were central correspondents. On 30 November 1946, Wallenberg's mother, Maj von Dardel, appealed to ER for help: "Knowing your warmheartedness and kindness to all those who suffer I have gathered courage to write to you." In response, ER galvanized State Department investigations and public outrage, which continued for decades. In 1948 ER, Albert Einstein, and others nominated Wallenberg for a Nobel Peace Prize, dead or alive. The entire Wallenberg file, classified secret, was finally declassified by the State Department on 17 August 1988. Marton, *Wallenberg*; Wallenberg, Soderlund, and Anger, *Letters and Dispatches*; State Department file 1945–47, BWC Collection.

Charles Taussig, a State Department adviser to the San Francisco delegation, whom both FDR and ER trusted. He wanted her advice on FDR's trusteeship policy. Their conversation was interrupted by an urgent call from Warm Springs: FDR had "fainted," Polly Delano said. ER called Dr. McIntire, who was not alarmed and suggested she go to her scheduled address at the Sulgrave Club and leave with him later. There Steve Early called and asked her to return immediately. "I did not even ask why. . . . In my heart I knew what had happened, but one does not actually formulate these terrible thoughts until they are spoken." In ER's sitting room, with Anna and John Boettiger, Early said that "the President had slipped away." She cabled her sons: HE DID HIS JOB TO THE END AS HE WOULD WANT YOU TO DO! Harry Truman was summoned to the White House, and ER told him, "Harry, the President is dead." There was a moment of silence, and then Harry asked ER: "Is there anything I can do for you?" She replied: "Is there anything we can do for you? For you are the one in trouble now."

Shortly after Harry S. Truman took the oath of office, ER, Early, and Dr. McIntire flew to Warm Springs. They arrived before midnight and made funeral arrangements with Grace Tully, Polly Delano, and Daisy Suckley. ER, Hassett, Steve Early, and others "decided what to do," said Daisy. "The undertakers waited. We leave at ten tomorrow morning. ER sent us off to bed . . . even if we don't sleep."

Perhaps that night, or on the train from Warm Springs to Washington, Polly told ER the truth about FDR's last visit, and other visits, with Lucy Mercer Rutherfurd. There is no record of ER's reaction. Perhaps she was silent. ER II observed that Polly was often critical and occasionally nasty, even cruel. At one dinner party ER's niece saw Polly furtively "pour a generous jigger of sherry in 'dear Eleanor's' soup"—even though she was fully aware of ER's feelings about alcohol. "It was then that I suspected [Polly] felt threatened by a power she could not match." That was "only embarrassing and rather sad, but eventually she revealed true malice." ER's niece believed ER "had not known until that moment that FDR had continued his relationship with Lucy Mercer. But Aunt Eleanor did not allow the revelation to destroy her. She simply had too much good work to do."

According to White House assistant chief usher J. B. West, ER entered the White House "tall and stately in black . . . with the flag-draped casket, which had been drawn on a caisson from Union Station by six white horses. . . . The undertaker placed the President's body on a catafalque in the East Room, where the honor guard [waited]." ER asked the ushers to have the casket, which had been sealed at Warm Springs, reopened: "Can you dispense with the Honor Guard for a few moments . . . ? I would like to have a few moments alone with my husband."

ER "waited in our office while we called the undertaker to open the casket." When it was ready, she requested complete privacy: "'Please do not let anybody come in.'" Chief Usher Howell Crim "asked the military honor guard to leave the room, and he stationed himself at one door"; his assistant, Charles Claunch, blocked the other door. From where he "stood guard inside the third door," West observed ER, who "stood at the casket, against the east wall, gazing down into her husband's face. Then she took a gold ring from her finger and tenderly placed it on the President's hand. She straightened, eyes dry, and left the room. The coffin was never opened again."*

Later that afternoon, at her husband's crowded funeral in the East Room, ER remained solemn and dignified, comforting others and offering support. During the train ride to Hyde Park for the burial, she saw America in mourning. Huge crowds turned out at every railroad siding, shedding tears of grief. ER recalled Millard Lampell's funeral poem for Abraham Lincoln, shot on 13 April 1865: "A lonesome train on a lonesome track / Seven coaches painted black / A slow train, a quiet train."

On the train to Hyde Park, she had time to read the last words FDR wrote on 11 April, which were to have been delivered the next day. This message remained for her his most profound legacy:

Today this nation which Jefferson helped so greatly to build is playing a tremendous part in the battle for the rights of man all over the world. . . .

But the mere conquest of our enemies is not enough. We must go on to do all in our power to conquer the doubts and fears, the

---

*There is disagreement about when Polly Delano revealed to ER the truth of FDR's relationship with Lucy Mercer—not at Warm Springs before the casket was sealed, but on the train ride to the White House. I have concluded that that train ride was the site of their conversation.

ignorance and the greed which made this horror possible. . . . Today we are faced with the pre-eminent fact that, if civilization is to survive, we must cultivate the science of human relationships—the ability of all peoples, of all kinds, to live together and work together in the same world, at peace. . . .

The work, my friends, is peace. More than an end of this war—an end . . . of all wars. Yes, an end, forever, to this impractical, unrealistic settlement of the differences between governments by the mass killing of peoples.

To all dedicated "to the making of an abiding peace, I say: The only limit to our realization of tomorrow will be our doubts of today. Let us move forward with strong and active faith."

Galvanized by these words, so reminiscent of his first inaugural address, ER wanted them included in the funeral tribute. Bishop Angus Dun acceded to her request, and FDR's earlier words, "the only thing we have to fear is fear itself," ended his final prayer.

For the rest of her life ER devoted herself to fulfilling the legacy she shared with her husband: the quest for peace in a world united for justice. She never criticized him or revealed her hurt. She "did not tell anyone" about Lucy Mercer's frequent presence in his life, observed Lash. Nor did she reveal her feelings about Anna's involvement in FDR's many meetings with Lucy Mercer. Anna subsequently referred to her mother's anguish and hurt, and their early-afternoon conversation at the White House shortly before the four p.m. funeral. ER wrote only of how comforted she was by the presence of Anna and John, and all the children present during FDR's final journey home.

ER wrote Joe Lash on 16 April: "I know you would do anything to help but somehow I am very calm. Only a little keyed up because there is so much to do & to think about! I don't need much sleep luckily." For the future, she wrote, "I count on you & Trude for much happiness and don't ever lets be sad about anything as long as we can be together! I want to cling to those I love because I find that mentally I counted so much on Franklin I feel a bit bereft."

Daisy Suckley, who knew most of FDR's secrets, affirmed that ER "loved him more deeply than she knows herself, and his feeling for her was deep & lasting. The fact that they could not relax together, or play together, is the tragedy of their joint lives, for I believe . . . they had everything else in common. It was probably a matter of personalities or a certain lack of humor on her part. I cannot blame either of them. They are both remarkable."

Esther Lape also believed that ER always loved and forgave FDR: "I don't think she ever stopped loving someone she loved." After his death ER wrote Lape, "You have an understanding heart dear, but you should know it is more shock & a sense of unreality than loneliness. I think we had all come to think of him as able to carry the world's problems & now we must carry them ourselves."

She wrote on the same theme in her notes to all her beloveds who rallied around her, including Hick, Joe in Virginia, Trude in New York, Bernard Baruch, who returned from London in time for the funeral and remained by her side throughout, and her aunt Maude in Ireland.

Subsequently, ER wrote more fully:

All human beings have failings . . . needs and temptations and stresses. Men and women who live together through long years get to know one another's failings; but they also come to know what is worthy of respect and admiration. . . . If at the end one can say: "This man used to the limit the powers that God granted him; he was worthy of love and respect and of the sacrifices of many people, made in order that he might achieve what he deemed to be his task," then that life has been lived well and there are no regrets. . . .

He might have been happier with a wife who was completely uncritical. That I was never able to be, and he had to find it in other people. Nevertheless, I think I sometimes acted as a spur, even though the spurring was not always wanted or welcome. I was one of those who served his purposes.

On 20 April 1945 she left the White House for the last time, having packed twenty trucks of Roosevelt possessions. Upon her arrival in New York, she dismissed the reporters assembled in her Washington Square lobby: "The story is over." Now free and "on her own," she embarked on a new chapter of service for peace and worldwide human rights.

ER's Legacy: Human Rights

ER began her emotional journey into widowhood with deep insights and surprising candor in *You Learn by Living*, published in 1960. "Like countless other women, I had to face the future alone after the death of my husband, making the adjustment to being by myself, to planning without someone else as the center of my world. . . . But I discovered that by keeping as busy as possible I could manage increasingly to keep my loneliness at bay." That was in fact how ER had lived her entire adult life. After 12 April 1945, however, she felt independent, relieved from political restraints.

ER returned to writing her daily column within a week of FDR's passing. In her 17 April memorial for her husband, she called for a people's movement to create a United Nations dedicated to a future of peace and human rights: Today grief "pervades the world, [and] personal sorrow seems to be lost in the general sadness of humanity. . . . There is only one way in which those of us who live can repay the dead who have given their utmost for the cause of liberty and justice." FDR's goal had been to build an organization "to prevent future wars," and that was now ER's quest.

After she completed her White House chores and packed belongings that filled twenty trucks, ER held a farewell tea for the sixty women of her press corps. She confided to them that her present work plans were limited to writing her columns; she would not accept public office, and she rejected Congresswoman Mary Norton's (D-NJ) intention to name her special delegate to the San Francisco Conference to establish the UN organization. Although ER had considered FDR's decision to convene the first UN meeting before war's end "a stroke of genius" and actively lobbied for women representatives, she mysteriously held back: "Nothing would induce me to run for public office or to accept an appointment to any office at the present time." Subsequently, she told her allies and most insistent promoters that she "would rather be chloroformed" than accept any political nomination. She was pleased, however, to continue her writing career—as a magazine journalist and daily columnist. "Because I was the wife of the President, certain restrictions were imposed upon me. Now I am on my own, and I hope to write as a newspaper woman." That spring she wrote Trude Lash, "I'm glad you like my columns; they are more fun to do now that I am freer."

Although ER refused to attend the UN conference of 25 April–26 June for "reasons of protocol," she was entirely committed to its success in creating the UN Charter. It was, after all, an extension of her intense efforts on behalf of U.S. involvement in the World Court and League of Nations after World War I and the fulfillment of her appeals to FDR to go beyond Churchill's limited vision of Anglo-American leadership and build a real international alliance for world peace.*

ER never took any credit for her husband's decision regarding the UN and repeatedly explained that she worked only to promote his vision, fulfill his legacy. That was her theme both in public and in her intimate correspondence. In her last White House letter to Hick, she wrote, "The Trumans have been to lunch & nearly all that I can do is done. The upstairs looks desolate & I will be glad to leave tomorrow. . . . Franklin's death ended [an era] in history & now in its wake for lots of us who lived in his shadow . . . we have to start again under our own momentum & wonder what we can achieve."

To lift ER's self-imposed veil of modesty, however, is to reveal a different reality. Eleanor Roosevelt promoted her unique vision of decency in world affairs from a variety of public positions—as lobbyist, critic, and insider. She did not become the "First Lady of the World" solely as a result of her role as the most public, active, and popular of all U.S. first ladies. Rather, her diplomatic interests and skills, and her involvement in U.S. international affairs, began during World War I and continued until her death. She was a key, if often unrecognized, figure in activist international circles.

---

*According to Dan Plesch, director of international studies at SOAS, University of London, "Churchill hankered for the vision of an Anglo-Saxon world Empire," defined by "an alliance of the English speaking peoples." Plesch credited ER for splendid lobbying efforts, in alliance with Clark Eichelberger, formerly of the League of Nations Association. Eichelberger had founded the United Nations Association in 1943, and with ER he created UN committees all across the United States. See Plesch, *America, Hitler, and the U.N.: How the Allies Won WW II and Forged a Peace* (L.B. Tauris, 2011) pp. 165–68.

ER imagined a world without war, and understood that peace would remain a chimera so long as entire nations and subject peoples were denied access to economic security: food, clothing, education, work, health, comfort. She understood power, sought power, and influenced policy from positions of power. She was a practical idealist who understood the complexities of colonial privilege and revolution and the vagaries of competition and compromise. She was committed to the precepts of America as codified in the Declaration of Independence and the United States Bill of Rights. But she also believed that no individual, community, or nation could be truly free so long as others were fettered.

On 30 April 1945, she wrote in support of Congresswoman Norton's efforts for a Fair Employment Practices Committee bill, to end race and gender discrimination in every workplace. This bill, ER wrote, would benefit the entire nation:

> If we do not see that equal opportunity, equal justice and equal treatment are [granted] to every citizen, the very basis on which this country can hope to survive with liberty and justice for all will be wiped away.
>
> Are we learning nothing from the horrible pictures of the concentration camps which have been appearing in our papers day after day? Are our memories so short that we do not recall how in Germany this unparalleled barbarism started by discrimination directed against Jewish people? It has ended in brutality and cruelty meted out to all people, even to our own boys who have been taken prisoner. This bestiality could not exist if the Germans had not allowed themselves to believe in a master race. . . .
>
> There is nothing, given certain kinds of leadership, which could prevent our falling prey to this same kind of insanity, much as it shocks us now. The idea of superiority of one race over another must not continue within our own country, nor must it grow up in our dealings with the rest of the world.

As we survey "the war-torn world," ER concluded, our struggle is "to find a way [to live] peacefully and cooperatively . . . internationally and within our own borders." We must boldly create a new system of equality, fairness, and dignity "through our government and as individuals. . . . Where the theory of a master race is accepted, there is danger to all progress in civilization." Her April 1945 call to create a new world defined by respect and equal opportunity for all became the core of her postwar efforts, which began on 8 May, V-E Day.

ER's important correspondence with President Harry Truman also began on 8 May, when she wrote to congratulate him on his V-E Day broadcast: "I listened to your Proclamation this morning and I was deeply moved. I am so happy that this day has come and the war in Europe is over." But, as she wrote in her column, there was nothing as yet to celebrate, since so many continued to die in the Pacific war. "Some of my own sons with millions of others are still in danger."

On 10 May the president wrote a ten-page letter that began with a note of appreciation—"the whole family was touched by your thoughtfulness"—and explained the international situation:

> I noticed in your good column today you expressed some surprise at the Russian attitude on the close of the European War. I think that I should explain the situation to you. On Wednesday, April 25, our Minister to Sweden sent a message to me saying that Himmler wanted to surrender to General Eisenhower all their troops facing the western front and that the Germans would continue to fight the Russians. . . . The matter was discussed with our staff and the offer was very promptly refused. . . . Negotiations went on for two more days— we always insisting on complete, unconditional surrender on all fronts. . . . Germans delayed and delayed, trying all the time to quit only on the western front. . . . Our commanding general [Eisenhower] finally told them that he would turn loose all we had and drive them into the Russians. They finally signed at Rheims the terms of unconditional surrender effective at 12:01 midnight of May 8-9. . . .
>
> I have been trying very carefully to keep all my engagements with the Russians because they are touchy and suspicious of us. The difficulties with Churchill are very nearly as exasperating as they are with the Russians. But patience I think must be our watchword if we are to have world peace. To have it we must have the wholehearted support of Russia, Great Britain and the United States.

ER agreed and told him she hoped FDR's commitment to the Grand Alliance might prevail: "Your experience with Mr. Churchill is not at all surprising. He is suspicious of the Russians and they know it. If you will remember, he said some pretty rough things about them years ago and they do not forget. Of course, we will have to be patient, and any lasting peace will have to have the Three Great Powers behind it." She suggested that Truman "get on a personal basis" with Churchill: "If you talk to him about books and let him quote to you from his marvelous memory everything on earth from Barbara Fritche to the Nonsense Rhymes and Greek tragedy, you will find him easier to deal with on political subjects. He is a gentleman to whom the personal element means a great deal." She also had practical advice about how he might approach the Russians during the Potsdam Conference, 17 July–2 August 1945.

Truman was grateful for her suggestions and courted her support. She did not criticize his most controversial decision to use the new atomic weapons against Hiroshima and Nagasaki in August, but subsequently wrote: "The day the atomic bomb was dropped we came into a new world—a world in which we had to learn to live in friendship with our neighbors of every race and creed and color, or face the fact that we might be wiped off the face of the earth. . . . Either we do have friendly relations, or we do away with civilization." ER's 12 October column was forevermore part of the movement for global disarmament.

On 20 November 1945 she wrote a long letter of opinion to Truman on a variety of troubling issues. "We have an obligation first of all, to solve our own problems at home," she urged, since U.S. failures had an impact on the rest of the world. She hoped that all postwar planning would be fair to labor and business interests alike and would take into account the United States' growing responsibilities in the world.

The issues were complex, and ER wanted people she trusted, notably Bernard Baruch, to be involved in investigations and analyses. She did not approve of Truman's initial lending policies: "If we lend only to Great Britain, we enter into an economic alliance against other nations, and our hope for the future lies in joint cooperation." With 400,000 Jewish survivors of death camps and hiding places now stranded in displaced-persons camps and unwanted everywhere, ER specifically opposed the formation of the Anglo-American Committee of Inquiry into Palestine:

I am very much distressed that Great Britain has made us take a share in another investigation of the few Jews remaining in Europe. If they are not to be allowed to enter Palestine, then certainly they could have been apportioned among the different United Nations and we would not have to continue to have on our consciences, the death of at least fifty of these poor creatures daily.

The question between Palestine and the Arabs, of course, has always been complicated by the oil deposits, and I suppose it always will. . . .

Lastly, I am deeply troubled about China. Unless we can stop the civil war there by moral pressure and not by the use of military force, and insist that Generalissimo Chiang give wider representation to all Chinese groups . . . I am very much afraid that continued war there may lead us to general war again.

Being a strong nation and having the greatest physical, mental and spiritual strength today, gives us a tremendous responsibility. We cannot use our strength to coerce, but if we are big enough, I think we can lead.

Their robust correspondence forged an alliance. Truman said he trusted her judgment and relied on her advice. He was so pleased by some of her columns he had them entered in the *Congressional Record*. Nevertheless she was amazed when Truman called her Washington Square apartment to appoint her to the U.S. delegation for the first session of the United Nations General Assembly in London.

Initially, she hesitated and demurred, saying she knew nothing about international affairs or parliamentary procedure. Her friends and family reminded her of all her previous contributions, and although she still felt "very inadequate," she accepted Truman's offer. Only Senator Theodore Bilbo (D-MS) voted against her confirmation.

She would lend considerable dash to the bipartisan and rather conservative first UN team. Former secretary of state Edward Stettinius was designated principal representative to the Security Council. The other members were Senator Tom Connally (D-TX), chair of the Foreign Relations Committee; Senator Arthur Vandenberg (R-MI); and Secretary of State James Byrnes, whom she had distrusted and disliked for many years. In addition there were five alternates: John Foster Dulles, a Wall Street lawyer and veteran Republican diplomat who had been at Versailles with Wilson and served as an adviser to the drafting conference for the UN Charter at San Francisco in April 1945; Representative Sol Bloom

(D-NY), chair of the House Foreign Affairs Committee; Representative Charles Eaton (R-NJ); former postmaster general Frank Walker; and former senator John Townsend, now chair of the Republican Senatorial Campaign Committee.

By appointing ER to the U.S. delegation to the UN, President Truman gave her the chance to fight for her vision of the future from an official position of leadership for over six years. She considered her appointment a great victory for women and a great opportunity. She would lobby and cajole, compromise and go to battle. She would be an earnest diplomat who frequently succeeded. When she lost, she would return fighting. Convinced that pessimism was politically incorrect, she would never give up.

ER sailed on the *Queen Elizabeth* on 30 December 1945.

Before she left for London, ER requested that the friends and allies she had depended upon for information and advice for decades send her suggestions. As she sailed across the ocean, she studied their reports.

Carrie Chapman Catt wrote that as far as she was concerned, women wanted peace: "War must be abolished. During the last two thousand years nearly every war has developed new and more destructive weapons. . . . The cost of the war just closed, for the first time, will be counted in trillions. Since wars have thus increased their wickedness and destruction . . . no nation which calls itself civilized should consider [this] question . . . debatable."

Walter White, Mary McCleod Bethune, and Dr. W. E. B. Du Bois sent her the "desires of American Negroes," which included the abolition of the entire colonial system, citing it as one of the chief causes of war, poverty, and disease; a world campaign of education for the uneducated colonial and other peoples; a world campaign to utilize all the resources of science, government, and philanthropy to abolish poverty for all people in our time; freedom for the native people of South Africa; democracy for China; withdrawal of recognition of Franco's Spain.

Esther Lape sent ER a list of very practical concerns. "The important thing about the UNO will be *who makes the agenda*. . . . An international debating society is *some* good; but not much. It won't avert wars.

Many international questions require domestic legislation. For example: How could we be a parry to international agreements regarding refugees so long as we keep our immigration quota system . . . which is really an incorporation of racial discrimination. How could we be a party to international agreements designed to make the raw materials of the earth more equitably available (and this is one of the promises of the Atlantic Charter) unless we are prepared to transfer to an international economic and scientific and allocating body the resources we now hold under strong national possessive control.

Lape was convinced that national legislation would be forthcoming if and when international agreements required it, especially laws concerning "raw materials, trade routes and policies, citizenship, immigration (which can no longer be a purely national question)." Moreover, economic issues were key, and the problem was less "what authority is to handle the atomic bomb" than how we "handle the economic questions that produce the wars of which the atomic bomb is a final form. . . . I hope all of your magnificent courage will be expended in this direction."

Much alone aboard the *Queen Elizabeth*, she was surprised during one afternoon walk to be stopped by Senator Vandenberg, who "said in his rather deep voice, 'we would like to know if you would serve on Committee 3,'" the social, humanitarian, and cultural committee. ER wondered why that decision was made without her but assumed that the men, who clearly resented her presence, had decided it was an appropriate place for a woman, and not especially important. But on the voyage out she remembered that she enjoyed a good fight, and that she was prepared to compete.

Once they were all in London, her competitive instincts would serve her well regarding the men of her delegation. Unused to a woman participating in decision making on important international issues, her colleagues met without her and awarded the tougher tasks to themselves. John Foster Dulles, for one, sat on the Trusteeship Committee, which negotiated the future of League of Nations–mandated territories and the controversial new U.S. trust territories in the Pacific—the Caroline and Marshall islands, which the United States had taken over as military bases and subsequently used as atomic test sites.

ER was puzzled by Dulles's apparent unconcern regarding South Africa's refusal to discuss conditions in its territories. She protested his calm and pointed out that the Union of South Africa clearly "believed a govern-

ment had the right to discriminate in any way against any part of its population." She thought the United States should support changes to "improve
the colonies," whether South African or British. Indeed, she noted, conditions in "places where the UK had been for a hundred years" were dreadful, and she "could not help wondering what the UK had been doing there
for a hundred years." ER sought a full discussion, but Dulles disagreed.

In London at meetings of the U.S. delegation, her convictions frequently got nowhere. Her male colleagues regarded her as an interloper
and treated her with crude misogyny. They tried to use the old boys' ploy
of listening politely to the lone woman in the room, then moving on—
never addressing her words, however apt or significant. Even in the official publication of State Department papers, *Foreign Relations of the
United States*, references to ER bear a tone of lofty condescension within
otherwise colorless reports. Her voice is reported to have been shrill; she
was called strident and schoolmarmish.

But she was insistent and would not be ignored. She banged the table
and repeated her words, patiently and frequently, until they were acknowledged. Undoubtedly it drove her colleagues, especially John Foster Dulles,
wild. And when the delegation failed to listen, she could take her percep-
tions to the public. The world's press was more interested in her views
than in theirs. Day after day her words were quoted in newspaper articles,
while she expressed her views directly in her daily column, her own radio
program and those of others, and the Voice of America. She was a political pro, agile at the political game as well as the game of nations.

ER was happy to hear the news that Norway's Trygve Lie was elected
secretary general. He was a compromise candidate whom the United States
and the USSR could agree upon. But she was critical of her fellow delegates as self-involved, legalistic, and wordy beyond belief. They strutted
and preened, generally careless about the sensibilities of other countries—
she was frankly surprised at how undiplomatic some diplomats could be.
They seemed to her without serious convictions and in many ways
thoughtless: "I like the Vandenbergs more than I do the Connallys but I
don't like any of them much." She was somewhat appalled at Senator
Connally's initial response to England during the drive to London: He
"kept repeating: 'Where is all this destruction I've heard so much about,
things look all right to me.' I started to point out bombed spots but soon
found he just wasn't interested."

ER appraised her colleagues most explicitly in a letter to Elinor Morgenthau: Senator Arthur Vandenberg "is smart & hard to get along with
and does not say what he feels. Byrnes is much too small for the job & . . .
can never give any inspiration. . . . Tom Connally is nicer than I thought
but he has no real sensitivity. . . . J. Foster Dulles I like not at all."

ER was more impressed with the State Department staff—Alger Hiss,
Dr. Ralph Bunche, Adlai Stevenson, Ben Cohen, and Durward Sandifer.
They had influence and a sense of responsibility, and she regularly spoke
with them at length: "I said many things which I hope go back to the
Secretary and the President." But she was critical of James Byrnes, whom
she had disliked for years.*

She reported in her London Diary, "The papers should not be pessi-
mistic, progress is being made here. Vandenberg and Dulles are largely
responsible for pessimism, I think. These representatives of ours do not
build friendships for us. . . . They have no confidence so they are rude
and arrogant and create suspicion. Honesty with friendliness [is needed,]
but they haven't the technique." By contrast, ER had faith in the importance of personal diplomacy. Face-to-face contacts mattered:

> At the Assembly sessions, our delegation is seated next to the Rus-
> sians. On the first day I was delighted to find that next to me was
> V. V. Kuznetsov, president of the All Union Council of Trade Unions
> of the USSR. He greeted me in a most friendly fashion, and I

---

*ER had long distrusted James Byrnes and was offended by his bossy and presump-
tive behavior during FDR's funeral at Hyde Park. Trude Lash took notes: Byrnes
wanted it understood that he was Truman's trusted intimate and he gave the orders.
Subsequently ER told Trude that "Byrnes was extremely difficult about the arrangements. . . . He told her to ride in the same car with the new President which she
refused to do. He protested vigorously" and, ER confided to Trude, "proved himself
a very small human being, indeed." Trude Lash notes, 15 April 1945, in Lash, *World
of Love*, pp. 184–85. ER had never understood FDR's reliance on the former South
Carolina senator, whom he named to the Supreme Court (1941–42) and then asked
to leave to become his principal aide. During the war, Byrnes was widely acknowledged as FDR's "assistant president." He attended important meetings, including
Yalta; was put in charge of the Office of War Mobilization, and the home front. Truman appointed him his first secretary of state in 1945, but to ER's relief, in January
1947, the president replaced him with George Marshall. Her feelings about Byrnes
were confirmed after 1954, when as governor of South Carolina he vowed to close
public schools rather than integrate them.

remembered that he had come to my apartment in NY one after-noon to interpret for a group of Russian women, part of a workers' delegation. . . . It's funny how a little opportunity like this of seeing someone in your own home, even for a little while, makes you feel much more friendly.

ER worked long and exhausting days, as she wrote on 31 January:

Yesterday was the usual pattern. 9:30 delegates meeting; at office, 10:30 committee meeting. Ate and dictated column, saw a doctor on national health organization, went to BBC and did two recordings, one for Infantile [Paralysis] and one for American Broadcasting pro-gram. Had tea for a Swedish woman and a Jewish refugee; went to Port of London Authority tea and Turkish Embassy. Frieda Miller dined with me and I had all the women delegates here in my room.

She was pleased that eighteen women, including the Soviet delegate, accepted this first of her many invitations.

Other days were packed with social events about which ER wrote very little. Her London diary for 23 January, for example, included these tan-talizing details: "The afternoon session was cancelled," so she saw many people, including her young friend Louise Morley and the suffragist and peace activist Lady Emmeline Pethick-Lawrence ("nice old lady"), who arrived with her houseguest, the U.S. feminist Betty Gram Swing ("very high powered"). They arrived to try "to persuade me" to support the establishment of the Commission on the Status of Women at the UN. Although "non-committal," ER promised to "look into it."*

That evening ER dined at the home of Vera Brittain and her husband, George Catlin: "A pleasant dinner, usual three courses and a very cold house. Lots of people in afterwards." One can only wonder about ER's conversation with Brittain, the most severe critic of mass bombings and

---

*ER's reluctance to support a separate women's commission reflected her convic-tion that women should have equal power in all UN committees. If separated, their interests could be more easily ignored. But she was pleased in June 1946 when the Women's Commission and the Human Rights Commission were created with equal powers. Ultimately, her work benefited profoundly from the Commission on the Status of Women, whose members were invited to all human rights discussions.

atomic weapons, whose pacifist-feminist-socialist books and articles had generated vigorous opposition. ER considered her first international assignment a remarkable learning experience. "It is a liberal education in background and personalities" to meet people with vast differences in vision and goals.

Constrained by State Department protocol and advice, ER was far less free than she had hoped to be. Nevertheless, she had much to contribute since her committee was concerned with all issues relating to human rights, fundamental freedoms, social progress, and world development. It was the committee that witnessed the first substantial confrontation between the United States and the USSR relating to refugees. Thirteen million displaced persons remained in temporary German domiciles and camps after V-E Day—"Ukrainians, Belorussians, Poles, Czechoslovaks, Latvians, Lithuanians, Estonians, and others . . . because they did not want to return to live under Communist rule. . . . There also were the pitiful Jewish survivors of the German death camps," unwanted every-where, with no haven in sight.

ER's opponent on the issue was the formidable Andrei Vishinsky, Sta-lin's chief prosecutor in the Moscow purge trials. The Russians accused Western propagandists of fomenting fear and hatred of the Soviet Union in the DP camps, discouraging Central European refugees from return-ing to their homelands now under Soviet rule. The Russians claimed that those who refused to return were quislings, traitors, and fascists.

ER, outraged by that accusation, called for universal recognition of the right of political asylum and freedom of movement. In a momentous speech to the General Assembly, she asked if the Soviets would really pre-fer to see "political refugees forcibly repatriated to Franco's Spain?" Eager to achieve the support of "our South American colleagues," she spoke about the great liberator Simón Bolívar "and his stand for the freedom of the people of Latin America." It worked, and the General Assembly voted for the right of refugees to choose their destinations. The victory was, however, a hollow one: no Western European country, nor Canada or the United States, welcomed the refugees, and Britain prohibited additional Jews from going to Palestine. The fight at the UN continued for years, while the refugees languished in camps.

ER's capacity to debate and best the Soviets pleased her State Depart-ment advisers and impressed even her Republican colleagues. At one in the morning, after exhausting meetings, she encountered Vandenberg and Dulles on the steps of the Claridge's Hotel. They told her frankly that they had been appalled by her appointment and had done "all we could to keep you off the United States delegation." They wanted now to acknowledge that they "found [her] good to work with. And we will be happy to do so again." ER noted in her diary, "So—against odds, the women move forward, but I'm rather old to be carrying on this fight!"

Despite her debates with Vishinsky, she made every effort to remain cordial with him and with the increasingly combative Soviet delegation. ER had met Ambassador Andrei Gromyko in Washington. Now during these meetings she "had the pleasure of sitting next to him at lunch. All these little contacts do develop better understanding," she concluded.

Personal diplomacy and institutional processes were needed to secure the future peace. She was gratified that fifteen "well distributed" judges were elected to the International Court of Justice, representing the United States, the UK, Russia, France, China, Belgium, Norway, Yugoslavia, Poland, Egypt, Canada, Mexico, Chile, and El Salvador. Since her post–World War I efforts to secure U.S. adherence to the World Court had failed, she was particularly pleased with the willingness of these nations to deal seriously with the hardest political questions. She hoped that spirit of cooperation could be maintained.

As the UN's first session came to an end, ER was optimistic. The greatest accomplishment, she wrote, was that "at the end we still are a group of 58 nations working together." The United States had not been in the League of Nations, but it was in the UN, and from the beginning Republicans and Democrats actively participated. She was also pleased that the UN decided to locate its permanent headquarters in the United States. As international host, the American public, ER believed, would be more responsive to it and actively support this "last and best hope for our civilization."

After the first session ended, ER toured the devastated European continent. She wrote in *My Day* that she dreaded the journey, knowing that the tragic sights would "fill our souls." In Germany, she visited two camps for displaced persons. At Zeilsheim, a camp for Jewish DPs, she answered their greetings "from an aching heart" and wondered, "When will our

consciences grow so tender that we will act to prevent human misery
rather than avenge it?" One man told her that his entire family had been
"made into soap." She met a boy of ten who looked six, who "had wandered into camp one day with his brother, so he was the head of his family" and "the camp singer."

> He sang for me—a song of his people—a song of freedom. Your
> heart cried out that there was no freedom—and where was hope,
> without which human beings cannot live? There is a feeling of des-
> peration and sorrow in this camp which seems beyond expression.
> An old woman knelt on the ground grasping my knees. I lifted her
> up, but could not speak. What could one say in the end of a life
> which had brought her such complete despair?
> "Israel," she murmured, over and over. "Israel! Israel!"
> As I looked at her weather beaten face . . . I knew for the first
> time what that small land meant to so many.

From Zeilsheim, ER went to Wiesbaden and visited a camp of "Poles
and Balts," refugees from Estonia, Latvia, and Lithuania. "These are refugees who, because of political differences with their present governments,
cannot see their way to return to their own countries, and yet they fought
against the Nazis, and many of them spent long years in concentration or
forced labor camps."

The political complexities of these refugees as well as the Jewish refugees haunted the early years of the UN. For years the debate went on as
the people continued to weaken and die, or subsisted in wretched or
underfunded UN Relief and Rehabilitation Administration camps.
What, ER asked in 1946, was the "ultimate answer"? The General Assembly created a Special Committee on Refugees and Displaced Persons to
meet in April 1946 to study the problem. ER predicted it "will tear at
their hearts" and recommended all due speed. But it was a dreary and
protracted process, complicated by disagreements over Palestine, political
distrust, pervasive bigotry—and the demands of the intensified Cold War.

When ER returned to the United States, she was invited to serve on a
commission to create "the structure and functions of the permanent
Commission on Human Rights," to convene at Hunter College in the
Bronx [subsequently Lehman College] on 29 April 1946. She accepted
but was perplexed by the fearful climate Truman seemed to endorse when

he accompanied Winston Churchill on 5 March to Westminster College in Fulton, Missouri. There the former prime minister declared: "From Stettin in the Baltic to Trieste in the Adriatic, an iron curtain has descended across the [European] continent." Churchill's bellicose speech was a call to arms and an appeal for an Anglo-American military alliance. ER was relieved to learn that Truman had not known what Churchill intended to say and believed he was to speak constructively "about the sinews of peace."

Armed with that information, ER felt free to disagree with Churchill in *My Day*:

> Instead of running an armament race against each other and building up trade cartels and political alliances, we the nations of the world should join together . . . [to] use the forum of the United Nations to discuss our difficulties and our grievances. . . . I do not wonder that the elderly statesmen think this a new and revolutionary move in the international situation. I will grant that there are two possibilities here, the old way and the new way. We have seen the results of the old way, however, in war and destruction and we may still see starvation and pestilence stalk the earth as a result of the old way. Might it be wise to try the new way?

ER spoke against Churchill's speech several times and was cheered by a note from her friend Arthur Murray, Lord Elibank, who was closely allied to Lady Stella Reading and John Winant. He wanted her to know that British "men of all parties" considered Churchill's "utterance one of great unwisdom, and a source of embarrassment." Just as the UN embarked on its difficult journey, there "plunges like a bull in a china shop, Winston Churchill."

Unanimously elected chair of the committee that founded the Human Rights Commission, ER was part of an extraordinary team that agreed their first project would be to write an International Bill of Human Rights. The other members of the committee were John P. Humphrey, Canadian international lawyer; Peng-chun (P. C.) Chang, a Chinese scholar, playwright, musician, and leading diplomat; and Lebanon's learned Dr. Charles

Habbib Malik. This leadership group was subsequently joined by France's René Cassin, who had spent the war years in London as Charles de Gaulle's legal adviser. He had lost his sister and more than twenty-five other relatives in Nazi concentration camps. By 1947 Cassin and ER supported a Jewish homeland, while Malik emerged as a leader of the Arab League. Their ability to work together, to negotiate across all their differences, made possible the creation of the Universal Declaration of Human Rights (UDHR).

They, along with India's Hansa Mehta, laid the unfinished ethical agenda of our time before the world. And Mehta, president of the All India Women's Conference and a leader of the independence movement— and the only other woman on the commission—significantly transformed the document by her insistence that the words "all men" would in much of the world be taken to exclude women. Hansa Mehta influenced ER in many ways. The commission adopted her inclusive formula, "all human beings," during its June 1948 session, and women's equality was forevermore affirmed in UN literature.

ER's imaginative and steadfast personal diplomacy helped ensure the passage of the UDHR by the UN General Assembly on 10 December 1948. Consisting of a preamble and thirty articles, the declaration was to serve "as a common standard of achievement for all peoples and all nations," a yardstick by which to measure decency and human dignity. Since 1948 it has continued to be the most significant of all UN declarations on behalf of fundamental political freedoms as well as economic and social rights:

> –All human beings are born free and equal in dignity and rights. . . .
> –Everyone is entitled to all the rights and freedoms set forth . . . without distinction of any kind, such as race, color, sex, language, religion, political or other opinion, national or social origin, property, birth or other status. . . .
> –No one shall be held in slavery or servitude.
> –No one shall be subjected to torture or to cruel, inhuman or degrading treatment or punishment. . . .
> –All are equal before the law. . . .
> –No one shall be subjected to arbitrary arrest, detention or exile. . . .
> –No one shall be subjected to arbitrary interference with privacy, family, home or correspondence, nor to attacks upon honor and reputation. . . .

–Everyone has the right to freedom of movement and residence
within the borders of each State. . . .
–Everyone has the right to leave any country, and to return. . . .
–The will of the people shall be the basis of the authority of the government, involving free and secret ballots based on equal and
universal suffrage.

In its first twenty-two articles the UDHR detailed political and civil
rights: freedom of assembly, opinion, and expression and "the right to
seek, receive and impart information and ideas through any media and
regardless of frontiers"; the right to religion and to change religion; the
right to marriage and divorce, and the right to be secure and protected
within the family unit.

Articles 23 to 30 detailed the economic and social rights and obligations of the human community to ensure the free and full development
of personality:

–Everyone has the right to work, to free choice of employment, . . .
and to protection against unemployment.
–Everyone, without any discrimination, has the right to equal pay
for equal work. . . .
–Everyone has the right to form and to join trade unions.
–Everyone has the right to rest and leisure, including periodic holiday with pay.
–Everyone has the right to a standard of living adequate for health
and well-being including food, clothing, housing, medical care
and necessary social services, and the right to security in the event
of unemployment, sickness, disability, widowhood, old age. . . .
–Motherhood and childhood are entitled to special care and assistance. All children, whether born in or out of wedlock, shall
enjoy the same social protection.
–Everyone has the right to education. Education shall be free, at least
in the elementary and fundamental stages . . . and higher education shall be equally accessible to all on the basis of merit.

ER believed that the kind of New Deal agencies created within the
United States to limit and prevent so many of the personal tragedies
engendered by the Great Depression might be applied to the entire postwar world. She championed the various agencies the UN created or

strengthened, notably the United Nations Educational, Scientific and Cultural Organization (UNESCO), the World Health Organization (WHO), the Food and Agriculture Organization (FAO), and the International Labor Organization (ILO). The work of each of these agencies supported the UDHR. But ER never underestimated the political differences and disagreements that limited its scope and endangered its future.

The UDHR was a compromise. At first ER was instructed to limit the principles to civil and political rights. This she refused to do. And the woman who always advised her friends, "If you have to compromise— compromise up," succeeded in persuading her delegation, as well as Truman and Secretary of State George Marshall, of the importance of including the Soviet-originated demands for economic and social rights. ER understood the need for an all-embracing document: "You cannot talk civil rights to people who are hungry." Moreover, in 1941 FDR's Four Freedoms had promised freedom from want as well as freedom from fear. ER believed in the connectedness of the economic, civil, political, and social aspects of human rights. When she offered to resign rather than forgo economic and social rights, President Truman told her to follow her conscience.

After eighty-five meetings, at three a.m. on 10 December 1948, the UN General Assembly finally approved the Universal Declaration of Human Rights. Forty-eight voted in favor; Honduras and Yemen were absent; and eight abstained: the six Soviet bloc nations (Byelorussia, Czechoslovakia, Poland, the Ukraine, the USSR, and Yugoslavia), Saudi Arabia, and South Africa. ER was relieved that the Soviets did not vote against it, a testimony to her remarkable personal diplomacy. She was also impressed that when each article was polled separately, twenty-three of thirty achieved unanimous approval. The General Assembly gave her an unprecedented standing ovation, and she left the Great Hall profoundly moved by the warmth and solidarity displayed that night. From that day to this, the declaration stands as a beacon, to stir our imaginations and prod us on. ER considered it a "first step" and went to work to negotiate enabling covenants.

ER initially hoped that the UDHR would quickly be followed by binding covenants—treaties "for the implementation of human rights," to be ratified by the Senate and rendered law. In the United States, the Senate would have to approve it. But hopes for ratification were soon shattered, domestically and worldwide, by the intensification of Cold

War realities, the Truman Doctrine, the Marshall Plan, the creation of NATO in April 1949, Russia's successful atomic explosion during that summer, and Mao Tse-tung's victorious announcement of the People's Republic of China in October. At home, McCarthyism and Truman's "Loyalty Oath" program (which ER deplored) contributed to opposition to the covenant. The president of the American Bar Association led a right-wing assault against the UN and the UDHR as a Communist threat to globalize the New Deal. Still negotiating and compromising, on 27 March 1950 ER called for a limited political and civil rights covenant, one that the Senate might actually ratify. In 1951 she accepted Hansa Mehta's suggestion that there be two covenants, one for political and civil rights, the other for economic and social rights.

In 1947 Dr. W. E. B. Du Bois protested to the UN against U.S. racism. But "An Appeal to the World: A Statement of Denial of Human Rights to Minorities in the Case of Citizens of Negro Descent" was derailed by President Truman's own actions on behalf of civil rights. Alongside ER, Truman was the first president to address the NAACP. On 27 June, their appearance at the closing meeting of the NAACP convention at the Lincoln Memorial before ten thousand people was historic. The United States had "reached a turning point in the long history of its efforts to guarantee freedom and equality to all Americans," he announced. "And when I say all Americans, I mean all Americans." All discrimination "because of ancestry, or religion, or race, or color" must be removed. "We can no longer afford the luxury of a leisurely attack upon prejudice and discrimination. . . . Our national government must show the way." ER spoke about the "blot of lynching." The racial tragedies faced by veterans and families of color, she said, destroyed the meaning of democracy as we sought to impress the world with promises of human rights.

In October 1947, Truman's civil rights vision, "To Secure These Rights," boldly promised real change. The president proposed the creation of a permanent civil rights commission to ensure voting rights, end segregation in the military, and ensure a federal anti-lynching law finally to end state-sanctioned violence. ER and Truman seemed allied in 1947 and 1948.

For the 1948 presidential election, when Truman ran for reelection as the Democratic candidate, several states broke away from the party to form a segregationist split-off known as the Dixiecrats, running South

Carolina governor Strom Thurmond as their candidate. ER hoped the Dixiecrat leaders of Alabama, Louisiana, Mississippi, and South Carolina would remain adrift. It was time, she wrote, for the Democratic Party to renounce racism and become a truly liberal party. Subsequently, she would deplore Truman's hypocritical preference for a unified Democratic Party—which reestablished the status quo as the Dixiecrats returned to their positions of congressional committee leadership, and Truman ended his pledge in "To Secure These Rights."

Then, in December 1951, civil rights attorney William Patterson, executive of the Civil Rights Congress, and singer Paul Robeson introduced to the UN a petition called "We Charge Genocide: The Crime of Government Against the Negro People." ER rejected it as the work of Communists and part of the Soviet assault that hurt the United States at the UN "in so many little ways." Blindsided by her Cold War priorities, she dismissed the charge of genocide as "perfect nonsense" yet insisted the future required an end to white supremacy: an end to segregation, discrimination, poverty, and violence. Limited by her own virulent anti-Communism, she would continue to challenge Soviet propaganda—and also to struggle for racial justice.

One of her colleagues on the Human Rights Commission, Dr. John Humphrey, wrote in his journal that ER's "role will embarrass her biographer." No longer the champion of democratic participation, she actually obstructed progress toward a strong human rights covenant. Humphrey believed that ER had become a State Department functionary and "one of the most reactionary forces" at the UN. But Harvard Law professor Mary Ann Glendon considers Humphrey's judgment "harsh and naive. Eleanor Roosevelt was a practical politician as well as a visionary statesperson." She juggled as she had learned so well to do; she fought for what was possible and considered what the Senate might ratify. It was limited, and ER acknowledged that hers were only tentative first steps in rapidly shifting sands. In the spring of 1951 she turned the chairmanship of the Human Rights Commission over to Lebanon's Charles Malik but continued to struggle for human rights covenants.

Progress was slow, and then Eisenhower's 1952 victory all but ended U.S. support for human rights and UN leadership on the issue. Eisenhower accepted ER's resignation with cold alacrity. In April 1953 Secretary of State John Foster Dulles told the Senate that the State Department no longer cared to pursue either the civil and political covenant or the economic and social covenant. The department was also uninterested in the Genocide Convention and intended to take no part in the effort to secure a UN treaty on the rights of women. ER's State Department adviser, Durward Sandifer, told ER that the United States' human rights position at the UN was now limited to issuing "reports and studies on the status of such human rights issues as slavery; and the creation of an advisory service which would fund seminars and fellowships on human rights." ER replied: "You will excuse me if I think these [efforts] are really comic."

After ER's official tour of duty at the UN ended, she walked across First Avenue and offered her time and energy to Clark Eichelberger's American Association of the United Nations. From 1953 to 1962 she traveled across the United States and around the world with her message of peace and human rights. She went door to door, town by town, insisting that the fight for a global standard of human rights, the inclusion of morality and decency in the international arena, must be on the agenda. ER understood that to win a war for human rights would take as much energy and vision, as much money and dedication, as it took to win any other kind of war.

On 27 March 1958, she celebrated the tenth anniversary of the UDHR with a UN speech that inspired and propelled the global human rights movement:

> Where, after all, do universal human rights begin? In small places, close to home—so close and so small that they cannot be seen on any maps of the world. Yet they *are* the world of the individual persons; the neighborhood . . . ; the school or college . . . ; the factory, farm or office. . . . Such are the places where every man, woman and child seeks equal justice, equal opportunity, equal dignity without discrimination. Unless these rights have meaning there, they have little meaning anywhere. Without concerned citizen action to uphold them close to home, we shall look in vain for progress in the larger world.

Personally, ER was nourished and fortified by her extended family of allies and beloveds. She cherished time with her grandchildren and supported her children through their multiple divorces. The intimate circle of friends she relied on changed over the years. She was bereft when her longtime great friend, secretary, traveling companion, and primary editor Tommy Thompson died suddenly on 12 April 1953. While Esther Lape, Lorena Hickok, Earl Miller, and Bernard Baruch remained her steadies, her time was more completely devoted to Dr. David Gurewitsch. After Joe and Trude Lash left Hyde Park to live in Martha's Vineyard, ER's primary affections turned to David and Edna Gurewitsch, with whom she bought an Upper East Side town house. An ISS associate of Trude, who introduced them, David became ER's intimate friend and traveling companion to many countries including India, Pakistan, Israel, and the Soviet Union. They were generally accompanied by hard-working congenial assistant, Maureen Corr, who had replaced Tommy.

Politically, race remained in the forefront of ER's efforts as she worked for a future defined by human rights. Her young friends Pauli Murray and Harry Belafonte fortified these efforts. ER predicted that the United States would lose to Communism unless it ended racial injustice: "Our great struggle today is to prove to the world that democracy has more to offer than communism"—but it could not do that as long as bigotry, segregation, and unemployment remained. The United States could not have it both ways: world leadership and domestic sloth.

She challenged the public to organize, to show what it could do: "We have to develop courage and a staunchness that perhaps we have never had." Civil rights was no longer a "domestic question." It was, she believed, "the question which may decide whether democracy or communism wins out in the world." "We cannot be complacent about unemployment . . . , about injustices." We have to be able to talk with each other and disagree, to "learn from each other, and contemplate new ideas." There were new friendships to be forged, intensified struggles under way. Throughout the 1950s ER campaigned for integrated housing, integrated schools, voting rights, and the end of discrimination and bigotry.

ER defended her friends in public and in print. Already outraged by the extremism of Senator Joseph McCarthy (R-WI) and the "Gestapo tactics" used by his Senate committee and HUAC's (House Un-American Activities Committee) crusade against subversives, she was further appalled when her dear friend, educator Mary McLeod Bethune, was accused of "association" with allegedly Communist organizations. ER told her *My Day* readers that a New Jersey school had disinvited Bethune—a most heroic "leader among the American colored citizens and loved and admired by all . . . who know her." Mary Mcleod Bethune was "the kindest, gentlest person I have ever met. . . . If it were not so sad to have respected and beloved American citizens insulted and slighted, it would be funny." The Red Scare threatened American traditions of freedom and civil liberties. She hoped a bold movement for justice and fairness would arise to "save us" from McCarthyite demands for "complete conformity which kills originality and truth."

When Paul Robeson was attacked by rioters during a concert in Peekskill, she defended him. She deplored his Communist sympathies, but she deplored violent repression that threatened democracy even more. In an extraordinary column she asserted that Robeson had the right to perform unmolested—even though he turned his concerts into forums for Communist propaganda. Moreover, ER thought it important to understand why such a talented star would praise the USSR and choose to reside there for several years. "He wanted to find something he did not find here. He was a brilliant law student," who graduated from Columbia Law School, "but there was no equality of opportunity for educated men of his race." He became a singer, "a gain for art—but perhaps there was some bitterness in his heart." He took his family to the USSR so that his son would not suffer as he did. "Others might feel the same way. In the USSR he was recognized as an educated man, as an artist and as an equal. We disapprove of his speeches, but we must also understand him and above all . . . we must [work] to preserve the liberties that are inherent in true democracy." Since the USSR "does not permit real democratic freedom," she subsequently chided Robeson for his failure to see that everyone had a better chance of achieving equality "in the US than anywhere else in the world."

By 1954 all white integrationists were accused of being Communists. ER remained allied with such southern race radicals as Jim Dombrowski and Myles Horton of Tennessee's Highlander Folk School, Aubrey Williams, Virginia Durr, Anne Braden, and other activists of the Southern Conference Education Fund (SCEF), the successor to the Southern Conference for Human Welfare, founded in 1947. ER agreed to serve on SCEF's board, spoke often on its behalf, raised funds, and worked closely with Aubrey Williams, president of SCEF, and Dombrowski, its director, on projects "dedicated to the fight against racial segregation and discrimination in all fields of social endeavor."

In 1952 SCEF issued a stunning pamphlet, *The Untouchables*, that protested the death-dealing situation that people of color faced all across the country when they were in need of emergency medical attention. Illustrated by Ben Shahn, with text by New Orleans journalist Alfred Maund—who edited *The Southern Patriot*, SCEF's monthly magazine—*The Untouchables* was part of SCEF's campaign to end hospital segregation and medical neglect, which ER supported financially and through several public events. In her 17 October column, she asked her white readers to imagine what might happen to them in Asia or the Middle East if such "segregation were practiced against us . . . because we would be in the minority, since two-thirds of the world's people are colored." ER concluded on a note of hope, since SCEF had inspired a citizens' movement to replace "Jim Crow medical care" with comprehensive health services for all, under way in many states including New York and Kentucky.

Our leadership of "the free world," she wrote in 1956, depended on our realization that "the white race is a minority race." Around the world "colored people have been exploited by white people and they are suspicious of us." Every time we "deny to any of our citizens equal rights it is proof . . . that freedom is no more real in the United States than it is in the Soviet Union. . . . We must face the facts," and make significant changes. As white supremacists organized to resist the Supreme Court's 1954 school desegregation decision in *Brown v. Board of Education of Topeka*, and as Dixiecrats returned to positions of congressional dominance, ER had no illusions, but she did have specific suggestions: "In the North . . . before integrating our schools we must get rid of segregated housing, and that is not easy. We can do it but it will take determined" and persistent citizen action. "In the South the first problem is the right to vote. Until we have that we cannot do anything. This is a Federal right and the Federal government can do something." Republican rule and partisan compromise had suspended all promises, and ER hoped that a victory for Adlai Stevenson would change that. But above all she called for an activist movement—to give people hope, to work to end disease and poverty, and thereby to maintain "our prestige in the world."

In 1958 ER attended Harry Belafonte's concert in Brussels that, as he said, "inaugurated the American pavilion of the World's Fair." She wrote a stunning review and visited Harry, his wife, Julie, and their baby David at their hotel. She held little David "as she discussed world affairs," whereupon he wet her lap. ER just laughed and said, "Well, little man! Thank you for your opinion!" Their friendship flourished, and the Belafontes made many visits to Val-Kill and dined with ER in New York City. In addition to Harry Belafonte's civil rights work, he increased his support for the Wiltwyck School for troubled black and white youth—which ER and their mutual friend Dr. Viola Bernard, a New York social worker and integration leader, supported. Belafonte was outraged by his inability to rent an apartment in New York City. He filed a complaint against the city and called a press conference. ER wrote on 20 October 1958,

I am sure that every New Yorker was shocked . . . to read that Harry Belafonte and his charming wife and baby were finding it practically impossible to get an apartment. . . . I have long been saying that in the North we have only one step to take to meet the Supreme Court order of nonsegregation in schools, and that is nonsegregation in housing. . . . We are a mixture of races in New York City, and every neighborhood should in normal course become a mixed neighborhood.

Personally, ER said, she would enjoy nothing more than having the Belafontes as her neighbors, and she hoped they found "a home shortly where they and their enchanting little boy can grow up without feeling the evils of the segregation pattern. Discrimination does something intangible and harmful to the souls of both white and colored people." The next day ER invited the Belafontes to move in with her. Although delighted, they refused, since they and several friends had decided to purchase a building at 300 West End Avenue, one that had refused to rent to him, and create an integrated cooperative. As their friendship grew, ER introduced Harry to many of the new African leaders she worked with through the UN Association, including Achar Maroff, the UN ambassador from Guinea; the son of Habib Bourgiba, Tunisia's first president; and Tom Mboya of Kenya. She also offered him profound advice: occasional demonstrations were not enough to achieve civil rights for blacks in the United States—it would require a nationally organized, vigorous, and persistent movement. As FDR had told A. Philip Randolph, "Go out and make me do it." Harry Belafonte believed that ER had become a "socialist" and that government needed to do more to confront "race . . . the greatest barrier to that more equitable vision" that promised "social benefits and job opportunities" for all.

Belafonte was correct about ER. She was a revolutionary who believed everybody should have equal opportunity, excellent education, and the comforts of life in a community that cared. She had devoted her life's work to the achievement of security for all. During the 1930s she had insisted that everyone must have enough means to enjoy the benefits of "graciousness and freedom." The New Deal promised an end to poverty and the pattern of "building a civilization on human suffering." Achieving this goal required imposing higher taxes and limitations upon the irresponsible, greedy actual "restrictions on their freedom to make fortunes." When in 1960 the sit-ins for integration began, ER urged college students everywhere to "go South for freedom." She lived to see a new day dawn, and see her work for universal human rights become a worldwide movement.

In January 1961, John F. Kennedy named her chair of the President's Committee on the Status of Women and reappointed her to the U.S. delegation to the UN. There she worked closely with her friend Adlai Stevenson—now UN ambassador—to renegotiate human rights covenants. She was gratified by the changed UN environment. Among the representatives of the many new nations, freed from colonial domination, the idea of human rights had spirited support. She was proud to be part of the global "social revolution" for civil rights and human rights that was under way.*

---

*As she had foreseen in 1948, the UDHR had "moral force" and was perceived as the international promissory note for human dignity, democracy, and freedom, in the tradition of the 1215 Magna Carta, long before the covenants were finally drafted. On 16 December 1966, after decades of delay, the UN General Assembly voted for the International Covenant on Civil and Political Rights (ICCPR) and the International Covenant on Economic, Social, and Cultural Rights (ICESCR); they entered into force in 1976, but the United States ignored them until President Jimmy Carter signed them in 1977. George H. W. Bush secured Senate ratification of the Civil and Political Rights Covenant on 8 September 1992. The U. S. Congress has still not considered the Economic and Social Rights Covenant, although the National Economic and Social Rights Initiative (NESRI) exists finally to put it on

On 5 November 1961 ER endorsed the American Friends Service Committee's declaration of conscience to protest "the present drift toward war." She affirmed her conviction that "freedom and democracy could not survive nuclear war" and called for a popular movement to demand disarmament.

Long before most of America's leadership appreciated the changing needs of this planet, ER did. In September 1962, she wrote a column that anticipated the primary challenge of our time:

> It has always seemed to me that we never present our case to the smaller nations in either a persuasive or interesting way. I think most people will acknowledge . . . that we have given far more military aid to these nations than economic aid. It is not very pleasant to palm off this military equipment on people who really are not looking for it. The fiction is that they are being given military aid so that they will be better able to cope with any Communist attack. But all the nations where we do this know quite well that it is pure fiction. . . .
>
> In view of this, why don't we offer them something they really want? For one thing, most of them would like food. Many of them, as they watch the development of the bigger nations, want to establish the beginnings of industry. But they know that wider training of their people is essential . . . and hence a primary need is aid to their education system.

Until her death on 7 November 1962, ER was committed to a liberal vision and to hope. In *Tomorrow Is Now*, her last book, published three months after her death, she looked to the future with genuine optimism. With "proper education . . . a strong sense of responsibility for our own actions, with a clear awareness that our future is linked with the welfare

---

the U.S. agenda. See nesri.org. Moreover, the United States ignores or violates several other UN covenants regarding human rights, notably the Convention on the Elimination of All Forms of Discrimination Against Women (CEDAW), entered into force 8 September 1981 and still not signed by the United States; the Convention on the Elimination of All Forms of Racial Discrimination, entered into force in 1969 and signed by the United States in 1994; and the Convention Against Torture and Other Cruel, Inhuman or Degrading Treatment or Punishment, entered into force 26 June 1987 and ratified by the United States 20 November 1994—and violated. See esp. Browne-Marshall, *Race, Law and American Society*, pp. 232–48, 346–50.

of the world as a whole, we may justly anticipate that the life of the next generation will be richer, more peaceful, more rewarding than any we have ever known." For the future the United States needed to resurrect with conviction and daring the good American word *liberal*, "which derives from the word *free*. . . . We must cherish and honor the word *free* or it will cease to apply to us."

Eleanor Roosevelt's international journey reflects the full range of the complex tides of the twentieth century. Committed to improving the quality of life, she made the noblest values seem globally achievable. She believed in the power of ideas to transform society. In *Tomorrow Is Now*, she wrote that social change required that ideas be faced with imagination, integrity, and courage. That was how she lived her life and pursued the most controversial and complex issues of state, none of which have become any less controversial. Ultimately, she embodied her own creed: "The influence you exert is through your own life, and what you've become yourself."

Adlai Stevenson, in his eulogies for ER both at the UN General Assembly on 9 November, and at New York's Cathedral of Saint John the Divine on 17 November, most eloquently defined that legacy:

> Her life was crowded, restless, and fearless. Perhaps she pitied most not those whom she aided in the struggle, but the more fortunate who were preoccupied with themselves and cursed with the self-deceptions of private success. She walked in the slums and the ghettos of the world, not on a tour of inspection . . . but as one who could not feel complacent while others were hungry, and who could not find contentment while others were in distress. This was not sacrifice; this, for Eleanor Roosevelt, was the only meaningful way of life. . . .
>
> Like so many others, I have lost more than a beloved friend. I have lost an inspiration. She would rather light a candle than curse the darkness, and her glow has warmed the world.

More than half a century later, ER's glow continues to warm the world with the hope that human rights will be observed in every home and village—and increasingly be accepted as women's rights and children's rights. The world movement to achieve the conception of human rights that ER advanced is under way. Someday poverty will be replaced by dignity and respect, and we will unite to save our small blue endangered water planet—which we all do happen to share.

List of Archives

Anna Roosevelt Halsted Papers, FDRL
Arizona Collection
David Gray Collection
Edith Nourse Rogers Papers, Schlesinger Library, Radcliffe College, Cambridge, MA
Eleanor Roosevelt Papers Project, www.gwu.edu (*My Day* columns)
Franklin D. Roosevelt Library (FDRL), Hyde Park, NY
Glenn Horowitz Collection, New York
Grace Tully Collection, FDRL
Henry Morgenthau Papers
Joseph P. Lash Papers, FDRL
Lorena Hickok Papers, FDRL
Martha Gellhorn Collection, Washington University, St. Louis, MO
NAACP Papers, Library of Congress, Washington, DC
Pauli Murray Papers, Schlesinger Library, Radcliffe College, Cambridge, MA
Peter Pratt Papers
President's Personal File, FDRL
President's Secretary's File, FDRL
Sumner Welles Papers, FDRL
WILPF Archive, Geneva
Woody Guthrie Archives, New York

Note on Sources and Selected Bibliography

The Eleanor Roosevelt Papers at the Franklin Delano Roosevelt Library (FDRL) at Hyde Park are in several collections, as cited in the notes. Series 70 largely includes correspondence with public officials and citizens; series 100 includes more personal correspondence and papers of the Roosevelt family, donated by the children. Basic to this work are several individual collections, notably the Molly Dewson, Marion Dickerman, Lorena Hickok, Esther Lape, Joseph Lash, Henry and Elinor Morgenthau, Aubrey Williams, and FDR papers. Anna Roosevelt Halsted papers donated by the children are in the ER and FDR Library. Although Earl Miller's papers are missing, his later correspondence and reflections upon the past are in the Miriam and Robert Abelow papers at the FDR Library.

ER's correspondence with Jane Addams is at the FDRL and at the Swarthmore College Peace Collection (SCPC). I am grateful to Mary Lynn McCree Bryan for documents from the Jane Addams Papers Project. See Mary Lynn McCree Bryan, *The Jane Addams Papers Guide* (Ann Arbor, University Microfilms, 1985).

Carrie Chapman Catt's papers are at the New York Public Library, including the file on the Christian Women's Protest Against Germany's Treatment of the Jews. Her letters to ER are at the FDRL.

Gertrude Ely's papers have not yet been located. Although there is correspondence with ER at the FDRL, her life story has yet to be told. I am grateful to Lorett Treese for biographical memorabilia on Ely in the Bryn Mawr College Archives, to Anonymous of Fowler's Beach for letters and memories of Ely, and to Rodney H. Clurman.

Isabella Greenway's Papers are in the Arizona Historical Society, Tucson.

Alice Hamilton's correspondence with ER is at the FDRL and in the Jane Addams Papers Project. I am grateful to Barbara Sicherman for excerpts from Hamilton's daybook and Hamilton's articles on Germany: "An Inquiry into the Nazi Mind," *NY Times Sunday Magazine,* 6 August 1933; "The Youth Who Are Hitler's Strength," *NY Times Sunday*

Magazine, 8 October 1933; "Hitler Speaks," *Atlantic,* October 1933; "Below the Surface," *Survey Graphic,* September 1933; "Sound and Fury in Germany," *Survey Graphic,* November 1933; "The Plight of the German Intellectuals," *Harper's,* January 1934; "German Intellectuals," *NY Times,* 7 January 1934.

ER's correspondence with Fannie Hurst is mostly in the Fannie Hurst Papers, in the Harry Ransom Collection, Humanities Research Center, University of Texas at Austin. Hurst's correspondence with Ruth Bryan Owen in this collection is significant.

The Helen Rogers Reid, Harold Ickes, and NAACP Papers are at the Library of Congress. ER's correspondence with Molly Dewson, Hilda Worthington Smith, and Charlotte Everett Hopkins is at the FDRL and the Schlesinger Library. Other significant collections at the Schlesinger Library are Pauli Murray, Pauline Newman, Barbara Deming, and Edith Sampson's important UN file, and ER correspondence. Frances Perkins's lecture notes are at Cornell. Frances Perkins's papers and oral history are at Columbia University. The Lillian Wald Papers are at the New York Public Library and at Columbia University. The Varian Fry Papers are at Columbia and the offices of the International Rescue Committee.

ER's monthly columns in New York State's *Women's Democratic News* were folded into the national *Democratic Digest* in 1936. In 1938, ER selected her favorite daily columns and published them in *My Days.* These are undated except by month and year. Now, thanks to Allida Black and her staff, they are all online. The *New York Times* and the NAACP's *Crisis Magazine* were basic to this study.

Also in the Franklin D. Roosevelt Library: the Anna Roosevelt Halsted papers (ARH), David Gray (ER's uncle) Collection, and the Grace Tully Collection. In addition to the Grace Tully Papers in the FDRL, I am grateful to Glenn Horowitz for use of the Grace Tully and Missy LeHand papers in his collection. The Martha Gellhorn Collection is at Washington University, St. Louis, Missouri. The Women's International League for Peace and Freedom (WILPF) Archive is in Geneva and at the Swarthmore College Peace Collection, and the Woody Guthrie Archive is in New York. The Glenn Horowitz Collection is in New York. I am profoundly grateful to Peter Pratt (Trude Lash's oldest son) and Elaine Pratt for the ten boxes of Trude and Joe Lash's papers, and to Franklin Roosevelt III and Nina Roosevelt Gibson for access to familial archives.

Selected Bibliography

Adamic, Louis. *Dinner at the White House*. New York: Harper & Bros., 1946.

Alsop, Joe, with Adam Platt. *I've Seen the Best of It*. New York: W. W. Norton, 1992.

Anderson, Carol. *Bourgeois Radicals: The NAACP & the Struggle for Colonial Liberation, 1941–1960*. Cambridge: Cambridge University Press, 2015.

———. *Eyes Off the Prize: The UN & the African-American Struggle for Human Rights, 1944–1955*. Cambridge: Cambridge University Press, 2005.

Anderson, Mark. *Hitler's Exiles: Personal Stories of the Flight from Nazi Germany to America*. New York: New Press, 2000.

Arsenault, Raymond. *The Sound of Freedom: Marian Anderson, the Lincoln Memorial, and the Concert That Awakened America*. New York: Bloomsbury Press, 2009.

Asbell, Bernard, ed. *Mother and Daughter: The Letters of Eleanor and Anna Roosevelt*. New York: Coward McCann, 1982.

Bach, Steven. *Marlene Dietrich: Life and Legend*. New York: William Morrow, 1992.

Baird, A. Craig, ed. *Representative American Speeches, 1939–40*. n.p.: H. W. Wilson, 1940.

Baker, Leonard. *Brandeis and Frankfurter: A Dual Biography*. New York: Harper & Row, 1984.

Baruch, Bernard. *Baruch: The Public Years*. New York: Holt, Rinehart & Winston, 1960.

———. *My Own Story*. 2 vols. New York: Henry Holt, 1957.

Baum, Charlotte, Paula Hyman, and Sonya Michel. *The Jewish Woman in America*. New York: New American Library, 1975.

Beasley, Maurine. *Eleanor Roosevelt and the Media: A Public Quest for Self-Fulfillment*. Urbana: University of Illinois Press, 1987.

———. *Eleanor Roosevelt: Transformative First Lady*. Lawrence: University Press of Kansas, 2010.

———. *The White House Press Conferences of Eleanor Roosevelt*. New York: Garland, 1983.

Beasley, Maurine, Holly Shulman, and Henry Beasley, eds. *The Eleanor Roosevelt Encyclopedia*. Westport, CT: Greenwood Press, 2001.

Belafonte, Harry. *My Song: A Memoir*. New York: Alfred A. Knopf, 2011.

Bell-Scott, Patricia. *The Firebrand and the First Lady: Pauli Murray, ER, and the Struggle for Social Justice*. New York: Alfred A. Knopf, 2016.

Bellush, Bernard. *He Walked Alone: A Biography of John Gilbert Winant*. Netherlands: Mouton, 1968.

Berenbaum, Michael. *The World Must Know: The History of the Holocaust as Told in the United States Holocaust Memorial Museum*. Baltimore: Johns Hopkins University Press, 1981.

Bernstein, Alison. *American Indians and World War II*. Norman: University of Oklahoma Press, 1999.

Beschloss, Michael. *Kennedy and Roosevelt: The Uneasy Alliance*. New York: W. W. Norton, 1980.

Bhagavan, Manu. *The Peacemakers: India and the Quest for One World*. New York: HarperCollins, 2012.

Biddle, Francis. *In Brief Authority*. New York: Doubleday, 1962.

Black, Allida, ed. *Courage in a Dangerous World: The Political Writings of Eleanor Roosevelt*. New York: Columbia University Press, 2000.

———, ed. *The Eleanor Roosevelt Papers: The Human Rights Years*. 2 vols. Charlottesville: University of Virginia Press, 2012.

———, ed. *What I Hope to Leave Behind: The Essential Essays of Eleanor Roosevelt*. n.p.: Carlson, 1995.

Black, George. *The Good Neighbor*. New York: Pantheon, 1988.

Black, Ruby. *Eleanor Roosevelt: A Biography*. New York: Duell, Sloan & Pearce, 1940.

Bliss, Michael. *Harvey Cushing: A Life in Surgery*. Oxford: Oxford University Press, 2005.

Bloch, Marc. *Strange Defeat: A Statement of Evidence, 1940*. W. W. Norton, 1968.

Blum, John Morton. *Roosevelt and Morgenthau*. Boston: Houghton Mifflin, 1970.

Blum, John Morton, ed. *From the Morgenthau Diaries.* 3 vols. Boston: Houghton Mifflin, 1959–67.

———, ed. *The Price of Vision: The Diary of Henry Wallace, 1942–1946.* Boston: Houghton Mifflin, 1973.

Boothe, Clare. *Europe in the Spring.* New York: Alfred A. Knopf, 1940.

Bowles, Chester. *Promises to Keep: My Years in Public Life, 1941–1969.* New York: Harper, 1971.

Braden, Anne. *The Wall Between,* 2nd ed. Knoxville: University of Tennessee Press, 1958.

Brands, H. W. *Traitor to His Class: The Privileged Life and Radical Presidency of Franklin Delano Roosevelt.* New York: Anchor Books, 2009.

Breitman, Richard. *Official Secrets.* New York: Hill & Wang, 1998.

Breitman, Richard and Alan Kraut. *American Refugee Policy and European Jewry, 1933–54.* Bloomington: Indiana University Press, 1988.

Breitman, Richard, Barbara McDonald Stewart, and Severin Hochberg, eds. *Refugees and Rescue: The Diaries & Papers of James G. McDonald, 1935–1945.* Bloomington: Indiana University Press, in association with the U.S. Holocaust Memorial Museum, 2009.

Bridenthal, Renate, Atina Grossmann, and Marion Kaplan, eds. *When Biology Becomes Destiny: Women in Weimar and Nazi Germany.* New York: Monthly Review Press, 1984.

Brittain, Vera. *Envoy Extraordinary: A Study of Vijaya Lakshmi Pandit and Her Contribution to Modern India.* London: George Allen, 1965.

———. *One Voice: Pacifist Writings from World War II.* New York: Bloomsbury Academic, 2005.

———. *Pethick-Lawrence: A Portrait.* London: George Allen & Unwin, 1963

———. *Testament of Experience.* New York: Macmillan, 1957.

Brockington, Lee. *Plantation Between the Waters: A Brief History of Hobcaw Barony.* Charleston: Historical Press of South Carolina, 2006.

Browne-Marshall, Gloria J. *Race, Law, and American Society: 1607–Present.* Abingdon, UK: Routledge, 2007.

Brysac, Shareen Blair. *Resisting Hitler: Mildred Harnack and the Red Orchestra.* New York: Oxford University Press, 2000.

Buckley, Gail. *American Patriots: The Story of Blacks in the Military from the Revolution to Desert Storm.* New York: Random House, 2002.

———. *The Hornes.* Montclair, NJ: Applause Books, 1986.

Buhite, Russell D., and David W. Levy. *FDR's Fireside Chats.* Norman: University of Oklahoma Press, 1992.

Bullitt, Orville, ed. *For the President, Personal and Secret: The Letters of William Bullitt.* Boston: Houghton Mifflin, 1972.

Bunch, Charlotte, and Roxanna Carrilo. "Women's Rights Are Human Rights: A Concept in the Making," in Ellen Chesler and Terry McGovern, eds., *Women and Girls Rising: Progress and Resistance Around the World.* New York: Routledge, 2015.

Burns, James MacGregor. *Roosevelt: The Soldier of Freedom, 1940–1945.* New York: Harcourt Brace, 1970.

Burns, James MacGregor, and Susan Dunn. *The Three Roosevelts: Patrician Leaders Who Transformed America.* New York: Grove Press, 2001.

Bussey, Gertrude, and Margaret Tims. *Women's International League for Peace and Freedom, 1915–1965: A Record of Fifty Years' Work.* London: George Allen & Unwin, 1965.

Callil, Carmen. *Bad Faith: A Forgotten History of Family, Fatherland and Vichy France.* New York: Vintage, 2007.

Catherwood, Christopher. *Churchill's Folly: How Winston Churchill Created Modern Iraq.* London: Carroll & Graf, 2004.

Chace, James. *Acheson: The Secretary of State Who Created the American World.* New York: Simon & Schuster, 1998.

Chavkin, Wendy, and Ellen Chesler. *Where Human Rights Begin: Health, Sexuality and Women in the New Millennium.* New Brunswick, NJ: Rutgers University Press, 2005.

Churchill, Sarah. *Keep On Dancing.* New York: Coward, McCann, 1981.

Churchill, Winston S. *Alone, 1932–1940.* Boston: Little, Brown, 1988.

———. *The Gathering Storm,* vol. 1 of *The Second World War.* Boston: Houghton Mifflin, 1948.

Clarke, Jeanne Nienaber. *Roosevelt's Warrior: Harold Ickes and the New Deal.* Baltimore: Johns Hopkins University Press, 1996.

Cloud, Stanley, and Lynne Olson. *The Morrow Boys: Pioneers on the Front Lines of Broadcast Journalism.* Boston: Houghton Mifflin, 1996.

Cohen, Robert. *When the Old Left Was Young: Student Radicals and America's First Mass Student Movement, 1929–41.* Oxford: Oxford University Press, 1993.

Coit, Margaret. *Mr. Baruch.* 1957; reprint, Fairless Hills, PA: Beard Books, 2000.

Cook, Blanche Wiesen. *Eleanor Roosevelt,* vols. 1 and 2. New York: Penguin, 1993, 2000.

———. *The Declassified Eisenhower.* New York: Penguin, 1984.

Cook, Blanche Wiesen, ed. *Crystal Eastman: On Women and Revolution.* New York: Oxford University Press, 1978.

Cornwell, John. *Hitler's Pope: The Secret History of Pius XII.* New York: Viking, 1999.

Costiglio, Frank. *Roosevelt's Lost Alliances: How Personal Politics Helped Start the Cold War.* Princeton: Princeton University Press, 2012.

Crane, John O., and Sylvia E. Crane. *Czechoslovakia: Anvil of the Cold War.* New York: Praeger, 1991.

Crum, Bartley. *Behind the Silken Curtain.* New York: Simon & Schuster, 1947.

Curtin, Kaier. *"We Can Always Call Them Bulgarians": The Emergence of Lesbians and Gay Men on the American Stage.* New York: Alyson Books, 1987.

Dallek, Robert. *FDR and American Foreign Policy, 1932–45.* Oxford: Oxford University Press, 1979.

Davis, Kenneth. *FDR: Into the Storm, 1937–1940.* New York: Random House, 1993.

Dinnerstein, Leonard. *America and the Survivors of the Holocaust.* New York: Columbia University Press, 1982.

Divine, Arthur D. *The Nine Days of Dunkirk.* New York: W. W. Norton, 1959.

Douglas, Helen Gahagan. *A Full Life.* New York: Doubleday, 1982.

———. *The Eleanor Roosevelt We Remember.* New York: Hill & Wang, 1963.

Douglas, Melvyn, and Tom Arthur. *See You at the Movies: The Autobiography of Melvyn Douglas.* Lanham, MD: University Press of America, 1986.

Drayer, Ruth A. *Nicholas and Helena Roerich.* Wheaton, IL: Theosophical Publishing House, 2005.

Drinnon, Richard. *Keeper of Concentration Camps: Dillon Meyer & American Racism.* Oakland: University of California Press, 1987.

Du Bois, Rachel Davis. *All This and Something More: Pioneering in Intercultural Education.* Bryn Mawr, PA: Dorrance, 1984.

Durr, Virginia. *Outside the Magic Circle: The Autobiography of Virginia Foster Durr,* edited by Holinger Barnard. Tuscaloosa: University of Alabama Press, 1985.

Eddy, William A. *FDR Meets Ibn Saud.* American Friends of the Middle East, 1954.

Egerton, John. *Speak Now Against the Day: The Generation Before the Civil Rights Movement in the South.* New York: Alfred A. Knopf, 1995.

Ehrenburg, Ilya. *Memoirs: 1921–1941.* Cleveland: World, 1964.

———. *The War: 1941–1945.* Cleveland: World, 1964.

Eisenhower, Milton S. *The President Is Calling.* New York: Doubleday, 1974.

Ernst, Jimmy. *A Not-So-Still Life.* New York: St. Martin's, 1984.

Faircloth, Adam. *Better Day Coming: Blacks and Equality, 1890–2000.* New York: Viking, 2001.

Feingold, Henry. *The Politics of Rescue: The Roosevelt Administration and the Holocaust, 1938–1945.* Washington, DC: U.S. Holocaust Memorial Museum, 1970.

Felsenthal, Carol. *Alice Roosevelt Longworth.* New York: Putnam, 1988.

Felstiner, Mary Lowenthal. *To Paint Her Life: Charlotte Salomon in the Nazi Era*. New York: HarperCollins, 1994.

Fink, Carole. *Marc Bloch: A Life in History*. New York: Cambridge University Press, 1991.

Fischer, Louis. *The Life of Mahatma Gandhi*. New York: Collier Books, 1962.

Flanagan, Hallie. *Arena: The History of the Federal Theatre*. 1940; reprint, New York: Limelight Editions, 1985.

Flanner, Janet. *Paris Was Yesterday, 1925–1939*. Edited by Irving Drutman. New York: Viking, 1972.

Fleming, Candace. *Our Eleanor: A Scrapbook*. New York: Simon & Schuster, 2005.

Fosl, Catherine. *Subversive Southerner: Anne Braden and the Struggle for Racial Justice in the Cold War South*. London: Palgrave Macmillan, 2002.

Fox, Richard. *Reinhold Niebuhr: A Biography*. New York: Pantheon, 1985.

Freedman, Max, ed. *Roosevelt and Frankfurter: Their Correspondence, 1928–1945*. Boston: Little, Brown, 1967.

Friedrich, Otto. *Before the Deluge: A Portrait of Berlin in the 1920s*. 1972; reprint, New York: HarperCollins, 1995.

Fromkin, David. *A Peace to End All Peace: The Fall of the Ottoman Empire and the Creation of the Modern Middle East*. New York: Henry Holt, 1989.

Fry, Varian. *Surrender on Demand*. 1945; reprint, Boulder, CO: Johnson Books, 1997. Published in conjunction with the U.S. Holocaust Memorial Museum.

Gellhorn, Martha. *The Face of War*. 1959; reprint, New York: Atlantic Monthly Press, 1994.

Gellman, Irwin. *Secret Affairs: FDR, Cordell Hull, and Sumner Welles*. Baltimore: Johns Hopkins University Press, 1995.

Geselbracht, Raymond H. *The Civil Rights Legacy of Harry S. Truman*. Kirksville, MO: Truman State University Press, 2007.

Gilbert, Martin. *Auschwitz and the Allies*. New York: Holt, Rinehart & Winston, 1981.

———. *Churchill and America*. New York: Free Press, 2005.

———. *Finest Hour: 1939–1941*. Vol. 6 of *Winston S. Churchill*. Boston: Houghton Mifflin, 1983.

———. *History of the Twentieth Century*. New York: William Morrow, 1998.

———. *The Second World War: A Complete History*. New York: Henry Holt, 1989.

Glendon, Mary Ann. *A World Made New: Eleanor Roosevelt and the Universal Declaration of Human Rights*. New York: Random House, 2002.

Gold, Mary Jane. *Crossroads Marseille, 1940*. New York: Doubleday, 1980.

Goodwin, Doris Kearns. *No Ordinary Time—Franklin and Eleanor Roosevelt: The Home Front in World War II*. New York: Simon & Schuster, 1994.

Gould, Leslie. *American Youth Today*. New York: Random House, 1940.

Grafton, David. *The Sisters: The Lives and Times of the Fabulous Cushing Sisters*. New York: Villard Books, 1992.

Grayling, A. C. *Among the Dead Cities*. New York: Walker & Co, 2006.

Greenberg, Karen J., ed. *Archives of the Holocaust, vol. 5: The Varian Fry Papers and the Fort Ontario Emergency Refugee Shelter Papers*, from the Columbia University Library. New York: Garland, 1990.

Grose, Peter. *Israel in the Mind of America*. New York: Schocken, 1984.

Gruber, Ruth. *Ahead of Time: My Early Years as a Foreign Correspondent*. New York: Carroll & Graf, 1991, 2001.

———. *Exodus, 1947: The Ship That Launched a Nation*. New York: Random House, Times, 1948. Published with an introduction by Bartley Crum. New York: Crown, 1999.

———. *Haven: The Story of 1,000 World War II Refugees and How They Came to America*. New York: Putnam, 1983. Republished 1994, Oswego Anniversary edition. New York: Three Rivers Press, 2000.

————. *Inside of Time: My Journey from Alaska to Israel: A Memoir with Eleanor Roosevelt, Harold Ickes, Golda Meir, and other Friends.* New York: Carroll & Graf, 2003.

————. *I Went to the Soviet Arctic.* New York: Viking, 1944.

————. *Witness.* New York: Schocken Books, 2007. Foreword by Richard Holbrook.

Gurewitsch, Edna. *Kindred Souls: The Devoted Friendship of Eleanor Roosevelt and Dr. David Gurewitsch.* New York: St. Martin's Press, 2002.

Hanak, Werner, ed. *The World of Ili Kronstein.* Vienna: Judisches Museum, 2000.

Harris, Mark Jonathan, and Deborah Oppenheimer. *Into the Arms of Strangers: Stories of the Kindertransport.* New York: Bloomsbury, 2000.

Harrity, Richard, and Ralph Martin. *Eleanor Roosevelt: Her Life in Pictures.* New York: Duell, Sloan & Pearce, 1958.

Hecht, Ben. *A Child of the Century.* New York: Simon & Schuster, 1954.

Height, Dorothy. *Open Wide the Freedom Gates: A Memoir.* New York: PublicAffairs, 2003.

Heilbut, Anthony. *Exiled in Paradise.* New York: Viking, 1983.

————. *Thomas Mann.* New York: Alfred A. Knopf, 1995.

Heinrichs, Waldo. *American Ambassador: Joseph Grew and the Development of the United States Diplomatic Tradition.* Boston: Little, Brown, 1966.

————. *Threshold of War: Franklin D. Roosevelt and American Entry into World War II.* New York: Oxford University Press, 1988.

Hitchcock, William. *The Bitter Road to Freedom: A New History of the Liberation of Europe.* New York: Free Press, 2008.

Hoff-Wilson, Joan, and Marjorie Lightman, eds. *Without Precedent: The Life and Career of Eleanor Roosevelt.* Bloomington: Indiana University Press, 1984.

Hunt, John Gabriel, ed. *The Essential Franklin Delano Roosevelt.* New York: Gramercy, 1995.

Hurok, Sol. *Impresario: A Memoir.* New York: Random House, 1946.

Ickes, Harold. *The Secret Diary of Harold L. Ickes.* 3 vols. New York: Simon & Schuster, 1953–54.

Isaacs, Stephen. *Jews and American Politics.* New York: Doubleday, 1974.

Isenberg, Sheila. *The Story of Varian Fry: A Hero of Our Own.* New York: Random House, 2001.

James, C. L. R., et al. *Fighting Racism in World War II.* New York: Pathfinder Press, 2001.

Jonas, Manfred. *Isolationism in America, 1935–1941.* Ithaca, NY: Cornell University Press, 1966.

Jungk, Robert. *Brighter Than a Thousand Suns.* New York: Harcourt Brace, 1958.

Kaplan, Marion A. *Dominican Haven: The Jewish Refugee Settlement in Sosua, 1940–1945.* New York: Museum of Jewish Heritage, 2008.

Katz-Nelson, Ira. *Fear Itself: The New Deal and the Origins of Our Time.* New York: W. W. Norton, 2013.

Keegan, Susanne. *The Bride of the Wind: The Life of Alma Mahler.* New York: Viking, 1992.

Keiler, Allen. *Marian Anderson: A Singer's Journey.* New York: Scribner, 2000.

Kennedy, David M. *Freedom from Fear: The American People in Depression and War, 1929–1945.* New York: Oxford University Press, 1999.

Klarsfeld, Serge, Susan Cohen, and Howard Epstein, eds. *French Children of the Holocaust.* New York: New York University Press, 1996.

Koonz, Claudia. *Mothers in the Fatherland: Women, the Family and Nazi Politics.* New York: St. Martin's, 1987.

Kushner, Tony. *The Holocaust and the Liberal Imagination.* London: Blackwell, 1994.

Lachmann, Vera. *Homer's Sun Still Shines: Ancient Greece in Essays, Poems and Translations.* Edited by Charles A. Miller. Blowing Rock, NC: Trackaday, 2004.

LaFeber, Walter. *Inevitable Revolutions: The United States in Central America.* New York: W. W. Norton, 1993.

Lash, Joseph P. *Dealers and Dreamers: A New Look at the New Deal.* New York: Doubleday, 1988.

————. *Eleanor and Franklin: The Story of their Relationship, Based on Eleanor Roosevelt's Private Papers.* New York: W. W. Norton, 1971.

————. *Eleanor Roosevelt: A Friend's Memoir.* New York: Doubleday, 1964.

————. *Eleanor: The Years Alone.* New York: W. W. Norton, 1972.

————. *"Life Was Meant to Be Lived." A Centenary Portrait.* New York: Norton, 1984.

————. *Love, Eleanor: Eleanor Roosevelt and Her Friends.* New York: Doubleday, 1982.

————. *Roosevelt and Churchill, 1939–1941: The Partnership That Saved the West.* New York: Norton, 1976.

————. *A World of Love: Eleanor Roosevelt and Her Friends, 1943–1962.* New York: Doubleday, 1987.

Lattimore, Owen. *Ordeal By Slander,* introduction by Blanche Wiesen Cook. New York: Carroll & Graf, l950, 2004.

Lerner, Gerda. *Fireweed.* Philadelphia: Temple University Press, 2002.

Leuchtenburg, William. *FDR and the New Deal.* New York: HarperPerennial, 1963.

Levine, Lawrence and Cornelia. *The People and the President: America's Conversation with FDR.* Boston: Beacon Press, 2002.

Levy, William Turner. *The Extraordinary Mrs. R: A Friend Remembers Eleanor Roosevelt.* New York: John Wiley, 1999.

Lewis, David Levering. *W. E. B. Du Bois, 1919–1963.* New York: Henry Holt, 2000.

Liggio, Leonard, and James Martin, eds. *Watershed of Empire: Essays on New Deal Foreign Policy.* Colorado Springs, CO: Ralph Myles, 1976.

Lippman, Thomas. *Inside the Mirage: America's Fragile Partnership with Saudi Arabia.* New York: Basic Books, 2005.

Littell, Norman. *My Roosevelt Years.* Seattle: University of Washington Press, 1987.

Lockwood, Bert, ed. *Women's Rights: A Human Rights Quarterly Reader.* Baltimore: Johns Hopkins University Press, 2006.

Loewenheim, Francis, Harold Langley, and Manfred Jonas, eds. *Roosevelt and Churchill: Their Secret Wartime Correspondence.* New York: Da Capo Press, 1990.

Lomazow, Steven, and Eric Fettmann. *FDR'S Deadly Secret.* New York: PublicAffairs, 2009.

Long, Breckenridge. *The War Diary of Breckenridge Long: 1939–1944.* Edited by Fred L. Israel. Lincoln: University of Nebraska Press, 1966.

Lowdermilk, Walter Clay. *Palestine: Land of Promise.* London: Victor Gollancz, 1944.

Lukacs, John. *Five Days in London.* New Haven, CT: Yale University Press, 1999.

MacAdams, William. *Ben Hecht: The Man Behind the Legend.* New York: Scribner, 1990.

Macgregor, Frances Cooke. *Twentieth Century Indians.* New York: Putnam, 1941.

Mahler, Alma. *And the Bridge Is Love.* New York: Harcourt Brace, 1958.

Manchester, William. *The Last Lion: William Spencer Churchill.* 2 vols. Boston: Little, Brown, 1983, 1988.

Manchester, William, and Paul Reid. *The Last Lion: Winston Spencer Churchill, Defender of the Realm.* Boston: Little, Brown, 2012.

Mann, Klaus. *The Turning Point.* Princeton, NJ: Markus Wiener, 1942.

Marcantonio, Vito. *I Vote My Conscience.* Edited by Annette Rubinstein. New York: Vito Marcantonio Memorial, 1956.

Marino, Andy. *A Quiet American: The Secret War of Varian Fry.* New York: St. Martin's, 1999.

Marrus, Michael, and Robert Paxton. *Vichy France and the Jews.* New York: Basic Books, 1981.

Marzani, Carl, and W. E. B. Du Bois, *We Can Be Friends.* New York: Topical Book, 1952.

Marton, Kati. *Wallenberg: Missing Hero.* New York: Ballantine, 1995.

Mathews, Jane DeHart. *The Federal Theatre, 1935–1939: Plays, Relief and Politics.* Princeton, NJ: Princeton University Press, 1967.

Medoff, Rafael. *Blowing the Whistle on Genocide: Josiah E. Du Bois and the Struggle for a U.S. Response to the Holocaust.* West Lafayette, IN: Purdue University Press, 2009.

Merry, Robert. *Taking on the World: Joseph and Stewart Alsop, Guardians of the American Century.* New York: Viking, 1996.

Millay, Edna St. Vincent. *The Murder of Lidice*. New York: Harper & Bros., 1942.

Miller, Charles A. *A Catawba Assembly*. Blowing Rock, NC: Trackaday, 1973.

Miller, Kristie, *Isabella Greenway: An Enterprising Woman*. Tucson: University of Arizona Press, 2004.

Miller, Kristie, and Robert H. McGinnis, eds. *A Volume of Friendship: The Letters of Eleanor Roosevelt and Isabella Greenway, 1904–1953*. Tucson: Arizona Historical Society, 2008.

Miller, Mary. *Baroness of Hobcaw: The Life of Belle W. Baruch*. Charleston: University of South Carolina Press, 2006.

Miller, Merle. *Ike the Soldier: As They Knew Him*. New York: Perigee, 1988.

Moore, Christopher Paul. *Black Soldiers: The Unsung Heroes of World War II*. New York: Ballantine, 2004.

Moorehead, Caroline, ed. *Selected Letters of Martha Gellhorn*. New York: Henry Holt, 2006.

Morgan, Ted. *FDR: A Biography*. New York: Simon & Schuster, 1985.

Morgenthau, Henry. *Mostly Morgenthaus: A Family History*. New York: Ticknor & Fields, 1991.

Morse, Arthur. *While Six Million Died: A Chronicle of American Apathy*. New York: Overlook Books, 1983.

Mosel, Tad, and Gertrude Macy. *Leading Lady: The World and Theatre of Katharine Cornell*. Boston: Little, Brown, 1978.

Mukerjee, Madhusree. *Churchill's Secret War: The British Empire and the Ravaging of India During World War II*. New York: Basic Books, 2010.

Murphy, Robert. *Diplomat Among Warriors*. New York: Doubleday, 1964.

Murray, Pauli. *Song in a Weary Throat: An American Pilgrimage*. New York: Harper & Row, 1987. Republished as *The Autobiography of a Black Activist, Feminist, Lawyer, Priest, and Poet*. Knoxville: University of Tennessee, 1989.

Nagorski, Tom. *Miracles on the Water*. New York: Hyperion, 2006.

Neal, Steve. *Dark Horse: A Biography of Wendell Willkie*. Lawrence: University of Kansas Press, 1984.

Neal, Steve, ed. *Eleanor and Harry: The Correspondence of Eleanor Roosevelt and Harry S. Truman*. New York: Scribner, 2002.

Nelson, Anne. *Red Orchestra: The Story of the Berlin Underground and the Circle of Friends Who Resisted Hitler*. New York: Random House, 2009.

Nesbitt, Henrietta. *White House Diary: F.D.R.'s Housekeeper*. New York: Doubleday, 1948.

Neumann, William L. *America Encounters Japan*. Baltimore: Johns Hopkins University Press, 1963.

Newman, Robert P., *Owen Lattimore and the "Loss" of China*. Berkeley: University of California Press, 1992.

Nicolson, Nigel, ed. *Diaries and Letters of Harold Nicolson*. 3 vols. New York: Atheneum, 1966, 1967, 1968.

Nissenson, Marilyn. *The Lady Upstairs: Dorothy Schiff and the* New York Post. New York: St. Martin's, 2007.

Norman, Dorothy. *Encounters: A Memoir*. New York: Harcourt, 1987.

Norman, Jessye. *Stand Up Straight and Sing! A Memoir*. Boston: Houghton Mifflin, 2014.

O'Farrell, Brigid. *She Was One of Us: Eleanor Roosevelt and the American Worker*. Ithaca, NY: Cornell University Press, 2010.

Olson, Lynne. *Citizens of London: The Americans Who Stood with Britain in Its Darkest, Finest Hour*. New York: Random House, 2010.

Pandit, Vijaya Lakshmi. *The Scope of Happiness: A Personal Memoir*. New York: Crown, 1979.

Papandreou, Margarita. *Nightmare in Athens*. Englewood Cliffs, NJ: Prentice Hall, 1970.

Parks, Lillian Rogers. *The Roosevelts: A Family in Turmoil*. Englewood Cliffs, NJ: Prentice Hall, 1981.

Peare, Catherine Owens. *Mary McLeod Bethune*. New York: Vanguard Press, 1951.

Pedersen, Susan. *Eleanor Rathbone and the Politics of Conscience*. New Haven, CT: Yale University Press, 2004.

Perkins, Frances. *The Roosevelt I Knew*. New York: Viking, 1946.

Persico, Joseph. *Franklin & Lucy: Mrs. Rutherford, and the Other Remarkable Women in Roose-velt's Life*. New York: Random House, 2008.

Plesch, Dan. *America, Hitler and the UN: How the Allies Won World War II and Forged a Peace*. London: I. B. Tauris, 2011.

Proctor, Robert. *Racial Hygiene: Medicine Under the Nazis*. Cambridge, MA: Harvard University Press, 1988.

Rauch, Basil, ed. *Franklin D. Roosevelt: Selected Speeches, Messages, Press Conferences, and Letters*. New York: Holt, Rinehart & Winston, 1964.

Reed, Linda. *Simple Decency and Common Sense: The Southern Conference Movement, 1938–1963*. Bloomington: Indiana University Press, 1991.

Reeves, Richard. *Infamy: The Shocking Story of Japanese-American Internment in World War II*. New York: Henry Holt, 2015.

Reitman, Alan, ed. *The Pulse of Freedom: American Liberties, 1920s–1970s*. New York: W. W. Norton, 1975.

Robinson, Greg. *After Camp: Portraits in Midcentury Japanese American Life and Politics*. Oakland: University of California Press, 2012.

———. *By Order of the President: FDR and the Internment of Japanese Americans*. Cambridge, MA: Harvard University Press, 2001.

———. *A Tragedy of Democracy: Japanese Confinement in North America*. New York: Columbia University Press, 2009.

———, and Elena Tajima Creef, eds. Miné Okubo: Following Her Own Road. Seattle: University of Washington Press, 2008.

Roeger, Harry N. *Minnie of Hobcaw*. n.p.: Xlibris, 2007.

Roosevelt, Eleanor. *Autobiography*. New York: HarperCollins, 1961.

———. *India and the Awakening East*. New York: Harper, 1953.

———. *My Day*. Eleanor Roosevelt Papers Project, www.gwu.edu.

———. *On My Own: The Years Since the White House*. London: Hutchinson, 1959.

———. *The Moral Basis of Democracy*. New York: Howell, Soskin, 1940.

———. *This I Remember*. New York: Harper & Bros., 1949.

———. *Tomorrow Is Now*. New York: Penguin, 1963.

———. *You Learn by Living*. New York: Harper & Bros., 1960.

Roosevelt, Eleanor, and Helen Ferris. *Partners: The UN and Youth*. New York: Doubleday, 1950.

Roosevelt, Eleanor, and Lorena A. Hickok. *Ladies of Courage*. New York: Putnam, 1954.

Roosevelt, Eleanor, and Frances Cooke Macgregor. *This Is America*. New York: G. P. Putnam's Sons, 1942.

Roosevelt, Eleanor, II. *With Love, Aunt Eleanor: Stories from My Life with the First Lady of the World*. Petaluma, CA: Scrapbook Press, 2004.

Roosevelt, Elliott, ed. *FDR: His Personal Letters*. 4 vols. New York: Duell, Sloan & Pearce, 1947–50.

Rosen, Robert. *Saving the Jews: Franklin D. Roosevelt and the Holocaust*. n.p.: Thunder's Mouth Press, 2006.

Rosenman, Samuel. *Working with Roosevelt*. New York: Harper & Bros., 1952.

Rowan, Carl. *Dream Makers, Dream Breakers: The World of Justice Thurgood Marshall*. Boston: Little, Brown, 1993.

Rukeyser, Muriel. *One Life*. New York: Simon & Schuster, 1957.

Russell, Jan Jarboe. *The Train to Crystal City: FDR's Secret Prisoner Exchange Program and America's Only Family Internment Camp During World War II*. New York: Scribner, 2015.

Sargent, Shirley. *Yosemite's Famous Guests*. n.p.: Flying Spur Press, 1970.

Schapsmeier, Edward, and Frederick Schapsmeier. *Henry Wallace of Iowa: The Agrarian Years, 1910–1940*. Ames: Iowa State University Press, 1968.

Scholl, Inge. *The White Rose*. Middletown, CT: Wesleyan University Press, 1983.

Schrecker, Ellen. *Many Are the Crimes: McCarthyism in America*. Boston: Little, Brown, 1998.

———. *No Ivory Tower: McCarthyism and the Universities*. Oxford: Oxford University Press, 1986.

Schwarz, Jordan A. *The Speculator, Bernard M. Baruch in Washington, 1917–1965*. Chapel Hill: University of North Carolina Press, 1981.

Scobie, Ingrid. *Center Stage: Helen Gahagan Douglas, A Life*. New York: Oxford University Press, 1992.

Scott, Anne Firor, ed. *Pauli Murray and Caroline Ware: Forty Years of Letters in Black and White*. Chapel Hill: University of North Carolina Press, 2006.

Seeger, Pete. *Hard Hitting Songs for Hard-Hit People*. Lincoln: University of Nebraska Press, 2012.

———. *Where Have All the Flowers Gone: A Singalong Memoir*. New York: W. W. Norton, 2009.

Selser, Gregorio. *Sandino*. New York: Monthly Review Press, 1981.

Sherwin, Martin. *A World Destroyed: The Atomic Bomb and the Grand Alliance*. New York: Knopf, 1975. Republished as *A World Destroyed: Hiroshima and Its Legacies*. Palo Alto, CA: Stanford University Press, 2003.

Shoumatoff, Elizabeth. *FDR's Unfinished Portrait: A Memoir*. Pittsburgh: University of Pittsburgh Press, 1990.

Sicherman, Barbara, Carol Hurd Green, et al., eds. *Notable American Women: The Modern Period*. Cambridge, MA: Harvard University Press, 1980.

Sherwood, Robert E. *Roosevelt and Hopkins: An Intimate History*. New York: Harper, 1948.

Shirer, William. *Berlin Diary: The Journal of a Foreign Correspondent, 1934–1941*. New York: Alfred A. Knopf, 1941.

Sifton, Elisabeth. *The Serenity Prayer*. New York: W. W. Norton, 2005.

Smedley, Agnes. *The Great Road: The Life and Times of Chu Teh*. New York: Monthly Review Press, 1956.

Smith, Amanda. *Hostage to Fortune: The Letters of Joseph P. Kennedy*. New York: Viking, 2001.

Smith, Gaddis. *American Diplomacy During the Second World War, 1941–1945*. New York: Wiley, 1967.

Smith, Jean Edward. *Eisenhower in War and Peace*. New York: Random House, 2013.

———. *FDR*. New York: Random House, 2007.

Smith, Margaret Chase. *Declaration of Conscience*. Edited by William C. Lewis. New York: Doubleday, 1972.

Smith, Neil. *American Empire: Roosevelt's Geographer and the Prelude to Globalization*. Berkeley: University of California Press, 2003.

Smith, Roger W., ed. *Genocide: Essays Toward Understanding*. n.p.: Association of Genocide Scholars, 1999.

Soames, Mary. *A Daughter's Tale: The Memoir of Winston Churchill's Youngest Child*. New York: Random House, 2011.

Somerville, Mollie D. *Eleanor Roosevelt As I Knew Her*. n.p.: Howell Press, 1996.

Spender, Dale, ed. *Feminist Theorists: Three Centuries of Women's Intellectual Traditions*. n.p.: Women's Press, 1983.

Stettinius, Edward, Jr. "Roosevelt and the Russians: The Yalta Conference." *American Political Science Review*, vol. 44, no. 2 (June 1950).

Straight, Michael. *After Long Silence*. New York: W. W. Norton, 1983.

Streitmatter, Rodger, ed. *Empty Without You: The Intimate Letters of Eleanor Roosevelt and Lorena Hickok*. New York: Free Press, 1998.

Sullivan, Patricia. *Lift Every Voice: The NAACP and the Making of the Civil Rights Movement*. New York: New Press, 2010.

Sullivan, Patricia, ed. *Freedom Writer: Virginia Foster Durr, Letters from the Civil Rights Years*. Abingdon, UK: Routledge, 2003.

Sullivan, Rosemary. *Villa Air-Bel: World War II, Escape, and a House in Marseille*. New York: HarperCollins, 2007.

Suyin, Han. *Eldest Son: Zhou Enlai and the Making of Modern China, 1898–1976*. New York: Hill & Wang, 1994.

———. *The Morning Deluge: Mao Tsetung and the Chinese Revolution, 1893–1954*. Boston: Little, Brown, 1972.

Swift, Will. *The Roosevelts and the Royals: Franklin and Eleanor, the King and Queen of England, and the Friendship that Changed History*. Hoboken, NJ: John Wiley, 2004.

Taylor, Myron, ed. *Wartime Correspondence Between President Roosevelt and Pope Pius XII*. New York: Macmillan, 1947.

Theoharis, Athan. *Spying on Americans: Political Surveillance from Hoover to the Houston Plan*. Philadelphia: Temple University Press, 1978.

Theoharis, Athan, ed. *From the Secret Files of J. Edgar Hoover*. Chicago: Ivan R. Dee, 1991.

Thomas, Gordon, and Max Morgan-Witts. *Voyage of the Damned*. 1974; reprint, London: Dalton Watson, 1994.

Thorpe, Frances Wills. *Navy Blue and Other Colors: A Memoir of Adventure and Happiness*. n.p.: Xlibris, 2007.

Troper, Harold, and Irving Abella. *None Is Too Many: Canada and the Jews of Europe, 1933–1948*. Toronto: University of Toronto Press, 1983.

Truman, Margaret. *Harry S. Truman*. New York: William Morrow, 1973.

Tuchman, Barbara. *Stilwell and the American Experience in China*. New York: Macmillan, 1971.

U.S. Holocaust Memorial Council. *Fifty Years After the Eve of Destruction*. Washington, DC: U.S. Holocaust Memorial Council, 1989.

Vaill, Amanda. *Hotel Florida: Truth, Love, and Death in the Spanish Civil War*. New York: Farrar, Strauss & Giroux, 2014.

Vanderbilt, Cornelius, Jr. *Man of the World: My Life on Five Continents*. New York: Crown, 1959.

Vickers, Hugo. *Elizabeth: The Queen Mother*. London: Hutchinson/Random House, 2005.

Villard, Oswald Garrison. *Oswald Garrison Villard: The Dilemmas of an Absolute Pacifist in Two World Wars*. Edited by Anthony Gronowicz. New York: Garland, 1983.

Vinke, Hermann. *The Short Life of Sophie Scholl*. New York: Harper, 1984.

Wall, Irwin. *The United States and the Making of Postwar France, 1945–1954*. Cambridge: Cambridge University Press, 1991.

Wallace, Henry. *The Price of Vision: The Diary of Henry A. Wallace, 1942–1946*. Boston: Houghton Mifflin, 1973.

Wallenberg, Raoul. *Letters and Dispatches, 1924–1944*. n.p.: Arcade and U.S. Holocaust Memorial Museum, 1987, 1995.

Ward, Geoffrey C. *Closest Companion: The Unknown Story of the Intimate Friendship Between Franklin Roosevelt and Margaret Suckley*. New York: Simon & Schuster, 2009.

Ward, Patricia Spain. "In Recognition of Esther Everett Lape," *Women and Health* (Summer 1980)

———. "US vs American Medical Association, et al. The Medical Anti-Trust Case of 1938–1943" *American Studies* (Fall 1989)

Ware, Susan. *Partner and I: Molly Dewson, Feminism, and New Deal Politics*. New Haven, CT: Yale University Press, 1987.

Susan Ware. *Letter to the World: Seven Women Who Shaped the American Century*. New York: W. W. Norton, 1998.

Ware Susan, ed., *Notable American Women: A Biographical Dictionary*. Cambridge, MA: Belknap Press of Harvard University Press, 2004.

Watkins, T. H. *Righteous Pilgrim: The Life and Times of Harold Ickes, 1874–1952*. New York: Henry Holt, 1990.

Weinberg, Gerhard. *A World at Arms: A Global History of World War II*. New York: Cambridge University Press, 1994.

Weiner, Tim. *Enemies: A History of the FBI.* New York: Random House, 2012.

Weitz, John. *Hitler's Banker: Hjalmar Horace Greeley Schacht.* Boston: Little, Brown, 1987.

Welles, Benjamin. *Sumner Welles: FDR's Global Strategist.* New York: St. Martin's, 1997.

Werth, Alexander. *Russia at War, 1941–1944.* New York: E. P. Dutton, 1964.

West, J. B. *Upstairs at the White House: My Life with the First Ladies, 1941–1969.* New York: Coward, McCann & Geoghegan, 1973.

White, Walter. *A Man Called White.* Atlanta: University of Georgia Press, 1948.

Whitman, Alden. *The Obituary Book.* New York: Stein & Day, 1971.

Whitman, Alden, ed. *American Reformers: A Biographical Dictionary.* New York: H. W. Wilson, 1985.

Whitman, Alden, and the *New York Times.* *Portrait: Adlai Stevenson: Politician, Diplomat, Friend.* New York: Harper & Row, 1965.

Williams, William A. *American-Russian Relations, 1781–1947.* New York: Holt, Rinehart & Co., 1952.

Wyman, David. *The Abandonment of the Jews: America and the Holocaust, 1941–1945.* New York: New Press, 1984.

———. *Paper Walls: America and the Refugee Crisis, 1938–1941.* New York: Pantheon, 1985.

Wyman, David, and Rafael Medoff. *A Race Against Death: Peter Bergson, America and the Holocaust.* New York: New Press, 2002.

Zangrando, Robert. *The NAACP Crusade Against Lynching, 1909–1950.* Philadelphia: Temple University Press, 1980.

Zevin, B. D., ed. *Nothing to Fear: The Selected Addresses of Franklin Delano Roosevelt, 1932–1945.* Boston: Houghton Mifflin, 1946.

Notes

Introduction: "Lady Great Heart"

1 **"No woman has ever"**: Clare Boothe Luce, 21 May 1950, presenting ER with the Williamsburg Settlement's annual gold medal for aid to the underprivileged at the Waldorf Astoria Hotel. Allida Black, in *ER*, 2:412, 282.

1 **"The First Lady of"**: Pauli Murray's 1984 centennial celebration of ER, in Bell-Scott, *Firebrand and First Lady*, 357.

2 **"Attention and admiration"**: Cook, *ER*, 1:100. There is to date no biography of Marie Souvestre.

2 **"Whatever I have become"**: Cook, *ER*, see Allenswood chapter, 1:102ff.

2 **"the happiest day"**: Ibid.

3 **"Eleanor Roosevelt cares"**: Lady Stella Reading interviewed for and quoted in Harrity and Martin, *ER in Pictures*, 208.

3 **"apostle of good-will"**: The 135th celebration, *The Churchman*, chapter VII.

4 **one of history's most powerful**: Cook, *ER*, 1:227–32, 235–36, 245–48, 379–80.

5 **Learning and living**: ER, *You Learn by Living*, foreword.

6 **"self-absorbed snobs"**: Cook, *ER*, 1, Val-Kill chapter.

6 **"her face to the wall"**: Ibid.

7 **"is so completely changed"**: For ER's happy days at Todhunter, purchased in 1927, see Cook, *ER*, 1, chapter 16; for the bitter end of the friendship, see Cook, *ER*, 2:525–37.

7 **"has every right"**: Tommy to Trude Pratt, 13 October 1944.

7 **"chiselers and users"**: Cook, *ER*, 1, chapter 18, 429–47.

7 **"for purely sentimental"**: Ibid.

8 **"full of warmth"**: Ibid.

8 **packet of "endearing"**: Ibid.

8 **"Navy Commander's wife"**: Ibid.

8 **"You are right"**: ER to Hick, 19–20 November 1934, in Cook, *ER*, 2:229.

8 **"Have you heard"**: ER to Lape, as recorded by Maureen Corr. For ER's friendship with Laura (Polly) Delano, Levy, *Extraordinary Mrs. R*, 178–84.

10 **"both grew individually"**: Polier, oral history, FDRL.

10 **"I have learned"**: Bowles, *Promises to Keep*, 121–25.

10 **"remarkable wife" were**: Ibid.

10 **"Imagine me Feigele"**: Baum, Hyman, and Michel, *Jewish Woman in America*, 160.

10 **"her labor colleagues"**: O'Farrell, *She Was One of Us*, 187. For Gila and other Japanese internment camps, I am grateful to Al Vinck for his interviews with former Gila residents.

11 **990 Tuskegee Airmen:** Buckley, *American Patriots*, 286–94, 311–12; Buckley, *Hornes*, 178–80. On the Tuskegee Airmen, I am grateful to Dr. Roscoe Brown of CUNY and to Percy Heath. See also Frances Wills Thorpe, *Navy Blue and Other Colors*.

12 **"Lady Big Heart":** Rowan, *Dream Makers,* 131–42.

14 **displaced persons camps:** In *My Day*, 16 February 1946, she detailed her visit to Zeilsheim: "They made me a speech at a monument . . . to the six million dead Jewish people. I answered from an aching heart. When will our consciences grow so tender that we will act to prevent human misery rather than avenge it?"

14 **"we let our consciences":** ER, speech to women's division of the United Jewish Appeal, New York, 20 February 1946, in Black, *ER Papers,* 1:257.

14 **"rescue the perishing":** See Pedersen, *Rathbone and Conscience*, 328ff, 411. Rathbone's biographer, Susan Pedersen, points out that no study has yet been written to detail her work for refugees and rescue. Britain's Tony Kushner dedicated his book *The Holocaust and the Liberal Imagination* in part "to Eleanor Rathbone who knew, cared and acted."

14 **"The truth is":** ER, on Palestinian refugees, *India and East*, 24–34.

15 **"We will have a":** FDR, 1940 speech.

15 **"To deny any part":** *My Day*, 16 April 1943.

15 **"We all go ahead together":** ER's 11 May 1934 speech against discrimination, in *Journal of Negro Education* (10/1934); Cook; *ER*, 2:185, reprinted in Black, *What I Hope to Leave Behind*, 141ff.

Chapter One: "We All Go Ahead Together, or We Will All Go Down Together"

17 **congressional opposition to:** FDR to Josephus Daniels, 14 November 1938, in *FDR: Personal Letters*, 4:827–28; Leuchtenburg, *FDR and New Deal*, 271–74.

18 **"sparkling east ballroom":** ER II, *Aunt Eleanor,* 30–36. I am grateful to ER's nieces Diana Roosevelt Jaicks and Janet R. Katten for press reports of ER's party.

18 **"a feeling of injustice":** ER to Charles Graves, 21 January 1939, box 1519, ER Papers.

19 **detailing various outings:** FDR to King of England, 18 January 1939, collected letters.

19 **"I hope adults everywhere":** *New York Times*, 1 January 1939.

19 **ER II chose to watch:** ER to Lape and Elizabeth Read, 1 January 1939, BWC.

19 **"Aunt Eleanor proposed":** ER II, *Aunt Eleanor,* 36.

19 **"I never saw such nerve":** ER, press conference, 5 January 1939, in Beasley, *ER Press Conferences,* 67–69. See also *My Day*, 3 January 1939.

20 **"I said I would tell you":** *My Day*, 5 January 1939. This stunning Broadway success was intensely controversial. Morley received the Drama Critics' Best Actor award for his portrayal of Oscar Wilde. See Kaier Curtin, *We Can Always Call Them Bulgarians*, 237–49.

20 **"Bill was so fond of you":** ER to Hick, 3 January 1939.

20 **"I'm playing a rather mean"**: Ibid.

21 **"made Pa very cheerful"**: ER to Anna, 22 January 1939, Asbell, ed., *Mother and Daughter*, 107.

21 **"And through the streets"**: Neruda quoted in Ehrenburg, *Memoirs*, 344. For Ehrenburg's extraordinary eyewitness account of Spain's fall, see 340ff.

21 **"Father is very gloomy"**: ER to Anna, 22 January 1939, Asbell, *Mother and Daughter*.

21 **"At the moment your mother"**: Tommy to Anna, 2 February 1939, Anna Roosevelt Halsted Papers, box 75.

21 **"I bobbed my hair"**: ER to Anna, 22 January 1939, Asbell, 107; ER to J. H. Cairns, Los Angeles, on women's rights and birth control information, 28 February 1938, box 1452.

22 **"Of course the trouble is"**: *My Day*, 5 April 1938.

23 **"our neutrality laws may"**: FDR, "Annual Message to Congress" (A Warning to Dictator Nations), January 4, 1939, in Zevin, *Nothing to Fear*, 162–73. FDR worked on this speech for months. He assigned an aide to find Lincoln's words, FDR to William D. Hassett, 22 October 1938, in *FDR: Personal Letters*, 4:820. See also Davis, *FDR: Into the Storm*, 387–90.

23 **"a solid block of people"**: *My Day*, 5 January 1939.

24 **"there can be no real democracy"**: Bess Furman's notes, press conference, 17 January 1939, Beasley, 71.

24 **"Where you have no official"**: Ibid., 70–72.

24 **Stunned, Frankfurter whispered:** Lash suggested that Frankfurter was not surprised at all, since his former students Tom Corcoran and Ben Cohen orchestrated the lobby for Frankfurter and persuaded progressive Senator George Norris (R-NE) to join their effort. According to them, when Norris agreed, FDR acted. Corcoran and Cohen, Lash wrote, were in daily communication with Frankfurter; see *Dealers and Dreamers*, 385–88.

24 **"mother had been alive"**: Felix Frankfurter to FDR, 4 January 1939, in Freedman, *Roosevelt and Frankfurter*, 482–83.

25 **"two Jews on the train"**: Joseph Lash on Rosenman, in *Dealers and Dreamers*, 388. Ickes lobbied vigorously for Frankfurter's appointment; he believed that FDR was persuaded by Justice Harlan Fiske Stone, who argued that there were not that many "distinguished judges or lawyers in the US—men with lovely minds." When Ickes's friends learned of FDR's signed commission to the U.S. Senate, a champagne party convened with Tom Corcoran; FDR's new attorney general Frank Murphy; Harry Hopkins; U.S. solicitor general Robert Jackson; SEC chair William O. Douglas; WPA assistant administrator David Niles; Missy LeHand; and Peggy Dowd.

25 **"So you would create"**: Stephen Isaacs, *Jews and American Politics* (New York: Doubleday, 1974), 65.

25 **"were fanatical and"**: Acheson to George Rublee, 17 January 1939, in Chace, *Acheson*, 74–75.

25 **"a great roar of approval"**: Chace, *Acheson*, 75. See also Ickes, *Secret Diary*, 2:552.

26 **"That things should be"**: Baker, *Brandeis and Frankfurter*, 345.

26 **"was saving central Europe"**: Pound on Hitler, Baker, 349ff. In 1939 Frankfurter and Arthur Schlesinger, Sr., issued the "Committee of Eight" report on religious discrimination at leading universities. Astonishingly, Samuel Eliot Morison defended the need to "save some places at mother Yale for *our* boys," given that worthy sons of America's founders were "being hustled and shoved from every side, politically mainly by the Irish; economically, by the Jews." See Baker, passim.

26 **"with permission to quote"**: ER, press conference, 13 February 1939, in Beasley, *ER Press Conferences*.

27 **"at the present time"**: ER to Justine Wise Politer, 28 February 1939.

27 **"charming children" all too**: Feingold, *Politics of Rescue*, 150; Richard Breitman and Alan Krant, *American Refugee Policy and European Jewry 1933–1945* (Bloomington: Indiana University Press, 1988), 74.

27 **"poisonous" in tone**: Moffatt and Bullitt in ibid., and Morgan on Bullitt, *FDR: Biography*, 498–99.

28 **"to condemn whole groups"**: Appendix, *Congressional Record*, 1772, 2253.

28 **"American's children are"**: Reynolds statements, 26 May 1939.

29 **"a general feeling"**: Eddie Cantor to FDR, 12 January 1939; see Morse, *While Six Million Died*, 207–8.

30 **"They are not *our* Jews"**: Richard Lieberman to author on FDR to Caroline O'Day. I am grateful to Richard Lieberman for his work, still to come, on Senator Wagner and fate of his bill.

30 **"courage and zeal"**: ER celebrates Dorothy Thompson's event, *New York Times*, 25 January 1939.

30 **"Czech culture was"**: Gilbert, *History of Twentieth Century*, 2:230. See also Crane and Crane, *Czechoslovakia*, 174–78. For the British government response, see Churchill, *Gathering Storm*, 342–46. On 15 March William Shirer reported "complete apathy in Paris tonight about Hitler's latest coup. France will not move a finger." *Berlin Diary*, 160. On 27 May exiled Czechoslovak president Edvard Beneš visited Hyde Park to appeal to FDR to oppose Germany's aggression, which threatened "world peace and the very structure of modern civilization." This visit engendered ER's enduring concern for Beneš and Czechoslovakia's future; Sylvia Crane to author.

30 **ER had long argued**: ER's efforts with Lape and Read to promote the World Court were the first documents collected by the FBI to monitor her "subversive" activities. See Cook, *ER*, 2:236–37.

31 **"single infertile women"**: Proctor, *Racial Hygiene*, 195–96. See esp. Renata Bridenthal, Atina Grossmann, and Marion Kaplan, *When Biology Becomes Destiny*; Koonz, *Mothers in the Fatherland*; and *The Works of Sybil Milton*.

31 **"havens of refuge"**: Infantile Paralysis Program (transcript), NBC, 11 January 1939, in Edith Nourse Rogers Papers, box 9, Schlesinger.

32 **"on the clear understanding"**: "National Conference on Problems of the Negro," *New York Times*, 13 January 1939; *Crisis*, February 1939, 54.

32 **"a policy of which"**: *My Day*, February 27, 1939; "Mrs. Roosevelt Indicates She Has Resigned from DAR Over Refusal of Hall to Negro," *New York Times*, 28 February 1939. An American Institute of Public Opinion poll indicated that 67 percent approved of ER's action in resigning, and 33 percent disapproved.

Democrats approved by 68 percent, Republicans by 63 percent. Only 56 percent of southerners polled disapproved. *New York Times*, 19 March 1939.

33 **"Prejudice rules to"**: *Washington Herald* editorial.

33 **"How kind of you"**: ER to Dorothy Kemp Roosevelt, 3 March 1939, with gratitude for this correspondence to Diana Roosevelt Jaicks and Janet Roosevelt Katten.

33 **"I am not surprised"**: Anderson quoted in "Mrs. Roosevelt Indicates She Has Resigned from DAR Over Refusal of Hall to Negro," *New York Times*, 28 February 1939. Anderson's concert schedule is in Mary Maples Dunn, *Notable American Women*. See esp. Arsenault, *Sound of Freedom*.

33 **"one of the most hopeful signs"**: Hurok, *Impresario*, 245–55.

33 **"We will all go ahead"**: For ER's 11 May 1934 speech, see Cook, *ER*, 2:185.

34 **"I regret exceedingly"**: ER to Citizens' Committee.

34 **"Bully for Oscar!"**: Scott Sandage, notes from interview with Chapman's widow, 6 November 1989, used with gratitude.

35 **"one of the most impressive"**: Ickes, *Secret Diary*, 2:614.

35 **"she was almost overcome"**: Ibid., 614–15.

35 **"In this great auditorium"**: Clarke, *Roosevelt's Warrior*; and esp. Watkins, *Righteous Pilgrim*, 650–53. After Anderson sang, Ickes was ecstatic: she "sang magnificently. I have never heard such a voice. The whole setting was unique, majestic, and impressive and I could not help but feel thankful that the DAR and the school board had refused her the use of an auditorium." Ickes, *Secret Diary*, 2:615.

35 **"I am so overwhelmed"**: Keiler, *Marian Anderson*, 181–217; Arsenault, *Sound of Freedom*; Jessye Norman, *Stand Up Straight and Sing*, 135–45; *New York Times*, 10 April 1939.

36 **the segregated, and ongoing:** Real change did not occur until President Dwight Eisenhower integrated all federal spaces by executive order in 1954. Despite Ickes's commitment to the NAACP on racial justice, his efforts were curiously limited. When a delegation of "Washington Negroes" urged him to open "all playgrounds, golf courses, parks, and swimming pools . . . to Negroes and whites alike," he said there were adequate separate facilities for recreation and urged them to go slow. It was, he explained, a terrible time "to move too fast," given the prejudices of the moment. Ickes, *Secret Diary*, 2:561–62.

36 **"will sing for them"**: Article on the concert, *Time*, 17 April 1939.

36 **"No matter how many times"**: ER on childbirth and love, *My Day*, 1 April 1939.

36 **"Anna is doing very well"**: ER to Lape and Read, 2 April 1939, Arizona Collection.

37 **tragedy struck at:** Ruby Black, *ER: Biography*, 121; ER II to author; "Daniel S. Roosevelt Killed," 19 April 1939; Raymond Daniel, "Harvard Nephew . . . Killed with Classmate," *New York Times*, 19 April 1939; "Mrs. FDR at Nephew's Funeral," 23 April 1939; Lash, *Eleanor and Franklin*, 488.

Chapter Two: "You Cannot Just Sit and Talk About It, You Have to Do Something"

39 **"every other woman"**: Cook, *ER*, 1:233.

39 **"at the council table"**: FDR to Hitler, 14 April 1939, in Hunt, *Essential FDR*, 152–55.

40 **two-hour Reichstag rant:** Shirer, *Berlin Diary,* 165–67.

40 **Hungary, ethnically diverse:** Enmity among Central European states was enduring. Béla Kun's Communist Hungary might have survived had it not been for an Allied blockade and the intervention of Romanian troops with French support. In 1920 irredentist Hungarians, led by ex-king Charles of Hapsburg sought a resurrected empire that would absorb Slovakia, Transylvania (from Romania), areas of Yugoslavia, and Austria. Consequently, the First World War bled into the Second with all borders at risk. Crystal Eastman, "In Communist Hungary," in Cook, *On Women and Revolution,* 315–28, esp. 321, 325; and Crane and Crane, *Czechoslovakia,* 66–69.

42 **"do nothing that would entail":** FDR to Norman Davis.

42 **"the full co-operation of Russia":** Churchill's 4 May speech in Churchill, *Gathering Storm,* 327, 337, 374–77.

42 **"I fear this terribly":** Nicolson, *Diaries and Letters,* 4 May 1939, 1:401. Perhaps because he had negotiated the first trade agreements with Denmark, Norway, and Weimar Germany, which ended the blockade against the Soviet Union, Litvinov was not liquidated as so many of Stalin's former allies had been during the dreadful purges of 1937. Subsequently, in November 1940, he was named ambassador to the United States.

43 **"costumes and accessories":** "World of Tomorrow Dress Design," *New York Times,* 22 April 1939.

43 **"profusion of beauty":** *My Day,* 9 June 1939. ER was close to William Reeves, "a delightful man" who had been the White House's head gardener since Theodore Roosevelt's administration. ER, *Autobiography,* 73.

43 **"a tempest in a teapot":** ER on Herbert Hoover, *My Day,* 3 February 1939.

44 **"both unconventional and unpredictable":** Charles Hurd, "Rugged Roosevelt Individualists," *New York Times,* 23 April 1939.

44 **"Where is foreign policy made":** *Time,* 17 April 1939. This piece represented only the first departure from "Luce's past coverage of Eleanor." Subsequently *Time* announced that *My Day* was "required reading" for Wall Streeters and sided with ER against Westbrook Pegler; see *Time,* 3 March 1941. For ER's speech on U.S. economic needs, see *Time,* 6 March 1939.

46 **She deplored scholar-politicians:** 18 March 1939.

46 **bigotry, race hatred:** *New York Times,* 13 January 1939; *Crisis,* February 1939, 54.

46 **"Divorce is necessary and right":** *Time,* 14 March 1938.

47 **"the insane dogma":** Claudia Koonz, *Mothers in the Fatherland,* 53; Robert Proctor, *Racial Hygiene: Medicine Under the Nazis,* 123.

47 **"I have been a long time":** ER to Mrs. Charles A. Goetting, 28 March 1938, in box 1459; *New York Times,* 17 January 1940.

47 **"get the whole thing":** "Roman Catholics and Birth Control," *Churchman,* 15 March, 15 April, 15 May, and 17 June 1941, sent to ER by Mary Lasker.

47 **"Like your many other":** Rev. Maurice Sheehy to ER, 13 February 1939, in box 1525; ER to Sheehy, 15 February 1939. See esp. Ellen Chesler, *Woman of Valor: Margaret Sanger and the Birth Control Movement* (New York: Simon & Schuster, 1992, 2007). For Margaret Sanger and ER's correspondence, see 339–44, 387–90, afterword passim.

48 **"The president was in top"**: Katherine Littell to Anna, 23 March 1940, Anna Roosevelt Halsted Papers, box 36.

48 **"I wonder if you realize"**: Hick to ER, 27 January 1939, Hickok, box 6.

48 **"It is magnificent!"**: Hick to ER, 15 March 1939, Hickok, box 6.

49 **"Many a soldier has told me"**: "Conquer Fear and You Will Enjoy Living," *Look*, 23 May 1939.

50 **"a curious feeling"**: "ER Reveals Ghosts," *New York Times*, 19 March 1939.

50 **"There is nothing discomforting"**: "White House Shadows," *New York Times*, 20 March 1939.

50 **"laughingly admitted at"**: *New York Times*, 18 March 1939.

50 **"Any good things"**: *New York Times*, 13 March 1939.

51 **"I think my own real objection"**: ER to Roy V. Peel, 20 March 1939, box 1519.

51 **"Why do nations go to war"**: *Photoplay*, undated ms. in Hickok, box 6.

52 **"Your valentine came"**: Hick to ER, 15 February 1939, Hickok Papers.

52 **"Living—just going on living"**: Hick to ER, 19 January 1939.

52 **"Please take the 100"**: ER to Hick, 9 March 1939.

52 **"I'll not even pretend"**: Hick to ER, 24 January 1939.

53 **"I'm getting two more books"**: Hick to ER, 13 April 1939.

53 **"Things are a little better"**: "human dynamo," Hick to ER, 22 April 1939.

53 **of "government extravagance"**: ER, graduation ms. April 1939.

55 **"Do you know, my dear"**: Hick to ER, 26–27 April 1939.

56 **"in a costume of printed silk"**: Kathleen McLaughlin, "Many Feminine Touches Revealed," *New York Times*, 1 May 1939. Over five thousand women volunteers representing forty-eight states were at the reception, McLaughlin reported, observing that women "unconditionally and instantly loved the Fair."

56 **"as a symbol of peace"**: FDR, speech opening World's Fair, 30 April 1939, was the first televised speech, *New York Times*, May 1939.

56 **"its formal bow"**: *New York Times*, 1 May 1939.

Chapter Three: **Tea and Hot Dogs: The Royal Visit**

58 **"Each American family must snap"**: "Headlines from Headliners," *Democratic Digest*, March 1939.

58 **"private non-profit religious"**: See Ira Katz-Nelson, *Fear Itself*, for the congressional war against the New Deal.

59 **"all services and supplies"**: Virginia Cocalis, "Medical Care for Farmers," *Democratic Digest*, February 1939; "New Deal in Health," *Democratic Digest*, February 1939.

60 **"Of all the programs"**: See Genevieve Forbes Herrick, "Congress Will Consider," *Democratic Digest*, January 1939; FDR's $525 million defense program, *Democratic Digest*, February 1939; Ellen S. Woodward, "Next Steps in Social Security," *Democratic Digest*, February 1939; "Congress Considers/Congress Enacts," *Democratic Digest*, April 1939; "Farm Poverty Giving Way to Security," *Democratic Digest*, January 1939; Wagner on Housing, "Headlines from Headliners," *Democratic Digest*, April 1939.

60 **"human side of government"**: "Mrs. R Counsels Women," January 1939, ER's Jackson Day speech, in *Democratic Digest*.

60 **dictator Anastasio Somoza**: *TIR*, 182; Cook, *ER*, 1:365; *Congressional Record*, 5 May 1939, 5163–64; Gregorio Selser, *Sandino*, passim; and Walter LaFeber, *Inevitable Revolutions*, passim. FDR biographers generally ignored Somoza's visit, which curiously is referred to almost nowhere.

61 **In a published photo**: George Black, *The Good Neighbor*, 71–72.

61 **"Just received wire"**: ER to FDR, 1 April 1939, and FDR to ER, 1 April 1939, in *FDR: Personal Letters*, 4:875.

62 **"The truth is"**: ER to Nan Honeyman, 14 February 1939, Nan Honeyman to ER, 11 February 1939; Cordell Hull to Honeyman constituent rescuer, Robert Auxier, 8 December 1938, ER Papers, box 1505. Honeyman and ER agreed to meet at Anna's during her spring visit.

62 **"It can happen here"**: *Congressional Record*, debate on Hobbs bill, HR 5643, 5 May 1939, 5161–92; O'Day on 5164.

63 **"the American people do not want"**: Ibid., Marcantonio on 5167; Dickstein on 5171; Ludlow and Celler on 5172; list of nations on 5180.

63 **"the big thing we talked about"**: FDR to Bernard Baruch, 18 April 1939, in *FDR: Personal Letters*, 4:879–80.

63 **"of all faiths and nationalities"**: Baruch's plan was endorsed by FDR's friends, and enemies, notably Sam Rosenman who, like Baruch, sought an alternative to a "world ghetto" for Jews. Hamilton Fish, although a fervent isolationist, campaigned for Baruch's plan in 1939. Baruch, *My Own Story*, 2:273–74; Jordan Schwarz, *The Speculator*, 564.

64 **"national home for the Jewish"**: FDR to Cordell Hull, 17 May 1939, in *FDR: Personal Letters*, 4:885–86. For the Balfour Declaration, see esp. Peter Grose, *Israel in the Mind of America*, 65.

64 **"I have been admonishing"**: ER to Hick, 20 May 1939.

65 **behaved . . . "as though"**: *TIR*, 184. See also Davis, *FDR: Into the Storm*, 446–49.

65 **"Pa was annoyed"**: ER to Anna, 31 May 1939, Asbell, 118.

66 **"air our minds"**: Cook, *ER*, 2:73.

66 **"sense of humor"**: *TIR*, 185.

66 **"we should give"**: ER, press conferences, 5 May, 22 May, and 29 May 1939, in Beasley, *ER Press Conferences*; *TIR*, 187.

66 **discuss than "etiquette"**: ER, press conference, ibid., 111–15.

67 **"Hyde Park is no castle"**: "Hyde Park," *Life*, 29 May 1939.

67 **"British men of war"**: *New York Times*, 4 March 1939, 4; "Hyde Park," *Life*, 29 May 1939; *Time*, 15 May 1939; "FDR Checks Home for Royalty," *New York Times*, 28 May 1939. For decisions over protocol, see Davis, *FDR: Into the Storm*, 145, and *TIR*, 184.

67 **celebrated her "energy"**: S. J. Woolf, "Energy: Mrs. Roosevelt Tells How She Conserves It," *New York Times*, 28 May 1939.

68 **radio press dispatches**: There were also strikes, forest fires, and baseball scores. Johnstown won the Kentucky Derby, and public health replaced education as the foremost issue of concern among U.S. foundations. In Washington,

Congress reconsidered the Neutrality Act, and there was hope that FDR would receive "more discretionary power" to sell arms on a "cash and carry" basis. Radio Press News, 8 May 1939, Tully Papers.

69 **"in the tropic heat"**: "Unwanted Refugees," *New York Times,* 4 June 1939, reported travail of SS *St. Louis.*

70 **The stirring speech:** ER, press conference, 29 May 1939, in Beasley, *ER Press Conferences,* 114–15; "News of Week," *New York Times,* 4 June 1939.

70 **"Like all other disappointments":** *My Day,* 3 June 1939.

70 **"mourning the loss":** Mollie Somerville, *Eleanor As I Knew Her,* 37.

70 **been "carefully coached":** *My Day,* 6 and 7 June 1939. The story of Billy Nelson and King Albert is in Cook, *ER,* 2:205–6. Carl Sharsmith and Elizabeth Stone O'Neill to author.

71 **"If you want a press conference":** ER, press conference, 7 June 1939, in Beasley, *ER Press Conferences,* 118–21.

71 **"Delegates from all parts":** ER's speech to Workers' Alliance, *New York Times,* 8 June 1939. Arthur Krock condemned ER's speech; see "The Non-Recoverable Relief Bill," *New York Times,* 9 June 1939.

71 **"At last I greet you":** FDR, *Time,* 19 June 1939. According to *Time,* five hundred people collapsed in the heat along the royal route. Sixty Girl Scouts were also felled by the heat as they waited for the procession at the White House gates, *My Day,* 8 June 1939. For Ickes's account of the royals' Washington visit, see *Secret Diary,* 2:642–51.

71 **"It was a gay and happy":** ER, *My Day,* 8 June 1939.

71 **"According to press stories":** Anna to Missy LeHand, 11 June 1939, Glenn Horowitz Collection.

73 **"a few harrowing moments":** *TIR,* 191; Ickes, *Secret Diary,* 2:646–47; Tommy wrote Esther Lape that there were no mishaps in Washington, although some tension between the royal staff and the White House staff arose—since "the King's valet was all prepared to get well saturated with W.H. whiskey, and the Q's maid requisitioned three quarts of gin in two days." Tommy to Lape, 13 June 1939, Arizona Collection.

73 **"Well, one day is over":** ER to Hick, 8 June 1939.

73 **"The Queen seems to be":** ER, press conference, 9 June 1939, in Beasley, *ER Press Conferences,* 122–25; *My Day,* 9 June 1939; Arlington, *My Day,* 13 June 1939.

73 **"crown and scepter":** *My Day,* 9 June 1939; *TIR,* 195.

74 **"There are a lot of them":** ER, press conference, 9 June 1939, in Beasley, *ER Press Conferences.*

74 **"I was not the only one":** *My Day,* 12 June 1939; *New York Times,* 13 June 1939; *TIR,* 193.

74 **"Dearest, This day":** ER to Hick, 8, 9 June 1939.

74 **"You know, Anna":** Jane Ickes to Anna, 14–15 June 1939, Anna Roosevelt Halsted Papers, box 32; Ickes on dinner and Garner, *Secret Diary,* 2:642–51.

74 **"My husband always loved":** *My Day, New York Times,* 13 June 1939, *TIR.*

75 **"heard that the White House butlers":** *TIR,* 196; *My Day,* 14 June 1939; *New York Times,* 13 June 1939.

75 **Meanwhile the king and queen:** Swift, *Roosevelts and Royals*, 130–31; "British Genealogist Finds Queen Is Kin to Washington and Lee," *New York Times*, 15 June 1939.

75 **Nicholas Murray Butler:** *Time*, 19 June 1939.

75 **"We sat in the library":** *TIR*, 195–96.

76 **"I must tell you first":** Tommy to Lape.

76 **"Mama tried in the best":** *TIR*, 196.

76 **"fell down the two steps":** Ibid., 196–97.

76 **"their Majesties remained":** *My Day*, 14 June 1939.

76 **"Why don't my ministers":** *TIR*, 197.

77 **"I think the service":** FDR to Henry St. George Tucker, 16 June 1939, in *FDR: Personal Letters*, 4:897.

77 **"cannot run the risk":** *TIR*, 197; *My Day*, 13–14 June 1939.

77 **After a quiet dinner:** Missy LeHand, Laura Delano, and Tracy Dows, FDR's aunt, were also at SDR's farewell dinner for twenty-one; *New York Times*, 12 June 1939; *My Day*, 12 June 1939; *New York Times*, 14 June 1939.

77 **"a very heavy thunderstorm":** *My Day*, 13 June 1939.

78 **As they departed:** *Time*, 19 June 1939; *TIR*, 198; *My Day*, 12 June 1939; *New York Times*, 12 and 14 June.

78 **"Such fun yesterday":** Harold Nicolson, *Diaries and Letters*, 14 June 1939, 1:403–5; 23 June 1939, 1:405.

78 **"the changed conditions":** *My Day*, 13 June 1939.

78 **"this country will have":** Ibid.

78 **"FDR was satisfied":** ER to Hick, 12 June 1939.

79 **"your father particularly":** Norman Littell to Anna, 21 June 1939, Anna Roosevelt Halsted Papers, box 36.

79 **"are very delightful":** FDR to Nicholas Roosevelt, 15 June 1939, in *FDR: Personal Letters*, 4:893. The quoted phrase is a reference to Elizabeth Dilling's 1934 screed *The Red Network*, filled with vitriol against liberals.

80 **The *Liesel*, with:** Joseph Levy, "906 Seized in Palestine," *New York Times*, 2 June 1939.

80 **"to the President and Congress":** 1 June, 2 June 1939, *New York Times*. Daily through June details of ships afloat were published in newspapers across the United States.

81 **"appeal to President Roosevelt":** *New York Times*, 7 June 1939.

81 **The State Department rejected:** *New York Times*, 1 and 2 June 1939.

81 **"could see the shimmering towers":** "The Saddest Ship Afloat Today," *New York Times*, 8 June 1939.

81 **inaction and cruelty:** See especially "Man's Inhumanity" (editorial), *New York Times*, 9 June 1939; "Victims of a Plague," *Baltimore Sun*, 3 June 1939, "There is something hideously wrong with a world in which there is no longer any sanctuary for the oppressed."

82 **referred to that event:** Earl Miller to Joseph Lash, 1968, Lash Papers and Earl Miller in Miriam Abelow Papers, FDRL; daily *New York Times* coverage of the SS *St. Louis* continued from 6–21 June.

82 **"to leave or go"**: *New York Times,* 11 June 1939. On the *St. Louis,* see Morse, *While Six Million Died,* 219–34; Morse, "Voyage to Doom," *Look,* 28 November 1967; and Gordon Thomas and Max Morgan-Witts, *Voyage of the Damned.* On the fiftieth (1989) and seventieth (2009) anniversaries of the voyage, ceremonies were held at Eden Roc, Miami; see survivors' interviews at www .stlouislegacyproject.org, notably that of Herbert Karliner.

82 **"the inviolability of the right"**: On 20 June the French steamer *Flandre* was allowed to land in France with 97 refugees, including 20 children. They had been "barred by Cuba and Mexico" and had been afloat since 16 May. On arrival they "danced down the gang plank, weeping for joy. . . . The majority of the men were shopkeepers, lawyers, doctors and engineers in their old homes," *New York Times,* 21 June 1939.

82 **China announced plans:** China's community was to be built with support from Jacob Berglas and the Chinese central government in Chungking. *New York Times,* 21 June 1939.

83 **"all parts of the world"**: Morse, *While Six Million Died,* 262–300.

Chapter Four: "We Must Think of the Greatest Good for the Greatest Number"

84 **"by Jane H. Todd, Republican"**: *My Day,* 14 June 1939.

84 **fifty-fifty rules:** Dorothy McAllister, "Fifty-Fifty—The First Step for '40," *Democratic Digest,* February 1939, 22.

84 **"basic right of"**: *My Day,* 16 June 1939.

84 **"as soon as you discriminate"**: ER at Town Hall forum, *New York Times,* 3 February 1936, ban "fascistic," *New York Times,* 20 June 1939; 25 July 1939; *My Day,* 14 June 1939; Helen Rogers Reid, *New York Times,* 3 June 1939.

84 **"the children are grown"**: ER at Town Hall forum, *New York Times,* 3 February 1936.

84 **Florence Birmingham, president:** *New York Times,* 4 June 1939. For ER's refusal and court decision on 18 and 20 July 1939, see *Democratic Digest,* August 1939; *New York Times,* 12 August 1939; on Felker, *New York Times,* 22 July 1939.

85 **"if not for your own sakes"**: Reid, *New York Times,* 3 June 1939.

85 **"attend to your own knitting"**: *New York Times,* 22 July 1939; supportive editorial is in *New York Times,* 24 July 1939; ER to Junior League, 28 November 1939.

85 **unavailable for fun:** ER to Hick, 9 March 1939.

85 **splendid color films:** Earl's film, Tommy to Anna, 8 May 1939.

85 **"the Cook and the Dickerman"**: Tommy to Lape and Read, 1939, Arizona Collection.

85 **to be "very ill"**: Tommy to Anna, 8 May 1939.

86 **essay on religious freedom:** Draft, for *Liberty,* March 1939, in Hickok, box 6.

86 **was "playing politics"**: Marcantonio, *I Vote My Conscience,* 16 June, 20 July, 3 August 1939, 108–9.

86 **Federal Theatre Project:** Jane DeHart Mathews, *Federal Theatre,* 122–25.

87 **"handed me a newspaper"**: Flanagan, *Arena*, 202–5.

88 **"Somehow we must build"**: ER's broadcast is quoted in Flanagan, *Arena*, 206.

88 **"I must say that talking"**: *My Day*, 24 June 1939.

88 **vigorously defended the theater**: Caroline O'Day in *Congressional Record*; Shaw and O'Neill in Flanagan, *Arena*, 192–93.

89 **lewd and "salacious"**: Flanagan, *Arena*, 355–60; and Mathews, *Federal Theatre*, 290–94.

89 **"having conquered selfishness"**: Flanagan, *Arena*, 364–65; and Mathews, *Federal Theatre*, 236–95; see esp. T. H. Watkins, *The Hungry Years*, 510–11.

90 **A pacifist but never an isolationist**: There is no biography of Caroline O'Day, and her papers have been lost. See Jonas, *Isolationism in America*, 189–93 and passim; and Marion Dickerman on Caroline Love Goodwin O'Day, in *Notable American Women*, 648–50.

90 **"The more we see"**: ER went on to say that economic waste and distress anywhere affect people everywhere. In military carnage, "the effects are just the same whether you win or whether you lose. . . . As the rest of the world suffers, so eventually do we." ER, "Because the War Idea Is Obsolete," reprinted in Black, *Courage*, 85.

90 **"We must find a way whereby"**: ER, "Three Americans Plead for Peace," *Democratic Digest*, May 1937, 17.

91 **"I think it may interest you"**: FDR to Caroline O'Day, 1 July 1939, in *FDR: Personal Letters*, 4:900–1.

92 **she rejected the proposed Ludlow Amendment**: ER, "Three Americans Plead for Peace," *Democratic Digest*, May 1937, and *Time*, 17 April 1939.

92 **"Protect our Mrs. Catt"**: Elizabeth N. Baker to ER, 1 February 1939; ER to Baker, 6 February 1939, ER Papers; "Because the War Idea Is Obsolete," in Catt's *Why Wars Must Cease*, 20ff, quote on 28.

93 **Her talk at the convention**: ER was accompanied by Tommy and Elinor Morgenthau. White noted that they had "reserve seats on the platform" since the mosque, which seated 5,200 people, was sold out. Walter White to ER, 13 June 1939; ER to White, 19 June 1939; White to ER, 20 June 1939, ER Papers.

93 **a powerful speech**: ER's presentation of Spingarn Medal, *Crisis*, April, June, July, September, for ER-related notations.

94 **"The courage to meet many difficulties"**: *Crisis*, September 1939, 265, 285; "First Lady Honors Marian Anderson," *New York Times*, 3 July 1939.

94 **"Speaking in the very stronghold"**: Editorial of the Month, Mrs. Roosevelt's speech, reprinted from *Chicago Defender* in *Crisis*, August 1939, 243; lunch with Virginia's governor James Prince, *My Day*, 3 July 1939.

95 **"Nothing finer could come out"**: ER to AYC, remarks and broadcast, 21 February 1939, in Hickok, box 6; "Anti-Red Resolution," *New York Times*, 4 July 1939. See also Lash, *Friend's Memoir*, 51; "First Lady Accused," *New York Times*, 6 July 1939.

95 **to "guard against"**: ER to WILPF on freedom of the press, *New York Times*, 17 January 1939. At the sixtieth anniversary luncheon of the Ethical Culture Schools on 21 January, she addressed more than a thousand educators and

parents with a similar speech. ER to Ethical Culture, *New York Times,* 22 January 1939.

96 **"the root problem":** In this "nation afflicted at the moment with astigmatic near-sightedness," wrote Fannie Hurst to ER, "your remarks last night were splendid, and the phrase 'We have bought time to think' is perfect—I hope you use it wherever possible." Fannie Hurst to ER, 22 February 1939. ER replied to Hurst on 25 February, "How much I appreciate all you say," Hurst Papers.

96 **"Democracy must have":** ER to Democratic Women, and Fannie Hurst, *New York Times,* 16 June 1939.

97 **"damned kike coward":** Hick to ER, 8 and 9 February 1939; 17 February 1939, Hickok, box 6.

97 **"If anything is evident today":** "Mrs. R Asks for Interfaith Amity," *New York Times,* 3 July 1939.

97 **"educational opportunities is":** *My Day,* 1 July 1939. ER's Independence Day theme was "unity of spirit and a determination to find a way to share our wealth." *My Day,* 3–5 July 1939.

97 **"impromptu press conference":** *New York Times,* 5 July 1939; *My Day,* 6 July 1939.

98 **"I left in my own car":** *My Day,* 7 July 1939; FDR boarded his special train, *New York Times,* 5 July 1939.

98 **"Pat, old dear":** FDR to Pat Harrison, 6 July 1939, in *FDR: Personal Letters,* 4:902.

98 **"ought to understand clearly":** *My Day,* 8 July 1939.

98 **"These gentlemen must":** *My Day,* 13 July 1939.

99 **anti-Jewish laws . . . Gypsies:** U.S. Holocaust Memorial Council, *Fifty Years After the Eve of Destruction,* 9.

99 **"The amount they say will feed":** *My Day,* 18 July 1939.

99 **"indiscriminate bombing":** FDR to Cordell Hull, 7 July 1939, in *FDR: Personal Letters,* 4:903–4. On Ambassador Johnson, see Heinrichs, *Threshold of War,* 288, Oumansley in Ickes, *Secret Diary,* 2:670–71.

99 **predicting a long, intense war:** Ickes, *Secret Diary,* 2:669–70, 675–77, 685.

100 **"because of its neutrality laws":** See Gerhard Weinberg, *A World at Arms,* 1013.

100 **"he sounded very cheerful":** *My Day,* 18 July 1939.

101 **"to open this meeting with a prayer":** Davis, *FDR: Into the Storm,* 457–58. David Kennedy, *Freedom from Fear,* 425. On Borah, see Carol Felsenthal, *Alice Longworth,* chapters 8 and 9.

102 **"perhaps, hangs the fate":** *My Day,* 21 July 1939.

102 **continued to fight:** Davis, *FDR: Into the Storm,* 453. A *Democratic Digest* editorial for "executive powers" regarding international relations, dated February 1939, 26, read: "In this vast external realm . . . the President [has] a degree of discretion and freedom from statutory restriction which would not be admissible were domestic affairs alone involved." Unattributed, it is possible that ER, as founder and contributing editor, was involved in the drafting of this editorial.

102 **"I finished the mail":** *My Day,* 24 July 1939.

102 **"His fund of tales"**: Ibid.

103 **"the most liberal administration"**: Norman Littell to Anna, 21 July 1939, Anna Roosevelt Halsted Papers, box 36. For a discussion of the role played by Corcoran and Cohen, see Lash, *Dealers and Dreamers*, 366–69, 390–92; and Littell, *My Roosevelt Years*.

103 **"all bets will be off"**: FDR recounted his meeting with Farley to Ickes in detail; see Ickes, *Secret Diary*, 2:691–92. See also Anna to Katherine and Norman Littell, 8 August 1939, Anna Roosevelt Halsted Papers, box 36.

104 **"was very useful in making"**: ER to Anna, 17 July 1939, Anna Roosevelt Halsted Papers, box 57; *My Day*, 25 July 1939; *My Day*, 28 July 1939; Roosevelt Deed Library Site, *New York Times*, 25 July 1939; Anna to Katherine and Norman Littell, 8 August 1939.

104 **"played so beautifully"**: *My Day*, 27 July 1939.

104 **"I suppose I had better"**: *My Day*, 29 July 1939.

104 **"Your car was stopped"**: *My Day*, 31 July 1939.

105 **"It is wearisome to read"**: *My Day*, 1 August 1939. She had read Graham Hutton's *Atlantic Monthly* article, "The Next War," which illustrated how "we are duplicating our behavior of before the 1914 cataclysm."

105 **"No other contribution"**: Ickes, *Secret Diary*, 2:689–90. See also William Preston, "Shadow of War and Fear," in Reitman, *Pulse of Freedom*, 105–53; Schrecker, *Many Are the Crimes*, 95 and passim; and Theoharis, *Spying on Americans*, 197–98, 201–6. Martin Dies was already compiling lists of alleged subversives and federally employed "political undesirables" to be investigated under the Hatch Act, which in 1940 morphed into the Smith Act. Subsequently the federal loyalty program was dominated by Joseph McCarthy and the McCarran Act.

106 **"I am sore and bruised of spirit"**: See also Ickes, *Secret Diary*, 2:668, 680–84, 693–94.

106 **to "Dearest Franklin"**: ER to FDR, 5 August 1939, box 177. At the end, the typed word "Affectionately" was crossed out and signed in pen, "Much Love, ER."

106 **"I wish the Congressmen"**: *My Day*, 8 August 1939.

107 **"their sporting disposition"**: *My Day*, 9 August 1939.

107 **"let his wife join in"**: "Off the Floor," *Time*, 21 August 1939; FDR to James Roosevelt, 11 August 1939, in *FDR: Personal Letters*, 4:912.

108 **"a silent, empty place"**: *My Day*, 14 August 1939.

108 **She tried to work on her new book**: ER to Anna, 17 July 1939, Anna Roosevelt Halsted Papers, box 57.

108 **"I can't say that"**: *My Day*, 14 August 1939.

108 **"war would leave no victors"**: *My Day*, 12 and 14 August 1939.

108 **"I lay the other night"**: *My Day*, 15 August 1939.

109 **"plain, insecure, lonely little girl"**: For Corinne, ER, and Marie Souvestre, see Merry, *Taking on the World*, 65–66.

109 **"Auntie Bye had a tongue"**: Alsop, *I've Seen the Best of It*, 30.

110 **"light, cheerful sort of piece"**: Ibid., 10–12.

110 **"Joe Alsop was here"**: ER to FDR, 14 August 1939, box 16. In that letter ER also noted that she had a "nice picnic" for newspaper people, mostly editors:

she and Heywood Broun were "the only columnists." The two events were unrelated.

110 **"glowing" family profile:** Joseph Alsop, "The President's Family Album," *Life.*

110 **"When I was connected with":** *My Day,* 17 August 1939.

110 **"I do not understand Nancy":** ER to Mary Dreier, 29 August 1939, Schlesinger Library, Radcliffe Institute.

111 **a "little cottage":** *My Day,* 18 August 1939.

111 **Cornelius "Neil" Vanderbilt:** Vanderbilt, *Man of the World,* 204–6, 210–13. Raconteur, reporter, and FDR's occasional spy, Neil Vanderbilt wrote much-admired and equally dismissed adventures in many worlds that evoked the eponymous hero of Upton Sinclair's Lanny Budd novels.

111 **"The mother of my President":** Carmel Offie to LeHand, 9 August 1939, Grace Tully Collection. Offie sent a running river of gossip and news from the Paris embassy to Missy LeHand, Mary Eben, and other White House administrators.

112 **"*Oh, comme le president*":** Neil Vanderbilt, *Cornelius Vanderbilt: Man of the World,* 204–6, 210–13.

Chapter Five: "If They Perish, We Perish Sooner or Later"

114 **Nazi-Soviet Pact:** Churchill, *Gathering Storm,* 374–81, 389–95; Manchester, *Last Lion,* 2:470–90.

114 **"All talk of appeasement":** Nicolson, *Diaries and Letters,* 21 August 1939, 1:411.

114 **"friendship cemented with blood":** Ehrenburg, *Memoirs,* 472–75.

114 **defenses along the Maginot Line:** Manchester, *Last Lion,* 2:492–96.

114 **"grim and preoccupied":** "Americans Abroad Urged to Return," *New York Times,* 25 August 1939.

114 **"probably means a partition":** Ickes, *Secret Diary,* 2:703.

115 **"dispatched three appeals":** "President Appeals to Poles and Reich," *New York Times,* 25 August 1939.

115 **"to go into Siberia":** For the international situation leading to this, see esp. Williams, *American-Russian Relations,* 247–54; Neumann, *America Encounters Japan,* 244–55; and Ickes, *Secret Diary,* 2:700–7.

116 **"in order not unnecessarily":** Ickes, *Secret Diary,* 2:700.

116 **"who stays on in Paris":** SDR and Aunt Dora, *My Day,* 24 August 1939.

117 **"one man may decide":** *My Day,* 25 August 1939.

117 **"the newspapers these days":** *My Day,* 24 August 1939.

117 **an "excellent lunch":** *My Day,* 22 August 1939.

117 **"I sank into bed last night":** *My Day,* 25 August 1939.

118 **"I talked to the President":** *My Day,* 26 August 1939.

118 **"Both the Pope and the President":** *My Day,* 26 August 1939.

118 **"What ghastly hours":** Sackville-West to Nicolson, 24 August 1939, in Nicolson, *Diaries and Letters,* 1:413.

118 **"I feel that every day":** *My Day,* 30 August 1939.

119 **"lies and invented incidents"**: Shirer, *Berlin Diary*, 177–93.

119 **"riding around on"**: Ibid., 183, 185.

119 **her lifelong friend**: Alice Kidd, later Huntington, was "a great influence" on ER in the early years. See Cook, *ER*, 1:95.

119 **"boys and girls, Jews, Catholics"**: *My Day*, 30 August 1939.

120 **"moccasins made me think"**: *My Day*, 31 August 1939.

120 **"Germany had invaded Poland"**: *My Day*, 2 September 1939.

120 **"sense of impending disaster"**: *TIR*, 207.

121 **"when hate was rampant"**: Carola von Schaeffer-Bernstein to ER, 19 August 1939. On Carola de Passavant at Allenswood, see Cook, *ER*, 1:108; Lash, *Eleanor and Franklin*, 75–76, 561, 567, 574–75, 583–84.

121 **"As I listened to Hitler's speech"**: *My Day*, 2 September 1939.

121 **"I could not help remembering"**: Ibid.

122 **"From London, Birmingham"**: "British Children Taken from Cities," *New York Times*, 1 September 1939, 1.

122 **"Even the highest Nazis"**: Nicolson, *Diaries and Letters*.

122 **"War will be declared"**: Ickes, *Secret Diary*, 2:712–13.

123 **"through your radios "**: FDR, "Reaction to War in Europe: Preparing for Cash-and-Carry," 3 September 1939, in Buhite and Levy, *Fireside Chats*, 148–51.

124 **"a bad proclamation"**: Nicolson, *Diaries and Letters*, 4 September 1939, 2:30.

124 **"It is curious when"**: *My Day*, 5 September 1939.

124 **"met the steamer"**: *My Day* 2 September 1939.

125 **"always enjoys" this**: *My Day*, 5 September 1939.

125 **"We were discussing the 1914"**: *My Day*, 7 September 1939.

126 **"I cannot say"**: ER to Carola von Schaeffer-Bernstein, 6 September 1939.

127 **"always remain a nation within a nation"**: "On Jews" (ER's unpublished essay), 25 November 1938.

128 **"This will be a happy day"**: *My Day*, 9 September 1939.

128 **"We awoke," ER wrote**: *My Day*, 6 September 1939.

128 **Morgenthaus' voyage**: *New York Times*, 9 September 1939.

129 **"the most beautiful drive"**: *My Day*, 9 September 1939.

129 **"We cooked our lunch"**: Ibid.

129 **"sight of domestic problems"**: *My Day*, 11 September 1939.

130 **"in time to greet"**: *My Day*, 9 September 1939.

130 **"all the little tag ends"**: *My Day*, 12 September 1939.

Chapter Six: "We Have to Fight with Our Minds"

131 **"in the present crisis"**: *Democratic Digest*, October 1939, 25, 33.

132 **"a good shield"**: *My Day*, 13 September 1939.

132 **"We must not forget"**: Ibid.

132 **of "racial extermination"**: Gilbert, *Second World War*, 6–10; Gilbert, *History of Twentieth Century*, 2:271.

132 **"Every soldier feels disgusted"**: Weitz, *Hitler's Banker*, 254.

133 **"of the infantile paralysis"**: *My Day,* 15 September 1939. There is no evidence ER knew anything about Tuskegee's racist and deadly syphilis experiment, which continued from 1932 to 1972.

133 **"gout hospital for colored veterans"**: *My Day,* 13, 14, 15, 16, and 18 September 1939.

133 **"a very pleasant beginning"**: Ibid.

133 **"Soviet Russia stabs Poland"**: Shirer, *Berlin Diary,* 199–212; *New York Times.*

133 **"the attack on Poland by Russia"**: ER to Maude Gray, in Lash, *Eleanor and Franklin,* 584.

133 **"I think this pact"**: Anna Louise Strong to ER, 24 August 1939.

134 **"A curious way"**: *My Day,* 18 September 1939.

134 **"I know that you"**: ER to Strong, 27 September, ER Papers.

134 **"piece of anti-aircraft shell"**: Offie to LeHand, 9 September 1939.

134 **From Paris, Carmel**: Cudahy to LeHand, 11 September 1939, Glenn Horowitz Collection.

134 **"The war continues"**: ER to Mary Dreier, 18 September 1939.

135 **through "beautiful country"**: *My Day,* 19 September 1939.

135 **"any effective help"**: Werth, *Russia at War,* 56–59.

135 **"Human life has been"**: Anne O'Hare McCormick, *New York Times,* 16 and 18 September 1939.

135 **"in this war the seeds"**: *My Day,* 19 September 1939.

136 **"to maintain a fighting front"**: "Week in Review," *New York Times,* 10 September 1939.

136 **his "appalling depression"**: Nicolson, *Diaries and Letters,* 16–20 September 1939, 2:33–36.

136 **"America's splendid isolationism"**: *My Day,* 19 September 1939.

136 **"hysterical with joy"**: Gilbert, *Second World War,* 11.

137 **as Operation T4**: Ibid.

137 **"any war anywhere"**: FDR, "Message to Congress Urging the Extraordinary Session to Repeal the Embargo Provision of the Neutrality Law," 21 September 1939, in Zevin, *Nothing to Fear,* 183-92; *Essential FDR,* 173–80.

138 **"Your message was grand"**: ER to FDR, 21 September 1939; *My Day,* 22 September 1939.

139 **"I have never been a pacifist"**: *New York Times,* 28 September 1939; ER, press conference, 27 September 1939, in Beasley, *ER Press Conferences,* 126–29.

139 **Warsaw fell to the Nazis**: Gilbert, *Second World War,* 12–16.

139 **"If you feel sad, think of me"**: Cudahy to LeHand, 10 October 1939, Glenn Horowitz Collection.

140 **"300,000 tons of"**: Gilbert, *Second World War,* 16. The German Soviet Accord was signed on 29 September 1939. See also Werth, *Russia at War,* 59–62.

140 **"even sadder" than**: Anne O'Hare McCormick, *New York Times,* 25 September and 30 September 1939.

140 **"go down fighting"**: Joseph Kennedy to FDR, 30 September 1939; Kennedy to Cordell Hull, 2 October 1939.

141 **his friend Nancy Astor:** Joseph Kennedy to Rose Kennedy, 2 October 1939, in Amanda Smith, *Hostage to Fortune,* 391. See also Kennedy Diary, 5 October 1939, ibid., 382–393.

141 **"I agree with you in theory":** ER to Mrs. Barmore, 3 October 1939, in Lash, *Eleanor and Franklin,* 584.

142 **"We passed first":** *My Day,* 20 September 1939.

142 **"two very kind":** *My Day,* 23 September 1939.

142 **learn "various handicrafts":** *My Day,* 26 September 1939.

143 **"The pool is one":** Ibid.

143 **"voice on its natural pitch":** *My Day,* 29 September 1939.

143 **"the most encouraging thing":** *My Day,* 2 October 1939.

144 **"People ask me":** ER to Anna, 23 September 1939, Asbell, 112.

144 **"It certainly is fun":** *My Day,* 4 October 1939.

144 **"1. What are the goals of our schools?":** *My Day,* 4 October 1939.

145 **Her son James:** James Roosevelt filed for divorce from Betsey on 16 February 1940. On 7 October 1939, Betsey's father, Dr. Harvey Cushing, died suddenly. See esp. Michael Bliss, *Harvey Cusing: A Life in Surgery,* and David Gratton, *The Sisters: The Lives and Times of the Fabulous Cushing Sisters* [Babe Mortimer Paley, Betsey R. Whitney, Minnie Astor Fosburgh].

146 **"It seems to me that the unexpected":** *My Day,* 10 October 1939.

146 **"in a great music center":** *My Day,* 10 October 1939.

146 **"May you be spared":** Bernard Baruch to ER, 11 October 1939.

147 **"very jittery about":** ER to Anna, 20 October 1939, in Asbell, 113; *My Day,* 13 October 1939.

147 **"Committee has been running":** Ickes, *Secret Diary,* 3:33.

147 **"under the pretense":** Ibid.

147 **"an actual menace":** Ibid., 3:35.

147 **relief to Chinese and Spanish:** *My Day,* 12 October 1939.

147 **"E.R.: Many Happy Returns":** FDR to ER, 11 October 1939, in *FDR: Personal Letters,* 4:937.

149 **"In the course of the last four months":** Einstein to FDR. See Robert Jungk, *Brighter Than a Thousand Suns*; Robert Jay Lifton and Greg Mitchell, *Hiroshima in America.*

150 **Poland's "General-Government":** Gilbert, *Second World War,* 18–24.

150 **"Extraordinary Pacification Program":** Hans Frank in Manchester, *Last Lion,* 2:591.

150 **"so poor the Poles":** Astor Drayton Phillips Diary.

150 **The "methods employed":** Ibid.

150 **"captured in Hamburg":** Ibid.

150 **Many Jews:** Gilbert, *Second World War,* 22–24.

150 **"I go, not without fear":** Caroline D. Phillips Diary, October–November 1939, esp. 17, 24–26, with gratitude to Kathleen Dalton.

151 **"Dreadful reprisals by the Germans":** Ibid. Over 100,000 Polish soldiers and pilots escaped to Romania, and then to England—where they subsequently fought alongside British and Allied troops in Free Polish battalions;

and a significant number of Polish destroyers and submarines "reached the Orkneys and joined the Royal Navy." Manchester, *Last Lion*, 2:591.

151 **"peasants working in the fields":** Caroline D. Phillips Diary, 17, 24–26, great gratitude to Kathleen Dalton.

151 **his "original" observation:** FDR to Hull, 2 October 1939, in *FDR: Personal Letters*, 4:930–31.

151 **"the whole refugee problem":** Feingold, *Politics of Rescue*, 83.

152 **"before the European war was over":** FDR to Sumner Welles, 4 December 1939, in *FDR: Personal Letters*, 4:963.

152 **"to speak of small settlements":** FDR, statement on political refugees, 17 October 1939.

152 **"lift a lamp":** Ibid.

153 **"within a very few days":** Ickes, *Secret Diary*, 2:720.

153 **"espionage and subversive propaganda":** *Democratic Digest*, October 1939, 19. Three other executive orders followed the outbreak of war. FDR increased troop strength among enlisted personnel—army, navy, Marine Corps, and National Guard; he created a three-hundred-mile offshore patrol perimeter and recommissioned 110 destroyers for "sea-going intelligence service"; and he created a State Department fund to help Americans "endangered in foreign countries" return to the United States.

153 **knew "as individuals":** ER insisted that Bill Hinckley, Abbott Simon, and especially Joseph Cadden were not Communists.

153 **was nothing "reprehensible":** ER, press conference, 10 October 1939, in Beasley, *ER Press Conferences*, 130–39.

154 **"purge the Federal payroll":** "No Red Purge Order Yet," *New York Times*, 28 September 1939.

154 **"no evidence of un-American activities":** *Democratic Digest*, October 1939, *New York Times*, 14 September 1939.

Chapter Seven: Red Scare, Refugees, and Racism

157 **"first allegiance":** On Browder, see ER to Clarence Gurewitz, 30 November 1939. For ER's criticism of Browder, with Robert Minor's lament that she was being "victimized by sinister reactionaries" who sought to drag the United States into war, see "Young Reds Defy . . . ," *New York Times*, 25 November 1939.

157 **"impossible to remain neutral":** ER to Jerome Davis, 27 September 1939, cf. Lash, *Eleanor and Franklin*, 594; ER to Irene Nelson, 12 September 1939.

157 **"I told them that since":** *TIR*, 200.

158 **"These attacks never hurt me":** Baruch, *My Own Story*, 1:48–52.

158 **its most generous supporter:** Clarence Pickett to Tommy, 12 January 1939, regarding contributions ER collected from Josephine Morgenthau ($150) and Mrs. George Backer [Dorothy Schiff] ($1,000) for the AYC, and ER's check for $500. Tommy to Pickett, 24 June 1939, with ER's check for $812, "earned on the last broadcast with Kate Smith." ER to Pickett, 25 June 1939: "Mr. Baruch is ill . . . and I am wondering how my account stands? I think Mr. B

would be much happier to give me for next year whatever we needed for the Arthurdale school." ER to Pickett, 5 July 1939: "Will you please send $3000 at once to the AYC. . . . I do not want the balance . . . they need sent until I get a check from Mr. B for the school." Pickett to ER, 8 September 1939: "We have just received $5,096.19 from Mr. Baruch. Do you still wish us to send the balance to the AYC?" ER to Pickett, 11 September 1939: "Yes." 25 September 1939, Pickett to ER: "The additional $3500 was sent to Cadden, for the AYC."

158 **published their names, positions:** "High Government Employees Linked to Reds," *New York Times*, October 26, 1939.

158 **"we fall far short":** "Liberty Plea Made by Mrs. Roosevelt," *New York Times*, 25 October 1939.

158 **"Pa agrees wholeheartedly":** ER to Anna, 20 and 29 October 1939, in Absell, 113.

160 **"a little chapel":** *My Day*, 3 November 1939.

160 **"A Typical Day":** ER "was every inch a queen herself," and "completely captivated her audience." *Lasso*, Texas State College for Women at Denton's college paper, 3 November 1939. I am grateful to the faculty and administration for photos and information about ER's visit and their splendid hospitality during my visit in 1999.

160 **"congenial home":** *My Day*, 11 November 1939.

160 **"Delighted all went well":** ER to FDR, 28 October 1939.

161 **"would suck the war":** See esp. Hank Meijer, "Arthur Vandenberg and the Fight for Neutrality, 1939," *Michigan Historical Review* (Fall 1990).

161 **"war refugees in different":** *My Day*, 8 November 1939.

161 **"It is of these Poles":** Ann Cardwell, aka (Mrs. Paul) Margaret L. Super, to ER, 26 October 1939.

163 **"I was very glad to see":** *My Day*, 14 November 1939.

163 **"would be glad to receive":** FDR to Hull, 19 October 1939, in *FDR: Personal Letters*, 4:941–42.

163 **"In view of the fact":** FDR to Hull, 11 November 1939, in *FDR: Personal Letters*, 4:952.

163 **"Mrs. Roosevelt and I would gladly":** FDR to King Leopold and FDR to Queen Wilhelmina, drafts, 11 November 1939, in *FDR: Personal Letters*, 4:953.

163 **"We were very glad":** Offie to LeHand, 15 November 1939, 9 December 1939, Glenn Horowitz Collection. William Shirer was told that Hitler planned for a five-year war, and was ready to release "a mass air attack on England," or drive through Holland and Belgium, or through Switzerland. No small country was safe. *Berlin Diary*, 248.

163 **"we will ever return":** *My Day*, 15 November 1939.

163 **"the Jewish ghetto in Warsaw":** Shirer, *Berlin Diary*, 250.

164 **"unchecked Nazism":** Morse, *While Six Million Died*, 242.

164 **"Margaret has been [wonderful]":** Offie to LeHand, 9 December 1939.

164 **"on the outside":** *My Day*, 16 and 17 October 1939.

165 **"poise and patience":** William Mulvey, Jr., to ER, 15 November 1938.

165 **"I think we are in grave danger":** ER to Mulvey, 26 November 1938.

165 **"the brawls of busy little men"**: Mulvey to ER, 19 September 1939.

166 **"Most of the educated ones"**: ER to Mulvey, 26 September 1939.

166 **"to make the labor unions"**: ER to Admiral Land, 27 August 1939.

166 **"It is our conviction that"**: Walter White to ER, 21 September 1939; ER to White, 26 September 1939.

167 **their private grievances**: For FDR and ER's cuisine battles, see Henrietta Nesbitt, *White House Diary*, chapter II.

167 **The cornerstone was laid**: "Placed in Cornerstone," *New York Times*, 20 November 1939.

167 **the "very simple"**: *My Day*, 21 November 1939.

167 **"We had a funny time"**: Tommy to Anna, ca. 22 November 1939, Anna Roosevelt Halsted Papers.

168 **"I am thankful"**: *My Day*, 23 November 1939.

169 **"where the patients needing"**: *My Day*, 25 November 1939. Racial divides did not disappear quickly in Warm Springs. When Clare Coss and I visited in 1996, we interviewed a retired teacher who had worked for decades in the school FDR built. She disparaged ER, "who cared so much more about Tuskegee and was always running off there when she was scheduled to be here. And then she built the Eleanor Roosevelt School for black children. . . . And it was built in brick too."

169 **"to introduce practical steps"**: *My Day*, 25 November 1939. See also *My Day*, 23, 24, and 27 November 1939. On Rachel Davis DuBois, see David Levering Lewis, *Du Bois 1919–1963*, 189–90, 270–72; and Rachel Davis DuBois, *All This and Something More: Pioneering in Intercultural Education*; *New York Times*, "Educator Who Promoted Diversity," 2 April 1993.

170 **"the refugee problem from"**: *My Day*, 30 November 1939.

171 **"disgrace to their calling"**: All quotes from the Churchman dinner are from *New York Times*.

172 **"courage to keep on trying"**: *My Day*, 1 December 1939.

172 **"Franklin and I got particular"**: *TIR*, 203.

173 **"denounced the committee's methods"**: FDR, Elliott Roosevelt, "Lauds Two Years of Dies," *New York Times*, 25 October 1939.

173 **Starnes announced a lunch break**: Charles Hurd, "ER Visits Dies Committee," *New York Times*, 1 December 1939; Lash, *Friend's Memoir*, 8–10.

174 **He "chuckled, roared"**: Lash, *Friend's Memoir*, 11.

174 **"One girl, Dolores"**: On the Soviet invasion of Finland, see Gilbert, *Second World War*, 31; Werth, *Russia at War*; and Gellhorn's *Collier's* articles and correspondence with ER.

174 **"a terrible thing"**: *My Day*, 2 December 1939.

175 **"down to earth"**: Lash, *Friend's Memoir*, 12.

175 **"Don't let her down"**: Ibid., 15.

175 **"piled high with mail"**: Ibid., 10–12.

175 **"All of us on the left"**: Lash, *Friend's Memoir*, 12–14.

175 **"with a divided soul"**: Ibid.

176 **"Well, they can't predict"**: Lash, *Love, Eleanor*, 285.

176 **"I took a pencil":** *TIR*, 202; *My Day*, 2 December 1939.

176 **the "profit system":** *New York Times*, 2 December 1939.

177 **"your great kindness":** Lash to ER, 6 December 1939.

177 **"I appreciate your note":** ER to Lash, 11 December 1939.

177 **"free speech for Reds":** *New York Times*, 4 December 1939.

178 **Loyalty oaths for:** *New York Times*, 26 October 1939.

179 **"Please always be frank":** Baruch to ER, 14 December 1939; ER to Baruch, 2 December 1939, box 1485.

179 **AFSC Humanitarian Award:** *New York Times*, 5 December 1939; "Humanitarian Award Announced," *New York Times,* 21 October 1939; 4 December 1939 in Philadelphia, presented by Curtis Bok, for ER's "devoted and self-sharing efforts in the cause of humanity"; *My Day*, 6 December 1939.

179 **"says that he does not":** ER to Lape, 2 and 6 December 1939, BWC, Arizona Collection.

179 **"whoopee 1940 roundup":** Margaret Hart, *Washington Sun*, 10 December 1939; "Is He or Ain't He? Gridiron Club Asks," *New York Times*, 10 December 1939.

180 **"we have developed a little":** *My Day*, 12 December 1939.

180 **"I hope that every citizen":** *My Day*, 13 December 1939.

181 **"joined the President today":** "Dies Report Scored by Mrs. R," *New York Times,* 14 December 1939. ER had not mentioned Mathews's report in her Bill of Rights column.

181 **"We have before us":** "Warning Sounded," *New York Times,* 14 December 1939.

182 **"the domination of un-Americanism":** *New York Times*, 11 December 1939; *New York Times*, 15 December 1939.

182 **the loss of "personal pride":** ER on WPA and Hollywood, *My Day*, 14, 15, 17, 18 December 1939.

182 **"On the Problems of American Youth":** "Hollywood, ER at Town Hall," *New York Times*, 17 December 1939; *My Day*, 18 December 1939.

182 **"not the only one having troubles":** Lash, *Friend's Memoir*, 19.

183 **"I think my daughter":** *My Day*, 18 December 1939.

183 **four generations of family:** "I think this old house likes the sound of children's voices. It is certainly an ideal place for children of every age to play in." Besides eighty-five-year-old SDR, who enjoyed every event, four grandchildren and little Diana Hopkins romped and played: Anna Eleanor (Sistie); Curtis; baby John; and FDR III. Time was set aside for telephone visits with the other cousins, the children of James and Betsey Cushing, Sara and Kate (who were to be with their maternal grandmother, in New Haven); Ruth Chandler and Elliott Jr. at home in Fort Worth, and William Donner Roosevelt, in Philadelphia.

183 **"I needed reassurance":** Hick to ER, 1 November 1939.

184 **"It's sweet of you":** ER to Hick, 30 November and 1 December 1939.

184 **"funny not to have":** Lash, *Love, Eleanor*, 285.

184 **"It has done more":** "Lauds Two Years of Dies," *New York Times*, 25 October 1939.

184 **her growing disappointment**: *My Day*, 11 December 1939.

184 **"deep respect and genuine"**: *My Day*, 20 December 1939.

185 **"Drink ye all of it"**: *My Day*, 25 December 1939.

185 **"Peace on earth"**: "A Vision for Today," *New York Times*, 24 December 1939.

185 **"right in the middle"**: *My Day*, 26 December 1939; "Four Generations Gather," *New York Times*, 24 December 1939.

186 **"Absolutely impossible for"**: "First Lady Declines," *New York Times*, 31 December 1939; *New York Times*, 20 December 1939.

187 **"meet the needs"**: "ER's 1940 Wish, and School Tolerance Program," *New York Times*, 31 December 1939.

Chapter Eight: The Politician and the Agitator: New Beginnings

187 **"The New Year is a time"**: *My Day*, 1 January 1940.

187 **"The old year is foul"**: Nicolson, *Diaries and Letters*, 31 December 1939, 2:52.

187 **"to destroy a free"**: Caroline D. Phillips Diary, December 1939, courtesy Kathleen Dalton.

187 **"Praise be, and"**: Edna Gellhorn to ER, 2, 3, and 21 December 1939; ER to Edna Gellhorn, 12 December 1939, Martha Gellhorn Collection, Washington University, St. Louis, Missouri.

187 **"dropped propaganda leaflets"**: Gellhorn to Ernest Hemingway, 30 November 1939, in Caroline Moorehead, *Letters of Gellhorn*, 77. See also Gellhorn, *Face of War*, 52ff. The *Collier's* article is "Bombs from a Low Sky: Why the Finns Are Getting Angry," *Collier's,* January 27, 1940, 12–13ff.

188 **"War in the arctic"**: Gellhorn to Ernest Hemingway, 4 December 1939, in Moorehead, *Letters of Gellhorn*, 76–80. For Finland, see also Carl Marzani, *We Can Be Friends*, 136–40, and Martha Gellhorn, *The Face of War*.

188 **In fact, the Russians:** Werth, *Russia at War*, 66–70; Manchester, *Last Lion*, 2:598–99.

189 **"to be anti-German"**: Caroline D. Phillips Diary, December 1939, courtesy of Kathleen Dalton.

189 **"efforts have saved"**: Ibid.

189 **"restore and ennoble"**: Pope Pius XII, *Summi Pontificatus,* new advent.org/library. According to John Cornwell, the encyclical was a powerful propaganda effort. It was published in Italy, scattered by the French air force over Germany, and read widely. The Nazis reproduced it, substituting the word *Germany* for *Poland*, and air-dropped copies over Poland; see Cornwell, *Hitler's Pope*, 233–34.

191 **"Your Holiness: Because"**: FDR to Pope Pius XII, 14 February, 1940, P1000.

192 **"very fine letter"**: Caroline D. Phillips Diary, courtesy of Kathleen Dalton.

192 **"freedom of religion"**: FDR to Taylor, 22 December 1939, in Taylor, *Wartime Correspondence*.

192 **letter of gratitude:** Cornwell, *Hitler's Pope*, 230.

192 **"to jam them all"**: O. G. Villard, "The Latest Anti-Jewish Horror," *Nation*, 30 December 1939, reprinted in Anthony Gronowicz, ed., *Oswald Garrison Villard: The Dilemma of an Absolute Pacifist in Two World Wars*, 572.

193 **"Just in case you missed"**: I am grateful to Cornelia Jane Strawser, for her mother's letter with W. L. White's 16 December article. Ruby Black to ER, 27 December 1939; Strawser to author, 6 April 2005.

195 **"to spend the night"**: FDR to William A. White, 14 December 1939, in *FDR: Personal Letters*, 4:967–68, cf. 1106.

195 **"is indeed in peril"**: Ibid.

197 **a "breathtaking affair"**: Lash, *Friend's Memoir*, 25.

197 **"Mrs. Roosevelt wondered"**: Kathrine Kressmann Taylor's *Address Unknown* (1938) was banned in Germany but became a film released by Columbia Pictures in 1944. The discussion is recounted in Lash, *Friend's Memoir*, 25–26, 29–30.

198 **the German socialist leader:** Richard W. Fox, *Reinhold Niebuhr*, 201.

198 **"At this the president"**: The dinner table discussion is recounted in Lash, *Friend's Memoir*, 25–26.

199 **"a haven for a few weeks"**: Ibid., 22, 29, 33.

199 **"anti-Semitic and anti-Catholic"**: Ibid., 32.

199 *Nacht und Nebel*: Gilbert, *Second World War*, 32.

199 **"a holy struggle"**: Shirer, *Berlin Diary*, 275–77, 9 and 18 January 1940.

199 **"without proper trials"**: Gilbert, *History of Twentieth Century*, 2:292.

200 **"found he had company"**: Lash's account of his stay at Val-Kill is in *Friend's Memoir*, 37–38; see *TIR*, 202.

201 **"plea for funds for Finland"**: Lash, *Friend's Memoir*, 47.

Chapter Nine: Radical Youth and Refugees: Winter–Spring 1940

202 **"This is a book"**: ER, foreword to Gould, *American Youth*.

203 **"cots for 150 boys"**: ER's press conference, in Beasley, *ER Press Conferences*, 150.

203 **She arranged for a fleet of buses:** Ibid.

203 **"believe in the communistic"**: *New York Times*, 6 February 1940.

204 **"a brief wrestling match"**: This account is from the *New York Times*.

206 **"was booed for fifteen minutes"**: *TIR*, 205.

207 **"Deep in the dream"**: Gould, *American Youth*, 10.

208 **but "a spanking"**: FDR's speech is recalled and paraphrased in Lash, *Friend's Memoir*, 56–58; Lash, *Eleanor and Franklin*, 603–4; and Gould, *American Youth*, 10–13. I am grateful to Vivian Cadden for her many memories regarding these events.

209 **My own friends:** For Amy Swerdlow, Victor Teisch, Bella Abzug, Mim Kelber, this was a defining political moment. In conversations with the author.

209 **"hopeful and constructive"**: Straight, *After Long Silence*.

209 **"The young people had begun"**: Lash, *Eleanor and Franklin*, 603–4.

209 **"It was raining mighty hard"**: I am grateful to Ronnie Gilbert for the lyrics and publishing context for "Standing in the Rain," reprinted in Seeger, *Where Have All the Flowers Gone* and *Hard Hitting Songs*. It was initially published as

sheet music, "Why Do You Stand There in the Rain," and in the *Daily Worker*, 18 April 1940. I am also profoundly grateful to Ronald Cohen for related information, especially Pete Seeger's draft essay, "An Informal Account of the Almanac Singers, December 1940–July 1942"; *Songs for Political Action: Folkmusic, Topical Songs and the American Left, 1926–1953* (CD); and the Woody Guthrie Archives, 250 W. Fifty-seventh Street, New York, N.Y. 10107.

210 **"Oh, Franklin Roosevelt":** I am grateful to Victor Teisch for "I Hate War," and the ditty heard frequently during and after the February conference, in FDR's "distinctive voice": "I hate war. Eleanor hates war. . . (pause). I hate Eleanor."

210 **"I felt as you did":** ER to Anna, 21 February 1940.

211 **"citizenship and voting rights":** Lash, *Friend's Memoir*, 61.

211 **"war is an outrage":** Gould, *American Youth*, 18. Dorothy Height's account of ER is in Height, *Open Wide the Freedom Gates*, 82–91.

211 **"Tactics of anti-Jewish":** Gould, *American Youth*, 18.

212 **Frances Williams's concluding:** Ibid., 29.

212 **"a semifascist state":** Lash, *Friend's Memoir*, 62–63.

212 **"When I rose to speak":** *TIR*, 205.

212 **"made it a giant boo":** Gould, *American Youth*, 34.

212 **"on the sore spot":** Ibid., 25–28.

213 **"I want you neither to clap":** Lash, *Friend's Memoir*, 63.

213 **"Don't you think":** The questions and answers in this and the following paragraphs are drawn from the accounts in Lash, *Friend's Memoir*, 63–68; Gould, *American Youth*, 27; Lash, *Eleanor and Franklin*, 605–7; Straight, *After Long Silence*, 150; and *New York Times*, 12 February 40.

214 **"in a way which":** ER to Hick, Lash, *Love, Eleanor*, 294.

215 **"after all you have done":** Hick to ER, ibid., 295.

215 **"The nation probably":** Dewey Fleming, *Baltimore Sun*, February 1940.

215 **"I went to all the sessions":** Betty Lindley to Anna, 13 February 1940, Anna Roosevelt Halsted Papers, box 36.

215 **"Our problem children":** Lash, *Eleanor and Franklin*, 607.

215 **"Here I am installed":** *My Day*, 20 February 1940.

216 **"I'm getting a good tan":** ER to Anna, 21 February 1940.

216 **"My husband likes":** *My Day*, 21 February 1940.

217 **"There is nothing which gives":** *My Day*, 22 February 1940.

217 **as "well done":** *My Day*, 23 February 1940.

217 **"in the midst of a world":** Ibid.

217 **"a zest for life":** *My Day*, 24 February 1940.

218 **"needed special education":** *My Day*, 28 February 1939.

218 **to "inspect the Atlantic":** FDR to ER, 17 February 1940; FDR to SDR, 27 February 1940, both in *FDR: Personal Letters*, 4:1002–3.

219 **"arrogant and brutal":** Nicolson, *Diaries and Letters*, 29 February 1940, Von Sittart on Joe Kennedy's defeatism, 2:6–16 March 1940, on Welles in Berlin, 2:62–63.

219 **"In this he will have":** Ibid., 29 February 1940.

219 **"faithfully followed Moscow's":** Murphy, *Diplomat Among Warriors*, 34–36.

219 **"die for Danzig":** Ehrenberg, *Memoirs*, 476.

220 **"various ideals and":** *My Day*, 29 February 1940.

220 **"defeating England":** For poll results, see Boothe, *Europe in Spring*, 4–5n1.

220 **"It was difficult to breathe":** Ehrenberg, *Memoirs*, 351–52.

221 **"conception of the good teacher":** *My Day*, 1 March 1940.

222 **"Dr. Lachmann, who":** Henry MacCracken to ER, 28 August 1939.

222 **"the academic board":** Dean W. K. Jordan to Mr. Warner, U.S. Consulate, Berlin, 16 August 1939.

223 **"published works and":** Erika Weigand's parents, Frances Rhoades Weigand and Dr. Hermann Weigand, to chair of Yale German department.

223 **"Vera Lachmann is":** Frances Rhoades Weigand to Henry MacCracken, 25 August 1939.

223 **"I believe Dr. Lachmann":** Hermann Weigand to MacCracken, 25 August 1939.

223 **"to do all they can":** ER to MacCracken 31 August 1939.

223 **"Dear Sumner: Thank you":** ER to Sumner Welles, 11 September 1939.

223 **"I feel sick":** ER to Anna, 11 September 1939, 111.

224 **a legendary American classicist:** Vera Regina Lachmann's vita, b. 23 June 1904, d. 1985. I am grateful to Renate Bridenthal, Eva Kollish, and especially Naomi Replansky for their memories and assistance researching Lachmann.

224 **"Another heavenly day":** *My Day*, 1 March 1940.

224 **Royal Palm Club:** *My Day*, 2 March 1940.

224 **"the day has come":** *My Day*, 4 March 1940.

225 **"will be starving":** Ibid.

225 **"so you can see for yourself":** Tommy to Lape, 2 March 1940, Arizona Collection.

225 **"I would not have had":** Ibid.

226 **"Our father, who hast set":** *My Day*, 6 March 1940.

Chapter Ten: "When You Go to War, You Cease to Solve the Problems of Peace": March–June 1940

227 **"small frontier rectification":** Werth, *Russia at War*, 75–79.

227 **"from the dust":** *My Day*, 11 March 1940.

228 **"a musical awakening":** *My Day*, 12 March 1940.

228 **"but in misfortune":** Ehrenburg, *Memoirs*, 477.

228 **"no other President's wife":** *New York Times*, 8 March 1940.

228 **"not only gladden":** *New York Times*, 2 March 1940.

229 **Foster Parents Plan:** Other supporters included Herbert Hoover, Helen Hayes, the Duchess of Atholl, Sara Delano Roosevelt, Helen Keller, and Thomas Mann.

229 **"with Catholic, Protestant":** *New York Times*, 13 March, 17 March, and 18 April 1940. ER agreed to be an honorary vice-president for this refugee children's group, with Herbert Lehman, Dorothy Canfield Fisher, Albert Einstein, and the Rev. Henry St. George Tucker.

229 **During the hectic:** *My Day*, 14 and 15 March 1940; ER, press conference, in Beasley, *ER Press Conferences*, 163.

229 **in "on business":** *My Day*, 16 March 1940.

230 **"undaunted" by all:** Tommy to Lape, 27 February 1940.

230 **"These youngsters work hard":** *My Day,* 16 March 1940.

230 **"which emphasize the liberty":** ER, "Civil Liberties—The Individual and the Community," in Baird, *Representative American Speeches,* 173–82.

232 **"No real teacher can ever":** *My Day,* 18 March 1940.

233 **"in a damp and fairly dark":** *My Day,* 19 March 1940.

233 **"small hospital on the lake":** *My Day,* 16 March 1940.

233 **"For the first time in some years":** *My Day,* 17 March 1940.

234 **"greeted them under":** *My Day,* 23 and 27 March 1940.

234 **"a huge vase of daffodils":** *My Day,* 23 March 1940.

234 **"upset us all considerably":** *My Day,* 21 March 1940.

235 **"I suppose weeks in bed":** Ibid.

235 **"the coldest" Easter:** *My Day,* 26 March 1940.

235 **"Why, I do nothing":** *My Day,* 29 March 1940.

235 **"These homeless people":** Ibid.

236 **senior State Department officials:** FDR to Cordell Hull, 7 March 1940, in *FDR: Personal Letters,* 4:1004–5; Morse, *While Six Million Died,* 261.

236 **In Seattle, Anna:** *My Day,* 30 March, 1 April 1940.

236 **"with the press stalking":** Tommy to Lape, n.d., ca. March 1940, BWC.

237 **"our friend, Hick":** Ibid.

237 **"ragged starving people":** Douglas, *Full Life,* 148, see also 142–44. See also John Steinbeck to ER, 20 June 1939; ER to Steinbeck, 30 June 1939.

237 **"DEAR YOU MUST":** Hick to ER, 13 May 1939, with two pages of quotes.

238 **"Squatters pay no rent":** *My Day,* 4 April 1940.

238 **"an electric light":** Ibid.

238 **had not exaggerated:** Douglas, *Full Life,* 154–55; "Mecca of Reports . . . Says Steinbeck Told the Truth," *New York Times,* 3 April 1940; *My Day,* 4, 5, and 6 April 1940.

238 **"the county authorities":** *My Day,* 5 April 1940.

239 **"standards for decent":** Ibid.

239 **"must be proud":** Ibid.

239 **"I know the president":** ER to Douglas, in Scobie, *Center Stage,* 113.

239 **"filled with apprehension":** Douglas, *Full Life,* 155–56.

239 **in San Francisco:** *My Day,* 8 and 9 April 1940.

240 **"Miss Chaney, just *who*":** Mayris Chaney memoir (unpublished ms.), 1–10, 49–50. I am grateful to Anna Eleanor Martin and Michele Martin, Mayris Chaney's daughters, for access to Tiny's memoir. See also Tommy to Lape on Chaney, 6 April 1940.

240 **"good audiences and":** Tommy to Lape, 6 April 1940.

241 **"The waterfalls are":** Sargent, *Yosemite's Famous,* 34.

241 **"after leading the boycott":** Chaney memoir (unpublished ms.), 45–50, with *San Francisco Chronicle* clip, and *New York Times,* 7 April 1940.

241 **Grim news arrived:** Davis, *FDR: Into the Storm,* 539–42. Norwegian minister of war Vidkun Quisling, whose surname is forever after a word for traitor, had worked with Berlin to plan the Nazi occupation of Norway.

241 **of "emerald green":** *My Day,* 11 April 1940.

241 **"It is all horrible":** ER to FDR, 11 April 1940.

242 **"think of anything":** *My Day*, 12 April 1940.

242 **"must keep out of war":** *New York Times* 15 April 1940.

243 **"group from the crippled":** *My Day*, 15 April 1940.

243 **"She is very much":** *My Day*, 13 April 1940.

243 **Dr. Will Alexander:** ER to Alexander, 10 April 1940; Alexander to ER, 16 April 1940; ER to Alexander, 12 March 1940; Egerton, *Speak Now*, 47–50. ER had a significant correspondence regarding the future of the SCHW. They worked closely together with the Julius Rosenwald Fund.

244 **"an equal opportunity":** Reed, *Simple Decency,* 21–27; *Baltimore African-American,* 13 April 1940; *New York Times,* 16 April 1940.

244 **"Communist aggression":** Egerton, *Speak Now*, 133, 297–98.

244 **"rise in net profits":** *My Day*, 17 April 1940.

244 **a message from Judge Charlton**: ER to Robert Jackson, 1 May 1940; Jackson to ER, 24 October 1940.

245 **She sent a sizable check:** During the election campaign, in October and November, the conservative Constitutional League would use ER's 23 April check to Highlander, for $100 (about $1,000 today), to discredit FDR throughout the South. See Joseph Kemp, *The Fifth Column in the South* (pamphlet), in *Nashville Tennessean,* leading Democratic newspaper, 1 November 1940, and widely reprinted.

245 **exhibited "bad manners":** "Why I Still Believe in the Youth Congress," *Liberty,* 20 April 1940, in Black, *Courage*, 125–29. "We have been the stupid ones," to argue: "Don't go near that group, they are controlled by Communists," she said. "Jobs to Balk Reds, First Lady's Plea," *New York Times,* 1 April 1940. In an address to over one thousand social workers, broadcast nationally, she said that unless youth had the means to lead "independent, creative lives," they would be prey to any stray idea. "The best thing we can do to help youth is to give youth the feeling they are needed in every community. . . . We say youth has failed. Perhaps they think we have failed. . . . Perhaps we all need a change." "First Lady Pleads for Aid to Youth," *New York Times,* 21 March 1940. In an address to 150 foreign correspondents and their guests, she said, "The only way to fight communism is to give youth something vital to solve their problems." "First Lady Denies Youth Group Is Red," *New York Times,* 22 March 1940.

246 **"It is nice to be home":** *My Day*, 18 April 1940.

246 **"The news from Norway":** David Gray to ER, 16 April 1940, David Gray Collection.

246 **"In the very heart":** "Appeal to Eleanor Roosevelt," *New York Times,* 10 March 1940.

247 **"our basic liberties":** "Save Our Liberties, First Lady Urges," *New York Times,* 24 April 1940.

247 **our "regularly constituted":** *My Day*, 23 April 1940.

247 **were "sadly needed":** *My Day*, 19 April 1940.

247 **"with the ladies of the 75th":** *My Day*, 20 April 1940.

248 **"believes she can tell":** Ibid.

248 **"forgotten to mention"**: *My Day*, 19 April 1940.

248 **"if you have enjoyed"**: *My Day*, 24 April 1940.

248 **"Such a week"**: Tommy to Lape, 21 April 1940.

249 **"to see some of the Farm Security"**: *My Day*, 25 and 26 April 1940.

249 **to the Carolinas**: *My Day*, 28 and 29 April 1940. In Asheville ER visited "Rabbit"—Louis Howe's assistant, Margaret Durand—who was recovering from TB. See *My Day*, 27–30 April 1940.

249 **"What is going to happen"**: *My Day*, 1 May 1940.

250 **"democracy a reality"**: *New York Times*, 2 May 1940.

250 **"has stood for freedom"**: Ibid.; *My Day*, 3 May 1940.

250 **Her old allies**: Scobie, *Center Stage*, 114; Ware, *Partner and I*, 139–40; Helen Gahagan, "FSA Aids Migratory Worker," *Democratic Digest*, February 1940, 11.

250 **of "solid, tweedy"**: "Women: Voters and Party Workers," *Time*, 13 May 1940.

250 **"a committee of Negro"**: All April 1940 memos in Democratic National Committee Institute file, FDRL.

251 **"What will keep peace"**: "Women Democrats Hear Peace Pleas," *New York Times*, 5 May 1940; see also *My Day*, 6 and 7 May 1940.

251 **"a beautiful idea"**: "Mrs Roosevelt's Three Ideas," *New York Times*, 7 May 1940.

251 **"Do you think the poll"**: *Democratic Digest*, June 1940, 24.

251 **"I would like to tell you"**: *My Day*, 7 May 1940.

252 **"One cannot help"**: *My Day*, 9 May 1940.

252 **a "terrific attack"**: Nicolson, *Diaries and Letters*, 7 May 1940, 2:77. For Churchill's message, see Gilbert, *Finest Hour: 1939–1941*, 638. See Nicolson, 14 April–10 May 1940, 71–85.

252 **refuge for the royal**: FDR to John Cudahy, 8 May 1940, in *FDR: Personal Letters*, 4:1024–25. Also see FDR to ER, 1022–23.

253 **"All these young things"**: *My Day*, 10 and 12 May 1940.

253 **"Altogether," ER wrote**: *My Day*, 14 May 1940.

253 **"so vile that it would"**: FDR to ER, 4 May 1940, in *FDR: Personal Letters*, 4:1022–23. FDR's memo to Sumner Welles, 4 May 1940; Welles to FDR, 6 May 1940.

253 **do "something worthwhile"**: ER to Hick, 11 May 1940.

253 **200,000 Belgian and Dutch refugee**: *New York Times*, 16 May 1940.

254 **International Child Service Committee**: "New Group to Aid Child Refugees Here," *New York Times*, 18 April 1940. See Catt to ER, 3 May 1940, and ER to Catt, 6 May 1940, regarding homes for refugees established by Louise Wise.

254 **Children's Crusade drives**: "75 Educators Back Children's Crusade," *New York Times*, 24 March 1940; *New York Times*, 1 April 1940.

254 **"Every child in American ought"**: *Time*, 13 May 1940, and *New York Times*, 18 April 1940.

254 **"Darkness is only"**: *My Day*, 14 May 1940.

Chapter Eleven: "If Democracy Is to Survive, It Must Be
Because It Meets the Needs of the People"

255 **"I have nothing":** Gilbert, *Second World War,* 64. See also Manchester, *Last Lion,* 2:682–83.

255 **"It must be a most":** *My Day,* 15 May 1940.

255 **"But what if the Nazis":** Lash, *Friend's Memoir,* 89–90.

255 **"My heart sank":** *My Day,* 15 May 1940.

255 **"The small countries":** Gilbert, *Finest Hour: 1939–1941,* 345-46.

256 **"the latest type":** Ibid., 355. See also Manchester, *Last Lion,* 64–67.

256 **"far more personal":** *My Day,* 17 May 1940.

256 **"If democracy is to survive":** Ibid.

257 **"a nation of healthy":** *My Day,* 18 May 1940.

257 **"facing a sinister power":** "Sinister Power Hit by Mrs. Roosevelt," *New York Times,* 18 May 1940.

257 **"one cannot live in a Utopia":** *My Day,* 17 May 1940,

258 **"for the succor":** Bullitt to FDR, 20 May 1940, telegrams, Orville H. Bullitt, ed., *For the President: Personal & Secret,* 428–29.

258 **"the Jew Prime Minister":** Murphy, *Diplomat,* 34; Bullitt to FDR, 27 May 1940, *For the President,* 432.

258 **"My friends . . . Tonight":** FDR, "Deepening Crisis in Europe and American Military Readiness," 26 May 1940, in Buhite and Levy, *Fireside Chats,* 152–62.

261 **"You don't want to go":** Lash, *Friend's Memoir,* 92.

261 **who "went overseas":** Ibid., 153n.

261 **"a Nazi-dominated":** "First Lady's Plea Ignored by Youth," *New York Times,* 27 May 1940.

261 **"temper of the delegates":** Lash, *Friend's Memoir,* 92; Marcantonio, *I Vote.*

261 **"wanted to listen":** "First Lady's Plea Ignored by Youth," *New York Times,* 27 May 1940.

262 **"her sensible words":** Lash, *Friend's Memoir,* 92–93.

262 **"addressed the brattish":** Snorted the testy journalist, Frank Kent, *Time,* 3 June 1940, editorial; and Bullitt, *For the President,* 28 May 1940, 433–35.

262 **"no longer existed":** Gilbert, *Second World War,* 77.

262 **"It seems incredible":** *My Day,* 29 May 1940.

263 **"which came from":** Fink, *Marc Bloch,* 229. See also Divine, *Nine Days of Dunkirk.* Dunkirk's equipment losses included 475 tanks, 38,000 vehicles, 12,000 motorcycles, thousands of heavy guns, 90,000 rifles, and 7,000 tons of ammunition.

263 **an evacuation is:** Gilbert, *Finest Hour: 1939–1941,* 86; Gilbert, *Second World War,* 81–83; Nicolson, *Diaries and Letters,* 92; cf. David Divine, *The Nine Days of Dunkirk*; and Shirer, *Berlin Diary,* 363.

263 **Clare Boothe Luce:** Ehrenburg, *Memoirs,* 489; Luce, *Europe in the Spring,* 270–71.

263 **"but their courage":** Bullitt to FDR, 4–5 June 1940, *For the President,* 449–51.

263 **that substantial American:** Both Churchill and Reynaud were hopeful that equipment FDR promised would in fact arrive in time, but the planes did not.

263 **"What a life!":** ER to Anna, 17 May 1940; ER "Links Relief to Defense," *New York Times,* 21 May 1940.

263 **"Today there are more":** ER, radio address, 26 May 1940.

264 **"flooding down across the country":** Hamilton Fish Armstrong, "Asks Unstinted US Aid," *New York Times,* 28 May 1940. ER "Pleas for War Refugees," *New York Times,* 27 May 1940.

264 **the "People's Common":** "People's Common Dedicated," *New York Times,* 2 June 1940; "Labor Unity Urged" and "120,000 Garment Workers Swell Fair Crowd," *New York Times,* 3 June 1940.

265 **"an art which has":** *My Day,* 3 June 1940.

265 **"through every experience":** Ibid.

265 **"Some of us forget":** *My Day,* 4 June 1940.

266 **"with the other boatmen":** Cook, *ER,* 1:58.

266 **"very miserable childhood":** Lash, *Friend's Memoir,* 108.

268 **"You are right":** ER to Anna, 17 May, 4 June 1940, Asbell, 117–18; *My Day,* 5 June 1940.

268 **On 5 June, the President:** Lash, *Friend's Memoir,* 98–106.

271 **"Every patriotic citizen":** *My Day,* 6 June 1940.

271 **"where the Negro people":** Ibid.

271 **"some rather nice pieces":** *My Day,* 7 June 1940.

271 **"always an exciting":** Haven's birth is announced in *New York Times,* 6 June 1940. See also *My Day,* 7, 8, and 10 June.

271 **"the only reality":** *My Day,* 11 June 1940.

271 **now surrounded France:** For the Nazi invasion of France, see Gilbert, *Second World War,* 85–90.

272 **"The times were fraught":** *TIR,* 211–12.

272 **"a lone island":** FDR, "Stab in the Back" speech, 10 June 1940, Miller Center of Public Affairs, Scripps Library; *New York Times,* 11 June 1940.

273 **"When the soldiers":** *My Day,* 12 June 1940.

273 **"whose lives can be saved":** Bullitt to FDR, 9–11 June 1940, *For the President,* 456–65. See also Shirer, *Berlin Diary,* "June," 399; Jean Edward Smith, *FDR,* 448–9.

273 **Burke-Wadsworth bill:** Smith, *FDR,* 464–66.

274 **"We have never thought of ourselves":** "Scores Forced Enlisting," *My Day,* 14 June 1940.

274 **"Personally I would rather":** Ibid.

274 **"A national mobilization":** *My Day,* 28 August 1940. See also *My Day,* 29 July 1940.

274 **NYA and CCC:** *My Day,* 21 August 1940.

274 **"sense of national purpose":** ER, press conference, 4 June 1940, in Beasley, *ER Press Conferences; New York Times,* 4 June 1940.

275 **"the jobless and needy":** Ibid.

275 **a "class ruling":** "Scores Forced Enlisting," *My Day,* 14 June 1940.

275 **"sat out on":** *My Day,* 15 June 1940.

276 **"It isn't only the shock":** Anne O'Hare McCormick, "Europe," *New York Times,* 15 June 1940.

276 **"The Germans have learned":** *My Day*, 25 June 1940.

276 **"from the women":** *My Day*, 17 June 1940.

277 **"I'm not going abroad":** ER to Lape and Read, BWC collection.

277 **"She has wanted desperately":** Tommy to Anna, 17 June 1940.

278 **"dressed in a pink-and-black":** "Opens Drive to Aid China," *New York Times,* 19 June 1940.

278 **"women in every country":** *My Day*, 20 June 1940.

Chapter Twelve: **"The World Rightly Belongs to Those Who Really Care": The Convention of 1940**

279 **Gurs in the Pyrenees:** Felstiner, *To Paint Her Life*; Lerner, *Fireweed*; Hanak, *World of Ili Kronstein*, 32–33; Paxton; Genet's "Exodus: Spanish Civil War," in Drutman, *Flanner's Paris*, 201–3.

279 **"It looks to me as if":** Ickes, *Secret Diary,* 3:207. For Ickes's frustration with the State Department, see 3:216–17. See also Smith, *FDR*, 449–52.

280 **And Henry Stimson:** FDR to Harry H. Woodring, 19 June 1940, in *FDR: Personal Letters*, 4:1041.

280 **"As to Frank Knox":** Ickes, *Secret Diary,* 3:215, see also 204–15.

280 **a "new order":** C. Brooks Peters, *New York Times*, 22 June to 7 July 1940.

281 **"We may find ourselves":** Nicolson, *Diaries and Letters,* 4 July 1940, 2:100. See also C. Brooks Peters, *New York Times,* 5 July. For context, see Gilbert, *Finest Hour: 1939–1941*, 628–44.

281 **the Smith Act:** Because Frances Perkins had opposed the deportation of Harry Bridges, the Australian-born head of the International Longshoremens Union, and was perceived to be concerned about the rights of aliens and the needs of refugees, all immigration issues were shifted from the Department of Labor to the Justice Department. Immigrant issues, along with the details of the Smith Act. now belonged to the attorney general. Schrecker, *Many Are the Crimes*, 92–98,

283 **The Court's majority issued:** Justice Felix Frankfurter's decision in *Minersville School District v. Gobitis,* 310 U.S. 586 (1940), was deplored by ER.

283 **"And to think":** Ickes, *Secret Diary,* 15 June 1940, 3:211.

283 **"were dragged from":** *My Day*, 21 June 1940. See also Baker, *Brandeis and Frankfurter*, 399–409.

283 **"People are breaking":** Ickes, *Secret Diary,* 3:211.

283 **"the hysteria that is sweeping":** Ibid.

283 **"Felix's Fall of France":** Frankfurter to FDR, 3, 4, and 5 June 1940.

284 **"We have been remarkably fortunate":** *My Day*, 24 June 1940. See *My Day*, 22 June 1940 for WPA and NYA training.

284 **"I never asked":** *TIR*, 212.

284 **a heart attack:** *Time*, 27 May 1940.

285 **"I drove through the woods":** *My Day*, 25 June 1940.

285 **Gertrude von Adam Wenzel:** On Trude Lash, see Adam Fifield, "A Living Primer of 20th Century Causes: Trude Lash, a Lifetime on the Barricades," *New York Times,* 3 June 2001; Wolfgang Saxon, "Trude Wenzel Lash," *New*

York Times, 5 February 2004; "Trude Wenzel Lash, Children's Advocate," *Vineyard Gazette,* 6 February 2004. TWL said her dissertation was burned during WWII.

286 **"more than casually attracted"**: ER to Lash, in Lash, *Love, Eleanor,* 305; Trude Lash to author, July 2002: "I would not want to tell what I know or hurt those still alive—so I'm caught in a trap of my own making." Subsequently I understood that she referred to her family of origin.

286 **"Washington had moved away"**: Bellush, *He Walked Alone,* 137. See also Perkins, *Roosevelt I Knew,* 300, 341–46.

287 **"twenty-four of the best members"**: Bellush, *He Walked Alone,* 150. For Winant's efforts after 1939 and especially between May and June 1940, see 140–48.

287 **"convinced" FDR to:** *New York Times,* 6 June 1938, quoted in Bellush, *He Walked Alone,* 134–40. The office escape after the armistice and FDR's about-face is recounted on 149–51. At McGill, Dr. Wilder Penfield of the Montreal Neurological Institute was Winant's intermediary. Fifteen ILO members and their dependents left Geneva 7 August. I am grateful to Carol Riegelman Lubin for this book, and for her memories of her ILO boss Winant, and to Jewel Bellush.

287 **"the three houses"**: *My Day,* 25 June and 3 July 1940. See also *Hitler's Exiles,* 226.

288 **Emergency Rescue Committee:** For the 25 June meeting, see Lash, *Friend's Memoir,* 112–13, and Lash Diary, 25 June 1940, Lash Papers. See also Fry, *Surrender on Demand,* 247–48; Berenbaum, *World Must Know,* 60; Michael Berenbaum on Varian Fry in Beasley, *ER Encyclopedia,* 198–201; Lash thought Joseph Buttinger (aka Hubert Richter), his wife, heiress Muriel Gardiner Buttinger, "the daring and glamorous" couple. Lash, *Friend's Memoir,* 112; Isenberg, *Hero of Our Own,* 6.

289 **"always said it was possible"**: Lash, *Friend's Memoir,* 111–12.

289 **"The President has seen"**: ER to Fry, 8 July 1940.

290 **"Under the quota"**: *My Day,* 26 June 1940.

290 **"I love my porch"**: ER to Anna, 26 June 1940.

290 **"The children are temporary"**: "Lift Bar to Children, ER Urges," *New York Times,* 7 July 1940. ER depended on the activist members of this splendid committee: Katherine Lenroot, head of the Federal Children's Bureau, Marshall Field, Bishop Bernard J. Sheil of Chicago, Dorothy Bellanca, Dr. Frank Kingdon, Shepard Morgan, Clarence Pickett of the AFSC, and Agnes King Inglis among others. The committee was a massive undertaking of several organizations, including the American Committee for Christian Refugees, the Friends of Children, the German-Jewish Children's Aid, the Catholic Youth Organization, the American Joint Distribution Committee, the English-Speaking Union, the Foster Home Department of New York's Children's Aid, the Non-Sectarian Foundation for Refugee Children, the Allied Relief Fund, the Unitarian Service Committee, the Committee for Catholic Refugees, the National Council of Jewish Women, the Dominican Republic Settlement Association, and the Queen Wilhelmina Fund, among others. This committee

represented all faiths, and was "in the truest sense a nonsectarian, nonpartisan movement inspired solely by the desire to rescue children." They intended to "coordinate all resources"; cooperate with Canada; aid children directly everywhere in danger; provide care in family homes for those children admitted to the United States. "U.S. Groups Formed," 21 June, "Many Offer Homes to Refugee Children," 22 June, "Saving Democracy's Children," editorial, 22 June 1920, *New York Times*.

291 **Christian Action Committee:** *My Day*, 9 July 1940.

291 **"the years of depression":** *My Day*, 28 June 1940.

292 **"Sometimes I wonder":** *My Day*, 1 July and 29 June 1940. On the 1940 Republican convention, see also Neal, *Dark Horse*, 86, 99; Smith, *FDR*, 451–55; *My Day*, 29 June, 1 July 1940.

292 **"I don't care":** Hick to ER, 2 July 1940, in Streitmatter, *Empty Without You*, 229.

292 **"This job is such fun":** Hick to ER.

292 **"corporate, entrenched wealth":** Ickes, *Secret Diary*, 29 June, 3:220–21.

292 **nobody in FDR's inner circle:** *TIR*, 212–13; Lash, *Friend's Memoir*, 127.

293 **"I personally want":** *My Day*, 4 July 1940. See also *My Day*, 6 July; *New York Times*, "Hyde Park Library," 5 July 1940.

293 **"my husband had":** *My Day*, 8 July 1940.

293 **"essential indifference to labor":** Lash, *Love, Eleanor*, 304–5.

293 **"Don't get tired":** ER to Hick, July 1940.

294 **"had a gay time":** Lash, *Friend's Memoir*, 128.

294 **"was in trouble":** Ibid.

294 **she "turned shy":** Lash, *Love, Eleanor,* 308.

294 **"in a mess":** Ibid., 309–10.

295 **"every effort to improve":** Ibid.

295 **in his words, "spry":** Lash, *Friend's Memoir*, 130; Lash journals, 15 July 1940.

295 **"The President has never":** Alben Barkley, speech at 1940 Democratic Convention.

295 **"shook her head resignedly":** Lash, *Friend's Memoir,* 131.

295 **"led the procession":** Ickes, *Secret Diary,* 3:240, 243, 247.

296 **"convention is bleeding":** Ickes, *Secret Diary,* 3:249.

296 **"men who are determined":** Ickes, *Secret Diary,* 3:249–50. See also Smith, *FDR*, 458–60.

296 **"get promises out":** Perkins, *Roosevelt I Knew*, 128–132.

297 **"I certainly am not":** *TIR*, 214.

297 **"overcome with emotion":** ER and Hickok, *Ladies of Courage*, 282.

297 **"Jim Farley really":** *TIR*, 215.

297 **"Tell Jim to meet me":** ER and Hickok, *Ladies of Courage*, 281–84; Black, *ER*, 150.

297 **"We sat thru":** Lash journal, 17–18 July 1940.

298 **"allowed me to fly the plane":** *TIR*, 215.

298 **"an unusual gravity":** Kathleen McLaughlin, "No Campaigning . . . ," *New York Times*, 19 July 1940.

298 **"Jim Farley drove":** *TIR*, 216.

299 **"It must be Wallace":** *TIR*, 216–17.

299 **"sweetened the convention":** Perkins, *Roosevelt I Knew*, 133.

299 **"The Stadium was packed":** ER and Hickok, *Ladies of Courage*, 283.

299 **"the State delegations":** *New York Times*, 19 July 1940.

299 **She "moved forward":** ER and Hickok, *Ladies of Courage*, 283.

299 **"For many years":** ER, speech to 1940 Democratic Convention.

300 **"It was striking":** *TIR*, 217.

300 **"the first wife of a president":** Kathleen McLaughlin, "No Campaigning . . . ," *New York Times*, 19 July 1940.

300 **"For God's sake":** Smith, *FDR*, 463.

300 **"had done a very good":** *TIR*, 218.

300 **"The perfect, gentle knight":** Senator George W. Norris to ER, 19 July 1940.

301 **"I listened over the radio":** Ibid. See also *TIR*, 214–18; Smith, *FDR*, 458–63; *New York Times*, 19 July 1940.

301 **"we will not participate":** Democratic Party platform, 1940, criticized for failure to grasp realities, *Sydney Herald*.

302 **seemed a "retreat":** "Hits at Foreign Plank," *New York Times,* 20 July 1940.

Chapter Thirteen: War and *The Moral Basis of Democracy*

303 **her remarkable meditation:** ER had begun the year with four book contracts: *The Story of the White House* (never written); a collection of essays on the meaning of Christmas around the world; a book for children, *Christmas: A Story of Hope*, which would be illustrated by Fritz Kredel and published by Knopf; and her essay on citizenship, which became *The Moral Basis of Democracy*. See Black, *ER: Biography*, 117.

303 **"stimulate the thoughts":** ER, *Moral Basis*, 11–14. Quotes from this book in the following paragraphs are from pages 26, 33–37, and 42–82.

308 **"strengthen the ticket":** *My Day,* 20 July 1940.

308 **she had deplored:** For Wallace's 1933 programs, see Cook, *ER*, 2:81–82, 412; ER to Lape, 22 September 1933, Arizona Collection.

309 **to "humanize capitalism":** Wallace's *Paths to Plenty* and other works in Schapsmeier and Schapsmeier, *Wallace of Iowa*, 250–55 and passim.

309 **"To me there is":** *My Day*, 20 July 1940.

309 **"the growth of three":** *My Day*, 17, 18, and 19 July 1940.

310 **"on the saddle":** Death of Aunt Dora, 21 July 1940. *My Day*, 22, 23, and 25 July 1940; *New York Times* obituary of Dora Delano Forbes, 22 July 1940.

310 **"is always happier":** Tommy to Anna, 12 July 1940.

310 **she worked closely:** Mary McLeod Bethune: Joanna Schneider Zangrando and Robert Zangrando, "ER and Black Civil Rights," in Hoff-Wilson and Lightman, *Without Precedent*, 96–98.

311 **"to eliminate racial":** Neal, *Dark Horse*, 146; "White House Blesses Jim Crow," *Crisis*, November 1940; Burke-Wadsworth in Smith, *FDR*, 464–66.

311 **"the horrid legal details":** *My Day*, 13 July 1940.

311 **was "very impatient":** When ER called from 20 June 1940 meeting with Lash and Karl Frank (aka Paul Hagen), then met with Joseph Battinger, Clarence

Pickett, and Varian Fry and others, 27 June 1940. There is, however, no record of this meeting.

311 **"I know it is due":** Lash, *Friend's Memoir*, 113n.

312 **"to tie up the ship":** "Family Separated by Stern Laws of US," *Norfolk Virginia Pilot*, 12 September 1940. The *Quanza* story was revived by Jacob L. Morewitz's son David and his grandson Stephen. See Stephen J. Morewitz, "The Saving of the SS *Quanza*," *William and Mary Magazine*, Summer 1991; Stephen Morewitz and Susan Lieberman, *Steamship Quanza*, a play reviewed in the *Chicago Tribune* on 29 May 1991; and Rebecca Zweifler, "Where Are They Now? Survivors of the SS *Quanza*," interviews for a traveling exhibit of Yeshiva University Museum, at the Cardozo School of Law, November 1994.

313 **officials granted permits:** Sumner Welles to ER, 12 September 1940; Eliot B. Coulter to ER, 19 September 1940/R 70, both in Sumner Welles Papers, box 793; Breckinridge Long to Prichard, Department of Justice, and Lemuel B. Schofield, Special Assistant to the Attorney General, 12 September 1940, FDRL, copies from David Morewitz; Stephen J. Morewitz and Susan B. Lieberman, "The Saving of the SS *Quanza* in Hampton Roads," 14 September 1940; and David Morewitz to author.

313 **"very generous in offering":** Bellush, *He Walked Alone*, 152. It is not clear whether FDR's former World War I boss, Ambassador to Mexico Josephus Daniels, who likened the *Quanza* situation to Edward Everett Hale's "Man Without a Country," communicated his distress about the refugees to his one-time assistant. Nor is it clear why Long's antagonism to Winant's endangered ILO colleagues in Geneva did not give FDR pause.

313 **"young and old":** *My Day*, 20 September 1940.

313 **"music is a universal":** *My Day*, 26 July, 12 August, and 8 August 1940.

313 **"Their performances," ER was:** *My Day*, 18 September 1940.

314 **On 15 August:** Gilbert, *Finest Hour: 1939–1941*, 734–35.

314 **"Never in the field":** Ibid., 736.

314 **"I looked at the moon":** *My Day*, 14 August 1940.

315 **"The horror grows":** *My Day*, 7 September 1940.

315 **Hitler's "cruel, wanton":** Gilbert, *Finest Hour: 1939–1941*, 778–79.

315 **"calmness and great":** *My Day*, 14 September 1940.

316 ***City of Benares*:** Nagorski, *Miracles on the Water*.

316 **Women's Committee for Mercy:** Mercy Ship Bill and Yorkshire mothers letter, *New York Times*, 9 August 1940.

316 **"We want American ships":** Foster Parent Plan for 32,250 children at the Children's Sanctuary, *New York Times*, 22 September 1940. Long Committee meetings, *My Day*, 16 August 1940; ER to Eric Biddle, 21 September 1940; "Child Refugee Aid to Continue," *New York Times*, 10 October 1940; Ruth Gage-Colby to author. In addition to rescue efforts, ER organized relief efforts for the 30,000 Belgian refugees in Britain, as well as Bundles for Britain. See *New York Times*, 18 August 1940.

316 **"I used to pray":** *My Day*, 23 September 1940.

317 **Reverend Martin Niemöller:** Berenbaum, *World Must Know*, 40–41; Gilbert, *Second World War*, 685–86; and Gilbert, *History of Twentieth Century*, 17,

39–40, 174, 719–20. In 1941 Thomas Mann published Niemöller's sermons, which Reinhold Niebuhr praised for their "thrilling note . . . of urgency," despite their "grave differences" on key issues, according to Niebuhr's daughter. Elizabeth Sifton, *Serenity Prayer*, 244–45.

318 **The fictionalized version:** "JR Gets British Film," *New York Times*, 16 July 1940; "ER Filmed for Anti-Nazi Picture," *New York Times*, 18 July 1940.

318 **"achieves a moment":** Bosley Crowther, review of *Pastor Hall*, *New York Times*.

318 **"I am glad to introduce":** Virtually lost to history, I was unable to find ER's prologue, written in part by Robert Sherwood—until my friend WNYC archivist Andy Lancet put out an international call. We learned that for Toller's centennial in Berlin in 1993, Jeanpaul Goergen had presented *Pastor Hall* and published a pamphlet, "Ernst Toller: Schallplatte, Rundfunk, Film," which included ER's words; and the producer Roy Boulting's essay, 21–25. I am grateful to Jeanpaul Goergen; to Leo Enticknap, University of Leeds; and to David Pierce, Association of Moving Image Archivists.

318 **"Not even the oldest":** *New York Sunday Mirror*, 22 September 1940, with gratitude to Peter Smith for this reference; Lash Diary, 21 September 1940, Lash Papers.

318 **"It seemed strange":** *My Day*, 23 September 1940.

319 **"applauded vigorously":** "President's Mother Backs Anti–Nazi film," *New York Times*, 3 October 1940.

Chapter Fourteen: **"Defense Is Not a Matter of What You Get, But of What You Give"**

322 **"so many things":** ER, review of *Lillian Wald: Neighbor and Crusader*, in *Survey Graphic* (December 1938).

322 **"I always fall":** *My Day*, 19 August 1940.

322 **"spray of white dahlias":** "Thousands Mourn Lillian Wald," *New York Times*, 5 September 1940.

322 **"the most alarming situation":** Gertrude Baer's WILPF circular letter and bulletins, from Geneva's WILPF Archive, 1940–45. I am grateful to Felicity Hill for these extraordinary documents. See also Gertrude Bussey and Margaret Tims, *WILPF, 1915–1965*.

323 **"American Women: Listen":** Lida Gustava Heymann, "From Europe to Women in America," WILPF Archive.

323 **Some objected to:** *My Day*, 16 August 1940. On Burke-Wadsworth, see Smith, *FDR*, 464–66.

323 **"conscientious objectors should":** *My Day*, 7 August 1940.

324 **"No one hearing him":** *My Day*, 6 September 1940.

324 **"may prove to be wrong":** *My Day*, 7 August 1940.

324 **"business and government":** *My Day*, 31 July 1940.

324 **"it is one thing":** *My Day*, 6 August 1940.

324 **"national defense is a matter":** *My Day*, 28 August 1940.

324 **and "morale" as:** Lash, *Friend's Memoir*, 154–56.

325 **"youth occupation trips"**: *My Day,* 12 August 1940. See also *My Day,* 2 August 1940.

325 **"I have yet to see anywhere"**: *My Day,* 28 August 1940. See also *My Day,* 20 August 1940.

325 **Children's Crusade for:** *My Day,* 31 August 1940.

325 **"Everyone who believes"**: *My Day,* 30 August 1940. See also Smith, *FDR,* 466.

325 **"a particularly happy time"**: Diana R. Jaicks and Janet R. Katten remembered their time with Aunt Eleanor as entirely enchanting, to author.

326 **"We could hardly be blamed"**: *My Day,* 10 August 1940.

326 **"When bombing begins"**: Nicolson, *Diaries and Letters,* 3 and 12 July 1940, 98–101.

327 **"the nation has changed"**: *My Day,* 3 September 1940.

327 **"There were too many"**: *My Day,* 2 September 1940.

328 **"every non-citizen"**: Alien Registration Act, Public Law 76-680.

329 **"Why, they are"**: "Three Making Negro Film Held as Fifth Columnists," *New York Herald Tribune,* 18 June 1940.

329 **"At a time when"**: Jane Sommerich to ER, 18 June 1940, with *Herald Tribune* clip. See also Tommy to Sommerich, 24 June 1940; Schrecker, *Many Are the Crimes,* 92–98.

329 **"It is estimated"**: Marcantonio, *I Vote My Conscience,* 129–30. See also *Congressional Record,* 9 February 1940, 1345–46, and broadcast on 30 July, opposing Smith Act. I am grateful to Annette Rubinstein for these sources and many suggestions over time.

330 **"Several people have"**: *My Day,* 22 August 1940.

331 **"If eight million"**: Gilbert, *Second World War,* 125.

331 **"mixed up together"**: Gilbert, *Finest Hour,* 671 and 832. The president made this extraordinary swap on his own authority as commander in chief, bypassing Congress since opposition there was so great. See Smith, *FDR,* 470–72.

331 **"It is hard even"**: *My Day,* 24 July 1940.

332 **"Our course is clear"**: Gilbert, *Second World War,* 131.

333 **"know it is not"**: ER and Walter White's speeches to 16 September 1940 banquet are in *Proceedings of the First Biennial Convention of the Ladies' Auxiliary,* 40–45. I am grateful to Mindy Chateauvert for this document. On Harriet Pickens, Lash, *Friend's Memoir,* 61, 122–24; Bill Pickens on his aunt's Smith College honors, to BWC; ER and Bethune at Pullman confab, *Chicago Defender,* 28 September 1940.

335 **"Here in our own country"**: Ibid.

337 **"forced him to reveal"**: Sullivan, *Lift Every Voice,* 237–42.

337 **"If Elbert Williams"**: *Pittsburgh Courier,* 10 August 1940.

338 **"mum as the Sphinx"**: "Willkie Promises Everything," *Chicago Defender,* 21 September 1940.

338 **if there were more Nazis:** *Baltimore Afro-American,* 17 February 1940.

338 **"there is a growing"**: ER to FDR, 16 September 1940 in Buckley, *American Patriots,* 263.

338 **"an ally of the NAACP"**: Ibid., 292.

339 **"This is for"**: White to ER, 17 September 1940; ER to FDR, 21 September 1940; ER serves 100, box 1584.

340 **"The policy of the War"**: FDR, press release, 9 October 1940.

340 **"been proven satisfactory"**: White, Randolph, and Hill to FDR, 10 October 1940.

341 **"it is the policy of the"**: "White House Blesses Jim Crow," *Crisis*, November 1940, 350–57.

342 **"one could not have"**: Lash Diary, 11 August 1940, Lash Papers.

342 **"statement on Negroes"**: Harriet Pickens, 20 October 1940, *Baltimore African-American*; White to ER, 4, 7, and 12 October 1940. ER sent all to FDR. FDR to ER with Steve Early's apology, 29 October 1940.

342 **"I regret that"**: General Davis, 375; FDR to White, Randolph, and Hill, 25 October 1940, in *Crisis*, November 1940, 350–57; Buckley, *American Patriots*, 63–65.

343 **were "mainly Republicans"**: Lash, *Love, Eleanor,* 316. See also Lash, *Eleanor and Franklin*, 531.

343 **"Friday afternoon, at"**: *My Day*, 28 October 1940.

343 **"constantly around headquarters"**: Lash Diary, end of August–early September 1940, Lash Papers.

344 **the "indefatigable women"**: *Democratic Digest,* January 1941, 18, 21.

344 **"someday we will reach"**: *My Day,* 16 October 1940.

344 **"will be intelligently"**: FDR, press release on Selective Service Act, 16 September 1940, Grace Tully Papers.

345 **"on her old friends"**: *Time*, 30 September 1940.

345 **she was "unruffled"**: "Eleanor Buttons," *New York Times,* 26 October 1940. See also *My Day*, 21 and 22 October 1940.

345 **"he will not discuss"**: Willkie, speech, 16 October 1940, Neal, *Dark Horse*, 154–60.

345 **"The people have a right"**: Lash, *Roosevelt and Churchill*, 236. See also Neal, ibid.

346 **"loved a good fight"**: FDR, speech in Philadelphia, 23 October 1940; *My Day*, 24 and 25 October 1940.

346 **"I hope that everyone"**: *My Day*, 25 October 1940.

346 **"Martin, Barton and Fish!"**: FDR, "Campaign Address at Madison Square Garden, New York," 28 October 1940, in Zevin, *Nothing to Fear*, 233–42.

346 **"It seemed to us"**: *My Day*, 30 October 1940. See also Smith, *FDR*, 476.

347 **"If anybody thinks"**: Buckley, *American Patriots,* 265. See also Lash, *Eleanor and Franklin*, 531–32.

347 **"I have said this"**: FDR, in Boston, 30 October 1940.

347 **"The President really"**: Kathleen Kennedy to Joseph Kennedy, 30 October 1940, in Smith, *Hostage to Fortune*, 489.

347 **"put 25 million"**: Joseph Kennedy to Clare Boothe Luce. Luce asked what changed Joe's mind, *Life* noted, which had saved FDR's election. He told her FDR promised to support Joe Jr. for governor. See Neal, *Dark Horse*, 169.

347 **was "very gracious"**: Joseph Kennedy Diary, 27 October 1940, in Smith, *Hostage to Fortune*, 481.

348 **"It is true":** Joseph Kennedy, radio address, 29 October 1940, ibid., 482–89.

348 **"We have all":** FDR to Joseph Kennedy, 29 October 1940, ibid., 489.

348 **she wondered what:** *My Day,* 1 November 1940.

348 **"Today no one":** *My Day,* 2 November 1940.

349 **Irita Van Doren:** Neal, *Dark Horse,* 37–44.

349 **These "guru letters":** Schapsmeier and Schapsmeier, *Wallace of Iowa,* 273–75. See also Ruth Drayer. *Nicholas and Helena Roerich.*

349 **"Both sides agreed":** Neal, *Dark Horse,* 144–45.

349 **"soothsayers" that no:** Lash, *Love, Eleanor,* 308.

349 **"Let us show":** *Democratic Digest,* January 1914.

349 **"It is the destiny":** FDR, Campaign Address at Cleveland, Ohio, 2 November 1940, in *FDR, The American Way,* 16–18, 24. See also www.presidency.ucsb .edu/ws/?pid=15893. He closed by saying, "Always the heart and soul of our country will be the heart and soul of the common man—the men and women who never have ceased to believe in democracy."

350 **speech "was grand":** ER to Anna, 3 November 1940, Asbell, 127; *My Day,* 4 November 1940.

350 **"We in this nation":** FDR, Cleveland speech. See also Smith, *FDR,* 478–79.

350 **"I would be grateful":** Walter White to ER, 4 November 1940; White, *Man Called White,* 198–99.

351 **seemed "particularly bright":** *My Day,* 5 and 6 November 1940.

351 **"comical silver donkey":** *New York Times,* 6 November 1940.

351 **"confident of victory":** Lash, *Friend's Memoir,* 187.

352 **"We are facing":** Ibid., 192–94; ER to Anna, 15 November 1940, Asbell, 127. See also *My Day,* 7 November 1940.

Chapter Fifteen: **"Heroism Is Always a Thrilling Thing":** The Politics of Race

353 **"one of the clearest":** Charles Poore's "Books of the Times," *New York Times,* 2 November 1940; ER to Anna, 3 November 1940.

354 **reading the "interesting":** *My Day,* 23 October 1940.

354 **"She walks as":** Black, *ER: Biography.*

354 **"the President stopped":** Ruby Black to ER, 1 November 1940.

354 **"I felt you had done":** ER to RB, 13 November 1940.

355 **"1. Her personality":** Ruby Black, "Can Eleanor Roosevelt Stop Wendell Willkie," *Look,* 8 October 1940. I am grateful to Black's daughter Cornelia Jane Strawser for this article and for many insights over the years, esp. "ER, Ruby Black and Me," to author, 8 August 1999. See also Anne Cottrell Free, "Ruby Black," *ER Encyclopedia,* 62–66.

356 **"Anybody will tell":** Ruby Black, "How and Why ER Does It," *Democratic Digest,* October–November 1940, 16, 51.

357 **ever-expanding Black Cabinet:** This group of Washington insiders and New Deal officials changed over time. It initially included Robert Vann (attorney, editor, and publisher of the *Pittsburgh Courier,* and special assistant to the attorney general, who supported Willkie but died shortly before the election),

Judge William Hastie, Dr. Robert Weaver (housing administrator and the first black Harvard PhD in economics), Lawrence Oxley (social worker who became chief of Division of Negro Labor), and Dr. Frank Horne (physician and college president, Lena Horne's uncle, who worked for several New Deal agencies, most notably the Federal Housing Administration).

357 **"they appeared so often"**: Peare, *Bethune*, 165.

358 **"always went running"**: West, *Upstairs*, 31–32.

358 **"Together, as war needs"**: In the coming years Bethune, with the support and assistance of ER, would expand Bethune-Cookman College. In 1941 she opened a new library, and in 1942 she added a Trades Building for National Defense, financed by NYA with new programs in mechanics, masonry, electricity, and engineering. Also in 1942 Bethune-Cookman became a four-year senior college. Eventually it would have 32 buildings on 52 acres to serve scores of thousands of U.S. and international students with 25 major degree programs for women and men, in teaching, nursing, business, engineering, and law, among others. See Gerda Lerner, ed., *Black Women in America*, on Mary McLeod Bethune, Bethune-Cookman College, and National Council of Negro Women. I am grateful to Harry Gurney for the current works of Bethune-Cookman College.

358 **"I'm willing to spend"**: "Kennedy Says Democracy All Done in Britain, Maybe Here," *Boston Globe*, 9 November 1940. For Kennedy's 6 November interview with FDR, see Amanda Smith, ed., 491–92. Asked specifically about ER, Kennedy called her a "wonderful woman. And marvelously helpful and full of sympathy." In Washington and London she was always after him "to take care of the poor little nobodies who hadn't any influence. . . . She's always sending me a note to have some little Susie Glotz to tea at the embassy."

359 **"threw the fear of God"**: Beschloss, *Kennedy and Roosevelt*, 226. Douglas Fairbanks to FDR, in Will Swift, *The Roosevelts and the Royals*, 227; Frankfurter to FDR on Kennedy's words, 11 November 1940, in Max Freedman, *Roosevelt and Frankfurter*, 559–60. See also Smith, *FDR*, 491–92.

359 **"bidding to ask"**: MacAdams, *Ben Hecht*, 225.

359 **"we thought were"**: John Boettiger to FDR, in Beschloss, *Kennedy and Roosevelt*, 228.

359 **"is out to do"**: Beschloss, *Kennedy and Roosevelt*, 229, 302. FDR and Kennedy met again at the White House on 1 December, when the ambassador's resignation was officially and cordially accepted and then announced. Over the years, reports of a bitter break, misremembered by ER as reported by Gore Vidal, have been repeated in many books. Until a new ambassador could be appointed, FDR dispatched his two trusted emissaries, Wendell Willkie and Harry Hopkins, to London. By February, at Esther Lape's suggestion, John Gilbert Winant was named the new ambassador. See Smith, *Hostage to Fortune*, 495–97.

359 **"there was not a sign"**: Ickes, *Secret Diary*, December 1940, 3:386–87.

359 **"has always been"**: ER to Alice Huntington, 12 December 1940, ER box 1555/100.

360 **"we have been on this"**: Tommy to Anna, 18 November 1940.

360 **"She fought with everyone"**: Tommy to Anna, 18 November 1940.

361 **the largest turnout by women**: In some states women voters had "actually outnumbered the men": Illinois, 56 percent; California, 54 percent; Montana, 53 percent; Missouri, 51 percent. ER's team was particularly satisfied that in New York City over 300,000 more women voted than in 1936. *Democratic Digest*, December 1940–January 1941.

361 **"just the way the president"**: ER to FDR, 11 November 1940.

361 **"make a magnificent job"**: Molly Dewson to ER, 10 November 1940; ER to Dewson, 15 November 1940.

361 **"with unusual and wide"**: "Lorena Hickok, Executive Secretary; Gladys Tillett, The Future Program for Democratic Women," *Democratic Digest*, January 1941, 5, 9.

362 **"Party politics had always"**: ER, "Women Must Learn to Play the Game As Men Do," *Redbook*, 1928. See also Dewson to Hick, 14 January 1941.

362 **to "gently urge"**: Tommy to Anna, 18 November 1940.

362 **"My trouble, I suspect"**: Hick to ER, 7 November 1940; ER to Hick, 8 November 1940; Hick to ER, 11 November 1940.

362 **"You are wrong"**: Lash, *Love, Eleanor,* 278.

363 **Earl continued regularly:** Lash Diary, 4 August 1940, Lash Papers.

363 **"Now we've stopped"**: ER to FDR, 12 November 1940; FDR to ER, 13 November 1940, with Sumner Welles's memo to FDR, 1 November 1940, in answer to ER's "request for facts on the subject of scrap iron exports to Japan . . . and Sino-Japanese trade." See also *FDR: Personal Letters*, 4:1077.

364 **Maternally she sought:** Lash Diary, 2, 17, and 28 March 1940, Lash Papers.

364 **"two of the pleasantest"**: *My Day*, 14 November 1940. See also ER to Florence Kerr, 16 December 1940; Kerr to ER, 20 December 1940. Kerr sent the information to George Foster, national director of the WPA music program about Florence Rush's new symphony, "rendered beautifully" by his splendid orchestra, to make final arrangements with Tommy.

364 **"You will do"**: ER to Lash, in Lash, *Love, Eleanor,* 321–22.

365 **"Heroism is always"**: *My Day*, 16 November 1940. See also *My Day*, 18 and 20 November 1940.

365 **"The family is so scattered"**: *My Day*, 22 November 1940.

365 **"Today as a nation"**: *My Day*, 21 November 1940.

365 **"We are free to register"**: Ibid.

366 **On Saturday ER:** *My Day,* 26 and 27 November 1940; Lash, *Love, Eleanor,* 322.

366 **"compelling" because the:** *My Day*, 26 November 1940. See also *My Day*, 23 and 25 November 1940.

366 **"little bronze boy"**: Lash, *Love, Eleanor,* 327.

366 **"the first birthday letter"**: ER to Lash, 2 December 1940, in Lash, *Love, Eleanor,* 323.

367 **"a wonderful birthday week"**: Ibid., 323–24; Lash Diary, 8 December 1940, Lash Papers.

367 **"Ever since our talk"**: ER to Trude Pratt, n.d., in Lash, *Love, Eleanor,* 66.

367 **"sense of being driven"**: Ibid.; Lash Diary, 4 January 1941, Lash Papers.

368 **"Of course I knew"**: Trude Pratt to author, 15 July 2000.

Chapter Sixteen: **"Isolationism Is Impossible": The Politics of Rescue**

369 **"immediately endangered political"**: Varian Fry's Papers are at the Rare Book and Manuscript Library at Columbia University; see esp. Karen Greenberg, ed., *Archives of the Holocaust*, vol. 5, Columbia University Library, selected documents from the Varian Fry Papers and the Fort Critario Emergency Refugee Shelter Papers.

369 **"Is there no way"**: ER to Sumner Welles, 6 September 1940. See also correspondence from Karl Frank to ER, 15, 21, and 30 August 1940, box 1551.

369 **"is holding up"**: Frank Kingdon to ER, 20 September 1940.

370 **"disloyal to the Reich"**: In 1934, ER read Lion Feuchtwanger's prophetic book about the Nazi regime *The Oppermanns*, published in English by Ben Huebsch of Viking, and in ten other languages. Written to stir concerned people beyond indifference and passivity to the most intense Nazi cruelties faced by Jews and anti-Hitler democrats, it was a highly regarded best-seller—which failed nevertheless to diminish the appeasement policies that insured Hitler's unimpeded march across Europe for six years.

371 **They had left Marseilles**: Alma Mahler described their journey in *And the Bridge Is Love*; see Keegan, *Bride of the Wind*, 279–80. See also Peter Jungk, *Franz Werfel*, 154–64, 170–73; Marino, *Quiet American*, 68–76.

372 *The Blue Angel*: Steven Bach, *Marlene Dietrich*, 6–7, 106–21.

372 **But Heinrich Mann**: Retirement folder, Peter Pratt Papers.

372 **"pioneers" at Sosúa**: Marian Kaplan, *Dominican Haven*, 49–54. See "On Arrivals," *New York Tribune*, 14 October 1940, "Writers Fleeing Nazis Here by 'Under ground,'" in Werfel, "Heinrich Mann, Golo Mann, among 15 Who Escaped France"; *New York Times*, 14 October 1940, "Authors Who Fled Nazis Arrive."

374 **"get this cleared up"**: ER to FDR, 28 September 1940, in Breitman and Kraut, *American Refugee Policy*, 129–33.

374 **"At a stroke"**: Marc Bloch, *Strange Defeat*. See Carole Fink, *Marc Bloch: A Life in History*. See also Carmen Callil, *Bad Faith*.

375 **"The war is won!"** Gilbert, *Second World War*, 130–34; and Gilbert, *Finest Hour: 1939–1941*, 888.

375 **"The world Cause"**: Churchill cable to FDR, 27 October 1940.

375 **"Suppose my neighbor's"**: FDR, Press Conference on Lend-Lease, 17 December 1940, in Rauch, *FDR: Selected Speeches*, 268–71.

375 **"The Nazi masters"**: FDR, "Fireside Chat on National Security" ("Arsenal of Democracy" speech), 29 December 1940, in Zevin, *Nothing to Fear*, 247–58.

376 **Some of his staff**: FDR told speechwriter Sam Rosenman to ignore the State Department's request to remove the line. Smith, *FDR*, 487.

377 **"a running argument"**: Lash, *Eleanor and Franklin*, 636–37, 747. See also ER to FDR, 7 November 1940, and ER to Welles, 11 December 1940.

377 **"As a human"**: Hans Lustig's lament to Kingdon, 13 September 1940, Kingdon to ER, 4 October 1940, 102/box 1808.

378 **"MGM may itself"**: Long to ER, 11 October 1940.

378 **"Mrs. R is sorry"**: Tommy to Kingdon, 22 October 1940, 102/box 1808.

378 **"I am just reading"**: Charlotte Lustig to ER, 1 September, 54/box 4157.

379 **"Can't something be"**: ER to FDR, December 1940.

379 **"Is there anything"**: ER to Sumner Welles.

380 **"everything in its"**: *New York Times*, 10 December 1940. See also Ickes, *Secret Diary*, 13 December 1940, 3:389–90.

381 **"There are 12,000"**: Breckinridge Long Diary, 13 November–12 December 1940, 151–61.

381 **"working at cross"**: Ibid., 27 November, 1940.

381 **"rather slapped my ears"**: Ickes, 21 December, *Secret Diary*.

381 **"Varian Fry's arrest"**: ER to Welles, 9 December 1940, FDRL.

381 **"no physical harm"**: Welles to ER, 11 December 1940, FDRL. On 10 December Fry wrote to Frank Kingdon detailing the appalling circumstances of his arrest in a surprise raid on their rented commune, Villa Air-Bel. Detectives had arrived without a search warrant, confiscated their papers and typewriters, accused them of nothing, and transported them to the SS *Sinaia*. They were held from Monday night until Thursday noon, then released as they had been arrested, with no word of explanation. Kingdon shared the letter with ER. Fry, *Surrender on Demand*, 130–31, 146–49.

382 **"Franklin, you know"**: Justine Wise Polier, oral history, 19, 20, FDRL. Around this time Judge Polier's father, Rabbi Stephen Wise, had learned that "affidavits he had sent to get people out were being held up by the U.S. Consul in Marseilles." When Rabbi Wise confronted the consul—"I understand you are not honoring my affidavits"—the consul replied: "Rabbi Wise, nobody could honor as many affidavits as you have given." According to Polier, her father insisted the consul call FDR "to find out whether you are to honor my word or not." The consul yielded, and that group "was cleared for admission to the United States and saved."

382 **never referred to her:** Years later, on 17 May 1960, Marta Feuchtwanger (wife of Lion, who died in 1958) wrote to ER that Hiram Bingham had told her husband that "you [ER] were instrumental in his visa at a moment of ultimate danger." ER replied, "It was really my husband. . . . I could have done nothing except when he asked me to do it and I had his backing." Lash, *Eleanor and Franklin*, 637.

383 **"a kind of world"**: FDR, "Four Freedoms" Speech, Annual Message to Congress, 6 January 1941, in Zevin, *Nothing to Fear*, 258–66.

383 **"saddened to notice"**: *My Day*, 7 January 1941.

383 **from Thomas Mann:** *My Day*, 14 January 1941. See also Klaus Mann, *The Turning Point*, 322ff, and chapters 14 and 15.

383 **"The Thomas Manns"**: ER to Lash, January 1941.

384 **was "the busiest"**: Fry, *Surrender on Demand*, 186–88.

384 **"important enough and"**: Ernst, *Not So Still Life*, 199; Rosemary Sullivan, *Villa Air-Bel*, 339–42.

384 **"Eleanor right about"**: Jimmy and Dallas Ernst to BWC, 1940–46, 1966 affidavits.

385 **"It was wonderful"**: *My Day,* 14 January 1941.

385 **"be sensitive to"**: Lash Diary, 16 January 1941, Lash Papers.

385 **"The Mrs. came into"**: Ickes, *Secret Diary,* 3:396–97. See also Lash, *Friend's Memoir,* 213–14.

386 **"is defense housing"**: "Housing Lag Seen Slowing Defense," *New York Times,* 26 January 1941.

387 **"the Number 1"**: *Time,* 3 February 1941, 59.

387 **"never went home"**: West, *Upstairs,* 19–24.

387 **first lady's "closest confidante"**: Ibid.

388 **"Crown Princess Martha"**: Ibid.

388 **"In contrast to"**: Ibid.

388 **"It is wonderful"**: ER to Lash, 6 January 1941 Lash, *Love, Eleanor,* 336.

389 **"did not like"**: Tommy to Lape, March 1941, Arizona Collection.

389 **"I am sorry"**: ER to Eileen Fry, 13 May 1941, 100/box 1607.

389 **"suicides will increase"**: Frank Kingdon to ER, 2 July 1941.

390 **Winant was an:** Olson, *Citizens of London,* 23–24.

390 **"had been thrown"**: Lady Florence Willert to ER; Lash Diary, 5 January 1941, Lash Papers.

390 **closest school chum:** Bennett to ER, 1 Janaury 1941, 100/box 1625. See also ER to Bennett, 25 February 1941.

390 **"Suddenly he opened one eye"**: Lash, *Friend's Memoir,* 208; Lash Diary, 27 February 1941, Lash Papers.

391 **nineteenth-century plantation:** Roegner, *Minnie of Hobcaw.*

391 **"her beautiful horses"**: See also *My Day,* 26 March 1941.

391 **Belle "liked Eleanor"**: Mary Miller, *Baroness of Hobcaw,* 115.

391 **associates urged decisive action:** Olson, *Citizens of London,* 86–90, 116.

391 **"snatch at beauty"**: Lash, *Love, Eleanor,* 338–39.

391 **her "empty heart"**: Lash Diary, 30 March 1941, Lash Papers.

392 **"mood of lonely despair"**: ER to Lash.

392 **"Time with you"**: Lash Diary, April 1941.

392 **with "great applause"**: Ibid., 20 April 1940, Lash Papers; Lash, *Friend's Memoir,* 214–15.

393 **a "social fascist"**: Joe Cadden to ER, 5 and 6 May 1941.

393 **"immediately to range"**: Loewenheim, Langley, and Jonas, *Roosevelt and Churchill Correspondence,* 83 and passim.

393 **"naval and military"**: FDR, "Fireside Chat Outlining American Policy in the World Crisis," 27 May 1941, in Zevin, *Nothing to Fear,* 271–83. See also Sherwood, *Roosevelt and Hopkins,* 293–300. See also *FDR: Personal Letters,* 4: 1154–55.

394 **"None of us saw him"**: Lash, Diary, 4 June 1941, Lash Papers.

394 **Missy LeHand believed:** Cook, *ER,* 1:314–17.

394 **"be surprised at"**: ER on Missy to Lash, Lash Diary, 20 March 1941, 20 April 1941, Lash Papers.

394 **"assigning students"**: Lash, *Friend's Memoir,* 236–54.

395 **"did most to fire"**: Ibid., 251.

395 **"*very* quiet life"**: FDR to SDR, 2 August 1941, in *FDR: Personal Letters,* 4:1196–97.

396 **"Early in August":** *TIR,* 224.

396 **when Franklin Jr.:** *TIR,* 225–26.

396 **the Atlantic Charter:** Loewenheim, Langley, and Jonas, *Roosevelt and Churchill Correspondence,* 152–55; Brands, *Traitor,* 597, 603–11.

396 **"reaffirmed faith in":** Plesch, *America, Hitler and the UN,* 24–27. The Atlantic Charter defined Allied goals for the postwar world. By this charter, Roosevelt and Churchill agreed: (1) to seek "no aggrandizement territorial or other"; (2) to seek "no territorial changes that do not accord with the freely expressed wishes of the people concerned"; (3) to "respect the right of all peoples to choose [their own] form of government . . . ; and wish to see sovereign rights and self-government restored" wherever it has been forcibly denied; (4) to "endeavor" to create a system of equal access to all states "to the trade and raw materials of the world" needed for economic prosperity [a caveat that exempted "existing obligations" suggested historical and imperial limitations]; (5) to seek "to bring about the fullest collaboration between all nations" and to secure "for all, improved labor standards, economic advancement and social security"; (6) after "the final destruction of the Nazi tyranny," to seek a peace for all nations and that provides all inhabitants therein with "freedom from fear and want"; (7) to seek a peace that would "enable all" to travel everywhere "without hindrance"; and (8) to strive for "all nations of the world, for realistic as well as spiritual reasons," to abandon "the use of force," since pending a "permanent system of general security . . . disarmament . . . is essential."

397 **"honestly faced my":** Lash, *Love, Eleanor,* 352–53.

397 **"An anxious 24":** *My Day,* 7 September 1941.

399 **"I see. So you":** When ER II told me that story, she said, "If you join the growing group that argues SDR was historically mistreated, I will never speak to you again."

399 **"My idea of hell":** ER to Lash, 25 September 1941.

399 **"It's such an":** ER to Anna, 17 September 1941.

400 **"Pale, but stately":** "G. Hall Roosevelt Dies," *New York Times,* 26 September 1941. "Rites," 27 September 1941; "Burial," 28 September 1941.

401 **She intended to build:** John Winant, Esther Lape, and others in ER's circle often discussed the various roles women played in Britain. Eugene Meyer, publisher of the *Washington Post,* had recently visited London and seen that women were "really a part of the armed forces with rank and recognition." He returned home filled with admiration for women volunteers. He met with ER and encouraged her to help build something similar. Ickes, *Secret Diary,* 25 October 1941, 3:634. Meyer thought La Guardia as OCD director was "a joke."

402 **"The loss of someone":** *TIR,* 230.

402 **"I will carry on here":** Tommy to Anna, 2 October 1941.

402 **"One morning my":** *TIR,* 231.

402 **"Her friends and family":** Lash, *Friend's Memoir,* 259–60.

403 **"I feel as you":** Lash, *Love, Eleanor,* 361.

403 **"for the honor":** Ickes, *Secret Diary,* 3:654–55; 7 December 1941, 3:661–66. See also Gilbert, *Second World War,* 262–64, 268–73.

403 **"when one of the ushers":** *TIR,* 232–35.

404 **"Yesterday, 7 December"**: FDR, "War Message to Congress," 8 December 1941, in Zevin, *Nothing to Fear*, 301-3. See also *TIR*, 232–35. FDR's speech was accepted without "a peep from an appeaser or an isolationist anywhere." Ickes, *Secret Diary*, 3:665.

Chapter Seventeen: "To Know Me Is a Terrible Thing": Friendship, Loyalties, and Alliances

405 **"a curious sense"**: *My Day*, 9 December 1941.

405 **"trend of thought"**: *My Day*, 16 December 1941.

405 **"The crops were ready"**: Tommy to Lape, 16 December 1941.

406 **"The greatest test"**: *My Day*, 16 December 1941.

406 **"if we are going to keep"**: *My Day*, 27 and 28 November 1941.

406 **"I hope every person"**: *My Day*, 3 December 1941.

406 **"an amazing letter"**: Tommy to Lape, 16 December 1941; see also Greg Robinson, *By Order*, 75.

406 **"more basic than"**: Pearl Buck to ER, 18 December 1941, in Lash, *Eleanor and Franklin*, 669. See also ER's draft of review for Pearl Buck's "American Unity and Asia," *New Republic*, 3 August 1942. I am grateful to Greg Robinson for this reference.

407 **"ER said she"**: Tommy to Lape, 16 December 1941.

407 **"comprehensive community"**: *My Day*, 27 November 1941.

407 **"health is a stepping stone"**: *My Day*, 6 December 1941.

407 **"in the operating policy"**: ER to National Council of Negro Women, press clip 20 October 1941 in NAACP Papers, Library of Congress.

408 **"maternal, child health"**: *TIR*, 235–40.

408 **"inspiring"** . . . **"her passionate integrity"**: Lash, *Eleanor and Franklin*, 646.

408 **"had a strictly"**: *My Day*, 20 December 1941.

408 **"Her voice did not"**: Lash Diary, 26 December 1941, Lash Papers.

409 **"the favorite of most"**: West, *Upstairs*, 38–40.

409 **His "most colorful"**: Ibid.

409 **disregard for public opinion**: Parks, *Family in Turmoil*, 98–100; Smith, *FDR*, 543–44.

409 **"the best Christmas"**: Coit, *Baruch*, 491–94.

410 **"I don't trust"**: ER to Anna, 23 December 1941 and 4 January 1942, Asbell, 140–41.

410 **"talked much with"**: ER to Hick, 26 December 1941, quoted in Gilbert, *Churchill and America*, 249–50.

410 **"loveable and emotional"**: ER to Anna, 23 December 1941; 4 January 1942, 140–41, Asbell. According to John Lukacs, ER "had gone so far as to ask a friend to impress that upon her husband." Lukacs, *Five Days in London*, 72.

410 **"The United Nations"**: *My Day*, 2 January 1942.

410 **"I did not open"**: Lash Diary, 1 January 1942, Lash Papers.

411 **of "other authorities"**: The Big Four were the United States, Britain, USSR, and China. They would have twenty-two allies: Australia, Belgium, Canada, Costa Rica, Cuba, Czechoslovakia, Dominican Republic, El Salvador, Greece,

Guatemala, Haiti, Honduras, India, Luxembourg, Netherlands, New Zealand, Nicaragua, Norway, Panama, Poland, South Africa, and Yugoslavia.

411 **"gotten as far"**: Lash, *Roosevelt and Churchill*, 16–20.

411 **"was upstairs pacing"**: Lash, *Roosevelt and Churchill*, 19. On the negotiations over Christmas week, see Sherwood, *Roosevelt and Hopkins*, 444–69, Plesch, *America, Hitler and the UN*, 31–38, and James MacGregor Burns, *Roosevelt: Soldier of Freedom*, 483–89.

412 **"Here, where the"**: Lash, *Roosevelt and Churchill*, 18n.

412 **"Four fifths of the human"**: Ibid., 20.

412 **"prelude to a"**: Sherwood, *Roosevelt and Hopkins*.

412 **"group activities, especially"**: *My Day*, 25 and 29 December 1941.

413 enjoy **"physical exercise"**: See also Mayris Chaney memoir (unpublished ms.), 57–58; 93–99.

413 **"largely in the mountain"**: *My Day*, 12 January 1942.

413 **"most moving and"**: *My Day*, 13 January 1942.

413 **"information and propaganda"**: Douglas, *Autobiography*, 116–23.

414 **"To know me"**: Lash, *Eleanor and Franklin*, 651.

414 **"ferried planes to"**: *My Day*, 27 and 28 January 1942.

414 **"freedom for every"**: *My Day*, 4 February 1942.

415 **"not quite moral"**: *My Day*, 13 February 1942.

415 **"I do not think"**: *TIR*, 249–50.

415 **"Eat it up"**: *My Day*, 21 February 1942.

415 **"I am not"**: Lash, *Eleanor and Franklin*, 651.

416 **"it was a Declaration"**: Ibid.

416 **"small and very vocal"**: ER broadcast, 22 February 1942. Tiny was also grateful to Eddie Cantor, who organized a group of performer friends in her defense, and for two significant columns: Sam Grafton, "I'd Rather Be Right," *New York Post*, 11 February 1942; and John D. Barry, "Ways of the World," 26 February 1942.

416 **"more recognition" to**: *Daily Mirror*, 21 February 1942.

416 **hero Doris "Dorie" Miller**: See Marcantonio, *I Vote*, 155–56. Miller had started out as the ship's cook, had not been trained as a machine gunner. "I just pulled the trigger, and she worked fine," he explained. In May 1942 he received the Navy Cross "for courage under fire." On 24 November 1943 he died when his ship was torpedoed in the South Pacific.

417 **"no law-abiding aliens"**: ER, broadcast, 4 December 1941.

417 **to "do something"**: In 1940 Churchill had detained 74,000 "enemy aliens." Britain subsequently released them since most were Jewish refugees from Germany and Austria, as well as antifascist allies, grateful and entirely loyal to Britain.

417 **The author Louis Adamic**: ER was subsequently shocked by Louis Adamic's distortions in his 1946 book *Dinner at the White House*, which misrepresented her convictions and denounced Winston Churchill so vigorously, he "hotly resented it," sued for libel—and won. *TIR*, 245. See esp. Robinson, *By Order*, 93–94 passim; and Kennedy, *Freedom from Fear*, 749–60.

418 **"photographed and examined"**: *My Day*, 15 January 1942.

418 **"to avoid mass internment"**: Biddle, *In Brief Authority*, 207–11. ER agreed with Biddle's determination.

418 **by EO 9066**: Burns, *Soldier of Freedom*, 209 and map; Smith, *FDR*, 494.

418 **"I see absolutely no"**: Milton Eisenhower, *President Is Calling*, 99–127, esp. 100.

419 **"virtually all permanent"**: Robinson, *By Order*, 108.

419 **"thousands of small"**: Eisenhower, *President Is Calling*, 99.

419 **"behind barbed wire"**: Morgenthau quoted ibid., 99.

419 **"brooded about this"**: Ibid., 125.

419 **"for mass internments"**: Ibid., 99, 125–26.

420 **"prisoners of war"**: *My Day*, 19 February 1942.

420 **as "smoothly, quickly"**: Eisenhower, *President Is Calling*, 95–125.

420 **"I'm afraid no one"**: ER to Elinor Morgenthau, 24 March 1942.

420 **"These are days"**: *My Day*, 21 March 1942.

421 **"secure fair prices"**: Morgenthau's conversation with FDR, 5 March 1942, in Smith, *FDR*, 552. See also Robinson, *By Order*, 75, 134–45, 176, 249.

421 **$400 million in:** After the war, Congress paid $37 million in reparations and in 1980 Ronald Reagan allocated an additional $20,000 for each surviving refugee.

421 **"You know I am"**: Memorandum of conversation, 15 May 1942, Morgenthau Papers, quoted in Gellman, *Secret Affairs*, 293. See also Blum, *Price of Vision*, 79–80.

422 **"It did your mother"**: Tommy to Anna, 1 April 1942, Anna Roosevelt Halsted Papers, box 75.

422 **"Many times I wanted"**: Lash Diary, March 1942, Lash Papers.

422 **everybody "chatted amiably"**: Ibid.

422 **"the linen and silver"**: ER to Anna, 27 April, 7 May, 19 May 1942.

422 **"very comfortable, there is"**: Tommy to Anna.

423 **"they don't make things"**: ER to Anna, 27 April, 7 May, 19 May 1942.

423 **"the summer with us"**: Tommy to Anna.

423 **"to please your mother"**: Tommy to Anna.

423 **"Elliott dropped from"**: ER to Anna, 27 April, 7 May, 19 May 1942.

423 **"I shall return"**: For the Pacific situation, and Douglas MacArthur's longtime friendship with Quezon, independence leader and first president of the Philippines, see Burns, *Soldier of Freedom*, 205–9.

423 **"Pa says Johnnie"**: ER to Anna, 27 April, 7 May, 19 May 1942.

424 **"people of the world"**: "Race, Religion and Prejudice" for the *New Republic*, 11 May 1942.

424 **"The pictures in"**: ER and Frances Cooke Macgregor, *This Is America*.

425 **"fleeing from oppression"**: Ibid. It is unclear how ER came to write this book or the origins of her friendship with Macgregor, a pioneering photographer who also published *Twentieth Century Indians*. See ER to Anna, 7 May 1942.

425 **"Freedom to live"**: ER, "What We Are Fighting For," *American Magazine* 134 (July 1942), 16-17, 60-62.

425 **"in its truest sense"**: Ibid.

425 **"Some have spoken"**: Henry Wallace, "The Price of Free World Victory," speech to the Free World Association, New York, 8 May 1942.

426 **"the Americanization of"**: Henry Luce, "The American Century," *Life*, February 17, 1941.

426 **"a voluntary registration"**: ER, press conference, 5 May 1942, in Beasley, *ER Press Conferences*.

427 **"This memo is"**: Wise to ER, 1 April 1942, and ER to Welles, in Welles, *FDR's Global Strategist*, 226–27. See also Feingold, *Politics of Rescue*, 170–73; and Gilbert, *Auschwitz and Allies*, 21–24, 32–36.

427 **"for fear of Arab"**: Welles to ER, in Welles, *FDR's Global Strategist*, 226–27.

428 **"not allowed to marry"**: ER, press conference, 5 and 14 May 1942, in Beasley, *ER Press Conferences*, 289–95.

428 **Oveta Culp Hobby:** Bill Hobby to author; Celia Morris and Sissy Farenthold to author.

428 **"I'm rather tired"**: ER to Anna, 19 May 1942.

428 **"If only the war"**: ER to Lape, 14 June 1942; *TIR*, 250–51; Sherwood, *Roosevelt and Hopkins*, 556–79.

428 **"There is a great"**: Tommy to Lape, 21 July 1942; see also letters from June and August 1942, esp. 24 August.

429 **"thought through what"**: *TIR*, 256–57.

429 **"I am very glad"**: ER, press conference, in Beasley, *ER Press Conferences*. See also "Hopkins Wedding," *New York Times*, 5 July 1942.

429 **"which meant she"**: *TIR*, 257.

429 **"best big party"**: Flanner, *Paris Was Yesterday*, 220–21.

430 **rigid "old dragons"**: Mosel and Macy, *Leading Lady*.

430 **"Harry Hopkins and"**: Anna to ER, 27 July 1942.

430 **"Vichy has agreed"**: Varian Fry to ER, 27 August 1942, with 25 August report, ER box 853. On 22 July 2012, French president François Hollande commemorated the seventieth anniversary of the 16–17 July 1942 Vélodrome d'Hiver roundup. See also Hollande, "The Crime Committed in France by France," *New York Review of Books*, 27 September 2012.

430 **"The U.S. Committee"**: ER to Norman Davis, 4 September 1942, box 1637.

430 **"I was very sorry"**: *My Day*, 5 September 1942.

431 **Vichy France denied them:** Marrus and Paxton, *Vichy France*, 261–70; Wyman, *Paper Walls*, 133–34. The State Department limited an effort to save 200 children who were already across the Pyrenees in Spain. Ultimately, 76,000 French Jews were deported to death camps; of them, only 2,500 returned.

431 **"Naturally we should"**: ER to FDR; FDR to ER.

431 **"I am firmly"**: ER speech, June 1942. Democracy in Action was supported by Wendell Willkie, Mary McLeod Bethune, Tallulah Bankhead, Herbert Agar, Lyman Beecher Stowe, Carl Van Doren, Daisy Harriman, and other notables, *New York Times*, 2 June 1942.

432 **"the propaganda campaign"**: Murray, *Song*.

432 **"tried to evade us"**: Ibid., 166–76.

432 **"in a voice that"**: Ibid.

432 **"four or five times"**: Harry Hopkins, memorandum, 1 July 1942.

433 **"the Government of the US"**: Murray's open letter to FDR (draft), 17 July 1942, Pauli Murray Papers. The letter was signed by A. Philip Randolph; Frank

Crosswaith, director the Negro Labor Committee and the New York Housing Authority; William Lloyd Imes, pastor of St. James Presbyterian Church in New York; Anna Arnold Hedgeman, Negro Women, Inc.; Layle Lane, vice-president of the American Federation of Teachers; Leon Ransom, acting dean of Howard University Law School; Pauli Murray, chair of the NAACP Student Conference; and Albert Hamilton of the Workers Defense League.

433 **"If Japanese-Americans"**: Murray to FDR.

434 **"I wonder if it"**: ER to Murray, 3 August 1942.

435 **"Today what concerns"**: *My Day*, 3 April 1942. In this column ER also cited Earl Brown's article "American Negroes in the War."

435 **"danced around"**: Lash Diary, 1 January 1942, Lash Papers.

435 **"One cannot help"**: *My Day*, 13 April 1942.

435 **"You are right"**: FDR to Ickes, 12 August 1942, Library of Congress. See William L. Neumann, "Roosevelt's Options and Evasions in Foreign Policy, 1940–1945," in Liggio and Martin, *Watershed of Empire*, 162–82; Fischer, *Life of Gandhi*, 360–65, 384ff; Gaddis Smith, 90; and Bhagavan, *Peacemakers*.

436 **"met us at the door"**: Murray, *Song*, 190–95.

436 **an ISS conference**: Ibid., and *New York Times*, 2 August 1942, to announce the ISS World Council, 2–5 September 1942.

437 **"Fairness gives you"**: For the Tuskegee Airmen in combat from 1943 to 1945, I am grateful to Dr. Roscoe Brown and Percy Heath for their memories, and to Dr. Brown for the Tuskegee Airmen history. See *Redtails*, the book and the film; and Henry Louis Gates, "3 Women 'Red Tails' Left Out," *Root*, posted 25 January 2012; I am grateful to Louise Bernikow for this last reference.

438 **pilot Jacqueline Cochran**: *My Day*, 16 September 1942.

438 **"We opened our"**: *My Day*, 14 and 16 September 1942. On the Battle of Stalingrad, see Ehrenburg, *War*, and Werth, *Russia at War*, 441ff. The Soviet victory was achieved after almost two million deaths.

438 **"FDR read. It is horrible."**: ER to FDR, 9 October 1942. The article was Paul Winterton, *News Chronicle*, London.

Chapter Eighteen: "Golden Footprints": A Permanent Bond in War and Peace

440 **persuaded Roland Hayes**: Olson, *Citizens of London*, 289.

440 **"across what has now"**: *My Day*, 24 October 1942.

440 **"by the queen"**: *TIR*, 263.

441 **"grew more and more nervous"**: *TIR*, 263–64.

441 **"We welcome you"**: Lash, *Eleanor and Franklin*, 659. See also Tania Long, *New York Times*, 24 October 1942.

441 **"various women's services"**: Tommy to Lape, 7 May 1942.

441 **"blocks upon blocks"**: *TIR*, 261–65; Lash, *Eleanor and Franklin*, 658–61; *My Day*, 24–26 October 1942.

441 **"in no way prepared"**: *My Day*, 27 October 1942.

442 **"with Sir Stafford"**: ER to Lash, 29 October and 5 November 1942; Lash, *Love Eleanor*, 411–12; Tommy to Lape, 14 November and 21 December 1942.

442 **"At the White House"**: William Phillips Diary, May–September 1943, 253–73. See also Caroline D. Phillips Diary, 7 May 1942, 215–16; 23 June 1942, 225ff; 5 November 1942, 235; 6 January 1943–May 1943. I am grateful to Kathleen Dalton for these journals.

442 **"she ran nine canteens"**: Olson, *Citizens of London*, 107–9.

443 **"it was a little too late"**: *TIR*, 275.

443 **"Mrs. Churchill is"**: Ibid., 267.

444 **"a Woman's Land Army"**: *My Day*, 4 December 1941.

444 **talking "without faltering"**: Tania Long, "Calmly Ignores First Genuine Air Raid Alarm," *New York Times*, 27 October 1942.

444 **"every type of army"**: *My Day*, 29 October 1942.

444 **"a delightful place"**: *TIR*, 267–68; *My Day*, 27 and 28 October 1942.

445 **"side by side"**: *TIR*, 273–74.

445 **"We used to look down"**: Ibid.

445 **"erotic frenzy of"**: Olson, *Citizens of London*, 98–104.

445 **"Randolph Churchill's"**: Lash, *Eleanor and Franklin*, 662. Duncan Sandys, Diana Churchill's husband, believed everybody knew of the affair. Hopkins told FDR, and he "got a big kick out of it." Olson, *Citizens of London*, 103.

445 **Norway's Princess Martha**: Lash, *Eleanor and Franklin*, 677–79.

445 **"Rover has lost"**: *TIR*, 268.

445 **"young colored trainees"**: *My Day*, 4 November 1942. See also *My Day*, 3 November 1942, Lash, *Eleanor and Franklin*, 662–66, Christopher Paul Moore, *Black Soldiers*, 29–30.

447 **"in some ways"**: *TIR*, 269–71.

447 **was "not . . . hilarious"**: Ibid. See also *My Day*, 3 and 4 November 1942, ER to FDR in Lash, *Eleanor and Franklin*, 622, and Tommy to Lape, 14 November 1942.

447 **"I liked her very much"**: Swift, *Roosevelts and Royals*, 199–201.

447 **"very much the same"**: *My Day*, 5 November 1942. See also *My Day*, 6 and 8 November 1942.

447 **for "country nurseries"**: *My Day*, 9 November 1942.

448 **"the British people"**: *My Day*, 10 November 1942.

448 **"We come among you"**: Rosenman, *Working with Roosevelt*, 364.

448 **"we assured that"**: *My Day*, 9 November 1942.

449 **"Are we fighting"**: Smith, *Eisenhower in War*, 239. See also Nicolson, *Diaries and Letters*, 9–27 November, 2:261–67.

449 **"felt betrayed and"**: Plesch, *America, Hitler and the UN*, 78.

449 **on the "futility"**: *My Day*, 12 November 1942.

449 **"a big gathering"**: *My Day*, 14 November 1942; Lash, *Eleanor and Franklin*, 667–68. See also *My Day*, 11–13 November 1942.

449 **"it was good to have a bath"**: *My Day*, 14 November 1942; ER Diary, 11–12 November 1942.

450 **"very old Allenswood"**: *My Day*, 15–17 November 1942; *TIR*, 176.

450 **"I suppose I look"**: ER Diary, 13 November 1942, 79–83.

450 **"a delightful evening"**: *My Day*, 17 November 1942.

450 **"You certainly have left"**: Lash, *Eleanor and Franklin*, 668.

450 **"has done more"**: Ibid.

450 **"I don't care how"**: Ibid.

450 **"surprised to see"**: *My Day,* 19 November 1942.

450 **"I really think Franklin"**: Lash, *Eleanor and Franklin,* 668.

451 only **"buy refreshments"**: Buckley, *American Patriots,* 260–61.

451 **"fight for freedom"**: Dwight Eisenhower in Sherwood, *Roosevelt and Hopkins,* 243–44.

451 **"I do not want us"**: Nicolson, *Diaries and Letters,* 26 November 1942, 2:263–64.

451 **"I have not become"**: Winston Churchill, "The Bright Gleam of Victory," speech, 9 November 1942, 2544–46.

451 **"more than anyone"**: Blum, *Morgenthau Diaries*; ER to Anna, 24 October 1942.

452 **"was a most ruthless"**: Blum, *Roosevelt and Morgenthau,* 495.

452 **"something that affects"**: Ibid., 497.

452 **"We are opposed"**: FDR, "Statement on Political Arrangements in North Africa," 17 November 1942.

452 **Bonnier de la Chapelle**: Nicolson, *Diaries and Letters,* 6 December 1942, 2:269.

453 **"none of us will ever forget"**: *My Day,* 13 June 1942. Lidice was remembered in Germany and Czechoslovakia in June 2012, with panels and the film *Lidice, In the Shadow of Memory* by Alan Teller and Jerry Zbiral.

453 **"resolved to do all"**: Writers' War Board introduction to Edna St. Vincent Millay, *Murder of Lidice.* See also Gilbert, *Second World War,* 332.

453 **"1,000,000 Jews slain"**: *New York Times,* 30 June 1942.

453 **"This morning I saw"**: *My Day,* 5 December 1942.

454 **"a message transmitted"**: *My Day,* 10 December 1942.

454 **"Letters, reports, cables"**: Varian Fry, "The Massacre of the Jews," *New Republic,* 21 December 1942.

455 **"any statement to make"**: Plesch, *America, Hitler and the UN,* 104–6.

456 **"we gathered at midnight"**: *My Day,* 2 January 1943.

456 **"To the person"**: Rosenman, *Working with Roosevelt,* 364–65.

456 **"to the women"**: *My Day,* 2 January 1943.

456 **"I'm sure the kids"**: ER to Anna, 21 December, 2 and 3 January 1943.

456 **"I don't know if I"**: Lash, *Love, Eleanor,* 416–18.

457 **"motioned for me"**: Eisenhower, *President Is Calling,* 143–44. For C. D. Vackson's contributions to propaganda and political warfare, see Blanche Wiesen Cook, *The Declassified Eisenhower.*

458 **"the French empire"**: Olson, *Citizens of London,* 221.

458 **"Roosevelt was familiar"**: Ibid., 217.

458 **"the only man"**: The day after Peyrouton's appointment was announced, Henry Wallace phoned Milton Eisenhower for his views "and found him very much disturbed about it." Wallace, *Price of Vision,* 167–68.

458 **"mean to maintain"**: Brands, *Traitor,* 700–2; Sherwood, *Roosevelt and Hopkins,* 274–98.

459 **"to overcrowd the"**: Grose, *Israel,* 123–33; Neil Smith, *American Empire.*

459 **"a politician and a fanatic"**: *TIR,* 281.

460 **"97% of the political prisoners"**: Lash, *Love Eleanor,* 423.

460 **to "trouble spots"**: *TIR,* 284.

460 **"The world of war"**: *My Day,* 1 April 1942. Mayling Soong Chiang's letter, dated 12 January 1942, was delivered by China scholar Owen Lattimore. For Lattimore's efforts in China see Robert Newman, *The Loss of China,* and BWC introduction to Lattimore, *Ordeal by Slander.*

461 **"seemed so small"**: *TIR,* 283; *My Day,* 1 and 15 April 1942.

461 **"mingled fire and ice"**: Lash, *Eleanor and Franklin,* 676.

461 **"sensitive to the global"**: Ibid.

462 **"I think she is able"**: Tommy to Lape, 25 February 1943.

462 **"a great feeling of pride"**: *My Day,* 19 February 1943.

462 **"I feel strongly"**: ER, press conference, 24 February 1943, in Beasley, *ER Press Conferences,* 325–28.

463 **"a sweet, gentle"**: *TIR,* 283–84.

463 **"extravagance and arrogance"**: Tommy to Lape, 14 April, 26 April, and 6 May 1943.

463 **"The President . . . is"**: Tuchman, *Stilwell and China,* 352.

463 **"F. said one"**: Lash, *Love, Eleanor,* 431.

464 **"The imprisonment of"**: George Bernard Shaw, "From a Message to the Tagore Society," reprinted in *Twice a Year,* 26 February 1943, 60–64.

464 **"Please read this"**: FDR to Hopkins, 19 March 1943.

464 **"To throw [the Congress activists]"**: Lash, *World of Love,* 8.

464 **was "very complimentary"**: FDR to Phillips.

464 **"Phillips returned to"**: Breckinridge Long Diary, 13 May 1943.

465 **"the great man thumped"**: Caroline D. Phillips Diary, 6 January–17 March, 16 May, 24 May 1943, courtesy of Kathleen Dalton. On Churchill meeting, 241–63. See also Fischer, *Life of Gandhi,* 391–96.

465 **"Loewe and Pollock"**: Wallace, *Price of Vision,* 184. See also Lash, *Love, Eleanor,* 428.

465 **"the loneliest man"**: Daisy Suckley, 14 February 1943, in Geoffrey Ward, *Closest Companion,* 201.

466 **"G-2 operatives had"**: Lash, *Love, Eleanor,* 450.

466 **"what the hotel people thought"**: Tommy to Lape, 14 and 26 April 1943; Lash, *Love, Eleanor,* 450–54.

466 **a "gigantic conspiracy"**: For the invasive file, zealously compiled on Joe, Trude, and ER, March 1943, see Lash, *Love, Eleanor,* 459–91.

466 **"I spent a rather terrible"**: Lash, *Love, Eleanor,* 446.

467 **"I'm sorry that I"**: Ibid., 450.

467 **"insist that Army intelligence"**: Ibid., 451.

467 **"isn't playing straight"**: Tommy to Lape.

467 **FDR gave Hoover:** On Hoover's unlimited authority, unchecked wiretaps, and routine discrimination against Spanish Civil War veterans, see Schrecker, *Many Are the Crimes,* 104–15; Athan Theoharis, *From the Secret Files of J. Edgar Hoover,* 59–65; and Tim Weiner, *Enemies,* 74–108.

467 **"would make her appear"**: Henry Wallace, oral history, 11 March 1944. Wallace noted that Hoover's agents revealed "stupendous ignorance" and used

as a "trust barometer" an individual's view of ER and himself: "If they thought highly of [ER or me] that made them suspicious characters," 3174.

468 **leaflets saying "Freedom!":** Gilbert, *Second World War*, 412.

468 **"There is a great ferment":** Hermann Vinke, *Short Life of Scholl*, 15–118, 154–56.

468 **"The world is deeply moved":** Scholl, *White Rose*, 148–59. See also Anne Nelson, *Red Orchestra*, 275–89; Shareen Brysac, *Resisting Hitler*.

468 **a political warfare campaign:** Paul Hagen, "How to Prepare Collaboration with the Anti-Nazi Underground Movement," *Twice a Year*, X–XI, 1943, 102–9; Dorothy Norman, "Editor's Statement," 21.

469 **"a mass memorial":** *My Day*, 14 April 1943.

469 **"Do all we possibly can":** *My Day*, 16 April 1943.

470 **the "moving, exciting":** Kurt Grossmann, August 1943 to Sophie Scholl. After the war Sophie Scholl's sister, Inge Aicher-Scholl, visited New York, and on 29 April 1957 she and Grossmann had tea with ER at her apartment.

470 **"Today is the 10th":** *My Day*, 11 May 1943.

470 **was "highly educated":** Ibid.

471 **"North African territory":** Breckenridge Long Diary 20 April, 22 April, 7 May, and 12 May 1943, 306–8; 29 January 1942, 246–47; and 23 June 1943, 316.

472 **It accomplished nothing:** For Bermuda, see Wyman, *Abandonment*, 104–23, 341–3. Wyman points out that Long appointed State Department advisers to Bermuda who opposed rescue efforts, led by R. Borden Reams—who had sought to silence publicity about exterminations, and opposed the 17 December 1942 UN war crimes declaration.

472 **"flashed news of":** Gilbert, *Second World War*, 421, 428; Wyman, *Abandonment*, 123.

473 **"Morale is disturbed":** Buckley, *American Patriots*, 288.

473 **"the 99th was off":** Ibid., 282–94. See also *Redtails*. I am grateful to Dr. Roscoe Brown for his memories and for the Tuskegee Airmen Chronology.

473 **"Lady Big Heart":** Ibid., 266–67, 272.

473 **"hotbed of racial hatred":** Rowan, *Dream Makers*, 99–102 See also Lash, *Eleanor and Franklin*, 675.

474 **"Dearest Franklin, I've":** ER to FDR, 9 July 1943, family archive, box 16.

474 **Frankie "is o.k.":** Lash, *World of Love*, 50–51.

475 **"The State Department":** Max Lerner, "What About the Jews, FDR?" *PM*, 22 July 1943.

475 **"I will be glad to say":** Wyman, *Abandonment*, 145.

475 **"extermination list," and:** *New York Times*, August 1943.

475 **"I do not know":** *My Day*, 13 August 1943.

475 **"You know better":** Stella Reading to Churchill, 16 January 1943; ER to Lash and Trude Pratt, 25 July 1943; ER to Hick, 26 July 1943; Lash, *World of Love* 45–52.

476 *Rescue the Perishing*: Breitman, *Official Secrets*, 171ff; Feingold, *Politics of Rescue*, 209. See also Nicolson. *Diaries and Letters*, 35, 2:343; and Susan Pedersen, *Eleanor Rathbone and the Politics of Conscience*.

476 **"Like everybody else":** *My Day*, 27 July 1943.

476 **"Death stares them"**: *My Day*, 2 August 1943.

476 **"was turning red"**: Churchill to FDR, 5 August 1943; see also *My Day*, 27 July and 2 August 1943; BWC, *Declassified Eisenhower*, 21–24; Burns, *Soldier of Freedom*, 382–92.

477 **"was kindness itself"**: Soames, *Daughter's Tale*, 247–48.

477 **to eliminate "destitution"**: *My Day*, 14 August 1943. See FDR, "Statement on the Second Anniversary of the Atlantic Charter," 14 August 1943.

478 **"the P was very sweet"**: Tommy to Lape, 18 August 1943.

Chapter Nineteen: "The White Heron of the One Flight": Travels in the Pacific and Beyond

479 **"I hate to see"**: Tommy to Lape, n.d., postmarked 18 August, 23 August, and 25 August 1943, BWC Arizona Collection.

479 **"representative of the"**: *My Day*, 28 August 1943.

480 **"was a wonderful"**: *TIR*, 303.

480 **"is seen but once"**: Lash, *Eleanor and Franklin*, 685.

480 **"as bad as bullets"**: ER to Hick, 1 September 1943, in Lash, *World of Love*, 62.

480 **"The people here"**: Ibid., 61–62.

480 **"did a magnificent job"**: Durno to Tommy, n.d., in Lash, *World of Love*, 62–63.

480 **her "first encounter"**: *TIR*, 299.

480 **"seemed to be no"**: Lash, *Eleanor and Franklin*, 683.

481 **"Last night four men"**: ER to Tommy, n.d., in Lash, *World of Love*, 59.

481 **"dreaded" ER's arrival**: Lash, *Eleanor and Franklin*, 684.

481 **"When I say"**: Ibid., 685.

481 **"she wanted to see"**: Robert M. White, "A Mother at the Front," *Christian Advocate*, 30 December 1943, in Lash, *Eleanor and Franklin*, 687.

481 **"When she came"**: Calvin Thompson in Fleming, *Our Eleanor*, 101.

482 **"The natives of Guadalcanal"**: *My Day*, 23 September 1943. ER's daughter Anna and Hick considered this column "one of the best you have ever written." Hick to ER, 24 September 1943; ER to Anna, 27 September 1943. See also *My Day*, 1, 3, 13, 18, and 24 September 1943.

482 **"I shall have"**: *TIR*, 309.

482 **"How I hated"**: ER to Joe, 18 September 1943, in Lash, *World of Love*, 71.

482 **"it was impossible"**: Lash, *Eleanor and Franklin*, 691.

482 **"I was ashamed"**: Ibid.

482 **"hospitals and cemeteries"**: Hick to ER, 24 September 1943.

483 **"Men not chief"**: Lash, *Eleanor and Franklin*, 691.

483 **"I talked to her"**: Lash, *World of Love*, 74.

483 **"seemed pretty feeble"**: Ibid.; Lape to ER, Tommy to Hick, 22 September 1943.

483 **who was "happy"**: ER to Lash, 22 September 1943, in Lash, *World of Love*, 74.

483 **"Pa asked me more"**: ER to Anna, 27 September 1943, in Lash, *World of Love*, 77.

483 "the onset of a": Lash, *World of Love*, 75.

483 "the men had been mentally": *TIR*, 311.

484 "I know that the Army": FDR to Henry Stimson and Frank Knox, 20 September 1943, in *FDR: Personal Letters*, 4:1443.

485 "some Rabbis sobbed": Wyman, *Abandonment*, 148–53.

485 "In a democracy": Heschel, to his classes, which I attended, 1961–62.

485 his attitude "perfect": *My Day*, 9 October 1943.

485 message of encouragement: ER's broadcasts with Peter Bergson for OWI, 18 and 29 October 1943, in Wyman, *Race Against Death*, 139.

485 by Eleanor Rathbone: See Pedersen, *Rathbone and Conscience*; Kushner, *Holocaust and Liberal Imagination*. Britain's Tony Kushner dedicated his book to Eleanor Rathbone, who knew, cared, and acted.

485 "The Boss was very": Trude to Lash, 9 October 1943, in Lash, *World of Love*, 80–81.

486 "As long as she": Trude to Joe, 9, 10, 11 October 1943, ibid., 81.

486 and "brushed aside": Daisy Suckley Diary, 8 and 11 October 1943, in Ward, *Closest Companion*, 248–49.

486 ER's "terrible sorrow": Lash to Trude, 28 October 1943, in Lash, *World of Love*, 81.

486 "find out whether": Henry Wallace Diary, 30 September 1943, 21 October 1943. FDRM, IV, 1391, 1530f.

486 "waste spaces for": For Bowman's 1938–1940 reports, see Cook, *ER*, 2:560–62. For the M Project, see Smith, *American Empire*, 301ff.

487 "from the Mediterranean": Wallace, *Price of Vision*, 276–77.

487 The first lady was impressed: Ibid., 210–11; at this meeting Churchill spoke about the "development of trans-Jordania for the Jews, which Wallace agreed with. ER to Lash on Baruch, in Lash, *World of Love*, 88–90; Baruch and King Leopold, Baruch, *Public Years*, 2:274; Baruch to Wallace, *Price of Vision*, 279.

488 "questions beyond her": Smith, *American Empire*, 305–6.

488 akin to the Nazis': Ibid., 306. See also Wallace, *Price of Vision*, 263–65, 269–70.

488 the President told: FDR, 22 May 1943, Wallace Diary.

488 "some Zionist ladies": ER to Lash, 16 November 1943, in Lash, *World of Love*, 91.

489 "to gas chambers, probably": Henry Morgenthau.

489 "The British say": *Morgenthau Diaries*, 519–29; Wyman, *Abandonment*, 178–85.

490 was "very happy": Trude to Lash, in Lash, *World of Love*, 88.

490 "Today in the East Room": *My Day*, 10 November 1943.

490 "something great may": ER to Lash, 9 November 1943, in Lash, *World of Love*, 88.

490 that two women: *My Day*, 4 December 1943. See also Morgenthau, *Mostly Morgenthaus*, 225.

490 all "abominable deeds": Gilbert, *Auschwitz and Allies*, 160.

491 "commission of diplomatic": Medoff, *Blowing the Whistle*, 56.

491 "Bestial and abominable": *New York Times*, 5 November 1943; Wyman, *Abandonment*, 154–55; ER to Bergson, 139; Morgenthau, *Mostly Morgenthaus*, 323; Ben Hecht, *Child of the Century*, 576–82. Although his chronology is inaccurate for "My Uncle Abraham," his details about the Bergson group,

Romania's offer, and related issues are stunning, 521ff. I am grateful to Mim Kelber for this book.

491 **"I've been amused"**: ER to FDR; Weinberg, *World at Arms*, 493; Gilbert, *History of Twentieth Century*, 521–22.

491 **to be "sidelined"**: Tommy to Lape, ca. October 1943, BWC Arizona Collection.

492 **FDR became "furious"**: ER to Lash, in Lash, *World of Love*, 101.

492 **"had a liking"**: *My Day*, 24 November 1943.

493 **"I find it hard"**: ER to Lape, 19 November 1943; BWC Arizona Collection.

493 **because of political "realities"**: For the work of the American Foundation, see Cook, *ER*, vols. 1–2; and for Lape and Elizabeth Read's influence on ER, see 11, 97, 294–95, and passim. On Esther Lape, see Susan Ware, ed., *Notable American Women* (2004 ed.).

493 **"Life without Lizzie"**: ER to Lape, 14 December 1943, in Lash, *World of Love*, 100.

494 **"I am sorry"**: ER to FDR, 5 December 1943.

494 **"Day by day news"**: *My Day*, 8 December 1943.

494 **"Those four powers"**: FDR, Christmas Eve Fireside Chat on Teheran and Cairo Conferences, 24 December 1943, in Rosenman, *FDR Public Papers*, 12:558ff.

495 **"Though two of our"**: *My Day*, 27 December 1943.

495 **"I guess one"**: ER to Lash, 25 December 1943, in Lash, *World of Love*, 104.

495 **"I want to tell you"**: ER to Lash and Trude Pratt, ca. 1 January 1944, ibid., 105.

495 **"There is one thing"**: ER to Lash, 21 January 1944, ibid., 116.

496 **"the most radical speech"**: Burns and Dunn, *Three Roosevelts*, 483; cf. Brands, *Traitor to His Class*, 733–34.

496 **"We have come to a clear"**: FDR, State of the Union address, 11 January 1944, in Rosenman, *FDR Public Papers*, 13:41–42.

496 **"WAVES at their"**: *My Day*, 13 January 1944.

496 **"complete, unified social"**: *My Day*, 19 January 1944.

497 **"social insurance measures"**: *My Day*, 20 January 1944.

497 **"the colored residents"**: *My Day*, 5 January 1944. See also *My Day*, 22 and 25 January 1944.

497 **"wipe out illiteracy"**: *My Day*, 24 January 1944.

498 **"to the limit of their"**: *My Day*, 14 January 1944. See ER to Lash, 18 January 1944, *World of Love*, 111.

498 **copy two cables**: Gruber, *Haven*, 16–19. See also Medoff, *Blowing the Whistle*.

498 **"One of the greatest"**: Gruber, *Haven*, 24.

498 **"the tragic bottleneck"**: Ibid., 25–26.

499 **"failed to use"**: Ibid., 24.

499 **president "listened attentively"**: See Medoff, *Blowing the Whistle*, for the fullest account.

499 **"placed in the same"**: Ibid.

500 **draft for a WRB "wonderful"**: Ibid.

500 **"Those terrible eighteen"**: *Morgenthau Diaries*, 531–33; Morgenthau, *Mostly Morgenthaus*, 321–35.

500 **"immediate rescue and"**: FDR executive order, 22 January 1944.

500 **"was withdrawn from"**: Gruber, *Haven*, 26–27.

500 **Raoul Wallenberg, a young**: See Marton, *Wallenberg*; Wallenberg, *Letters and Dispatches*.

501 **"none is too many"**: Troper and Abella, *None Is Too Many*.

501 **FDR was "cordial"**: Morgenthau, *Mostly Morgenthaus*, 333.

501 **"Anna's presence was"**: *TIR*, 319.

502 **"be conquered by"**: ER's initial response to Anna as told to Ward, *Closest Companion*, 285.

502 **ER graciously "greeted"**: Daisy Suckley Diary, 30 January, 273.

502 **he had surgery**: Ibid., 2 February, 275–76; *My Day*, 3 February 1944.

502 **"not for the needy"**: ER to Lash, ca. 23 February 1944, in Lash, *World of Love*, 112.

503 **a "fighting liberal"**: Lash, *Eleanor and Franklin*, 695.

503 **she said, "Now, Franklin"**: Anna, in Asbell, 177.

503 **"In continuing to"**: Lash, *Eleanor and Franklin*, 693.

503 **"What fun our"**: ER to Elinor Morgenthau, ca. 6 March 1944, in Lash, *World of Love*, 113.

503 **"Trude and I talk"**: ER to Lash, 27 April 1944, ibid., 120.

503 **"felt they were in"**: *TIR*, 319.

504 **"a real weariness"**: Tommy to Lape, ca. 14 March 1944, in Lash, *World of Love*, 112–13.

504 **"Many happy returns"**: ER to FDR, 10, 13 and 17 March 1944. ER reflected on her trip in *My Day*, daily from 7 March to 7 April 1944.

504 **"flying from Recife"**: ER to FDR, 17 March 1944.

504 **"cheered the men"**: "First Lady Visits Brazil," *New York Times*, 16, 17 March 1944.

504 **"The trip did"**: Tommy to Lape, ca. April 1944, in Lash, *World of Love*, 115.

504 **diagnosed with "hypertension"**: Lash, *World of Love*, 114–116.

505 **"Hobcaw was just"**: *TIR*, 328.

505 **"knew that Franklin"**: Ibid., 329. ER's visit 24 April 1944, to Lash, *World of Love*, 118–19; *My Day*, 27 April 1944. See also Brockington, *Plantation*, 95; Miller, *Baroness of Hobcaw*, 134–41. Photographs of FDR without his blemish, thought by many a melanoma, occur after his Hobcaw visit. See Harry S. Goldsmith, MD, "Unanswered Mysteries in the Death of FDR," *Surgeon's Library* (December 1979), 899–908; Lomazow and Fettmann, *FDR's Deadly Secret*. Thanks to ELR, MD, and MDWL. To date there is no evidence of FDR's surgery at Hobcaw, although James MacGregor Burns refers to a rumor that circulated "even in the White House" that FDR had had a "secret operation at Hobcaw." Burns, *Soldier of Freedom*, 507.

505 **"I am more worried"**: Daisy Suckley Diary, April 1944, 292; 4–9 May 1944, 294–98; 26 March 1944 at Hyde Park, 287–88.

506 **"shorten the war"**: See Y. Aleksandra Bennett, introduction to Brittain, *One Voice*; Brittain, *Testament of Experience*; Brittain, *Seed of Chaos*, 324–36.

506 **"the callous cruelty"**: Brittain, *Seed of Chaos*, 324–36.

506 **"their facts are wrong!"**: "Mass Bombing Foes Rebuked by Roosevelt," *Tribune*, 26 April 1944; "FDR Defends Mass Raids," *New Chronicle*, 27 April 1944.

506 **"I must really live"**: ER to Lash, 19 May 1944, in Lash, *World of Love,* 118.

506 **"is so fine"**: Daisy Suckley Diary, 19–24 May 1944, 300–3.

507 **"very good orientals"**: Daisy Suckley Diary, 19–24 May 1944, 300–3.

507 **"was composed of"**: *My Day,* 23 May 1944.

507 **"more serious subjects"**: Daisy Suckley Diary, 19–24 May 1944, 300–3.

507 **"Was this a war"**: *My Day,* 30 May 1944. ER's last words here suggest that she had not dismissed *Seed of Chaos* as merely "sentimental nonsense" as was reported.

508 **"the foundations of"**: FDR, "Fireside Chat on the Fall of Rome," 5 June 1944, in Rosenman, *FDR Public Papers,* 13:148, 151.

508 **"Soldiers, sailors, and"**: Eisenhower, 6 June 1944.

508 **"went off with some"**: Daisy Suckley Diary, 7–8 June 1944, 309–10.

508 **"So at last"**: *My Day,* 7 June 1944.

509 **"Last night, when I"**: FDR, D-Day prayer.

509 **"a good prayer"**: *My Day,* 8 June 1944.

509 **"I hope that many people"**: Ibid.

510 **Oswego, New York**: Gruber, *Haven,* 117ff.

510 **"ER is trying to force"**: *Morgenthau Diaries,* 6 July 1944; other conversation materials, thanks to Bill Hannegan. On Wallace, Pendergast, and Truman, see Wallace, *Price of Vision,* 395.

510 **"Labor is firmly"**: Trude to Lash, 14 July 1944, in Lash, *World of Love,* 129.

510 **"The future belongs"**: Wallace, *Price of Vision,* "Recollections of the Chicago 1944 Convention," 367–74.

510 **"but F says"**: ER to Lash, ca. 16 July 1944, in Lash, *World of Love,* 129. As requested, ER did not publish the column until 24 July.

511 **"Hannegan came to"**: ER to Hick, 16 July 1944, ibid., 130.

511 **"I don't know that"**: ER to Trude, 16 July 1944, ibid., 129.

511 **"I am no politician"**: ER to Lash, 16 July 1944, ibid., 130.

511 **"shot and killed"**: *Crisis* editorial, August 1944, 249.

512 **"There has been"**: ER to Lash, 18 July 1944, in Lash, *World of Love,* 131.

512 **"dancing in a little"**: *My Day,* 28 July 1944.

512 **"has spoiled me"**: ER to Anna, 16 July 1944, Halsted Papers.

512 **"Wallace did not lose"**: *Crisis* editorial, August 1944, 249.

512 promised **"progressive leadership"**: FDR, address broadcast from a naval base on the Pacific Coast to the Democratic National Convention in Chicago, 20 July 1944, in Rosenman, *FDR Public Papers,* 13:204–5. See also Wallace's detailed convention notes, *Price of Vision,* 360–81, 413–14.

513 note: **"Dearest Babs"**: FDR to ER, 21 July 1944, *FDR: Personal Letters,* 4:1525. ER to FDR, 30 July 44, family archive, box 16, mentions FDR's colly-wobbles, with no indication it might have been a heart attack. ER to Lash, 29 July, 132–33.

513 **"There is integrity"**: *My Day,* 24 July 1944.

513 **"who think first of"**: *My Day,* 10 August 1944.

513 **"year of extra training"**: *My Day,* 24 August 1944.

513 **"was sad, but"**: ER to FDR, 6 August 1944. Missy died on 2 August.

513 **"valiant and important"**: *My Day,* 4 August 1944.

514 **"subject the nations"**: Burns, *Soldier of Freedom,* 516.

514 **"The ladies have"**: ER to Trude, 12 September 1944, in Lash, *World of Love*, 137.

514 **"It seems such a waste"**: ER to Elinor Morgenthau, ibid., 137.

514 **"particularly along the"**: *TIR*, 335–36.

515 **"I don't know what"**: ER to Hick, in Lash, n.d., *World of Love*, 138.

515 **"a Russian propaganda"**: BBC, rejected Werth's "Reports from Lublin."

515 **await "further corroboration"**: *New York Herald Tribune*. Werth, *Russia at War*, 884–899, esp. 890, 898; Gilbert, *Second World War*, 559. One reason for disbelief was that the Nazis destroyed and buried Sobibor and Treblinka before the Soviets arrived. See Manchester, *Last Lion*, 2:873.

516 **"the French people"**: *My Day*, 26 August 1944.

516 **"through the woods"**: ER to Lash, ca. 16 September 1944, in Lash, *World of Love*, 139.

516 **"My time slips"**: ER to Lash, 18 September 1944, ibid., 139–40.

517 **"rather fun really"**: Clementine Churchill's "high praise," Manchester, *Last Lion*, 2:876.

517 **prime minister "twitted"**: *My Day*, 14 September 1944. See also ER to Lash, 18 September 1944, in Lash, *World of Love*, 140.

517 **Leahy was riveted**: Burns, *Soldier of Freedom*, 521.

517 **"We can establish"**: ER's now much-quoted sentiment on love, with gratitude to Frazer Doughtery for his New Year message, 2014.

517 **"direct aid of"**: Bhagavan, *Peacemakers*, 23–25, 30–31ff. For the Bengal famine and Churchill's "will to punish" the people of India, see Mukerjee, *Churchill's Secret War*. Mukerjee revised the death toll to over five million. See also John Newsinger, "Britain's Noxious History of Imperial Warfare," *Global Research*, 19 November 2013.

518 **divided the Balkans**: Breckinridge Long, Diary, 6 June 1944, 352; William Neumann, *After Victory: Churchill, Roosevelt, Stalin and the Making of the Peace*, 130; Manchester, *Last Lion*, 2:877–82. The Moscow meetings lasted until 27 October to deal with Poland, and Stalin's desire to recognize Charles de Gaulle, which FDR agreed to do, eventually.

518 **"Half my mail"**: ER to Lash, 14 September 1944, in Lash, *World of Love*, 139.

518 **"colored WACs are going"**: ER to Oveta Culp Hobby, 4 May 1944.

518 **colored WACs assigned**: Colonel William Scobey, executive assistant to McCloy, secretary of war, to ER, 24 June 1943. Scobey reported Hobby's decision that assignments to Camp Shelby "will not be made" and other locations would be investigated; "Colonel Hobby shares Mrs. Roosevelt's feeling concerning overseas service for Negro members of our Corps." But we send only "personnel requisitioned by the theatre commanders" and no Negro WAC "has been requisitioned." See ER to Alston, 8 November 1944.

518 **"Why do Northern Negro"**: ER to McCloy, December 1944.

519 **"fit only to do"**: Moore, *Fighting for America*, 292.

519 **"Our people are greatly"**: Lillian Jackson to ER, 24 March 1945.

519 **of "rampant discrimination"**: See Moore, *Fighting for America*, 201–3; James, *Fighting Racism*, 321–23.

520 **"special care in"**: ER to James Forrestal, 8 April 1945, with NAACP pamphlet "Mutiny"; Forrestal to ER, 12 April 1945.

520 **"Partitions have been"**: *My Day*, 22 September 1944.

520 **"character which has"**: Ibid.

521 **"Storm in the Shelter"**: Gruber, *Haven*, 199.

521 **"your world-known humanity"**: Ernst Wolff to ER, 1 February 1945, enclosing "Storm in the Shelter"; Morgenthau to ER, 20 February 1945; Morgenthau to Wolff, 19 February 1945; Elinor Morganthau and sleepless nights, 217.

521 **"to culminate in"**: FBI report on "Refugees At Oswego," S. S. Allen to D. M. Ladd, 27 February 1945.

521 **"admissible under the"**: Gruber, *Haven*, 238–45.

522 **"the Old World's"**: Wendell Willkie, "Cowardice at Chicago," and "Citizens of Negro Blood," *Collier's*, 7 September and 7 October 1944; Neal, *Dark Horse*, 315–23. See also Muriel Rukeyser, *One Life*.

522 his **"great leadership"**: *My Day*, 12 October 1944.

522 **"You are still my"**: Hick to ER, ca. 11 October 1944, ibid., 142.

522 **"the ornamental office"**: Lash to ER, 1 October 1944, ibid., 143.

522 **"if I don't deserve"**: ER to Lash, 22 October 1944, ibid., 144.

523 of **"re-homing people"**: Lady Reading to ER, 10 October 1944, box 1739; ER replied to this letter and to Lady Reading's cable of congratulations on FDR's election on 18 November 1944. For V1s and V2s see Olson, *Citizens of London*, 323–26.

523 **"Republican leaders have"**: FDR, Address at Dinner of International Brotherhood of Teamsters, Chauffeurs, . . . Washington, DC, 23 September 1944, in Rosenman, *FDR Public Papers*, 13:290.

524 **"The right to vote"**: FDR, radio address from the White House, 5 October 1944, in Rosenman, *FDR Public Papers*, 13:317.

524 vigorously slammed **"propagandists"**: Ibid.

524 to **"this land"**: FDR, campaign address at Soldiers' Field, Chicago, 28 October 1944, ibid., 13:3670.

524 **"change into dry"**: *TIR*, 337.

524 **"I was really worried"**: *TIR*, 337.

524 **"prudence" in riding**: Churchill to FDR, 23 October 1944.

525 **"does not hurt"**: FDR to Churchill, 24 October 1944.

525 **"very peaceful and"**: Daisy Suckley Diary, 7 November 1944, 140–41.

525 **"the leaves crackling"**: Lash, *World of Love*, 145–47.

525 **"an unusually nice"**: Daisy Suckley Diary, 7 November 1944, 140–41.

525 the president toasted: Lash, *World of Love*, 146.

525 **"winning the war"**: ER, press conference, 9 November 1944, in Beasley, *ER Press Conferences*. See also C. B. Powell, "FDR or Governor Dewey," *Crisis*, October 1944, 315.

526 wanted all **"pussyfooting"**: Sherwood, *Roosevelt and Hopkins*, 831; Lash, *Eleanor and Franklin*, 712, 713.

526 **"had their lunch"**: Daisy Suckley Diary, 23–27 November, 346–47.

526 **"I received yesterday"**: *My Day*, 4 December 1944. John Groth, ER's source, was a correspondent and artist for the *Chicago Sun*. "The Camp of Disappear-

ing Men" was based on reports from the Polish underground labor movement; the pamphlet may have been in part a product of the Office of War Information director Elmer Davis. It was published before the Soviets liberated Auschwitz on 27 January 1945 and was distributed by the CIO War Relief Committee. It has been digitized by the University of Michigan.

527 **"It seems to me"**: ER to FDR, 4 December 1944, in Lash, *Eleanor and Franklin*, 713–14. ER's worries about FDR's State Department shared by Wallace, see Diary, 11–20 December 1944, 400–9, and Waldo Heinrichs on Joseph Grew.

527 **and "treacherous aggressors"**: For Greece, see Wittner, *American Intervention in Greece*, 23–35, 322–23; Papandreou, *Nightmare in Athens*, 20–26. For Sforza and Italy, see Cook, *Eisenhower*, 21–37.

527 **"The composition of"**: Stettinius, statement, 5 December 1944.

527 **"I like the statement"**: ER to FDR, 6 December 1944, in Lash, *Eleanor and Franklin*, 714.

528 **be a "pest"**: Lash, *World of Love*, 159.

528 **"suspicious of this"**: ER to Trude, 5 December 1944, in Lash, *World of Love*, 159.

528 **"wrote a column"**: ER to FDR, 6 December 1944, ibid.

528 **ER's phone calls**: Daisy Suckley Diary, 28 November–17 December 1944, 347–66.

528 **"You will . . . I believe"**: FDR, Fourth Inaugural Address, 20 January 1945, in Rosenman, *FDR Public Papers*, 13:523.

529 **"evening when we"**: ER to Lash, 11 January 1945, in Lash, *World of Love*, 164.

529 **"I am tired"**: ER to Lash, 21 January 1945, ibid., 165.

529 **"Franklin felt that"**: ER to Florence Willert, 8 February 1945.

530 **"territorial trusteeships and"**: Stettinius, *Roosevelt and Russians*, 236–39.

531 **"I have never met"**: FDR's visit with King Ibn Sand in Colonel William Eddy's memo of conversations aboard USS *Quincy*. The Lebanon-born U.S. minister to Saudi Arabia, Marine Colonel William Eddy, translated and documented these meetings; see Eddy, *FDR Meets Ibn Saud*. For Eddy's memo of conversations and related *FRUS* documents and *State Department Bulletin*, 25 February 1945, I am grateful to Karl Meyer. *FRUS*, 1945, vol. 8, 1–9.

532 **"his one complete failure"**: ER to Lash, 28 February 1945, in Lash, *World of Love*, 172; also Lash, *Eleanor and Franklin*, 717. See also Thomas W. Lippman, "The Day FDR Met Saudi Arabia's Ibn Saud," *The Link* (Ameu.org), April–May 2005, 1–12; and Thomas Lippman, *Inside the Mirage: America's Fragile Partnership with Saudi Arabia*.

532 **"Many people in"**: *My Day*, 26 February 1945. For changes in Middle East policy, see Catherwood, *Churchill's Folly*, and Fromkin, *Peace to End All Peace*.

532 **great "personal loss"**: *TIR*, 342.

532 **"Franklin feels his"**: Daisy Suckley Diary, 27 February 1945, 397.

533 **"I come from the"**: FDR, address to Congress on Yalta, 1 March 1945, in Rosenman, *FDR Public Papers*.

533 **"He says he felt"**: ER to Lash, 28 February 1945, in Lash, *World of Love*, 172.

533 **"thin and worn and gray"**: Margaret Fayerweather Diary, in Lash, *Eleanor and Franklin*, 718–19.

534 **"I found him less"**: *TIR*, 342–43.

534 **"they would not"**: Ibid.

534 **"settled in Warm"**: Lash, *Eleanor and Franklin*, 719.

534 **"great meeting at"**: ER press conference, 2 April 1945, in Beasley, *ER Press Conferences*, 331–32.

535 **"We are now talking"**: Ibid.

535 **"whether colonial empires"**: Bhagavan, *Peacemakers*, 34–41, 49–53. See also Brittain, *Envoy Extraordinary*; Pandit, *Scope of Happiness*.

536 **"so as not to stir"**: ER to Stettinius, 4 April 1945, in Bhagavan, *Peacemakers*.

536 **"Dearest Franklin, I"**: ER to FDR, 8 April 1945.

537 **"most interesting speeches"**: *My Day*, 11 April 1945.

537 was **"terribly shocked"**: *Morgenthau Diaries*, 11 April 1945, 1499–1503, with gratitude to Bill Hannegan.

538 **"real knowledge" of**: ER, press conference, 12 April 1945, in Beasley, *ER Press Conferences*, 334–36.

538 **"in a sea of misery"**: For U.S.-U.K. reaction to the camps, 11–15 April, and Eisenhower's tour, see Hitchcock, *Bitter Road*, 295ff, and Cook, *Eisenhower*, 33–35. The night Eisenhower learned that FDR was dead, he resolved to honor all agreements made at Yalta. For ER's tour of Zeilsheim, see the epilogue.

539 **FDR had "fainted"**: *TIR*, 343–44.

539 **"the President had slipped"**: Laura (Polly) Delano's call.

539 **"pour a generous jigger"**: ER II, *With Love*, 84–85; ER II to author.

539 **"tall and stately"**: West, *Upstairs*, 55–56.

540 **"waited in our office"**: West, *Upstairs*. In *TIR*, ER says she asked to have the casket opened "so that I could go in alone to put a few flowers in it," 345.

540 **"Today this nation"**: FDR's final speech, ms.

541 **"did not tell anyone"**: Lash, *World of Love*, 183.

541 **"I know you"**: ER to Lash, 16 April 1945, ibid., 188.

542 **"loved him more deeply"**: Daisy Suckley Diary, 420–21.

542 **"I don't think she ever"**: Lape to Lash and many others.

542 **"You have an understanding"**: ER to Lape, 25 April 1945, in Lash, *World of Love*, 190. See *Eleanor and Franklin*, 720–23; *World of Love*, 183–90; Burns, *Soldier of Freedom*, 601–6.

542 **"All human beings have"**: *TIR*, 349.

542 **"The story is over"**: Lash, *World of Love*, 191.

Epilogue: ER's Legacy: Human Rights

543 **"Like countless other women"**: ER, *You Learn by Living*, 55.

543 **"pervades the world"**: *My Day*, 17 April 1945.

543 **"a stroke of genius"**: Black, ed., *ER Papers*, 1:16.

543 **"Nothing would induce me"**: *My Day*, 19 April 1945.

544 **"Because I was the wife"**: *My Day*, 19 April 1945.

544 **"I'm glad you like"**: ER to Trude Lash, n.d., in Lash, *World of Love*, 192.

544 **"The Trumans have"**: ER to Hick, 19 April 1945, ibid., 189.

545 **"If we do not"**: *My Day*, 30 April 1945.

546 **"I listened to your"**: ER to Truman, 8 May 1945, in Neal, *Eleanor and Harry*, 25.

546 **"the whole family"**: Truman to ER, 10 May 1945, ibid., 26–27.

546 **"Your experience with"**: ER to Truman, 14 May 1945, ibid., 28–29.

547 **"The day the atomic"**: *My Day*, 12 October 1945.

547 **"We have an obligation"**: ER to Truman, 20 November 1945, in Neal, *Eleanor and Harry*, 45–46.

548 felt **"very inadequate"**: ER to Anna, 20 December 1945, in Lash, *World of Love*, 207.

548 **"first UN team"**: *New York Times*, 20 December 1945.

549 **"War must be abolished"**: Carrie Chapman Catt to ER, 28 December 1945, box 4561, ER Papers.

549 **"the desires of American Negroes"**: Walter White, Mary McLeod Bethune, and Dr. W. E. B. Du Bois to ER, December 1945, box 4561.

549 **"The important thing"**: Lape to ER, December 1945, box 4562, ER papers.

550 **"said in his rather deep"**: ER, *On My Own*, 41–42.

551 **her words were quoted**: *New York Times*, 8 January 1946; *FRUS*, I, 1947, 304ff; *FRUS*, I, 1948, 278–79.

551 **"I like the Vandenbergs"**: ER, London Diary, 2, 6, 7, and 27 January 1946.

552 **"is smart & hard"**: ER to Elinor Morgenthau, 20 January 1946, in Lash, *World of Love*, 214. ER told Hick, "Byrnes is a curious study, when I come home I'm going to give you thumbnail sketches of my playmates that I don't dare put on paper." ER to Hick, 22 January 1946, in Lash, *World of Love*, 215–16.

552 **"I said many things"**: ER, London Diary, 16 January 1946.

552 **"The papers should not"**: Ibid.

552 **"At the Assembly"**: Ibid.

553 **"Yesterday was the"**: ER, London Diary, 31 January 1946.

553 **"The afternoon session"**: Ibid., 23 January 1946.

553 **"a pleasant dinner"**: Ibid., in Black, ed., *ER Papers*, 1:221. In 1947, when Brittain was on a ten-week tour of the United States, ER invited her to Hyde Park. Again, we have no details of their discussions, although Brittain noted that ER was "now informal and unintimidating." Brittain, *Testament of Experience*, 407. A lifelong member of WILPF, she subsequently wrote a biography of its illustrious British founder Emmeline Pethick-Lawrence, whose favorite expression after the war was "It's women for women now!" See Brittain, *Pethick-Lawrence*; Brittain, *Envoy Extraordinary*; and Muriel Mellown, "Vera Brittain: Feminist in a New Age (1896–1970)," in Spender, ed., *Feminist Theorists*, 313–44.

554 **"It is a liberal"**: Ibid.

555 **"Ukrainians, Belorussians"**: ER, *On My Own*, 49–50.

555 **"all we could"**: ER, *On My Own*, 49–53.

555 **"So—against odds"**: ER, London Diary, 6 and 8 February 1946.

555 **"had the pleasure"**: *My Day*, 11 and 13 February 1946.

555 **"at the end"**: ER, London Diary, 29 January 1946 and passim.

555 **"fill our souls"**: *My Day*, 16 February 1946. See also *On My Own*, 55–56; Black, *ER Papers*, 1:252–59.

556 **"Poles and Balts"**: *My Day*, 16 February 1946.

556 the **"ultimate answer?"**: *My Day*, 16 February 1946.

556 **"the structure and functions"**: Glendon, *A World Made New*, 30.

557 **"From Stettin in the Baltic":** Churchill, Iron Curtain speech, 5 March 1946. See YouTube, with dramatic details. Also see *My Day*, 7 March 1946. Margaret Truman, who wrote her father's speech, was not prepared for Churchill's bellicose declaration, although the prime minister had sent the president an "Iron Curtain" telegram on 12 May 1945. See *Churchill, Taken from the Diaries of Lord Moran: The Struggle for Survival*, 1940–65, 311–314.

557 **"Instead of running":** *My Day*, 7 March 1946.

557 **"men of all parties":** Arthur Murray to ER, 19 March 1946, in Black, *ER Papers*, 1:279–281. ER to Murray, 13 April 1946.

557 **the committee that:** Mary Ann Glendon details the work and vision of the key members of the team that drafted and lobbied for the Declaration from its first meetings in January 1947 at Lake Success, New York, to its final meetings in Geneva and Paris. Glendon, *A World Made New*, 32–35, 53. The contributions of John Humphrey, Charles Malik, P. C. Chang, and René Cassin were mostly forgotten and uncelebrated until Glendon's book; see 126–30.

558 **the words "all men":** Ibid., 90–92. For Hansa Mehta's role, see Bhagavan, *Peacemakers*, 137–46.

558 **"All human beings":** UN Declaration of Human Rights.

560 **a "first step":** Glendon, *A World Made New*, 139.

561 **Hansa Mehta's suggestion:** Bhagavan, *Peacemakers*, 137–43, 204.

561 **"reached a turning point":** Truman, "Address Before the NAACP," 29 June 1947, in Geselbracht, *Legacy of Truman*, 152–55. For 29 June 1947, see Neal, *Eleanor and Harry*, 88, 105–6.

561 **"blot of lynching":** Geselbracht, *Legacy of Truman*, 96.

561 **"To Secure These Rights":** ER to Truman, 23 December 1947, in Neal, *Eleanor and Harry*, 117; *New York Times*, 19 June, 29 June, and 30 June 1947.

562 **"We Charge Genocide":** Black, *ER Papers*, 2:855–58.

562 **"role will embarrass":** Glendon, *A World Made New*, 195.

562 **"harsh and naïve":** Ibid., 199. Republican Ambassador to the Holy See under George W. Bush, Prof. Glendon's views are tempered and complex.

563 **"reports and studies":** The UN adopted the Convention on the Prevention and Punishment of the Crime of Genocide on 9 December 1948, and it entered into force on 8 September 1951. The United States did not ratify the Genocide Convention until 1988. Browne-Marshall, *Race, Law, and American Society*, 234–35.

563 **she traveled across:** See ER, *India and the Awakening East*.

563 **"Where, after all":** ER to United Nations, 27 March 1958, in Black, *ER Papers*. In 1980 the human rights case *Filártiga v Peña-Irala*, 630 F.2d 876 (2d Cir. 1980), brought by the Center for Constitutional Rights, globalized the Universal Declaration. For ER's human rights legacy, see Beth Van Schaack, "The Anatomy of Torture: A Documentary History of *Filártiga v Peña-Irala*" (review), *Human Rights Quarterly* 30, no. 4 (November 2008). See also Bert Lockwood, ed., *Women's Rights: A Human Rights Reader*; Wendy Chavkin and Ellen Chesler, *Where Human Rights Begin: Health, Sexuality, and Women*; and Amnesty International, Outright, Human Rights Watch.

564 **"our great struggle":** ER, *Congressional Record*, 19 April 1950, A-2802.

565 **"leader among the American"**: *My Day*, 3 May 1952.

565 **"save us" from**: *My Day*, 22 May 1952.

565 **"He wanted to find"**: *My Day*, 3 September 1949.

565 **"does not permit"**: ER, "Some of My Best Friends Are Negro," *Ebony*, February 1953, in Black, *What I Hope to Leave Behind*, 171–78.

566 **"dedicated to the fight"**: For ER and Anne Braden, see Catherine Fosl, *Subversive Southerner*. Anne Braden became editor of *The Southern Patriot* in 1957; her memoir, *The Wall Between*, which ER hoped everyone would read, was published in 1958.

566 **"segregation were practiced"**: *My Day*, 17 October 1952. See also Black, *ER Papers*, 2:956–59.

566 **"the white race"**: ER's campaign addresses for Adlai Stevenson, Detroit, 3 October 1956, in Black, *What I Hope to Leave Behind*, 441–42; see esp. Charleston, WV, 1 October 1956, 437–39.

567 **"inaugurated the American"**: Belafonte, *My Song*, 188.

567 **"Well, little man"**: Ibid., 189.

567 **"I am sure"**: Ibid., 191–92.

567 **"to move in"**: Ibid., 192.

568 **"race . . . the greatest"**: Ibid., 188–197.

569 **"freedom and democracy"**: *My Day*, 3 November 1961.

569 **"It has always seemed"**: *My Day*, 14 September 1962.

569 **With "proper education"**: ER, *Tomorrow Is Now*.

570 **"The influence you exert"**: Ibid.

570 **"Her life was crowded"**: Adlai Stevenson, 9 and 17 November 1962, Memorial Address at the UN and St. John the Divine.

Index

Acheson, Dean, 25, 527
Addams, Jane, 59n, 90, 169,
    321, 322
African Americans, 93, 96,
    165–67, 169, 204,
    216–17, 333–43, 566
  in armed forces, 11–12,
    338, 339–43, 345,
    338–43, 350, 416, 431,
    437, 439–40, 446,
    450–51, 472–73, 511,
    518–19, 535
  education of, 216,
    328–29
  lynchings of, 54, 166, 243
  violence against, 204,
    336–37
  voting rights of,
    336–37, 357
  see also racism
Allenswood School, 2, 109,
    121, 144, 450
Alsop, Joseph, 109–10
American Friends of
    German Freedom, 198,
    289, 468–70
American Friends Service
    Committee (AFSC),
    26, 62, 83, 134, 179,
    229, 242, 288, 323,
    370, 421, 431, 505,
    521–22, 569
American Red Cross,
    430, 444–45, 451,
    479–80
American Student Union
    (ASU), 95n, 174,
    175–76, 177, 182, 183,
    197, 208
American Youth Congress
    (AYC), 94–95, 109,
    117, 158, 196–97, 201,
    202–5, 210, 211, 219,
    245, 261–62, 285,
    324, 342

Communist members of,
    153, 157, 172, 175–76,
    177, 197, 203, 208, 230,
    282, 330, 360, 393
  Dies Committee hearings
    on, 172–79, 182, 184
  ER and, 95, 153, 157,
    212–15, 229–30, 330,
    334, 356, 360
Amery, Leo, 182–83, 252
Anderson, Charles Alfred,
    11, 437
Anderson, Marian, 33,
    34–35, 36, 57, 66, 73,
    93–94, 159
anti-colonialism, 436, 439,
    459, 464, 535–36,
    537, 549
anti-Communism, 157, 281,
    328, 360, 561, 564–65
  see also Red Scare
anti-lynching laws,
    31–32, 166
anti-Nazi films, 316,
    318–19, 359
anti-Semitism, 25, 26,
    27–28, 29, 92, 96–97,
    100, 126–27, 156, 171,
    192, 258, 321, 406,
    426–27, 449, 451–52,
    459, 486n
appeasement, 30, 41, 45,
    124, 136, 269
Arendt, Hannah, 179
armed forces, U.S.:
  Blacks in, 11–12, 338,
    339–43, 345, 338–43,
    350, 416, 431, 437,
    439–40, 446, 450–51,
    472–73, 511,
    518–19, 535
  women in, 426, 427–28,
    437–38, 444, 450–51
arms embargo, 86, 90,
    91–93, 97, 98,

    100–102, 101n, 123,
    124, 134, 137–38,
    160–61
Arthurdale, W.Va., 59, 68,
    142, 157–58, 230–31,
    243, 414
Atlantic Charter, 396, 411,
    418, 448, 461, 464,
    477, 550
Atomic Age Begins,
    147–49
Auden, W. H., 383
Augsberg, Anita, 323
Auschwitz-Birkenau, 431,
    453, 454, 516, 526
Australia, 302, 465, 479,
    480, 483
Austria, 26, 41, 99, 131

Backer, Dorothy Schiff, 168,
    351, 401, 474n
Baldwin, Joseph, 490–91
Baldwin, Roger,
    283–84, 395
Baruch, Belle, 505
Barr, Alfred, 384
Baruch, Bernard, 8, 63–64,
    146, 157–58, 175,
    178–79, 293, 363–64,
    390, 391, 407, 409,
    429, 483, 505, 542,
    547, 564
Belafonte, Harry, 512n,
    564, 566–68
Belgium, 81, 140, 163, 252,
    253–54
  Nazi invasion of, 255,
    257–58, 262
Bengal Famine, 492, 517
Bergen-Belsen, 516, 538
Bergson, Peter, 469, 474–75,
    484, 485, 487
Bermuda Conference
    (1943), 470–72, 474
Bernard, Viola, 567

Bethune, Mary McLeod,
211, 215–16, 250, 271,
336, 339, 343, 401, 407,
428, 432, 518–19, 549
ER and, 34, 156, 310,
333, 357–58, 564–65
Bhagavan, Manu, 536–647
Biddle, Anthony J. Drexel,
120, 139, 316
Biddle, Francis, 27, 337n,
417, 418, 420
Biddle, Margaret, 164,
316, 444
Bill of Rights, 180–81, 304,
321, 406, 417, 545
Bingham, Hiram, 371, 373,
381, 384, 389
Black, Ruby, 193,
353–57, 362
Blitz, 241, 314–15, 330–31,
375, 390, 392, 412,
441, 442, 506, 507
Boas, Franz, 181
Bond, Horace Mann, 244
Borah, William, 101
Boettiger, Anna Roosevelt,
48, 74, 79, 103, 183,
215, 352, 359, 474,
539, 541
ER's correspondence
with, 65–66, 71–72,
159, 210, 263, 268,
290, 351, 360, 399,
410, 423–24, 428,
430, 456, 483, 512
ER's visits with, 36–37,
53, 61, 144, 235, 236,
385, 402–3, 420,
422, 495
as FDR's aide, 501–2,
503, 504–5, 529
Tommy and, 167–68,
277–78, 310, 362,
422, 430
Boettiger, John Jr., 36, 37,
72, 359, 385, 430, 508,
533, 539
Boettiger, Johnnie (ER's
grandson), 53, 144, 236
Bowman, Isaiah, 459,
486–88
Braden, Ann, 565
British Empire, 212, 439,
458–59
Brittain, Vera, 316n, 505–6,
553–54

Brotherhood of Sleeping
Car Porters, 333,
334–35
Broun, Heywood,
184–85, 354
Brown, Roscoe, and the
Tuskegee Airmen, 437
Buck, Pearl S., 30, 278,
406–7, 517
Bullitt, William, 27, 37,
112, 120, 134, 139,
163, 219, 258, 263,
273, 316, 394
Bunche, Ralph, 552
Burke-Wadsworth bill,
323–24, 332,
338–39
Burma Road, 331–32, 492
Buttinger, Joseph, 288,
289, 379
Byrnes, James, 298, 300,
347, 511, 512, 548, 552

Cadden, Joseph, 94n, 173,
174, 204, 212,
261–62, 393
Cairo Conference, 483, 491,
492, 494
Catlin, George, 553
Catlin, Shirley Vivian, 316
California, 236, 238–41
Campobello, 393, 394–95,
396, 397
Cardwell, Ann, 161–63
Carlson, Evans, 460,
461, 512
Casablanca Conference
(1943), 452, 457,
458–59, 461
Cassin, René, 557–58
Catholics, Catholic Church,
41, 47, 151, 189–92, 360
Catt, Carrie Chapman, 90,
92, 321, 497, 549
Celler, Emanuel, 63, 498–99
Chamberlain, Neville, 113,
115, 218, 252, 347
Chaney, Mayris "Tiny," 7,
145, 236, 239–40, 241,
412, 414, 415, 416, 512
Chang, Peng-chun (P. C.)
557–58
Chapman, Oscar, 34, 35, 159
Chiang, Madame Mayling
Soong, 424, 460,
460–63, 491, 517

Chiang Kai-shek, 331, 460,
461–63, 465, 474, 483,
491, 494, 548
China, 41–42, 82, 99, 116,
203, 210, 213, 254,
278, 331–32, 460, 461,
463, 548, 549, 561
Churchill, Clementine,
442–43, 445, 450,
476, 514, 517
Churchill, Randolph, and
Pamela Digby
Churchill
Harriman, 445
Churchill, Sarah, 529
Churchill, Winston, 40,
114, 136, 140, 151,
252, 255, 263, 314,
315, 332, 375, 390,
393, 438, 442, 472,
474, 490, 515, 524–25
at Cairo Conference, 492
at Casablanca
Conference, 458–59
and cross-channel
invasion plan, 477, 494
delays in opening second
European front urged
by, 492
destruction of French
fleet ordered by, 281
ER and, 443, 450, 491,
516, 517, 557
in first wartime meeting
with FDR, 395–96
Greece and, 527–28
Hyde Park visits of,
476–77, 516–17
Ibn Saud's meeting
with, 531
imperialism of, 451, 458,
535, 544n
Indian independence and,
434–35, 439, 459,
463–65, 491–92, 517,
535, 536
"iron curtain" speech of,
556–57
Italy and, 527
Jewish refugees and,
475–76, 484,
500–501
as monarchist, 527
in Quebec Conference,
484, 514, 516,
517, 518

Soviets and, 42, 546–47
"sphere of influence"
policy of, 517–18
in Tehran Conference,
483, 492
Truman and, 546–47
U.S. destroyers requested
by, 256, 331
in White House meetings
with FDR,
408–12, 417
at Yalta Conference, 530
Citizenship Institute,
202–205, 210, 216
Civilian Conservation
Corps (CCC), 23, 54,
63, 74, 87n, 160
civil liberties, 157, 178, 230,
232, 244, 257, 268,
281–83, 406, 417, 418,
419, 565
civil rights, 9, 11, 13, 204,
211, 304, 310–11, 321,
334, 336–37, 561
civil rights movement, 243,
425, 431–32, 436,
522, 568
Cockburn, Claude, 100
Cohen, Ben, 102, 103, 105,
123, 205, 206n, 552
Cold War, 556, 560–61, 562
Communism, Communists,
24, 88, 92, 96, 135,
141, 156, 159, 178,
210, 219, 245, 247,
258, 269, 460, 463,
523, 525
AYC and, 153, 157, 172,
175–77, 197, 203, 208,
230, 282, 330, 360, 393
Dies Committee and, 69,
153–54, 181–84
see also anti-Communism;
Red Scare
concentration camps, 81,
99, 126, 198, 199,
452–53, 454, 515–16,
538, 558
Congress, U.S., 58, 31, 63,
79, 91, 98, 102, 113,
196, 270, 346–47, 375,
391, 396, 404, 408,
415, 437
anti-alien bills in, 27–28
anti-New Deal legislation
in, 86–93

Churchill's address to, 410
draft bill in, 273–74
ER's criticisms of,
106–7
FDR's post-Yalta address
to, 533
FDR's relations with,
270, 502–3
Madame Chiang's
address to, 462
Neutrality Acts in,
137–38
opposition to WPA in, 60
refugee issue in, 82
Congress Party, India, 434,
435, 491–92
Connally, Tom, 548,
551–52
"Conquer Fear and You
Will Enjoy Living" (E.
Roosevelt), 48–50
Constitution, U.S., 92,
180–81, 230, 304
Cook, Nancy, 6, 85, 97, 110,
125, 168, 360
Corcoran, Tom, 102, 105,
123, 205, 394
Coughlin, Charles, 41, 156,
158, 321
Crim, Howell, 387–88, 540
Cripps, Stafford, and Lady
Isobel, 434–35, 442
Cudahy, John, 139–40
Cushing, Dr. Harvey, 143
Czechoslovakia, 18, 29, 41,
58, 113, 115, 131,
148n–49n, 210, 213,
232, 254

Dachau, 317, 516, 538
Daily Worker, 135, 176, 182
Daladier, Édouard, 164,
218, 280
Danzig, 112, 113, 136
Darlan, François, 448–49,
451–52
Darlan Deal, 449,
451–52, 457
Davis, Norman, 41, 42,
138, 253, 277, 430,
451, 481
D-Day, 501, 508–9
death camps, 515–16, 538,
547, 554
Declaration of
Independence, 304, 545

de Gaulle, Charles, 411,
449, 451, 458–61,
508, 516
Delano, Laura "Polly," 8,
401, 502, 526, 528,
534, 537, 539, 540n
democracy, 24, 231, 303–7,
333, 341, 358–60
Democratic Digest, 251, 356,
360–61
Democratic National
Committee, 236
Women's Division of,
250, 309, 343, 356,
360–61
Democratic National
Convention, 292
of 1940, 295–302, 353
of 1944, 512
Democratic Party,
Democrats, 1, 6, 17,
84, 102–3, 107,
303–8, 521
Dewey, Thomas, 291, 488,
514, 522
in 1944 election, 513,
518, 523, 525
Dickerman, Marion, 6, 85,
97, 110, 125, 168
Dies, Martin, 41, 69–70,
147, 153, 154, 158,
260, 469
Dies Committee, 69–70,
86, 147, 153, 158–59,
172–74, 175–76,
178–79, 181–82, 184,
197, 202, 204, 244,
281, 469
Displaced Persons, 547, 554,
555–56
Dixiecrats, 13, 167, 216,
510, 561–62, 566
Dombrowski, James, 243,
565–66
Dominican Republic, 236,
372, 373
Douglas, Helen Gahagan,
174, 175, 237–38, 239,
250, 402, 413
Douglas, Melvyn, 174, 175,
237–38, 413, 414,
415, 416
draft, 55, 273–74,
280, 323–24, 332,
344–45
DuBois, Joseph E., 489, 498

Dubois, Rachel Davis, 169–70, 186
Du Bois, W. E. B., 549, 561
Dulles, John Foster, 514, 548, 550–51, 552, 554–55, 562–63
Dumbarton Oaks Conference, 513–14, 534
Durno, Major George, 479
Durr, Virginia, 251, 321, 565

Early, Steve, 122, 340, 346–47, 358, 539
Eden, Anthony, 455, 458, 490
Edison, Charles, 120, 122, 280
education, 28, 33–34, 59, 93, 97, 144–45, 160, 169–70
Ehrenburg, Ilya, 114, 219, 220–21, 228
Eichelberger, Clark, 554, 563
Einstein, Albert, 30, 148–49, 383
Eisenhower, Dwight, 439, 440, 449, 459, 494, 508, 516, 538, 562
Eisenhower, Milton S., 418, 419, 420, 457
Eleanor Roosevelt (Ruby Black biography), 353–57
elections, U.S.:
    of 1938, 17
    of 1940, 96, 103, 131, 164, 168, 178, 251, 284, 291–92, 295–302, 343–52, 360–61
    of 1944, 510, 512, 513, 518, 521, 523–24
    of 1948, 561–62
    of 1952, 562
Elizabeth, the Queen Mother, 43, 44, 65–79, 441, 450
Emergency Committee to Save the Jews of Europe, 485, 488, 490, 501
Emergency Rescue Committee (ERC), 288–90, 311, 368, 369, 373, 377, 379–80, 383, 384, 389, 430
Ernst, Max, and Dr. Lou Straus-Ernst, Jimmy, 384–89

Ethiopia, 203, 213, 269
Europe, 161
    Displaced Persons in, 547, 554, 555–56
    ER's travels in, 266
    Normandy invasion in, 501, 508–9
Farley, James, 102–3, 104, 267, 292, 296, 297, 298–300, 309, 355
Farm Security Administration (FSA), 59, 142, 237, 239, 243
fascists, fascism, 24, 41, 69–70, 156, 159, 172, 220, 247, 310, 320, 321, 358
Federal Bureau of Investigation (FBI), 73, 153, 172, 337, 466, 467, 492
    ER investigated by, 521
Federal Theatre Project, 86–90, 97
Feuchtwanger, Lion, 368, 370–71
Field, Marshall, 229, 288, 290, 312, 430
Finland, 114, 178, 203, 208, 210, 221, 225, 254
    Soviet invasion of, 174, 187–88, 197, 204, 213, 219, 227
Fisher, Dorothy Canfield, 53, 225, 254, 325
Flynn, Ed, 309, 343, 351, 352, 360, 361
Food and Agriculture Organization (FAO), 474, 477, 560
Forbes, Dora Delano, 103–4, 116, 128, 163, 279, 284, 310
Foreign Office, British, 476, 500, 536
Fort Devens, Negro WACs nurses demeaned, 519
Four Freedoms, 56, 382–83, 411, 461, 494, 496, 560
France, 141, 153, 203, 219, 227, 229, 247, 252, 254, 280, 373, 374, 431, 448
    anti-Semitism in, 258

colonial empire of, 212, 458–59
Communists is, 154, 214, 219, 258
    in early stages of war, 154, 214, 252
    fall of, 276, 279, 280, 302, 310, 327, 328, 348, 370
    German invasion of, 257–58, 262–63, 271, 276, 286, 302, 327, 328
    German occupation of, 286, 448–49
    internment camps in, 221, 275, 279, 370
    Jews in, 374, 430, 431, 451, 489, 499
    lack of preparedness in, 114, 154, 219
    refugees in, 81, 147, 152, 164, 229, 253–54, 258, 273, 275–77, 369–70, 374, 381, 384
    rescue of Jews and antifascists in, 288–89, 368, 369
    in run-up to war, 21, 40, 41–42, 99, 112–15
    sale of planes to, 43–44
    U.S. aid to, 43–44, 115, 134, 136, 161, 163, 219, 257, 273
Franco, Francisco, 17, 21, 37, 68, 91, 100, 443, 527
Frank, Karl, *see* Hagen, Paul
Frankfurter, Felix, 24–26, 283–84, 394
Fry, Varian, 9n, 289–90, 311, 368, 369, 370–71, 373, 377, 381, 384, 389, 430, 454
Gage-Colby, Ruth, 316
Gandhi, Mohandas K., 434, 435, 437, 464, 491–92
Garner, John Nance, 21, 101–2, 184, 295, 298
Gellhorn, Martha, 187, 220–21, 232, 275
George VI, King of England, 19, 43, 65–79, 441
Germany, Nazi, 126, 136, 187, 189, 221, 222, 229, 241, 246, 314,

317n, 323, 328, 330,
332, 375, 376, 391, 404
Allied bombing of, 438,
505, 533n
book burning in, 470
France invaded by,
257–58, 262–63, 286
French armistice with,
276, 279, 280, 370
Hitler's purification
of, 320
murder of Jews by, see
Jews, Nazi slaughter of
in nonaggression pact
with Soviets, see
Nazi-Soviet pact
Poland invaded by, 120
Poles massacred by,
199, 452
Polish Jews expelled by, 82
propaganda of, 199
"resisters" in, 198
in run-up to World War
II, 119–20
Soviet Union invaded
by, 389
unconditional surrender
of, 546
GI Bill of Rights, 477, 483,
489, 524
Goebbels, Josef, 38, 119,
150, 153
Graham, Frank, 28, 244, 415
Gray, David, 98, 128,
246, 450
Gray, Maude, 98, 119, 120,
133, 143, 450, 534, 542
Great Britain, 78, 81, 113,
136, 141, 152, 153,
161, 163, 195, 196,
212, 219, 227, 246,
252, 254, 327, 332,
358, 391, 401, 403
American racism and,
439–40
anticipated Nazi attack
on, 255, 280–81, 290
in Battle of Britain,
314–15; see also Blitz
ER's 1942 mission to,
437, 440–47
imperialism of, 212, 439,
458–59
Jewish immigration to
Palestine blocked
by, 427

as not prepared for
war, 136
oil and, 471, 531
refugee children from, 316
Soviet Union and, 40, 42,
99, 140
U.S. aid to, 137, 161, 263,
287, 376, 393
U.S. public opinion on,
18–19, 65, 320
U.S. relations with,
471–72
Greece, 332, 346, 365, 391,
518, 533n
Greenway, Isabella, 34, 56,
291, 293, 456
Gruber, Ruth, 14, 500,
510, 521
Guadalcanal, 482
Gurewitsch, David, 7, 14, 564

Hagen, Paul (Karl Frank),
465, 198, 199, 288,
311, 368, 369, 465
Halsey, William, 481,
482, 513
Hannegan, William, 510–11
Hastie, William H., 340,
342, 473
health care, 23, 93, 179,
233, 497, 566
Hecht, Ben, 359, 378–79,
469, 474–75
Hedgeman, Anna Arnold,
432, 436, 470
Height, Dorothy, 211
Helm, Edith, 66, 167, 179,
351, 466
Heschel, Abraham
Joshua, 485
Heymann, Lida Gustava, 323
Hickok, Lorena "Hick," 20,
55, 64, 73, 74, 78, 85,
120, 143, 237, 241,
250, 253, 292, 299,
343–44, 389, 399,
406, 410, 480, 483,
485, 510, 511, 515,
528, 542, 544, 564
bigotry of, 96–97, 293
DNC work of, 236, 292,
297, 361
ER's friendship with, 6, 7,
8, 43, 48, 52–53, 109,
183–84, 214–15, 293,
361–63, 403, 516, 522

Tommy and, 236–37, 423
as White House resident,
236–37, 362, 363, 387,
423, 456, 457
World's Fair work of, 55,
85, 120, 143
Highlander Folk School,
243, 245, 565
Hill, T. Arnold, 106, 339,
340, 342–43
Hiss, Alger, 552
Hiss, Donald, 498
Hitler, Adolf, 17, 31, 56, 61,
68, 69, 78, 91, 93, 100,
108, 113–14, 115, 116,
119, 120, 125–26, 131,
135, 140, 150, 157, 163,
172, 195, 198, 218–19,
227, 242, 252, 255,
286, 315, 317n, 322,
325, 331, 367, 370,
372, 454, 468, 470
character of, 122
Communists and, 30, 41,
92, 154, 327
and creation of Master
Race, 320, 321
Czechoslovakia and, 18,
29, 30, 148n–49n
edicts of, 150, 199, 320
eugenics program of,
136–37
FDR's messages to,
39–40, 63
France and, 276, 279–81,
327, 374
Jews and, 46–47, 82, 99,
132, 155, 192, 199,
374, 453, 469, 491,
498, 499
lack of opposition to, 26,
27, 30, 41, 90, 92, 359
Mussolini and, 21,
39, 375
Poland and, 40, 149,
155, 262
women as viewed by,
46–47
Hobbs, Sam and the Alien
Detention bill 62–63
Hobby, Oveta Culp, 428,
440, 443–44, 518
Hooker, Harry, 185, 318,
325, 534
Hoover, Herbert, 26, 43,
61n, 64, 210, 225, 475

Hoover, J. Edgar, 153, 157,
      159, 337n, 419, 466,
      467–68
Hopkins, Diana, 73, 106,
      143, 267, 422, 423,
      428, 429
Hopkins, Harry, 73, 268,
      284–85, 295–96, 308,
      343, 391, 411, 422,
      423, 459, 464, 477
   ER and, 267, 277, 300,
      401, 432, 467, 526
   failing health of, 143, 532
   FDR and, 267, 297, 351,
      387, 390, 403, 428–29,
      452, 491, 501, 532
   marriage of, 428–29, 430
   stomach cancer of,
      106, 267
Hopkins, Louise Macy,
      428–30
Horton, Myles, 243, 565
House of Representatives,
      U.S., 62–63, 86–90,
      105, 138, 161, 282,
      489, 564
   see also Dies Committee
housing:
   affordable, 9, 53, 54,
      59–60, 90, 93, 237,
      238–39, 385–87
   discrimination in, 406,
      497, 564, 566–67
Howard University, 32–33,
      34, 310, 473
Howe, Louis, 225, 267,
      362–63
Hull, Cordell, 42, 64, 99,
      99n, 101, 114, 115,
      116, 120, 138, 163,
      164, 272, 287,
      298, 403, 490,
      491, 499
"Humanistic Democracy—
      The American Ideal"
      (E. Roosevelt), 159
human rights, 9, 11, 13
   ER's crusade for, 542,
      545, 549–71
Humphrey, John,
      557–58, 562
Hungary, 40, 92, 99, 114,
      135, 164, 500, 518
Huntington, Alice,
      119, 120, 293,
      346, 359

Ibn Saud, King of Saudi
      Arabia, 529, 530–32
Ickes, Harold, 34, 35, 74,
      99, 99n–100n, 100,
      105, 106, 114, 122,
      123, 147, 256, 279,
      280, 283, 292,
      295–96, 298, 359, 381,
      385–86, 435, 475
   refugees supported by, 27,
      379–80, 381, 501,
      510, 521
immigrants, immigration,
      190, 222, 328, 329,
      330, 369, 372–73,
      379–80
   quotas for, 27–30, 83
   suspicion and fear of,
      260–61, 417–18, 498
India:
   famine in, 477, 492, 517
   independence movement
      in, 434–35, 436–37,
      439, 441–42, 459,
      463–65, 491–92, 517,
      535–36, 558
Intergovernmental
      Committee on
      Refugees, 152,
      236, 471
International Labor
      Organization (ILO),
      322, 376, 560
International Ladies
      Garment Workers
      Union (ILGWU), 11,
      265, 497
International Student
      Service (ISS), 286,
      364–65, 394–95, 415,
      428, 436
isolationism, 18–19, 22–23,
      29, 40, 45, 65, 91, 101,
      136, 141, 156, 161,
      164, 220, 255, 261–62,
      269, 274, 279, 280,
      291, 358, 376, 393, 396
Israel, 14, 556, 558
Italy, 40, 68, 100n, 114, 115,
      189, 204, 218, 255,
      269, 271–72, 331, 332,
      346, 365, 404

Jackson, C. D. 457
Jackson, Robert, 122,
      205–6, 245, 283, 330

Japan, 40, 41–42, 61, 99,
      115, 241, 331–32, 363,
      396, 403, 533n
   China invaded by, 269.
      278, 460
   early victories of, 405,
      409, 418
Japanese-Americans, 11
   fear and suspicion about,
      405, 407, 417–18, 420
   internment of, 416–21
Jews, 47, 64, 80, 82, 96–97,
      100, 126–27, 152, 157,
      163–64, 192, 193, 194,
      222, 312, 317, 358–59,
      369, 374–75, 430, 451
   Arab enmity toward,
      530–31
   Nazi slaughter of, 199,
      452–53, 469, 475,
      490–91, 498, 499–500,
      515, 530, 538
   in Poland, 132, 150
   as refugees, see refugees,
      Jewish
Justice Department, U.S.,
      137, 154, 204, 205,
      244, 337

Kellogg, Paul, 407, 408,
      415, 535
Kennedy, Joseph P., 100,
      140–41, 219, 258,
      347–48, 358, 359,
      376, 390
King, Mackenzie, 71, 75,
      76, 78
Kingdon, Frank, 171, 249,
      253–54, 289, 290,
      369–70, 373, 377, 378,
      389, 431
Kirchwey, Freda, and the
      Nation, 249
Kiskadden, Peggy Bok, 328
Knox, Frank, 11, 172, 280,
      289, 339, 340, 341–42
Ku Klux Klan, 158, 204,
      205, 243, 473

Lachmann, Vera, 222–24
LaGuardia, Fiorello, 75,
      87n, 333, 401, 405,
      408, 475
Lape, Esther, 41, 104, 179,
      248–49, 286, 292, 293,
      328n, 394, 507, 564

American Foundation
and, 5, 59, 376
ER's correspondence
with, 8, 36–37, 277,
428, 477, 483, 493–94,
542, 549–50
as ER's mentor and
confidant, 5, 20, 85,
129, 493
Tommy and, 6, 7, 60, 76,
110, 225, 236, 237,
240, 271, 405, 428,
442, 462, 478, 479,
504, 528
World Court and, 5,
128–29, 300, 493
Lash, Joseph, 7, 211, 212,
255, 265, 268–69, 288,
293–95, 297, 318, 334,
342, 343, 390, 394,
401, 402, 407, 410,
423, 435, 460, 461,
463, 528, 542
in Army Air Force,
422–23, 482, 516, 525
Army Intelligence
investigation of,
466–67
ASU and, 95n, 174,
175–76, 177, 182,
183, 208
AYC and, 8–9, 174, 206,
285, 334
on ER, 9, 175, 197, 262,
402, 486, 495, 522
ER and, 9, 176–77,
182–83, 196–201, 253,
266–67, 293–95,
297–98, 351, 364–68,
387–88, 391–92, 397,
398, 399–400, 408,
422, 456, 474, 495, 525
on ER-FDR relationship,
209, 377, 385, 422, 503
ER's correspondence
with, 286, 383, 398,
442, 474, 482, 488,
490, 492, 495, 506,
510, 511, 512, 516, 518,
522, 529, 533, 541
Spanish Civil War and,
176, 220, 366, 466
Trude and, see Lash,
Trude Pratt, Joe and
Lash, Trude Pratt, 7, 344,
360, 361, 389, 423,

460, 465, 482, 510,
528, 542, 552n
ER and, 14, 294, 295,
366, 394, 396–97,
428, 436, 446, 456,
467, 468, 469, 474,
486, 503, 516, 517,
525, 541
ER's correspondence
with, 367, 495, 511,
514, 544
Joe and, 9, 285, 286, 288,
294, 295, 364,
367–68, 388, 391–92,
397, 466, 485–86,
490, 491, 516, 525, 564
marriage of Eliot Pratt
and, 286, 367–68, 396
Latin America, 61, 421,
501, 554
Lattimore, Owen, 461, 479,
486n, 536
Leach, Agnes Brown, 168,
343, 351, 360
League of Nations, 31, 40,
287, 300, 322, 490,
544, 555
Leahy, William, 377,
513, 517
LeHand, Missy, 134, 139,
163, 167, 267, 347,
394, 401, 501, 502
death of, 513
Leopold, King of Belgium,
64, 163, 262
Lewis, John L., 210–11,
214–15, 337, 462
Lincoln, Abraham, 23,
200, 203
Lisbon, 311, 312,
369–70, 371
Lithuania, 114, 436, 556
Littell, Katherine,
47–48, 79
Littell, Norman, 47, 79, 103,
104, 174
Litvinov, Ivy Low, 40–41
Litvinov, Maxim, 27,
40–41, 42, 68, 113,
133, 411
London, 112, 122, 198, 219,
314–15, 330–31, 332,
347, 375, 390, 523
Blitz in, see Blitz
UN session in, 548,
551–55

Long, Breckenridge, 426,
442, 464–65, 486n,
489, 498–500
rescue of Jews blocked by,
200, 312–13, 369, 373,
377–78, 380–81,
389–90, 471, 489,
498–99
Longworth, Alice Roosevelt,
101, 484
Lowdermilk, Walter
Clay, 487
loyalty oaths, 86, 89, 561
Luce, Clare Boothe, 1, 34n,
44, 263, 277, 292
Luce, Henry, 44, 292, 426
Lustig, Hans (Bohumil) and
Charlotte, 377–79
Luxembourg, 252, 254,
258, 262
lynchings, 54, 166, 243

Mahler, Franz, and Alma
Mahler Werfel, 371
McAllister, Dorothy, 131,
250, 361
MacArthur, Douglas, 423,
481, 513
McCarthyism, 561,
564–65
McCormick, Anne O'Hare,
135, 140, 275–76
MacCracken, Henry, 163,
222–23
MacDonald, James G.,
373–74
McIntire, Ross, 47, 122, 539
MacLeish, Archibald,
395, 452
McMichael, Jack, 173, 174,
204, 205, 207
Malik, Charles Habbib,
557–58, 562
Mann, Heinrich, 370,
371, 372
Mann, Klaus and Erika,
383
Mann, Thomas, 368, 371,
372, 373, 377, 383, 468
Marcantonio, Vito, 86,
261, 329
Marseilles, 368, 369–71,
374, 381, 384
Marshall, George, 274, 446,
459, 467, 491, 518,
519–20, 552n, 560

Marshall, Thurgood, 12, 337, 473
Martha, Crown Princess of Norway, 56, 325, 388, 401, 423, 446, 502
Mary of Teck, Queen Consort of England, 65, 111–12, 446–47
Matthews, J. B., 175, 181–82
Mehta, Hansa, 558, 561
Mercer, Lucy, *see* Rutherfurd, Lucy Mercer
Michelson, Charles, 292, 297, 355
Miller, Earl, 6, 7–8, 21, 82, 85, 97, 109, 145, 200, 215, 216, 225, 239–40, 293–94, 351, 363, 366, 387, 388, 389, 456, 528, 564
Molotov, Vyacheslav, 42, 113–14, 140, 227, 438, 439, 490
Moral Basis of Democracy, The (E. Roosevelt), 108, 302, 303–8, 319, 353, 382
Morgenthau, Elinor, 7, 102, 128, 179, 271, 293, 326, 343, 351, 360, 401, 420, 451, 456, 495, 503, 514, 520, 536, 552
Morgenthau, Henry, 34n, 77, 100n, 102, 116, 128, 405, 419, 421, 443, 451–52, 460, 463, 466, 467, 475, 477, 485, 495, 499, 502, 521, 537–38
and rescue of Jews, 488–89, 498–99, 501, 510
Morley, Louise, 553
Morrow, Janet and Edward R., 440, 449
Munich Agreement, 114–15
Munich Conference (1938), 40
Murphy, Robert, 205n, 219, 258, 448
Murray, Arthur Lord Elibank, 557–58
Murray, Pauli, 1, 431, 432, 433, 435–37, 564
Mussolini, Benito, 21, 39–40, 63, 78, 91, 115,

116, 148n–49n, 204, 218, 255, 271–72, 285, 332, 346, 375, 476

NAACP, 34, 86, 92–94, 156, 170, 211, 250, 292, 310, 333, 334, 336–37, 357, 395, 428, 431, 437, 463, 510, 511, 517, 521, 536
anti-lynching law and, 31–32, 166
in campaign against racial discrimination, 338, 341, 472, 519
conventions of, 86, 92–93, 94, 561
Legal Defense and Education Fund of, 12, 473, 519
Spingarn Medal and, 36, 93
Nagasaki, 547
Nation, 192, 193, 249–50, 380
National Council of Negro Women (NCNW), 211, 343, 407
National Youth Administration (NYA), 54, 86, 117, 142, 160, 213, 228, 239, 249, 271, 310, 325, 339, 357, 426
Nazi-Soviet Pact, 113–15, 117, 133–34, 135, 140, 153, 172, 178, 195, 196, 201, 203, 210, 219, 247, 257, 321, 393
Nehru, Jawaharlal, 434, 435, 437, 491–92, 517, 535
Neilson, William Allan, 221–22, 395
Netherlands, 81, 140, 163, 252–54
Nazi invasion of, 255–56, 262
Neutrality Acts, 22, 42, 79, 90, 98, 102, 123, 136, 137–38, 161, 269, 280, 393
New Deal, 23, 53, 58–59, 93, 96, 105, 141–42, 154, 156, 167, 173, 175, 178, 200, 201, 204, 206, 229, 237, 269,

279, 300, 302, 305, 308, 309, 321, 342, 343, 345, 346, 356, 376, 387, 425, 559, 568
opposition to, 17, 32, 59, 69, 71, 86, 90, 93, 94, 96, 105, 147, 156, 158, 167, 172, 412
see also Works Progress Administration
New Republic, 380, 424, 454
Newspaper Guild, 10, 184, 186, 360
New York Herald Tribune, 85, 370, 506, 515
New York Times, 24, 38, 43, 50, 57, 67, 78, 81, 85, 114, 135, 136, 158–59, 171, 173, 175, 176, 181, 185, 228–29, 241, 264, 275–76, 284, 300, 318, 319, 353, 400, 444, 474–75, 504
New York World's Fair (1939), 43, 55–56, 71, 85, 104, 120, 143, 264, 265–66, 316n
New Zealand, 465, 479, 480, 483
Nicolson, Harold, 40, 42, 78, 114, 118, 122, 124, 136, 187, 219, 281, 326–27, 451
Niebuhr, Reinhold, 198, 289, 465
Niemöller, Martin, and *Pastor Hall* (film) 317–19
North Africa, 280
Allied invasion of, 431, 438, 446, 448
Darlan Deal and, 449, 451–52, 457
Vichy regime in, 280, 448–49, 451–52, 458, 460, 466
Norton, Mary, 56, 543, 545
Norway, 56, 246, 252, 254
Nazi invasion of, 241
neutrality of, 227
Nye, Gerald, 90, 101, 101n

O'Day, Caroline, 6, 26, 29–30, 34, 35, 62–63, 85, 88, 90–91, 92, 161, 229, 321, 360, 404

Office of Civilian Defense (OCD), 401, 402, 405, 407–8, 412–15

Office of War Information and Psychological Warfare (OWI), 450, 454, 457, 485

Offie, Carmel, 112, 134, 139, 163

oil, 471, 531, 532, 548

"On Jews" (E. Roosevelt), 127–28

Osthagen, Henry, 6, 215, 216, 293, 351, 389

Oswego, N.Y., refugee camp at, 510, 520–21

Pacific Theater, ER's tour of, 465, 479–84

Palestine, 26, 64, 79–80, 152, 157, 311, 427, 486–88, 501, 530, 532, 547–48, 554, 556

Pandit, Madame Vijaya Lakshmi, 517, 535–36

Palmer, Charles F., 385, 386, 387

Paris, 112, 134, 273, 516
   Nazi occupation of, 275–76, 279

Parliament, British, 113, 115, 219, 252, 314, 375

Patterson, William, 562

Patterson, Robert, 339, 340, 483

Patton, George S., 203, 448, 538

Paul, Randolph, 489

Paulino, Edward, 236

Peare, Catherine Owens, 357

Pearl Harbor, Japanese attack on, 403–4, 416, 419

Pehle, John, 489, 498, 499, 500, 501

Perkins, Frances, 26, 27, 123, 147, 287, 296–97, 299, 376–77

Pétain, Henri-Philippe, 271, 276, 280–81

Pethick-Lawrence, Lady Emmeline, 553

Phillips, Caroline Astor Drayton, 150–51, 187, 189, 191–92, 442

Phillips, William, 150–51, 189, 191–92, 271–72, 442, 463–64

Pickens, Harriet Ida, 11, 95n, 211, 334, 342

Pickens, William, 12, 211, 334

Pickett, Clarence, 26, 62, 83, 155, 229, 321, 421

Pinchot, Cornelia Bryce "Leila," 31, 34, 408, 437

Pinchot, Gifford, 31, 34, 437

Pius XII, Pope, 69, 189–92, 199, 228

Poland, Poles, 40, 69, 92, 115, 119, 135, 149, 153, 178, 189, 194, 199, 203, 210, 225, 229, 246–47, 498, 518, 533n, 556, 163–64, 254
   lack of Western aid to, 135–36
   massacres in, 132–33, 139–40, 151, 199, 452, 515, 530
   Nazi air raids on, 174
   Nazi invasion of, 120, 131, 139–40, 150–51, 262
   partition of, 114
   refugee crisis in, 161–63
   refugees from, 236
   "resettlement" camps in, 152
   resistance movement in, 453–54
   Soviet invasion of, 133–34, 135–36

Polier, Justine Wise, 9–10, 27, 382, 407

poll taxes, 93, 96, 156, 251

Port Chicago, munitions explosion at, 511–12, 519–20

Potsdam Conference (1945), 547

poverty, 28, 86, 160

Pratt, Eliot, 286, 367, 388, 397

President's Advisory Committee on Political Refugees (PACPR), 312, 313, 369, 373

press, freedom of, 95–96

Price, Florence, 364

public health, 59, 247–48, 251

Quakers, 34, 169, 170, 179, 321, 489

Quanza, SS, 82n, 311–13, 369

Quebec Conference (1944), 484, 514, 516, 517, 518

"Race, Religion and Prejudice" (E. Roosevelt), 424

racial violence, 204, 243, 336, 473, 511

racism, 11, 54, 96–97, 155, 156, 166, 169, 204, 310–11, 321, 329, 333–36, 338, 340, 350, 357–58, 413, 414–15, 416, 424, 431–34, 435, 436, 439–40, 446, 450–51, 472–73, 497, 518–21, 535, 545, 561, 564, 566

Randolph, A. Philip, 333, 339, 340, 342–43, 432–33, 568

Raset, Zena, 398, 399, 423

Rathbone, Eleanor, 14, 476, 485

Read, Elizabeth, 5, 6, 7, 20, 36, 60, 85, 128–29, 179, 225, 237, 271, 277, 286, 293, 328n, 493–94

Reading, Stella, 3, 14, 141, 390, 401, 440, 443–44, 445, 475–76, 485, 522–23, 557

Red Cross, 138, 253, 263, 264, 273, 430, 444–45, 451, 479–80, 483, 507

Red Scare, 39, 147, 153–54, 155, 281–83, 328–30

refugee children, 253–54

Refugee Facts, 83

refugees, 61, 63–64, 92, 99, 120, 138, 151–52, 161–64, 258, 276–77, 287–91
   Churchill and, 475–76, 484, 500–501
   ER and, see Roosevelt, Eleanor, refugees and

refugees *(cont.)*
  in France, 164, 258, 273, 276–77, 369–70, 374, 381, 384
  Jewish, 13–14, 26, 62, 69, 79–83, 189, 427, 455, 470–71, 472, 474–76, 484–85, 486, 488, 489, 498–99, 500–501, 520–21, 530, 547, 554, 555–56
Reid, Helen Rogers, 84–85, 159, 291, 370
religious freedom, 96, 238
Republican Party, Republicans, 1, 17, 23, 107, 203, 291, 346, 349
Reynaud, Paul, 258, 263, 271, 273, 276, 280
Reynolds, Agnes, 182, 267, 294, 318
Robeson, Paul, 562, 565
Rogers, Edith Nourse, 26, 31, 393
Romania, 40, 92, 114, 135, 140, 161–62, 498, 518, 533*n*
  rescue of Jews from, 488–89
Roosevelt, Amy, 325, 364, 400
Roosevelt, Anna Eleanor "Sistie," 144, 185, 196, 236, 483
Roosevelt, Anna Rebecca Hall (ER's mother), 2, 21, 266
Roosevelt, Anne Clark, 70, 103–4, 112, 116, 125, 271, 512
Roosevelt, Archibald, 204, 213
Roosevelt, Belle, 391
Roosevelt, Curtis "Buzzy," 144, 196, 236
Roosevelt, Daniel Stewart, 37–38, 43
Roosevelt, Diana, 325, 364, 400
Roosevelt, Dorothy Kemp, 33, 364, 400
Roosevelt, Eleanor, 110, 129
  activism of, 171, 229, 355
  affinity for people, 2–3

"air our minds" luncheons of, 66
America christened by, 125
anti-Asian racial discrimination deplored by, 424
anti-Communism of, 154, 157, 562, 564, 565
on anti-immigrant feelings, 405–6
anti-lynching laws and, 31–32
arms embargo and, 91, 98, 102, 138–39
article to graduates of 1939 by, 53–55
attacks on, 182–83, 412, 413–14, 415–16, 469
AYC and, 94–95, 157–58, 173–79, 202–5, 209, 210, 211–15, 229–30, 245, 261–62
and backlash against New Deal, 59
Baruch and, 363–64
Belafonte and, 567–68
Bethune and, 357–58
birth control supported by, 47
Black's biography of, 353–57, 362
boundaries of, 246
California trip of, 236, 237–41
in campaign for FDR's reelection, 333
as chair of President's Committee on the Status of Women, 568
Chaney and, 239–40
charity given by, 356–57
childhood of, 266
Churchill and, 443, 450, 491, 516, 517, 557
Churchill's White House visit and, 408–12
civil liberties and, 257, 268, 282, 283, 406–7, 414, 417
civil liberties defended by, 177–78
civil rights movement and, 431–32, 436, 568
competitiveness of, 550, 551

compulsory universal service proposed by, 274–75
Congress criticized by, 106–7
contempt for Wallace's early policies, 308
critics of, 21–22, 46
DAR resigned by, 32–33
defense buildup and, 256–57
on democracy, 303, 304–8, 333
depressions of, 4, 6, 290, 402–3, 483, 486, 492
dismal state of mind of, 234–35
Displaced Persons and, 554
on education, 144–45, 232–33
education of, 2
in efforts to save British children, 316
Eleventh Street apartment of, 288
face-to-face diplomacy of, 552, 555, 558
FBI/Army Intelligence investigation of, 466–67
FBI investigation of, 521
in FDR's 1940 reelection campaign, 251, 295–302, 343–52, 355, 360–61, 373
on FDR's 1940 State of the Union address, 196
FDR's death and, 539–41, 543, 544
and FDR's failing health, 504–5, 533–34
FDR's flu and, 233–34, 241–42
on FDR's military segregation, 341–42
on FDR speech to AYC, 210
FDR's policies as influenced by, 10, 357, 382–83
Federal Theatre Project and, 87
fifty-fifth birthday of, 146–47

fifty-seventh birthday
of, 402
first 1940 campaign
speech of, 96
as "First Lady of the
World," 544
Florida vacation of,
215–18, 220, 221, 224
Four Freedoms and, 496
freedom as core principle
of, 425
friendships of, 5–9, 85,
178, 236–37, 293, 294,
493, 564
Goya prints given to, 37–38
Greenwich Village
apartment of, 20, 70,
422, 436, 524
Hick and, 6, 8, 43, 48,
52–53, 183–84, 214–15,
293, 361–63, 403
Hitler's barbarism and,
246–47
and Hitler's Reichstag
address, 120–21
housing and, 238–39,
385–87
Human Rights
Commission and,
557–58, 562
human rights crusade of,
542, 545, 549–71
humility of, 3
impact of, 1–2
Indian independence and,
441–42, 535–36
influence on public
opinion of, 50–51
and internment of
Japanese-Americans,
416–21
on isolationism, 136
Israel and, 556, 558
labor ties of, 10–11
Lash and, see Lash,
Joseph, ER and
in Latin America tour,
503–4
in lead in to World War
II, 117–30
legacy of, 570–71
London mission of, 438
loneliness of, 392
love of nature and, 309
Manhattan townhouse
of, 422

Mann on, 317n
melancholy of, 108–9
military draft and, 274,
323–24, 345
missing Miller
correspondence of, 8
in movement for racial
justice, 310–11, 321,
333–39, 350
at NAACP conference,
92–94
on national defense,
324–25
national health program
upset by, 407
as nationally beloved
person, 249
national unity campaign
of, 257, 412–13, 485
Nazi atrocities and,
453–54
on Nazi-Soviet Pact, 117
on Neutrality Act, 22–23
New Year's Day message
of, 19
niece's debutante dance
planned by, 18
at 1940 Democratic
Convention, 353
in 1942 mission to
England, 337, 440–47
at OCD, 405, 407–8,
412–15
in OCD resignation, 415
optimism of, 569–70
outfits of, 173, 228–29
Pacific Theater tour of,
465, 479–84
Palestine and, 487–88,
547–48
Pastor Hall and, 316,
318–19
as political pro, 551
on possibility of FDR's
third term, 551
post-1940 election tour
of, 359–60, 364–65
power of, elements of,
355–56
praise for, 171–72
public approval for, 228
public health and,
247–48
racism deplored by,
166–67, 357–58, 413,
414–15, 416, 424, 427,

435, 440, 446, 450–51,
472–73, 518–21, 535,
545, 561, 564, 566
radio broadcasts of, 416
radio series of, 242
Rearmament Act and, 58
Red Scare and, 153–54,
328–30
refugees and, 26–30,
61–62, 63–64,
161–62, 170–71, 188,
190, 192–93, 195,
199–200, 222–24,
229, 235–36, 253–54,
263–64, 276–77,
287–91, 311–13, 316,
325, 368, 369–74,
377–82, 383–84, 389,
427, 470–71, 472, 475,
485, 489, 555–56
Robeson defended
by, 565
Royal visit and, 65–79
on SDR, 397–98
second child lost by, 70
"secret plan" of, 392–93
self-deprecating nature of,
172, 357
self-perception of, 355
as serial romantic,
363–64
as sickened by Hitler,
320–21
sixtieth birthday of,
522–23
Smith Act and, 282, 330
social agenda of, 256–57,
265, 274, 469, 477–78,
496–98, 513, 525–26,
535, 547, 569–70
and sons' military service,
408, 420, 423, 428,
483, 508, 534, 536
Southern speaking tour
of, 133–34
Soviet invasion of Finland
and, 187–88
speaking tours of,
229–33, 239, 240,
242–45, 249,
414–15, 535
speech/voice lessons for,
240, 248
speeding stop of, 104–5
sports and music
education and, 313–14

Roosevelt, Elliott
  Bulloch *(cont.)*
  on State of the Union
    (1939), 23–24
  Time article on, 44–46
  in tour of post-war
    Europe, 555–56
  Trude and, *see* Lash,
    Trude Pratt
  Truman and, 546–49
  UN and, 13, 15, 538,
    548, 549–55, 557–58,
    559–60, 568
  UN founding conference
    and, 533, 536,
    543, 544
  and U.S. aid to
    Britain, 287
  in U.S. delegation to UN,
    548, 549–55, 568
  Wald and, 322
  Wallace and, 308–9
  on war, 51–52, 90,
    152–53, 164
  war information received
    by, 134
  as WILPF member,
    322–23
  women's rights and,
    84–85, 426, 427–28,
    437, 447, 450, 462,
    535, 545
  Woolf interview of,
    67–68
  at World's Fair (1939),
    56–57
  world citizenship
    championed by, 535,
    545–46
  on World War II, 314,
    315, 327–28
  writing of, 50, 86, 108
  writing skills of, 48–49
  Youth Act and,
    198–99, 203
  youth and, 356
Roosevelt, Eleanor, FDR's
  relationship with,
    9–10, 107–8, 139,
    169, 246, 294,
    296–97, 466
  arguments in, 381–82,
    385–86, 387
  ER's defense of FDR
    and, 2123
  ER's view of, 542

FDR's affairs and, 3–5,
    367, 401, 446, 502, 541
  growing distance in,
    429, 474
  after Hall's death, 400
  internment of
    Japanese-Americans
    as turning point in,
    419, 421
  marital partnership in,
    382, 387, 388
  policy issues in, 284, 426,
    431, 437, 442, 460,
    465, 521
  political distance in, 167
  renewed mutual respect
    in, 456, 457
  Suckley on, 541–42
  thirty-fifth wedding
    anniversary of, 233
Roosevelt, Eleanor, II, 18,
    19, 43, 56, 104, 400
Roosevelt, Elliott Bulloch
  (father), 2, 399
  alcoholism of, 239, 266
  death of, 314
  ER's relationship
    with, 266
Roosevelt, Elliott (son), 72,
    145, 147, 184, 268,
    316, 345, 352, 396,
    408, 423, 446, 458,
    495, 528, 534
Roosevelt, Franklin Delano,
    1, 3, 5, 6, 8, 9, 12–13,
    15, 48, 86, 97, 99*n*,
    100, 100*n*, 172–73,
    174, 179, 181, 185,
    200, 215, 246, 252,
    253, 254, 281, 291,
    292–93, 295–96, 297,
    317*n*, 326, 345–46,
    361, 363, 375–77,
    378–79, 381, 387,
    390–91, 395, 397,
    402–3, 456, 490
  in address to Youth
    Council, 206–10, 214
  agriculture policy of,
    489–90
  anti-colonialism of, 459,
    463, 531, 535, 537
  anti-lynching laws and, 32
  on arms embargo, 98
  arms embargo and, 91,
    100–102

on birth control, 47
  Black Cabinet of, 357
  on Black's biography of
    ER, 354
  Britain aided by, 393
  Britain supplied with
    destroyers by, 331
  at Cairo Conference, 483,
    491, 492, 494
  campaign for war
    preparation, 178
  and Casablanca
    Conference, 458–59
  China and, 461
  Churchill's White House
    meeting with,
    408–12, 417
  Congress and, 270
  Congress's relations with,
    502–3
  criticism of, 204
  Darlan Deal and, 457
  death of, 539–41,
    543, 544
  declaration of war
    and, 404
  defense buildup and,
    256–57, 259–60, 272
  Einstein letter to,
    148–49
  on ER, 356
  ER's impact on policies
    of, 10, 357, 382–83
  European leaders offered
    refuge by, 163
  failing health of, 495–96,
    501, 504–5, 533–34
  "Fala" speech of, 523
  FBI wiretaps condoned
    by, 467
  fighting mood of, 22
  in first wartime meeting
    with Churchill,
    395–96
  flu of, 233–34, 241–42
  Four Freedoms and,
    382–83, 494, 496, 560
  fourth inaugural address
    of, 528–29
  Frankfurter and, 283–84
  Frankfurter nomination
    and, 24–26
  GI Bill and, 489
  handicap of, 169, 242
  Hatch Act and, 105–6
  at Hobcaw, 505

honorary degree received
by, 316
Ibn Saud's meetings with,
530–32
imperialist tendencies of,
457–58
inconsistent policies of,
421–22
Indian independence and,
435, 437, 459, 464–65
infidelities of, 146
and internment of
Japanese-Americans,
416–21
Jefferson Day speech of,
540–41
Jewish quotas supported
by, 459
J. Kennedy and, 347–48,
358, 359
Lash on, 200–201
lend-lease act proposed
by, 375
May 1940 radio address
of, 258–61
in meeting with young
people, 268–70
Mercer's affair with, *see*
Rutherfurd, Lucy
Mercer
Middle East and, 486
military draft and, 332
Nazi–Soviet Pact and, 195
Nazi attrocities and,
455–56
Nazi-Soviet Pact and,
114–15, 198–99
Neutrality Act (1939)
signed by, 161
neutrality proclamation
of, 123–24
New Deal and, 178,
205–6
Nicaragua policy of,
60–61
1940 reelection campaign
of, 251, 284, 295–302,
343–52, 360–61, 373
in 1944 election, 521,
523–24
1944 State of the Union
address of, 496
Open Door concept
of, 531
Palestine and, 486–88,
530–31, 532

Pearl Harbor attack and,
403–4
Philippines independence
and, 535, 537
pledge to keep U.S. out of
war by, 346, 347,
348–49
presidential archive
of, 167
proclamation of "limited
national emergency"
issued by, 137–38
public message to Hitler
and Mussolini from,
39–40
purge of conservative
Democrats for, 17
in Quebec Conference
(1944), 484, 514, 516,
517, 518
race issues and, 337–38,
339–43
Rearmament Act of, 58
Red Scare and, 153–54
refugees and, 13–14,
27–30, 61–62, 190,
199–200, 236,
253–54, 289, 311, 312,
313, 369, 373–74,
377–78, 381, 471, 475,
484–85, 486, 530–31
Royal visit and, 65–79
Sachs meeting of, 147–50
St. Louis affair and,
80–82
silence and inaccessibility
of, 393
Smith Act and, 328, 330
southern strategy of,
311, 333
Soviet invasion of Finland
and, 174, 187–88
spend-lend bill of, 90
State of the Union
Address (1939) of,
22–24
State of the Union
address (1940) of, 196
at Tehran Conference,
483, 491, 492, 494
third inauguration of, 353
third term debate of,
50–51
Tuscaloosa vacation
of, 218
UN and, 410–11

and UN founding
conference, 533
and U.S.-U.K. relations,
18–19
"Vichy gamble" of,
448, 466
Virginia Law School
address of, 272–73, 285
Wallace as running mate
of, 298–99
in Warm Springs, 365,
526, 528, 534, 535,
536, 537, 539
on war profiteering,
122–24
White House Conference
on Political Refugees
held by, 151–52
Willkie's nomination
and, 292
and World's Fair (1939),
56–57
at Yalta Conference,
530, 533
Roosevelt, Franklin Delano,
Jr., 72, 212, 234, 272,
310, 343, 344, 352,
385, 394, 408, 423,
428, 474, 495
Roosevelt, Franklin Delano,
III, 19, 310, 351
Roosevelt, Hall, 18, 20, 33,
37, 43, 111, 133, 147,
325, 364, 393, 397,
398–401, 402
Roosevelt, James "Jimmy,"
72, 125, 145, 147, 229,
236, 318, 344, 352,
399, 400, 402, 408,
424, 428, 460,
483, 512
Roosevelt, Janet, 325,
364, 400
Roosevelt, John, 70, 103–4,
112, 116, 125, 271,
402–3, 408, 423
Roosevelt, Kate and
Sara, 495
Roosevelt, Sara Delano,
19–20, 44, 65, 66, 76,
102, 163, 167, 168,
172–73, 186, 196, 225,
284, 295, 319, 351,
365, 375, 385, 399,
401, 402, 446,
492–93, 495

Roosevelt, Sara
    Delano *(cont.)*
    death of, 397–98
    European trip of, 97–98,
        111–12, 116
    health of, 235, 393,
        395, 397
Rosenman, Sam, 25,
    452, 456
Royal Navy, 252, 331, 375
Rutherfurd, Lucy Mercer,
    3–4, 8, 367, 401, 528,
    537, 539, 540*n*, 541

Sachs, Alexander, 147–50,
    148*n*–49*n*
St. Louis, USS, 69, 80–82,
    81*n*, 90, 312
Sandifer, Durward, 552
Saudi Arabia, 486
    oil deposits in, 531
    U.S. as favored trading
        partner of, 532
Save the Children Fund,
    413, 253, 517
Schiffrin, Jacques, 384
Scholl, Hans and Sophie,
    the White Rose,
    468–70
Schröder, Gustav, 69, 80, 81*n*
segregation, 9, 10, 34,
    35–36, 93, 156, 169,
    216, 497, 566–67
    in military, *see* armed
        forces, Blacks in
    of schools, 33–34, 358,
        566–67
    see also racism
Selective Service Act, 332,
    344–45, 396
Senate, U.S., 21, 32, 88, 97,
    105, 160, 246
    Foreign Relations
        Committee of, 98, 269
Sharp, Reverend Waitstill
    and Martha, 371
Sheppard-Towner Infant
    and Maternity Health
    care Act, 58–59
Sherwood, Robert, 265,
    412, 525–26
Shirer, William, 119, 133,
    163–64, 199, 284, 396
Shoumatoff, Elizabeth, 537
Sicily, Allied invasion of,
    459, 476

Simon, Abbott, 197,
    198–99, 212, 214, 219
Smith Act, 281–82, 321,
    328–30
Smith Act and Alien
    Registration 281–84
Soames, Mary Churchill,
    472, 476–77
Socialist Party, 175,
    176, 324
Social Security, 23, 412,
    469, 496–97
Social Security Act (1935),
    58–59, 59*n*, 179,
    477–78, 496
Social Security Board, 59,
    286, 496, 497
Sosúa, refugees settlement,
    Dominican Republic,
    372–73
Soul of Chaos (Brittain),
    505–6
South, 166, 308, 321
South Africa, 69, 549,
    550–51
Southern Conference for
    Human Welfare
    (SCHW), 34, 242,
    243, 244, 321
Souvestre, Marie, 2, 3, 5,
    109, 144, 221, 233, 275
Soviet Union, 40, 41, 42,
    99, 208, 212, 411, 439,
    492, 554
    Churchill and, 546–47
    Finland invaded by, 174,
        187–88, 197, 204, 213,
        219, 227
    Nazi invasion of, 389
    in nonaggression pact
        with Germany, *see*
        Nazi-Soviet pact
    Poland invaded by,
        133–34, 151
    Truman and, 546, 547
    Warsaw uprising and, 515
Spain, 17, 21, 26, 37–38, 41,
    42, 58, 91, 100, 101*n*,
    131, 176, 203, 210,
    213, 220–21, 254, 549
Spanish Civil War, 91, 157,
    176, 221, 255, 269,
    366, 443, 466
Stalin, Joseph, 42, 113–14,
    115, 134, 157, 172, 195,
    411, 439, 455, 465,

474, 483, 490, 491,
    515, 518
State Department, U.S., 27,
    30, 41, 61*n*, 65, 66, 82,
    99, 99*n*–100*n*, 101,
    116, 120, 164, 219,
    348, 403, 431, 476,
    526–27, 528, 529, 55,
    562–63
    aid to refugees blocked
        by, 62, 81, 199–200,
        222, 287, 290, 311,
        312–13, 369, 373, 389,
        427, 455, 488–89,
        498–99
Stettinius, Edward, 280*n*,
    484, 499–500, 526–27,
    536, 537, 548
Stevenson, Adlai, 552, 566,
    568, 570
Stimson, Henry L., 172,
    274, 280, 310, 440,
    446, 451, 473, 499
Stokowski, Leopold, 146,
    228, 313
Straight, Michael, 206*n*,
    208, 209
Strawser, Cornelia Jane,
    353–54
Strong, Anna Louise,
    133–34
Suckley, Margaret "Daisy,"
    401, 465–66, 477, 495,
    502, 504, 505, 506–7,
    525, 526, 528, 532,
    534, 539, 541–42
Supreme Court, U.S., 12,
    21, 24–26, 432, 566
Swing, Betty Gram, 553
Szold, Henrietta, 532

Tagore, Rabindranath, 492
Tehran Conference, 483,
    491, 492, 494
Tennessee Valley Authority
    (TVA), 21, 244,
    291, 301
This Is America (E. Roosevelt
    and Macgregor),
    424–25
This Troubled World (E.
    Roosevelt), 86, 91, 116
Thomas, Norman, 175, 176,
    198, 324
Thompson, Geraldine
    Preston, 247

Thompson, Dorothy, 3, 30, 135, 171
Thompson, Malvina "Tommy," 5, 21, 67, 98, 104, 108, 120, 129, 133, 138, 179, 215, 216, 229–30, 239, 242, 247, 248–49, 265, 293, 295, 297, 318, 326, 351, 363, 378, 387, 389, 397, 398, 399, 402, 456, 466, 480, 481, 483, 485–86, 495, 511, 525, 536
  Anna Boettiger and, 167–68, 277–78, 310, 362, 422, 430
  death of, 564
  on ER, 6–7, 68, 277–78, 290, 310, 360, 407, 422, 428, 479, 504
  in ER's British trip, 440, 442, 445, 447, 449, 450
  on ER's friends, 7, 85, 110, 168, 225, 236, 360, 423
  Hick and, 236–37, 423
  Lape and, 6, 7, 60, 76, 110, 225, 236, 237, 240, 271, 405, 428, 442, 462, 478, 479, 504, 528
Thompson, Mildred, 507
Thompson, Private Calvin, 481–82
Time, 44–46, 107, 242, 250, 254, 284, 345, 387, 515
Toller, Ernst, 316, 316n–17n, 383
Tomorrow Is Now (E. Roosevelt), 569–70
Toscanini, Arturo, 33, 417–18
Treasury Department, U.S., 405, 421
Truman, Harry S., 511, 521, 560, 561
  Churchill and, 546–47
  ER and, 546–49
  in 1944 election, 510–11, 512
  in 1948 election, 561–62
  Soviets and, 546, 547, 556–57, 561
  swearing in of, 539

Tully, Grace, 167, 394, 422, 485, 507, 539
Tuskegee Airmen, 11, 437, 472, 473
Tuskegee Institute, 133, 169, 310, 437

U-boats, 128, 316, 332, 375, 391
unemployment, 49, 59, 60, 182, 210, 245, 251, 345
UNESCO, 507, 560
United Nations, 13, 15, 456, 461, 490, 512, 514, 526, 527, 543, 555
  Charter of, 548
  Displaced Persons and, 556
  Dumbarton Oaks Conference and, 513–14
  ER and, 538, 548, 549–55, 557–58, 559–60, 568
  FDR and, 410–11
  founding conference of, 530, 533, 534–35, 536, 543, 544, 548
  London session of, 548, 551–55
  Security Council of, 548
  U.S. delegation to, 548–55, 568
  "We Charge Genocide" petition to, 562
United Nations, General Assembly of, 556, 558, 560
  ER's speeches to, 554, 563
  Soviet delegation to, 554–55
  U.S. delegation to, 554–55
United Nations Human Rights Commission, 553n, 557–58, 562
United States:
  British relations with, 471–72
  China aided by, 331
  German POWs in, 472
  immigration to, 311, 312–13, 320

isolationism in, *see* isolationism
military buildup of, 256–57, 259–60, 272, 280
United States of Africa, 63–64
Universal Declaration of Human Rights (UDHR), 13, 15, 558–61, 563, 568n
U.S. Committee for the Care of European Children, 288, 290, 311, 312, 316, 325, 426–27, 430–31

Vandenberg, Arthur, 161, 291, 522, 534, 548, 550, 551–52, 554–55
Vanderbilt, Cornelius (Neil) and Grace, 111
Van Doren, Irita, 349
Van Waters, Miriam, 247
Vatican, 190, 192, 199
Versailles Treaty (1919), 51, 114, 119, 131, 136
Villard, Oswald Garrison, 91, 161, 192–93
Vishinsky, Andrei, 554
Virgin Islands, 379, 380, 381
Voorhis, Jerry, 63, 173, 176
voting rights, 336–37, 357, 524

Wagner, Robert F., Jr., 26, 30, 31, 59–60, 90, 105, 117, 265, 338, 509
Wagner-Rogers bill, 26–30, 214
Wald, Lillian, 59n, 90, 321, 322, 535
Wallace, Henry, 28, 297–99, 300, 301, 308–9, 326, 349, 425–26, 432, 437, 465, 466, 467, 485, 487, 488, 510, 512, 513, 521
Wallenberg, Raoul, 500, 538
Waller, Odell, 431–33
War Department, U.S., 339, 340, 341, 403, 519
War Refugee Board (WRB), 499, 521, 537–38

War Relocation Authority,
418, 420, 421
Warsaw, 150, 139,
163–64, 515,
bombing of, 131, 132
1944 uprising of, 515
siege of, 135–36, 139
Soviets in, 521, 538
Warsaw Ghetto, 453,
472, 509
Watson, Edwin, 122,
149, 532
Wechsler, James, 175,
182, 395
Weigand, Erika, 223
Weigand Dr. Hermann and
Frances Rhoades, 223
Welles, Sumner, 115, 120,
218–19, 223, 369, 379,
381, 427, 484
Werfel, Franz, 371–73
Werth, Alexander, 135,
515–16
West, J. B., 358, 387, 409,
539–40
White, Walter, 32, 93, 156,
166, 333, 335–36,
337, 338, 339, 340,
341–42, 350–51, 395,
401, 407, 440, 463,
517, 549
White, William Allen, 193,
195–96, 249
White, W. L., 193–96
White House Conference
on Political Refugees,
151–52
White Rose, 468, 470
white supremacism, 58–59,
321, 328, 333, 343,
357, 358, 566
Whitney, Betsey Cushing
Roosevelt, 145,
429–30
Whitney, Jock and Betsey
Cushing Roosevelt,
429–30

Williams, Aubrey, 117, 174,
175, 209, 229, 325,
333, 343, 565–66
Williams, Frances, 95n,
212, 230
Willkie, Wendell, 293,
301, 321, 337–38,
342, 345–46, 347,
349, 350–51, 352,
355, 360, 449, 463,
475, 488
death of, 522
in 1940 election, 291–92,
311, 332, 343
1942 world tour of, 439
race issues and, 311, 333,
433–34
Wilson, Woodrow, 342, 548
Wiltwyck School, 567
Winant, John, 376–77, 390,
439, 440, 442–43, 451,
453, 557
Wise, Stephen, 287, 378,
427, 488
women:
in armed forces, 426,
427–28, 437–38, 444
Nazi assaults on, 47
in public life, 362
rights of, 21, 84–85,
426, 427–28, 437, 447,
450, 462, 535, 545,
558, 563
Women's Army Corps
(WAC), 427–28, 444
Blacks in, 518–19
Women's International
League for Peace and
Freedom (WILPF), 58,
90, 95, 170, 199, 321,
322–23
Women's Land Army,
British, 443, 447
Women's Voluntary Service
(WVS), British, 390,
440, 443–44,
445, 476

Woodring, Harry, 120,
279, 280
Woodward, Ellen, 56,
321, 490
Woollcott, Alexander, 102,
396, 453
Workers' Alliance,
70–71, 360
Works Progress
Administration
(WPA), 21, 54, 60, 70,
71, 86, 87, 89, 106,
160, 174, 182, 205,
213, 230, 231, 249,
267, 364
World Court, 30–31, 90,
128, 300, 544, 555
World War I, 131, 146, 243,
310, 338
World War II, 5, 11, 131,
314–19, 320, 322–23,
327–28, 330–32,
358–59, 390, 404
Allied defeats in, 405,
409, 418, 428
opposition to U.S.
involvement in, see
isolationism

Yalta Conference, 528, 529,
530, 533
Yard, Molly, 95n, 175, 182,
183, 197
Yosemite National Park, 70,
240–41
You Learn By Living
(E. Roosevelt), 543
Youth Act, 198–99, 207
youth movement,
54–55,
156–57
Yugoslavia, 114, 391,
518, 533n
YWCA, 211, 342, 497

Zeilsheim DP Camp,
555–56

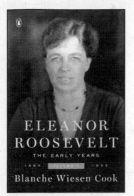
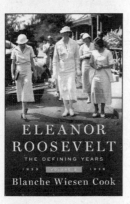
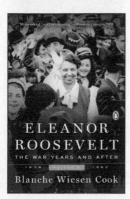